The Editor

PHILLIP MALLETT is Senior Lecturer in English at the University of St Andrews. He is the author of chapters and articles on a number of Victorian and earlier writers, and editor of several texts and collections of essays, including *Kipling Considered*, *Satire*, *The Achievement of Thomas Hardy*, *Palgrave Advances in Thomas Hardy Studies*, *Thomas Hardy: The Woodlanders*, and the Norton Critical Edition of *The Mayor of Casterbridge*. His *Rudyard Kipling: A Literary Life* appeared in 2003.

W. W. NORTON & COMPANY, INC.
Also Publishes

A NORTON CRITICAL EDITION

Thomas Hardy

THE RETURN OF THE NATIVE

SECOND EDITION

Edited by

PHILLIP MALLETT

UNIVERSITY OF ST ANDREWS

W. W. NORTON & COMPANY

New York • London

W. W. Norton & Company has been independent since its founding in 1923, when William Warder Norton and Mary D. Herter Norton first published lectures delivered at the People's Institute, the adult education division of New York City's Cooper Union. The Nortons soon expanded their program beyond the Institute, publishing books by celebrated academics from America and abroad. By mid-century, the two major pillars of Norton's publishing program— trade books and college texts—were firmly established. In the 1950s, the Norton family transferred control of the company to its employees, and today—with a staff of four hundred and a comparable number of trade, college, and professional titles published each year—W. W. Norton & Company stands as the largest and oldest publishing house owned wholly by its employees.

The text of this book is composed in Fairfield Medium
with the display set in Bernhard Modern.
Composition by PennSet, Inc.
Manufacturing by the Maple-Vail Book Group, Binghamton.
Production Manager: Benjamin Reynolds.

Library of Congress Cataloging-in-Publication Data
Hardy, Thomas, 1840–1928.
The return of the native: authoritative text, backgrounds and
contexts, criticism / Thomas Hardy; edited by Phillip Mallett.— 2nd ed.
p. cm. — (A Norton critical edition)
Includes bibliographical references.

ISBN 0–393–92787–3 (pbk.)

1. Wessex (England—Fiction. 2. Hardy, Thomas, 1840–1928. Return
of the native. 3. People with visual disabilities—Fiction. 4. Mothers
and sons—Fiction. 5. Mate selection—Fiction. 6. Heathlands—
Fiction. 7. Adultery—Fiction. I. Mallett, Phillip, 1946–
II. Title. III. Series.

PR4747.A2M35 2005
823'.8—dc22

2005053925

W. W. Norton & Company, Inc., 500 Fifth Avenue, New York, N.Y. 10110-0017
www.wwnorton.com

W. W. Norton & Company Ltd., Castle House,
75/76 Wells Street, London W1T 3QT

1   2   3   4   5   6   7   8   9   0

In Memoriam
Edward Craven

Contents

Preface to the Second Edition   ix
A Note on the Text   xiii

The Text of *The Return of the Native*

Facsimile title page of the first edition   3
Sketch map of the Scene of the Story   4
Preface   5
Contents   6
The Return of the Native   8

Backgrounds and Contexts

Map of the Wessex of the Novels and Poems   338
Glossary of Dialect Words   340
COMPOSITION   343
     Simon Gatrell • The Textual History of *The Return of*
       the Native   343
     Andrew Nash • *The Return of the Native* and
       Belgravia   363
     The Serialization of *The Return of the Native*   371
     Phillip Mallett • Hardy's 1912 Note to Book VI,
       Chapter III   372
HARDY'S NONFICTIONAL WRITINGS   375
     From Hardy's Letters   375
     From *The Life and Works of Thomas Hardy*   383
     Two Letters on Dialect in the Novel   392
     From The Profitable Reading of Fiction   394
     From Candour in English Fiction   394
     From General Preface to the Novels and Poems   397

Criticism

CONTEMPORARY RECEPTION   403
     Unsigned Review • *The Athenaeum*   406
     W. E. Henley • *The Academy*   408
     Unsigned Review • *The Saturday Review*   409

R. H. Hutton • *The Spectator*   414
Unsigned Review • *Harper's New Monthly Magazine*   417
MODERN CRITICISM   418
D. H. Lawrence • From *Study of Thomas Hardy*   418
Donald Davidson • The Traditional Basis of Thomas
    Hardy's Fiction   427
John Paterson • *The Return of the Native* as
    Antichristian Document   439
Richard Swigg • Thomas Hardy and the Problem of
    the "Middle Distance"   454
Michael Wheeler • The Defects of the Real   463
Rosemarie Morgan • Conflicting Courses in
    The Return of the Native   474
Pamela Dalziel • Anxieties of Representation: The
    Serial Illustrations to Hardy's *The Return of*
    the Native   489
Gillian Beer • Can the Native Return?   504
Jennifer Gribble • The Quiet Women of Egdon Heath   524

Thomas Hardy: A Chronology   543
Selected Bibliography   549

Preface to the Second Edition

In 1879 the reviewer in the *New Quarterly Magazine* noted, astutely, that *The Return of the Native*, Hardy's sixth published novel, presented "a new phase, and perhaps a new departure in the development of Mr. Hardy's genius." So it has seemed to most later readers. Since its first publication in 1878, it has been widely translated, re-edited, dramatized, and adapted for film and television; it has even inspired a piece of music, Gustav Holst's symphonic "Egdon Heath." It remains both a popular classic—it is, like *Wuthering Heights* or *Jane Eyre*, one of those novels that seems to excite a passion for reading in those who discover it—and a favorite set text for book clubs, schools, and colleges. *The Return of the Native*, wrote D. H. Lawrence in his *Study of Thomas Hardy* (1912), was Hardy's "first tragic and important novel."

Hardy probably began work on *The Return* toward the end of 1876, after he and his wife Emma had moved to Sturminster Newton in Dorset; it may well have been completed by the time they moved to London in March 1878. Despite the somber tone of the novel, this was a period he remembered later as the happiest time of their marriage, but he was in his thirty-seventh year, his previous novel, *The Hand of Ethelberta*, had been neither a popular nor a critical success, and his standing as a full-time writer was still not wholly secure. Nor, perhaps, was he himself quite sure of the direction he wished to take. After his first, unpublished attempt at prose fiction, *The Poor Man and the Lady*, he had written five novels in as many years. *Desperate Remedies*, published in 1871, is an exercise in sensation fiction, with a plot that includes illegitimacy, a lesbian scene, a fire, murder, and attempted rape. *Under the Greenwood Tree*, published a year later, is a much quieter book, pastoral and self-consciously charming, which traces Dick Dewy's only slightly troubled courtship of Fancy Day, one rung above him on the social ladder. *A Pair of Blue Eyes* (1873) is a romance, albeit one tinged with tragedy; like much of Hardy's fiction, it explores the trials of a woman wooed by several men, and the demands on her to meet male expectations. *Far from the Madding Crowd* (1874), solicited by Leslie Stephen for the prestigious *Cornhill Magazine*, brought a return to the pastoral, as Stephen had required, but with a deeper

exploration of love, and a darker treatment of rural life; the plot includes the death in childbirth of an unmarried woman, as well as a
murder and a mental breakdown. *The Hand of Ethelberta* (1875),
also written for the *Cornhill*, was an experiment in a very different
direction: a comedy of social manners, satirical rather than pastoral
or tragic, but with elements of disguised autobiography in a plot
that explores the boundaries between a rural working world like
that in which Hardy had grown up, and the urban middle and upper class to which his success was beginning to win him the right of
entry.

The Hand of Ethelberta disappointed the critics, who would have
settled for another novel in the style of *Far from the Madding
Crowd*. The literary marketplace was as competitive as any other,
and Hardy must have known that he had ground to make up, but
rather than return to the pastoral mode he determined upon another change of direction. His next novel, *The Return of the Native*,
was to be an ambitious attempt at high tragedy. During 1877, with
a substantial part of the novel written—a different version of what
came to form the first two books of the published text—he offered
it unsuccessfully to a number of magazines, including the *Cornhill*,
Blackwood's, and *Temple Bar*, before finding a home for it in the far
from prestigious *Belgravia* and at a significantly lower price than he
had received for *Ethelberta*. It appeared in serial form through
1878, with illustrations by Arthur Hopkins, and in America in
Harper's New Monthly Magazine from February 1878 to January
1879. As was customary, the first volume publication came just before the completion of the serial, in November 1878. The reviews
were mixed, and the note of metropolitan condescension never far
to seek, but they were by no means so unfavourable as has sometimes been assumed; a selection is included in this edition. There
were objections, from one quarter or another, to almost everything—to the language, characterization, setting, mood, and tone;
yet most critics, even those who least liked the novel, continued to
place Hardy alongside George Eliot and the young Henry James as
an author to be reckoned with. In 1879 the *New Quarterly Magazine* published the first article that set out to survey Hardy's work in
its entirety, and did so sympathetically (though with some reservations about *The Return*). Others were soon to follow: among them
Havelock Ellis in the *Westminster Review* in 1883, J. M. Barrie in
the *Contemporary Review* in 1889, Edmund Gosse a year later in
The Speaker. By now it was clear that Hardy was to be thought of
as a "tragic novelist," and the importance in his development of *The
Return of the Native* was widely acknowledged. Its status as one of
the half-dozen books on which Hardy's reputation as a novelist
chiefly rests is now beyond question.

The first aim of this Norton Critical Edition has been to provide a reliable text. Here I have agreed with James Gindin, who edited *The Return of the Native* for Norton in 1969, in basing the text on that of the Wessex Edition of 1912; my reasons for doing so are set out in the Note on the Text. This edition, however, unlike its predecessor, includes the illustrations that accompanied the novel's first, serial publication, as well as the sketch map of the scene of the story drawn by Hardy himself for the 1878 volume edition; neither the illustrations nor this map were included in the Wessex Edition. In preparing the annotation, I have drawn on Gindin's work and on that of other editors of the novel, in particular Simon Gatrell and Tony Slade, but at times I have differed from all of them, both in matters of substance, and in the choice of what to annotate and what to leave without comment. Such decisions inevitably reflect our varied experiences as readers of Hardy, and as teachers of English literature, as well perhaps as cultural differences between the two sides of the Atlantic. Further remarks on the notes may be found in the Note on the Text.

The other main difference between this and the earlier Norton edition is to be found in the selection of modern criticism of the novel, where I have included a number of essays written after 1969, including work by Gillian Beer, Pamela Dalziel, Jennifer Gribble, Simon Gatrell, Rosemarie Morgan, Andrew Nash, Richard Swigg, and Michael Wheeler. Three of the essays are, in their present form, published for the first time in this edition. Rosemarie Morgan revisits questions raised in an earlier chapter on the novel, in *Women and Sexuality in the Novels of Thomas Hardy*, first published in 1988; Simon Gatrell draws together work done in his introductions to the Garland edition of the manuscripts of *The Return of the Native*, and to the World's Classics edition of the novel, and in two monographs, *Hardy the Creator: A Textual Biography* (1988) and *Thomas Hardy's Vision of Wessex* (2003); Andrew Nash has revised an article originally published in *The Library* in 2001 to take account of Gatrell's essay in the form in which it appears here. Inevitably, in order to make room for the new material I have had to exclude some pieces that Gindin included; I have done so with regret, but in the confidence that many of the issues they addressed are taken up and re-examined by the critics represented here. I have also included a rather larger selection of Hardy's nonfictional writing, including letters, and his third-person autobiography. Here I have had the advantage, as Gindin did not, of being able to consult the seven volumes of Hardy's *Collected Letters*, edited for the Clarendon Press by Richard Purdy and Michael Millgate.

I owe thanks to a number of people. The community of Hardy

scholars is a wide and generous one; I have sought and received advice from, in particular, Pamela Dalziel, Kathleen Huggett, Caroline Jackson-Houlston, Peter Millington, Birgit Plietzsch, Martin Ray, Angelique Richardson, Peter Robson, and Terry Wright. To all of them, my thanks.

Lilian Swindall, at the Dorset County Museum in Dorchester, has been, as always, unfailingly welcoming, resourceful, and informed; there could be no better guide to the Museum's collection of Hardy materials. Everyone I have dealt with at Norton has been friendly, patient (above all, patient), and efficient, and it is a pleasure to say so here; I am grateful especially to Brian Baker.

I should not have completed the work on this edition without the support, quietly, graciously, and generously given, of Margaret Craven. I owe her more than she would ever allow me to say.

A Note on the Text

Like its predecessor, this Norton edition of *The Return of the Native* is based on the Macmillan Wessex Edition of 1912. In the General Preface he wrote at the time, Hardy described this as the "definite edition." Most readers have taken this to mean definitive, following Richard L. Purdy in his influential *Thomas Hardy: A Bibliographical Study* (1954), and definitive has been taken to mean authoritative—authoritative enough to provide the base text for most of the editions currently available. This seems uncontroversial: we expect to read, say, *Great Expectations* with the ending Dickens finally chose for it, not the one he rejected on the advice of his friend Bulwer Lytton; or George Eliot's *Middlemarch* in the revised edition of 1874, rather than in the 1872 first edition. But with the exception of *Desperate Remedies* and *Under the Greenwood Tree*, all of Hardy's novels, including *The Return of the Native*, had a complicated publishing history, allowing for significant changes to be made at a number of different stages. These stages typically include a serial version, often substantially revised from the manuscript to comply with the demands of editors, or Hardy's guesses as to what those demands might be; a first volume edition, in which the text was revised back toward its pre-serial form; and then the two collected editions, the "Wessex Novels" from Osgood, McIlvaine in 1895, and the "Wessex Edition" from Macmillan in 1912, each marked by extensive revisions. This is complex enough, but the issues are often further involved by substantial differences between the first English and the first American book versions, as is the case with *The Mayor of Casterbridge*, or between first and second volume editions, as with the 1891 and 1892 editions of *Tess of the d'Urbervilles*.

There are at least three orders of change here, overlapping but still analytically distinct. There are, first, those made by Hardy's own decision, most of them for the 1895 and 1912 editions, in an effort to impose, retrospectively, a unified idea of "Wessex," which had in fact developed in piecemeal fashion. Second, there are those that were forced on Hardy by the need to avoid offending the more prudish sections of his audience. This was a pressure he came increasingly to resent, and one that contributed to his decision to abandon prose fiction after the hostile reception given in some quarters to *Jude the Obscure*: the chapter of the *Life* which deals with *Jude* is called "Another Novel Finished, Mutilated, and Restored." Third, and often most fascinating, there are those that reflect a refueling of Hardy's creative energies as he worked on the texts and felt compelled to re-imagine and re-write characters and situations.

Each kind of change is apparent in the textual history of *The Return of the Native*. When Hardy began work on the novel, probably toward the end of 1876, he had no reason to suppose that he would for the next twenty years restrict his focus to the southwestern counties of England. But "Wessex" soon became an expected, and marketable, feature of his fiction, and in the process of revising the novel for the Osgood, McIlvaine edition of 1895 he incorporated a number of place-names which were by now familiar to his readers—Anglebury (Wareham), Casterbridge (Dorchester), and Weatherbury (Puddletown)—which he had not included in 1878. These serve to locate Egdon Heath, the arena of the novel's action, and to D. H. Lawrence "the great, tragic power in the book," more precisely in relation to other parts of Wessex, but they also qualify the sense of its size, age, and remoteness, and not all readers have welcomed the change.

The interview between Wildeve and Eustacia in Book First, Chapter VI, provides an example of the kinds of change associated with (self)-censorship, interwoven with others that signal a deeper re-thinking of the novel. Eustacia protests against Wildeve's abandonment of her in favor of Thomasin. In 1878, in the first volume edition, the passage reads:

> "you . . . deserted me entirely, as if I had never been yours!"

This leaves open the question of what degree of sexual intimacy there has been between them. In the 1895 edition, the text is seemingly more explicit:

> "you . . . deserted me entirely, as if I had never been yours body and soul so irretrievably!"

It seems reasonable to assume that Hardy was now making clear what he had felt obliged to veil in 1878, that Eustacia and Wildeve had been lovers. But for the 1912 edition he made another change:

> "you . . . deserted me entirely, as if I had never been yours life and soul so irretrievably!"

Whatever one takes to be the effect of substituting "life and soul" for "body and soul"—perhaps an emphasis on the emotional rather than the sexual aspects of the relationship—this later change clearly owes little to editorial pressure and much to Hardy's renewed engagement with the novel, as "revising" modulated into "revisioning."

This is revision on a local scale; other and larger changes more obviously affected plot and characterization. Two examples must suffice, one made early on, between the spring of 1878, when Hardy probably completed work on the serial version, and the publication of the first volume edition on 4 November the same year, and the other after an interval of seventeen years, for the Osgood, McIlvaine edition of 1895. The first concerns the episode of the misdirected guineas. In the *Belgravia*, Book Third closes with a scene deleted from the book versions, in which Venn, having won back the guineas gambled away by Christian, tells him to assure Mrs. Yeobright that the money has been "safe delivered . . . into the proper hands." Taking this to mean that both Clym and Thomasin have received their share, Mrs. Yeobright is puzzled not to hear from her son, and visits his cottage hoping for an explanation. Her opening comment to Eustacia, though "coldly" spoken, is not in itself offensive: "I was coming on business only . . . If you or my son had acknowledged the receipt of the money, it would not have been necessary for me to have come at all." Eustacia replies, truthfully, "We have received nothing"; the ensuing quarrel turns not on questions of money, but on her mortification at Mrs. Yeobright's refusal to attend the wedding. In the 1878 and all subsequent editions, however, Christian admits to Mrs. Yeobright that he has gambled away the guineas to Wildeve, including those intended for Clym; in this revised version of events, he knows nothing of Venn's intervention and can merely hope that Wildeve will have restored to Clym the fifty he is due. Mrs. Yeobright's question to Eustacia now is very different: "Will you excuse my asking this—Have you received a gift from Thomasin's husband?" This question, coming without explanation, *is* offensive, and Eustacia's anger is wholly understandable. As rewritten, the scene does much to justify Eustacia's unwillingness to come to terms with her mother-in-law, and, with fatal consequences, her reluctance to open the door to her on her second visit.

The second example concerns the relation between Wildeve and Eustacia toward the close of the novel. Wildeve's conduct during their final interview, in Book Fifth, Chapter V, is more scrupulous in 1878 than in the 1895 edition. Eustacia worries that in accepting help from him she might lay herself open to gossip. In 1878 he replies:

> "Well, there's no preventing slanderers from having their fill at any time; but as there will be no evil in it you need not be

afraid. I believe I am now a sobered man, and whatever I may feel I promise you on my word of honour never to speak to you about—what might have been. Thomasin is quite helplessly dependent on me now; and I know my duty to her quite as well as I know my duty to you as a woman unfairly treated. I will assist you without prejudice to her. What shall I assist you in?"

In 1895 this is more ambiguously worded:

"Well, there's no preventing slanderers from having their fill at any time; but you need not be afraid. Whatever I may feel I promise you on my word of honour never to speak to you about—or act upon—until you say I may. I know my duty to Thomasin quite as well as I know my duty to you as a woman unfairly treated. What shall I assist you in?"

Eustacia is correspondingly more alive to Wildeve's continued sexual interest in her in the 1895 edition. In 1878 she tells him that she needs time to consider:

"I will think of this," she said hurriedly. "Whether I can honestly make use of you as a friend—that is what I must ask myself."

In 1895 this becomes:

"I will think of this," she said hurriedly. "Whether I can honestly make use of you as a friend, or must close with as a lover—that is what I must ask myself."

The significance of these changes is underscored by others in Chapter VII, as Eustacia crouches in the rain on the heath. The 1878 text reads:

To ask Wildeve for pecuniary aid was impossible to a woman with the shadow of pride left in her: his assistance in driving her to Budmouth had become almost distasteful to her during the last few hours, and was of the nature of humiliation.

In 1895 this becomes:

To ask Wildeve for pecuniary aid without allowing him to accompany her was impossible to a woman with the shadow of pride left in her: to fly as his mistress—and she knew that he loved her—was of the nature of humiliation.

In effect, in the 1878 edition Eustacia is beaten down by the thought of leaving alone, and without money, for an uncertain future; in 1895, what defeats her is the recognition that if she leaves she will do so as Wildeve's mistress.

Whether the later version provides a clue to what Hardy had always intended, but in 1878 had not dared present to the public, or whether it reflects a change in his view of Eustacia, or of the dynamics of the novel, must remain an open question. The mere fact of such a question, however, makes it difficult to consider any text as "definite," or fixed. The 1912 text, it might be argued, rather than being definitive, should be seen as the last-produced layer in a record or palimpsest of Hardy's creative moods and decisions at different phases of his working life: as a relative newcomer to novel-writing, still, as he acknowledged, unsure of his way, and constrained by the need to write nothing that might alarm the publishers and reviewers (1878); as an experienced hand at the form, grown impatient with the demands of his audience, and emboldened by the sexual radicalism of the 1890s (1895); and as the Grand Old Man of Letters, the author of three volumes of poetry and a verse-epic, *The Dynasts*, who had long since turned his back on prose fiction (1912).

This might suggest an argument for using the first volume edition as the base text: free from the constraints of serial publication, but free too from later accretions. There are, however, countervailing arguments, not least that Hardy did not always return to his original conception in the first volume edition. In the serial version of *The Mayor of Casterbridge*, for example, Henchard and Lucetta marry on the mistaken assumption that Henchard is a widower; in the first book version, they have a nonsexual relationship; and it was not until the Osgood, McIlvaine edition that they have the irregular sexual liaison Hardy seems initially to have intended. It is at least possible, as suggested above, that a similar case might be made about the 1895 edition of *The Return of the Native*. Fortunately, unlike (say) architectural restoration, revisions to the text of a novel do not involve the destruction of its previous forms, and those who wish to consult earlier versions of Hardy's novels are able to do so. In the absence of a variorum edition, however, an editor must choose the text as it stood at one moment in time, and the decision has been taken here to use the 1912 edition, though regarding it as rather the closing than the culminating stage in the evolution of the novel. This, it is true, is not the edition the reviewers had before them in 1878; but it is the text most often cited in contemporary critical discussion, and, more important, the form in which the novel has been read, adapted, loved, and hated for the best part of a century.

There is a strong case for incorporating manuscript readings at one or two points where it seems likely that the printed text reflects compositorial errors made at an early stage and subsequently overlooked. To do so, however, would be to produce an eclectic text, one that Hardy himself never saw, and on these grounds the temptation has been resisted. These instances, and some of the more significant differences between editions, are mentioned in the notes; a fuller account of the publication and textual history of the novel is given in the essays by Andrew Nash and Simon Gatrell later in this volume. A few obvious slips, in the form of omitted speech marks or full stops, have been silently corrected.

It remains to add that the illustrations included here are from the first, serial publication, in (to give its full title) *Belgravia: An Illustrated London Magazine*, but omitted from all later editions; they are discussed in the essay by Pamela Dalziel, also included in this volume. The Map of Wessex (pp. 338–39) comes from the Macmillan Wessex edition of 1912; Hardy's sketch-map of the action of the novel (p. 4) formed the basis of the frontispiece of the 1878 volume but was not included in later editions.

A Note on the Notes

There are some 500 notes in this edition of *The Return of the Native*. About one in ten of these are glosses of dialect words, ranging from the relatively familiar, if still potentially misleading—"ballet" for ballad, "chiel" for child, "tatie" for potato—to the decidedly rare: "mollyhorning," for example, meaning idling, wasting one's time, seems to be unique to Hardy, while he himself was doubtful about the origin of "chips-in-porridge," used to denote someone or something of no significance. In the General Preface of 1912, he insisted on the accuracy of his representation of Wessex life: "things were like that in Wessex; the inhabitants lived in certain ways, engaged in certain occupations, kept alive certain customs." But ways, occupations and customs were all changing, and the local dialect along with them; one of the impulses behind Hardy's fiction was to preserve a record of a world that would soon be gone. The dialect scenes helped to anchor the story in the location he knew best, and loved most.

The reviewers of his previous novel, *The Hand of Ethelberta* (1875), had been dismissive of his knowledge of London life and urged him to keep to the rural world, or, as the *London* put it, offensively, "the world of boors" rather than "society." The dialect scenes were one way of meeting that criticism. But the suggestion that Hardy lacked formal education, made by these same reviewers, clearly rankled. He was in any case unsure about the direction he wanted to take as a novelist. In March 1876 he told the publisher George Smith that he intended to pause "for a few months, until I can learn the best line to take for the future"; around the same time he sought advice from Leslie Stephen, the editor of his two previous novels, on what to read in order to improve his writing.

Stephen replied, wisely, that he had no need to emulate anyone, but over the next year or so Hardy undertook a deliberate course of reading and note-taking, which can now be traced in *The Literary Notebooks of Thomas Hardy*, edited by Lennart Björk (1985). Twenty or more of these notes, as Björk points out, are used in *The Return of the Native*. It is possible, just, that Hardy intended his reading to lend him the cultural authority that his reviewers—for the most part London-based and Oxbridge-educated—assumed as their birthright. The effect, however, in *The Return of the Native*, is to disintegrate (say) Matthew Arnold's unitary Culture, defined as "the best that is known and thought in the world," into a series of fragments, as diverse as the marital adventures of the actress Lavinia Fenton, the animation of a brass statue by Albertus Magnus, and the appearance under bright light of the tiger-beetle. Hardy's reading included such works as Cassell's *Popular Educator*, Charles Mackay's *Memoirs of Extraordinary Popular Delusions*, and J. G. Woods's *Insects at Home*, as well as "the great writers—Shakespeare, Goethe, Scott, &c. &c" recommended by Leslie Stephen. Stephen's confidence is implicit in that "&c. &c"; but like Ethelberta in his previous novel, Clym in this, or Jude in his last, Hardy saw Culture as contested ground. It is unlikely that any reader, of his time or later, would have been fully at ease with the assortment of ideas Hardy draws upon in the novel; it would be rash to assume that he blunderingly supposed otherwise.

Other notes in this edition address more familiar cultural territory, including Hardy's numerous references to artists (among them Pheidias, Raphael, Perugino, Dürer, Antoon Sallaert, Denis Van Alsloot, and Rembrandt), and to such writers as Homer, Sappho, Vergil, Dante, Petrarch, Shakespeare, Milton, Dryden, Thomson, Gray, Wordsworth, Byron, and Keats. But here too Hardy disrupts the notion of Culture, with upper case C, by interspersing allusions to these canonical figures with others from the popular literary tradition, including ballads and songs such as "Earl Marshall," "As Down among the Meadows," and "The Foggy, Foggy Dew." It is to neither the high nor the popular tradition, however, that Clym turns for a song when he is working as a furze-cutter, but to a little-known French comic opera, *Gulistan*, with music by Nicolas-Marie Dalayrac and a libretto by Charles-Guillaume Etienne and A.-E.-X. de la Chabeaussière. Clearly such matters have a bearing on how the reader responds to Clym's aspirations to "educate" the inhabitants of Egdon.

One other cluster of allusions deserves particular notice. There are more than fifty references to or quotations from the Bible in the novel. Strikingly, in Books I and II, there is only one clear allusion to the New Testament—Eustacia's schoolgirl question whether

Pontius Pilate was "as handsome as he was frank and fair"—while the same two Books yield some twenty references to the Old Testament. Many of these are insignificant in themselves: for example, Psalm 133 is mentioned only as a means to recount the musicianship of Thomasin's long-dead father. But the cumulative effect of a series of such references, to Goliath's greaves of brass, Belshazzar's feast, the Witch of Endor, the mark of Cain, Nebuchadnezzar's dreams, and the belief systems of the ancient Chaldeans, casually mingled with others to classical literature and mythology—the overthrow of the Titans, Scylla and Charybdis, Tantalus, the Cretan labyrinth, the blinding of Oedipus—is to suggest both the extreme ancientness of Egdon Heath and its isolation from those progressive tendencies of nineteenth-century thought that Clym encounters in Paris. Conversely, after Clym's emergence as a main character, and the elaborate description of him at the opening of Book Third, references to the New Testament predominate: Clym is likened to John the Baptist by the narrator, and to St. Paul by Eustacia; he himself quotes or alludes to the epistles (Romans, Galatians, and 2 Corinthians) as well as the Sermon on the Mount, the parable of Dives and Lazarus, and even Christ's words on the Cross; he is, in later editions, thirty-three years of age when the novel ends, traditionally the age at which Christ died. Readers will draw their own inferences from this; but the shift of mood and tone, between the first two Books and the later ones, is palpable. The immediate purpose of the notes is of course to identify or elucidate passages that might otherwise be unfamiliar or unclear, but taken as a whole they suggest areas for further critical inquiry.

References to Shakespeare are to *The Complete Works of William Shakespeare*, edited by Stanley Wells and others for Oxford University Press (1988); references to the Bible are to the Authorized King James's Version of 1611. The two volumes of *The Literary Notebooks of Thomas Hardy*, edited by Lennart A. Björk (London: Macmillan, 1985), are cited as *Literary Notebooks*. The seven volumes of the *Collected Letters of Thomas Hardy*, edited by R. L. Purdy and Michael Millgate (Oxford: Clarendon Press, 1978–88), are cited as *Letters*.

The Text of
THE RETURN OF THE
NATIVE

THE

RETURN OF THE NATIVE

BY

THOMAS HARDY

AUTHOR OF

'FAR FROM THE MADDING CROWD' 'A PAIR OF BLUE EYES ETC.

' To sorrow
I bade good morrow,
And thought to leave her far away behind ;
But cheerly, cheerly,
She loves me dearly ;
She is so constant to me, and so kind.
I would deceive her,
And so leave her,
But ah ! she is so constant and so kind

IN THREE VOLUMES — VOL. I.

LONDON

SMITH, ELDER, & CO., 15 WATERLOO PLACE

1878

† Facsimile title page of the first edition, courtesy of the Rare Books Division, the New York Public Library, Astor, Lenox, and Tilden Foundations. The lines of poetry are from John Keats's *Endymion* (1818), IV.173–81.

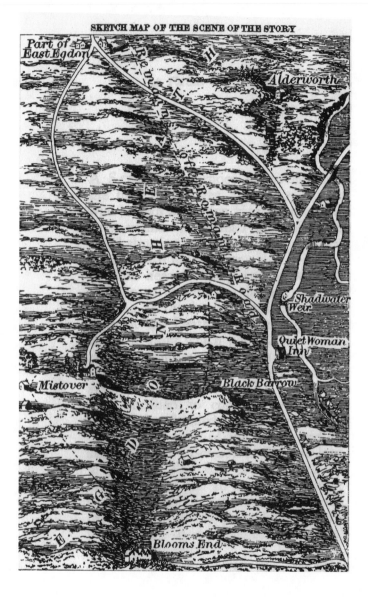

SKETCH MAP OF THE SCENE OF THE STORY

Preface

The date at which the following events are assumed to have occurred may be set down as between 1840 and 1850, when the old watering-place herein called 'Budmouth' still retained sufficient afterglow from its Georgian gaiety and prestige to lend it an absorbing attractiveness to the romantic and imaginative soul of a lonely dweller inland.

Under the general name of 'Egdon Heath,' which has been given to the sombre scene of the story, are united or typified heaths of various real names, to the number of at least a dozen; these being virtually one in character and aspect, though their original unity, or partial unity, is now somewhat disguised by intrusive strips and slices brought under the plough with varying degrees of success, or planted to woodland.

It is pleasant to dream that some spot in the extensive tract whose south-western quarter is here described, may be the heath of that traditionary King of Wessex—Lear.

July 1895.

Postscript

To prevent disappointment to searchers for scenery it should be added that though the action of the narrative is supposed to proceed in the central and most secluded part of the heaths united into one whole, as above described, certain topographical features resembling those delineated really lie on the margin of the waste, several miles to the westward of the centre. In some other respects also there has been a bringing together of scattered characteristics.

The first edition of this novel was published in three volumes in 1878.

T. H.

April 1912.

Contents

Book First. The Three Women

		PAGE
1.	A FACE ON WHICH TIME MAKES BUT LITTLE IMPRESSION	8
2.	HUMANITY APPEARS UPON THE SCENE, HAND IN HAND WITH TROUBLE	11
3.	THE CUSTOM OF THE COUNTRY	16
4.	THE HALT ON THE TURNPIKE ROAD	34
5.	PERPLEXITY AMONG HONEST PEOPLE	38
6.	THE FIGURE AGAINST THE SKY	49
7.	QUEEN OF NIGHT	60
8.	THOSE WHO ARE FOUND WHERE THERE IS SAID TO BE NOBODY	66
9.	LOVE LEADS A SHREWD MAN INTO STRATEGY	71
10.	A DESPERATE ATTEMPT AT PERSUASION	79
11.	THE DISHONESTY OF AN HONEST WOMAN	86

Book Second. The Arrival

1.	TIDINGS OF THE COMER	93
2.	THE PEOPLE AT BLOOMS-END MAKE READY	97
3.	HOW A LITTLE SOUND PRODUCED A GREAT DREAM	101
4.	EUSTACIA IS LED ON TO AN ADVENTURE	105
5.	THROUGH THE MOONLIGHT	113
6.	THE TWO STAND FACE TO FACE	118
7.	A COALITION BETWEEN BEAUTY AND ODDNESS	128
8.	FIRMNESS IS DISCOVERED IN A GENTLE HEART	135

Book Third. The Fascination

1.	'MY MIND TO ME A KINGDOM IS'	143
2.	THE NEW COURSE CAUSES DISAPPOINTMENT	147
3.	THE FIRST ACT IN A TIMEWORN DRAMA	154
4.	AN HOUR OF BLISS AND MANY HOURS OF SADNESS	166
5.	SHARP WORDS ARE SPOKEN, AND A CRISIS ENSUES	172
6.	YEOBRIGHT GOES, AND THE BREACH IS COMPLETE	178
7.	THE MORNING AND THE EVENING OF A DAY	183
8.	A NEW FORCE DISTURBS THE CURRENT	194

Book Fourth. The Closed Door

1. The Rencounter by the Pool 201
2. He is set upon by Adversities; but he sings a Song . . 206
3. She goes out to Battle against Depression . . . 215
4. Rough Coercion is employed 224
5. The Journey across the Heath 230
6. A Conjuncture, and its Result upon the
   Pedestrian 233
7. The Tragic Meeting of Two Old Friends . . . 242
8. Eustacia hears of Good Fortune, and beholds
   Evil 248

Book Fifth. The Discovery

1. 'Wherefore is Light given to him that is in Misery?' . 255
2. A Lurid Light breaks in upon a Darkened
   Understanding 261
3. Eustacia dresses herself on a Black Morning . . 269
4. The Ministrations of a Half-forgotten One . . 275
5. An Old Move inadvertently repeated . . . 280
6. Thomasin argues with her Cousin, and he writes
   a Letter 285
7. The Night of the Sixth of November . . . 290
8. Rain, Darkness, and Anxious Wanderers . . . 296
9. Sights and Sounds draw the Wanderers together . . 305

Book Sixth. Aftercourses

1. The Inevitable Movement Onward 314
2. Thomasin walks in a Green Place by the Roman
   Road 321
3. The Serious Discourse of Clym with his Cousin . 323
4. Cheerfulness again asserts itself at Blooms-End,
   and Clym finds his Vocation 328

Book First. The Three Women

A Face on Which Time Makes but Little Impression

I

A Saturday afternoon in November was approaching the time of twilight, and the vast tract of unenclosed wild known as Egdon Heath embrowned itself moment by moment. Overhead the hollow stretch of whitish cloud shutting out the sky was as a tent which had the whole heath for its floor.

The heaven being spread with this pallid screen and the earth with the darkest vegetation, their meeting-line at the horizon was clearly marked. In such contrast the heath wore the appearance of an instalment of night which had taken up its place before its astronomical hour was come: darkness had to a great extent arrived hereon, while day stood distinct in the sky. Looking upwards, a furze-cutter[1] would have been inclined to continue work; looking down, he would have decided to finish his faggot[2] and go home. The distant rims of the world and of the firmament seemed to be a division in time no less than a division in matter. The face of the heath by its mere complexion added half an hour to evening; it could in like manner retard the dawn, sadden noon, anticipate the frowning of storms scarcely generated, and intensify the opacity of a moonless midnight to a cause of shaking and dread.

In fact, precisely at this transitional point of its nightly roll into darkness the great and particular glory of the Egdon waste began, and nobody could be said to understand the heath who had not been there at such a time. It could best be felt when it could not clearly be seen, its complete effect and explanation lying in this and the succeeding hours before the next dawn: then, and only then, did it tell its true tale. The spot was, indeed, a near relation of night, and when night showed itself an apparent tendency to gravitate together could be perceived in its shades and the scene. The sombre stretch of rounds and hollows seemed to rise and meet the evening gloom in pure sympathy, the heath exhaling darkness as rapidly as the heavens precipitated it. And so the obscurity in the air and the obscurity in the land closed together in a black fraternization towards which each advanced half-way.

The place became full of a watchful intentness now; for when

---

1. Furze, also needle-furze or gorse, is a spiny evergreen shrub that can be cut, dried, and used for fuel.
2. Bundle of twigs or sticks.

other things sank brooding to sleep the heath appeared slowly to awake and listen. Every night its Titanic[3] form seemed to await something; but it had waited thus, unmoved, during so many centuries, through the crises of so many things, that it could only be imagined to await one last crisis—the final overthrow.

It was a spot which returned upon the memory of those who loved it with an aspect of peculiar and kindly congruity. Smiling champaigns[4] of flowers and fruit hardly do this, for they are permanently harmonious only with an existence of better reputation as to its issues than the present. Twilight combined with the scenery of Egdon Heath to evolve a thing majestic without severity, impressive without showiness, emphatic in its admonitions, grand in its simplicity. The qualifications which frequently invest the façade of a prison with far more dignity than is found in the façade of a palace double its size lent to this heath a sublimity in which spots renowned for beauty of the accepted kind are utterly wanting. Fair prospects wed happily with fair times; but alas, if times be not fair! Men have oftener suffered from the mockery of a place too smiling for their reason than from the oppression of surroundings oversadly tinged. Haggard Egdon appealed to a subtler and scarcer instinct, to a more recently learnt emotion, than that which responds to the sort of beauty called charming and fair.

Indeed, it is a question if the exclusive reign of this orthodox beauty is not approaching its last quarter. The new Vale of Tempe may be a gaunt waste in Thule:[5] human souls may find themselves in closer and closer harmony with external things wearing a sombreness distasteful to our race when it was young. The time seems near, if it has not actually arrived, when the chastened sublimity of a moor, a sea, or a mountain will be all of nature that is absolutely in keeping with the moods of the more thinking among mankind. And ultimately, to the commonest tourist, spots like Iceland may become what the vineyards and myrtle-gardens of South Europe are to him now; and Heidelberg and Baden be passed unheeded as he hastens from the Alps to the sand-dunes of Scheveningen.[6]

The most thorough-going ascetic could feel that he had a natural right to wander on Egdon: he was keeping within the line of legitimate indulgence when he laid himself open to influences such as

---

3. Colossal. In Greek mythology, the Titans were the giant offspring of Uranus (the sky) and Ge (the earth); they deposed Uranus but were themselves overthrown and imprisoned by Zeus, who thus became king of the gods.
4. Open fields.
5. The Vale of Tempe, a valley in Thessaly in Greece, was cited by classical writers as an ideal of natural beauty; Thule was the name given by ancient geographers to a barren land six days' sail north of Britain, thought to be the most northerly habitable region.
6. Heidelberg and Baden-Baden are popular beauty-spots in Germany; Scheveningen is a bleak seaside resort in the Netherlands, characterized by sandhills and coarse grass. The Hardys traveled through Germany and the Netherlands in May 1876.

these. Colours and beauties so far subdued were, at least, the birthright of all. Only in summer days of highest feather did its mood touch the level of gaiety. Intensity was more usually reached by way of the solemn than by way of the brilliant, and such a sort of intensity was often arrived at during winter darkness, tempests, and mists. Then Egdon was aroused to reciprocity; for the storm was its lover, and the wind its friend. Then it became the home of strange phantoms; and it was found to be the hitherto unrecognized original of those wild regions of obscurity which are vaguely felt to be compassing us about in midnight dreams of flight and disaster, and are never thought of after the dream till revived by scenes like this.

It was at present a place perfectly accordant with man's nature—neither ghastly, hateful, nor ugly: neither commonplace, unmeaning, nor tame; but, like man, slighted and enduring; and withal singularly colossal and mysterious in its swarthy monotony. As with some persons who have long lived apart, solitude seemed to look out of its countenance. It had a lonely face, suggesting tragical possibilities.

This obscure, obsolete, superseded country figures in Domesday.[7] Its condition is recorded therein as that of heathy, furzy, briary wilderness—'Bruaria.' Then follows the length and breadth in leagues[8]; and, though some uncertainty exists as to the exact extent of this ancient lineal measure, it appears from the figures that the area of Egdon down to the present day has but little diminished. 'Turbaria[9] Bruaria'—the right of cutting heath-turf—occurs in charters relating to the district. 'Overgrown with heth and mosse,' says Leland[1] of the same dark sweep of country.

Here at least were intelligible facts regarding landscape—far-reaching proofs productive of genuine satisfaction. The untameable, Ishmaelitish[2] thing that Egdon now was it always had been. Civilization was its enemy; and ever since the beginning of vegetation its soil had worn the same antique brown dress, the natural and invariable garment of the particular formation. In its venerable one coat lay a certain vein of satire on human vanity in clothes. A person on a heath in raiment of modern cut and colours has more or less an anomalous look. We seem to want the oldest and simplest human clothing where the clothing of the earth is so primitive.

To recline on a stump of thorn in the central valley of Egdon, be-

---

7. The Domesday Book of 1086 surveyed the extent, value, and ownership of all the land of England.
8. A league is an old measure of distance, of about three miles (or 5000 meters).
9. Peat-bog, turf (medieval Latin).
1. John Leland (1503?–1552), poet, cleric, and historian, commissioned by Henry VIII to research English records and antiquities.
2. Outcast (Ishmael, Abraham's son by the bondservant Hagar, was banished after Abraham's wife Sarah gave birth to Isaac; see Genesis 21.9–21).

tween afternoon and night, as now, where the eye could reach
nothing of the world outside the summits and shoulders of heathland which filled the whole circumference of its glance, and to
know that everything around and underneath had been from prehistoric times as unaltered as the stars overhead, gave ballast to the
mind adrift on change, and harassed by the irrepressible New. The
great inviolate place had an ancient permanence which the sea
cannot claim. Who can say of a particular sea that it is old? Dis-
tilled by the sun, kneaded by the moon, it is renewed in a year, in a
day, or in an hour. The sea changed, the fields changed, the rivers,
the villages, and the people changed, yet Egdon remained. Those
surfaces were neither so steep as to be destructible by weather, nor
so flat as to be the victims of floods and deposits. With the exception of an aged highway, and a still more aged barrow[3] presently to
be referred to—themselves almost crystallized to natural products
by long continuance—even the trifling irregularities were not
caused by pickaxe, plough, or spade, but remained as the very
finger-touches of the last geological change.

The above-mentioned highway traversed the lower levels of the
heath, from one horizon to another. In many portions of its course
it overlaid an old vicinal way,[4] which branched from the great Western road of the Romans, the Via Iceniana, or Ikenild Street,[5] hard
by. On the evening under consideration it would have been noticed
that, though the gloom had increased sufficiently to confuse the
minor features of the heath, the white surface of the road remained
almost as clear as ever.

Humanity Appears upon the Scene, Hand in Hand with Trouble

II

Along the road walked an old man. He was white-headed as a
mountain, bowed in the shoulders, and faded in general aspect. He
wore a glazed hat, an ancient boat-cloak,[1] and shoes; his brass buttons bearing an anchor upon their face. In his hand was a silver-
headed walking-stick, which he used as a veritable third leg,
perseveringly dotting the ground with its point at every few inches'
interval. One would have said that he had been, in his day, a naval
officer of some sort or other.

Before him stretched the long, laborious road, dry, empty, and
white. It was quite open to the heath on each side, and bisected

3. Prehistoric mound of earth (sometimes of stones) over a grave.
4. By-road.
5. Ancient route between the eastern and south-western parts of England, the basis later of
   the Roman road usually known as Icknield Way.
1. Large cloak worn by naval officers.

that vast dark surface like the parting-line on a head of black hair, diminishing and bending away on the furthest horizon.

The old man frequently stretched his eyes ahead to gaze over the tract that he had yet to traverse. At length he discerned, a long distance in front of him, a moving spot, which appeared to be a vehicle, and it proved to be going the same way as that in which he himself was journeying. It was the single atom of life that the scene contained, and it only served to render the general loneliness more evident. Its rate of advance was slow, and the old man gained upon it sensibly.

When he drew nearer he perceived it to be a spring van,[2] ordinary in shape, but singular in colour, this being a lurid red. The driver walked beside it; and, like his van, he was completely red. One dye of that tincture covered his clothes, the cap upon his head, his boots, his face, and his hands. He was not temporarily overlaid with the colour: it permeated him.

The old man knew the meaning of this. The traveller with the cart was a reddleman—a person whose vocation it was to supply farmers with redding[3] for their sheep. He was one of a class rapidly becoming extinct in Wessex, filling at present in the rural world the place which, during the last century, the dodo occupied in the world of animals. He is a curious, interesting, and nearly perished link between obsolete forms of life and those which generally prevail.

The decayed officer, by degrees, came up alongside his fellow-wayfarer, and wished him good evening. The reddleman turned his head, and replied in sad and occupied tones. He was young, and his face, if not exactly handsome, approached so near to handsome that nobody would have contradicted an assertion that it really was so in its natural colour. His eye, which glared so strangely through his stain, was in itself attractive—keen as that of a bird of prey, and blue as autumn mist. He had neither whisker nor moustache, which allowed the soft curves of the lower part of his face to be apparent. His lips were thin, and though, as it seemed, compressed by thought, there was a pleasant twitch at their corners now and then. He was clothed throughout in a tight-fitting suit of corduroy, excellent in quality, not much worn, and well-chosen for its purpose; but deprived of its original colour by his trade. It showed to advantage the good shape of his figure. A certain well-to-do air about the man suggested that he was not poor for his degree. The natural query of an observer would have been, Why should such a promising being as this have hidden his prepossessing exterior by adopting that singular occupation?

2. Light, covered wagon, resting on springs.
3. Red ocher used to mark sheep; also known as "reddle."

After replying to the old man's greeting he showed no inclination to continue in talk, although they still walked side by side, for the elder traveller seemed to desire company. There were no sounds but that of the booming wind upon the stretch of tawny herbage around them, the crackling wheels, the tread of the men, and the footsteps of the two shaggy ponies which drew the van. They were small, hardy animals, of a breed between Galloway and Exmoor, and were known as 'heath-croppers' here.

Now, as they thus pursued their way, the reddleman occasionally left his companion's side, and, stepping behind the van, looked into its interior through a small window. The look was always anxious. He would then return to the old man, who made another remark about the state of the country and so on, to which the reddleman again abstractedly replied, and then again they would lapse into silence. The silence conveyed to neither any sense of awkwardness; in these lonely places wayfarers, after a first greeting, frequently plod on for miles without speech; contiguity amounts to a tacit conversation where, otherwise than in cities, such contiguity can be put an end to on the merest inclination, and where not to put an end to it is intercourse in itself.

Possibly these two might not have spoken again till their parting, had it not been for the reddleman's visits to his van. When he returned from his fifth time of looking in the old man said, 'You have something inside there besides your load?'

'Yes.'

'Somebody who wants looking after?'

'Yes.'

Not long after this a faint cry sounded from the interior. The reddleman hastened to the back, looked in, and came away again.

'You have a child there, my man?'

'No, sir, I have a woman.'

'The deuce you have![4] Why did she cry out?'

'Oh, she has fallen asleep, and not being used to travelling, she's uneasy, and keeps dreaming.'

'A young woman?'

'Yes, a young woman.'

'That would have interested me forty years ago. Perhaps she's your wife?'

'My wife!' said the other bitterly. 'She's above mating with such as I. But there's no reason why I should tell you about that.'

'That's true. And there's no reason why you should not. What harm can I do to you or to her?'

The reddleman looked in the old man's face. 'Well, sir,' he said at

4. The devil you have!

last, 'I knew her before to-day, though perhaps it would have been better if I had not. But she's nothing to me, and I am nothing to her; and she wouldn't have been in my van if any better carriage had been there to take her.'

'Where, may I ask?'

'At Anglebury.'

'I know the town well. What was she doing there?'

'Oh, not much—to gossip about. However, she's tired to death now, and not at all well, and that's what makes her so restless. She dropped off into a nap about an hour ago, and 'twill do her good.'

'A nice-looking girl, no doubt?'

'You would say so.'

The other traveller turned his eyes with interest towards the van window, and, without withdrawing them, said, 'I presume I might look in upon her?'

'No,' said the reddleman abruptly. 'It is getting too dark for you to see much of her; and, more than that, I have no right to allow you. Thank God she sleeps so well: I hope she won't wake till she's home.'

'Who is she? One of the neighbourhood?'

' 'Tis no matter who, excuse me.'

'It is not that girl of Blooms-End, who has been talked about more or less lately? If so, I know her; and I can guess what has happened.'

' 'Tis no matter. . . . Now, sir, I am sorry to say that we shall soon have to part company. My ponies are tired, and I have further to go, and I am going to rest them under this bank for an hour.'

The elder traveller nodded his head indifferently, and the reddleman turned his horses and van in upon the turf, saying, 'Good night.' The old man replied, and proceeded on his way as before.

The reddleman watched his form as it diminished to a speck on the road and became absorbed in the thickening films of night. He then took some hay from a truss which was slung up under the van, and, throwing a portion of it in front of the horses, made a pad of the rest, which he laid on the ground beside his vehicle. Upon this he sat down, leaning his back against the wheel. From the interior a low soft breathing came to his ear. It appeared to satisfy him, and he musingly surveyed the scene, as if considering the next step that he should take.

To do things musingly, and by small degrees, seemed, indeed, to be a duty in the Egdon valleys at this transitional hour, for there was that in the condition of the heath itself which resembled protracted and halting dubiousness. It was the quality of the repose appertaining to the scene. This was not the repose of actual stagnation, but the apparent repose of incredible slowness. A condition of healthy life so nearly resembling the torpor of death is a noticeable thing of its sort; to exhibit the inertness of the desert, and at the same time to be exercising powers akin to those of the meadow, and even of the forest, awakened in those who thought of it the attentiveness usually engendered by understatement and reserve.

The scene before the reddleman's eyes was a gradual series of ascents from the level of the road backward into the heart of the heath. It embraced hillocks, pits, ridges, acclivities, one behind the other, till all was finished by a high hill cutting against the still light sky. The traveller's eye hovered about these things for a time, and finally settled upon one noteworthy object up there. It was a barrow. This bossy[5] projection of earth above its natural level occupied the loftiest ground of the loneliest height that the heath contained. Although from the vale it appeared but as a wart on an Atlantean[6] brow, its actual bulk was great. It formed the pole and axis of this heathery world.

As the resting man looked at the barrow he became aware that its summit, hitherto the highest object in the whole prospect round, was surmounted by something higher. It rose from the semiglobular mound like a spike from a helmet. The first instinct of an imaginative stranger might have been to suppose it the person of one of the Celts[7] who built the barrow, so far had all of modern date withdrawn from the scene. It seemed a sort of last man among them, musing for a moment before dropping into eternal night with the rest of his race.

There the form stood, motionless as the hill beneath. Above the plain rose the hill, above the hill rose the barrow, and above the barrow rose the figure. Above the figure was nothing that could be mapped elsewhere than on a celestial globe.

Such a perfect, delicate, and necessary finish did the figure give to the dark pile of hills that it seemed to be the only obvious justification of their outline. Without it, there was the dome without the lantern; with it the architectural demands of the mass were satisfied. The scene was strangely homogeneous, in that the vale, the upland, the barrow, and the figure above it amounted only to unity. Looking at this or that member of the group was not observing a complete thing, but a fraction of a thing.

The form was so much like an organic part of the entire motionless structure that to see it move would have impressed the mind as a strange phenomenon. Immobility being the chief characteristic of that whole which the person formed portion of, the discontinuance of immobility in any quarter suggested confusion.

5. Rounded.
6. Atlas, one of the defeated Titans, was condemned by Zeus to support the heavens on his head and shoulders.
7. The ancient peoples of western Europe, including the Britons.

Yet that is what happened. The figure perceptibly gave up its fixity, shifted a step or two, and turned round. As if alarmed, it descended on the right side of the barrow, with the glide of a water-drop down a bud, and then vanished. The movement had been sufficient to show more clearly the characteristics of the figure, and that it was a woman's.

The reason of her sudden displacement now appeared. With her dropping out of sight on the right side, a new-comer, bearing a burden, protruded into the sky on the left side, ascended the tumulus,[8] and deposited the burden on the top. A second followed, then a third, a fourth, a fifth, and ultimately the whole barrow was peopled with burdened figures.

The only intelligible meaning in this sky-backed pantomime of silhouettes was that the woman had no relation to the forms who had taken her place, was sedulously avoiding these, and had come thither for another object than theirs. The imagination of the observer clung by preference to that vanished, solitary figure, as to something more interesting, more important, more likely to have a history worth knowing than these new-comers, and unconsciously regarded them as intruders. But they remained, and established themselves; and the lonely person who hitherto had been queen of the solitude did not at present seem likely to return.

The Custom of the Country

III

Had a looker-on been posted in the immediate vicinity of the barrow, he would have learned that these persons were boys and men of the neighbouring hamlets. Each, as he ascended the barrow, had been heavily laden with furze-faggots, carried upon the shoulder by means of a long stake sharpened at each end for impaling them easily—two in front and two behind. They came from a part of the heath a quarter of a mile to the rear, where furze almost exclusively prevailed as a product.

Every individual was so involved in furze by his method of carrying the faggots that he appeared like a bush on legs till he had thrown them down. The party had marched in trail, like a travelling flock of sheep; that is to say, the strongest first, the weak and young behind.

The loads were all laid together, and a pyramid of furze thirty feet in circumference now occupied the crown of the tumulus, which was known as Rainbarrow for many miles round. Some made themselves busy with matches, and in selecting the driest tufts of furze,

8. Barrow or burial-mound.

others in loosening the bramble bonds which held the faggots together. Others, again, while this was in progress, lifted their eyes and swept the vast expanse of country commanded by their position, now lying nearly obliterated by shade. In the valleys of the heath nothing save its own wild face was visible at any time of day; but this spot commanded a horizon enclosing a tract of far extent, and in many cases lying beyond the heath country. None of its features could be seen now, but the whole made itself felt as a vague stretch of remoteness.

While the men and lads were building the pile, a change took place in the mass of shade which denoted the distant landscape. Red suns and tufts of fire one by one began to arise, flecking the whole country round. They were the bonfires of other parishes and hamlets that were engaged in the same sort of commemoration. Some were distant, and stood in a dense atmosphere, so that bundles of pale strawlike beams radiated around them in the shape of a fan. Some were large and near, glowing scarlet-red from the shade, like wounds in a black hide. Some were Mænades,[1] with winy faces and blown hair. These tinctured the silent bosom of the clouds above them and lit up their ephemeral caves, which seemed thenceforth to become scalding caldrons. Perhaps as many as thirty bonfires could be counted within the whole bounds of the district; and as the hour may be told on a clock-face when the figures themselves are invisible, so did the men recognize the locality of each fire by its angle and direction, though nothing of the scenery could be viewed.

The first tall flame from Rainbarrow sprang into the sky, attracting all eyes that had been fixed on the distant conflagrations back to their own attempt in the same kind. The cheerful blaze streaked the inner surface of the human circle—now increased by other stragglers, male and female—with its own gold livery, and even overlaid the dark turf around with a lively luminousness, which softened off into obscurity where the barrow rounded downwards out of sight. It showed the barrow to be the segment of a globe, as perfect as on the day when it was thrown up, even the little ditch remaining from which the earth was dug. Not a plough had ever disturbed a grain of that stubborn soil. In the heath's barrenness to the farmer lay its fertility to the historian. There had been no obliteration, because there had been no tending.

It seemed as if the bonfire-makers were standing in some radiant upper storey of the world, detached from and independent of the dark stretches below. The heath down there was now a vast abyss, and no longer a continuation of what they stood on; for their eyes,

---

1. The priestesses of Bacchus, god of wine, usually pictured in frenzy with streaming hair.

adapted to the blaze, could see nothing of the deeps beyond its in-fluence. Occasionally, it is true, a more vigorous flare than usual from their faggots sent darting lights like aides-de-camp[2] down the inclines to some distant bush, pool, or patch of white sand, kin-dling these to replies of the same colour, till all was lost in darkness again. Then the whole black phenomenon beneath represented Limbo as viewed from the brink by the sublime Florentine[3] in his vision, and the muttered articulations of the wind in the hollows were as complaints and petitions from the 'souls of mighty worth' suspended therein.

It was as if these men and boys had suddenly dived into past ages, and fetched therefrom an hour and deed which had before been familiar with this spot. The ashes of the original British pyre which blazed from that summit lay fresh and undisturbed in the barrow beneath their tread. The flames from funeral piles long ago kindled there had shone down upon the lowlands as these were shining now. Festival fires to Thor and Woden[4] had followed on the same ground and duly had their day. Indeed, it is pretty well known that such blazes as this the heathmen were now enjoying are rather the lineal descendants from jumbled Druidical[5] rites and Saxon ceremonies than the invention of popular feeling about Gunpowder Plot.[6]

Moreover to light a fire is the instinctive and resistant act of man when, at the winter ingress, the curfew is sounded throughout Nature. It indicates a spontaneous, Promethean[7] rebelliousness against the fiat that this recurrent season shall bring foul times, cold darkness, misery and death. Black chaos comes, and the fet-tered gods of the earth say, Let there be light.[8]

The brilliant lights and sooty shades which struggled upon the skin and clothes of the persons standing round caused their lineaments and general contours to be drawn with Dureresque[9] vigour and dash. Yet the permanent moral expression of each face it was impossible to

2. Officers who assist at ceremonial functions (military).
3. In the *Inferno*, the first part of his *Divine Comedy*, the Florence-born poet Dante Alighieri (1265–1321) represents Limbo as the first circle of hell, where virtuous pagans and unbaptized children dwell after death. The "souls of mighty worth" come from the translation by H. F. Cary (rev. ed., 1844), Canto iv, lines 41–2.
4. Thor was the Norse god of thunder; Woden is the Saxon name for Odin, the Norse god of poetry, war, and the underworld.
5. Druids were the priests of pre-Roman Britain; their rites were supposedly conducted in oak groves, and involved human sacrifice.
6. The attempt by Catholic conspirators to blow up Parliament in 1605, commemorated each November 5 by the burning of an effigy of Guy Fawkes, one of those caught and ex-ecuted.
7. Prometheus was the Titan who stole fire from heaven to save the human race; he was punished by being chained to a rock, where a vulture preyed on his liver. He often ap-pears in nineteenth-century art, notably in P. B. Shelley's *Prometheus Unbound* (1820), as a type or figure of human aspiration.
8. God's command at the beginning of creation; see Genesis 1.3.
9. Dramatic or grotesque, like the work of the German artist Albrecht Dürer (1471–1528).

discover, for as the nimble flames towered, nodded, and swooped through the surrounding air, the blots of shade and flakes of light upon the countenances of the group changed shape and position endlessly. All was unstable; quivering as leaves, evanescent as lightning. Shadowy eyesockets, deep as those of a death's head, suddenly turned into pits of lustre: a lantern-jaw was cavernous, then it was shining; wrinkles were emphasized to ravines, or obliterated entirely by a changed ray. Nostrils were dark wells; sinews in old necks were gilt mouldings; things with no particular polish on them were glazed; bright objects, such as the tip of a furze-hook one of the men carried, were as glass; eyeballs glowed like little lanterns. Those whom Nature had depicted as merely quaint became grotesque, the grotesque became preternatural; for all was in extremity.

Hence it may be that the face of an old man, who had like others been called to the heights by the rising flames, was not really the mere nose and chin that it appeared to be, but an appreciable quantity of human countenance. He stood complacently sunning himself in the heat. With a speäker, or stake, he tossed the outlying scraps of fuel into the conflagration, looking at the midst of the pile, occasionally lifting his eyes to measure the height of the flame, or to follow the great sparks which rose with it and sailed away into darkness. The beaming sight, and the penetrating warmth, seemed to breed in him a cumulative cheerfulness, which soon amounted to delight. With his stick in his hand he began to jig a private minuet, a bunch of copper seals shining and swinging like a pendulum from under his waistcoat: he also began to sing, in the voice of a bee up a flue[1]—

> 'The king´ call'd down´ his nó-bles all´,
>   By one´, by two´, by three´;
> Earl Mar´-shal, I'll´ go shrive´ the queen´,
>   And thou´ shalt wend´ with me´.
>
> 'A boon´, a boon´, quoth Earl´ Mar-shal´,
>   And fell´ on his bend´-ded knee´,
> That what´-so-e'er´ the queen´ shall say´,
>   No harm´ there-of´ may be´.'[2]

Want of breath prevented a continuance of the song; and the breakdown attracted the attention of a firm-standing man of middle age, who kept each corner of his crescent-shaped mouth rigorously drawn back into his cheek, as if to do away with any suspicion of mirthfulness which might erroneously have attached to him.

1. Chimney.
2. From the traditional ballad "Queen Eleanor's Confession," also known as "Earl Marshall"; Cantle sings further verses in the chapter.

'A fair stave,[3] Grandfer Cantle; but I am afeard 'tis too much for the mouldy weasand[4] of such a old man as you,' he said to the wrinkled reveller. 'Dostn't wish th' wast three sixes again, Grandfer, as you was when you first learnt to sing it?'

'Hey?' said Grandfer Cantle, stopping in his dance.

'Dostn't wish wast young again, I say? There's a hole in thy poor bellows nowadays seemingly.'

'But there's good art in me? If I couldn't make a little wind go a long ways I should seem no younger than the most aged man, should I, Timothy?'

'And how about the new-married folks down there at the Quiet Woman Inn?' the other inquired, pointing towards a dim light in the direction of the distant highway, but considerably apart from where the reddleman was at that moment resting. 'What's the rights of the matter about 'em? You ought to know, being an understanding man.'

'But a little rakish, hey? I own to it. Master Cantle is that, or he's nothing. Yet 'tis a gay fault, neighbour Fairway, that age will cure.'

'I heard that they were coming home to-night. By this time they must have come. What besides?'

'The next thing is for us to go and wish 'em joy, I suppose?'

'Well, no.'

'No? Now, I thought we must. I must, or 'twould be very unlike me—the first in every spree that's going!

> "Do thou´ put on´ a fri´-ar's coat´,
>   And I'll´ put on´ a-no´-ther,
> And we´ will to´ Queen Ele´anor go´,
>   Like Fri´ar and´ his bro´ther."

I met Mis'ess Yeobright, the young bride's aunt, last night, and she told me that her son Clym was coming home a' Christmas. Wonderful clever, 'a[5] believe—ah, I should like to have all that's under that young man's hair. Well, then, I spoke to her in my well-known merry way, and she said, "O that what's shaped so venerable should talk like a fool!"—that's what she said to me. I don't care for her, be jowned[6] if I do, and so I told her. "Be jowned if I care for 'ee," I said. I had her there—hey?'

'I rather think she had you,' said Fairway.

'No,' said Grandfer Cantle, his countenance slightly flagging. ' 'Tisn't so bad as that with me?'

'Seemingly 'tis; however, is it because of the wedding that Clym

3. Verse or stanza.
4. Windpipe, throat (dialect).
5. I (dialect).
6. Mild oath (dialect: literally, "drowned").

is coming home a' Christmas—to make a new arrangement because his mother is now left in the house alone?'

'Yes, yes—that's it. But, Timothy, hearken to me,' said the Grandfer earnestly. 'Though known as such a joker, I be an understanding man if you catch me serious, and I am serious now. I can tell 'ee lots about the married couple. Yes, this morning at six o'clock they went up the country to do the job, and neither vell[7] nor mark have been seen of 'em since, though I reckon that this afternoon has brought 'em home again, man and woman—wife, that is. Isn't it spoke like a man, Timothy, and wasn't Mis'ess Yeobright wrong about me?'

'Yes, it will do. I didn't know the two had walked together since last fall, when her aunt forbad the banns.[8] How long has this new set-to been in mangling[9] then? Do you know, Humphrey?'

'Yes, how long?' said Grandfer Cantle smartly, likewise turning to Humphrey. 'I ask that question.'

'Ever since her aunt altered her mind, and said she might hae the man after all,' replied Humphrey, without removing his eyes from the fire. He was a somewhat solemn young fellow, and carried the hook and leather gloves of a furze-cutter, his legs, by reason of that occupation, being sheathed in bulging leggings as stiff as the Philistine's greaves of brass.[1] 'That's why they went away to be married, I count. You see, after kicking up such a nunny-watch[2] and forbidding the banns 'twould have made Mis'ess Yeobright seem foolish-like to have a banging[3] wedding in the same parish all as if she'd never gainsaid it.'

'Exactly—seem foolish-like; and that's very bad for the poor things that be so, though I only guess as much, to be sure,' said Grandfer Cantle, still strenuously preserving a sensible bearing and mien.

'Ah, well, I was at church that day,' said Fairway, 'which was a very curious thing to happen.'

'If 'twasn't my name's Simple,' said the Grandfer emphatically. 'I ha'n't been there to-year;[4] and now the winter is a-coming on I won't say I shall.'

'I ha'n't been these three years,' said Humphrey; 'for I'm so dead sleepy of a Sunday; and 'tis so terrible far to get there; and when you do get there 'tis such a mortal poor chance that you'll be chose

---

7. Trace or sign; literally, skin or hide (dialect).
8. The banns or proclamation of a forthcoming marriage are read in church so that anyone with an objection may voice it.
9. Going on (a set-to here is a situation or state of affairs).
1. Goliath, the Philistine giant slain by David, wore greaves or leggings of brass; see 1 Samuel 17.6.
2. Disturbance (dialect).
3. Impressive, first-class (dialect).
4. This year (dialect).

for up above, when so many bain't, that I bide at home and don't go at all.'

'I not only happened to be there,' said Fairway, with a fresh collection of emphasis, 'but I was sitting in the same pew as Mis'ess Yeobright. And though you may not see it as such, it fairly made my blood run cold to hear her. Yes, it is a curious thing; but it made my blood run cold, for I was close at her elbow.' The speaker looked round upon the bystanders, now drawing closer to hear him, with his lips gathered tighter than ever in the rigorousness of his descriptive moderation.

' 'Tis a serious job to have things happen to 'ee there,' said a woman behind.

' "Ye are to declare it," was the parson's words,' Fairway continued. 'And then up stood a woman at my side—a-touching of me. "Well, be damned if there isn't Mis'ess Yeobright a-standing up," I said to myself. Yes, neighbours, though I was in the temple of prayer that's what I said. 'Tis against my conscience to curse and swear in company, and I hope any woman here will overlook it. Still what I did say I did say, and 'twould be a lie if I didn't own it.'

'So 'twould, neighbour Fairway.'

' "Be damned if there isn't Mis'ess Yeobright a-standing up," I said,' the narrator repeated, giving out the bad word with the same passionless severity of face as before, which proved how entirely necessity and not gusto had to do with the iteration. 'And the next thing I heard was, "I forbid the banns," from her. "I'll speak to you after the service," said the parson, in quite a homely way—yes, turning all at once into a common man no holier than you or I. Ah, her face was pale! Maybe you can call to mind that monument in Weatherbury church—the cross-legged soldier that have had his arm knocked away by the school-children? Well, he would about have matched that woman's face, when she said, "I forbid the banns." '

The audience cleared their throats and tossed a few stalks into the fire, not because these deeds were urgent, but to give themselves time to weigh the moral of the story.

'I'm sure when I heard they'd been forbid I felt as glad as if anybody had gied me sixpence,' said an earnest voice—that of Olly Dowden, a woman who lived by making heath brooms, or besoms. Her nature was to be civil to enemies as well as to friends, and grateful to all the world for letting her remain alive.

'And now the maid have married him just the same,' said Humphrey.

'After that Mis'ess Yeobright came round and was quite agreeable,' Fairway resumed, with an unheeding air, to show that his words were no appendage to Humphrey's, but the result of independent reflection.

'Supposing they were ashamed, I don't see why they shouldn't have done it here-right,' said a widespread woman whose stays[5] creaked like shoes whenever she stooped or turned. ' 'Tis well to call the neighbours together and to hae a good racket[6] once now and then; and it may as well be when there's a wedding as at tide-times.[7] I don't care for close ways.'

'Ah, now, you'd hardly believe it, but I don't care for gay weddings,' said Timothy Fairway, his eyes again travelling round. 'I hardly blame Thomasin Yeobright and neighbour Wildeve for doing it quiet, if I must own it. A wedding at home means five and six-handed reels[8] by the hour; and they do a man's legs no good when he's over forty.'

'True. Once at the woman's house you can hardly say nay to being one in a jig, knowing all the time that you be expected to make yourself worth your victuals.'

'You be bound to dance at Christmas because 'tis the time o' year; you must dance at weddings because 'tis the time o' life. At christenings folk will even smuggle in a reel or two, if 'tis no further on than the first or second chiel.[9] And this is not naming the songs you've got to sing. . . . For my part I like a good hearty funeral as well as anything. You've as splendid victuals and drink as at other parties, and even better. And it don't wear your legs to stumps in talking over a poor fellow's ways as it do to stand up in hornpipes.'[1]

'Nine folks out of ten would own 'twas going too far to dance then, I suppose?' suggested Grandfer Cantle.

' 'Tis the only sort of party a staid man can feel safe at after the mug have been round a few times.'

'Well, I can't understand a quiet lady-like little body like Tamsin Yeobright caring to be married in such a mean way,' said Susan Nunsuch, the wide woman, who preferred the original subject. ' 'Tis worse than the poorest do. And I shouldn't have cared about the man, though some may say he's good-looking.'

'To give him his due he's a clever, learned fellow in his way— a'most as clever as Clym Yeobright used to be. He was brought up to better things than keeping the Quiet Woman. An engineer— that's what the man was, as we know; but he threw away his chance, and so 'a took a public-house to live. His learning was no use to him at all.'

'Very often the case,' said Olly, the besom-maker. 'And yet how people do strive after it and get it! The class of folk that couldn't

5. Corset, typically stiffened with strips of whalebone.
6. Party (dialect).
7. Religious festivals and holidays, such as Christmas.
8. Popular country dances for two or more couples.
9. Child (dialect).
1. A lively dance, performed as a solo.

use to make a round O to save their bones[2] from the pit can write their names now without a sputter of the pen, oftentimes without a single blot: what do I say?—why, almost without a desk to lean their stomachs and elbows upon.'

'True: 'tis amazing what a polish the world have been brought to,' said Humphrey.

'Why, afore I went a soldier in the Bang-up Locals[3] (as we was called), in the year four,' chimed in Grandfer Cantle brightly, 'I didn't know no more what the world was like than the commonest man among ye. And now, jown it all, I won't say what I bain't fit for, hey?'

'Couldst sign the book, no doubt,' said Fairway, 'if wast young enough to join hands with a woman again, like Wildeve and Mis'ess Tamsin, which is more than Humph there could do, for he follows his father in learning. Ah, Humph, well I can mind when I was married how I zid thy father's mark staring me in the face as I went to put down my name. He and your mother were the couple married just afore we were, and there stood thy father's cross with arms stretched out like a great banging scarecrow. What a terrible black cross that was—thy father's very likeness in en! To save my soul I couldn't help laughing when I zid[4] en, though all the time I was as hot as dog-days,[5] what with the marrying, and what with the woman a-hanging to me, and what with Jack Changley and a lot more chaps grinning at me through church window. But the next moment a strawmote[6] would have knocked me down, for I called to mind that if thy father and mother had had high words once, they'd been at it twenty times since they'd been man and wife, and I zid myself as the next poor stunpoll[7] to get into the same mess. . . . Ah—well, what a day 'twas!'

'Wildeve is older than Tamsin Yeobright by a good-few summers. A pretty maid too she is. A young woman with a home must be a fool to tear her smock[8] for a man like that.'

The speaker, a peat or turf-cutter, who had newly joined the group, carried across his shoulder the singular heart-shaped spade of large dimensions used in that species of labour; and its well-whetted edge gleamed like a silver bow in the beams of the fire.

'A hundred maidens would have had him if he'd asked 'em,' said the wide woman.

---

2. So in all editions; the manuscript here reads "souls."
3. Bang-up means first-rate; the Locals were the Dorset Yeomanry, a volunteer force raised in 1794 to meet the threat of war against France and called to readiness a number of times, especially in 1804 ("the year four").
4. Saw (dialect).
5. The hottest period of the summer.
6. Stalk of straw (dialect).
7. Blockhead, fool (dialect).
8. Give up her unmarried life (a smock is a woman's slip or chemise, so there is a mildly vulgar sense to the phrase).

'Didst ever know a man that no woman would marry?'

'Didst ever know a man, neighbour, that no woman at all would marry?' inquired Humphrey.

'I never did,' said the turf-cutter.

'Nor I,' said another.

'Nor I,' said Grandfer Cantle.

'Well, now, I did once,' said Timothy Fairway, adding more firmness to one of his legs. 'I did know of such a man. But only once, mind.' He gave his throat a thorough rake round, as if it were the duty of every person not to be mistaken through thickness of voice. 'Yes, I knew of such a man,' he said.

'And what ghastly gallicrow[9] might the poor fellow have been like, Master Fairway?' asked the turf-cutter.

'Well, 'a was neither a deaf man, nor a dumb man, nor a blind man. What 'a was I don't say.'

'Is he known in these parts?' said Olly Dowden.

'Hardly,' said Timothy; 'but I name no name. . . . Come, keep the fire up there, youngsters.'

'Whatever is Christian Cantle's teeth a-chattering for?' said a boy from amid the smoke and shades on the other side of the blaze. 'Be ye a-cold, Christian?'

A thin jibbering voice was heard to reply, 'No, not at all.'

'Come forward, Christian, and show yourself. I didn't know you were here,' said Fairway, with a humane look across towards that quarter.

9. Scarecrow (dialect).

Thus requested, a faltering man, with reedy hair, no shoulders, and a great quantity of wrist and ankle beyond his clothes, advanced a step or two by his own will, and was pushed by the will of others half a dozen steps more. He was Grandfer Cantle's youngest son.

'What be ye quaking for, Christian?' said the turf-cutter kindly.

'I'm the man.'

'What man?'

'The man no woman will marry.'

'The deuce you be!' said Timothy Fairway, enlarging his gaze to cover Christian's whole surface and a great deal more; Grandfer Cantle meanwhile staring as a hen stares at the duck she has hatched.

'Yes, I be he; and it makes me afeard,' said Christian. 'D'ye think 'twill hurt me? I shall always say I don't care, and swear to it, though I do care all the while.'

'Well, be damned if this isn't the queerest start ever I know'd,' said Mr. Fairway. 'I didn't mean you at all. There's another in the country, then! Why did ye reveal yer misfortune, Christian?'

''Twas to be if 'twas, I suppose. I can't help it, can I?' He turned upon them his painfully circular eyes, surrounded by concentric lines like targets.

'No, that's true. But 'tis a melancholy thing, and my blood ran cold when you spoke, for I felt there were two poor fellows where I had thought only one. 'Tis a sad thing for ye, Christian. How'st know the women won't hae thee?'

'I've asked 'em.'

'Sure I should never have thought you had the face. Well, and what did the last one say to ye? Nothing that can't be got over, perhaps, after all?'

' "Get out of my sight, you slack-twisted,[1] slim-looking maphrotight[2] fool," was the woman's words to me.'

'Not encouraging, I own,' said Fairway. ' "Get out of my sight, you slack-twisted, slim-looking maphrotight fool," is rather a hard way of saying No. But even that might be overcome by time and patience, so as to let a few grey hairs show themselves in the hussy's head. How old be you, Christian?'

'Thirty-one last tatie-digging,[3] Mister Fairway.'

'Not a boy—not a boy. Still there's hope yet.'

'That's my age by baptism, because that's put down in the great book of the Judgment[4] that they keep in church vestry; but mother told me I was born some time afore I was christened.'

1. Spineless, ineffectual (dialect).
2. Lacking virility (dialect or corrupt form of hermaphrodite).
3. Potato digging.
4. The register of baptisms.

'Ah!'

'But she couldn't tell when, to save her life, except that there was no moon.'

'No moon: that's bad. Hey, neighbours, that's bad for him!'

'Yes, 'tis bad,' said Grandfer Cantle, shaking his head.

'Mother know'd 'twas no moon, for she asked another woman that had an almanac, as she did whenever a boy was born to her, because of the saying, "No moon, no man," which made her afeard every man-child she had. Do ye really think it serious, Mister Fairway, that there was no moon?'

'Yes; "No moon, no man." 'Tis one of the truest sayings ever spit out. The boy never comes to anything that's born at new moon. A bad job for thee, Christian, that you should have showed your nose then of all days in the month.'

'I suppose the moon was terrible full when you were born?' said Christian, with a look of hopeless admiration at Fairway.

'Well, 'a was not new,' Mr. Fairway replied, with a disinterested gaze.

'I'd sooner go without drink at Lammas-tide[5] than be a man of no moon,' continued Christian, in the same shattered recitative. ' 'Tis said I be only the rames[6] of a man, and no good for my race at all; and I suppose that's the cause o't.'

'Ay,' said Grandfer Cantle, somewhat subdued in spirit; 'and yet his mother cried for scores of hours when 'a was a boy, for fear he should outgrow hisself and go for a soldier.'

'Well, there's many just as bad as he,' said Fairway. 'Wethers[7] must live their time as well as other sheep, poor soul.'

'So perhaps I shall rub on? Ought I to be afeard o' nights, Master Fairway?'

'You'll have to lie alone all your life; and 'tis not to married couples but to single sleepers that a ghost shows himself when 'a do come. One has been seen lately, too. A very strange one.'

'No—don't talk about it if 'tis agreeable of ye not to! 'Twill make my skin crawl when I think of it in bed alone. But you will—ah, you will, I know, Timothy; and I shall dream all night o't! A very strange one? What sort of a spirit did ye mean when ye said, a very strange one, Timothy?—no, no—don't tell me.'

'I don't half believe in spirits myself. But I think it ghostly enough—what I was told. 'Twas a little boy that zid it.'

'What was it like?—no, don't—'

'A red one. Yes, most ghosts be white; but this is as if it had been dipped in blood.'

---

5. August 1, celebrated in the early English church as a harvest festival.
6. Skeleton (dialect).
7. Castrated rams (and so unable to mate).

Christian drew a deep breath without letting it expand his body, and Humphrey said, 'Where has it been seen?'

'Not exactly here; but in this same heth. But 'tisn't a thing to talk about. What do ye say,' continued Fairway in brisker tones, and turning upon them as if the idea had not been Grandfer Cantle's—'what do you say to giving the new man and wife a bit of a song to-night afore we go to bed—being their wedding-day? When folks are just married 'tis as well to look glad o't, since looking sorry won't unjoin 'em. I am no drinker, as we know, but when the womenfolk and youngsters have gone home we can drop down across to the Quiet Woman, and strike up a ballet[8] in front of the married folks' door. 'Twill please the young wife, and that's what I should like to do, for many's the skinful I've had at her hands when she lived with her aunt at Blooms-End.'

'Hey? And so we will!' said Grandfer Cantle, turning so briskly that his copper seals swung extravagantly. 'I'm as dry as a kex[9] with biding up here in the wind, and I haven't seen the colour of drink since nammet-time[1] to-day. 'Tis said that the last brew at the Woman is very pretty drinking. And, neighbours, if we should be a little late in the finishing, why, to-morrow's Sunday, and we can sleep it off?'

'Grandfer Cantle! you take things very careless for an old man,' said the wide woman.

'I take things careless; I do—too careless to please the women! Klk! I'll sing the "Jovial Crew,"[2] or any other song, when a weak old man would cry his eyes out. Jown it; I am up for anything.

> "The king' look'd o'-ver his left' shoul-der',
>   And a grim' look look'-ed hee',
> Earl Mar'-shal, he said', but for' my oath'
>   Or hang'-ed thou' shouldst bee'." '

'Well, that's what we'll do,' said Fairway. 'We'll give 'em a song, an' it please the Lord. What's the good of Thomasin's cousin Clym a-coming home after the deed's done? He should have come afore, if so be he wanted to stop it, and marry her himself.'

'Perhaps he's coming to bide with his mother a little time, as she must feel lonely now the maid's gone.'

'Now, 'tis very odd, but I never feel lonely—no, not at all,' said Grandfer Cantle. 'I am as brave in the night-time as a' admiral!'

The bonfire was by this time beginning to sink low, for the fuel had not been of that substantial sort which can support a blaze

8. Ballad, popular song (dialect).
9. Dry hollow stem of a plant (dialect).
1. Lunch-time ("nammet" is a dialect form of noon-meat, the midday meal).
2. A popular drinking song, also known as "Joan's Ale," though what Cantle goes on to sing is another verse of "Earl Marshall."

long. Most of the other fires within the wide horizon were also dwindling weak. Attentive observation of their brightness, colour, and length of existence would have revealed the quality of the material burnt; and through that, to some extent the natural produce of the district in which each bonfire was situate. The clear, kingly effulgence that had characterized the majority expressed a heath and furze country like their own, which in one direction extended an unlimited number of miles: the rapid flares and extinctions at other points of the compass showed the lightest of fuel—straw, beanstalks, and the usual waste from arable land. The most enduring of all—steady unaltering eyes like planets—signified wood, such as hazel-branches, thorn-faggots, and stout billets.[3] Fires of the last-mentioned materials were rare, and, though comparatively small in magnitude beside the transient blazes, now began to get the best of them by mere long-continuance. The great ones had perished, but these remained. They occupied the remotest visible positions—sky-backed summits rising out of rich coppice and plantation districts to the north, where the soil was different, and heath foreign and strange.

Save one; and this was the nearest of any, the moon of the whole shining throng. It lay in a direction precisely opposite to that of the little window in the vale below. Its nearness was such that, notwithstanding its actual smallness, its glow infinitely transcended theirs.

This quiet eye had attracted attention from time to time; and when their own fire had become sunken and dim it attracted more; some even of the wood fires more recently lighted had reached their decline, but no change was perceptible here.

'To be sure, how near that fire is!' said Fairway. 'Seemingly, I can see a fellow of some sort walking round it. Little and good must be said of that fire, surely.'

'I can throw a stone there,' said the boy.

'And so can I!' said Grandfer Cantle.

'No, no, you can't, my sonnies. That fire is not much less than a mile off, for all that 'a seems so near.'

' 'Tis in the heath, but not furze,' said the turf-cutter.

' 'Tis cleft-wood, that's what 'tis,' said Timothy Fairway. 'Nothing would burn like that except clean timber. And 'tis on the knap[4] afore the old captain's house at Mistover. Such a queer mortal as that man is! To have a little fire inside your own bank and ditch, that nobody else may enjoy it or come anigh it! And what a zany an old chap must be, to light a bonfire when there's no youngsters to please.'

---

3. Billets, or cleft-wood (see below) are logs cut for firewood.
4. Knoll, small hill.

'Cap'n Vye has been for a long walk to-day, and is quite tired out,' said Grandfer Cantle, 'so 'tisn't likely to be he.'

'And he would hardly afford good fuel like that,' said the wide woman.

'Then it must be his grand-daughter,' said Fairway. 'Not that a body of her age can want a fire much.'

'She is very strange in her ways, living up there by herself, and such things please her,' said Susan.

'She's a well-favoured maid enough,' said Humphrey the furze-cutter; 'especially when she's got one of her dandy[5] gowns on.'

'That's true,' said Fairway. 'Well, let her bonfire burn an't will. Ours is well-nigh out by the look o't.'

'How dark 'tis now the fire's gone down!' said Christian Cantle, looking behind him with his hare eyes. 'Don't ye think we'd better get home-along, neighbours? The heth isn't haunted, I know; but we'd better get home. . . . Ah, what was that?'

'Only the wind,' said the turf-cutter.

'I don't think Fifth-of-Novembers ought to be kept up by night except in towns. It should be by day in outstep, ill-accounted[6] places like this!'

'Nonsense, Christian. Lift up your spirits like a man! Susy, dear, you and I will have a jig—hey, my honey?—before 'tis quite too dark to see how well-favoured you be still, though so many summers have passed since your husband, a son of a witch, snapped you up from me.'

This was addressed to Susan Nunsuch; and the next circumstance of which the beholders were conscious was a vision of the matron's broad form whisking off towards the space whereon the fire had been kindled. She was lifted bodily by Mr. Fairway's arm, which had been flung round her waist before she had become aware of his intention. The site of the fire was now merely a circle of ashes flecked with red embers and sparks, the furze having burnt completely away. Once within the circle he whirled her round and round in a dance. She was a woman noisily constructed; in addition to her enclosing framework of whalebone and lath, she wore pattens[7] summer and winter, in wet weather and in dry, to preserve her boots from wear; and when Fairway began to jump about with her, the clicking of the pattens, the creaking of the stays, and her screams of surprise, formed a very audible concert.

'I'll crack thy numskull[8] for thee, you mandy[9] chap!' said Mrs.

5. Fine, smart.
6. Remote, isolated (dialect); overlooked, not much thought of.
7. Overshoes, often with wooden soles.
8. A fool, or blockhead; here, the fool's actual head.
9. Cheeky (dialect).

Nunsuch, as she helplessly danced round with him, her feet playing like drumsticks among the sparks. 'My ankles were all in a fever before, from walking through that prickly furze, and now you must make 'em worse with these vlankers!'[1]

The vagary of Timothy Fairway was infectious. The turf-cutter seized old Olly Dowden, and, somewhat more gently, poussetted[2] with her likewise. The young men were not slow to imitate the example of their elders, and seized the maids; Grandfer Cantle and his stick jigged in the form of a three-legged object among the rest; and in half a minute all that could be seen on Rainbarrow was a whirling of dark shapes amid a boiling confusion of sparks, which leapt around the dancers as high as their waists. The chief noises were women's shrill cries, men's laughter, Susan's stays and pattens, Olly Dowden's 'heu-heu-heu!' and the strumming of the wind upon the furze-bushes, which formed a kind of tune to the demoniac measure they trod. Christian alone stood aloof, uneasily rocking himself as he murmured. 'They ought not to do it—how the vlankers do fly! 'tis tempting the Wicked one, 'tis.'

'What was that?' said one of the lads, stopping.

'Ah—where?' said Christian, hastily closing up to the rest.

The dancers all lessened their speed.

' 'T was behind you, Christian, that I heard it—down there.'

'Yes—'tis behind me!' Christian said. 'Matthew, Mark, Luke, and John, bless the bed that I lie on; four angels guard——'

'Hold your tongue. What is it?' said Fairway.

'Hoi-i-i-i!' cried a voice from the darkness.

'Halloo-o-o-o!' said Fairway.

'Is there any cart-track up across here to Mis'ess Yeobright's, of Blooms-End?' came to them in the same voice, as a long, slim, indistinct figure approached the barrow.

'Ought we not to run home as hard as we can, neighbours, as 'tis getting late?' said Christian. 'Not run away from one another, you know; run close together, I mean.'

'Scrape up a few stray locks of furze, and make a blaze, so that we can see who the man is,' said Fairway.

When the flame arose it revealed a young man in tight raiment, and red from top to toe. 'Is there a track across here to Mis'ess Yeobright's house?' he repeated.

'Ay—keep along the path down there.'

'I mean a way two horses and a van can travel over?'

'Well, yes; you can get up the vale below here with time. The track is rough, but if you've got a light your horses may pick along wi' care. Have ye brought your cart far up, neighbour reddleman?'

1. Sparks (dialect).
2. Danced round and round.

'I've left it in the bottom, about half a mile back. I stepped on in front to make sure of the way, as 'tis night-time, and I han't been here for so long.'

'Oh, well, you can get up,' said Fairway. 'What a turn it did give me when I saw him!' he added to the whole group, the reddleman included. 'Lord's sake, I thought, whatever fiery mommet[3] is this come to trouble us? No slight to your looks, reddleman, for ye bain't bad-looking in the groundwork, though the finish is queer. My meaning is just to say how curious I felt. I half thought 'twas the devil or the red ghost the boy told of.'

'It gied me a turn likewise,' said Susan Nunsuch, 'for I had a dream last night of a death's head.'

'Don't ye talk o't no more,' said Christian. 'If he had a handkerchief over his head he'd look for all the world like the Devil in the picture of the Temptation.'

'Well, thank you for telling me,' said the young reddleman, smiling faintly. 'And good night t'ye all.'

He withdrew from their sight down the barrow.

'I fancy I've seen that young man's face before,' said Humphrey. 'But where, or how, or what his name is, I don't know.'

The reddleman had not been gone more than a few minutes when another person approached the partially revived bonfire. It proved to be a well-known and respected widow of the neighbourhood, of a standing which can only be expressed by the word genteel. Her face, encompassed by the blackness of the receding heath, showed whitely, and without half-lights, like a cameo.

She was a woman of middle-age, with well-formed features of the type usually found where perspicacity is the chief quality enthroned within. At moments she seemed to be regarding issues from a Nebo[4] denied to others around. She had something of an estranged mien: the solitude exhaled from the heath was concentrated in this face that had risen from it. The air with which she looked at the heathmen betokened a certain unconcern at their presence, or at what might be their opinions of her for walking in that lonely spot at such an hour, thus indirectly implying that in some respect or other they were not up to her level. The explanation lay in the fact that though her husband had been a small farmer she herself was a curate's daughter, who had once dreamt of doing better things.

Persons with any weight of character carry, like planets, their atmospheres along with them in their orbits; and the matron who entered now upon the scene could, and usually did, bring her own

---

3. Puppet or effigy (dialect).
4. Mount Nebo, also known as Pisgah, from which just before his death Moses was allowed to see, but not to enter, the land God had promised to the Jews; see Deuteronomy 34.1–5.

tone into a company. Her normal manner among the heathfolk had that reticence which results from the consciousness of superior communicative power. But the effect of coming into society and light after lonely wandering in darkness is a sociability in the comer above its usual pitch, expressed in the features even more than in the words.

'Why, 'tis Mis'ess Yeobright,' said Fairway. 'Mis'ess Yeobright, not ten minutes ago a man was here asking for you—a reddleman.'

'What did he want?' said she.

'He didn't tell us.'

'Something to sell, I suppose; what it can be I am at a loss to understand.'

'I am glad to hear that your son Mr. Clym is coming home at Christmas, ma'am,' said Sam, the turf-cutter. 'What a dog he used to be for bonfires!'

'Yes. I believe he is coming,' she said.

'He must be a fine fellow by this time,' said Fairway.

'He is a man now,' she replied quietly.

''Tis very lonesome for 'ee in the heth to-night, mis'ess,' said Christian, coming from the seclusion he had hitherto maintained. 'Mind you don't get lost. Egdon Heth is a bad place to get lost in, and the winds do huffle[5] queerer to-night than ever I heard 'em afore. Them that know Egdon best have been pixy-led[6] here at times.'

'Is that you, Christian?' said Mrs. Yeobright. 'What made you hide away from me?'

''Twas that I didn't know you in this light, mis'ess; and being a man of the mournfullest make, I was scared a little, that's all. Oftentimes if you could see how terrible down I get in my mind, 'twould make 'ee quite nervous for fear I should die by my hand.'

'You don't take after your father,' said Mrs. Yeobright, looking towards the fire, where Grandfer Cantle, with some want of originality, was dancing by himself among the sparks, as the others had done before.

'Now, Granfer,' said Timothy Fairway, 'we are ashamed of ye. A reverent old patriarch man as you be—seventy if a day—to go hornpiping like that by yourself!'

'A harrowing[7] old man, Mis'ess Yeobright,' said Christian despondingly. 'I wouldn't live with him a week, so playward as he is, if I could get away.'

' 'Twould be more seemly in ye to stand still and welcome Mis'ess

5. Blow, gust (dialect).
6. Led astray by pixies or fairies.
7. Exasperating.

Yeobright, and you the venerablest here, Grandfer Cantle,' said the besom-woman.

'Faith, and so it would,' said the reveller, checking himself repentantly. 'I've such a bad memory, Mis'ess Yeobright, that I forget how I'm looked up to by the rest of 'em. My spirits must be wonderful good, you'll say? But not always. 'Tis a weight upon a man to be looked up to as commander, and I often feel it.'

'I am sorry to stop the talk,' said Mrs. Yeobright. 'But I must be leaving you now. I was passing down the Anglebury Road, towards my niece's new home, who is returning to-night with her husband; and seeing the bonfire and hearing Olly's voice among the rest I came up here to learn what was going on. I should like her to walk with me, as her way is mine.'

'Ay, sure, ma'am, I'm just thinking of moving,' said Olly.

'Why, you'll be safe to meet the reddleman that I told ye of,' said Fairway. 'He's only gone back to get his van. We heard that your niece and her husband were coming straight home as soon as they were married, and we are going down there shortly, to give 'em a song o' welcome.'

'Thank you indeed,' said Mrs. Yeobright.

'But we shall take a shorter cut through the furze than you can go with long clothes; so we won't trouble you to wait.'

'Very well—are you ready, Olly?'

'Yes, ma'am. And there's a light shining from your niece's window, see. It will help to keep us in the path.'

She indicated the faint light at the bottom of the valley which Fairway had pointed out; and the two women descended the tumulus.

The Halt on the Turnpike Road

IV

Down, downward they went, and yet further down—their descent at each step seeming to outmeasure their advance. Their skirts were scratched noisily by the furze, their shoulders brushed by the ferns, which, though dead and dry, stood erect as when alive, no sufficient winter weather having as yet arrived to beat them down. Their Tartarean[1] situation might by some have been called an imprudent one for two unattended women. But these shaggy recesses were at all seasons a familiar surrounding to Olly and Mrs. Yeobright; and the addition of darkness lends no frightfulness to the face of a friend.

---

1. Hellish, infernal (Tartarus was the underworld abyss where Zeus imprisoned the defeated Titans).

'And so Tamsin has married him at last,' said Olly, when the incline had become so much less steep that their footsteps no longer required undivided attention.

Mrs. Yeobright answered slowly, 'Yes: at last.'

'How you will miss her—living with 'ee as a daughter, as she always have.'

'I do miss her.'

Olly, though without the tact to perceive when remarks were untimely, was saved by her very simplicity from rendering them offensive. Questions that would have been resented in others she could ask with impunity. This accounted for Mrs. Yeobright's acquiescence in the revival of an evidently sore subject.

'I was quite strook to hear you'd agreed to it, ma'am, that I was,' continued the besom-maker.

'You were not more struck by it than I should have been last year this time, Olly. There are a good many sides to that wedding. I could not tell you all of them, even if I tried.'

'I felt myself that he was hardly solid-going enough to mate with your family. Keeping an inn—what is it? But 'a's clever, that's true, and they say he was an engineering gentleman once, but has come down by being too outwardly given.'

'I saw that, upon the whole, it would be better she should marry where she wished.'

'Poor little thing, her feelings got the better of her, no doubt. 'Tis nature. Well, they may call him what they will—he've several acres of heth-ground broke up here, besides the public-house, and the heth-croppers, and his manners be quite like a gentleman's. And what's done cannot be undone.'

'It cannot,' said Mrs. Yeobright. 'See, here's the waggon-track at last. Now we shall get along better.'

The wedding subject was no further dwelt upon; and soon a faint diverging path was reached, where they parted company, Olly first begging her companion to remind Mr. Wildeve that he had not sent her sick husband the bottle of wine promised on the occasion of his marriage. The besom-maker turned to the left towards her own house, behind a spur of the hill, and Mrs. Yeobright followed the straight track, which further on joined the highway by the Quiet Woman Inn, whither she supposed her niece to have returned with Wildeve from their wedding at Anglebury that day.

She first reached Wildeve's Patch, as it was called, a plot of land redeemed from the heath, and after long and laborious years brought into cultivation. The man who had discovered that it could be tilled died of the labour: the man who succeeded him in possession ruined himself in fertilizing it. Wildeve came like Amerigo

Vespucci,[2] and received the honours due to those who had gone before.

When Mrs. Yeobright had drawn near to the inn, and was about to enter, she saw a horse and vehicle some two hundred yards beyond it, coming towards her, a man walking alongside with a lantern in his hand. It was soon evident that this was the reddleman who had inquired for her. Instead of entering the inn at once, she walked by it and towards the van.

The conveyance came close, and the man was about to pass her with little notice, when she turned to him and said, 'I think you have been inquiring for me? I am Mrs. Yeobright of Blooms-End.'

The reddleman started, and held up his finger. He stopped the horses, and beckoned to her to withdraw with him a few yards aside, which she did, wondering.

'You don't know me, ma'am, I suppose?' he said.

'I do not,' said she. 'Why, yes, I do! You are young Venn—your father was a dairyman somewhere here?'

'Yes; and I knew your niece, Miss Tamsin, a little. I have something bad to tell you.'

'About her—no? She has just come home, I believe, with her husband. They arranged to return this afternoon—to the inn beyond here?'

'She's not there.'

'How do you know?'

'Because she's here. She's in my van,' he added slowly.

'What new trouble has come?' murmured Mrs. Yeobright, putting her hand over her eyes.

'I can't explain much, ma'am. All I know is that, as I was going along the road this morning, about a mile out of Anglebury, I heard something trotting after me like a doe, and looking round there she was, white as death itself. "O, Diggory Venn!" she said, "I thought 'twas you: will you help me? I am in trouble."'

'How did she know your Christian name?' said Mrs. Yeobright doubtingly.

'I had met her as a lad before I went away in this trade. She asked then if she might ride, and then down she fell in a faint. I picked her up and put her in, and there she has been ever since. She has cried a good deal, but she has hardly spoke; all she has told me being that she was to have been married this morning. I tried to get her to eat something, but she couldn't; and at last she fell asleep.'

'Let me see her at once,' said Mrs. Yeobright, hastening towards the van.

---

2. America takes its name from the Italian navigator Amerigo Vespucci (1451–1512), even though he was not the first to discover it.

The reddleman followed with the lantern, and; stepping up first, assisted Mrs. Yeobright to mount beside him. On the door being opened she perceived at the end of the van an extemporized couch, around which was hung apparently all the drapery that the reddleman possessed, to keep the occupant of the little couch from contact with the red materials of his trade. A young girl lay thereon, covered with a cloak. She was asleep, and the light of the lantern fell upon her features.

A fair, sweet, and honest country face was revealed, reposing in a nest of wavy chestnut hair. It was between pretty and beautiful. Though her eyes were closed, one could easily imagine the light necessarily shining in them as the culmination of the luminous workmanship around. The groundwork of the face was hopefulness; but over it now lay like a foreign substance a film of anxiety and grief. The grief had been there so shortly as to have abstracted nothing of the bloom, and had as yet but given a dignity to what it might eventually undermine. The scarlet of her lips had not had time to abate, and just now it appeared still more intense by the absence of the neighbouring and more transient colour of her cheek. The lips frequently parted, with a murmur of words. She seemed to belong rightly to a madrigal—to require viewing through rhyme and harmony.

One thing at least was obvious: she was not made to be looked at thus. The reddleman had appeared conscious of as much, and, while Mrs. Yeobright looked in upon her, he cast his eyes aside with a delicacy which well became him. The sleeper apparently thought so too, for the next moment she opened her own.

The lips then parted with something of anticipation, something more of doubt; and her several thoughts and fractions of thoughts, as signalled by the changes on her face, were exhibited by the light to the utmost nicety. An ingenuous, transparent life was disclosed; as if the flow of her existence could be seen passing within her. She understood the scene in a moment.

'O yes, it is I, aunt,' she cried. 'I know how frightened you are, and how you cannot believe it; but all the same, it is I who have come home like this!'

'Tamsin, Tamsin!' said Mrs. Yeobright, stooping over the young woman and kissing her. 'O my dear girl!'

Thomasin was now on the verge of a sob; but by an unexpected self-command she uttered no sound. With a gentle panting breath she sat upright.

'I did not expect to see you in this state, any more than you me,' she went on quickly. 'Where am I, aunt?'

'Nearly home, my dear. In Egdon Bottom. What dreadful thing is it?'

'I'll tell you in a moment. So near, are we? Then I will get out and walk. I want to go home by the path.'

'But this kind man who has done so much will, I am sure, take you right on to my house?' said the aunt, turning to the reddleman, who had withdrawn from the front of the van on the awakening of the girl, and stood in the road.

'Why should you think it necessary to ask me? I will, of course,' said he.

'He is indeed kind,' murmured Thomasin. 'I was once acquainted with him, aunt, and when I saw him to-day I thought I should pre- fer his van to any conveyance of a stranger. But I'll walk now. Red- dleman, stop the horses, please.'

The man regarded her with tender reluctance, but stopped them.

Aunt and niece then descended from the van, Mrs. Yeobright say- ing to its owner, 'I quite recognize you now. What made you change from the nice business your father left you?'

'Well, I did,' he said, and looked at Thomasin, who blushed a lit- tle. 'Then you'll not be wanting me any more to-night, ma'am?'

Mrs. Yeobright glanced around at the dark sky, at the hills, at the perishing bonfires, and at the lighted window of the inn they had neared. 'I think not,' she said, 'since Thomasin wishes to walk. We can soon run up the path and reach home: we know it well.'

And after a few further words they parted, the reddleman moving onwards with his van, and the two women remaining standing in the road. As soon as the vehicle and its driver had withdrawn so far as to be beyond all possible reach of her voice, Mrs. Yeobright turned to her niece.

'Now, Thomasin,' she said sternly, 'what's the meaning of this dis- graceful performance?'

Perplexity among Honest People

V

Thomasin looked as if quite overcome by her aunt's change of man- ner. 'It means just what it seems to mean: I am—not married,' she replied faintly. 'Excuse me—for humiliating you, aunt, by this mishap: I am sorry for it. But I cannot help it.'

'Me? Think of yourself first.'

'It was nobody's fault. When we got there the parson wouldn't marry us because of some trifling irregularity in the licence.'

'What irregularity?'

'I don't know. Mr. Wildeve can explain. I did not think when I went away this morning that I should come back like this.' It being dark, Thomasin allowed her emotion to escape her by the silent way of tears, which could roll down her cheek unseen.

'I could almost say that it serves you right—if I did not feel that you don't deserve it,' continued Mrs. Yeobright, who, possessing two distinct moods in close contiguity, a gentle mood and an angry, flew from one to the other without the least warning. 'Remember, Thomasin, this business was none of my seeking; from the very first, when you began to feel foolish about that man, I warned you he would not make you happy. I felt it so strongly that I did what I would never have believed myself capable of doing—stood up in the church, and made myself the public talk for weeks. But having once consented, I don't submit to these fancies without good reason. Marry him you must after this.'

'Do you think I wish to do otherwise for one moment?' said Thomasin, with a heavy sigh. 'I know how wrong it was of me to love him, but don't pain me by talking like that, aunt! You would not have had me stay there with him, would you?—and your house is the only home I have to return to. He says we can be married in a day or two.'

'I wish he had never seen you.'

'Very well; then I will be the miserablest woman in the world, and not let him see me again. No, I won't have him!'

'It is too late to speak so. Come with me. I am going to the inn to see if he has returned. Of course I shall get to the bottom of this story at once. Mr. Wildeve must not suppose he can play tricks upon me, or any belonging to me.'

'It was not that. The licence[1] was wrong, and he couldn't get another the same day. He will tell you in a moment how it was, if he comes.'

'Why didn't he bring you back?'

'That was me!' again sobbed Thomasin. 'When I found we could not be married I didn't like to come back with him, and I was very ill. Then I saw Diggory Venn, and was glad to get him to take me home. I cannot explain it any better, and you must be angry with me if you will.'

'I shall see about that,' said Mrs. Yeobright; and they turned towards the inn, known in the neighbourhood as the Quiet Woman, the sign of which represented the figure of a matron carrying her head under her arm, beneath which gruesome design was written the couplet so well known to frequenters of the inn:—

SINCE THE WOMAN'S QUIET
LET NO MAN BREED A RIOT.[2]

1. Document giving permission to marry, in lieu of the proclamation of banns.
2. The inn which really bore this sign and legend stood some miles to the northwest of the present scene, wherein the house more immediately referred to is now no longer an inn;

The front of the house was towards the heath and Rainbarrow, whose dark shape seemed to threaten it from the sky. Upon the door was a neglected brass plate, bearing the unexpected inscription, 'Mr. Wildeve, Engineer'—a useless yet cherished relic from the time when he had been started in that profession in an office at Budmouth by those who had hoped much from him, and had been disappointed. The garden was at the back, and behind this ran a still deep stream, forming the margin of the heath in that direction, meadow-land appearing beyond the stream.

But the thick obscurity permitted only sky-lines to be visible of any scene at present. The water at the back of the house could be heard, idly spinning whirlpools in its creep between the rows of dry feather-headed reeds which formed a stockade along each bank. Their presence was denoted by sounds as of a congregation praying humbly, produced by their rubbing against each other in the slow wind.

The window, whence the candlelight had shone up the vale to the eyes of the bonfire group, was uncurtained, but the sill lay too high for a pedestrian on the outside to look over it into the room. A vast shadow, in which could be dimly traced portions of a masculine contour, blotted half the ceiling.

'He seems to be at home,' said Mrs. Yeobright.

'Must I come in, too, aunt?' asked Thomasin faintly. 'I suppose not; it would be wrong.'

'You must come, certainly—to confront him, so that he may make no false representations to me. We shall not be five minutes in the house, and then we'll walk home.'

Entering the open passage she tapped at the door of the private parlour, unfastened it, and looked in.

The back and shoulders of a man came between Mrs. Yeobright's eyes and the fire. Wildeve, whose form it was, immediately turned, arose, and advanced to meet his visitors.

He was quite a young man, and of the two properties, form and motion, the latter first attracted the eye in him. The grace of his movement was singular: it was the pantomimic expression of a lady-killing career. Next came into notice the more material qualities, among which was a profuse crop of hair impending over the top of his face, lending to his forehead the high-cornered outline of an early Gothic shield; and a neck which was smooth and round as a cylinder. The lower half of his figure was of light build. Altogether he was one in whom no man would have seen anything to admire, and in whom no woman would have seen anything to dislike.

---

and the surroundings are much changed. But another inn, some of whose features are also embodied in this description, the *Red Lion* at Winfrith, still remains as a haven for the wayfarer (1912). [Hardy's note.]

He discerned the young girl's form in the passage, and said, 'Thomasin, then, has reached home. How could you leave me in that way, darling?' And turning to Mrs. Yeobright: 'It was useless to argue with her. She would go, and go alone.'

'But what's the meaning of it all?' demanded Mrs. Yeobright haughtily.

'Take a seat,' said Wildeve, placing chairs for the two women. 'Well, it was a very stupid mistake, but such mistakes will happen. The licence was useless at Anglebury. It was made out for Budmouth, but as I didn't read it I wasn't aware of that.'

'But you had been staying at Anglebury?'

'No. I had been at Budmouth—till two days ago—and that was where I had intended to take her; but when I came to fetch her we decided upon Anglebury, forgetting that a new licence would be necessary. There was not time to get to Budmouth afterwards.'

'I think you are very much to blame,' said Mrs. Yeobright.

'It was quite my fault we chose Anglebury,' Thomasin pleaded. 'I proposed it because I was not known there.'

'I know so well that I am to blame that you need not remind me of it,' replied Wildeve shortly.

'Such things don't happen for nothing,' said the aunt. 'It is a great slight to me and my family; and when it gets known there will be a very unpleasant time for us. How can she look her friends in the face to-morrow? It is a very great injury, and one I cannot easily forgive. It may even reflect on her character.'

'Nonsense,' said Wildeve.

Thomasin's large eyes had flown from the face of one to the face of the other during this discussion, and she now said anxiously. 'Will you allow me, aunt, to talk it over alone with Damon for five minutes? Will you, Damon?'

'Certainly, dear,' said Wildeve, 'if your aunt will excuse us.' He led her into an adjoining room, leaving Mrs. Yeobright by the fire.

As soon as they were alone, and the door closed, Thomasin said, turning up her pale, tearful face to him, 'It is killing me, this, Damon! I did not mean to part from you in anger at Anglebury this morning; but I was frightened, and hardly knew what I said. I've not let aunt know how much I have suffered to-day; and it is so hard to command my face and voice, and to smile as if it were a slight thing to me; but I try to do so, that she may not be still more indignant with you. I know you could not help it, dear, whatever aunt may think.'

'She is very unpleasant.'

'Yes,' Thomasin murmured, 'and I suppose I seem so now. . . . Damon, what do you mean to do about me?'

'Do about you?'

'Yes. Those who don't like you whisper things which at moments make me doubt you. We mean to marry, I suppose, don't we?'

'Of course we do. We have only to go to Budmouth on Monday, and we may marry at once.'

'Then do let us go!—O Damon, what you make me say!' She hid her face in her handkerchief. 'Here am I asking you to marry me; when by rights you ought to be on your knees imploring me, your cruel mistress, not to refuse you, and saying it would break your heart if I did. I used to think it would be pretty and sweet like that; but how different!'

'Yes, real life is never at all like that.'

'But I don't care personally if it never takes place,' she added with a little dignity; 'no, I can live without you. It is aunt I think of. She is so proud, and thinks so much of her family respectability, that she will be cut down with mortification if this story should get abroad before—it is done. My cousin Clym, too, will be much wounded.'

'Then he will be very unreasonable. In fact, you are all rather un-reasonable.'

Thomasin coloured a little, and not with love. But whatever the momentary feeling which caused that flush in her, it went as it came, and she humbly said, 'I never mean to be, if I can help it. I merely feel that you have my aunt to some extent in your power at last.'

'As a matter of justice it is almost due to me,' said Wildeve. 'Think what I have gone through to win her consent; the insult that it is to any man to have the banns forbidden: the double insult to a man unlucky enough to be cursed with sensitiveness, and blue demons, and Heaven knows what, as I am. I can never forget those banns. A harsher man would rejoice now in the power I have of turning upon your aunt by going no further in the business.'

She looked wistfully at him with her sorrowful eyes as he said those words, and her aspect showed that more than one person in the room could deplore the possession of sensitiveness. Seeing that she was really suffering he seemed disturbed and added, 'This is merely a reflection, you know. I have not the least intention to re-fuse to complete the marriage, Tamsie mine—I could not bear it.'

'You could not, I know!' said the fair girl, brightening. 'You, who cannot bear the sight of pain in even an insect, or any disagreeable sound, or unpleasant smell even, will not long cause pain to me and mine.'

'I will not, if I can help it.'

'Your hand upon it, Damon.'

He carelessly gave her his hand.

'Ah, by my crown, what's that?' he said suddenly.

There fell upon their ears the sound of numerous voices singing in front of the house. Among these, two made themselves prominent by their peculiarity: one was a very strong bass, the other a wheezy thin piping. Thomasin recognized them as belonging to Timothy Fairway and Grandfer Cantle respectively.

'What does it mean—it is not skimmity-riding,[3] I hope?' she said, with a frightened gaze at Wildeve.

'Of course not; no, it is that the heath-folk have come to sing to us a welcome. This is intolerable!' He began pacing about, the men outside singing cheerily—

> 'He told´ her that she´ was the joy´ of his life´,
> And if´ she'd con-sent´ he would make´ her his wife´;
> She could´ not refuse´ him; to church´ so they went´,
> Young Will was forgot´, and young Sue´ was content´;
> And then´ was she kiss'd´ and set down´ on his knee´,
> No man´ in the world´ was so lov´-ing as he´!'[4]

Mrs. Yeobright burst in from the outer room. 'Thomasin, Thomasin!' she said, looking indignantly at Wildeve; 'here's a pretty exposure! Let us escape at once. Come!'

It was, however, too late to get away by the passage. A rugged knocking had begun upon the door of the front room. Wildeve, who had gone to the window, came back.

'Stop!' he said imperiously, putting his hand upon Mrs. Yeobright's arm. 'We are regularly besieged. There are fifty of them out there if there's one. You stay in this room with Thomasin; I'll go out and face them. You must stay now, for my sake, till they are gone, so that it may seem as if all was right. Come, Tamsie dear, don't go making a scene—we must marry after this; that you can see as well as I. Sit still, that's all—and don't speak much. I'll manage them. Blundering fools!'

He pressed the agitated girl into a seat, returned to the outer room and opened the door. Immediately outside, in the passage, appeared Grandfer Cantle singing in concert with those still standing in front of the house. He came into the room and nodded abstractedly to Wildeve, his lips still parted, and his features excruciatingly strained in the emission of the chorus. This being ended, he said heartily, 'Here's welcome to the new-made couple, and God bless 'em!'

'Thank you,' said Wildeve, with dry resentment, his face as gloomy as a thunderstorm.

3. A skimmington-ride, or charivari: a procession with effigies and raucous music, used to express popular disapproval at adultery or at the ill-treatment by a husband or wife of the partner. The custom was made illegal in 1882, but took some time to die out.
4. From a version of the popular song "As Down in the Meadows."

At the Grandfer's heels now came the rest of the group, which included Fairway, Christian, Sam the turf-cutter, Humphrey, and a dozen others. All smiled upon Wildeve, and upon his tables and chairs likewise, from a general sense of friendliness towards the articles as well as towards their owner.

'We be not here afore Mrs. Yeobright after all,' said Fairway, recognizing the matron's bonnet through the glass partition which divided the public apartment they had entered from the room where the women sat. 'We struck down across, d'ye see, Mr. Wildeve, and she went round by the path.'

'And I see the young bride's little head!' said Grandfer, peeping in the same direction, and discerning Thomasin, who was waiting beside her aunt in a miserable and awkward way. 'Not quite settled in yet—well, well, there's plenty of time.'

Wildeve made no reply; and probably feeling that the sooner he treated them the sooner they would go, he produced a stone jar, which threw a warm halo over matters at once.

'That's a drop of the right sort, I can see,' said Grandfer Cantle, with the air of a man too well-mannered to show any hurry to taste it.

'Yes,' said Wildeve, ' 'tis some old mead. I hope you will like it.'

'O ay!' replied the guests, in the hearty tones natural when the words demanded by politeness coincide with those of deepest feeling. 'There isn't a prettier drink under the sun.'

'I'll take my oath there isn't,' added Grandfer Cantle. 'All that can be said against mead is that 'tis rather heady, and apt to lie about a man a good while. But to-morrow's Sunday, thank God.'

'I feel'd for all the world like some bold soldier after I had had some once,' said Christian.

'You shall feel so again,' said Wildeve, with condescension. 'Cups or glasses, gentlemen?'

'Well, if you don't mind, we'll have the beaker, and pass 'en round; 'tis better than heling[5] it out in dribbles.'

'Jown the slippery glasses,' said Grandfer Cantle. 'What's the good of a thing that you can't put down in the ashes to warm, hey, neighbours; that's what I ask?'

'Right, Grandfer,' said Sam; and the mead then circulated.

'Well,' said Timothy Fairway, feeling demands upon his praise in some form or other, ' 'tis a worthy thing to be married, Mr. Wildeve; and the woman you've got is a dimant, so says I. Yes,' he continued, to Grandfer Cantle, raising his voice so as to be heard through the partition; 'her father (inclining his head towards the inner room) was as good a feller as ever lived. He always had his great indignation ready against anything underhand.'

5. Pouring (dialect).

'Is that very dangerous?' said Christian.

'And there were few in these parts that were upsides with him,'[6] said Sam. 'Whenever a club[7] walked he'd play the clarinet in the band that marched before 'em as if he'd never touched anything but a clarinet all his life. And then, when they got to church-door he'd throw down the clarinet, mount the gallery, snatch up the bass-viol, and rozum away[8] as if he'd never played anything but a bass-viol. Folk would say—folk that knowed what a true stave was—"Surely, surely that's never the same man that I saw handling the clarinet so masterly by now!" '

'I can mind it,' said the furze-cutter. ' 'Twas a wonderful thing that one body could hold it all and never mix the fingering.'

'There was Kingsbere church likewise,' Fairway recommenced, as one opening a new vein of the same mine of interest.

Wildeve breathed the breath of one intolerably bored, and glanced through the partition at the prisoners.

'He used to walk over there of a Sunday afternoon to visit his old acquaintance Andrew Brown, the first clarinet there; a good man enough, but rather screechy in his music, if you can mind?'

' 'A was.'

'And neighbour Yeobright would take Andrey's place for some part of the service, to let Andrey have a bit of a nap, as any friend would naturally do.'

'As any friend would,' said Grandfer Cantle, the other listeners expressing the same accord by the shorter way of nodding their heads.

'No sooner was Andrey asleep and the first whiff of neighbour Yeobright's wind had got inside Andrey's clarinet than every one in church felt in a moment there was a great soul among 'em. All heads would turn, and they'd say, "Ah, I thought 'twas he!" One Sunday I can well mind—a bass-viol day that time, and Yeobright had brought his own. 'Twas the Hundred-and-thirty-third to "Lydia";[9] and when they'd come to "Ran down his beard and o'er his robes its costly moisture shed," neighbour Yeobright, who had just warmed to his work, drove his bow into them strings that glorious grand that he e'en a'most sawed the bass-viol into two pieces. Every winder in church rattled as if 'twere a thunderstorm. Old Pa'son Williams lifted his hands in his great holy surplice as natural as if

---

6. Equal to him.
7. Local benefit societies, or clubs, held annual ceremonies that included a walk or procession.
8. Work away (dialect).
9. Psalm 133 in *A New Version of the Psalms* (1696), put into metrical form by Nahum Tate and set to music by Nicholas Brady; "Lydia" was among the most popular of these tunes. Known as "Tate and Brady," the *New Version* was widely used in Anglican churches until the mid-nineteenth century.

he'd been in common clothes, and seemed to say to hisself, "O for such a man in our parish!" But not a soul in Kingsbere could hold a candle to Yeobright.'

'Was it quite safe when the winder shook?' Christian inquired.

He received no answer; all for the moment sitting rapt in admiration of the performance described. As with Farinelli's singing[1] before the princesses, Sheridan's renowned Begum Speech,[2] and other such examples, the fortunate condition of its being for ever lost to the world invested the deceased Mr. Yeobright's *tour de force* on that memorable afternoon with a cumulative glory which comparative criticism, had that been possible, might considerably have shorn down.

'He was the last you'd have expected to drop off in the prime of life,' said Humphrey.

'Ah, well: he was looking for the earth some months afore he went. At that time women used to run for smocks and gown-pieces at Greenhill Fair, and my wife that is now, being a long-legged slittering[3] maid, hardly husband-high, went with the rest of the maidens, for 'a was a good runner afore she got so heavy. When she came home I said—we were then just beginning to walk together— "What have ye got, my honey?" "I've won—well, I've won—a gownpiece," says she, her colours coming up in a moment. 'Tis a smock for a crown,[4] I thought; and so it turned out. Ay, when I think what she'll say to me now without a mossel of red in her face, it do seem strange that 'a wouldn't say such a little thing then. . . . However, then she went on, and that's what made me bring up the story, "Well, whatever clothes I've won, white or figured, for eyes to see or for eyes not to see" ('a could do a pretty stroke of modesty in those days), "I'd sooner have lost it than have seen what I have. Poor Mr. Yeobright was took bad directly he reached the fair ground, and was forced to go home again." That was the last time he ever went out of the parish.'

' 'A faltered on from one day to another, and then we heard he was gone.'

'D'ye think he had great pain when 'a died?' said Christian.

'O no: quite different. Nor any pain of mind. He was lucky enough to be God A'mighty's own man.'

'And other folk—d'ye think 'twill be much pain to 'em, Mister Fairway?'

1. The Italian castrato Carlo Broschi (1705–82), known as Farinelli, was forbidden from singing in public by his employer Philip V of Spain.
2. An extemporized speech in Parliament by Richard Brinsley Sheridan (1751–1816), accusing Warren Hastings of extorting money from Indian princesses, or begums; though it was much admired, no full text survived.
3. Carefree, skipping (dialect).
4. Five-shilling coin (a pound was twenty shillings).

'That depends on whether they be afeard.'

'I bain't afeard at all, I thank God!' said Christian strenuously. 'I'm glad I bain't, for then 'twon't pain me. . . . I don't think I be afeard—or if I be I can't help it, and I don't deserve to suffer. I wish I was not afeard at all!'

There was a solemn silence, and looking from the window, which was unshuttered and unblinded, Timothy said, 'Well, what a fess[5] little bonfire that one is, out by Cap'n Vye's! 'Tis burning just the same now as ever, upon my life.'

All glances went through the window, and nobody noticed that Wildeve disguised a brief, tell-tale look. Far away up the sombre valley of heath, and to the right of Rainbarrow, could indeed be seen the light, small, but steady and persistent as before.

'It was lighted before ours was,' Fairway continued; 'and yet every one in the country round is out afore 'n.'

'Perhaps there's meaning in it!' murmured Christian.

'How meaning?' said Wildeve sharply.

Christian was too scattered to reply, and Timothy helped him.

'He means, sir, that the lonesome dark-eyed creature up there that some say is a witch—ever I should call a fine young woman such a name—is always up to some odd conceit or other; and so perhaps 'tis she.'

'I'd be very glad to ask her in wedlock, if she'd hae me, and take the risk of her wild dark eyes ill-wishing me,' said Grandfer Cantle staunchly.

'Don't ye say it, father!' implored Christian.

'Well, be dazed[6] if he who do marry the maid won't hae an uncommon picture for his best parlour,' said Fairway in a liquid tone, placing down the cup of mead at the end of a good pull.

'And a partner as deep as the North Star,' said Sam, taking up the cup and finishing the little that remained.

'Well, really, now I think we must be moving,' said Humphrey, observing the emptiness of the vessel.

'But we'll gie 'em another song?' said Grandfer Cantle. 'I'm as full of notes as a bird!'

'Thank you, Grandfer,' said Wildeve. 'But we will not trouble you now. Some other day must do for that—when I have a party.'

'Be jown'd if I don't learn ten new songs for't, or I won't learn a line!' said Grandfer Cantle. 'And you may be sure I won't disappoint ye by biding away, Mr. Wildeve.'

'I quite believe you,' said that gentleman.

All then took their leave, wishing their entertainer long life and happiness as a married man, with recapitulations which occupied

5. Vigorous; also proud, conceited (dialect).
6. Polite form of damned (dialect).

some time. Wildeve attended them to the door, beyond which the deep-dyed upward stretch of heath stood awaiting them, an amplitude of darkness reigning from their feet almost to the zenith, where a definite form first became visible in the lowering forehead of Rainbarrow. Diving into the dense obscurity in a line headed by Sam the turf-cutter, they pursued their trackless way home.

When the scratching of the furze against their leggings had fainted upon the ear, Wildeve returned to the room where he had left Thomasin and her aunt. The women were gone.

They could only have left the house in one way, by the back window; and this was open.

Wildeve laughed to himself, remained a moment thinking, and idly returned to the front room. Here his glance fell upon a bottle of wine which stood on the mantelpiece. 'Ah—old Dowden!' he murmured; and going to the kitchen door shouted, 'Is anybody here who can take something to old Dowden?'

There was no reply. The room was empty, the lad who acted as his factotum[7] having gone to bed. Wildeve came back, put on his hat, took the bottle, and left the house, turning the key in the door, for there was no guest at the inn to-night. As soon as he was on the road the little bonfire on Mistover Knap again met his eye.

'Still waiting, are you, my lady?' he murmured.

However, he did not proceed that way just then; but leaving the hill to the left of him, he stumbled over a rutted road that brought him to a cottage which, like all other habitations on the heath at this hour, was only saved from being invisible by a faint shine from its bedroom window. This house was the home of Olly Dowden, the besom-maker, and he entered.

The lower room was in darkness; but by feeling his way he found a table, whereon he placed the bottle, and a minute later emerged again upon the heath. He stood and looked north-east at the undying little fire—high up above him, though not so high as Rainbarrow.

We have been told what happens when a woman deliberates;[8] and the epigram is not always terminable with woman, provided that one be in the case, and that a fair one. Wildeve stood, and stood longer, and breathed perplexedly, and then said to himself with resignation, 'Yes—by Heaven, I must go to her, I suppose!'

Instead of turning in the direction of home he pressed on rapidly by a path under Rainbarrow towards what was evidently a signal light.

---

7. General servant.
8. "The woman that deliberates is lost," from Joseph Addison's play *Cato*, IV.1 (1713).

The Figure against the Sky

VI

When the whole Egdon concourse had left the site of the bonfire to its accustomed loneliness, a closely wrapped female figure approached the barrow from that quarter of the heath in which the little fire lay. Had the reddleman been watching he might have recognized her as the woman who had first stood there so singularly, and vanished at the approach of strangers. She ascended to her old position at the top, where the red coals of the perishing fire greeted her like living eyes in the corpse of day. There she stood still, around her stretching the vast night atmosphere, whose incomplete darkness in comparison with the total darkness of the heath below it might have represented a venial beside a mortal sin.

That she was tall and straight in build, that she was ladylike in her movements, was all that could be learnt of her just now, her form being wrapped in a shawl folded in the old cornerwise fashion, and her head in a large kerchief, a protection not superfluous at this hour and place. Her back was towards the wind, which blew from the north-west; but whether she had avoided that aspect because of the chilly gusts which played about her exceptional position, or because her interest lay in the south-east, did not at first appear.

Her reason for standing so dead still as the pivot of this circle of heath-country was just as obscure. Her extraordinary fixity, her conspicuous loneliness, her heedlessness of night, betokened among other things an utter absence of fear. A tract of country unaltered from that sinister condition which made Cæsar[1] anxious every year to get clear of its glooms before the autumnal equinox, a kind of landscape and weather which leads travellers from the South to describe our island as Homer's Cimmerian land,[2] was not, on the face of it, friendly to women.

It might reasonably have been supposed that she was listening to the wind, which rose somewhat as the night advanced, and laid hold of the attention. The wind, indeed, seemed made for the scene, as the scene seemed made for the hour. Part of its tone was quite special; what was heard there could be heard nowhere else. Gusts in innumerable series followed each other from the northwest, and when each one of them raced past the sound of its progress resolved into three. Treble, tenor, and bass notes were to be found therein. The general ricochet of the whole over pits and

1. Julius Caesar invaded Britain in 55 and 54 B.C.E. but retired across the Channel before the autumn equinox (September 23); neither invasion, however, took him near Hardy's Egdon Heath.
2. Land of perpetual darkness in Homer's *Odyssey* (Book XI).

prominences had the gravest pitch of the chime. Next there could be heard the baritone buzz of a holly tree. Below these in force, above them in pitch, a dwindled voice strove hard at a husky tune, which was the peculiar local sound alluded to. Thinner and less immediately traceable than the other two, it was far more impressive than either. In it lay what may be called the linguistic peculiarity of the heath; and being audible nowhere on earth off a heath, it afforded a shadow of reason for the woman's tenseness, which continued as unbroken as ever.

Throughout the blowing of these plaintive November winds that note bore a great resemblance to the ruins of human song which remain to the throat of fourscore and ten. It was a worn whisper, dry and papery, and it brushed so distinctly across the ear that, by the accustomed, the material minutiæ in which it originated could be realized as by touch. It was the united products of infinitesimal vegetable causes, and these were neither stems, leaves, fruit, blades, prickles, lichen, nor moss.

They were the mummied heath-bells of the past summer, originally tender and purple, now washed colourless by Michaelmas[3] rains, and dried to dead skins by October suns. So low was an individual sound from these that a combination of hundreds only just emerged from silence, and the myriads of the whole declivity reached the woman's ear but as a shrivelled and intermittent recitative. Yet scarcely a single accent among the many afloat to-night could have such power to impress a listener with thoughts of its origin. One inwardly saw the infinity of those combined multitudes; and perceived that each of the tiny trumpets was seized on, entered, scoured and emerged from by the wind as thoroughly as if it were as vast as a crater.

'The spirit moved them.'[4] A meaning of the phrase forced itself upon the attention; and an emotional listener's fetichistic mood might have ended in one of more advanced quality.[5] It was not, after all, that the left-hand expanse of old blooms spoke, or the right-hand, or those of the slope in front; but it was the single person of something else speaking through each at once.

Suddenly, on the barrow, there mingled with all this wild rhetoric of night a sound which modulated so naturally into the rest that its beginning and ending were hardly to be distinguished. The bluffs, and the bushes, and the heather-bells had broken silence; at last, so did the woman; and her articulation was but as another phrase

---

3. Michaelmas, the feast of St. Michael, is on September 29.
4. The spirit of God several times moves people in the Bible, e.g., Samson at Judges 13.25, and holy men more generally at 2 Peter 1.21, but the phrase is not an exact quotation.
5. Nineteenth-century thinkers usually regarded fetichism, or the tendency to reverence inanimate objects, as a primitive phase of belief that would give way to more advanced opinions.

of the same discourse as theirs. Thrown out on the winds it became twined in with them, and with them it flew away.

What she uttered was a lengthened sighing, apparently at something in her mind which had led to her presence here. There was a spasmodic abandonment about it as if, in allowing herself to utter the sound, the woman's brain had authorized what it could not regulate. One point was evident in this; that she had been existing in a suppressed state, and not in one of languor, or stagnation.

Far away down the valley the faint shine from the window of the inn still lasted on; and a few additional moments proved that the window, or what was within it, had more to do with the woman's sigh than had either her own actions or the scene immediately around. She lifted her left hand, which held a closed telescope. This she rapidly extended, as if she were well accustomed to the operation, and raising it to her eye directed it towards the light beaming from the inn.

'She lifted her left hand.'

The handkerchief which had hooded her head was now a little thrown back, her face being somewhat elevated. A profile was visible against the dull monochrome of cloud around her; and it was as though side shadows from the features of Sappho[6] and Mrs. Siddons[7] had converged upwards from the tomb to form an image like

6. Greek lyric poet from Lesbos, working around 600 B.C.E. and reputed to have thrown herself into the sea in despair at her unrequited love.
7. The actress Sarah Siddons, née Kemble (1755–1831), renowned for the intensity of her roles; Hardy was familiar with Sir Joshua Reynolds's 1784 portrait of her as "The Tragic Muse."

neither but suggesting both. This, however, was mere superficiality. In respect of character a face may make certain admissions by its outline; but it fully confesses only in its changes. So much is this the case that what is called the play of the features often helps more in understanding a man or woman than the earnest labours of all the other members together. Thus the night revealed little of her whose form it was embracing, for the mobile parts of her countenance could not be seen.

At last she gave up her spying attitude, closed the telescope, and turned to the decaying embers. From these no appreciable beams now radiated, except when a more than usually smart gust brushed over their faces and raised a fitful glow which came and went like the blush of a girl. She stooped over the silent circle, and selecting from the brands a piece of stick which bore the largest live coal at its end, brought it to where she had been standing before.

She held the brand to the ground, blowing the red coal with her mouth at the same time; till it faintly illuminated the sod, and revealed a small object, which turned out to be an hour-glass, though she wore a watch. She blew long enough to show that the sand had all slipped through.

'Ah!' she said, as if surprised.

The light raised by her breath had been very fitful, and a momentary irradiation of flesh was all that it had disclosed of her face. That consisted of two matchless lips and a cheek only, her head being still enveloped. She threw away the stick, took the glass in her hand, the telescope under her arm, and moved on.

Along the ridge ran a faint foot-track, which the lady followed. Those who knew it well called it a path; and, while a mere visitor would have passed it unnoticed even by day, the regular haunters of the heath were at no loss for it at midnight. The whole secret of following these incipient paths, when there was not light enough in the atmosphere to show a turnpike-road, lay in the development of the sense of touch in the feet, which comes with years of night-rambling in little-trodden spots. To a walker practised in such places a difference between impact on maiden herbage, and on the crippled stalks of a slight footway, is perceptible through the thickest boot or shoe.

The solitary figure who walked this beat took no notice of the windy tune still played on the dead heath-bells. She did not turn her head to look at a group of dark creatures further on, who fled from her presence as she skirted a ravine where they fed. They were about a score of the small wild ponies known as heath-croppers. They roamed at large on the undulations of Egdon, but in numbers too few to detract much from the solitude.

The pedestrian noticed nothing just now, and a clue to her abstraction was afforded by a trivial incident. A bramble caught hold of her skirt, and checked her progress. Instead of putting it off and hastening along, she yielded herself up to the pull, and stood passively still. When she began to extricate herself it was by turning round and round, and so unwinding the prickly switch. She was in a desponding reverie.

Her course was in the direction of the small undying fire which had drawn the attention of the men on Rainbarrow and of Wildeve in the valley below. A faint illumination from its rays began to glow upon her face, and the fire soon revealed itself to be lit, not on the level ground, but on a salient corner or redan of earth, at the junction of two converging bank fences. Outside was a ditch, dry except immediately under the fire, where there was a large pool, bearded all round by heather and rushes. In the smooth water of the pool the fire appeared upside down.

The banks meeting behind were bare of a hedge, save such as was formed by disconnected tufts of furze, standing upon stems along the top, liked impaled heads above a city wall. A white mast, fitted up with spars and other nautical tackle, could be seen rising against the dark clouds whenever the flames played brightly enough to reach it. Altogether the scene had much the appearance of a fortification upon which had been kindled a beacon fire.

Nobody was visible; but ever and anon a whitish something moved above the bank from behind, and vanished again. This was a small human hand, in the act of lifting pieces of fuel into the fire; but for all that could be seen the hand, like that which troubled Belshazzar,[8] was there alone. Occasionally an ember rolled off the bank, and dropped with a hiss into the pool.

At one side of the pool rough steps built of clods enabled any one who wished to do so to mount the bank; which the woman did. Within was a paddock in an uncultivated state, though bearing evidence of having once been tilled; but the heath and fern had insidiously crept in, and were reasserting their old supremacy. Further ahead were dimly visible an irregular dwelling-house, garden, and outbuildings, backed by a clump of firs.

The young lady—for youth had revealed its presence in her buoyant bound up the bank—walked along the top instead of descending inside, and came to the corner where the fire was burning. One reason for the permanence of the blaze was now manifest: the fuel consisted of hard pieces of wood, cleft and sawn—the knotty boles of old thorn trees which grew in twos and threes about the hillsides. A yet unconsumed pile of these lay in the inner angle of the

8. Babylonian king who saw a disembodied hand write a message on his palace wall announcing God's judgment against him; see Daniel 5.24–31.

bank; and from this corner the upturned face of a little boy greeted her eyes. He was dilatorily throwing up a piece of wood into the fire every now and then, a business which seemed to have engaged him a considerable part of the evening, for his face was somewhat weary.

'I am glad you have come, Miss Eustacia,' he said, with a sigh of relief. 'I don't like biding by myself.'

'Nonsense. I have only been a little way for a walk. I have been gone only twenty minutes.'

'It seemed long,' murmured the sad boy. 'And you have been so many times.'

'Why, I thought you would be pleased to have a bonfire. Are you not much obliged to me for making you one?'

'Yes; but there's nobody here to play wi' me.'

'I suppose nobody has come while I've been away?'

'Nobody except your grandfather: he looked out of doors once for 'ee. I told him you were walking round upon the hill to look at the other bonfires.'

'A good boy.'

'I think I hear him coming again, miss.'

An old man came into the remoter light of the fire from the direction of the homestead. He was the same who had overtaken the reddleman on the road that afternoon. He looked wistfully to the top of the bank at the woman who stood there, and his teeth, which were quite unimpaired, showed like parian[9] from his parted lips.

'When are you coming indoors, Eustacia?' he asked. ' 'Tis almost bedtime. I've been home these two hours, and am tired out. Surely 'tis somewhat childish of you to stay out playing at bonfires so long, and wasting such fuel. My precious thorn roots, the rarest of all firing, that I laid by on purpose for Christmas—you have burnt 'em nearly all!'

'I promised Johnny a bonfire, and it pleases him not to let it go out just yet,' said Eustacia, in a way which told at once that she was absolute queen here. 'Grandfather, you go in to bed. I shall follow you soon. You like the fire, don't you, Johnny?'

The boy looked up doubtfully at her and murmured, 'I don't think I want it any longer.'

Her grandfather had turned back again, and did not hear the boy's reply. As soon as the white-haired man had vanished she said in a tone of pique to the child, 'Ungrateful little boy, how can you contradict me? Never shall you have a bonfire again unless you keep it up now. Come, tell me you like to do things for me, and don't deny it.'

9. White marble used for statuary, from the Greek island of Paros.

The repressed child said, 'Yes, I do, miss,' and continued to stir the fire perfunctorily.

'Stay a little longer and I will give you a crooked sixpence,' said Eustacia, more gently. 'Put in one piece of wood every two or three minutes, but not too much at once. I am going to walk along the ridge a little longer, but I shall keep on coming to you. And if you hear a frog jump into the pond with a flounce like a stone thrown in, be sure you run and tell me, because it is a sign of rain.'

'Yes, Eustacia.'

'Miss Vye, sir.'

'Miss Vy—stacia.'

'That will do. Now put in one stick more.'

The little slave went on feeding the fire as before. He seemed a mere automaton, galvanized into moving and speaking by the wayward Eustacia's will. He might have been the brass statue which Albertus Magnus[1] is said to have animated just so far as to make it chatter, and move, and be his servant.

Before going on her walk again the young girl stood still on the bank for a few instants and listened. It was to the full as lonely a place as Rainbarrow, though at rather a lower level; and it was more sheltered from wind and weather on account of the few firs to the north. The bank which enclosed the homestead, and protected it from the lawless state of the world without, was formed of thick square clods, dug from the ditch on the outside, and built up with a slight batter or incline, which forms no slight defence where hedges will not grow because of the wind and the wilderness, and where wall materials are unattainable. Otherwise the situation was quite open, commanding the whole length of the valley which reached to the river behind Wildeve's house. High above this to the right, and much nearer thitherward than the Quiet Woman Inn, the blurred contour of Rainbarrow obstructed the sky.

After her attentive survey of the wild slopes and hollow ravines a gesture of impatience escaped Eustacia. She vented petulant words every now and then; but there were sighs between her words, and sudden listenings between her sighs. Descending from her perch she again sauntered off towards Rainbarrow, though this time she did not go the whole way.

Twice she reappeared at intervals of a few minutes and each time she said—

'Not any flounce into the pond yet, little man?'

'No, Miss Eustacia,' the child replied.

---

1. German monk and scholar (1206–1280). Hardy found this and several other little-known facts or stories referred to in the novel in Charles Mackay's *Memoirs of Extraordinary Popular Delusions, and the Madness of Crowds*, first published in three volumes in 1841.

'Well,' she said at last, 'I shall soon be going in, and then I will give you the crooked sixpence,[2] and let you go home.'

'Thank'ee, Miss Eustacia,' said the tired stoker, breathing more easily. And Eustacia again strolled away from the fire, but this time not towards Rainbarrow. She skirted the bank and went round to the wicket before the house, where she stood motionless, looking at the scene.

Fifty yards off rose the corner of the two converging banks, with the fire upon it: within the bank, lifting up to the fire one stick at a time, just as before, the figure of the little child. She idly watched him as he occasionally climbed up in the nook of the bank and stood beside the brands. The wind blew the smoke, and the child's hair, and the corner of his pinafore, all in the same direction: the breeze died, and the pinafore and hair lay still, and the smoke went up straight.

While Eustacia looked on from this distance the boy's form visibly started: he slid down the bank and ran across towards the white gate.

'Well?' said Eustacia.

'A hop-frog have jumped into the pond. Yes, I heard 'en!'

'Then it is going to rain, and you had better go home. You will not be afraid?' She spoke hurriedly, as if her heart had leapt into her throat at the boy's words.

'No, because I shall hae the crooked sixpence.'

'Yes, here it is. Now run as fast as you can—not that way— through the garden here. No other boy in the heath has had such a bonfire as yours.'

The boy, who clearly had had too much of a good thing, marched away into the shadows with alacrity. When he was gone Eustacia, leaving her telescope and hour-glass by the gate, brushed forward from the wicket towards the angle of the bank, under the fire.

Here, screened by the outwork, she waited. In a few moments a splash was audible from the pond outside. Had the child been there he would have said that a second frog had jumped in; but by most people the sound would have been likened to the fall of a stone into the water. Eustacia stepped upon the bank.

'Yes?' she said, and held her breath.

Thereupon the contour of a man became dimly visible against the low-reaching sky over the valley, beyond the outer margin of the pool. He came round it and leapt upon the bank beside her. A low laugh escaped her—the third utterance which the girl had indulged in to-night. The first, when she stood upon Rainbarrow, had ex-

---

2. A bent sixpenny piece was considered a lucky charm, especially against witchcraft.

pressed anxiety; the second, on the ridge, had expressed impatience; the present was one of triumphant pleasure. She let her joyous eyes rest upon him without speaking, as upon some wondrous thing she had created out of chaos.

'I have come,' said the man, who was Wildeve. 'You give me no peace. Why do you not leave me alone? I have seen your bonfire all the evening.' The words were not without emotion, and retained their level tone as if by a careful equipoise between imminent extremes.

At this unexpectedly repressing manner in her lover the girl seemed to repress herself also. 'Of course you have seen my fire,' she answered with languid calmness, artificially maintained. 'Why shouldn't I have a bonfire on the Fifth of November, like other denizens of the heath?'

'I knew it was meant for me.'

'How did you know it? I have had no word with you since you—you chose her, and walked about with her, and deserted me entirely, as if I had never been yours life and soul[3] so irretrievably!'

'Eustacia! could I forget that last autumn at this same day of the month and at this same place you lighted exactly such a fire as a signal for me to come and see you? Why should there have been a bonfire again by Captain Vye's house if not for the same purpose?'

'Yes, yes—I own it,' she cried under her breath, with a drowsy fervour of manner and tone which was quite peculiar to her. 'Don't begin speaking to me as you did, Damon; you will drive me to say words I would not wish to say to you. I had given you up, and resolved not to think of you any more; and then I heard the news, and I came out and got the fire ready because I thought that you had been faithful to me.'

'What have you heard to make you think that?' said Wildeve, astonished.

'That you did not marry her!' she murmured exultingly. 'And I knew it was because you loved me best, and couldn't do it. . . . Damon, you have been cruel to me to go away, and I have said I would never forgive you. I do not think I can forgive you entirely, even now—it is too much for a woman of any spirit to quite overlook.'

'If I had known you wished to call me up here only to reproach me, I wouldn't have come.'

'But I don't mind it, and I do forgive you now that you have not married her, and have come back to me!'

---

3. Revised from the 1895 edition, which has "body and soul," itself revised from the less sexually explicit 1878 edition, where the sentence ends at "as if I had never been yours."

'Who told you that I had not married her?'

'My grandfather. He took a long walk to-day, and as he was coming home he overtook some person who told him of a broken-off wedding: he thought it might be yours; and I knew it was.'

'Does anybody else know?'

'I suppose not. Now Damon, do you see why I lit my signal fire? You did not think I would have lit it if I had imagined you to have become the husband of this woman. It is insulting my pride to suppose that.'

Wildeve was silent: it was evident that he had supposed as much.

'Did you indeed think I believed you were married?' she again demanded earnestly. 'Then you wronged me; and upon my life and heart I can hardly bear to recognize that you have such ill thoughts of me! Damon, you are not worthy of me: I see it, and yet I love you. Never mind: let it go—I must bear your mean opinion as best I may. . . . It is true, is it not,' she added with ill-concealed anxiety, on his making no demonstration, 'that you could not bring yourself to give me up, and are still going to love me best of all?'

'Yes; or why should I have come?' he said touchily. 'Not that fidelity will be any great merit in me after your kind speech about my unworthiness, which should have been said by myself if by anybody, and comes with an ill grace from you. However, the curse of inflammability is upon me, and I must live under it, and take any snub from a woman. It has brought me down from engineering to innkeeping: what lower stage it has in store for me I have yet to learn.' He continued to look upon her gloomily.

She seized the moment, and throwing back the shawl so that the firelight shone full upon her face and throat, said with a smile, 'Have you seen anything better than that in your travels?'

Eustacia was not one to commit herself to such a position without good ground. He said quietly, 'No.'

'Not even on the shoulders of Thomasin?'

'Thomasin is a pleasing and innocent woman.'

'That's nothing to do with it,' she cried with quick passionateness. 'We will leave her out; there are only you and me now to think of.' After a long look at him she resumed with the old quiescent warmth: 'Must I go on weakly confessing to you things a woman ought to conceal; and own that no words can express how gloomy I have been because of that dreadful belief I held till two hours ago—that you had quite deserted me?'

'I am sorry I caused you that pain.'

'But perhaps it is not wholly because of you that I get gloomy,' she archly added. 'It is in my nature to feel like that. It was born in my blood, I suppose.'

'Hypochondriasis.'[4]

'Or else it was coming into this wild heath. I was happy enough at Budmouth. O the times, O the days at Budmouth! But Egdon will be brighter again now.'

'I hope it will,' said Wildeve moodily. 'Do you know the consequence of this recall to me, my old darling? I shall come to see you again as before, at Rainbarrow.'

'Of course you will.'

'And yet I declare that until I got here to-night I intended, after this one good-bye, never to meet you again.'

'I don't thank you for that,' she said, turning away, while indignation spread through her like subterranean heat. 'You may come again to Rainbarrow if you like, but you won't see me; and you may call, but I shall not listen; and you may tempt me, but I won't give myself[5] to you any more.'

'You have said as much before, sweet; but such natures as yours don't so easily adhere to their words. Neither, for the matter of that, do such natures as mine.'

'This is the pleasure I have won by my trouble,' she whispered bitterly. 'Why did I try to recall you? Damon, a strange warring takes place in my mind occasionally. I think when I become calm after your woundings, "Do I embrace a cloud of common fog after all?" You are a chameleon, and now you are at your worst colour. Go home, or I shall hate you!'

He looked absently towards Rainbarrow while one might have counted twenty, and said, as if he did not much mind all this, 'Yes, I will go home. Do you mean to see me again?'

'If you own to me that the wedding is broken off because you love me best.'

'I don't think it would be good policy,' said Wildeve, smiling. 'You would get to know the extent of your power too clearly.'

'But tell me!'

'You know.'

'Where is she now?'

'I don't know. I prefer not to speak of her to you. I have not yet married her: I have come in obedience to your call. That is enough.'

'I merely lit that fire because I was dull, and thought I would get a little excitement by calling you up and triumphing over you as the Witch of Endor[6] called up Samuel. I determined you should come;

4. A term used by Victorian doctors to describe a condition of morbid melancholy and irritability, supposed to be especially common in women.
5. Revised in 1895; the 1878 text has the less compromising "I won't encourage you any more."
6. The night before a battle against the Philistines, Saul required the Witch of Endor to summon the spirit of the prophet Samuel, who foretold Saul's death on the following day (1 Samuel 28.7–19).

and you have come! I have shown my power. A mile and half hither, and a mile and half back again to your home—three miles in the dark for me. Have I not shown my power?'

He shook his head at her. 'I know you too well, my Eustacia; I know you too well. There isn't a note in you which I don't know; and that hot little bosom couldn't play such a cold-blooded trick to save its life. I saw a woman on Rainbarrow at dusk looking down towards my house. I think I drew out you before you drew out me.'

The revived embers of an old passion[7] glowed clearly in Wildeve now; and he leant forward as if about to put his face towards her cheek.

'O no,' she said, intractably moving to the other side of the decayed fire. 'What did you mean by that?'

'Perhaps I may kiss your hand?'

'No, you may not.'

'Then I may shake your hand?'

'No.'

'Then I wish you good-night without caring for either. Good-bye, good-bye.'

She returned no answer, and with the bow of a dancing-master he vanished on the other side of the pool as he had come.

Eustacia sighed: it was no fragile maiden sigh, but a sigh which shook her like a shiver. Whenever a flash of reason darted like an electric light upon her lover—as it sometimes would—and showed his imperfections, she shivered thus. But it was over in a second, and she loved on. She knew that he trifled with her; but she loved on. She scattered the half-burnt brands, went indoors immediately, and up to her bedroom without a light. Amid the rustles which denoted her to be undressing in the darkness other heavy breaths frequently came; and the same kind of shudder occasionally moved through her when, ten minutes later, she lay on her bed asleep.

Queen of Night

VII

Eustacia Vye was the raw material of a divinity. On Olympus[1] she would have done well with a little preparation. She had the passions and instincts which make a model goddess, that is, those which make not quite a model woman. Had it been possible for the earth and mankind to be entirely in her grasp for a while, had she

---

7. The words translate Vergil's "veteris vestigia flammae" in the *Aeneid* (IV.23), which Hardy later used as the epigraph to his "Poems of 1912–13."
1. Mount Olympus, the highest mountain in Greece, and after the defeat of the Titans the home of the gods.

handled the distaff, the spindle, and the shears[2] at her own free will, few in the world would have noticed the change of government. There would have been the same inequality of lot, the same heaping up of favours here, of contumely there, the same generosity before justice, the same perpetual dilemmas, the same captious alteration of caresses and blows that we endure now.

She was in person full-limbed and somewhat heavy; without ruddiness, as without pallor; and soft to the touch as a cloud. To see her hair was to fancy that a whole winter did not contain darkness enough to form its shadow: it closed over her forehead like nightfall extinguishing the western glow.

Her nerves extended into those tresses, and her temper could always be softened by stroking them down. When her hair was brushed she would instantly sink into stillness and look like the Sphinx.[3] If, in passing under one of the Egdon banks, any of its thick skeins were caught, as they sometimes were, by a prickly tuft of the large *Ulex Europæus*[4]—which will act as a sort of hairbrush—she would go back a few steps, and pass against it a second time.

She had Pagan eyes, full of nocturnal mysteries, and their light, as it came and went, and came again, was partially hampered by their oppressive lids and lashes; and of these the under lid was much fuller than it usually is with English women. This enabled her to indulge in reverie without seeming to do so: she might have been believed capable of sleeping without closing them up. Assuming that the souls of men and women were visible essences, you could fancy the colour of Eustacia's soul to be flame-like. The sparks from it that rose into her dark pupils gave the same impression.

The mouth seemed formed less to speak than to quiver, less to quiver than to kiss. Some might have added, less to kiss than to curl. Viewed sideways, the closing-line of her lips formed, with almost geometric precision, the curve so well known in the arts of design as the cima-recta, or ogee.[5] The sight of such a flexible bend as that on grim Egdon was quite an apparition. It was felt at once that that mouth did not come over from Sleswig[6] with a band of Saxon pirates whose lips met like the two halves of a muffin. One had fancied that such lip-curves were mostly lurking underground in the South as

2. In Greek mythology the distaff, spindle, and shears are the emblems of the three Fates, Clotho, Lachesis, and Atropos, who spin, measure out, and cut the thread of human lives.
3. In Greek mythology, an enigmatic monster with the head of a woman, body of a lion, and wings of a bird; in Egypt, a lion with a pharaoh's head, as in the giant statue at Gizeh, and a symbol of royal power. Hardy perhaps had both in mind.
4. Botanical name for gorse (Latin).
5. An S-shaped curve, used in architectural moldings.
6. City in northwest Germany, from which Saxon tribes invaded Britain.

fragments of forgotten marbles. So fine were the lines of her lips that, though full, each corner of her mouth was as clearly cut as the point of a spear. This keenness of corner was only blunted when she was given over to sudden fits of gloom, one of the phases of the night-side of sentiment which she knew too well for her years.

Her presence brought memories of such things as Bourbon roses,[7] rubies, and tropical midnights; her moods recalled lotus-eaters[8] and the march in 'Athalie';[9] her motions, the ebb and flow of the sea; her voice, the viola. In a dim light, and with a slight re-arrangement of her hair, her general figure might have stood for that of either of the higher female deities. The new moon behind her head, an old helmet upon it, a diadem of accidental dewdrops round her brow, would have been adjuncts sufficient to strike the note of Artemis, Athena, or Hera[1] respectively, with as close an approximation to the antique as that which passes muster on many respected canvases.

But celestial imperiousness, love, wrath, and fervour had proved to be somewhat thrown away on netherward Egdon. Her power was limited, and the consciousness of this limitation had biassed her development. Egdon was her Hades,[2] and since coming there she had imbibed much of what was dark in its tone, though inwardly and eternally unreconciled thereto. Her appearance accorded well with this smouldering rebelliousness, and the shady splendour of her beauty was the real surface of the sad and stifled warmth within her. A true Tartarean dignity sat upon her brow, and not factitiously or with marks of constraint, for it had grown in her with years.

Across the upper part of her head she wore a thin fillet of black velvet, restraining the luxuriance of her shady hair, in a way which added much to this class of majesty by irregularly clouding her forehead. 'Nothing can embellish a beautiful face more than a narrow band drawn over the brow,' says Richter.[3] Some of the neighbouring girls wore coloured ribbon for the same purpose, and sported metallic ornaments elsewhere; but if any one suggested coloured ribbon and metallic ornaments to Eustacia Vye she laughed and went on.

7. Hybrid roses grown on the Isle de Bourbon (now Réunion). Bourbon was also the name of the French royal family; both associations may be present.
8. Mythical people living on the fruit of the lotus-plant, which induces lethargy and forget-fulness (Homer, *Odyssey*, Book 9).
9. A play by Jean Racine (1639–99); music written for the play by Mendelssohn in 1843 ends with the "War March of the Priests."
1. The "higher female deities": Artemis, the Greek goddess of hunting and of women, had the moon as symbol; Athena, goddess of war, was usually depicted fully armed; Hera, wife of Zeus and queen of the heavens, usually wears a crown or diadem.
2. The underworld of Greek mythology. Though a place of gloom, it was not necessarily a place of punishment.
3. Johann Paul Richter (1763–1825), German writer; if this is a quotation, it has not been identified.

Why did a woman of this sort live on Egdon Heath? Budmouth was her native place, a fashionable seaside resort at that date. She was the daughter of the bandmaster of a regiment which had been quartered there—a Corfiote[4] by birth, and a fine musician—who met his future wife during her trip thither with her father the captain, a man of good family. The marriage was scarcely in accord with the old man's wishes, for the bandmaster's pockets were as light as his occupation. But the musician did his best; adopted his wife's name, made England permanently his home, took great trouble with his child's education, the expenses of which were defrayed by the grandfather, and throve as the chief local musician till her mother's death, when he left off thriving, drank, and died also. The girl was left to the care of her grandfather, who, since three of his ribs became broken in a shipwreck, had lived in this airy perch on Egdon, a spot which had taken his fancy because the house was to be had for next to nothing, and because a remote blue tinge on the horizon between the hills, visible from the cottage door, was traditionally believed to be the English Channel. She hated the change; she felt like one banished; but here she was forced to abide.

Thus it happened that in Eustacia's brain were juxtaposed the strangest assortment of ideas, from old time and from new. There was no middle distance in her perspective: romantic recollections of sunny afternoons on an esplanade, with military bands, officers, and gallants around, stood like gilded letters upon the dark tablet of surrounding Egdon. Every bizarre effect that could result from the random intertwining of watering-place glitter with the grand solemnity of a heath, was to be found in her. Seeing nothing of human life now, she imagined all the more of what she had seen.

Where did her dignity come from? By a latent vein from Alcinous'[5] line, her father hailing from Phæacia's isle?—or from Fitzalan and De Vere,[6] her maternal grandfather having had a cousin in the peerage? Perhaps it was the gift of Heaven—a happy convergence of natural laws. Among other things opportunity had of late years been denied her of learning to be undignified, for she lived lonely. Isolation on a heath renders vulgarity well-nigh impossible. It would have been as easy for the heath-ponies, bats, and snakes to be vulgar as for her. A narrow life in Budmouth might have completely demeaned her.

The only way to look queenly without realms or hearts to queen

---

4. Native of the Ionian island of Corfu, at the entrance to the Adriatic; it was under British control at the time of the action of the novel.
5. King of the Phaeacians and ruler of Scheria (Corfu), where Odysseus recovers after he is shipwrecked (*Odyssey*, Book VI).
6. Aristocratic families of the sixteenth century who acquired a reputation for haughtiness. In the first, 1878 edition, the possibility raised here, that Eustacia has aristocratic forebears, is explicitly set aside.

it over is to look as if you had lost them; and Eustacia did that to a triumph. In the captain's cottage she could suggest mansions she had never seen. Perhaps that was because she frequented a vaster mansion than any of them, the open hills. Like the summer condition of the place around her, she was an embodiment of the phrase 'a populous solitude'[7]—apparently so listless, void, and quiet, she was really busy and full.

To be loved to madness—such was her great desire. Love was to her the one cordial which could drive away the eating loneliness of her days. And she seemed to long for the abstraction called passionate love more than for any particular lover.

She could show a most reproachful look at times, but it was directed less against human beings than against certain creatures of her mind, the chief of these being Destiny, through whose interference she dimly fancied it arose that love alighted only on gliding youth—that any love she might win would sink simultaneously with the sand in the glass. She thought of it with an ever-growing consciousness of cruelty, which tended to breed actions of reckless unconventionality, framed to snatch a year's, a week's, even an hour's passion from anywhere while it could be won. Through want of it she had sung without being merry, possessed without enjoying, outshone without triumphing. Her loneliness deepened her desire. On Egdon, coldest and meanest kisses were at famine prices; and where was a mouth matching hers to be found?

Fidelity in love for fidelity's sake had less attraction for her than for most women: fidelity because of love's grip had much. A blaze of love, and extinction, was better than a lantern glimmer of the same which should last long years. On this head she knew by prevision what most women learn only by experience: she had mentally walked round love, told the towers thereof, considered its palaces;[8] and concluded that love was but a doleful joy. Yet she desired it, as one in a desert would be thankful for brackish water.

She often repeated her prayers; not at particular times, but, like the unaffectedly devout, when she desired to pray. Her prayer was always spontaneous, and often ran thus, 'O deliver my heart from this fearful gloom and loneliness: send me great love from somewhere, else I shall die.'

Her high gods were William the Conqueror, Strafford, and Napoleon Buonaparte,[9] as they had appeared in the Lady's History

---

7. From Lord Byron's *Childe Harold's Pilgrimage*, Canto III, stanza 101 (1816).
8. Alluding to Psalm 48.12–13, where it is Mount Zion, not sexual love, that is being explored.
9. Ruthless and ambitious men. William (c. 1027–87) invaded England in 1066; Thomas Wentworth, Earl of Strafford (1593–1641), ruled Ireland on behalf of Charles I and was executed by the King's opponents; Napoleon (1769–1821) became Emperor of the French, but died in exile.

used at the establishment in which she was educated. Had she been a mother she would have christened her boys such names as Saul or Sisera[1] in preference to Jacob or David,[2] neither of whom she admired. At school she had used to side with the Philistines[3] in several battles, and had wondered if Pontius Pilate[4] were as handsome as he was frank and fair.

Thus she was a girl of some forwardness of mind, indeed, weighed in relation to her situation among the very rereward of thinkers, very original. Her instincts towards social nonconformity were at the root of this. In the matter of holidays, her mood was that of horses who, when turned out to grass, enjoy looking upon their kind at work on the highway. She only valued rest to herself when it came in the midst of other people's labour. Hence she hated Sundays when all was at rest, and often said they would be the death of her. To see the heathmen in their Sunday condition, that is, with their hands in their pockets, their boots newly oiled, and not laced up (a particularly Sunday sign), walking leisurely among the turves and furze-faggots they had cut during the week, and kicking them critically as if their use were unknown, was a fearful heaviness to her. To relieve the tedium of this untimely day she would overhaul the cupboards containing her grandfather's old charts and other rubbish, humming Saturday-night ballads of the country people the while. But on Saturday nights she would frequently sing a psalm, and it was always on a week-day that she read the Bible, that she might be unoppressed with a sense of doing her duty.

Such views of life were to some extent the natural begettings of her situation upon her nature. To dwell on a heath without studying its meanings was like wedding a foreigner without learning his tongue. The subtle beauties of the heath were lost to Eustacia; she only caught its vapours. An environment which would have made a contented woman a poet, a suffering woman a devotee, a pious woman a psalmist, even a giddy woman thoughtful, made a rebellious woman saturnine.[5]

Eustacia had got beyond the vision of some marriage of inexpressible glory; yet, though her emotions were in full vigour, she cared for no meaner union. Thus we see her in a strange state of isolation. To have lost the godlike conceit that we may do what we

1. Saul, the first king of Israel, killed himself after defeat in battle (see 1 Samuel 9–31); Sisera fought against the Israelites, but was killed when Jael drove a tent spike into his head (Judges 4.12–22). Both were victims of divine displeasure.
2. Jacob used craft and patience to become successful (see Genesis 25–35); David followed Saul as king of Israel. Both had God's support.
3. Enemies of the Israelites, God's chosen people.
4. The Roman governor Pontius Pilate ordered Christ to be crucified (see Matthew 27).
5. Cold or gloomy in temperament.

will, and not to have acquired a homely zest for doing what we can, shows a grandeur of temper which cannot be objected to in the abstract, for it denotes a mind that, though disappointed, forswears compromise. But, if congenial to philosophy, it is apt to be dangerous to the commonwealth. In a world where doing means marrying, and the commonwealth is one of hearts and hands, the same peril attends the condition.

And so we see our Eustacia—for at times she was not altogether unlovable—arriving at that stage of enlightenment which feels that nothing is worth while, and filling up the spare hours of her existence by idealizing Wildeve for want of a better object. This was the sole reason of his ascendency: she knew it herself. At moments her pride rebelled against her passion for him, and she even had longed to be free. But there was only one circumstance which could dislodge him, and that was the advent of a greater man.

For the rest, she suffered much from depression of spirits, and took slow walks to recover them, in which she carried her grandfather's telescope and her grandmother's hour-glass—the latter because of a peculiar pleasure she derived from watching a material representation of time's gradual glide away. She seldom schemed, but when she did scheme, her plans showed rather the comprehensive strategy of a general than the small arts called womanish, though she could utter oracles of Delphian[6] ambiguity when she did not choose to be direct. In heaven she will probably sit between the Héloïses and the Cleopatras.[7]

Those Who Are Found Where There Is Said to be Nobody

VIII

As soon as the sad little boy had withdrawn from the fire he clasped the money tight in the palm of his hand, as if thereby to fortify his courage, and began to run. There was really little danger in allowing a child to go home alone on this part of Egdon Heath. The distance to the boy's house was not more than three-eighths of a mile, his father's cottage, and one other a few yards further on, forming part of the small hamlet of Mistover Knap: the third and only remaining house was that of Captain Vye and Eustacia, which stood quite away from the small cottages, and was the loneliest of lonely houses on these thinly populated slopes.

---

6. The messages given by the oracle at Delphi, one of the holiest sites in ancient Greece, were notoriously capable of opposing interpretations.
7. Héloise (c. 1098–1164) secretly married her tutor Peter Abelard, and entered a convent after their forced separation: Cleopatra, Queen of Egypt (69–30 B.C.E.), was renowned for passionate rather than faithful love. Despite the contrast in their natures, both brought harm to the men who loved them.

He ran until he was out of breath, and then, becoming more courageous, walked leisurely along, singing in an old voice a little song about a sailor-boy and a fair one, and bright gold in store. In the middle of this the child stopped: from a pit under the hill ahead of him shone a light, whence proceeded a cloud of floating dust and a smacking noise.

Only unusual sights and sounds frightened the boy. The shrivelled voice of the heath did not alarm him, for that was familiar. The thorn-bushes which arose in his path from time to time were less satisfactory, for they whistled gloomily, and had a ghastly habit after dark of putting on the shapes of jumping madmen, sprawling giants, and hideous cripples. Lights were not uncommon this evening, but the nature of all of them was different from this. Discretion rather than terror prompted the boy to turn back instead of passing the light, with a view of asking Miss Eustacia Vye to let her servant accompany him home.

When the boy had reascended to the top of the valley he found the fire to be still burning on the bank, though lower than before. Beside it, instead of Eustacia's solitary form, he saw two persons, the second being a man. The boy crept along under the bank to ascertain from the nature of the proceedings if it would be prudent to interrupt so splendid a creature as Miss Eustacia on his poor trivial account.

After listening under the bank for some minutes to the talk he turned in a perplexed and doubting manner and began to withdraw as silently as he had come. That he did not, upon the whole, think it advisable to interrupt her conversation with Wildeve, without being prepared to bear the whole weight of her displeasure, was obvious.

Here was a Scyllæo-Charybdean[1] position for a poor boy. Pausing when again safe from discovery he finally decided to face the pit phenomenon as the lesser evil. With a heavy sigh he retraced the slope, and followed the path he had followed before.

The light had gone, the rising dust had disappeared—he hoped for ever. He marched resolutely along, and found nothing to alarm him till, coming within a few yards of the sandpit, he heard a slight noise in front, which led him to halt. The halt was but momentary, for the noise resolved itself into the steady bites of two animals grazing.

'Two he'th-croppers down here,' he said aloud. 'I have never known 'em come down so far afore.'

---

1. Faced with a choice between two equally unpleasant possibilities. In classical myth Scylla and Charybdis are respectively a rock and a whirlpool on opposite sides of the Strait of Messina, both inhabited by or identified with monsters; sailors trying to avoid the one ran the risk of being destroyed by the other.

The animals were in the direct line of his path, but that the child thought little of; he had played round the fetlocks of horses from his infancy. On coming nearer, however, the boy was somewhat surprised to find that the little creatures did not run off, and that each wore a clog, to prevent his going astray; this signified that they had been broken in. He could now see the interior of the pit, which, being in the side of the hill, had a level entrance. In the innermost corner the square outline of a van appeared, with its back towards him. A light came from the interior, and threw a moving shadow upon the vertical face of gravel at the further side of the pit into which the vehicle faced.

The child assumed that this was the cart of a gipsy, and his dread of those wanderers reached but to that mild pitch which titillates rather than pains. Only a few inches of mud wall kept him and his family from being gipsies themselves. He skirted the gravel-pit at a respectful distance, ascended the slope, and came forward upon the brow, in order to look into the open door of the van and see the original of the shadow.

The picture alarmed the boy. By a little stove inside the van sat a figure red from head to heels—the man who had been Thomasin's friend. He was darning a stocking, which was red like the rest of him. Moreover, as he darned he smoked a pipe, the stem and bowl of which were red also.

At this moment one of the heath-croppers feeding in the outer shadows was audibly shaking off the clog attached to its foot. Aroused by the sound the reddleman laid down his stocking, lit a lantern which hung beside him, and came out from the van. In sticking up the candle he lifted the lantern to his face, and the light shone into the whites of his eyes and upon his ivory teeth, which, in contrast with the red surrounding, lent him a startling aspect enough to the gaze of a juvenile. The boy knew too well for his peace of mind upon whose lair he had lighted. Uglier persons than gipsies were known to cross Egdon at times, and a reddleman was one of them.

'How I wish 'twas only a gipsy!' he murmured.

The man was by this time coming back from the horses. In his fear of being seen the boy rendered detection certain by nervous motion. The heather and peat stratum overhung the brow of the pit in mats, hiding the actual verge. The boy had stepped beyond the solid ground; the heather now gave way, and down he rolled over the scarp of grey sand to the very foot of the man.

The red man opened the lantern and turned it upon the figure of the prostrate boy.

'Who be ye?' he said.

'Johnny Nunsuch, master!'

'What were you doing up there?'

'I don't know.'

'Watching me, I suppose?'

'Yes, master.'

'What did you watch me for?'

'Because I was coming home from Miss Vye's bonfire.'

'Beest hurt?'

'No.'

'Why, yes, you be: your hand is bleeding. Come under my tilt and let me tie it up.'

'Please let me look for my sixpence.'

'How did you come by that?'

'Miss Vye gied it to me for keeping up her bonfire.'

The sixpence was found, and the man went to the van, the boy behind, almost holding his breath.

The man took a piece of rag from a satchel containing sewing materials, tore off a strip, which, like everything else, was tinged red, and proceeded to bind up the wound.

'My eyes have got foggy-like—please may I sit down, master?' said the boy.

'To be sure, poor chap. 'Tis enough to make you feel fainty. Sit on that bundle.'

The man finished trying up the gash, and the boy said, 'I think I'll go home now, master.'

'You are rather afraid of me. Do you know what I be?'

The child surveyed his vermilion figure up and down with much misgiving, and finally said, 'Yes.'

'Well, what?'

'The reddleman!' he faltered.

'Yes, that's what I be. Though there's more than one. You little children think there's only one cuckoo, one fox, one giant, one devil, and one reddleman, when there's lots of us all.'

'Is there? You won't carry me off in your bags, will ye, master? 'Tis said that the reddleman will sometimes.'

'Nonsense. All that reddlemen do is sell reddle. You see all these bags at the back of my cart? They are not full of little boys—only full of red stuff.'

'Was you born a reddleman?'

'No, I took to it. I should be as white as you if I were to give up the trade—that is, I should be white in time—perhaps six months: not at first, because 'tis grow'd into my skin and won't wash out. Now, you'll never be afraid of a reddleman again, will ye?'

'No, never. Willy Orchard said he seed a red ghost here t'other day—perhaps that was you?'

'I was here t'other day.'

'Were you making that dusty light I saw by now?'[2]

'O yes: I was beating out some bags. And have you had a good bonfire up there? I saw the light. Why did Miss Vye want a bonfire so bad that she should give you sixpence to keep it up?'

'I don't know. I was tired, but she made me bide and keep up the fire just the same, while she kept going up across Rainbarrow way.'

'And how long did that last?'

'Until a hopfrog jumped into the pond,'

The reddleman suddenly ceased to talk idly. 'A hopfrog?' he inquired. 'Hopfrogs don't jump into ponds this time of year.'

'They do, for I heard one.'

'Certain-sure?'

'Yes. She told me afore that I should hear'n; and so I did. They say she's clever and deep, and perhaps she charmed 'en to come.'

'And what then?'

'Then I came down here, and I was afeard, and I went back; but I didn't like to speak to her, because of the gentleman, and I came on here again.'

'A gentleman—ah! What did she say to him, my man?'

'Told him she supposed he had not married the other woman because he liked his old sweetheart best; and things like that.'

'What did the gentleman say to her, my sonny?'

'He only said he did like her best, and how he was coming to see her again under Rainbarrow o' nights.'

'Ha!' cried the reddleman, slapping his hand against the side of his van so that the whole fabric shook under the blow. 'That's the secret o't!'

The little boy jumped clean from the stool.

'My man, don't you be afraid,' said the dealer in red, suddenly becoming gentle. 'I forgot you were here. That's only a curious way reddlemen have of going mad for a moment; but they don't hurt anybody. And what did the lady say then?'

'I can't mind. Please, Master Reddleman, may I go home-along now?'

'Ay, to be sure you may. I'll go a bit of ways with you.'

He conducted the boy out of the gravel-pit and into the path leading to his mother's cottage. When the little figure had vanished in the darkness the reddleman returned, resumed his seat by the fire, and proceeded to darn again.

2. Just now (dialect).

Love Leads a Shrewd Man into Strategy

IX

Reddlemen of the old school are now but seldom seen. Since the introduction of railways Wessex farmers have managed to do without these Mephistophelian[1] visitants, and the bright pigment so largely used by shepherds in preparing sheep for the fair is obtained by other routes. Even those who yet survive are losing the poetry of existence which characterized them when the pursuit of the trade meant periodical journeys to the pit whence the material was dug, a regular camping out from month to month, except in the depth of winter, a peregrination among farms which could be counted by the hundred, and in spite of this Arab existence the preservation of that respectability which is insured by the never-failing production of a well-lined purse.

Reddle spreads its lively hues over everything it lights on, and stamps unmistakably, as with the mark of Cain,[2] any person who has handled it half an hour.

A child's first sight of a reddleman was an epoch in his life. That blood-coloured figure was a sublimation of all the horrid dreams which had afflicted the juvenile spirit since imagination began. 'The reddleman is coming for you!' had been the formulated threat of Wessex mothers for many generations. He was successfully supplanted for a while, at the beginning of the present century, by Buonaparte; but as process of time rendered the latter personage stale and ineffective the older phrase resumed its early prominence. And now the reddleman has in his turn followed Buonaparte to the land of worn-out bogeys, and his place is filled by modern inventions.

The reddleman lived like a gipsy; but gipsies he scorned. He was about as thriving as travelling basket and mat makers; but he had nothing to do with them. He was more decently born and brought up than the cattle-drovers who passed and repassed him in his wanderings; but they merely nodded to him. His stock was more valuable than that of pedlars; but they did not think so, and passed his cart with eyes straight ahead. He was such an unnatural colour to look at that the men of roundabouts and wax-work shows[3] seemed gentlemen beside him; but he considered them low company, and remained aloof. Among all these squatters and folks of the road the reddleman continually found himself; yet he was not of them. His

---

1. In German legend Mephistopheles is the evil spirit to whom Faust sold his soul; he appears both in Christopher Marlowe's *Dr. Faustus* (*c.* 1592) and Johann Wolfgang von Goethe's *Faust* (1808, 1832).
2. Cain, the first son of Adam and Eve, was banished for killing his brother Abel; God "set a mark upon Cain," so that nobody would kill him (Genesis 4.15).
3. Exhibitions of lifelike wax figures.

occupation tended to isolate him, and isolated he was mostly seen to be.

It was sometimes suggested that reddlemen were criminals for whose misdeeds other men had wrongfully suffered: that in escaping the law they had not escaped their own consciences, and had taken to the trade as a lifelong penance. Else why should they have chosen it? In the present case such a question would have been particularly apposite. The reddleman who had entered Egdon that afternoon was an instance of the pleasing being wasted to form the ground-work of the singular, when an ugly foundation would have done just as well for that purpose. The one point that was forbidding about this reddleman was his colour. Freed from that he would have been as agreeable a specimen of rustic manhood as one would often see. A keen observer might have been inclined to think—which was, indeed, partly the truth—that he had relinquished his proper station in life for want of interest in it. Moreover, after looking at him one would have hazarded the guess that good-nature, and an acuteness as extreme as it could be without verging on craft, formed the frame-work of his character.

While he darned the stocking his face became rigid with thought. Softer expressions followed this, and then again recurred the tender sadness which had sat upon him during his drive along the highway that afternoon. Presently his needle stopped. He laid down the stocking, arose from his seat, and took a leathern pouch from a hook in the corner of the van. This contained among other articles a brown-paper packet, which, to judge from the hinge-like character of its worn folds, seemed to have been carefully opened and closed a good many times. He sat down on a three-legged milking-stool that formed the only seat in the van, and, examining his packet by the light of a candle, took thence an old letter and spread it open. The writing had originally been traced on white paper, but the letter had now assumed a pale red tinge from the accident of its situation; and the black strokes of writing thereon looked like the twigs of a winter hedge against a vermilion sunset. The letter bore a date some two years previous to that time, and was signed 'Thomasin Yeobright.' It ran as follows:—

> DEAR DIGGORY VENN,—The question you put when you overtook me coming home from Pond-close gave me such a surprise that I am afraid I did not make you exactly understand what I meant. Of course, if my aunt had not met me I could have explained all then at once, but as it was there was no chance. I have been quite uneasy since, as you know I do not wish to pain you, yet I fear I shall be doing so now in contradicting what I seemed to say then. I cannot, Diggory, marry you, or think of letting you call me your sweetheart. I could

'The reddleman re-reads an old love letter.'

not, indeed, Diggory. I hope you will not much mind my saying this, and feel in a great pain. It makes me very sad when I think it may, for I like you very much, and I always put you next to my cousin Clym in my mind. There are so many reasons why we cannot be married that I can hardly name them all in a letter. I did not in the least expect that you were going to speak on such a thing when you followed me, because I had never thought of you in the sense of a lover at all. You must not becall[4] me for laughing when you spoke; you mistook when

4. Blame (dialect).

you thought I laughed at you as a foolish man. I laughed because the idea was so odd, and not at you at all. The great reason with my own personal self for not letting you court me is, that I do not feel the things a woman ought to feel who consents to walk with you with the meaning of being your wife. It is not as you think, that I have another in my mind, for I do not encourage anybody, and never have in my life. Another reason is my aunt. She would not, I know, agree to it, even if I wished to have you. She likes you very well, but she will want me to look a little higher than a small dairy-farmer, and marry a professional man. I hope you will not set your heart against me for writing plainly, but I felt you might try to see me again, and it is better that we should not meet. I shall always think of you as a good man, and be anxious for your well-doing. I send this by Jane Orchard's little maid,—And remain Diggory, your faithful friend,

THOMASIN YEOBRIGHT.

To Mr. VENN, Dairy-farmer.

Since the arrival of that letter, on a certain autumn morning long ago, the reddleman and Thomasin had not met till to-day. During the interval he had shifted his position even further from hers than it had originally been, by adopting the reddle trade; though he was really in very good circumstances still. Indeed, seeing that his expenditure was only one-fourth of his income, he might have been called a prosperous man.

Rejected suitors take to roaming as naturally as unhived bees; and the business to which he had cynically devoted himself was in many ways congenial to Venn. But his wanderings, by mere stress of old emotions, had frequently taken an Egdon direction, though he never intruded upon her who attracted him thither. To be in Thomasin's heath, and near her, yet unseen, was the one ewe-lamb[5] of pleasure left to him.

Then came the incident of that day, and the reddleman, still loving her well, was excited by this accidental service to her at a critical juncture to vow an active devotion to her cause, instead of, as hitherto, sighing and holding aloof. After what had happened it was impossible that he should not doubt the honesty of Wildeve's intentions. But her hope was apparently centred upon him; and dismissing his regrets Venn determined to aid her to be happy in her own chosen way. That this way was, of all others, the most distressing to himself, was awkward enough; but the reddleman's love was generous.

---

5. Sent by God to warn King David against adultery, the prophet Nathan tells him a parable about a rich man with many flocks who steals a poor man's "one little ewe lamb"; see I Samuel 12.1–5.

His first active step in watching over Thomasin's interests was taken about seven o'clock the next evening, and was dictated by the news which he had learnt from the sad boy. That Eustacia was somehow the cause of Wildeve's carelessness in relation to the marriage had at once been Venn's conclusion on hearing of the secret meeting between them. It did not occur to his mind that Eustacia's love-signal to Wildeve was the tender effect upon the deserted beauty of the intelligence which her grandfather had brought home. His instinct was to regard her as a conspirator against rather than as an antecedent obstacle to Thomasin's happiness.

During the day he had been exceedingly anxious to learn the condition of Thomasin; but he did not venture to intrude upon a threshold to which he was a stranger, particularly at such an unpleasant moment as this. He had occupied his time in moving with his ponies and load to a new point in the heath, eastward to his previous station; and here he selected a nook with a careful eye to shelter from wind and rain, which seemed to mean that his stay there was to be a comparatively extended one. After this he returned on foot some part of the way that he had come; and, it being now dark, he diverged to the left till he stood behind a holly-bush on the edge of a pit not twenty yards from Rainbarrow.

He watched for a meeting there, but he watched in vain. Nobody except himself came near the spot that night.

But the loss of his labour produced little effect upon the reddleman. He had stood in the shoes of Tantalus,[6] and seemed to look upon a certain mass of disappointment as the natural preface to all realizations, without which preface they would give cause for alarm.

The same hour the next evening found him again at the same place; but Eustacia and Wildeve, the expected trysters, did not appear.

He pursued precisely the same course yet four nights longer, and without success. But on the next, being the day-week of their previous meeting, he saw a female shape floating along the ridge and the outline of a young man ascending from the valley. They met in the little ditch encircling the tumulus—the original excavation from which it had been thrown up by the ancient British people.

The reddleman, stung with suspicion of wrong to Thomasin, was aroused to strategy in a moment. He instantly left the bush and crept forward on his hands and knees. When he had got as close as he might safely venture without discovery he found that, owing to a cross-wind, the conversation of the trysting pair could not be overheard.

6. In Greek mythology, Tantalus was condemned to stand up to his neck in water which receded when he tried to drink it, beneath a tree hung with clusters of fruit just out of reach.

Near him, as in divers places about the heath, were areas strewn with large turves, which lay edgeways and upside-down awaiting removal by Timothy Fairway, previous to the winter weather. He took two of these as he lay, and dragged them over him till one covered his head and shoulders, the other his back and legs. The reddleman would now have been quite invisible, even by daylight; the turves, standing upon him with the heather upwards, looked precisely as if they were growing. He crept along again, and the turves upon his back crept with him. Had he approached without any covering the chances are that he would not have been perceived in the dusk; approaching thus, it was as though he burrowed underground. In this manner he came quite close to where the two were standing.

'Wish to consult me on the matter?' reached his ears in the rich, impetuous accents of Eustacia Vye. 'Consult me? It is an indignity to me to talk so: I won't bear it any longer!' She began weeping. 'I have loved you, and have shown you that I loved you, much to my regret; and yet you can come and say in that frigid way that you wish to consult with me whether it would not be better to marry Thomasin. Better—of course it would be. Marry her: she is nearer to your own position in life than I am!'

'Yes, yes; that's very well,' said Wildeve peremptorily. 'But we must look at things as they are. Whatever blame may attach to me for having brought it about, Thomasin's position is at present much worse than yours. I simply tell you that I am in a strait.'

'But you shall not tell me! You must see that it is only harassing me. Damon, you have not acted well; you have sunk in my opinion. You have not valued my courtesy—the courtesy of a lady in loving you—who used to think of far more ambitious things. But it was Thomasin's fault. She won you away from me, and she deserves to suffer for it. Where is she staying now? Not that I care, nor where I am myself. Ah, if I were dead and gone how glad she would be! Where is she, I ask?'

'Thomasin is now staying at her aunt's shut up in a bedroom, and keeping out of everybody's sight,' he said indifferently.

'I don't think you care much about her even now,' said Eustacia with sudden joyousness; 'for if you did you wouldn't talk so coolly about her. Do you talk so coolly to her about me? Ah, I expect you do! Why did you originally go away from me? I don't think I can ever forgive you, except on one condition, that whenever you desert me, you come back again, sorry that you served me so.'

'I never wish to desert you.'

'I do not thank you for that. I should hate it to be all smooth. Indeed, I think I like you to desert me a little once now and then. Love is the dismallest thing where the lover is quite honest. O, it is a shame to say so; but it is true!' She indulged in a little laugh. 'My low spirits begin at the very idea. Don't you offer me tame love, or away you go!'

'I wish Tamsie were not such a confoundedly good little woman,' said Wildeve, 'so that I could be faithful to you without injuring a worthy person. It is I who am the sinner after all; I am not worth the little finger of either of you.'

'But you must not sacrifice yourself to her from any sense of justice,' replied Eustacia quickly. 'If you do not love her it is the most merciful thing in the long run to leave her as she is. That's always the best way. There, now I have been unwomanly, I suppose. When you have left me I am always angry with myself for things that I have said to you.'

Wildeve walked a pace or two among the heather without replying. The pause was filled up by the intonation of a pollard thorn a little way to windward, the breezes filtering through its unyielding twigs as through a strainer. It was as if the night sang dirges with clenched teeth.

She continued, half sorrowfully, 'Since meeting you last, it has occurred to me once or twice that perhaps it was not for love of me you did not marry her. Tell me, Damon: I'll try to bear it. Had I nothing whatever to do with the matter?'

'Do you press me to tell?'

'Yes, I must know. I see I have been too ready to believe in my own power.'

'Well, the immediate reason was that the licence would not do for the place, and before I could get another she ran away. Up to that point you had nothing to do with it. Since then her aunt has spoken to me in a tone which I don't at all like.'

'Yes, yes! I am nothing in it—I am nothing in it. You only trifle with me. Heaven, what can I, Eustacia Vye, be made of to think so much of you!'

'Nonsense; do not be so passionate. . . . Eustacia, how we roved among these bushes last year, when the hot days had got cool, and the shades of the hills kept us almost invisible in the hollows!'

She remained in moody silence till she said, 'Yes; and how I used to laugh at you for daring to look up to me! But you have well made me suffer for that since.'

'Yes, you served me cruelly enough until I thought I had found some one fairer than you. A blessed find for me, Eustacia.'

'Do you still think you found somebody fairer?'

'Sometimes I do, sometimes I don't. The scales are balanced so nicely that a feather would turn them.'

'But don't you really care whether I meet you or whether I don't?' she said slowly.

'I care a little, but not enough to break my rest,' replied the

young man languidly. 'No, all that's past. I find there are two flowers where I thought there was only one. Perhaps there are three, or
four, or any number as good as the first. . . . Mine is a curious fate.
Who would have thought that all this could happen to me?'

She interrupted with a suppressed fire of which either love or
anger seemed an equally possible issue, 'Do you love me now?'

'Who can say?'

'Tell me; I will know it!'

'I do, and I do not,' said he mischievously. 'That is, I have my
times and my seasons. One moment you are too tall, another moment you are too do-nothing, another too melancholy, another too
dark, another I don't know what, except—that you are not the
whole world to me that you used to be, my dear. But you are a
pleasant lady to know, and nice to meet, and I dare say as sweet as
ever—almost.'

Eustacia was silent, and she turned from him, till she said, in a
voice of suspended mightiness, 'I am for a walk, and this is my way.'

'Well, I can do worse than follow you.'

'You know you can't do otherwise, for all your moods and
changes!' she answered defiantly. 'Say what you will; try as you may;
keep away from me all that you can—you will never forget me. You
will love me all your life long. You would jump to marry me!'

'So I would!' said Wildeve. 'Such strange thoughts as I've had
from time to time, Eustacia; and they come to me this moment. You
hate the heath as much as ever; that I know.'

'I do,' she murmured deeply. ' 'Tis my cross, my shame, and will
be my death!'

'I abhor it too,' said he. 'How mournfully the wind blows round
us now!'

She did not answer. Its tone was indeed solemn and pervasive.
Compound utterances addressed themselves to their senses, and it
was possible to view by ear the features of the neighbourhood.
Acoustic pictures were returned from the darkened scenery; they
could hear where the tracts of heather began and ended; where the
furze was growing stalky and tall; where it had been recently cut; in
what direction the fir-clump lay, and how near was the pit in which
the hollies grew; for these differing features had their voices no less
than their shapes and colours.

'God, how lonely it is!' resumed Wildeve. 'What are picturesque
ravines and mists to us who see nothing else? Why should we stay
here? Will you go with me to America? I have kindred in Wiscon-
sin.'

'That wants consideration.'

'It seems impossible to do well here, unless one were a wild bird
or a landscape-painter. Well?'

'Give me time,' she softly said, taking his hand. 'America is so far away. Are you going to walk with me a little way?'

As Eustacia uttered the latter words she retired from the base of the barrow, and Wildeve followed her, so that the reddleman could hear no more.

He lifted the turves and arose. Their black figures sank and disappeared from against the sky. They were as two horns which the sluggish heath had put forth from its crown, like a mollusc, and had now again drawn in.

The reddleman's walk across the vale, and over into the next where his cart lay, was not sprightly for a slim young fellow of twenty-four. His spirit was perturbed to aching. The breezes that blew around his mouth in that walk carried off upon them the accents of a commination.[7]

He entered the van, where there was a fire in a stove. Without lighting his candle he sat down at once on the three-legged stool, and pondered on what he had seen and heard touching that still loved-one of his. He uttered a sound which was neither sigh nor sob, but was even more indicative than either of a troubled mind.

'My Tamsie,' he whispered heavily. 'What can be done? Yes, I will see that Eustacia Vye.'

A Desperate Attempt at Persuasion

X

The next morning, at the time when the height of the sun appeared very insignificant from any part of the heath as compared with the altitude of Rainbarrow, and when all the little hills in the lower levels were like an archipelago in a fog-formed Ægean,[1] the reddleman came from the brambled nook which he had adopted as his quarters and ascended the slopes of Mistover Knap.

Though these shaggy hills were apparently so solitary, several keen round eyes were always ready on such a wintry morning as this to converge upon a passer-by. Feathered species sojourned here in hiding which would have created wonder if found elsewhere. A bustard haunted the spot, and not many years before this five and twenty might have been seen in Egdon at one time. Marsh-harriers looked up from the valley by Wildeve's. A cream-coloured courser[2] had used to visit this hill, a bird so rare that not more than a dozen

---

7. The threats of divine anger against sinners in the Anglican liturgy for Ash Wednesday.
1. An archipelago is a group of islands; the Aegean is the sea east of Greece.
2. The ground-dwelling Little Bustard is a native of contintental Europe, rarely seen in Britain; the Marsh Harrier is a medium-sized, long-winged bird of prey, no longer found in "Wessex"; the Cream-coloured Courser, a slim fast-running bird, is a very rare visitor from North Africa.

have ever been seen in England; but a barbarian rested neither night nor day till he had shot the African truant, and after that event cream-coloured coursers thought fit to enter Egdon no more.

A traveller who should walk and observe any of these visitants as Venn observed them now could feel himself to be in direct communication with regions unknown to man. Here in front of him was a wild mallard—just arrived from the home of the north wind. The creature brought within him an amplitude of Northern knowledge. Glacial catastrophes, snowstorm episodes, glittering auroral effects, Polaris in the zenith, Franklin[3] underfoot,—the category of his commonplaces was wonderful. But the bird, like many other philosophers, seemed as he looked at the reddleman to think that a present moment of comfortable reality was worth a decade of memories.

Venn passed on through these towards the house of the isolated beauty who lived up among them and despised them. The day was Sunday; but as going to church, except to be married or buried, was exceptional at Egdon, this made little difference. He had determined upon the bold stroke of asking for an interview with Miss Vye—to attack her position as Thomasin's rival either by art or by storm, showing therein, somewhat too conspicuously, the want of gallantry characteristic of a certain astute sort of men, from clowns to kings. The great Frederick making war on the beautiful Archduchess,[4] Napoleon refusing terms to the beautiful Queen of Prussia,[5] were not more dead to difference of sex than the reddleman was, in his peculiar way, in planning the displacement of Eustacia.

To call at the captain's cottage was always more or less an undertaking for the inferior inhabitants. Though occasionally chatty, his moods were erratic, and nobody could be certain how he would behave at any particular moment. Eustacia was reserved, and lived very much to herself. Except the daughter of one of the cotters,[6] who was their servant, and a lad who worked in the garden and stable, scarcely any one but themselves ever entered the house. They were the only genteel people of the district except the Yeobrights, and though far from rich, they did not feel that necessity for preserving a friendly face towards every man, bird, and beast which influenced their poorer neighbours.

When the reddleman entered the garden the old man was look-

---

3. Polaris is the North Star. The British explorer Sir John Franklin disappeared in the Arctic in 1845; despite numerous expeditions, the fact of his death, and that of all 129 of his crew, was not established until 1859.
4. Frederick the Great of Prussia emerged victorious from the Seven Years War (1756–63) against Austria, ruled by the Archduchess Maria Theresa.
5. Napoleon refused to make concessions after the defeat of the Prussian armies at Jena in 1806, despite a personal appeal from the Queen of Prussia.
6. A cotter is a laborer occupying a cottage belonging to a farm.

ing through his glass at the stain of blue sea in the distant landscape, the little anchors on his buttons twinkling in the sun. He
recognized Venn as his companion on the highway, but made no remark on that circumstance, merely saying, 'Ah, reddleman—you
here? Have a glass of grog?'[7]

Venn declined, on the plea of it being too early, and stated that
his business was with Miss Vye. The captain surveyed him from cap
to waistcoat and from waistcoat to leggings for a few moments, and
finally asked him to go indoors.

Miss Vye was not to be seen by anybody just then; and the reddleman waited in the window-bench of the kitchen, his hands
hanging across his divergent knees, and his cap hanging from his
hands.

'I suppose the young lady is not up yet?' he presently said to the
servant.

'Not quite yet. Folks never call upon ladies at this time of day.'

'Then I'll step outside,' said Venn. 'If she is willing to see me, will
she please send out word, and I'll come in.'

The reddleman left the house and loitered on the hill adjoining.
A considerable time elapsed, and no request for his presence was
brought. He was beginning to think that his scheme had failed,
when he beheld the form of Eustacia herself coming leisurely towards him. A sense of novelty in giving audience to that singular
figure had been sufficient to draw her forth.

She seemed to feel, after a bare look at Diggory Venn, that the
man had come on a strange errand, and that he was not so mean as
she had thought him; for her close approach did not cause him to
writhe uneasily, or shift his feet, or show any of those little signs
which escape an ingenuous rustic at the advent of the uncommon
in womankind. On his inquiring if he might have a conversation
with her she replied, 'Yes, walk beside me;' and continued to move
on.

Before they had gone far it occurred to the perspicacious reddleman that he would have acted more wisely by appearing less unim-
pressionable, and he resolved to correct the error as soon as he
could find opportunity.

'I have made so bold, miss, as to step across and tell you some
strange news which has come to my ears about that man.'

'Ah! what man?'

He jerked his elbow to south-east—the direction of the Quiet
Woman.

Eustacia turned quickly to him. 'Do you mean Mr. Wildeve?'

'Yes, there is trouble in a household on account of him, and I

7. Spirits, usually rum, served with hot water and sugar.

have come to let you know of it, because I believe you might have power to drive it away.'

'I? What is the trouble?'

'It is quite a secret. It is that he may refuse to marry Thomasin Yeobright after all.'

Eustacia, though set inwardly pulsing by his words, was equal to her part in such a drama as this. She replied coldly, 'I do not wish to listen to this, and you must not expect me to interfere.'

'But, miss, you will hear one word?'

'I cannot. I am not interested in the marriage, and even if I were I could not compel Mr. Wildeve to do my bidding.'

'As the only lady on the heath I think you might,' said Venn with subtle indirectness. 'This is how the case stands. Mr. Wildeve would marry Thomasin at once, and make all matters smooth, if so be there were not another woman in the case. This other woman is some person he has picked up with, and meets on the heath occasionally, I believe. He will never marry her, and yet through her he may never marry the woman who loves him dearly. Now, if you, miss, who have so much sway over us men-folk, were to insist that he should treat your young neighbour Tamsin with honourable kindness and give up the other woman, he would perhaps do it, and save her a good deal of misery.'

'Ah, my life!' said Eustacia, with a laugh which unclosed her lips so that the sun shone into her mouth as into a tulip, and lent it a similar scarlet fire. 'You think too much of my influence over men-folk indeed, reddleman. If I had such a power as you imagine I would go straight and use it for the good of anybody who has been kind to me—which Thomasin Yeobright has not particularly, to my knowledge.'

'Can it be that you really don't know of it—how much she has always thought of you?'

'I have never heard a word of it. Although we live only two miles apart I have never been inside her aunt's house in my life.'

The superciliousness that lurked in her manner told Venn that thus far he had utterly failed. He inwardly sighed and felt it necessary to unmask his second argument.

'Well, leaving that out of the question, 'tis in your power, I assure you, Miss Vye, to do a great deal of good to another woman.'

She shook her head.

'Your comeliness is law with Mr. Wildeve. It is law with all men who see 'ee. They say, "This well-favoured lady coming—what's her name? How handsome!" Handsomer than Thomasin Yeobright,' the reddleman persisted, saying to himself, 'God forgive a rascal for lying!' And she was handsomer, but the reddleman was far from thinking so. There was a certain obscurity in Eustacia's beauty, and

Venn's eye was not trained. In her winter dress, as now, she was like the tiger-beetle,[8] which, when observed in dull situations, seems to be of the quietest neutral colour, but under a full illumination blazes with dazzling splendour.

Eustacia could not help replying, though conscious that she endangered her dignity thereby. 'Many women are lovelier than Thomasin,' she said; 'so not much attaches to that.'

The reddleman suffered the wound and went on: 'He is a man who notices the looks of women, and you could twist him to your will like withywind,[9] if you only had the mind.'

'Surely what she cannot do who has been so much with him I cannot do living up here away from him.'

The reddleman wheeled and looked her in the face. 'Miss Vye!' he said.

'Why do you say that—as if you doubted me?' She spoke faintly, and her breathing was quick. 'The idea of your speaking in that tone to me!' she added, with a forced smile of hauteur. 'What could have been in your mind to lead you to speak like that?'

'Miss Vye, why should you make-believe that you don't know this man?—I know why, certainly. He is beneath you, and you are ashamed.'

'You are mistaken. What do you mean?'

The reddleman had decided to play the card of truth. 'I was at the meeting by Rainbarrow last night and heard every word,' he said. 'The woman that stands between Wildeve and Thomasin is yourself.'

It was a disconcerting lift of the curtain, and the mortification of Candaules' wife[1] glowed in her. The moment had arrived when her lip would tremble in spite of herself, and when the gasp could no longer be kept down.

'I am unwell,' she said hurriedly. 'No—it is not that—I am not in a humour to hear you further. Leave me, please.'

'I must speak, Miss Vye, in spite of paining you. What I would put before you is this. However it may come about—whether she is to blame, or you—her case is without doubt worse than yours. Your giving up Mr. Wildeve will be a real advantage to you, for how could you marry him? Now she cannot get off so easily—everybody will blame her if she loses him. Then I ask you—not because her right is best, but because her situation is worst—to give him up to her.'

---

8. A predatory beetle, frequently with striped wing-cases; Hardy found the detail in J. G. Wood's *Insects at Home* (1872).
9. Dialect name for bindweed, which grows by twining itself around other plants.
1. Candaules, King of Lydia (*c.* 710–688 B.C.E.), invited Gyges into his wife's chamber to witness her beauty; the insulted Queen had her husband murdered by Gyges, whom she then married.

'No—I won't, I won't!' she said impetuously, quite forgetful of her previous manner towards the reddleman as an underling. 'Nobody has ever been served so! It was going on well—I will not be beaten down—by an inferior woman like her. It is very well for you to come and plead for her, but is she not herself the cause of all her own trouble? Am I not to show favour to any person I may choose without asking permission of a parcel of cottagers? She has come between me and my inclination, and now that she finds herself rightly punished she gets you to plead for her!'

'Indeed,' said Venn earnestly, 'she knows nothing whatever about it. It is only I who ask you to give him up. It will be better for her and you both. People will say bad things if they find out that a lady secretly meets a man who has ill-used another woman.'

'I have *not* injured her: he was mine before he was hers! He came back—because—because he liked me best!' she said wildly. 'But I lose all self-respect in talking to you. What am I giving way to!'

'I can keep secrets,' said Venn gently. 'You need not fear. I am the only man who knows of your meetings with him. There is but one thing more to speak of, and then I will be gone. I heard you say to him that you hated living here—that Egdon heath was a jail to you.'

'I did say so. There is a sort of beauty in the scenery, I know; but it is a jail to me. The man you mention does not save me from that feeling, though he lives here. I should have cared nothing for him had there been a better person near.'

The reddleman looked hopeful: after these words from her his third attempt seemed promising. 'As we have now opened our minds a bit, miss,' he said, 'I'll tell you what I have got to propose. Since I have taken to the reddle trade I travel a good deal, as you know.'

She inclined her head, and swept round so that her eyes rested in the misty vale beneath them.

'And in my travels I go near Budmouth. Now Budmouth is a wonderful place—wonderful—a great salt sheening sea bending into the land like a bow—thousands of gentlepeople walking up and down—bands of music playing—officers by sea and officers by land walking among the rest—out of every ten folk you meet nine of 'em in love.'

'I know it,' she said disdainfully. 'I know Budmouth better than you. I was born there. My father came to be a military musician there from abroad. Ah, my soul, Budmouth! I wish I was there now.'

The reddleman was surprised to see how a slow fire could blaze on occasion. 'If you were, miss,' he replied, 'in a week's time you would think no more of Wildeve than of one of those he'th-croppers that we see yond. Now, I could get you there.'

'How?' said Eustacia, with intense curiosity in her heavy eyes.

'My uncle has been for five and twenty years the trusty man of a rich widow-lady who has a beautiful house facing the sea. This lady has become old and lame, and she wants a young company-keeper to read and sing to her, but can't get one to her mind to save her life, though she've advertised in the papers, and tried half a dozen. She would jump to get you, and uncle would make it all easy.'

'I should have to work, perhaps?'

'No, not real work: you'd have a little to do, such as reading and that. You would not be wanted till New Year's Day.'

'I knew it meant work,' she said, drooping to languor again.

'I confess there would be a trifle to do in the way of amusing her; but though idle people might call it work, working people would call it play. Think of the company and the life you'd lead, miss; the gaiety you'd see, and the gentleman you'd marry. My uncle is to inquire for a trustworthy young lady from the country, as she don't like town girls.'

'It is to wear myself out to please her! and I won't go. O, if I could live in a gay town as a lady should, and go my own ways, and do my own doings, I'd give the wrinkled half of my life! Yes, reddle-man, that would I.'

'Help me to get Thomasin happy, miss, and the chance shall be yours,' urged her companion.

'Chance!—'tis no chance,' she said proudly. 'What can a poor man like you offer me, indeed?—I am going indoors. I have nothing more to say. Don't your horses want feeding, or your reddlebags want mending, or don't you want to find buyers for your goods, that you stay idling here like this?'

Venn spoke not another word. With his hands behind him he turned away, that she might not see the hopeless disappointment in his face. The mental clearness and power he had found in this lonely girl had indeed filled his manner with misgiving even from the first few minutes of close quarters with her. Her youth and situation had led him to expect a simplicity quite at the beck of his method. But a system of inducement which might have carried weaker country lasses along with it had merely repelled Eustacia. As a rule, the word Budmouth meant fascination on Egdon. That Royal port[2] and watering-place, if truly mirrored in the minds of the heath-folk, must have combined, in a charming and indescribable manner, a Carthaginian bustle of building with Tarentine luxuriousness and Baian[3] health and beauty. Eustacia felt little less

2. King George III (reigned 1760–1820) was a frequent visitor to Weymouth (Hardy's 'Budmouth') in his later years.
3. Carthage, near Tunis on the north coast of Africa, was a powerful commercial and cultural center from around 500 B.C.E. until about 150 B.C.E.; Tarentum (modern Taranto) was a rich Greek city on the Italian coast, famous for luxurious living; Baiae, a spa town near Naples, was a favorite resort of the Roman aristocracy.

extravagantly about the place; but she would not sink her independence to get there.

When Diggory Venn had gone quite away, Eustacia walked to the bank and looked down the wild and picturesque vale towards the sun, which was also in the direction of Wildeve's. The mist had now so far collapsed that the tips of the trees and bushes around his house could just be discerned, as if boring upwards through a vast white cobweb which cloaked them from the day. There was no doubt that her mind was inclined thitherward; indefinitely, fancifully—twining and untwining about him as the single object within her horizon on which dreams might crystallize. The man who had begun by being merely her amusement, and would never have been more than her hobby but for his skill in deserting her at the right moments, was now again her desire. Cessation in his love-making had revivified her love. Such feeling as Eustacia had idly given to Wildeve was dammed into a flood by Thomasin. She had used to tease Wildeve, but that was before another had favoured him. Often a drop of irony into an indifferent situation renders the whole piquant.

'I will never give him up—never!' she said impetuously.

The reddleman's hint that rumour might show her to disadvantage had no permanent terror for Eustacia. She was as unconcerned at that contingency as a goddess at a lack of linen. This did not originate in inherent shamelessness, but in her living too far from the world to feel the impact of public opinion. Zenobia[4] in the desert could hardly have cared what was said about her at Rome. As far as social ethics were concerned Eustacia approached the savage state, though in emotion she was all the while an epicure.[5] She had advanced to the secret recesses of sensuousness, yet had hardly crossed the threshold of conventionality.

The Dishonesty of an Honest Woman

XI

The reddleman had left Eustacia's presence with desponding views on Thomasin's future happiness; but he was awakened to the fact that one other channel remained untried by seeing, as he followed the way to his van, the form of Mrs. Yeobright slowly walking towards the Quiet Woman. He went across to her; and could almost perceive in her anxious face that this journey of hers to Wildeve was undertaken with the same object as his own to Eustacia.

4. Zenobia, Queen of Palmyra in the Syrian desert, sought to extend her power in the region, but was defeated and captured by the Romans in 272 C.E.
5. Person devoted to refined or sensuous pleasure.

She did not conceal the fact. 'Then,' said the reddleman, 'you may as well leave it alone, Mrs. Yeobright.'

'I half think so myself,' she said. 'But nothing else remains to be done besides pressing the question upon him.'

'I should like to say a word first,' said Venn firmly. 'Mr. Wildeve is not the only man who has asked Thomasin to marry him; and why should not another have a chance? Mrs. Yeobright, I should be glad to marry your niece, and would have done it any time these last two years. There, now it is out, and I have never told anybody before but herself.'

Mrs. Yeobright was not demonstrative, but her eyes involuntarily glanced towards his singular though shapely figure.

'Looks are not everything,' said the reddleman, noticing the glance. 'There's many a calling that don't bring in so much as mine, if it comes to money; and perhaps I am not so much worse off than Wildeve. There is nobody so poor as these professional fellows who have failed; and if you shouldn't like my redness—well, I am not red by birth, you know; I only took to this business for a freak; and I might turn my hand to something else in good time.'

'I am much obliged to you for your interest in my niece; but I fear there would be objections. More than that, she is devoted to this man.'

'True; or I shouldn't have done what I have this morning.'

'Otherwise there would be no pain in the case, and you would not see me going to his house now. What was Thomasin's answer when you told her of your feelings?'

'She wrote that you would object to me; and other things.'

'She was in a measure right. You must not take this unkindly: I merely state it as a truth. You have been good to her, and we do not forget it. But as she was unwilling on her own account to be your wife, that settles the point without my wishes being concerned.'

'Yes. But there is a difference between then and now, ma'am. She is distressed now, and I have thought that if you were to talk to her about me, and think favourably of me yourself, there might be a chance of winning her round, and getting her quite independent of this Wildeve's backward and forward play, and his not knowing whether he'll have her or no.'

Mrs. Yeobright shook her head. 'Thomasin thinks, and I think with her, that she ought to be Wildeve's wife, if she means to appear before the world without a slur upon her name. If they marry soon, everybody will believe that an accident did really prevent the wedding. If not, it may cast a shade upon her character—at any rate make her ridiculous. In short, if it is anyhow possible they must marry now.'

'I thought that till half an hour ago. But, after all, why should her going off with him to Anglebury for a few hours do her any harm? Anybody who knows how pure she is will feel any such thought to be quite unjust. I have been trying this morning to help on this marriage with Wildeve—yes, I, ma'am—in the belief that I ought to do it, because she was so wrapped up in him. But I much question if I was right, after all. However, nothing came of it. And now I offer myself.'

Mrs. Yeobright appeared disinclined to enter further into the question. 'I fear I must go on,' she said. 'I do not see that anything else can be done.'

And she went on. But though this conversation did not divert Thomasin's aunt from her purposed interview with Wildeve, it made a considerable difference in her mode of conducting that interview. She thanked God for the weapon which the reddleman had put into her hands.

Wildeve was at home when she reached the inn. He showed her silently into the parlour, and closed the door. Mrs. Yeobright began—

'I have thought it my duty to call to-day. A new proposal has been made to me, which has rather astonished me. It will affect Thomasin greatly; and I have decided that it should at least be mentioned to you.'

'Yes? What is it?' he said civilly.

'It is, of course, in reference to her future. You may not be aware that another man has shown himself anxious to marry Thomasin. Now, though I have not encouraged him yet, I cannot conscientiously refuse him a chance any longer. I don't wish to be short with you; but I must be fair to him and to her.'

'Who is the man?' said Wildeve with surprise.

'One who has been in love with her longer than she has with you. He proposed to her two years ago. At that time she refused him.'

'Well?'

'He has seen her lately, and has asked me for permission to pay his addresses to her. She may not refuse him twice.'

'What is his name?'

Mrs. Yeobright declined to say. 'He is a man Thomasin likes,' she added, 'and one whose constancy she respects at least. It seems to me that what she refused then she would be glad to get now. She is much annoyed at her awkward position.'

'She never once told me of this old lover.'

'The gentlest women are not such fools as to show *every* card.'

'Well, if she wants him I suppose she must have him.'

'It is easy enough to say that; but you don't see the difficulty. He wants her much more than she wants him; and before I can encourage anything of the sort I must have a clear understanding from you that you will not interfere to injure an arrangement which I promote in the belief that it is for the best. Suppose, when they are engaged, and everything is smoothly arranged for their marriage, that you should step between them and renew your suit? You might not win her back, but you might cause much unhappiness.'

'Of course I should do no such thing,' said Wildeve. 'But they are not engaged yet. How do you know that Thomasin would accept him?'

'That's a question I have carefully put to myself; and upon the whole the probabilities are in favour of her accepting him in time. I flatter myself that I have some influence over her. She is pliable, and I can be strong in my recommendations of him.'

'And in your disparagement of me at the same time.'

'Well, you may depend upon my not praising you,' she said drily. 'And if this seems like manœuvring, you must remember that her position is peculiar, and that she has been hardly used. I shall also be helped in making the match by her own desire to escape from the humiliation of her present state; and a woman's pride in these cases will lead her a very great way. A little managing may be required to bring her round; but I am equal to that, provided that you agree to the one thing indispensable; that is, to make a distinct declaration that she is to think no more of you as a possible husband. That will pique her into accepting him.'

'I can hardly say that just now, Mrs. Yeobright. It is so sudden.'

'And so my whole plan is interfered with! It is very inconvenient that you refuse to help my family even to the small extent of saying distinctly you will have nothing to do with us.'

Wildeve reflected uncomfortably. 'I confess I was not prepared for this,' he said. 'Of course I'll give her up if you wish, if it is necessary. But I thought I might be her husband.'

'We have heard that before.'

'Now, Mrs. Yeobright, don't let us disagree. Give me a fair time. I don't want to stand in the way of any better chance she may have; only I wish you had let me know earlier. I will write to you or call in a day or two. Will that suffice?'

'Yes,' she replied, 'provided you promise not to communicate with Thomasin without my knowledge.'

'I promise that,' he said. And the interview then terminated, Mrs. Yeobright returning homeward as she had come.

By far the greatest effect of her simple strategy on that day was, as often happens, in a quarter quite outside her view when arranging it. In the first place, her visit sent Wildeve the same evening after dark to Eustacia's house at Mistover.

At this hour the lonely dwelling was closely blinded and shuttered from the chill and darkness without. Wildeve's clandestine plan with her was to take a little gravel in his hand and hold it to the crevice at the top of the window-shutter, which was on the out-side, so that it should fall with a gentle rustle, resembling that of a mouse, between shutter and glass. This precaution in attracting her attention was to avoid arousing the suspicions of her grandfather.

The soft words, 'I hear; wait for me,' in Eustacia's voice from within told him that she was alone.

He waited in his customary manner by walking round the enclo-sure and idling by the pool, for Wildeve was never asked into the house by his proud though condescending mistress. She showed no sign of coming out in a hurry. The time wore on, and he began to grow impatient. In the course of twenty minutes she appeared from round the corner, and advanced as if merely taking an airing.

'You would not have kept me so long had you known what I come about,' he said with bitterness. 'Still, you are worth waiting for.'

'What has happened?' said Eustacia. 'I did not know you were in trouble. I too am gloomy enough.'

'I am not in trouble,' said he. 'It is merely that affairs have come to a head, and I must take a clear course.'

'What course is that?' she asked with attentive interest.

'And can you forget so soon what I proposed to you the other night? Why, take you from this place, and carry you away with me abroad.'

'I have not forgotten. But why have you come so unexpectedly to repeat the question, when you only promised to come next Satur-day? I thought I was to have plenty of time to consider.'

'Yes, but the situation is different now.'

'Explain to me.'

'I don't want to explain, for I may pain you.'

'But I must know the reason of this hurry.'

'It is simply my ardour, dear Eustacia. Everything is smooth now.'

'Then why are you so ruffled?'

'I am not aware of it. All is as it should be. Mrs. Yeobright—but she is nothing to us.'

'Ah, I knew she had something to do with it! Come, I don't like reserve.'

'No—she has nothing. She only says she wishes me to give up Thomasin because another man is anxious to marry her. The woman, now she no longer needs me, actually shows off!' Wildeve's vexation had escaped him in spite of himself.

Eustacia was silent a long while. 'You are in the awkward position of an official who is no longer wanted,' she said in a changed tone.

'It seems so. But I have not yet seen Thomasin.'

'And that irritates you. Don't deny it, Damon. You are actually nettled by this slight from an unexpected quarter.'

'Well?'

'And you come to get me because you cannot get her. This is certainly a new position altogether. I am to be a stop-gap.'

'Please remember that I proposed the same thing the other day.'

Eustacia again remained in a sort of stupefied silence. What curious feeling was this coming over her? Was it really possible that her interest in Wildeve had been so entirely the result of antagonism that the glory and the dream[1] departed from the man with the first sound that he was no longer coveted by her rival? She was, then, secure of him at last. Thomasin no longer required him. What a humiliating victory! He loved her best, she thought; and yet—dared she to murmur such treacherous criticism ever so softly?—what was the man worth whom a woman inferior to herself did not value? The sentiment which lurks more or less in all animate nature—that of not desiring the undesired of others—was lively as a passion in the supersubtle, epicurean[2] heart of Eustacia. Her social superiority over him, which hitherto had scarcely ever impressed her, became unpleasantly insistent, and for the first time she felt that she had stooped in loving him.

'Well, darling, you agree?' said Wildeve.

'If it could be London, or even Budmouth, instead of America,' she murmured languidly. 'Well, I will think. It is too great a thing for me to decide offhand. I wish I hated the heath less—or loved you more.'

'You can be painfully frank. You loved me a month ago warmly enough to go anywhere with me.'

'And you loved Thomasin.'

'Yes, perhaps that was where the reason lay,' he returned, with almost a sneer. 'I don't hate her now.'

'Exactly. The only thing is that you can no longer get her.'

'Come—no taunts, Eustacia, or we shall quarrel. If you don't agree to go with me, and agree shortly, I shall go by myself.'

'Or try Thomasin again. Damon, how strange it seems that you could have married her or me indifferently, and only have come to me because I am—cheapest! Yes, yes—it is true. There was a time when I should have exclaimed against a man of that sort, and been quite wild; but it is all past now.'

'Will you go, dearest? Come secretly with me to Bristol, marry me, and turn our backs upon this dog-hole of England for ever? Say Yes.'

'I want to get away from here at almost any cost,' she said with weariness, 'but I don't like to go with you. Give me more time to decide.'

1. An echo of Wordsworth's "Ode: Intimations of Immortality" (1807), line 57: "Where is it now, the glory and the dream?"
2. Delighting in pleasure.

'I have already,' said Wildeve. 'Well, I give you one more week.'

'A little longer, so that I may tell you decisively. I have to consider so many things. Fancy Thomasin being anxious to get rid of you! I cannot forget it.'

'Never mind that. Say Monday week. I will be here precisely at this time.'

'Let it be at Rainbarrow,' said she. 'This is too near home; my grandfather may be walking out.'

'Thank you, dear. On Monday week at this time I will be at the Barrow. Till then good-bye.'

'Good-bye. No, no, you must not touch me now. Shaking hands is enough till I have made up my mind.'

Eustacia watched his shadowy form till it had disappeared. She placed her hand to her forehead and breathed heavily; and then her rich, romantic lips parted under that homely impulse—a yawn. She was immediately angry at having betrayed even to herself the possible evanescence of her passion for him. She could not admit at once that she might have over-estimated Wildeve, for to perceive his mediocrity now was to admit her own great folly heretofore. And the discovery that she was the owner of a disposition so purely that of the dog in the manger, had something in it which at first made her ashamed.

The fruit of Mrs. Yeobright's diplomacy was indeed remarkable, though not as yet of the kind she had anticipated. It had appreciably influenced Wildeve, but it was influencing Eustacia far more. Her lover was no longer to her an exciting man whom many women strove for, and herself could only retain by striving with them. He was a superfluity.

She went indoors in that peculiar state of misery which is not exactly grief, and which especially attends the dawnings of reason in the latter days of an ill-judged, transient love. To be conscious that the end of the dream is approaching, and yet has not absolutely come, is one of the most wearisome as well as the most curious stages along the course between the beginning of a passion and its end.

Her grandfather had returned, and was busily engaged in pouring some gallons of newly arrived rum into the square bottles of his square cellaret.[3] Whenever these home supplies were exhausted he would go to the Quiet Woman, and, standing with his back to the fire, grog in hand, tell remarkable stories of how he had lived seven years under the water-line[4] of his ship, and other naval wonders, to the natives, who hoped too earnestly for a treat of ale from the teller to exhibit any doubts of his truth.

3. Cabinet holding bottles.
4. The surgery in a man-of-war was situated below the water-line, safe from enemy fire.

He had been there this evening. 'I suppose you have heard the Egdon news, Eustacia?' he said, without looking up from the bottles. 'The men have been talking about it at the Woman as if it were of national importance.'

'I have heard none,' she said.

'Young Clym Yeobright, as they call him, is coming home next week to spend Christmas with his mother. He is a fine fellow by this time, it seems. I suppose you remember him?'

'I never saw him in my life.'

'Ah, true; he left before you came here. I well remember him as a promising boy.'

'Where has he been living all these years?'

'In that rookery[5] of pomp and vanity, Paris, I believe.'

Book Second. The Arrival

Tidings of the Comer

I

On fine days at this time of the year, and earlier, certain ephemeral operations were apt to disturb, in their trifling way, the majestic calm of Egdon Heath. They were activities which, beside those of a town, a village, or even a farm, would have appeared as the ferment of stagnation merely, a creeping of the flesh of somnolence. But here, away from comparisons, shut in by the stable hills, among which mere walking had the novelty of pageantry, and where any man could imagine himself to be Adam[1] without the least difficulty, they attracted the attention of every bird within eyeshot, every reptile not yet asleep, and set the surrounding rabbits curiously watching from hillocks at a safe distance.

The performance was that of bringing together and building into a stack the furze-faggots which Humphrey had been cutting for the captain's use during the foregoing fine days. The stack was at the end of the dwelling, and the men engaged in building it were Humphrey and Sam, the old man looking on.

It was a fine and quiet afternoon, about three o'clock; but the winter solstice[2] having stealthily come on, the lowness of the sun caused the hour to seem later than it actually was, there being little here to remind an inhabitant that he must unlearn his summer experience of the sky as a dial. In the course of many days and weeks

5. Contemptuous term for an area of densely packed houses.
1. The first and for a time therefore the only man in the world.
2. The shortest day of the year: in the northern hemisphere, around December 22.

sunrise had advanced its quarters from north-east to south-east, sunset had receded from north-west to south-west; but Egdon had hardly heeded the change.

Eustacia was indoors in the dining-room, which was really more like a kitchen, having a stone floor and a gaping chimney-corner. The air was still, and while she lingered a moment here alone sounds of voices in conversation came to her ears directly down the chimney. She entered the recess, and, listening, looked up the old irregular shaft, with its cavernous hollows, where the smoke blundered about on its way to the square bit of sky at the top, from which the daylight struck down with a pallid glare upon the tatters of soot draping the flue as sea-weed drapes a rocky fissure.

She remembered: the furze-stack was not far from the chimney, and the voices were those of the workers.

Her grandfather joined in the conversation. 'That lad ought never to have left home. His father's occupation would have suited him best, and the boy should have followed on. I don't believe in these new moves in families. My father was a sailor, so was I, and so should my son have been if I had had one.'

'The place he's been living at is Paris,' said Humphrey, 'and they tell me 'tis where the king's head was cut off years ago.[3] My poor mother used to tell me about that business. "Hummy," she used to say, "I was a young maid then, and as I was at home ironing mother's caps one afternoon the parson came in and said, "They've cut the king's head off, Jane; and what 'twill be next God knows." '

'A good many of us knew as well as He before long,' said the captain, chuckling. 'I lived seven years under water on account of it in my boyhood—in that damned surgery of the *Triumph*, seeing men brought down to the cockpit with their legs and arms blown to Jericho.[4] . . . And so the young man has settled in Paris. Manager to a diamond merchant, or some such thing, is he not?'

'Yes, sir, that's it. 'Tis a blazing great business that he belongs to, so I've heard his mother say—like a king's palace, as far as diments go.'

'I can well mind when he left home,' said Sam.

' 'Tis a good thing for the feller,' said Humphrey. 'A sight of times better to be selling diments than nobbling[5] about here.'

'It must cost a good few shillings to deal at such a place.'

'A good few indeed, my man,' replied the captain. 'Yes, you may

3. Louis XVI was guillotined in 1793, during the French Revolution. From 1793 until 1815 Britain was almost continually at war with France.
4. (Here) blown to pieces; to "go to Jericho" is to go somewhere else, no matter where. From 1806–09 HMS *Triumph*, a 74-gun man-of-war, was commanded by a fellow Dorsetman, Sir Thomas Masterman Hardy (no relation); Hardy met his daughter while at work on the novel.
5. Idling (dialect).

make away with a deal of money and be neither drunkard nor glutton.'

'They say, too, that Clym Yeobright is become a real perusing man, with the strangest notions about things. There, that's because he went to school early, such as the school was.'

'Strange notions, has he?' said the old man. 'Ah, there's too much of that sending to school in these days! It only does harm. Every gatepost and barn's door you come to is sure to have some bad word or other chalked upon it by the young rascals: a woman can hardly pass for shame sometimes. If they'd never been taught how to write they wouldn't have been able to scribble such villainy. Their fathers couldn't do it, and the country was all the better for it.'

'Now, I should think, cap'n, that Miss Eustacia had about as much in her head that comes from books as anybody about here?'

'Perhaps if Miss Eustacia, too, had less romantic nonsense in her head it would be better for her,' said the captain shortly; after which he walked away.

'I say, Sam,' observed Humphrey when the old man was gone, 'she and Clym Yeobright would make a very pretty pigeon-pair[6]— hey? If they wouldn't I'll be dazed! Both of one mind about niceties for certain, and learned in print, and always thinking about high doctrine—there couldn't be a better couple if they were made o' purpose. Clym's family is as good as hers. His father was a farmer, that's true; but his mother was a sort of lady, as we know. Nothing would please me better than to see them two man and wife.'

'They'd look very natty, arm-in-crook together, and their best clothes on, whether or no, if he's at all the well-favoured fellow he used to be.'

'They would, Humphrey. Well, I should like to see the chap terrible much after so many years. If I knew for certain when he was coming I'd stroll out three or four miles to meet him and help carry anything for'n; though I suppose he's altered from the boy he was. They say he can talk French as fast as a maid can eat blackberries; and if so, depend upon it we who have stayed at home shall seem no more than scroff[7] in his eyes.'

'Coming across the water to Budmouth by steamer, isn't he?'

'Yes; but how he's coming from Budmouth I don't know.'

'That's a bad trouble about his cousin Thomasin. I wonder such a nice-notioned fellow as Clym likes to come home into it. What a nunnywatch[8] we were in, to be sure, when we heard they weren't married at all, after singing to 'em as man and wife that night! Be

6. Natural partners (pigeons produce two young at a time, supposedly one male and one female, from identical eggs).
7. Scraps of peat or wood, hence anything worthless (dialect).
8. State of confusion (dialect).

dazed if I should like a relation of mine to have been made such a fool of by a man. It makes the family look small.'

'Yes. Poor maid, her heart has ached enough about it. Her health is suffering from it, I hear, for she will bide entirely indoors. We never see her out now, scampering over the furze with a face as red as a rose, as she used to do.'

'I've heard she wouldn't have Wildeve now if he asked her.'

'You have? 'Tis news to me.'

While the furze-gatherers had desultorily conversed thus Eustacia's face gradually bent to the hearth in a profound reverie, her toe unconsciously tapping the dry turf which lay burning at her feet.

The subject of their discourse had been keenly interesting to her. A young and clever man was coming into that lonely heath from, of all contrasting places in the world, Paris. It was like a man coming from heaven. More singular still, the heathmen had instinctively coupled her and this man together in their minds as a pair born for each other.

That five minutes of overhearing furnished Eustacia with visions enough to fill the whole blank afternoon. Such sudden alternations from mental vacuity do sometimes occur thus quietly. She could never have believed in the morning that her colourless inner world would before night become as animated as water under a microscope, and that without the arrival of a single visitor. The words of Sam and Humphrey on the harmony between the unknown and herself had on her mind the effect of the invading Bard's prelude in the 'Castle of Indolence,'[9] at which myriads of imprisoned shapes arose where had previously appeared the stillness of a void.

Involved in these imaginings she knew nothing of time. When she became conscious of externals it was dusk. The furze-rick was finished; the men had gone home. Eustacia went upstairs, thinking that she would take a walk at this her usual time; and she determined that her walk should be in the direction of Blooms-End, the birthplace of young Yeobright and the present home of his mother. She had no reason for walking elsewhere, and why should she not go that way? The scene of a day-dream is sufficient for a pilgrimage at nineteen. To look at the palings before the Yeobrights' house had the dignity of a necessary performance. Strange that such a piece of idling should have seemed an important errand.

She put on her bonnet, and, leaving the house, descended the hill on the side towards Blooms-End, where she walked slowly along the valley for a distance of a mile and a half. This brought her to a spot in which the green bottom of the dale began to widen, the

9. In James Thomson's allegorical poem "The Castle of Indolence" (1748), the bard Philomelus helps raise those imprisoned in the Castle from their torpor.

furze bushes to recede yet further from the path on each side, till they were diminished to an isolated one here and there by the increasing fertility of the soil. Beyond the irregular carpet of grass was a row of white palings, which marked the verge of the heath in this latitude. They showed upon the dusky scene that they bordered as distinctly as white lace on velvet. Behind the white palings was a little garden; behind the garden an old, irregular, thatched house, facing the heath, and commanding a full view of the valley. This was the obscure, removed spot to which was about to return a man whose latter life had been passed in the French capital—the centre and vortex of the fashionable world.

The People at Blooms-End Make Ready

II

All that afternoon the expected arrival of the subject of Eustacia's ruminations created a bustle of preparation at Blooms-End. Thomasin had been persuaded by her aunt, and by an instinctive impulse of loyalty towards her cousin Clym, to bestir herself on his account with an alacrity unusual in her during these most sorrowful days of her life. At the time that Eustacia was listening to the rick-makers' conversation on Clym's return, Thomasin was climbing into a loft over her aunt's fuelhouse, where the store-apples were kept, to search out the best and largest of them for the coming holiday-time.

The loft was lighted by a semicircular hole, through which the pigeons crept to their lodgings in the same high quarters of the premises; and from this hole the sun shone in a bright yellow patch upon the figure of the maiden as she knelt and plunged her naked arms into the soft brown fern, which, from its abundance, was used on Egdon in packing away stores of all kinds. The pigeons were flying about her head with the greatest unconcern, and the face of her aunt was just visible above the floor of the loft, lit by a few stray motes of light, as she stood half-way up the ladder, looking at a spot into which she was not climber enough to venture.

'Now a few russets, Tamsin. He used to like them almost as well as ribstones.'

Thomasin turned and rolled aside the fern from another nook, where more mellow fruit greeted her with its ripe smell. Before picking them out she stopped a moment.

'Dear Clym, I wonder how your face looks now?' she said, gazing abstractedly at the pigeon-hole, which admitted the sunlight so directly upon her brown hair and transparent tissues that it almost seemed to shine through her.

'If he could have been dear to you in another way,' said Mrs. Yeobright from the ladder, 'this might have been a happy meeting.'

'Is there any use in saying what can do no good, aunt?'

'Yes,' said her aunt, with some warmth. 'To thoroughly fill the air with the past misfortune, so that other girls may take warning and keep clear of it.'

Thomasin lowered her face to the apples again. 'I am a warning to others, just as thieves and drunkards and gamblers are,' she said in a low voice. 'What a class to belong to! Do I really belong to them? 'Tis absurd! Yet why, aunt, does everybody keep on making me think that I do, by the way they behave towards me? Why don't people judge me by my acts? Now, look at me as I kneel here, picking up these apples—do I look like a lost woman? . . . I wish all good women were as good as I!' she added vehemently.

'Strangers don't see you as I do,' said Mrs. Yeobright; 'they judge from false report. Well, it is a silly job, and I am partly to blame.'

'How quickly a rash thing can be done!' replied the girl. Her lips were quivering, and tears so crowded themselves into her eyes that she could hardly distinguish apples from fern as she continued industriously searching to hide her weakness.

'As soon as you have finished getting the apples,' her aunt said, descending the ladder, 'come down, and we'll go for the holly. There is nobody on the heath this afternoon, and you need not fear being stared at. We must get some berries, or Clym will never believe in our preparations.'

Thomasin came down when the apples were collected, and together they went through the white palings to the heath beyond. The open hills were airy and clear, and the remote atmosphere appeared, as it often appears on a fine winter day, in distinct planes of illumination independently toned, the rays which lit the nearer tracts of landscape streaming visibly across those further off; a stratum of ensaffroned light was imposed on a stratum of deep blue, and behind these lay still remoter scenes wrapped in frigid grey.

They reached the place where the hollies grew, which was in a conical pit, so that the tops of the trees were not much above the general level of the ground. Thomasin stepped up into a fork of one of the bushes, as she had done under happier circumstances on many similar occasions, and with a small chopper that they had brought she began to lop off the heavily-berried boughs.

'Don't scratch your face,' said her aunt, who stood at the edge of the pit, regarding the girl as she held on amid the glistening green and scarlet masses of the tree. 'Will you walk with me to meet him this evening?'

'I should like to. Else it would seem as if I had forgotten him,'

'I wish all good women were as good as I!'

said Thomasin, tossing out a bough. 'Not that that would matter much; I belong to one man; nothing can alter that. And that man I must marry, for my pride's sake.'

'I am afraid——' began Mrs. Yeobright.

'Ah, you think, "That weak girl—how is she going to get a man to marry her when she chooses?" But let me tell you one thing, aunt: Mr. Wildeve is not a profligate man, any more than I am an improper woman. He has an unfortunate manner, and doesn't try to make people like him if they don't wish to do it of their own accord.'

'Thomasin,' said Mrs. Yeobright quietly, fixing her eye upon her niece, 'do you think you deceive me in your defence of Mr. Wildeve?'

'How do you mean?'

'I have long had a suspicion that your love for him has changed its colour since you have found him not to be the saint you thought him, and that you act a part to me.'

'He wished to marry me, and I wish to marry him.'

'Now, I put it to you: would you at this present moment agree to be his wife if that had not happened to entangle you with him?'

Thomasin looked into the tree and appeared much disturbed. 'Aunt,' she said presently, 'I have, I think, a right to refuse to answer that question.'

'Yes, you have.'

'You may think what you choose. I have never implied to you by word or deed that I have grown to think otherwise of him, and I never will. And I shall marry him.'

'Well, wait till he repeats his offer. I think he may do it, now that he knows—something I told him. I don't for a moment dispute that it is the most proper thing for you to marry him. Much as I have objected to him in bygone days, I agree with you now, you may be sure. It is the only way out of a false position, and a very galling one.'

'What did you tell him?'

'That he was standing in the way of another lover of yours.'

'Aunt,' said Thomasin, with round eyes, 'what *do* you mean?'

'Don't be alarmed; it was my duty. I can say no more about it now, but when it is over I will tell exactly what I said, and why I said it.'

Thomasin was perforce content.

'And you will keep the secret of my would-be marriage from Clym for the present?' she next asked.

'I have given my word to. But what is the use of it? He must soon know what has happened. A mere look at your face will show him that something is wrong.'

Thomasin turned and regarded her aunt from the tree. 'Now, hearken to me,' she said, her delicate voice expanding into firmness by a force which was other than physical. 'Tell him nothing. If he finds out that I am not worthy to be his cousin, let him. But, since he loved me once, we will not pain him by telling him my trouble too soon. The air is full of the story, I know; but gossips will not dare to speak of it to him for the first few days. His closeness to me is the very thing that will hinder the tale from reaching him early. If I am not made safe from sneers in a week or two I will tell him my-self.'

The earnestness with which Thomasin spoke prevented further objections. Her aunt simply said, 'Very well. He should by rights have been told at the time that the wedding was going to be. He will never forgive you for your secrecy.'

'Yes, he will, when he knows it was because I wished to spare him, and that I did not expect him home so soon. And you must not let me stand in the way of your Christmas party. Putting it off would only make matters worse.'

'Of course I shall not. I do not wish to show myself beaten before all Egdon, and the sport of a man like Wildeve. We have enough berries now, I think, and we had better take them home. By the time we have decked the house with this and hung up the mistletoe, we must think of starting to meet him.'

Thomasin came out of the tree, shook from her hair and dress the loose berries which had fallen thereon, and went down the hill with her aunt, each woman bearing half the gathered boughs. It was now nearly four o'clock, and the sunlight was leaving the vales. When the west grew red the two relatives came again from the house and plunged into the heath in a different direction from the first, towards a point in the distant highway along which the expected man was to return.

How a Little Sound Produced a Great Dream

III

Eustacia stood just within the heath, straining her eyes in the direction of Mrs. Yeobright's house and premises. No light, sound, or movement was perceptible there. The evening was chilly; the spot was dark and lonely. She inferred that the guest had not yet come; and after lingering ten or fifteen minutes she turned again towards home.

She had not far retraced her steps when sounds in front of her betokened the approach of persons in conversation along the same path. Soon their heads became visible against the sky. They were walking slowly; and though it was too dark for much discovery of character from aspect, the gait of them showed that they were not workers on the heath. Eustacia stepped a little out of the foot-track to let them pass. They were two women and a man; and the voices of the women were those of Mrs. Yeobright and Thomasin.

They went by her, and at the moment of passing appeared to discern her dusky form. There came to her ears in a masculine voice, 'Good night!'

She murmured a reply, glided by them, and turned round. She could not, for a moment, believe that chance, unrequested, had

brought into her presence the soul of the house she had gone to inspect, the man without whom her inspection would not have been
thought of.

She strained her eyes to see them, but was unable. Such was her
intentness, however, that it seemed as if her ears were performing
the functions of seeing as well as hearing. This extension of power
can almost be believed in at such moments. The deaf Dr. Kitto[1] was
probably under the influence of a parallel fancy when he described
his body as having become, by long endeavour, so sensitive to vibra-
tions that he had gained the power of perceiving by it as by ears.

She could follow every word that the ramblers uttered. They
were talking no secrets. They were merely indulging in the ordinary
vivacious chat of relatives who have long been parted in person
though not in soul. But it was not to the words that Eustacia listened; she could not even have recalled, a few minutes later, what
the words were. It was to the alternating voice that gave out about
one-tenth of them—the voice that had wished her good night.
Sometimes this throat uttered Yes, sometimes it uttered No; sometimes it made inquiries about a timeworn denizen of the place.
Once it surprised her notions by remarking upon the friendliness
and geniality written in the faces of the hills around.

The three voices passed on, and decayed and died out upon her
ear. Thus much had been granted her; and all besides withheld. No
event could have been more exciting. During the greater part of the
afternoon she had been entrancing herself by imagining the fascination which must attend a man come direct from beautiful
Paris—laden with its atmosphere, familiar with its charms. And this
man had greeted her.

With the departure of the figures the profuse articulations of the
women wasted away from her memory; but the accents of the other
stayed on. Was there anything in the voice of Mrs. Yeobright's
son—for Clym it was—startling as a sound? No: it was simply comprehensive. All emotional things were possible to the speaker of
that 'good night.' Eustacia's imagination supplied the rest—except
the solution to one riddle. What *could* the tastes of that man be
who saw friendliness and geniality in these shaggy hills?

On such occasions as this a thousand ideas pass through a highly
charged woman's head; and they indicate themselves on her face;
but the changes, though actual, are minute. Eustacia's features
went through a rhythmical succession of them. She glowed; re-
membering the mendacity of the imagination, she flagged; then she
freshened; then she fired; then she cooled again. It was a cycle of
aspects, produced by a cycle of visions.

1. John Kitto (1804–54), left stone-deaf by an accident at the age of twelve; his book, *The
Lost Senses* (1845), describes the lives of blind, deaf, and mute people.

Eustacia entered her own house; she was excited. Her grandfather was enjoying himself over the fire, raking about the ashes and exposing the red-hot surface of the turves, so that their lurid glare irradiated the chimney-corner with the hues of a furnace.

'Why is it that we are never friendly with the Yeobrights?' she said, coming forward and stretching her soft hands over the warmth. 'I wish we were. They seem to be very nice people.'

'Be hanged if I know why,' said the captain. 'I liked the old man well enough, though he was as rough as a hedge. But you would never have cared to go there, even if you might have, I am well sure.'

'Why shouldn't I?'

'Your town tastes would find them far too countrified. They sit in the kitchen, drink mead and elderwine, and sand the floor to keep it clean. A sensible way of life; but how would you like it?'

'I thought Mrs. Yeobright was a ladylike woman? A curate's daughter, was she not?'

'Yes; but she was obliged to live as her husband did; and I suppose she has taken kindly to it by this time. Ah, I recollect that I once accidentally offended her, and I have never seen her since.'

That night was an eventful one to Eustacia's brain, and one which she hardly ever forgot. She dreamt a dream; and few human beings, from Nebuchadnezzar[2] to the Swaffham tinker,[3] ever dreamt a more remarkable one. Such an elaborately developed, perplexing, exciting dream was certainly never dreamed by a girl in Eustacia's situation before. It had as many ramifications as the Cretan labyrinth,[4] as many fluctuations as the Northern Lights,[5] as much colour as a parterre[6] in June, and was as crowded with figures as a coronation. To Queen Scheherazade[7] the dream might have seemed not far removed from commonplace; and to a girl just returned from all the courts of Europe it might have seemed not more than interesting. But amid the circumstances of Eustacia's life it was as wonderful as a dream could be.

There was, however, gradually evolved from its transformation scenes[8] a less extravagant episode, in which the heath dimly appeared behind the general brilliancy of the action. She was dancing

2. King of Babylon (ruled 604–561 B.C.E.), whose elaborate dreams were interpreted by the prophet Daniel; see Daniel 2.
3. John Chapman, a pedlar of the fifteenth century, who according to legend learned through dreams of the treasure buried in his garden at Swaffham in East Anglia.
4. In Greek mythology, the maze constructed by Daedalus on the orders of Minos, King of Crete, to secure the Minotaur, a monstrous creature half-bull and half-man.
5. The aurora borealis, seen in the upper atmosphere in high northern latitudes.
6. An ornamental garden, laid out with paths.
7. In *The Arabian Nights' Entertainments*, ancient oriental tales introduced to Europe in the eighteenth century through French and English translations, Scheherazade saves herself from execution by each night amusing her husband, the Sultan, with a new story.
8. The technical term for rapid changes of stage scenery, especially in pantomimes.

to wondrous music, and her partner was the man in silver armour who had accompanied her through the previous fantastic changes, the visor of his helmet being closed. The mazes of the dance were ecstatic. Soft whispering came into her ear from under the radiant helmet, and she felt like a woman in Paradise. Suddenly these two wheeled out from the mass of dancers, dived into one of the pools of the heath, and came out somewhere beneath into an iridescent hollow, arched with rainbows. 'It must be here,' said the voice by her side, and blushingly looking up she saw him removing his casque to kiss her. At that moment there was a cracking noise, and his figure fell into fragments like a pack of cards.

She cried aloud, 'O that I had seen his face!'

Eustacia awoke. The cracking had been that of the window-shutter downstairs, which the maid-servant was opening to let in the day, now slowly increasing to Nature's meagre allowance at this sickly time of the year. 'O that I had seen his face!' she said again. ' 'Twas meant for Mr. Yeobright!'

When she became cooler she perceived that many of the phases of the dream had naturally arisen out of the images and fancies of the day before. But this detracted little from its interest, which lay in the excellent fuel it provided for newly kindled fervour. She was at the modulating point between indifference and love, at the stage called 'having a fancy for.' It occurs once in the history of the most gigantic passions, and it is a period when they are in the hands of the weakest will.

The perfervid[9] woman was by this time half in love with a vision. The fantastic nature of her passion, which lowered her as an intellect, raised her as a soul. If she had had a little more self-control she would have attenuated the emotion to nothing by sheer reasoning, and so have killed it off. If she had had a little less pride she might have gone and circumambulated the Yeobrights' premises at Blooms-End at any maidenly sacrifice until she had seen him. But Eustacia did neither of these things. She acted as the most exemplary might have acted, being so influenced; she took an airing twice or thrice a day upon the Egdon hills, and kept her eyes employed.

The first occasion passed, and he did not come that way.

She promenaded a second time, and was again the sole wanderer there.

The third time there was a dense fog: she looked around, but without much hope. Even if he had been walking within twenty yards of her she could not have seen him.

9. Impassioned.

At the fourth attempt to encounter him it began to rain in torrents, and she turned back.

The fifth sally was in the afternoon: it was fine, and she remained out long, walking to the very top of the valley in which Blooms-End lay. She saw the white paling about half a mile off; but he did not appear. It was almost with heart-sickness that she came home, and with a sense of shame at her weakness. She resolved to look for the man from Paris no more.

But Providence is nothing if not coquettish; and no sooner had Eustacia formed this resolve than the opportunity came which, while sought, had been entirely withholden.

Eustacia Is Led on to an Adventure

IV

In the evening of this last day of expectation, which was the twenty-third of December, Eustacia was at home alone. She had passed the recent hour in lamenting over a rumour newly come to her ears—that Yeobright's visit to his mother was to be of short duration, and would end some time the next week. 'Naturally,' she said to herself. A man in the full swing of his activities in a gay city could not afford to linger long on Egdon Heath. That she would behold face to face the owner of the awakening voice within the limits of such a holiday was most unlikely, unless she were to haunt the environs of his mother's house like a robin, to do which was difficult and unseemly.

The customary expedient of provincial girls and men in such circumstances is churchgoing. In an ordinary village or country town one can safely calculate that, either on Christmas-day or the Sunday contiguous, any native home for the holidays, who has not through age or *ennui* lost the appetite for seeing and being seen, will turn up in some pew or other, shining with hope, self-consciousness, and new clothes. Thus the congregation on Christmas morning is mostly a Tussaud[1] collection of celebrities who have been born in the neighbourhood. Hither the mistress, left neglected at home all the year, can steal and observe the development of the returned lover who has forgotten her, and think as she watches him over her prayer-book that he may throb with a renewed fidelity when novelties have lost their charm. And hither a comparatively recent settler like Eustacia may betake herself to scrutinize the person of a native son who left home before her ad-

---

1. Madame Tussaud, née Marie Grosholz (1761–1850), established in 1835 a permanent site in London for her Exhibition of life-size waxwork models of well-known figures.

vent upon the scene, and consider if the friendship of his parents be worth cultivating during his next absence in order to secure a knowledge of him on his next return.

But these tender schemes were not feasible among the scattered inhabitants of Egdon Heath. In name they were parishioners, but virtually they belonged to no parish at all. People who came to these few isolated houses to keep Christmas with their friends remained in their friends' chimney-corners drinking mead and other comforting liquors till they left again for good and all. Rain, snow, ice, mud everywhere around, they did not care to trudge two or three miles to sit wet-footed and splashed to the nape of their necks among those who, though in some measure neighbours, lived close to the church, and entered it clean and dry. Eustacia knew it was ten to one that Clym Yeobright would go to no church at all during his few days of leave, and that it would be a waste of labour for her to go driving the pony and gig over a bad road in hope to see him there.

It was dusk, and she was sitting by the fire in the dining-room or hall, which they occupied at this time of the year in preference to the parlour, because of its large hearth, constructed for turf-fires, a fuel the captain was partial to in the winter season. The only visible articles in the room were those on the window-sill, which showed their shapes against the low sky: the middle article being the old hour-glass, and the other two a pair of ancient British urns which had been dug from a barrow near, and were used as flower-pots for two razor-leaved cactuses. Somebody knocked at the door. The servant was out; so was her grandfather. The person, after waiting a minute, came in and tapped at the door of the room.

'Who's there?' said Eustacia.

'Please, Cap'n Vye, will you let us——'

Eustacia arose and went to the door. 'I cannot allow you to come in so boldly. You should have waited.'

'The cap'n said I might come in without any fuss,' was answered in a lad's pleasant voice.

'Oh, did he?' said Eustacia more gently. 'What do you want, Charley?'

'Please will your grandfather lend us his fuel-house to try over our parts in, to-night at seven o'clock?'

'What, are you one of the Egdon mummers for this year?'

'Yes, miss. The cap'n used to let the old mummers practise here.'

'I know it. Yes, you may use the fuel-house if you like,' said Eustacia languidly.

The choice of Captain Vye's fuel-house as the scene of rehearsal was dictated by the fact that his dwelling was nearly in the centre of the heath. The fuel-house was as roomy as a barn, and was a most desirable place for such a purpose. The lads who formed the company of players lived at different scattered points around, and by meeting in this spot the distances to be traversed by all the comers would be about equally proportioned.

For mummers and mumming Eustacia had the greatest contempt. The mummers themselves were not afflicted with any such feeling for their art, though at the same time they were not enthusiastic. A traditional pastime is to be distinguished from a mere revival in no more striking feature than in this, that while in the revival all is excitement and fervour, the survival is carried on with a stolidity and absence of stir which sets one wondering why a thing that is done so perfunctorily should be kept up at all. Like Balaam[2] and other unwilling prophets, the agents seem moved by an inner compulsion to say and do their allotted parts whether they will or no. This unweeting[3] manner of performance is the true ring by which, in this refurbishing age, a fossilized survival may be known from a spurious reproduction.

The piece was the well-known play of 'Saint George,'[4] and all who were behind the scenes assisted in the preparations, including the women of each household. Without the co-operation of sisters and sweethearts the dresses were likely to be a failure; but on the other hand, this class of assistance was not without its drawbacks. The girls could never be brought to respect tradition in designing and decorating the armour; they insisted on attaching loops and bows of silk and velvet in any situation pleasing to their taste. Gorget, gusset, basinet, cuirass,[5] gauntlet, sleeve, all alike in the view of these feminine eyes were practicable spaces whereon to sew scraps of fluttering colour.

It might be that Joe, who fought on the side of Christendom, had a sweetheart, and that Jim, who fought on the side of the Moslem, had one likewise. During the making of the costumes it would come to the knowledge of Joe's sweetheart that Jim's was putting brilliant silk scallops at the bottom of her lover's surcoat, in addition to the ribbons of the visor, the bars of which, being invariably formed of coloured strips about half an inch wide hanging before the face, were mostly of that material. Joe's sweetheart straight-way

2. Despite the promise of rewards if he would curse the Israelites, the prophet Balaam insisted that he could speak only "the word that God putteth into my mouth"; see Numbers 23.36–8.
3. Unknowing, unconsidered.
4. Patron saint of England (also of Portugal, and Venice). His identity is uncertain, but he was probably a Roman officer martyred at Nicomedia in 303. He appeared in a vision to the Christian forces during the First Crusade (1098), and was thereafter associated across Europe with the ideals of Christian chivalry.
5. Pieces of armor: the gorget protects the throat, the gusset covers joints in the armour, the basinet is a light helmet, while the cuirass is worn over the chest and back.

placed brilliant silk on the scallops of the hem in question, and, going a little further, added ribbon tufts to the shoulder pieces. Jim's, not to be outdone, would affix bows and rosettes everywhere.

The result was that in the end the Valiant Soldier, of the Christian army, was distinguished by no peculiarity of accoutrement from the Turkish Knight; and what was worse, on a casual view Saint George himself might be mistaken for his deadly enemy, the Saracen. The guisers[6] themselves, though inwardly regretting this confusion of persons, could not afford to offend those by whose assistance they so largely profited, and the innovations were allowed to stand.

There was, it is true, a limit to this tendency to uniformity. The Leech or Doctor preserved his character intact: his darker habiliments, peculiar hat, and the bottle of physic slung under his arm, could never be mistaken. And the same might be said of the conventional figure of Father Christmas, with his gigantic club, an older man, who accompanied the band as general protector in long night journeys from parish to parish, and was bearer of the purse.

Seven o'clock, the hour of the rehearsal, came round, and in a short time Eustacia could hear voices in the fuel-house. To dissipate in some trifling measure her abiding sense of the murkiness of human life she went to the 'linhay' or lean-to shed, which formed the root-store of their dwelling and abutted on the fuel-house. Here was a small rough hole in the mud wall, originally made for pigeons, through which the interior of the next shed could be viewed. A light came from it now; and Eustacia stepped upon a stool to look in upon the scene.

On a ledge in the fuel-house stood three tall rush-lights[7] and by the light of them seven or eight lads were marching about, haranguing, and confusing each other, in endeavours to perfect themselves in the play. Humphrey and Sam, the furze and turf cutters, were there looking on, so also was Timothy Fairway, who leant against the wall and prompted the boys from memory, interspersing among the set words remarks and anecdotes of the superior days when he and others were the Egdon mummers-elect that these lads were now.

'Well, ye be as well up to it as ever ye will be,' he said. 'Not that such mumming would have passed in our time. Harry as the Saracen should strut a bit more, and John needn't holler his inside out. Beyond that perhaps you'll do. Have you got all your clothes ready?'

'We shall by Monday.'

'Your first outing will be Monday night, I suppose?'

6. Mummers.
7. Tapers made by dipping the stem of a rush—a slender, cylindrical plant, used also in basket-weaving, etc.—in tallow.

'Yes. At Mrs. Yeobright's.'

'Oh, Mrs. Yeobright's. What makes her want to see ye? I should think a middle-aged woman was tired of mumming.'

'She's got up a bit of a party because 'tis the first Christmas that her son Clym has been home for a long time.'

'To be sure, to be sure—her party! I am going myself. I almost forgot it, upon my life.'

Eustacia's face flagged. There was to be a party at the Yeobright's; she, naturally, had nothing to do with it. She was a stranger to all such local gatherings, and had always held them as scarcely appertaining to her sphere. But had she been going, what an opportunity would have been afforded her of seeing the man whose influence was penetrating her like summer sun! To increase that influence was coveted excitement; to cast it off might be to regain serenity; to leave it as it stood was tantalizing.

The lads and men prepared to leave the premises, and Eustacia returned to her fireside. She was immersed in thought, but not for long. In a few minutes the lad Charley, who had come to ask permission to use the place, returned with the key to the kitchen. Eustacia heard him, and opening the door into the passage said, 'Charley, come here.'

The lad was surprised. He entered the front room not without blushing; for he, like many, had felt the power of this girl's face and form.

She pointed to a seat by the fire, and entered the other side of the chimney-corner herself. It could be seen in her face that whatever motive she might have had in asking the youth indoors would soon appear.

'Which part do you play, Charley—the Turkish Knight, do you not?' inquired the beauty, looking across the smoke of the fire to him on the other side.

'Yes, miss, the Turkish Knight,' he replied diffidently.

'Is yours a long part?'

'Nine speeches, about.'

'Can you repeat them to me? If so I should like to hear them.'

The lad smiled into the glowing turf and began—

> 'Here come I, a Turkish Knight,
> Who learnt in Turkish land to fight,'

continuing the discourse throughout the scenes to the concluding catastrophe of his fall by the hand of Saint George.

Eustacia had occasionally heard the part recited before. When the lad ended she began, precisely in the same words, and ranted on without hitch or divergence till she too reached the end. It was the same thing, yet how different. Like in form, it had the added softness and finish of a Raffaelle after Perugino,[8] which, while faithfully reproducing the original subject, entirely distances the original art.

Charley's eyes rounded with surprise. 'Well, you be a clever lady!' he said, in admiration. 'I've been three weeks learning mine.'

'I have heard it before,' she quietly observed. 'Now, would you do anything to please me, Charley?'

'I'd do a good deal, miss.'

'Would you let me play your part for one night?'

'O, miss! But your woman's gown—you couldn't.'

'I can get boy's clothes—at least all that would be wanted besides the mumming dress. What should I have to give you to lend me your things, to let me take your place for an hour or two on Monday night, and on no account to say a word about who or what I am? You would, of course, have to excuse yourself from playing that night, and to say that somebody—a cousin of Miss Vye's—would act for you. The other mummers have never spoken to me in their lives, so that it would be safe enough; and if it were not, I should not mind. Now, what must I give you to agree to this? Half a crown?'

The youth shook his head.

'Five shillings?'

He shook his head again. 'Money won't do it,' he said, brushing the iron head of the fire-dog with the hollow of his hand.

'What will, then, Charley?' said Eustacia in a disappointed tone.

'You know what you forbade me at the maypoling,[9] miss,' murmured the lad, without looking at her, and still stroking the fire-dog's head.

'Yes,' said Eustacia, with a little more hauteur. 'You wanted to join hands with me in the ring, if I recollect?'

'Half an hour of that, and I'll agree, miss.'

Eustacia regarded the youth steadfastly. He was three years younger than herself, but apparently not backward for his age. 'Half an hour of what?' she said, though she guessed what.

'Holding your hand in mine.'

She was silent. 'Make it a quarter of an hour,' she said.

'Yes, Miss Eustacia—I will, if I may kiss it too. A quarter of an hour. And I'll swear to do the best I can to let you take my place without anybody knowing. Don't you think somebody might know your tongue, miss?'

'It is possible. But I will put a pebble in my mouth to make it less

---

8. The Italian painter Raphael (Raffaello Sanzio, 1483–1520) was apprenticed to Perugino (Pietro Vannucci), but soon surpassed him.
9. Dance around the Maypole, set up to commemorate May Day (May 1).

likely. Very well; you shall be allowed to have my hand as soon as you bring the dress and your sword and staff. I don't want you any longer now.'

Charley departed, and Eustacia felt more and more interest in life. Here was something to do: here was some one to see, and a charmingly adventurous way to see him. 'Ah,' she said to herself, 'want of an object to live for—that's all is the matter with me!'

Eustacia's manner was as a rule of a slumberous sort, her passions being of the massive rather than the vivacious kind. But when aroused she would make a dash which, just for the time, was not unlike the move of a naturally lively person.

On the question of recognition she was somewhat indifferent. By the acting lads themselves she was not likely to be known. With the guests who might be assembled she was hardly so secure. Yet detection, after all, would be no such dreadful thing. The fact only could be detected, her true motive never. It would be instantly set down as the passing freak of a girl whose ways were already considered singular. That she was doing for an earnest reason what would most naturally be done in jest was at any rate a safe secret.

The next evening Eustacia stood punctually at the fuel-house door, waiting for the dusk which was to bring Charley with the trappings. Her grandfather was at home to-night, and she would be unable to ask her confederate indoors.

He appeared on the dark ridge of heathland, like a fly on a negro, bearing the articles with him, and came up breathless with his walk.

'Here are the things,' he whispered, placing them upon the threshold. 'And now, Miss Eustacia——'

'The payment. It is quite ready. I am as good as my word.'

She leant against the door-post, and gave him her hand. Charley took it in both his own with a tenderness beyond description, unless it was like that of a child holding a captured sparrow.

'Why, there's a glove on it!' he said in a deprecating way.

'I have been walking,' she observed.

'But, miss!'

'Well—it is hardly fair.' She pulled off the glove, and gave him her bare hand.

They stood together minute after minute, without further speech, each looking at the blackening scene, and each thinking his and her own thoughts.

'I think I won't use it all up to-night,' said Charley devotedly, when six or eight minutes had been passed by him caressing her hand. 'May I have the other few minutes another time?'

'As you like,' said she without the least emotion. 'But it must be over in a week. Now, there is only one thing I want you to do: to wait while I put on the dress, and then to see if I do my part properly. But let me look first indoors.'

She vanished for a minute or two, and went in. Her grandfather was safely asleep in his chair. 'Now, then,' she said, on returning, 'walk down the garden a little way, and when I am ready I'll call you.'

Charley walked and waited, and presently heard a soft whistle. He returned to the fuel-house door.

'Did you whistle, Miss Vye?'

'Yes; come in,' reached him in Eustacia's voice from a back quarter. 'I must not strike a light till the door is shut, or it may be seen shining. Push your hat into the hole through to the wash-house, if you can feel your way across.'

Charley did as commanded, and she struck the light, revealing herself to be changed in sex, brilliant in colours, and armed from top to toe. Perhaps she quailed a little under Charley's vigorous gaze, but whether any shyness at her male attire appeared upon her countenance could not be seen by reason of the strips of ribbon which used to cover the face in mumming costumes, representing the barred visor of the mediæval helmet.

'It fits pretty well,' she said, looking down at the white overalls, 'except that the tunic, or whatever you call it, is long in the sleeve. The bottom of the overalls I can turn up inside. Now pay attention.'

Eustacia then proceeded in her delivery, striking the sword against the staff or lance at the minatory phrases, in the orthodox mumming manner, and strutting up and down. Charley seasoned his admiration with criticism of the gentlest kind, for the touch of Eustacia's hand yet remained with him.

'And now for your excuse to the others,' she said. 'Where do you meet before you go to Mrs. Yeobright's?'

'We thought of meeting here, miss, if you have nothing to say against it. At eight o'clock, so as to get there by nine.'

'Yes. Well, you of course must not appear. I will march in about five minutes late, ready-dressed, and tell them that you can't come. I have decided that the best plan will be for you to be sent somewhere by me, to make a real thing of the excuse. Our two heath-croppers are in the habit of straying into the meads, and to-morrow evening you can go and see if they are gone there. I'll manage the rest. Now you may leave me.'

'Yes, miss. But I think I'll have one minute more of what I am owed, if you don't mind.'

Eustacia gave him her hand as before.

'One minute,' she said, and counted on till she reached seven or eight minutes. Hand and person she then withdrew to a distance of several feet, and recovered some of her old dignity. The contract completed, she raised between them a barrier impenetrable as a wall.

'There, 'tis all gone; and I didn't mean quite all,' he said, with a sigh.

'You had good measure,' said she, turning away.

'Yes, miss. Well, 'tis over, and now I'll get home-along.'

Through the Moonlight

V

The next evening the mummers were assembled in the same spot, awaiting the entrance of the Turkish Knight.

'Twenty minutes after eight by the Quiet Woman, and Charley not come.'

'Ten minutes past by Blooms-End.'

'It wants ten minutes to, by Grandfer Cantle's watch.'

'And 'tis five minutes past by the captain's clock.'

On Egdon there was no absolute hour of the day. The time at any moment was a number of varying doctrines professed by the different hamlets, some of them having originally grown up from a common root, and then become divided by secession, some having been alien from the beginning. West Egdon believed in Blooms-End time, East Egdon in the time of the Quiet Woman Inn. Grandfer Cantle's watch had numbered many followers in years gone by, but since he had grown older faiths were shaken. Thus, the mummers having gathered hither from scattered points, each came with his own tenets on early and late; and they waited a little longer as a compromise.

Eustacia had watched the assemblage through the hole; and seeing that now was the proper moment to enter, she went from the 'linhay' and boldly pulled the bobbin of the fuel-house door. Her grandfather was safe at the Quiet Woman.

'Here's Charley at last! How late you be, Charley.'

' 'Tis not Charley,' said the Turkish Knight from within his visor. ' 'Tis a cousin of Miss Vye's, come to take Charley's place from curiosity. He was obliged to go and look for the heath-croppers that have got into the meads, and I agreed to take his place, as he knew he couldn't come back here again to-night. I know the part as well as he.'

Her graceful gait, elegant figure, and dignified manner in general won the mummers to the opinion that they had gained by the exchange, if the newcomer were perfect in his part.

'It don't matter—if you be not too young,' said Saint George. Eustacia's voice had sounded somewhat more juvenile and fluty than Charley's.

'I know every word of it, I tell you,' said Eustacia decisively. Dash being all that was required to carry her triumphantly through, she adopted as much as was necessary. 'Go ahead, lads, with the try-over. I'll challenge any of you to find a mistake in me.'

The play was hastily rehearsed, whereupon the other mummers were delighted with the new knight. They extinguished the candles at half-past eight, and set out upon the heath in the direction of Mrs. Yeobright's house at Blooms-End.

There was a slight hoar-frost that night, and the moon, though not more than half full, threw a spirited and enticing brightness upon the fantastic figures of the mumming band, whose plumes and ribbons rustled in their walk like autumn leaves. Their path was not over Rainbarrow now, but down a valley which left that ancient elevation a little to the east. The bottom of the vale was green to a width of ten yards or thereabouts, and the shining facets of frost upon the blades of grass seemed to move on with the shadows of those they surrounded. The masses of furze and heath to the right and left were dark as ever; a mere half-moon was powerless to silver such sable features as theirs.

Half-an-hour of walking and talking brought them to the spot in the valley where the grass riband widened and led down to the front of the house. At sight of the place Eustacia, who had felt a few passing doubts during her walk with the youths, again was glad that the adventure had been undertaken. She had come out to see a man who might possibly have the power to deliver her soul from a most deadly oppression. What was Wildeve? Interesting, but inadequate. Perhaps she would see a sufficient hero to-night.

As they drew nearer to the front of the house the mummers became aware that music and dancing were briskly flourishing within. Every now and then a long low note from the serpent,[1] which was the chief wind instrument played at these times, advanced further into the heath than the thin treble part, and reached their ears alone; and next a more than usually loud tread from a dancer would come the same way. With nearer approach these fragmentary sounds became pieced together, and were found to be the salient points of the tune called 'Nancy's Fancy.'[2]

He was there, of course. Who was she that he danced with? Perhaps some unknown woman, far beneath herself in culture, was by that most subtle of lures sealing his fate this very instant. To dance with a man is to concentrate a twelvemonth's regulation fire upon

1. Large wooden wind instrument, about eight feet long; the name derives from its form, which consists of three U-shaped turns.
2. A dance for two lines of men and women.

him in the fragment of an hour. To pass to courtship without acquaintance, to pass to marriage without courtship, is a skipping of
terms reserved for those alone who tread this royal road. She would
see how his heart lay by keen observation of them all.

The enterprising lady followed the mumming company through
the gate in the white paling, and stood before the open porch. The
house was encrusted with heavy thatchings, which dropped between the upper windows: the front, upon which the moonbeams
directly played, had originally been white; but a huge pyracanth[3]
now darkened the greater portion.

It became at once evident that the dance was proceeding immediately within the surface of the door, no apartment intervening.
The brushing of skirts and elbows, sometimes the bumping of
shoulders, could be heard against the very panels. Eustacia, though
living within two miles of the place, had never seen the interior of
this quaint old habitation. Between Captain Vye and the Yeobrights
there had never existed much acquaintance, the former having
come as a stranger and purchased the long-empty house at Mistover Knap not long before the death of Mrs. Yeobright's husband;
and with that event and the departure of her son such friendship as
had grown up became quite broken off.

'Is there no passage inside the door, then?' asked Eustacia as they
stood within the porch.

'No,' said the lad who played the Saracen. 'The door opens right
upon the front sitting-room, where the spree's going on.'

'So that we cannot open the door without stopping the dance.'

'That's it. Here we must bide till they have done, for they always
bolt the back door after dark.'

'They won't be much longer,' said Father Christmas.

This assertion, however, was hardly borne out by the event. Again
the instruments ended the tune; again they recommenced with as
much fire and pathos as if it were the first strain. The air was now
that one without any particular beginning, middle, or end, which
perhaps, among all the dances which throng an inspired fiddler's
fancy, best conveys the idea of the interminable—the celebrated
'Devil's Dream.'[4] The fury of personal movement that was kindled
by the fury of the notes could be approximately imagined by these
outsiders under the moon, from the occasional kicks of toes and
heels against the door, whenever the whirl round had been of more
than customary velocity.

The first five minutes of listening was interesting enough to the
mummers. The five minutes extended to ten minutes, and these to

3. Thorny evergreen shrub of the rose family, with white flowers and red or yellow berries.
4. A six-handed reel, or dance for six couples.

a quarter of an hour; but no signs of ceasing were audible in the lively Dream. The bumping against the door, the laughter, the stamping, were all as vigorous as ever, and the pleasure in being outside lessened considerably.

'Why does Mrs. Yeobright give parties of this sort?' Eustacia asked, a little surprised to hear merriment so pronounced.

'It is not one of her bettermost parlour-parties. She's asked the plain neighbours and workpeople without drawing any lines, just to give 'em a good supper and such like. Her son and she wait upon the folks.'

'I see,' said Eustacia.

' 'Tis the last strain, I think,' said Saint George, with his ear to the panel. 'A young man and woman have just swung into this corner, and he's saying to her, "Ah, the pity; 'tis over for us this time, my own." '

'Thank God,' said the Turkish Knight, stamping and taking from the wall the conventional lance that each of the mummers carried. Her boots being thinner than those of the young men, the hoar had damped her feet and made them cold.

'Upon my song 'tis another ten minutes for us,' said the Valiant Soldier, looking through the keyhole as the tune modulated into another without stopping. 'Grandfer Cantle is standing in this corner, waiting his turn.'

' 'Twon't be long; 'tis a six-handed reel,' said the Doctor.

'Why not go in, dancing or no? They sent for us,' said the Saracen.

'Certainly not,' said Eustacia authoritatively, as she paced smartly up and down from door to gate to warm herself. 'We should burst into the middle of them and stop the dance, and that would be unmannerly.'

'He thinks himself somebody because he has had a bit more schooling than we,' said the Doctor.

'You may go to the deuce!' said Eustacia.

There was a whispered conversation between three or four of them, and one turned to her.

'Will you tell us one thing?' he said, not without gentleness. 'Be you Miss Vye? We think you must be.'

'You may think what you like,' said Eustacia slowly. 'But honourable lads will not tell tales upon a lady.'

'We'll say nothing, miss. That's upon our honour.'

'Thank you,' she replied.

At this moment the fiddles finished off with a screech, and the serpent emitted a last note that nearly lifted the roof. When, from the comparative quiet within, the mummers judged that the dancers had taken their seats, Father Christmas advanced, lifted the latch, and put his head inside the door.

'Ah, the mummers, the mummers!' cried several guests at once. 'Clear a space for the mummers.'

Hump-backed Father Christmas then made a complete entry, swinging his huge club, and in a general way clearing the stage for the actors proper, while he informed the company in smart verse that he was come, welcome or welcome not; concluding his speech with

> 'Make room, make room, my gallant boys,
>   And give us space to rhyme;
> We've come to show Saint George's play,
>   Upon this Christmas time.'

The guests were now arranging themselves at one end of the room, the fiddler was mending a string, the serpent-player was emptying his mouthpiece, and the play began. First of those outside the Valiant Soldier entered, in the interest of Saint George—

> 'Here come I, the Valiant Soldier;
>   Slasher is my name;'

and so on. This speech concluded with a challenge to the infidel, at the end of which it was Eustacia's duty to enter as the Turkish Knight. She, with the rest who were not yet on, had hitherto remained in the moonlight which streamed under the porch. With no apparent effort or backwardness she came in, beginning—

> 'Here come I, a Turkish Knight,
>   Who learnt in Turkish land to fight;
> I'll fight this man with courage bold:
>   If his blood's hot I'll make it cold!'

During her declamation Eustacia held her head erect, and spoke as roughly as she could, feeling pretty secure from observation. But the concentration upon her part necessary to prevent discovery, the newness of the scene, the shine of the candles, and the confusing effect upon her vision of the ribboned visor which hid her features, left her absolutely unable to perceive who were present as spectators. On the further side of a table bearing candles she could faintly discern faces, and that was all.

Meanwhile Jim Starks as the Valiant Soldier had come forward, and, with a glare upon the Turk, replied—

> 'If, then, thou art that Turkish Knight,
>   Draw out thy sword, and let us fight!'

And fight they did; the issue of the combat being that the Valiant Soldier was slain by a preternaturally inadequate thrust from Eustacia, Jim, in his ardour for genuine histrionic art, coming down

like a log upon the stone floor with force enough to dislocate his
shoulder. Then, after more words from the Turkish Knight, rather
too faintly delivered, and statements that he'd fight Saint George
and all his crew, Saint George himself magnificently entered with
the well-known flourish—

> 'Here come I, Saint George, the valiant man,
> With naked sword and spear in hand,
> Who fought the dragon and brought him to the slaughter,
> And by this won fair Sabra, the King of Egypt's daughter;
> What mortal man would dare to stand
> Before me with my sword in hand?'

This was the lad who had first recognised Eustacia; and when she
now, as the Turk, replied with suitable defiance, and at once began
the combat, the young fellow took especial care to use his sword as
gently as possible. Being wounded, the Knight fell upon one knee,
according to the direction. The Doctor now entered, restored the
Knight by giving him a draught from the bottle which he carried,
and the fight was again resumed, the Turk sinking by degrees until
quite overcome—dying as hard in this venerable drama as he is said
to do at the present day.[5]

This gradual sinking to the earth was, in fact, one reason why
Eustacia had thought that the part of the Turkish Knight, though
not the shortest, would suit her best. A direct fall from upright to
horizontal, which was the end of the other fighting characters, was
not an elegant or decorous part[6] for a girl. But it was easy to die
like a Turk, by a dogged decline.

Eustacia was now among the number of the slain, though not on
the floor, for she had managed to sink into a sloping position
against the clock-case, so that her head was well elevated. The play
proceeded between Saint George, the Saracen, the Doctor, and Father Christmas; and Eustacia, having no more to do, for the first
time found leisure to observe the scene around, and to search for
the form that had drawn her hither.

The Two Stand Face to Face

VI

The room had been arranged with a view to the dancing, the large
oak table having been moved back till it stood as a breastwork to
the fireplace. At each end, behind, and in the chimney-corner were
grouped the guests, many of them being warm-faced and panting,

5. The Turkish or Ottoman empire, which collapsed during World War I, was under threat
through much of the nineteenth century.
6. So in all editions; the manuscript has "feat."

among whom Eustacia cursorily recognized some well-to-do persons from beyond the heath. Thomasin, as she had expected, was not visible, and Eustacia recollected that a light had shone from an upper window when they were outside—the window, probably, of Thomasin's room. A nose, chin, hands, knees, and toes projected from the seat within the chimney opening, which members she found to unite in the person of Grandfer Cantle, Mrs. Yeobright's occasional assistant in the garden, and therefore one of the invited. The smoke went up from an Etna[1] of peat in front of him, played round the notches of the chimney-crook, struck against the salt-box, and got lost among the flitches.[2]

Another part of the room soon riveted her gaze. At the other side of the chimney stood the settle, which is the necessary supplement to a fire so open that nothing less than a strong breeze will carry up the smoke. It is, to the hearths of old-fashioned cavernous fire-places, what the east belt of trees is to the exposed country estate, or the north wall to the garden. Outside the settle candles gutter, locks of hair wave, young women shiver, and old men sneeze. Inside is Paradise. Not a symptom of a draught disturbs the air; the sitters' backs are as warm as their faces, and songs and old tales are drawn from the occupants by the comfortable heat, like fruit from melon-plants in a frame.

It was, however, not with those who sat in the settle that Eustacia was concerned. A face showed itself with marked distinctness against the dark-tanned wood of the upper part. The owner, who was leaning against the settle's outer end, was Clement Yeobright, or Clym, as he was called here; she knew it could be nobody else. The spectacle constituted an area of two feet in Rembrandt's intensest manner.[3] A strange power in the lounger's appearance lay in the fact that, though his whole figure was visible, the observer's eye was only aware of his face.

To one of middle age the countenance was that of a young man, though a youth might hardly have seen any necessity for the term of immaturity. But it was really one of those faces which convey less the idea of so many years as its age than of so much experience as its store. The number of their years may have adequately summed up Jared, Mahalaleel,[4] and the rest of the antediluvians, but the age of a modern man is to be measured by the intensity of his history.

1. Etna, in Sicily, is the highest active volcano in Europe.
2. Sides of an animal, hung up to be smoked and cured; usually, a side of bacon.
3. The Dutch painter Rembrandt van Ryn (1606–69) often employed extreme contrasts of light and dark in his portraits.
4. According to Genesis 5.15–20, Mahalaleel lived 895 years, and his son Jared 962 years; both lived before the flood that destroyed all the earth's inhabitants except for Noah and his family.

The face was well shaped, even excellently. But the mind within was beginning to use it as a mere waste tablet[5] whereon to trace its idiosyncrasies as they developed themselves. The beauty here visible would in no long time be ruthlessly overrun by its parasite, thought, which might just as well have fed upon a plainer exterior where there was nothing it could harm. Had Heaven preserved Yeobright from a wearing habit of meditation, people would have said, 'A handsome man.' Had his brain unfolded under sharper contours they would have said, 'A thoughtful man.' But an inner strenuousness was preying upon an outer symmetry, and they rated his look as singular.

Hence people who began by beholding him ended by perusing him. His countenance was overlaid with legible meanings. Without being thought-worn he yet had certain marks derived from a perception of his surroundings, such as are not unfrequently found on men at the end of the four or five years of endeavour which follow the close of placid pupilage. He already showed that thought is a disease of flesh, and indirectly bore evidence that ideal physical beauty is incompatible with emotional development and a full recognition of the coil of things. Mental luminousness must be fed with the oil of life, even though there is already a physical need for it; and the pitiful sight of two demands on one supply was just showing itself here.

When standing before certain men the philosopher regrets that thinkers are but perishable tissue, the artist that perishable tissue has to think. Thus to deplore, each from his point of view, the mutually destructive interdependence of spirit and flesh would have been instinctive with these in critically observing Yeobright.

As for his look, it was a natural cheerfulness striving against depression from without, and not quite succeeding. The look suggested isolation, but it revealed something more. As is usual with bright natures, the deity that lies ignominiously chained within an ephemeral human carcase shone out of him like a ray.

The effect upon Eustacia was palpable. The extraordinary pitch of excitement that she had reached beforehand would, indeed, have caused her to be influenced by the most commonplace man. She was troubled at Yeobright's presence.

The remainder of the play ended: the Saracen's head was cut off, and Saint George stood as victor. Nobody commented, any more than they would have commented on the fact of mushrooms coming in autumn or snowdrops in spring. They took the piece as phlegmatically as did the actors themselves. It was a phase of cheerfulness which was, as a matter of course, to be passed through every Christmas; and there was no more to be said.

5. Panel covered in wax, on which text could be inscribed or traced.

They sang the plaintive chant which follows the play, during which all the dead men rise to their feet in a silent and awful manner, like the ghosts of Napoleon's soldiers in the Midnight Review.[6] Afterwards the door opened, and Fairway appeared on the threshold, accompanied by Christian and another. They had been waiting outside for the conclusion of the play, as the players had waited for the conclusion of the dance.

'Come in, come in,' said Mrs. Yeobright; and Clym went forward to welcome them. 'How is it you are so late? Grandfer Cantle has been here ever so long, and we thought you'd have come with him, as you live so near one another.'

'Well, I should have come earlier,' Mr. Fairway said, and paused to look along the beam of the ceiling for a nail to hang his hat on; but, finding his accustomed one to be occupied by the mistletoe, and all the nails in the walls to be burdened with bunches of holly, he at last relieved himself of the hat by ticklishly balancing it between the candle-box and the head of the clock-case. 'I should have come earlier, ma'am,' he resumed, with a more composed air, 'but I know what parties be, and how there's none too much room in folks' houses at such times, so I thought I wouldn't come till you'd got settled a bit.'

'And I thought so too, Mrs. Yeobright,' said Christian earnestly; 'but father there was so eager that he had no manners at all, and left home almost afore 'twas dark. I told him 'twas barely decent in a' old man to come so oversoon; but words be wind.'

'Klk! I wasn't going to bide waiting about till half the game was over! I'm as light as a kite when anything's going on!' crowed Grandfer Cantle from the chimney-seat.

Fairway had meanwhile concluded a critical gaze at Yeobright. 'Now, you may not believe it,' he said to the rest of the room, 'but I should never have knowed this gentleman if I had met him anywhere off his own he'th: he's altered so much.'

'You too have altered, and for the better, I think, Timothy,' said Yeobright, surveying the firm figure of Fairway.

'Master Yeobright, look me over too. I have altered for the better, haven't I, hey?' said Grandfer Cantle, rising, and placing himself something above half a foot from Clym's eye, to induce the most searching criticism.

'To be sure we will,' said Fairway, taking the candle and moving it over the surface of the Grandfer's countenance, the subject of his scrutiny irradiating himself with light and pleasant smiles, and giving himself jerks of juvenility.

---

6. The English title of "Die nächtliche Heerschau," by the Austrian writer J. C. von Zedlitz (1790–1862), in which Napoleon's dead soldiers are called from their graves.

'If there's any difference, Grandfer is younger.'

'You haven't changed much,' said Yeobright.

'If there's any difference, Grandfer is younger,' appended Fairway decisively.

'And yet not my own doing, and I feel no pride in it,' said the pleased ancient. 'But I can't be cured of my vagaries; them I plead guilty to. Yes, Master Cantle always was that, as we know. But I am nothing by the side of you, Mister Clym.'

'Nor any o' us,' said Humphrey, in a low rich tone of admiration, not intended to reach anybody's ears.

'Really, there would have been nobody here who could have stood as decent second to him, or even third, if I hadn't been a soldier in the Bang-up Locals (as we was called for our smartness),' said Grandfer Cantle. 'And even as 'tis we all look a little scammish[7] beside him. But in the year four 'twas said there wasn't a finer figure in the whole South Wessex than I, as I looked when dashing past the shop-winders with the rest of our company on the day we ran out o' Budmouth because it was thought that Boney had landed round the point. There was I, straight as a young poplar, wi' my firelock, and my bagnet, and my spatterdashes,[8] and my stock sawing my jaws off, and my accoutrements sheening like the seven stars![9] Yes, neighbours, I was a pretty sight in my soldiering days. You ought to have seen me in four!'

7. Awkward (dialect).
8. A firelock is a musket, a bagnet is a bayonet; spatterdashes are leggings worn to protect against splashes of mud, etc; a stock is a high neckcloth, made of stiff material.
9. Either the Pleiades, also known as the Seven Sisters, the seven brightest stars in the constellation of Taurus, or the seven stars that make up the Great Bear.

''Tis his mother's side where Master Clym's figure comes from, bless ye,' said Timothy. 'I know'd her brothers well. Longer coffins were never made in the whole county of South Wessex, and 'tis said that poor George's knees were crumpled up a little e'en as 'twas.'

'Coffins, where?' inquired Christian, drawing nearer. 'Have the ghost of one appeared to anybody, Master Fairway?'

'No, no. Don't let your mind so mislead your ears, Christian; and be a man,' said Timothy reproachfully.

'I will,' said Christian. 'But now I think o't my shadder last night seemed just the shape of a coffin. What is it a sign of when your shade's like a coffin, neighbours? It can't be nothing to be afeard of, I suppose?'

'Afeard, no!' said the Grandfer. 'Faith, I was never afeard of nothing except Boney, or I shouldn't ha' been the soldier I was. Yes, 'tis a thousand pities you didn't see me in four!'

By this time the mummers were preparing to leave; but Mrs. Yeobright stopped them by asking them to sit down and have a little supper. To this invitation Father Christmas, in the name of them all, readily agreed.

Eustacia was happy in the opportunity of staying a little longer. The cold and frosty night without was doubly frigid to her. But the lingering was not without its difficulties. Mrs. Yeobright, for want of room in the larger apartment, placed a bench for the mummers half-way through the pantry-door, which opened from the sitting-room. Here they seated themselves in a row, the door being left open: thus they were still virtually in the same apartment. Mrs. Yeobright now murmured a few words to her son, who crossed the room to the pantry-door, striking his head against the mistletoe as he passed, and brought the mummers beef and bread, cake, pastry, mead, and elder-wine, the waiting being done by him and his mother, that the little maid-servant might sit as guest. The mummers doffed their helmets, and began to eat and drink.

'But you will surely have some?' said Clym to the Turkish Knight, as he stood before that warrior, tray in hand. She had refused, and still sat covered, only the sparkle of her eyes being visible between the ribbons which covered her face.

'None, thank you,' replied Eustacia.

'He's quite a youngster,' said the Saracen apologetically, 'and you must excuse him. He's not one of the old set, but have jined us because t'other couldn't come.'

'But he will take something?' persisted Yeobright. 'Try a glass of mead or elder-wine.'

'Yes, you had better try that,' said the Saracen. 'It will keep the cold out going home-along.'

Though Eustacia could not eat without uncovering her face she could drink easily enough beneath her disguise. The elder-wine was accordingly accepted, and the glass vanished inside the ribbons.

At moments during this performance Eustacia was half in doubt about the security of her position; yet it had a fearful joy.[1] A series of attentions paid to her, and yet not to her but to some imaginary person, by the first man she had ever been inclined to adore, complicated her emotions indescribably.[2] She had loved him partly because he was exceptional in this scene, partly because she had determined to love him, chiefly because she was in desperate need of loving somebody after wearying of Wildeve. Believing that she must love him in spite of herself, she had been influenced after the fashion of the second Lord Lyttleton[3] and other persons, who have dreamed that they were to die on a certain day, and by stress of a morbid imagination have actually brought about that event. Once let a maiden admit the possibility of her being stricken with love for some one at a certain hour and place, and the thing is as good as done.

Did anything at this moment suggest to Yeobright the sex of the creature whom that fantastic guise inclosed, how extended was her scope both in feeling and in making others feel, and how far her compass transcended that of her companions in the band? When the disguised Queen of Love appeared before Æneas[4] a preternatural perfume accompanied her presence and betrayed her quality. If such a mysterious emanation ever was projected by the emotions of an earthly woman upon their object, it must have signified Eustacia's presence to Yeobright now. He looked at her wistfully, then seemed to fall into a reverie, as if he were forgetting what he observed. The momentary situation ended, he passed on, and Eustacia sipped her wine without knowing what she drank. The man for whom she had predetermined to nourish a passion went into the small room, and across it to the further extremity.

The mummers, as has been stated, were seated on a bench, one end of which extended into the small apartment, or pantry, for want of space in the outer room. Eustacia, partly from shyness, had chosen the midmost seat, which thus commanded a view of the interior of the pantry as well as the room containing the guests. When Clym passed down the pantry her eyes followed him in the gloom which prevailed there. At the remote end was a door which, just as

1. Thomas Gray writes of a "fearful joy" in his "Ode on a Distant Prospect of Eton College" (1742), line 40.
2. The manuscript and serial continue here: "She had undoubtedly begun to love him." Some such sentence seems to be needed; it was probably omitted in error by the printer of the 1878 edition, and overlooked thereafter.
3. Three days before his death in 1779, Thomas, second Baron Lyttelton, dreamed that he had only three days to live.
4. In Book I of Vergil's *Aeneid*, Venus appears to her son Aeneas in disguise; he eventually recognizes her from her divine scent.

he was about to open it for himself, was opened by somebody within; and light streamed forth.

The person was Thomasin, with a candle, looking anxious, pale, and interesting. Yeobright appeared glad to see her, and pressed her hand. 'That's right, Tamsie,' he said heartily, as though recalled to himself by the sight of her: 'you have decided to come down. I am glad of it.'

'Hush—no, no,' she said quickly. 'I only came to speak to you.'

'But why not join us?'

'I cannot. At least I would rather not. I am not well enough, and we shall have plenty of time together now you are going to be home a good long holiday.'

'It isn't nearly so pleasant without you. Are you really ill?'

'Just a little, my old cousin—here,' she said, playfully sweeping her hand across her heart.

'Ah, mother should have asked somebody else to be present to-night, perhaps?'

'O no, indeed. I merely stepped down, Clym, to ask you——'
Here he followed her through the doorway into the private room beyond, and, the door closing, Eustacia and the mummer who sat next to her, the only other witness of the performance, saw and heard no more.

The heat flew to Eustacia's head and cheeks. She instantly guessed that Clym, having been home only these two or three days, had not as yet been made acquainted with Thomasin's painful situation with regard to Wildeve; and seeing her living there just as she had been living before he left home, he naturally suspected nothing. Eustacia felt a wild jealousy of Thomasin on the instant. Though Thomasin might possibly have tender sentiments towards another man as yet, how long could they be expected to last when she was shut up here with this interesting and travelled cousin of hers? There was no knowing what affection might not soon break out between the two, so constantly in each other's society, and not a distracting object near. Clym's boyish love for her might have languished, but it might easily be revived again.

Eustacia was nettled by her own contrivances. What a sheer waste of herself to be dressed thus while another was shining to advantage! Had she known the full effect of the encounter she would have moved heaven and earth to get here in a natural manner. The power of her face all lost, the charm of her emotions all disguised, the fascinations of her coquetry denied existence, nothing but a voice left to her: she had a sense of the doom of Echo.[5] 'Nobody

---

5. In Greek mythology the nymph Echo, in love with Narcissus, pined away until only her voice was left.

here respects me,' she said. She had overlooked the fact that, in coming as a boy among other boys, she would be treated as a boy. The slight, though of her own causing, and self-explanatory, she was unable to dismiss as unwittingly shown, so sensitive had the situation made her.

Women have done much for themselves in histrionic dress. To look far below those who, like a certain fair personator of Polly Peachum early in the last century, and another of Lydia Languish[6] early in this, have won not only love but ducal coronets into the bargain, whole shoals of them have reached to the initial satisfaction of getting love almost whence they would. But the Turkish Knight was denied even the chance of achieving this by the fluttering ribbons which she dared not brush aside.

Yeobright returned to the room without his cousin. When within two or three feet of Eustacia he stopped, as if again arrested by a thought. He was gazing at her. She looked another way, disconcerted, and wondered how long this purgatory was to last. After lingering a few seconds he passed on again.

To court their own discomfiture by love is a common instinct with certain perfervid women. Conflicting sensations of love, fear, and shame reduced Eustacia to a state of the utmost uneasiness. To escape was her great and immediate desire. The other mummers appeared to be in no hurry to leave; and murmuring to the lad who sat next to her that she preferred waiting for them outside the house, she moved to the door as imperceptibly as possible, opened it, and slipped out.

The calm, lone scene reassured her. She went forward to the palings and leant over them, looking at the moon. She had stood thus but a little time when the door again opened. Expecting to see the remainder of the band Eustacia turned; but no—Clym Yeobright came out as softly as she had done, and closed the door behind him.

He advanced and stood beside her. 'I have an odd opinion,' he said, 'and should like to ask you a question. Are you a woman—or am I wrong?'

'I am a woman.'

His eyes lingered on her with great interest. 'Do girls often play as mummers now? They never used to.'

'They don't now.'

'Why did you?'

'To get excitement and shake off depression,' she said in low tones.

6. Lavinia Fenton, who played Polly Peachum in John Gay's play *The Beggar's Opera* (1728), later married Charles Paulet, third duke of Bolton; Harriet Mellon, who played Lydia Languish in Richard Sheridan's *The Rivals* (1775), married William Aubrey de Vere Beauclerk, ninth duke of St. Albans, in 1827.

'What depressed you?'

'Life.'

'That's a cause of depression a good many have to put up with.'

'Yes.'

A long silence. 'And do you find excitement?' asked Clym at last.

'At this moment, perhaps.'

'Then you are vexed at being discovered?'

'Yes; though I thought I might be.'

'I would gladly have asked you to our party had I known you wished to come. Have I ever been acquainted with you in my youth?'

'Never.'

'Won't you come in again, and stay as long as you like?'

'No. I wish not to be further recognized.'

'Well, you are safe with me.' After remaining in thought a minute he added gently, 'I will not intrude upon you longer. It is a strange way of meeting, and I will not ask why I find a cultivated woman playing such a part as this.'

She did not volunteer the reason which he seemed to hope for, and he wished her good night, going thence round to the back of the house, where he walked up and down by himself for some time before re-entering.

Eustacia, warmed with an inner fire, could not wait for her companions after this. She flung back the ribbons from her face, opened the gate, and at once struck into the heath. She did not hasten along. Her grandfather was in bed at this hour, for she so frequently walked upon the hills on moonlight nights that he took no notice of her comings and goings, and, enjoying himself in his own way, left her to do likewise. A more important subject than that of getting indoors now engrossed her. Yeobright, if he had the least curiosity, would infallibly discover her name. What then? She first felt a sort of exultation at the way in which the adventure had terminated, even though at moments between her exultations she was abashed and blushful. Then this consideration recurred to chill her: What was the use of her exploit? She was at present a total stranger to the Yeobright family. The unreasonable nimbus of romance with which she had encircled that man might be her misery. How could she allow herself to become so infatuated with a stranger? And to fill the cup of her sorrow there would be Thomasin, living day after day in inflammable proximity to him; for she had just learnt that, contrary to her first belief, he was going to stay at home some considerable time.

She reached the wicket at Mistover Knap, but before opening it she turned and faced the heath once more. The form of Rainbarrow stood above the hills, and the moon stood above Rainbarrow.

The air was charged with silence and frost. The scene reminded
Eustacia of a circumstance which till that moment she had totally
forgotten. She had promised to meet Wildeve by the Barrow this
very night at eight, to give a final answer to his pleading for an
elopement.

She herself had fixed the evening and the hour. He had probably
come to the spot, waited there in the cold, and been greatly disappointed.

'Well, so much the better: it did not hurt him,' she said serenely.
Wildeve had at present the rayless outline of the sun through
smoked glass, and she could say such things as that with the greatest facility.

She remained deeply pondering; and Thomasin's winning manner towards her cousin arose again upon Eustacia's mind.

'O that she had been married to Damon before this!' she said.
'And she would if it hadn't been for me! If I had only known—if I
had only known!'

Eustacia once more lifted her deep stormy eyes to the moonlight,
and, sighing that tragic sigh of hers which was so much like a shudder, entered the shadow of the roof. She threw off her trappings in
the outhouse, rolled them up, and went indoors to her chamber.

A Coalition between Beauty and Oddness

VII

The old captain's prevailing indifference to his granddaughter's
movements left her free as a bird to follow her own courses; but it
so happened that he did take upon himself the next morning to ask
her why she had walked out so late.

'Only in search of events, grandfather,' she said, looking out of
the window with that drowsy latency of manner which discovered
so much force behind it whenever the trigger was pressed.

'Search of events—one would think you were one of the bucks I
knew at one-and-twenty.'

'It is so lonely here.'

'So much the better. If I were living in a town my whole time
would be taken up in looking after you. I fully expected you would
have been home when I returned from the Woman.'

'I won't conceal what I did. I wanted an adventure, and I went
with the mummers. I played the part of the Turkish Knight.'

'No, never? Ha, ha! Good gad! I didn't expect it of you, Eustacia.'

'It was my first performance, and it certainly will be my last. Now
I have told you—and remember it is a secret.'

'Of course. But, Eustacia, you never did—ha! ha! Dammy, how

'twould have pleased me forty years ago! But remember, no more of it, my girl. You may walk on the heath night or day, as you choose, so that you don't bother me; but no figuring in breeches again.'

'You need have no fear for me, grandpapa.'

Here the conversation ceased, Eustacia's moral training never exceeding in severity a dialogue of this sort, which, if it ever became profitable to good works, would be a result not dear at the price. But her thoughts soon strayed far from her own personality; and, full of a passionate and indescribable solicitude for one to whom she was not even a name, she went forth into the amplitude of tanned wild around her, restless as Ahasuerus the Jew.[1] She was about half a mile from her residence when she beheld a sinister redness arising from a ravine a little way in advance—dull and lurid like a flame in sunlight, and she guessed it to signify Diggory Venn.

When the farmers who had wished to buy in a new stock of reddle during the last month had inquired where Venn was to be found, people replied, 'On Egdon Heath.' Day after day the answer was the same. Now, since Egdon was populated with heath-croppers and furze-cutters rather than with sheep and shepherds, and the downs where most of the latter were to be found lay some to the north, some to the west of Egdon, his reason for camping about there like Israel in Zin[2] was not apparent. The position was central and occasionally desirable. But the sale of reddle was not Diggory's primary object in remaining on the heath, particularly at so late a period of the year, when most travellers of his class had gone into winter quarters.

Eustacia looked at the lonely man. Wildeve had told her at their last meeting that Venn had been thrust forward by Mrs. Yeobright as one ready and anxious to take his place as Thomasin's betrothed. His figure was perfect, his face young and well outlined, his eye bright, his intelligence keen, and his position one which he could readily better if he chose. But in spite of possibilities it was not likely that Thomasin would accept this Ishmaelitish creature while she had a cousin like Yeobright at her elbow, and Wildeve at the same time not absolutely indifferent. Eustacia was not long in guessing that poor Mrs. Yeobright, in her anxiety for her niece's future, had mentioned this lover to stimulate the zeal of the other. Eustacia was on the side of the Yeobrights now, and entered into the spirit of the aunt's desire.

'Good morning, miss,' said the reddleman, taking off his cap of hareskin, and apparently bearing her no ill-will from recollection of their last meeting.

---

1. The Wandering Jew, who according to the medieval legend insulted Christ on the road to Calvary and was condemned to roam the earth until Judgment Day.
2. In Numbers 33.36 the Israelites pitch camp in "the wilderness of Zin" during their journey from Egypt to Canaan.

'Good morning, reddleman,' she said, hardly troubling to lift her heavily shaded eyes to his. 'I did not know you were so near. Is your van here too?'

Venn moved his elbow towards a hollow in which a dense brake of purple-stemmed brambles had grown to such vast dimensions as almost to form a dell. Brambles, though churlish when handled, are kindly shelter in early winter, being the latest of the deciduous bushes to lose their leaves. The roof and chimney of Venn's caravan showed behind the tracery and tangles of the brake.

'You remain near this part?' she asked with more interest.

'Yes, I have business here.'

'Not altogether the selling of reddle?'

'It has nothing to do with that.'

'It has to do with Miss Yeobright?'

Her face seemed to ask for an armed peace, and he therefore said frankly, 'Yes, miss; it is on account of her.'

'On account of your approaching marriage with her?'

Venn flushed through his stain. 'Don't make sport of me, Miss Vye,' he said.

'It isn't true?'

'Certainly not.'

She was thus convinced that the reddleman was a mere *pis aller*[3] in Mrs. Yeobright's mind; one, moreover, who had not even been informed of his promotion to that lowly standing. 'It was a mere notion of mine,' she said quietly; and was about to pass by without further speech, when, looking round to the right, she saw a painfully well-known figure serpenting upwards by one of the little paths which led to the top where she stood. Owing to the necessary windings of his course his back was at present towards them. She glanced quickly round; to escape that man there was only one way. Turning to Venn, she said, 'Would you allow me to rest a few minutes in your van? The banks are damp for sitting on.'

'Certainly, miss; I'll make a place for you.'

She followed him behind the dell of brambles to his wheeled dwelling, into which Venn mounted, placing the three-legged stool just within the door.

'That is the best I can do for you,' he said, stepping down and retiring to the path, where he resumed the smoking of his pipe as he walked up and down.

Eustacia bounded into the vehicle and sat on the stool, ensconced from view on the side towards the trackway. Soon she heard the brushing of other feet than the reddleman's, a not very friendly 'Good day' uttered by two men in passing each other, and then the

3. A last resort, when other options have failed (French).

dwindling of the footfall of one of them in a direction onwards. Eustacia stretched her neck forward till she caught a glimpse of a receding back and shoulders; and she felt a wretched twinge of misery, she knew not why. It was the sickening feeling which, if the changed heart has any generosity at all in its composition, accompanies the sudden sight of a once-loved one who is beloved no more.

When Eustacia descended to proceed on her way the reddleman came near. 'That was Mr. Wildeve who passed, miss,' he said slowly, and expressed by his face that he expected her to feel vexed at having been sitting unseen.

'Yes, I saw him coming up the hill,' replied Eustacia. 'Why should you tell me that?' It was a bold question, considering the reddleman's knowledge of her past love; but her undemonstrative manner had power to repress the opinions of those she treated as remote from her.

'I am glad to hear that you can ask it,' said the reddleman bluntly. 'And, now I think of it, it agrees with what I saw last night.'

'Ah—what was that?' Eustacia wished to leave him, but wished to know.

'Mr. Wildeve stayed at Rainbarrow a long time waiting for a lady who didn't come.'

'You waited too, it seems?'

'Yes, I always do. I was glad to see him disappointed. He will be there again to-night.'

'To be again disappointed. The truth is, reddleman, that that lady, so far from wishing to stand in the way of Thomasin's marriage with Mr. Wildeve, would be very glad to promote it.'

Venn felt much astonishment at this avowal, though he did not show it clearly; that exhibition may greet remarks which are one remove from expectation, but it is usually withheld in complicated cases of two removes and upwards. 'Indeed, miss,' he replied.

'How do you know that Mr. Wildeve will come to Rainbarrow again to-night?' she asked.

'I heard him say to himself that he would. He's in a regular temper.'

Eustacia looked for a moment what she felt, and she murmured, lifting her deep dark eyes anxiously to his, 'I wish I knew what to do. I don't want to be uncivil to him; but I don't wish to see him again; and I have some few little things to return to him.'

'If you choose to send 'em by me, miss, and a note to tell him that you wish to say no more to him, I'll take it for you quite privately. That would be the most straightforward way of letting him know your mind.'

'Very well,' said Eustacia. 'Come towards my house, and I will bring it out to you.'

She went on, and as the path was an infinitely small parting in the shaggy locks of the heath, the reddleman followed exactly in her trail. She saw from a distance that the captain was on the bank sweeping the horizon with his telescope; and bidding Venn to wait where he stood she entered the house alone.

In ten minutes she returned with a parcel and a note, and said, in placing them in his hand, 'Why are you so ready to take these for me?'

'Can you ask that?'

'I suppose you think to serve Thomasin in some way by it. Are you as anxious as ever to help on her marriage?'

Venn was a little moved. 'I would sooner have married her myself,' he said in a low voice. 'But what I feel is that if she cannot be happy without him I will do my duty in helping her to get him, as a man ought.'

Eustacia looked curiously at the singular man who spoke thus. What a strange sort of love, to be entirely free from that quality of selfishness which is frequently the chief constituent of the passion, and sometimes its only one! The reddleman's disinterestedness was so well deserving of respect that it overshot respect by being barely comprehended; and she almost thought it absurd.

'Then we are both of one mind at last,' she said.

'Yes,' replied Venn gloomily. 'But if you would tell me, miss, why you take such an interest in her, I should be easier. It is so sudden and strange.'

Eustacia appeared at a loss. 'I cannot tell you that, reddleman,' she said coldly.

Venn said no more. He pocketed the letter, and, bowing to Eustacia, went away.

Rainbarrow had again become blended with night when Wildeve ascended the long acclivity at its base. On his reaching the top a shape grew up from the earth immediately behind him. It was that of Eustacia's emissary. He slapped Wildeve on the shoulder. The feverish young innkeeper and ex-engineer started like Satan at the touch of Ithuriel's spear.[4]

'The meeting is always at eight o'clock, at this place,' said Venn, 'and here we are—we three.'

'We three?' said Wildeve, looking quickly round.

'Yes; you, and I, and she. This is she.' He held up the letter and parcel.

Wildeve took them wonderingly. 'I don't quite see what this means,' he said. 'How do you come here? There must be some mistake.'

4. In Milton's *Paradise Lost* (1674), Satan disguises himself as a toad in order to gain access to Eve; he is returned to his proper form when the angel Ithuriel touches him with his spear (Book IV, lines 779–814).

'It will be cleared from your mind when you have read the letter. Lanterns for one.' The reddleman struck a light, kindled an inch of tallow-candle which he had brought, and sheltered it with his cap.

'Who are you?' said Wildeve, discerning by the candle-light an obscure rubicundity of person in his companion. 'You are the reddleman I saw on the hill this morning—why, you are the man who——'

'Please read the letter.'

'If you had come from the other one I shouldn't have been surprised,' murmured Wildeve as he opened the letter and read. His face grew serious.

To Mr. WILDEVE.

> After some thought I have decided once and for all that we must hold no further communication. The more I consider the matter the more I am convinced that there must be an end to our acquaintance. Had you been uniformly faithful to me throughout these two years you might now have some ground for accusing me of heartlessness; but if you calmly consider what I bore during the period of your desertion, and how I passively put up with your courtship of another without once interfering, you will, I think, own that I have a right to consult my own feelings when you come back to me again. That these are not what they were towards you may, perhaps, be a fault in me, but it is one which you can scarcely reproach me for when you remember how you left me for Thomasin.
>
> The little articles you gave me in the early part of our friendship are returned by the bearer of this letter. They should rightly have been sent back when I first heard of your engagement to her.
>
> EUSTACIA.

By the time that Wildeve reached her name the blankness with which he had read the first half of the letter intensified to mortification. 'I am made a great fool of, one way and another,' he said pettishly. 'Do you know what is in this letter?'

The reddleman hummed a tune.

'Can't you answer me?' asked Wildeve warmly.

'Ru-um-tum-tum,' sang the reddleman.

Wildeve stood looking on the ground beside Venn's feet, till he allowed his eyes to travel upwards over Diggory's form, as illuminated by the candle, to his head and face. 'Ha-ha! Well, I suppose I deserve it, considering how I have played with them both,' he said at last, as much to himself as to Venn. 'But of all the odd things that ever I knew, the oddest is that you should so run counter to your own interests as to bring this to me.'

'My interests?'

'Certainly. 'Twas your interest not to do anything which would send me courting Thomasin again, now she has accepted you—or something like it. Mrs. Yeobright says you are to marry her. 'Tisn't true, then?'

'Good Lord! I heard of this before, but didn't believe it. When did she say so?'

Wildeve began humming as the reddleman had done.

'I don't believe it now,' cried Venn.

'Ru-um-tum-tum,' sang Wildeve.

'O Lord—how we can imitate!' said Venn contemptuously. 'I'll have this out. I'll go straight to her.'

Diggory withdrew with an emphatic step, Wildeve's eye passing over his form in withering derision, as if he were no more than a heath-cropper. When the reddleman's figure could no longer be seen, Wildeve himself descended and plunged into the rayless hollow of the vale.

To lose the two women—he who had been the well-beloved of both—was too ironical an issue to be endured. He could only decently save himself by Thomasin; and once he became her husband, Eustacia's repentance, he thought, would set in for a long and bitter term. It was no wonder that Wildeve, ignorant of the new man at the back of the scene, should have supposed Eustacia to be playing a part. To believe that the letter was not the result of some momentary pique, to infer that she really gave him up to Thomasin, would have required previous knowledge of her transfiguration by that man's influence. Who was to know that she had grown generous in the greediness of a new passion, that in coveting one cousin she was dealing liberally with another, that in her eagerness to appropriate she gave way?

Full of this resolve to marry in haste, and wring the heart of the proud girl, Wildeve went his way.

Meanwhile Diggory Venn had returned to his van, where he stood looking thoughtfully into the stove. A new vista was opened up to him. But, however promising Mrs. Yeobright's views of him might be as a candidate for her niece's hand, one condition was indispensable to the favour of Thomasin herself, and that was a renunciation of his present wild mode of life. In this he saw little difficulty.

He could not afford to wait till the next day before seeing Thomasin and detailing his plan. He speedily plunged himself into toilet operations, pulled a suit of cloth clothes from a box, and in about twenty minutes stood before the van-lantern as a reddleman in nothing but his face, the vermilion shades of which were not to be removed in a day. Closing the door and fastening it with a padlock Venn set off towards Blooms-End.

He had reached the white palings and laid his hand upon the gate when the door of the house opened, and quickly closed again. A female form had glided in. At the same time a man, who had seemingly been standing with the woman in the porch, came forward from the house till he was face to face with Venn. It was Wildeve again.

'Man alive, you've been quick at it,' said Diggory sarcastically.

'And you slow, as you will find,' said Wildeve. 'And,' lowering his voice, 'you may as well go back again now. I've claimed her, and got her. Good night, reddleman!' Thereupon Wildeve walked away.

Venn's heart sank within him, though it had not risen unduly high. He stood leaning over the palings in an indecisive mood for nearly a quarter of an hour. Then he went up the garden-path, knocked, and asked for Mrs. Yeobright.

Instead of requesting him to enter she came to the porch. A discourse was carried on between them in low measured tones for the space of ten minutes or more. At the end of the time Mrs. Yeobright went in, and Venn sadly retraced his steps into the heath. When he had again regained his van he lit the lantern, and with an apathetic face at once began to pull off his best clothes, till in the course of a few minutes he reappeared as the confirmed and irretrievable reddleman that he had seemed before.

Firmness Is Discovered in a Gentle Heart

VIII

On that evening the interior of Blooms-End, though cosy and comfortable, had been rather silent. Clym Yeobright was not at home. Since the Christmas party he had gone on a few days' visit to a friend about ten miles off.

The shadowy form seen by Venn to part from Wildeve in the porch, and quickly withdraw into the house, was Thomasin's. On entering she threw down a cloak which had been carelessly wrapped round her, and came forward to the light, where Mrs. Yeobright sat at her work-table, drawn up within the settle, so that part of it projected into the chimney-corner.

'I don't like your going out after dark alone, Tamsin,' said her aunt quietly, without looking up from her work.

'I have only been just outside the door.'

'Well?' inquired Mrs. Yeobright, struck by a change in the tone of Thomasin's voice, and observing her. Thomasin's cheek was flushed to a pitch far beyond that which it had reached before her troubles, and her eyes glittered.

'It was *he* who knocked,' she said.

'I thought as much.'

'He wishes the marriage to be at once.'

'Indeed! What—is he anxious?' Mrs. Yeobright directed a searching look upon her niece. 'Why did not Mr. Wildeve come in?'

'He did not wish to. You are not friends with him, he says. He would like the wedding to be the day after to-morrow, quite privately; at the church of his parish—not at ours.'

'Oh! And what did you say?'

'I agreed to it,' Thomasin answered firmly. 'I am a practical woman now. I don't believe in hearts at all. I would marry him under any circumstances since—since Clym's letter.'

A letter was lying on Mrs. Yeobright's work-basket, and at Thomasin's words her aunt reopened it, and silently read for the tenth time that day:—

> What is the meaning of this silly story that people are circulating about Thomasin and Mr. Wildeve? I should call such a scandal humiliating if there was the least chance of its being true. How could such a gross falsehood have arisen? It is said that one should go abroad to hear news of home, and I appear to have done it. Of course I contradict the tale everywhere; but it is very vexing, and I wonder how it could have originated. It is too ridiculous that such a girl as Thomasin could so mortify us as to get jilted on the wedding-day. What has she done?

'Yes,' Mrs. Yeobright said sadly, putting down the letter. 'If you think you can marry him, do so. And since Mr. Wildeve wishes it to be unceremonious, let it be that too. I can do nothing. It is all in your own hands now. My power over your welfare came to an end when you left this house to go with him to Anglebury.' She continued, half in bitterness, 'I may almost ask, why do you consult me in the matter at all? If you had gone and married him without saying a word to me, I could hardly have been angry—simply because, poor girl, you can't do a better thing.'

'Don't say that and dishearten me.'

'You are right: I will not.

'I do not plead for him, aunt. Human nature is weak, and I am not a blind woman to insist that he is perfect. I did think so, but I don't now. But I know my course, and you know that I know it. I hope for the best.'

'And so do I, and we will both continue to,' said Mrs. Yeobright, rising and kissing her. 'Then the wedding, if it comes off, will be on the morning of the very day Clym comes home?'

'Yes. I decided that it ought to be over before he came. After that you can look him in the face, and so can I. Our concealments will matter nothing.'

Mrs. Yeobright moved her head in thoughtful assent, and pres-

ently said, 'Do you wish me to give you away? I am willing to undertake that, you know, if you wish, as I was last time. After once
forbidding the banns I think I can do no less.'

'I don't think I will ask you to come,' said Thomasin reluctantly,
but with decision. 'It would be unpleasant, I am almost sure. Better
let there be only strangers present, and none of my relations at all.
I would rather have it so. I do not wish to do anything which may
touch your credit, and I feel that I should be uncomfortable if you
were there, after what has passed. I am only your niece, and there
is no necessity why you should concern yourself more about me.'

'Well, he has beaten us,' her aunt said. 'It really seems as if he
had been playing with you in this way in revenge for my humbling
him as I did by standing up against him at first.'

'O no, aunt,' murmured Thomasin.

They said no more on the subject then. Diggory Venn's knock
came soon after; and Mrs. Yeobright, on returning from her interview with him in the porch, carelessly observed, 'Another lover has
come to ask for you.'

'No?'

'Yes; that queer young man Venn.'

'Asks to pay his addresses to me?'

'Yes; and I told him he was too late.'

Thomasin looked silently into the candle-flame. 'Poor Diggory!'
she said, and then aroused herself to other things.

The next day was passed in mere mechanical deeds of preparation, both the women being anxious to immerse themselves in
these to escape the emotional aspect of the situation. Some wearing apparel and other articles were collected anew for Thomasin,
and remarks on domestic details were frequently made, so as to obscure any inner misgivings about her future as Wildeve's wife.

The appointed morning came. The arrangement with Wildeve
was that he should meet her at the church to guard against any unpleasant curiosity which might have affected them had they been
seen walking off together in the usual country way.

Aunt and niece stood together in the bedroom where the bride
was dressing. The sun, where it could catch it, made a mirror of
Thomasin's hair, which she always wore braided. It was braided according to a calendric system: the more important the day the more
numerous the strands in the braid. On ordinary working-days she
braided it in threes; on ordinary Sundays in fours; at May-polings,
gipsyings,[1] and the like, she braided it in fives. Years ago she had
said that when she married she would braid it in sevens. She had
braided it in sevens to-day.

---

1. Picnics or dances held outdoors.

'I have been thinking that I will wear my blue silk after all,' she said. 'It *is* my wedding day, even though there may be something sad about the time. I mean,' she added, anxious to correct any wrong impression, 'not sad in itself, but in its having had great disappointment and trouble before it.'

Mrs. Yeobright breathed in a way which might have been called a sigh. 'I almost wish Clym had been at home,' she said. 'Of course you chose the time because of his absence.'

'Partly. I have felt that I acted unfairly to him in not telling him all; but, as it was done not to grieve him, I thought I would carry out the plan to its end, and tell the whole story when the sky was clear.'

'You are a practical little woman,' said Mrs. Yeobright, smiling. 'I wish you and he—no, I don't wish anything. There, it is nine o'clock,' she interrupted, hearing a whizz and a dinging downstairs.

'I told Damon I would leave at nine,' said Thomasin, hastening out of the room.

Her aunt followed. When Thomasin was going up the little walk from the door to the wicket-gate, Mrs. Yeobright looked reluctantly at her, and said, 'It is a shame to let you go alone.'

'It is necessary,' said Thomasin.

'At any rate,' added her aunt with forced cheerfulness, 'I shall call upon you this afternoon, and bring the cake with me. If Clym has returned by that time he will perhaps come too. I wish to show Mr. Wildeve that I bear him no ill-will. Let the past be forgotten. Well, God bless you! There, I don't believe in old superstitions, but I'll do it.' She threw a slipper at the retreating figure of the girl, who turned, smiled, and went on again.

A few steps further, and she looked back. 'Did you call me, aunt?' she tremulously inquired. 'Goodbye!'

Moved by an uncontrollable feeling as she looked upon Mrs. Yeobright's worn, wet face, she ran back, when her aunt came forward, and they met again. 'O—Tamsie,' said the elder, weeping, 'I don't like to let you go.'

'I—I am——' Thomasin began, giving way likewise. But, quelling her grief, she said 'Good-bye!' again and went on.

Then Mrs. Yeobright saw a little figure wending its way between the scratching furze-bushes, and diminishing far up the valley—a pale-blue spot in a vast field of neutral brown, solitary and undefended except by the power of her own hope.

But the worst feature in the case was one which did not appear in the landscape; it was the man.

The hour chosen for the ceremony by Thomasin and Wildeve had been so timed as to enable her to escape the awkwardness of meeting her cousin Clym, who was returning the same morning. To own to the partial truth of what he had heard would be distressing as long as the humiliating position resulting from the event was unimproved. It was only after a second and successful journey to the altar that she could lift up her head and prove the failure of the first attempt a pure accident.

She had not been gone from Blooms-End more than half an hour when Yeobright came by the meads from the other direction and entered the house.

'I had an early breakfast,' he said to his mother after greeting her. 'Now I could eat a little more.'

They sat down to the repeated meal, and he went on in a low, anxious voice, apparently imagining that Thomasin had not yet come downstairs, 'What's this I have heard about Thomasin and Mr. Wildeve?'

'It is true in many points,' said Mrs. Yeobright quietly; 'but it is all right now, I hope.' She looked at the clock.

'True?'

'Thomasin is gone to him to-day.'

Clym pushed away his breakfast. 'Then there is a scandal of some sort, and that's what's the matter with Thomasin. Was it this that made her ill?'

'Yes. Not a scandal: a misfortune. I will tell you all about it, Clym. You must not be angry, but you must listen, and you'll find that what we have done has been done for the best.'

She then told him the circumstances. All that he had known of the affair before he returned from Paris was that there had existed an attachment between Thomasin and Wildeve, which his mother had at first discountenanced, but had since, owing to the arguments of Thomasin, looked upon in a little more favourable light. When she, therefore, proceeded to explain all he was greatly surprised and troubled.

'And she determined that the wedding should be over before you came back,' said Mrs. Yeobright, 'that there might be no chance of her meeting you, and having a very painful time of it. That's why she has gone to him; they have arranged to be married this morning.'

'But I can't understand it,' said Yeobright, rising. ' 'Tis so unlike her. I can see why you did not write to me after her unfortunate return home. But why didn't you let me know when the wedding was going to be—the first time?'

'Well, I felt vexed with her just then. She seemed to me to be obstinate; and when I found that you were nothing in her mind I vowed that she should be nothing in yours. I felt that she was only my niece after all; I told her she might marry, but that I should take no interest in it, and should not bother you about it either.'

'It wouldn't have been bothering me. Mother, you did wrong.'

'I thought it might disturb you in your business, and that you might throw up your situation, or injure your prospects in some way because of it, so I said nothing. Of course, if they had married at that time in a proper manner, I should have told you at once.'

'Tamsin actually being married while we are sitting here!'

'Yes. Unless some accident happens again, as it did the first time. It may, considering he's the same man.'

'Yes, and I believe it will. Was it right to let her go? Suppose Wildeve is really a bad fellow?'

'Then he won't come, and she'll come home again.'

'You should have looked more into it.'

'It is useless to say that,' his mother answered with an impatient look of sorrow. 'You don't know how bad it has been here with us all these weeks, Clym. You don't know what a mortification anything of that sort is to a woman. You don't know the sleepless nights we've had in this house, and the almost bitter words that have passed between us since that Fifth of November. I hope never to pass seven such weeks again. Tamsin has not gone outside the door, and I have been ashamed to look anybody in the face; and now you blame me for letting her do the only thing that can be done to set that trouble straight.'

'No,' he said slowly. 'Upon the whole I don't blame you. But just consider how sudden it seems to me. Here was I, knowing nothing; and then I am told all at once that Tamsie is gone to be married. Well, I suppose there was nothing better to do. Do you know, mother,' he continued after a moment or two, looking suddenly interested in his own past history, 'I once thought of Tamsin as a sweetheart? Yes, I did. How odd boys are! And when I came home and saw her this time she seemed so much more affectionate than usual, that I was quite reminded of those days, particularly on the night of the party, when she was unwell. We had the party just the same—was not that rather cruel to her?'

'It made no difference. I had arranged to give one, and it was not worth while to make more gloom than necessary. To begin by shutting ourselves up and telling you of Tamsin's misfortunes would have been a poor sort of welcome.'

Clym remained thinking. 'I almost wish you had not had that party,' he said; 'and for other reasons. But I will tell you in a day or two. We must think of Tamsin now.'

They lapsed into silence. 'I'll tell you what,' said Yeobright again, in a tone which showed some slumbering feeling still. 'I don't think it kind to Tamsin to let her be married like this, and neither of us there to keep up her spirits or care a bit about her. She hasn't disgraced herself, or done anything to deserve that. It is bad enough that the wedding should be so hurried and unceremonious, without our keeping away from it in addition. Upon my soul, 'tis almost a shame. I'll go.'

'It is over by this time,' said his mother with a sigh; 'unless they were late, or he—'

'Then I shall be soon enough to see them come out. I don't quite like your keeping me in ignorance, mother, after all. Really, I half hope he has failed to meet her!'

'And ruined her character?'

'Nonsense: that wouldn't ruin Thomasin.'

He took up his hat and hastily left the house. Mrs. Yeobright looked rather unhappy, and sat still, deep in thought. But she was not long left alone. A few minutes later Clym came back again, and in his company came Diggory Venn.

'I find there isn't time for me to get there,' said Clym.

'Is she married?' Mrs. Yeobright inquired, turning to the reddle-man a face in which a strange strife of wishes, for and against, was apparent.

Venn bowed. 'She is, ma'am.'

'How strange it sounds,' murmured Clym.

'And he didn't disappoint her this time?' said Mrs. Yeobright.

'He did not. And there is now no slight on her name. I was hastening ath'art[2] to tell you at once, as I saw you were not there.'

'How came you to be there? How did you know it?' she asked.

'I have been in that neighbourhood for some time, and I saw them go in,' said the reddleman. 'Wildeve came up to the door, punctual as the clock. I didn't expect it of him.' He did not add, as he might have added, that how he came to be in that neighbourhood was not by accident; that, since Wildeve's resumption of his right to Thomasin, Venn, with the thoroughness which was part of his character, had determined to see the end of the episode.

'Who was there?' said Mrs. Yeobright.

'Nobody hardly. I stood right out of the way, and she did not see me.' The reddleman spoke huskily, and looked into the garden.

'Who gave her away?'

'Miss Vye.'

'How very remarkable! Miss Vye! It is to be considered an honour, I suppose?'

'Who's Miss Vye?' said Clym.

'Captain Vye's granddaughter, of Mistover Knap.'

'A proud girl from Budmouth,' said Mrs. Yeobright. 'One not much to my liking. People say she's a witch, but of course that's absurd.'

---

2. Athwart, across.

The reddleman kept to himself his acquaintance with that fair personage, and also that Eustacia was there because he went to fetch her, in accordance with a promise he had given as soon as he learnt that the marriage was to take place. He merely said, in continuation of the story—

'I was sitting on the churchyard-wall when they came up, one from one way, the other from the other; and Miss Vye was walking thereabouts, looking at the head-stones. As soon as they had gone in I went to the door, feeling I should like to see it, as I knew her so well. I pulled off my boots because they were so noisy, and went up into the gallery. I saw then that the parson and clerk were already there.'

'How came Miss Vye to have anything to do with it, if she was only on a walk that way?'

'Because there was nobody else. She had gone into the church just before me, not into the gallery. The parson looked round before beginning, and as she was the only one near he beckoned to her, and she went up to the rails. After that, when it came to signing the book, she pushed up her veil and signed; and Tamsin seemed to thank her for her kindness.' The reddleman told the tale thoughtfully, for there lingered upon his vision the changing colour of Wildeve, when Eustacia lifted the thick veil which had concealed her from recognition and looked calmly into his face. 'And then,' said Diggory sadly, 'I came away, for her history as Tamsin Yeobright was over.'

'I offered to go,' said Mrs. Yeobright regretfully. 'But she said it was not necessary.'

'Well, it is no matter,' said the reddleman. 'The thing is done at last as it was meant to be at first, and God send her happiness. Now I'll wish you good morning.'

He placed his cap on his head and went out.

From that instant of leaving Mrs. Yeobright's door, the reddleman was seen no more in or about Egdon Heath for a space of many months. He vanished entirely. The nook among the brambles where his van had been standing was as vacant as ever the next morning, and scarcely a sign remained to show that he had been there, excepting a few straws, and a little redness on the turf, which was washed away by the next storm of rain.

The report that Diggory had brought of the wedding, correct as far as it went, was deficient in one significant particular, which had escaped him through his being at some distance back in the church. When Thomasin was tremblingly engaged in signing her name Wildeve had flung towards Eustacia a glance that said plainly, 'I have punished you now.' She had replied in a low tone—and he little thought how truly—'You mistake; it gives me sincerest pleasure to see her your wife to-day.'

Book Third. The Fascination

'My Mind to Me A Kingdom Is'[1]

I

In Clym Yeobright's face could be dimly seen the typical countenance of the future. Should there be a classic period to art hereafter, its Pheidias[2] may produce such faces. The view of life as a
thing to be put up with, replacing that zest for existence which was
so intense in early civilizations, must ultimately enter so thoroughly
into the constitution of the advanced races that its facial expression
will become accepted as a new artistic departure. People already
feel that a man who lives without disturbing a curve of feature, or
setting a mark of mental concern anywhere upon himself, is too far
removed from modern perceptiveness to be a modern type. Physically beautiful men—the glory of the race when it was young—are
almost an anachronism now; and we may wonder whether, at some
time or other, physically beautiful women may not be an anachronism likewise.

The truth seems to be that a long line of disillusive centuries has
permanently displaced the Hellenic idea of life,[3] or whatever it may
be called. What the Greeks only suspected we know well; what
their Æschylus[4] imagined our nursery children feel. That old-
fashioned revelling in the general situation grows less and less possible as we uncover the defects of natural laws, and see the
quandary that man is in by their operation.

The lineaments which will get embodied in ideals based upon
this new recognition will probably be akin to those of Yeobright.
The observer's eye was arrested, not by his face as a picture, but by
his face as a page; not by what it was, but by what it recorded. His
features were attractive in the light of symbols, as sounds intrinsically common become attractive in language, and as shapes intrinsically simple become interesting in writing.

He had been a lad of whom something was expected. Beyond this
all had been chaos. That he would be successful in an original way,
or that he would go to the dogs in an original way, seemed equally

---

1. The title and first line of a poem of 1588, usually attributed to Sir Edward Dyer
(1543–1607), but sometimes to Edward de Vere, Earl of Oxford (1550–1604), which
celebrates mental rather than material wealth.
2. The leading architect and sculptor of Greece in the fifth century B.C.E., and the initiator
of the idealized, classical style.
3. Hellenism, the spirit of Greek culture, was associated by writers like Matthew Arnold,
especially in his *Culture and Society* (1869), with joyousness and spontaneity, and opposed to Hebraism, which emphasizes right conduct and strictness of conscience.
4. Aeschylus (525–456 B.C.E.), Greek tragic dramatist; Hardy owned and annotated a copy
of his play *Prometheus Bound*.

probable. The only absolute certainty about him was that he would not stand still in the circumstances amid which he was born.

Hence, when his name was casually mentioned by neighbouring yeomen, the listener said, 'Ah, Clym Yeobright: what is he doing now?' When the instinctive question about a person is, What is he doing? it is felt that he will not be found to be, like most of us, doing nothing in particular. There is an indefinite sense that he must be invading some region of singularity, good or bad. The devout hope is that he is doing well. The secret faith is that he is making a mess of it. Half a dozen comfortable market-men, who were habitual callers at the Quiet Woman as they passed by in their carts, were partial to the topic. In fact, though they were not Egdon men, they could hardly avoid it while they sucked their long clay tubes and regarded the heath through the window. Clym had been so inwoven with the heath in his boyhood that hardly anybody could look upon it without thinking of him. So the subject recurred: if he were making a fortune and a name, so much the better for him; if he were making a tragical figure in the world, so much the better for a narrative.

The fact was that Yeobright's fame had spread to an awkward extent before he left home. 'It is bad when your fame outruns your means,' said the Spanish Jesuit Gracian.[5] At the age of six he had asked a Scripture riddle: 'Who was the first man known to wear breeches?'[6] and applause had resounded from the very verge of the heath. At seven he painted the Battle of Waterloo with tiger-lily pollen and black-currant juice, in the absence of water-colours. By the time he reached twelve he had in this manner been heard of as artist and scholar for at least two miles round. An individual whose fame spreads three or four thousand yards in the time taken by the fame of others similarly situated to travel six or eight hundred, must of necessity have something in him. Possibly Clym's fame, like Homer's,[7] owed something to the accidents of his situation; nevertheless famous he was.

He grew up and was helped out in life. That waggery of fate which started Clive as a writing clerk, Gay as a linen-draper, Keats as a surgeon,[8] and a thousand others in a thousand other odd ways, banished the wild and ascetic heath lad to a trade whose sole concern was with the especial symbols of self-indulgence and vainglory.

---

5. Balthasar Gracian (1601–58), Spanish Jesuit; Hardy's notebooks contain a number of his maxims for conduct, transcribed from an article in the *Fortnightly Review* in 1877.
6. Adam, who made a covering for himself out of fig leaves (see Genesis 3.7).
7. In his *Social Dynamics*, Auguste Comte (1798–1857) argued that Homer's influence owed more to his situation, as one of the few known poets of his time, than to his genius.
8. Robert Clive (1725–74), soldier and administrator in India, John Gay (1685–1732), author of *The Beggar's Opera*, and the poet John Keats (1795–1821), all began life in relatively mundane occupations.

The details of this choice of a business for him it is not necessary to give. At the death of his father a neighbouring gentleman had kindly undertaken to give the boy a start; and this assumed the form of sending him to Budmouth. Yeobright did not wish to go there, but it was the only feasible opening. Thence he went to London; and thence, shortly after, to Paris, where he had remained till now.

Something being expected of him, he had not been at home many days before a great curiosity as to why he stayed on so long began to arise in the heath. The natural term of a holiday had passed, yet he still remained. On the Sunday morning following the week of Thomasin's marriage a discussion on this subject was in progress at a hair-cutting before Fairway's house. Here the local barbering was always done at this hour on this day; to be followed by the great Sunday wash of the inhabitants at noon, which in its turn was followed by the great Sunday dressing an hour later. On Egdon Heath Sunday proper did not begin till dinner-time, and even then it was a somewhat battered specimen of the day.

These Sunday-morning hair-cuttings were performed by Fairway; the victim sitting on a chopping-block in front of the house, without a coat, and the neighbours gossiping around, idly observing the locks of hair as they rose upon the wind after the snip, and flew away out of sight to the four quarters of the heavens. Summer and winter the scene was the same, unless the wind were more than usually blusterous, when the stool was shifted a few feet round the corner. To complain of cold in sitting out of doors, hatless and coat-less, while Fairway told true stories between the cuts of the scis-sors, would have been to pronounce yourself no man at once. To flinch, exclaim, or move a muscle of the face at the small stabs un-der the ear received from those instruments, or at scarifications of the neck by the comb, would have been thought a gross breach of good manners, considering that Fairway did it all for nothing. A bleeding about the poll on Sunday afternoons was amply accounted for by the explanation, 'I have had my hair cut, you know.'

The conversation on Yeobright had been started by a distant view of the young man rambling leisurely across the heath before them.

'A man who is doing well elsewhere wouldn't bide here two or three weeks for nothing,' said Fairway. 'He's got some project in 's head—depend upon that.'

'Well, 'a can't keep a diment shop here,' said Sam.

'I don't see why he should have had them two heavy boxes home if he had not been going to bide; and what there is for him to do here the Lord in heaven knows.'

Before many more surmises could be indulged in Yeobright had come near; and seeing the hair-cutting group he turned aside to join them. Marching up, and looking critically at their faces for a moment, he said, without introduction, 'Now, folks, let me guess what you have been talking about.'

'Ay, sure, if you will,' said Sam.

'About me.'

'Now, it is a thing I shouldn't have dreamed of doing, otherwise,' said Fairway in a tone of integrity; 'but since you have named it, Master Yeobright, I'll own that we was talking about 'ee. We were wondering what could keep you home here mollyhorning[9] about when you have made such a world-wide name for yourself in the nick-nack trade—now, that's the truth o't.'

'I'll tell you,' said Yeobright, with unexpected earnestness. 'I am not sorry to have the opportunity. I've come home because, all things considered, I can be a trifle less useless here than anywhere else. But I have only lately found this out. When I first got away from home I thought this place was not worth troubling about. I thought our life here was contemptible. To oil your boots instead of blacking them, to dust your coat with a switch instead of a brush: was there ever anything more ridiculous? I said.'

'So 'tis; so 'tis!'

'No, no—you are wrong; it isn't.'

'Beg your pardon, we thought that was your maning?'[1]

'Well, as my views changed my course became very depressing. I found that I was trying to be like people who had hardly anything in common with myself. I was endeavouring to put off one sort of life for another sort of life, which was not better than the life I had known before. It was simply different.'

'True; a sight different,' said Fairway.

'Yes, Paris must be a taking place,' said Humphrey. 'Grand shop-winders, trumpets, and drums; and here be we out of doors in all winds and weathers——'

'But you mistake me,' pleaded Clym. 'All this was very depressing. But not so depressing as something I next perceived—that my business was the idlest, vainest, most effeminate business that ever a man could be put to. That decided me: I would give it up and try to follow some rational occupation among the people I knew best, and to whom I could be of most use. I have come home; and this is how I mean to carry out my plan. I shall keep a school as near to Egdon as possible, so as to be able to walk over here and have a night-school in my mother's house. But I must study a little at first, to get properly qualified. Now, neighbours, I must go.'

And Clym resumed his walk across the heath.

---

9. Idling (a dialect word; it is not recorded elsewhere).
1. Meaning (dialect).

'He'll never carry it out in the world,' said Fairway. 'In a few weeks he'll learn to see things otherwise.'

' 'Tis good-hearted of the young man,' said another. 'But, for my part, I think he had better mind his business.'

The New Course Causes Disappointment

II

Yeobright loved his kind. He had a conviction that the want of most men was knowledge of a sort which brings wisdom rather than affluence. He wished to raise the class at the expense of individuals rather than individuals at the expense of the class. What was more, he was ready at once to be the first unit sacrificed.

In passing from the bucolic to the intellectual life the intermediate stages are usually two at least, frequently many more; and one of these stages is almost sure to be worldly advance. We can hardly imagine bucolic placidity quickening to intellectual aims without imagining social aims as the transitional phase. Yeobright's local peculiarity was that in striving at high thinking he still cleaved to plain living[1]—nay, wild and meagre living in many respects, and brotherliness with clowns.

He was a John the Baptist[2] who took ennoblement rather than repentance for his text. Mentally he was in a provincial future, that is, he was in many points abreast with the central town thinkers of his date. Much of this development he may have owed to his studious life in Paris, where he had become acquainted with ethical systems popular at the time.[3]

In consequence of this relatively advanced position, Yeobright might have been called unfortunate. The rural world was not ripe for him. A man should be only partially before his time: to be completely to the vanward in aspirations is fatal to fame. Had Philip's warlike son[4] been intellectually so far ahead as to have attempted civilization without bloodshed, he would have been twice the godlike hero that he seemed, but nobody would have heard of an Alexander.

In the interests of renown the forwardness should lie chiefly in the capacity to handle things. Successful propagandists have succeeded because the doctrine they bring into form is that which

1. An allusion to Wordsworth's sonnet "Written in London, September, 1802": "Plain living and high thinking are no more."
2. John is described in Matthew 3.3 as "a voice crying in the wilderness."
3. Probably Positivism, developed by Auguste Comte, in which traditional religion was rejected in favor of a "religion of humanity" and the improvement of the social condition of the human race.
4. Alexander the Great (356–323 B.C.E.), son of Philip of Macedon, conquered much of the known world.

their listeners have for some time felt without being able to shape.
A man who advocates æsthetic effort and deprecates social effort is
only likely to be understood by a class to which social effort has become a stale matter. To argue upon the possibility of culture before
luxury to the bucolic world may be to argue truly, but it is an attempt to disturb a sequence to which humanity has been long accustomed. Yeobright preaching to the Egdon eremites[5] that they
might rise to a serene comprehensiveness without going through
the process of enriching themselves, was not unlike arguing to
ancient Chaldeans[6] that in ascending from earth to the pure
empyrean it was not necessary to pass first into the intervening
heaven of ether.

Was Yeobright's mind well-proportioned? No. A well-
proportioned mind is one which shows no particular bias; one of
which we may safely say that it will never cause its owner to be
confined as a madman, tortured as a heretic, or crucified as a blas-
phemer. Also, on the other hand, that it will never cause him to be
applauded as a prophet, revered as a priest, or exalted as a king. Its
usual blessings are happiness and mediocrity. It produces the poetry of Rogers, the paintings of West, the statecraft of North, the
spiritual guidance of Tomline;[7] enabling its possessors to find their
way to wealth, to wind up well, to step with dignity off the stage, to
die comfortably in their beds, and to get the decent monument
which, in many cases, they deserve. It never would have allowed
Yeobright to do such a ridiculous thing as throw up his business to
benefit his fellow-creatures.

He walked along towards home without attending to paths. If any
one knew the heath well it was Clym. He was permeated with its
scenes, with its substance, and with its odours. He might be said to
be its product. His eyes had first opened thereon; with its appearance
all the first images of his memory were mingled; his estimate of life
had been coloured by it; his toys had been the flint knives and arrow-
heads which he found there, wondering why stones should 'grow' to
such odd shapes; his flowers, the purple bells and yellow furze; his
animal kingdom, the snakes and croppers; his society, its human
haunters. Take all the varying hates felt by Eustacia Vye towards the
heath, and translate them into loves, and you have the heart of Clym.
He gazed upon the wide prospect as he walked, and was glad.

5. Hermits.
6. Babylonians who practiced astronomy and astrology, as at Daniel 2.2. The empyrean, the
   highest of the heavens, was a region of pure fire, lying beyond the ether, the region immediately above the clouds (or, in some systems of thought, above the moon).
7. Sir George Tomline (1750–1827), Bishop of Winchester; Lord Frederick North
   (1732–92), Prime Minister from 1770 to 1782; Benjamin West (1738–1820), American
   painter and president of the Royal Academy; Samuel Rogers (1763–1855), poet, who
   was offered but declined the position of Poet Laureate in 1850. All were well regarded in
   their lifetimes, but are remembered as relative mediocrities.

To many persons this Egdon was a place which had slipped out of its century generations ago, to intrude as an uncouth object into this. It was an obsolete thing, and few cared to study it. How could this be otherwise in the days of square fields, plashed hedges,[8] and meadows watered on a plan so rectangular that on a fine day they look like silver gridirons? The farmer, in his ride, who could smile at artificial grasses,[9] look with solicitude at the coming corn, and sigh with sadness at the fly-eaten turnips, bestowed upon the distant upland of heath nothing better than a frown. But as for Yeobright, when he looked from the heights on his way he could not help indulging in a barbarous satisfaction at observing that, in some of the attempts at reclamation from the waste, tillage, after holding on for a year or two, had receded again in despair, the ferns and furze-tufts stubbornly reasserting themselves.

He descended into the valley, and soon reached his home at Blooms-End. His mother was snipping dead leaves from the window-plants. She looked up at him as if she did not understand the meaning of his long stay with her; her face had worn that look for several days. He could perceive that the curiosity which had been shown by the hair-cutting group amounted in his mother to concern. But she had asked no question with her lips, even when the arrival of his trunks suggested that he was not going to leave her soon. Her silence besought an explanation of him more loudly than words.

'I am not going back to Paris again, mother,' he said. 'At least, in my old capacity. I have given up the business.'

Mrs. Yeobright turned in pained surprise. 'I thought something was amiss, because of the boxes. I wonder you did not tell me sooner.'

'I ought to have done it. But I have been in doubt whether you would be pleased with my plan. I was not quite clear on a few points myself. I am going to take an entirely new course.'

'I am astonished, Clym. How can you want to do better than you've been doing?'

'Very easily. But I shall not do better in the way you mean; I suppose it will be called doing worse. But I hate that business of mine, and I want to do some worthy thing before I die. As a schoolmaster I think to do it—a schoolmaster to the poor and ignorant, to teach them what nobody else will.'

'After all the trouble that has been taken to give you a start, and when there is nothing to do but to keep straight on towards affluence, you say you will be a poor man's schoolmaster. Your fancies will be your ruin, Clym.'

8. Hedges interwoven to increase their effectiveness as barriers or windbreaks.
9. Hybrids produced by cross-breeding.

Mrs. Yeobright spoke calmly, but the force of feeling behind the words was but too apparent to one who knew her as well as her son did. He did not answer. There was in his face that hopelessness of being understood which comes when the objector is constitutionally beyond the reach of a logic that, even under favouring conditions, is almost too coarse a vehicle for the subtlety of the argument.

No more was said on the subject till the end of dinner. His mother then began, as if there had been no interval since the morning. 'It disturbs me, Clym, to find that you have come home with such thoughts as those. I hadn't the least idea that you meant to go backward in the world by your own free choice. Of course, I have always supposed you were going to push straight on, as other men do—all who deserve the name—when they have been put in a good way of doing well.'

'I cannot help it,' said Clym, in a troubled tone. 'Mother, I hate the flashy business. Talk about men who deserve the name, can any man deserving the name waste his time in that effeminate way, when he sees half the world going to ruin for want of somebody to buckle to and teach them how to breast the misery they are born to? I get up every morning and see the whole creation groaning and travailing in pain, as St. Paul says,[1] and yet there am I, trafficking in glittering splendours with wealthy women and titled libertines, and pandering to the meanest vanities—I, who have health and strength enough for anything. I have been troubled in my mind about it all the year, and the end is that I cannot do it any more.'

'Why can't you do it as well as others?'

'I don't know, except that there are many things other people care for which I don't; and that's partly why I think I ought to do this. For one thing, my body does not require much of me. I cannot enjoy delicacies; good things are wasted upon me. Well, I ought to turn that defect to advantage, and by being able to do without what other people require I can spend what such things cost upon anybody else.'

Now, Yeobright, having inherited some of these very instincts from the woman before him, could not fail to awaken a reciprocity in her through her feelings, if not by arguments, disguise it as she might for his good. She spoke with less assurance. 'And yet you might have been a wealthy man if you had only persevered. Manager to that large diamond establishment—what better can a man wish for? What a post of trust and respect! I suppose you will be like your father; like him, you are getting weary of doing well.'

1. See Romans 8.22: "the whole creation groaneth and travaileth in pain together until now."

'No,' said her son; 'I am not weary of that, though I am weary of what you mean by it. Mother, what is doing well?'[2]

Mrs. Yeobright was far too thoughtful a woman to be content with ready definitions, and, like the 'What is wisdom?' of Plato's Socrates, and the 'What is truth?' of Pontius Pilate,[3] Yeobright's burning question received no answer.

The silence was broken by the clash of the garden gate, a tap at the door, and its opening. Christian Cantle appeared in the room in his Sunday clothes.

It was the custom on Egdon to begin the preface to a story before absolutely entering the house, so as to be well in for the body of the narrative by the time visitor and visited stood face to face. Christian had been saying to them while the door was leaving its latch, 'To think that I, who go from home but once in a while, and hardly then, should have been there this morning!'

' 'Tis news you have brought us, then, Christian?' said Mrs. Yeobright.

'Ay, sure, about a witch, and ye must overlook my time o' day; for, says I, "I must go and tell 'em, though they won't have half done dinner." I assure ye it made me shake like a driven leaf. Do ye think any harm will come o't?'

'Well—what?'

'This morning at church we was all standing up, and the pa'son said, "Let us pray." "Well," thinks I, "one may as well kneel as stand;" so down I went; and, more than that, all the rest were as willing to oblige the man as I. We hadn't been hard at it for more than a minute when a most terrible screech sounded through church, as if somebody had just gied up their heart's blood. All the folk jumped up, and then we found that Susan Nunsuch had pricked Miss Vye with a long stocking-needle, as she had threatened to do as soon as ever she could get the young lady to church, where she don't come very often. She've waited for this chance for weeks, so as to draw her blood and put an end to the bewitching of Susan's children that has been carried on so long. Sue followed her into church, sat next to her, and as soon as she could find a chance in went the stocking-needle into my lady's arm.'

'Good heaven, how horrid!' said Mrs. Yeobright.

'Sue pricked her that deep that the maid fainted away; and as I was afeard there might be some tumult among us, I got behind the bass-viol and didn't see no more. But they carried her out into the

2. An echo of Galatians 6.9: "And let us not be weary in well doing: for in due season we shall reap, if we faint not."
3. Socrates asks his question in *Charmides*, an early dialogue by Plato (c. 428–c. 328 B.C.E.); the figure of Charmides, "a beautiful youth," may have influenced Hardy's account of Clym's thought-worn appearance. For Pontius Pilate's question, asked at Christ's trial, see John 18.38.

air, 'tis said; but when they looked round for Sue she was gone. What a scream that girl gied, poor thing! There were the pa'son in his surplice holding up his hand and saying, "Sit down, my good people, sit down!" But the deuce a bit[4] would they sit down. O, and what d'ye think I found out, Mrs. Yeobright? The pa'son wears a suit of clothes under his surplice!—I could see his black sleeve when he held up his arm.'

' 'Tis a cruel thing,' said Yeobright.

'Yes,' said his mother.

'The nation ought to look into it,' said Christian. 'Here's Humphrey coming, I think.'

In came Humphrey. 'Well, have ye heard the news? But I see you have. 'Tis a very strange thing that whenever one of Egdon folk goes to church some rum job or other is sure to be doing. The last time one of us was there was when neighbour Fairway went in the fall; and that was the day you forbad the banns, Mrs. Yeobright.'

'Has this cruelly treated girl been able to walk home?' said Clym.'

'They say she got better, and went home very well. And now I've told it I must be moving homeward myself.'

'And I,' said Humphrey. 'Truly now we shall see if there's anything in what folks say about her.'

When they were gone into the heath again Yeobright said quietly to his mother, 'Do you think I have turned teacher too soon?'

'It is right that there should be schoolmasters, and missionaries, and all such men,' she replied. 'But it is right, too, that I should try to lift you out of this life into something richer, and that you should not come back again, and be as if I had not tried at all.'

Later in the day Sam, the turf-cutter, entered. 'I've come a-borrowing, Mrs. Yeobright. I suppose you have heard what's been happening to the beauty on the hill?'

'Yes, Sam: half a dozen have been telling us.'

'Beauty?' said Clym.

'Yes, tolerably well-favoured,' Sam replied. 'Lord! all the country owns that 'tis one of the strangest things in the world that such a woman should have come to live up there.'

'Dark or fair?'

'Now, though I've seen her twenty times, that's a thing I cannot call to mind.'

'Darker than Tamsin,' murmured Mrs. Yeobright.

'A woman who seems to care for nothing at all, as you may say.'

'She is melancholy, then?' inquired Clym.

'She mopes about by herself, and don't mix in with the people.'

---

4. "Deuce" sometimes substitutes for "the devil" in exclamations: "the devil a bit."

'Is she a young lady inclined for adventures?'

'Not to my knowledge.'

'Doesn't join in with the lads in their games, to get some sort of excitement in this lonely place?'

'No.'

'Mumming, for instance?'

'No. Her notions be different. I should rather say her thoughts were far away from here, with lords and ladies she'll never know, and mansions she'll never see again.'

Observing that Clym appeared singularly interested Mrs. Yeo-bright said rather uneasily to Sam, 'You see more in her than most of us do. Miss Vye is to my mind too idle to be charming. I have never heard that she is of any use to herself or to other people. Good girls don't get treated as witches even on Egdon.'

'Nonsense—that proves nothing either way,' said Yeobright.

'Well, of course I don't understand such niceties,' said Sam, with-drawing from a possibly unpleasant argument; 'and what she is we must wait for time to tell us. The business that I have really called about is this, to borrow the longest and strongest rope you have. The captain's bucket has dropped into the well, and they are in want of water; and as all the chaps are at home to-day we think we can get it out for him. We have three cart-ropes already, but they won't reach to the bottom.'

Mrs. Yeobright told him that he might have whatever ropes he could find in the outhouse, and Sam went out to search. When he passed by the door Clym joined him, and accompanied him to the gate.

'Is this young witch-lady going to stay long at Mistover?' he asked.

'I should say so.'

'What a cruel shame to ill-use her! She must have suffered greatly—more in mind than in body.'

' 'Twas a graceless trick—such a handsome girl, too. You ought to see her, Mr. Yeobright, being a young man come from far, and with a little more to show for your years than most of us.'

'Do you think she would like to teach children?' said Clym.

Sam shook his head. 'Quite a different sort of body from that, I reckon.'

'O, it was merely something which occurred to me. It would of course be necessary to see her and talk it over—not an easy thing, by the way, for my family and hers are not very friendly.'

'I'll tell you how you mid[5] see her, Mr. Yeobright,' said Sam. 'We are going to grapple for the bucket at six o'clock to-night at her

5. Might (dialect).

house, and you could lend a hand. There's five or six coming, but the well is deep, and another might be useful, if you don't mind appearing in that shape. She's sure to be walking round.'

'I'll think of it,' said Yeobright; and they parted.

He thought of it a good deal; but nothing more was said about Eustacia inside the house at that time. Whether this romantic martyr to superstition and the melancholy mummer he had conversed with under the full moon were one and the same person remained as yet a problem.

The First Act in a Timeworn Drama

III

The afternoon was fine, and Yeobright walked on the heath for an hour with his mother. When they reached the lofty ridge which divided the valley of Blooms-End from the adjoining valley they stood still and looked round. The Quiet Woman Inn was visible on the low margin of the heath in one direction, and afar on the other hand rose Mistover Knap.

'You mean to call on Thomasin?' he inquired.

'Yes. But you need not come this time,' said his mother.

'In that case I'll branch off here, mother. I am going to Mistover.'

Mrs. Yeobright turned to him inquiringly.

'I am going to help them get the bucket out of the captain's well,' he continued. 'As it is so very deep I may be useful. And I should like to see this Miss Vye—not so much for her good looks as for another reason.'

'Must you go?' his mother asked.

'I thought to.'

And they parted. 'There is no help for it,' murmured Clym's mother gloomily as he withdrew. 'They are sure to see each other. I wish Sam would carry his news to other houses than mine.'

Clym's retreating figure got smaller and smaller as it rose and fell over the hillocks on his way. 'He is tender-hearted,' said Mrs. Yeobright to herself while she watched him; 'otherwise it would matter little. How he's going on!'

He was, indeed, walking with a will over the furze, as straight as a line, as if his life depended upon it. His mother drew a long breath, and, abandoning the visit to Thomasin, turned back. The evening films began to make nebulous pictures of the valleys, but the high lands still were raked by the declining rays of the winter sun, which glanced on Clym as he walked forward, eyed by every rabbit and fieldfare[1] around, a long shadow advancing in front of him.

1. Large gregarious thrush; mainly a winter visitor to Britain.

On drawing near to the furze-covered bank and ditch which fortified the captain's dwelling he could hear voices within, signifying that operations had been already begun. At the side-entrance gate he stopped and looked over.

Half a dozen able-bodied men were standing in a line from the well-mouth, holding a rope which passed over the well-roller into the depths below. Fairway, with a piece of smaller rope round his body, made fast to one of the standards, to guard against accidents, was leaning over the opening, his right hand clasping the vertical rope that descended into the well.

'Now, silence, folks,' said Fairway.

The talking ceased, and Fairway gave a circular motion to the rope, as if he were stirring batter. At the end of a minute a dull splashing reverberated from the bottom of the well; the helical twist he had imparted to the rope had reached the grapnel below.

'Haul!' said Fairway; and the men who held the rope began to gather it over the wheel.

'I think we've got sommat,' said one of the haulers-in.

'Then pull steady,' said Fairway.

They gathered up more and more, till a regular dripping into the well could be heard below. It grew smarter with the increasing height of the bucket, and presently a hundred and fifty feet of rope had been pulled in.

Fairway then lit a lantern, tied it to another cord, and began lowering it into the well beside the first. Clym came forward and looked down. Strange humid leaves, which knew nothing of the seasons of the year, and quaint-natured mosses were revealed on the well-side as the lantern descended; till its rays fell upon a confused mass of rope and bucket dangling in the dank, dark air.

'We've only got en by the edge of the hoop—steady, for God's sake!' said Fairway.

They pulled with the greatest gentleness, till the wet bucket appeared about two yards below them, like a dead friend come to earth again. Three or four hands were stretched out, then jerk went the rope, whizz went the wheel, the two foremost haulers fell backward, the beating of a falling body was heard, receding down the sides of the well, and a thunderous uproar arose at the bottom. The bucket was gone again.

'Damn the bucket!' said Fairway.

'Lower again,' said Sam.

'I'm as stiff as a ram's horn stooping so long,' said Fairway, standing up and stretching himself till his joints creaked.

'Rest a few minutes, Timothy,' said Yeobright. 'I'll take your place.'

The grapnel was again lowered. Its smart impact upon the distant water reached their ears like a kiss, whereupon Yeobright knelt down, and leaning over the well began dragging the grapnel round and round as Fairway had done.

'Tie a rope round him—it is dangerous!' cried a soft and anxious voice somewhere above them.

Everybody turned. The speaker was a woman, gazing down upon tne group from an upper window, whose panes blazed in the ruddy glare from the west. Her lips were parted and she appeared for the moment to forget where she was.

The rope was accordingly tied round his waist, and the work proceeded. At the next haul the weight was not heavy, and it was discovered that they had only secured a coil of the rope detached from the bucket. The tangled mass was thrown into the background. Humphrey took Yeobright's place, and the grapnel was lowered again.

Yeobright retired to the heap of recovered rope in a meditative mood. Of the identity between the lady's voice and that of the melancholy mummer he had not a moment's doubt. 'How thoughtful of her!' he said to himself.

Eustacia, who had reddened when she perceived the effect of her exclamation upon the group below, was no longer to be seen at the window, though Yeobright scanned it wistfully. While he stood there the men at the well succeeded in getting up the bucket without a mishap. One of them then went to inquire for the captain, to learn what orders he wished to give for mending the well-tackle. The captain proved to be away from home; and Eustacia appeared at the door and came out. She had lapsed into an easy and dignified calm, far removed from the intensity of life in her words of solicitude for Clym's safety.

'Will it be possible to draw water here to-night?' she inquired.

'No, miss; the bottom of the bucket is clean knocked out. And as we can do no more now we'll leave off, and come again to-morrow morning.'

'No water,' she murmured, turning away.

'I can send you up some from Blooms-End,' said Clym, coming forward and raising his hat as the men retired.

Yeobright and Eustacia looked at each other for one instant, as if each had in mind those few moments during which a certain moonlight scene was common to both. With the glance the calm fixity of her features sublimed itself to an expression of refinement and warmth: it was like garish noon rising to the dignity of sunset in a couple of seconds.

'Thank you; it will hardly be necessary,' she replied.

'But if you have no water?'

'Well, it is what I call no water,' she said, blushing, and lifting her

'Tie a rope around him; it is dangerous.'

long-lashed eyelids as if to lift them were a work requiring consideration. 'But my grandfather calls it water enough. I'll show you what I mean.'

She moved away a few yards, and Clym followed. When she reached the corner of the enclosure, where the steps were formed for mounting the boundary bank, she sprang up with a lightness which seemed strange after her listless movement towards the well. It incidentally showed that her apparent languor did not arise from lack of force.

Clym ascended behind her, and noticed a circular burnt patch at the top of the bank. 'Ashes?' he said.

'Yes,' said Eustacia. 'We had a little bonfire here last Fifth of November, and those are the marks of it.'

On that spot had stood the fire she had kindled to attract Wildeve.

'That's the only kind of water we have,' she continued, tossing a stone into the pool, which lay on the outside of the bank like the white of an eye without its pupil. The stone fell with a flounce, but no Wildeve appeared on the other side, as on a previous occasion there. 'My grandfather says he lived for more than twenty years at sea on water twice as bad as that,' she went on, 'and considers it quite good enough for us here on an emergency.'

'Well, as a matter of fact there are no impurities in the water of these pools at this time of the year. It has only just rained into them.'

She shook her head. 'I am managing to exist in a wilderness, but I cannot drink from a pond,' she said.

Clym looked towards the well, which was now deserted, the men having gone home. 'It is a long way to send for spring-water,' he said, after a silence. 'But since you don't like this in the pond, I'll try to get you some myself.' He went back to the well. 'Yes, I think I could do it by tying on this pail.'

'But, since I would not trouble the men to get it, I cannot in conscience let you.'

'I don't mind the trouble at all.'

He made fast the pail to the long coil of rope, put it over the wheel, and allowed it to descend by letting the rope slip through his hands. Before it had gone far, however, he checked it.

'I must make fast the end first, or we may lose the whole,' he said to Eustacia, who had drawn near. 'Could you hold this a moment, while I do it—or shall I call your servant?'

'I can hold it,' said Eustacia; and he placed the rope in her hands, going then to search for the end.

'I suppose I may let it slip down?' she inquired.

'I would advise you not to let it go far,' said Clym. 'It will get much heavier, you will find.'

However, Eustacia had begun to pay out. While he was trying she cried, 'I cannot stop it!'

Clym ran to her side, and found he could only check the rope by twisting the loose part round the upright post, when it stopped with a jerk. 'Has it hurt you?'

'Yes,' she replied.

'Very much?'

'No; I think not.' She opened her hands. One of them was bleeding; the rope had dragged off the skin. Eustacia wrapped it in her handkerchief.

'You should have let go,' said Yeobright. 'Why didn't you?'

'You said I was to hold on. . . . This is the second time I have been wounded to-day.'

'Ah, yes; I have heard of it. I blush for my native Egdon. Was it a serious injury you received in church, Miss Vye?'

There was such an abundance of sympathy in Clym's tone that Eustacia slowly drew up her sleeve and disclosed her round white arm. A bright red spot appeared on its smooth surface, like a ruby on Parian marble.[2]

'There it is,' she said, putting her finger against the spot.

'It was dastardly of the woman,' said Clym. 'Will not Captain Vye get her punished?'

'He is gone from home on that very business. I did not know that I had such a magic reputation.'

'And you fainted?' said Clym, looking at the scarlet little puncture as if he would like to kiss it and make it well.

'Yes, it frightened me. I had not been to church for a long time. And now I shall not go again for ever so long—perhaps never. I cannot face their eyes after this. Don't you think it dreadfully humiliating? I wished I was dead for hours after, but I don't mind now.'

'I have come to clean away these cobwebs,' said Yeobright. 'Would you like to help me—by high class teaching? We might benefit them much.'

'I don't quite feel anxious to. I have not much love for my fellow-creatures. Sometimes I quite hate them.'

'Still I think that if you were to hear my scheme you might take an interest in it. There is no use in hating people—if you hate anything, you should hate what produced them.'

'Do you mean Nature? I hate her already. But I shall be glad to hear your scheme at any time.'

The situation had now worked itself out, and the next natural thing was for them to part. Clym knew this well enough, and Eustacia made a move of conclusion; yet he looked at her as if he had one word more to say. Perhaps if he had not lived in Paris it would never have been uttered.

'We have met before,' he said, regarding her with rather more interest than was necessary.

'I do not own it,' said Eustacia, with a repressed, still look.

'But I may think what I like.'

'Yes.'

'You are lonely here.'

2. Fine white marble, from the Aegean island of Paros.

'I cannot endure the heath, except in its purple season. The heath is a cruel taskmaster to me.'

'Can you say so?' he asked. 'To my mind it is most exhilarating, and strengthening, and soothing. I would rather live on these hills than anywhere else in the world.'

'It is well enough for artists; but I never would learn to draw.'

'And there is a very curious Druidical stone[3] just out there.' He threw a pebble in the direction signified. 'Do you often go to see it?'

'I was not even aware that there existed any such curious Druidical stone. I am aware that there are Boulevards in Paris.'

Yeobright looked thoughtfully on the ground. 'That means much,' he said.

'It does indeed,' said Eustacia.

'I remember when I had the same longing for town bustle. Five years of a great city would be a perfect cure for that.'

'Heaven send me such a cure! Now, Mr. Yeobright, I will go in-doors and plaster my wounded hand.'

They separated, and Eustacia vanished in the increasing shade. She seemed full of many things. Her past was a blank, her life had begun. The effect upon Clym of this meeting he did not fully dis-cover till some time after. During his walk home his most intelligi-ble sensation was that his scheme had somehow become glorified. A beautiful woman had been intertwined with it.

On reaching the house he went up to the room which was to be made his study, and occupied himself during the evening in un-packing his books from the boxes and arranging them on shelves. From another box he drew a lamp and a can of oil. He trimmed the lamp, arranged his table, and said, 'Now, I am ready to begin.'

He rose early the next morning, read two hours before breakfast by the light of his lamp—read all the morning, all the afternoon. Just when the sun was going down his eyes felt weary, and he leant back in his chair.

His room overlooked the front of the premises and the valley of the heath beyond. The lowest beams of the winter sun threw the shadow of the house over the palings, across the grass margin of the heath, and far up the vale, where the chimney outlines and those of the surrounding tree-tops stretched forth in long dark prongs. Having been seated at work all day, he decided to take a turn upon the hills before it got dark; and, going out forthwith, he struck across the heath towards Mistover.

It was an hour and a half later when he again appeared at the garden gate. The shutters of the house were closed, and Christian

3. Prehistoric stones, supposed to have been used by Druid priests in their rites.

Cantle, who had been wheeling manure about the garden all day, had gone home. On entering he found that his mother, after waiting a long time for him, had finished her meal.

'Where have you been, Clym?' she immediately said. 'Why didn't you tell me that you were going away at this time?'

'I have been on the heath.'

'You'll meet Eustacia Vye if you go up there.'

Clym paused a minute. 'Yes, I met her this evening,' he said, as though it were spoken under the sheer necessity of preserving honesty.

'I wondered if you had.'

'It was no appointment.'

'No; such meetings never are.'

'But you are not angry, mother?'

'I can hardly say that I am not. Angry? No. But when I consider the usual nature of the drag which causes men of promise to disappoint the world I feel uneasy.'

'You deserve credit for the feeling, mother. But I can assure you that you need not be disturbed by it on my account.'

'When I think of you and your new crotchets,' said Mrs. Yeobright, with some emphasis, 'I naturally don't feel so comfortable as I did a twelvemonth ago. It is incredible to me that a man accustomed to the attractive women of Paris and elsewhere should be so easily worked upon by a girl in a heath. You could just as well have walked another way.'

'I had been studying all day.'

'Well, yes,' she added more hopefully, 'I have been thinking that you might get on as a schoolmaster, and rise that way, since you really are determined to hate the course you were pursuing.'

Yeobright was unwilling to disturb this idea, though his scheme was far enough removed from one wherein the education of youth should be made a mere channel of social ascent. He had no desires of that sort. He had reached the stage in a young man's life when the grimness of the general human situation first becomes clear; and the realization of this causes ambition to halt awhile. In France it is not uncustomary to commit suicide at this stage; in England we do much better, or much worse, as the case may be.

The love between the young man and his mother was strangely invisible now. Of love it may be said, the less earthly the less demonstrative. In its absolutely indestructible form it reaches a profundity in which all exhibition of itself is painful. It was so with these. Had conversations between them been overheard, people would have said, 'How cold they are to each other!'

His theory and his wishes about devoting his future to teaching had made an impression on Mrs. Yeobright. Indeed, how could it be otherwise when he was a part of her—when their discourses were as if carried on between the right and the left hands of the same body? He had despaired of reaching her by argument; and it was almost as a discovery to him that he could reach her by a magnetism which was as superior to words as words are to yells.

Strangely enough he began to feel now that it would not be so hard to persuade her who was his best friend that comparative poverty was essentially the higher course for him, as to reconcile to his feelings the act of persuading her. From every provident point of view his mother was so undoubtedly right, that he was not without a sickness of heart in finding he could shake her.

She had a singular insight into life, considering that she had never mixed with it. There are instances of persons who, without clear ideas of the things they criticize, have yet had clear ideas of the relations of those things. Blacklock,[4] a poet blind from his birth, could describe visual objects with accuracy; Professor Sanderson,[5] who was also blind, gave excellent lectures on colour, and taught others the theory of ideas which they had and he had not. In the social sphere these gifted ones are mostly women; they can watch a world which they never saw, and estimate forces of which they have only heard. We call it intuition.

What was the great world to Mrs. Yeobright? A multitude whose tendencies could be perceived, though not its essences. Communities were seen by her as from a distance; she saw them as we see the throngs which cover the canvases of Sallaert, Van Alsloot,[6] and others of that school—vast masses of beings, jostling, zigzagging, and processioning in definite directions, but whose features are indistinguishable by the very comprehensiveness of the view.

One could see that, as far as it had gone, her life was very complete on its reflective side. The philosophy of her nature, and its limitation by circumstances, was almost written in her movements. They had a majestic foundation, though they were far from being majestic; and they had a groundwork of assurance, but they were not assured. As her once elastic walk had become deadened by time, so had her natural pride of life been hindered in its blooming by her necessities.

The next slight touch in the shaping of Clym's destiny occurred a few days after. A barrow was opened on the heath, and Yeobright attended the operation, remaining away from his study during several hours. In the afternoon Christian returned from a journey in the same direction, and Mrs. Yeobright questioned him.

4. Thomas Blacklock (1721–91), Scottish poet, in fact lost his sight at six months after an attack of smallpox; he wrote an article on blindness for the *Encyclopaedia Britannica*.
5. Nicholas Sanderson, or Saunderson (1682–1739), Professor of Mathematics at Cambridge, lost his eyes, as well as his sight, from smallpox at the age of twelve.
6. Antoon Sallaert (1590–1657) and Denis Van Alsloot (c. 1570–1626), Flemish painters whose subjects included large gatherings of people at feasts, fairs, and the like.

'They have dug a hole, and they have found things like flower-
pots upside down, Mis'ess Yeobright; and inside these be real char-
nel bones. They have carried 'em off to men's houses; but I
shouldn't like to sleep where they will bide. Dead folks have been
known to come and claim their own. Mr. Yeobright had got one pot
of the bones, and was going to bring 'em home—real skellington
bones—but 'twas ordered otherwise. You'll be relieved to hear that
he gave away his, pot and all, on second thoughts; and a blessed
thing for ye, Mis'ess Yeobright, considering the wind o' nights.'

'Gave it away?'

'Yes. To Miss Vye. She has a cannibal taste for such churchyard
furniture seemingly.'

'Miss Vye was there too?'

'Ay, 'a b'lieve she was.'

When Clym came home, which was shortly after, his mother
said, in a curious tone, 'The urn you had meant for me you gave
away.'

Yeobright made no reply; the current of her feeling was too pronounced to admit it.

The early weeks of the year passed on. Yeobright certainly studied
at home, but he also walked much abroad, and the direction of his
walk was always towards some point of a line between Mistover and
Rainbarrow.

The month of March arrived, and the heath showed its first faint
signs of awakening from winter trance. The awakening was almost
feline in its stealthiness. The pool outside the bank by Eustacia's
dwelling, which seemed as dead and desolate as ever to an observer
who moved and made noises in his observation, would gradually
disclose a state of great animation when silently watched awhile. A
timid animal world had come to life for the season. Little tadpoles
and efts[7] began to bubble up through the water, and to race along
beneath it; toads made noises like very young ducks, and advanced
to the margin in twos and threes; overhead, bumble-bees flew
hither and thither in the thickening light, their drone coming and
going like the sound of a gong.

On an evening such as this Yeobright descended into the Blooms-
End valley from beside that very pool, where he had been standing
with another person quite silently and quite long enough to hear all
this puny stir of resurrection in nature; yet he had not heard it. His
walk was rapid as he came down, and he went with a springy tread.
Before entering upon his mother's premises he stopped and
breathed. The light which shone forth on him from the window revealed that his face was flushed and his eye bright. What it did not

7. Newts.

show was something which lingered upon his lips like a seal set there. The abiding presence of this impress was so real that he hardly dared to enter the house, for it seemed as if his mother might say, 'What red spot is that glowing upon your mouth so vividly?'

But he entered soon after. The tea was ready, and he sat down opposite his mother. She did not speak many words; and as for him, something had been just done and some words had been just said on the hill which prevented him from beginning a desultory chat. His mother's taciturnity was not without ominousness, but he appeared not to care. He knew why she said so little, but he could not remove the cause of her bearing towards him. These half-silent sittings were far from uncommon with them now. At last Yeobright made a beginning of what was intended to strike at the whole root of the matter.

'Five days have we sat like this at meals with scarcely a word. What's the use of it, mother?'

'None,' said she, in a heart-swollen tone. 'But there is only too good a reason.'

'Not when you know all. I have been wanting to speak about this, and I am glad the subject is begun. The reason, of course, is Eustacia Vye. Well, I confess I have seen her lately, and have seen her a good many times.'

'Yes, yes; and I know what that amounts to. It troubles me, Clym. You are wasting your life here; and it is solely on account of her. If it had not been for that woman you would never have entertained this teaching scheme at all.'

Clym looked hard at his mother. 'You know that is not it,' he said.

'Well, I know you had decided to attempt it before you saw her; but that would have ended in intentions. It was very well to talk of, but ridiculous to put in practice. I fully expected that in the course of a month or two you would have seen the folly of such self-sacrifice, and would have been by this time back again to Paris in some business or other. I can understand objections to the diamond trade—I really was thinking that it might be inadequate to the life of a man like you even though it might have made you a millionaire. But now I see how mistaken you are about this girl I doubt if you could be correct about other things.'

'How am I mistaken in her?'

'She is lazy and dissatisfied. But that is not all of it. Supposing her to be as good a woman as any you can find, which she certainly is not, why do you wish to connect yourself with anybody at present?'

'Well, there are practical reasons,' Clym began, and then almost broke off under an overpowering sense of the weight of argument which could be brought against his statement. 'If I take a school an educated woman would be invaluable as a help to me.'

'What! you really mean to marry her?'

'It would be premature to state that plainly. But consider what obvious advantages there would be in doing it. She——'

'Don't suppose she has any money. She hasn't a farthing.'

'She is excellently educated, and would make a good matron in a boarding-school. I candidly own that I have modified my views a little, in deference to you; and it should satisfy you. I no longer adhere to my intention of giving with my own mouth rudimentary education to the lowest class. I can do better. I can establish a good private school for farmers' sons, and without stopping the school I can manage to pass examinations.[8] By this means, and by the assistance of a wife like her——'

'O, Clym!'

'I shall ultimately, I hope, be at the head of one of the best schools in the county.'

Yeobright had enunciated the word 'her' with a fervour which, in conversation with a mother, was absurdly indiscreet. Hardly a maternal heart within the four seas could, in such circumstances, have helped being irritated at that ill-timed betrayal of feeling for a new woman.

'You are blinded, Clym,' she said warmly. 'It was a bad day for you when you first set eyes on her. And your scheme is merely a castle in the air built on purpose to justify this folly which has seized you, and to salve your conscience on the irrational situation you are in.'

'Mother, that's not true,' he firmly answered.

'Can you maintain that I sit and tell untruths, when all I wish to do is to save you from sorrow? For shame, Clym! But it is all through that woman—a hussy!'[9]

Clym reddened like fire and rose. He placed his hand upon his mother's shoulder and said, in a tone which hung strangely between entreaty and command, 'I won't hear it. I may be led to answer you in a way which we shall both regret.'

His mother parted her lips to begin some other vehement truth, but on looking at him she saw that in his face which led her to leave the words unsaid. Yeobright walked once or twice across the room, and then suddenly went out of the house. It was eleven o'clock when he came in, though he had not been further than the precincts of the garden. His mother was gone to bed. A light was left burning on the table, and supper was spread. Without stopping for any food he secured the doors and went upstairs.

8. In 1878 Clym continues: "Then I can take orders", i.e., become a clergyman in the Church of England—a familiar step for someone seeking a career as a teacher, but inconsistent with Clym's advanced views.
9. Literally a housewife, but generally used to signify a woman of low character.

An Hour of Bliss and Many Hours of Sadness

IV

The next day was gloomy enough at Blooms-End. Yeobright remained in his study, sitting over the open books; but the work of
those hours was miserably scant. Determined that there should be
nothing in his conduct towards his mother resembling sullenness,
he had occasionally spoken to her on passing matters, and would
take no notice of the brevity of her replies. With the same resolve to
keep up a show of conversation he said, about seven o'clock in the
evening, 'There's an eclipse of the moon to-night. I am going out to
see it.' And, putting on his overcoat, he left her.

The low moon was not as yet visible from the front of the house,
and Yeobright climbed out of the valley until he stood in the full
flood of her light. But even now he walked on, and his steps were in
the direction of Rainbarrow.

In half an hour he stood at the top. The sky was clear from verge
to verge, and the moon flung her rays over the whole heath, but
without sensibly lighting it, except where paths and water-courses
had laid bare the white flints and glistening quartz sand, which
made streaks upon the general shade. After standing awhile he
stooped and felt the heather. It was dry, and he flung himself down
upon the barrow, his face towards the moon, which depicted a
small image of herself in each of his eyes.

He had often come up here without stating his purpose to his
mother; but this was the first time that he had been ostensibly
frank as to his purpose while really concealing it. It was a moral situation which, three months earlier, he could hardly have credited
of himself. In returning to labour in this sequestered spot he had
anticipated an escape from the chafing of social necessities; yet behold they were here also. More than ever he longed to be in some
world where personal ambition was not the only recognized form of
progress—such, perhaps, as might have been the case at some time
or other in the silvery globe then shining upon him. His eye travelled over the length and breadth of that distant country—over the
Bay of Rainbows, the sombre Sea of Crises, the Ocean of Storms,
the Lake of Dreams, the vast Walled Plains, and the wondrous Ring
Mountains[1]—till he almost felt himself to be voyaging bodily
through its wild scenes, standing on its hollow hills, traversing its
deserts, descending its vales and old sea bottoms, or mounting to
the edges of its craters.

While he watched the far-removed landscape a tawny stain grew

---

1. Fanciful if unscientific names for areas of the moon's surface, widely used in the nineteenth century and still current.

into being on the lower verge: the eclipse had begun. This marked a preconcerted moment: for the remote celestial phenomenon had been pressed into sublunary service as a lover's signal. Yeobright's mind flew back to earth at the sight; he arose, shook himself, and listened. Minute after minute passed by, perhaps ten minutes passed, and the shadow on the moon perceptibly widened. He heard a rustling on his left hand, a cloaked figure with an upturned face appeared at the base of the Barrow, and Clym descended. In a moment the figure was in his arms, and his lips upon hers.

'My Eustacia!'

'Clym, dearest!'

Such a situation had less than three months brought forth.

They remained long without a single utterance, for no language could reach the level of their condition: words were as the rusty implements of a by-gone barbarous epoch, and only to be occasionally tolerated.

'I began to wonder why you did not come,' said Yeobright, when she had withdrawn a little from his embrace.

'You said ten minutes after the first mark of shade on the edge of the moon; and that's what it is now.'

'Well, let us only think that here we are.'

Then, holding each other's hand, they were again silent, and the shadow on the moon's disc grew a little larger.

'Has it seemed long since you last saw me?' she asked.

'It has seemed sad.'

'And not long? That's because you occupy yourself, and so blind yourself to my absence. To me, who can do nothing, it has been like living under stagnant water.'

'I would rather bear tediousness, dear, than have time made short by such means as have shortened mine.'

'In what way is that? You have been thinking you wished you did not love me.'

'How can a man wish that, and yet love on? No, Eustacia.'

'Men can, women cannot.'

'Well, whatever I may have thought, one thing is certain—I do love you—past all compass and description. I love you to oppressiveness—I, who have never before felt more than a pleasant passing fancy for any woman I have ever seen. Let me look right into your moonlit face, and dwell on every line and curve in it! Only a few hair-breadths make the difference between this face and faces I have seen many times before I knew you; yet what a difference— the difference between everything and nothing at all. One touch on that mouth again! there, and there, and there. Your eyes seem heavy, Eustacia.'

'No, it is my general way of looking. I think it arises from my feeling sometimes an agonizing pity for myself that I ever was born.'

'You don't feel it now?'

'No. Yet I know that we shall not love like this always. Nothing can ensure the continuance of love. It will evaporate like a spirit, and so I feel full of fears.'

'You need not.'

'Ah, you don't know. You have seen more than I, and have been into cities and among people that I have only heard of, and have lived more years than I; but yet I am older at this than you. I loved another man once, and now I love you.'

'In God's mercy don't talk so, Eustacia!'

'But I do not think I shall be the one who wearies first. It will, I fear, end in this way: your mother will find out that you meet me, and she will influence you against me!'

'That can never be. She knows of these meetings already.'

'And she speaks against me?'

'I will not say.'

'There, go away! Obey her. I shall ruin you. It is foolish of you to meet me like this. Kiss me, and go away for ever. For ever—do you hear?—for ever!'

'Not I.'

'It is your only chance. Many a man's love has been a curse to him.'

'You are desperate, full of fancies, and wilful; and you misunderstand. I have an additional reason for seeing you to-night besides love of you. For though, unlike you, I feel our affection may be eternal, I feel with you in this, that our present mode of existence cannot last.'

'Oh! 'tis your mother. Yes, that's it! I knew it.'

'Never mind what it is. Believe this, I cannot let myself lose you. I must have you always with me. This very evening I do not like to let you go. There is only one cure for this anxiety, dearest—you must be my wife.'

She started: then endeavoured to say calmly, 'Cynics say that cures the anxiety by curing the love.'

'But you must answer me. Shall I claim you some day—I don't mean at once?'

'I must think,' Eustacia murmured. 'At present speak of Paris to me. Is there any place like it on earth?'

'It is very beautiful. But will you be mine?'

'I will be nobody else's in the world—does that satisfy you?'

'Yes, for the present.'

'Now tell me of the Tuileries, and the Louvre,'[2] she continued evasively.

---

2. The Louvre, formerly a royal palace, was converted into a museum in 1793; the Tuileries Palace, also in Paris, was destroyed in 1871.

'I hate talking of Paris! Well, I remember one sunny room in the Louvre which would make a fitting place for you to live in—the Galerie d'Apollon. Its windows are mainly east; and in the early morning, when the sun is bright, the whole apartment is in a perfect blaze of splendour. The rays bristle and dart from the encrustations of gilding to the magnificent inlaid coffers, from the coffers to the gold and silver plate, from the plate to the jewels and precious stones, from these to the enamels, till there is a perfect network of light which quite dazzles the eye. But now, about our marriage——'

'And Versailles—the King's Gallery is some such gorgeous room, is it not?'

'Yes. But what's the use of talking of gorgeous rooms? By the way, the Little Trianon[3] would suit us beautifully to live in, and you might walk in the gardens in the moonlight and think you were in some English shrubbery; it is laid out in English fashion.'

'I should hate to think that!'

'Then you could keep to the lawn in front of the Grand Palace. All about there you would doubtless feel in a world of historical romance.'

He went on, since it was all new to her, and described Fontainebleau, St. Cloud, the Bois,[4] and many other familiar haunts of the Parisians; till she said—

'When used you to go to these places?'

'On Sundays.'

'Ah, yes. I dislike English Sundays. How I should chime in with their manners over there! Dear Clym, you'll go back again?'

Clym shook his head, and looked at the eclipse.

'If you'll go back again I'll—be something,' she said tenderly, putting her head near his breast. 'If you'll agree I'll give my promise, without making you wait a minute longer.'

'How extraordinary that you and my mother should be of one mind about this!' said Yeobright. 'I have vowed not to go back, Eustacia. It is not the place I dislike; it is the occupation.'

'But you can go in some other capacity.'

'No. Besides, it would interfere with my scheme. Don't press that, Eustacia. Will you marry me?'

'I cannot tell.'

'Now—never mind Paris; it is no better than other spots. Promise, sweet!'

'You will never adhere to your education plan, I am quite sure;

3. Small palace built between 1763 and 1768 by Louis XV at Versailles, itself the site of the palace and gardens of Louis XIV.
4. The Bois de Boulogne, a park on the edge of Paris. St. Cloud was a royal chateau; Fontainebleau was a royal hunting-lodge.

and then it will be all right for me; and so I promise to be yours for ever and ever.'

Clym brought her face towards his by a gentle pressure of the hand, and kissed her.

'Ah! but you don't know what you have got in me,' she said. 'Sometimes I think there is not that in Eustacia Vye which will make a good homespun wife. Well, let it go—see how our time is slipping, slipping, slipping!' She pointed towards the half eclipsed moon.

'You are too mournful.'

'No. Only I dread to think of anything beyond the present. What is, we know. We are together now, and it is unknown how long we shall be so: the unknown always fills my mind with terrible possibilities, even when I may reasonably expect it to be cheerful. . . . Clym, the eclipsed moonlight shines upon your face with a strange foreign colour, and shows its shape as if it were cut out in gold. That means that you should be doing better things than this.'

'You are ambitious, Eustacia—no, not exactly ambitious, luxurious. I ought to be of the same vein, to make you happy, I suppose. And yet, far from that, I could live and die in a hermitage here, with proper work to do.'

There was that in his tone which implied distrust of his position as a solicitous lover, a doubt if he were acting fairly towards one whose tastes touched his own only at rare and infrequent points. She saw his meaning, and whispered, in a low, full accent of eager assurance, 'Don't mistake me, Clym: though I should like Paris, I love you for yourself alone. To be your wife and live in Paris would be heaven to me; but I would rather live with you in a hermitage here than not be yours at all. It is gain to me either way, and very great gain. There's my too candid confession.'

'Spoken like a woman. And now I must soon leave you. I'll walk with you towards your house.'

'But must you go home yet?' she asked. 'Yes, the sand has nearly slipped away, I see, and the eclipse is creeping on more and more. Don't go yet! Stop till the hour has run itself out; then I will not press you any more. You will go home and sleep well; I keep sighing in my sleep! Do you ever dream of me?'

'I cannot recollect a clear dream of you.'

'I see your face in every scene of my dreams, and hear your voice in every sound. I wish I did not. It is too much what I feel. They say such love never lasts. But it must! And yet once, I remember, I saw an officer of the Hussars[5] ride down the street at Budmouth, and though he was a total stranger and never spoke to me, I loved him

5. Light cavalry regiments, typically with brilliant uniforms.

till I thought I should really die of love—but I didn't die, and at last I left off caring for him. How terrible it would be if a time should come when I could not love you, my Clym!'

'Please don't say such reckless things. When we see such a time at hand we will say, "I have outlived my faith and purpose," and die. There, the hour has expired: now let us walk on.'

Hand in hand they went along the path towards Mistover. When they were near the house he said, 'It is too late for me to see your grandfather to-night. Do you think he will object to it?'

'I will speak to him. I am so accustomed to be my own mistress that it did not occur to me that we should have to ask him.'

Then they lingeringly separated, and Clym descended towards Blooms-End.

And as he walked further and further from the charmed atmosphere of his Olympian girl[6] his face grew sad with a new sort of sadness. A perception of the dilemma in which his love had placed him came back in full force. In spite of Eustacia's apparent willingness to wait through the period of an unpromising engagement, till he should be established in his new pursuit, he could not but perceive at moments that she loved him rather as a visitant from a gay world to which she rightly belonged than as a man with a purpose opposed to that recent past of his which so interested her. Often at their meetings a word or a sigh escaped her. It meant that, though she made no conditions as to his return to the French capital, this was what she secretly longed for in the event of marriage; and it robbed him of many an otherwise pleasant hour. Along with that came the widening breach between himself and his mother. Whenever any little occurrence had brought into more prominence than usual the disappointment that he was causing her it had sent him on lone and moody walks; or he was kept awake a great part of the night by the turmoil of spirit which such a recognition created. If Mrs. Yeobright could only have been led to see what a sound and worthy purpose this purpose of his was and how little it was being affected by his devotion to Eustacia, how differently would she regard him!

Thus as his sight grew accustomed to the first blinding halo kindled about him by love and beauty, Yeobright began to perceive what a strait he was in. Sometimes he wished that he had never known Eustacia, immediately to retract the wish as brutal. Three antagonistic growths had to he kept alive: his mother's trust in him, his plan for becoming a teacher, and Eustacia's happiness. His fervid nature could not afford to relinquish one of these, though two

---

6. In Greek mythology Olympus is the home of the gods who succeeded the Titans; Clym is presumably thinking of Eustacia as goddess-like.

of the three were as many as he could hope to preserve. Though his love was as chaste as that of Petrarch for his Laura,[7] it had made fetters of what previously was only a difficulty. A position which was not too simple when he stood whole-hearted had become indescribably complicated by the addition of Eustacia. Just when his mother was beginning to tolerate one scheme he had introduced another still bitterer than the first, and the combination was more than she could bear.

Sharp Words Are Spoken and a Crisis Ensues

v

When Yeobright was not with Eustacia he was sitting slavishly over his books; when he was not reading he was meeting her. These meetings were carried on with the greatest secrecy.

One afternoon his mother came home from a morning visit to Thomasin. He could see from a disturbance in the lines of her face that something had happened.

'I have been told an incomprehensible thing,' she said mournfully. 'The captain has let out at the Woman that you and Eustacia Vye are engaged to be married.'

'We are,' said Yeobright. 'But it may not be yet for a very long time.'

'I should hardly think it *would* be yet for a very long time! You will take her to Paris, I suppose?' She spoke with weary hopelessness.

'I am not going back to Paris.'

'What will you do with a wife, then?'

'Keep a school in Budmouth, as I have told you.'

'That's incredible! The place is overrun with schoolmasters. You have no special qualifications. What possible chance is there for such as you?'

'There is no chance of getting rich. But with my system of education, which is as new as it is true, I shall do a great deal of good to my fellow-creatures.'

'Dreams, dreams! If there had been any system left to be invented they would have found it out at the universities long before this time.'

'Never, mother. They cannot find it out, because their teachers don't come in contact with the class which demands such a system—that is, those who have had no preliminary training. My plan

---

7. The *Sonnets* of the Italian poet Francesco Petrarca (1304–74) were inspired by his idealized love for Laura, whom he saw from afar but never met.

is one for instilling high knowledge into empty minds without first cramming them with what has to be uncrammed again before true study begins.'

'I might have believed you if you had kept yourself free from entanglements; but this woman—if she had been a good girl it would have been bad enough; but being——'

'She is a good girl.'

'So you think. A Corfu bandmaster's daughter! What has her life been? Her surname even is not her true one.'

'She is Captain Vye's granddaughter, and her father merely took her mother's name. And she is a lady by instinct.'

'They call him "captain," but anybody is captain.'

'He was in the Royal Navy!'

'No doubt he has been to sea in some tub or other. Why doesn't he look after her? No lady would rove about the heath at all hours of the day and night as she does. But that's not all of it. There was something queer between her and Thomasin's husband at one time—I am as sure of it as that I stand here.'

'Eustacia has told me. He did pay her a little attention a year ago; but there's no harm in that. I like her all the better.'

'Clym,' said his mother with firmness, 'I have no proofs against her, unfortunately. But if she makes you a good wife, there has never been a bad one.'

'Believe me, you are almost exasperating,' said Yeobright vehemently. 'And this very day I had intended to arrange a meeting between you. But you give me no peace; you try to thwart my wishes in everything.'

'I hate the thought of any son of mine marrying badly! I wish I had never lived to see this; it is too much for me—it is more than I dreamt!' She turned to the window. Her breath was coming quickly, and her lips were pale, parted, and trembling.

'Mother,' said Clym, 'whatever you do, you will always be dear to me—that you know. But one thing I have a right to say, which is, that at my age I am old enough to know what is best for me.'

Mrs. Yeobright remained for some time silent and shaken, as if she could say no more. Then she replied, 'Best? Is it best for you to injure your prospects for such a voluptuous, idle woman as that? Don't you see that by the very fact of your choosing her you prove that you do not know what is best for you? You give up your whole thought—you set your whole soul—to please a woman.'

'I do. And that woman is you.'

'How can you treat me so flippantly!' said his mother, turning again to him with a tearful look. 'You are unnatural, Clym, and I did not expect it.'

'Very likely,' said he cheerlessly. 'You did not know the measure you were going to mete me, and therefore did not know the measure that would be returned to you again.'[1]

'You answer me; you think only of her. You stick to her in all things.'

'That proves her to be worthy. I have never yet supported what is bad. And I do not care only for her. I care for you and for myself, and for anything that is good. When a woman once dislikes another she is merciless!'

'O Clym! please don't go setting down as my fault what is your obstinate wrong-headedness. If you wished to connect yourself with an unworthy person why did you come home here to do it? Why didn't you do it in Paris?—it is more the fashion there. You have come only to distress me, a lonely woman, and shorten my days! I wish that you would bestow your presence where you bestow your love!'

Clym said huskily, 'You are my mother. I will say no more—beyond this, that I beg your pardon for having thought this my home. I will no longer inflict myself upon you; I'll go.' And he went out with tears in his eyes.

It was a sunny afternoon at the beginning of summer, and the moist hollows of the heath had passed from their brown to their green stage. Yeobright walked to the edge of the basin which extended down from Mistover and Rainbarrow. By this time he was calm, and he looked over the landscape. In the minor valleys, between the hillocks which diversified the contour of the vale, the fresh young ferns were luxuriantly growing up, ultimately to reach a height of five or six feet. He descended a little way, flung himself down in a spot where a path emerged from one of the small hollows, and waited. Hither it was that he had promised Eustacia to bring his mother this afternoon, that they might meet and be friends. His attempt had utterly failed.

He was in a nest of vivid green. The ferny vegetation round him, though so abundant, was quite uniform: it was a grove of machine-made foliage, a world of green triangles with saw-edges, and not a single flower. The air was warm with a vaporous warmth, and the stillness was unbroken. Lizards, grasshoppers, and ants were the only living things to be beheld. The scene seemed to belong to the ancient world of the carboniferous period,[2] when the forms of plants were few, and of the fern kind; when there was neither bud

1. Clym is adapting Jesus' words at Matthew 7.1–2 (the Sermon on the Mount): "Judge not, that ye be not judged. For with what judgement ye judge, ye shall be judged; and with what measure ye mete, it shall be measured to you again."
2. Period from about 350 till 270 million years ago; Hardy is drawing on notes taken in 1877 from a review of O. Heer, *The Primeval World of Switzerland* (1876).

nor blossom, nothing but a monotonous extent of leafage, amid which no bird sang.[3]

When he had reclined for some considerable time, gloomily pondering, he discerned above the ferns a drawn bonnet of white silk approaching from the left, and Yeobright knew directly that it covered the head of her he loved. His heart awoke from its apathy to a warm excitement, and, jumping to his feet, he said aloud, 'I knew she was sure to come.'

She vanished in a hollow for a few moments, and then her whole form unfolded itself from the brake.[4]

'Only you here?' she exclaimed, with a disappointed air, whose hollowness was proved by her rising redness and her half-guilty low laugh. 'Where is Mrs. Yeobright?'

'She has not come,' he replied in a subdued tone.

'I wish I had known that you would be here alone,' she said seriously, 'and that we were going to have such an idle, pleasant time as this. Pleasure not known beforehand is half wasted; to anticipate it is to double it. I have not thought once to-day of having you all to myself this afternoon, and the actual moment of a thing is so soon gone.'

'It is indeed.'

'Poor Clym!' she continued, looking tenderly into his face. 'You are sad. Something has happened at your home. Never mind what is—let us only look at what seems.'

'But, darling, what shall we do?' said he.

'Still go on as we do now—just live on from meeting to meeting, never minding about another day. You, I know, are always thinking of that—I can see you are. But you must not—will you, dear Clym?'

'You are just like all women. They are ever content to build their lives on any incidental position that offers itself; whilst men would fain make a globe to suit them. Listen to this, Eustacia. There is a subject I have determined to put off no longer. Your sentiment on the wisdom of *Carpe diem*[5] does not impress me to-day. Our present mode of life must shortly be brought to an end.'

'It is your mother!'

'It is. I love you none the less in telling you; it is only right you should know.'

'I have feared my bliss,' she said, with the merest motion of her lips. 'It has been too intense and consuming.'

---

3. An echo of Keats's poem "La Belle Dame Sans Merci" (1819), in which a knight awakes from enchantment on a hillside where "The sedge has withered from the lake, / And no birds sing."

4. Clump of bushes or bracken.

5. Enjoy yourself while you can (literally, "seize the day"); now proverbial, but originally from Book I of the *Odes* of the Roman poet Horace (Quintus Horatius Flaccus, 65–8 B.C.E.).

'There is hope yet. There are forty years of work in me yet, and why should you despair? I am only at an awkward turning. I wish people wouldn't be so ready to think that there is no progress without uniformity.'

'Ah—your mind runs off to the philosophical side of it. Well, these sad and hopeless obstacles are welcome in one sense, for they enable us to look with indifference upon the cruel satires that Fate loves to indulge in. I have heard of people, who, upon coming suddenly into happiness, have died from anxiety lest they should not live to enjoy it. I felt myself in that whimsical state of uneasiness lately; but I shall be spared it now. Let us walk on.'

Clym took the hand which was already bared for him—it was a favourite way with them to walk bare hand in bare hand—and led her through the ferns. They formed a very comely picture of love at full flush, as they walked along the valley that late afternoon, the sun sloping down on their right, and throwing their thin spectral shadows, tall as poplar trees, far out across the furze and fern. Eustacia went with her head thrown back fancifully, a certain glad and voluptuous air of triumph pervading her eyes at having won by her own unaided self a man who was her perfect complement in attainments, appearance, and age. On the young man's part, the paleness of face which he had brought with him from Paris, and the incipient marks of time and thought, were less perceptible than when he returned, the healthful and energetic sturdiness which was his by nature having partially recovered its original proportions. They wandered onward till they reached the nether margin of the heath, where it became marshy, and merged in moorland.

'I must part from you here, Clym,' said Eustacia.

They stood still and prepared to bid each other farewell. Everything before them was on a perfect level. The sun, resting on the horizon line, streamed across the ground from between copper-coloured and lilac clouds, stretched out in flats beneath a sky of pale soft green. All dark objects on the earth that lay towards the sun were overspread by a purple haze, against which groups of wailing gnats shone out, rising upwards and dancing about like sparks of fire.[6]

'O! this leaving you is too hard to bear!' exclaimed Eustacia in a sudden whisper of anguish. 'Your mother will influence you too much; I shall not be judged fairly, it will get afloat that I am not a good girl, and the witch story will be added to make me blacker!'

'They cannot. Nobody dares to speak disrespectfully of you or of me.'

6. This and the penultimate paragraph in this chapter closely echo a passage in *Desperate Remedies* (1871), Volume II, Chapter IV.

'O how I wish I was sure of never losing you—that you could not be able to desert me anyhow!'

Clym stood silent a moment. His feelings were high, the moment was passionate, and he cut the knot.

'You shall be sure of me, darling,' he said, folding her in his arms. 'We will be married at once.'

'O Clym!'

'Do you agree to it?'

'If—if we can.'

'We certainly can, both being of full age. And I have not followed my occupation all these years without having accumulated money; and if you will agree to live in a tiny cottage somewhere on the heath, until I take a house in Budmouth for the school, we can do it at a very little expense.'

'How long shall we have to live in the tiny cottage, Clym?'

'About six months. At the end of that time I shall have finished my reading—yes, we will do it, and this heart-aching will be over. We shall, of course, live in absolute seclusion, and our married life will only begin to outward view when we take the house in Budmouth, where I have already addressed a letter on the matter. Would your grandfather allow you?'

'I think he would—on the understanding that it should not last longer than six months.'

'I will guarantee that, if no misfortune happens.'

'If no misfortune happens,' she repeated slowly.

'Which is not likely. Dearest, fix the exact day.'

And then they consulted on the question, and the day was chosen. It was to be a fortnight from that time.

This was the end of their talk, and Eustacia left him. Clym watched her as she retired towards the sun. The luminous rays wrapped her up with her increasing distance, and the rustle of her dress over the sprouting sedge and grass died away. As he watched, the dead flat of the scenery overpowered him, though he was fully alive to the beauty of that untarnished early summer green which was worn for the nonce[7] by the poorest blade. There was something in its oppressive horizontality which too much reminded him of the arena of life; it gave him a sense of bare equality with, and no superiority to, a single living thing under the sun.

Eustacia was now no longer the goddess but the woman to him, a being to fight for, support, help, be maligned for. Now that he had reached a cooler moment he would have preferred a less hasty marriage; but the card was laid, and he determined to abide by the game. Whether Eustacia was to add one other to the list of those

7. Temporarily, for the occasion.

who love too hotly to love long and well, the forthcoming event was certainly a ready way of proving.

Yeobright Goes, and the Breach Is Complete

VI

All that evening smart sounds denoting an active packing up came from Yeobright's room to the ears of his mother downstairs.

Next morning he departed from the house and again proceeded across the heath. A long day's march was before him, his object being to secure a dwelling to which he might take Eustacia when she became his wife. Such a house, small, secluded, and with its windows boarded up, he had casually observed a month earlier, about two miles beyond the village of East Egdon, and six miles distant altogether; and thither he directed his steps to-day.

The weather was far different from that of the evening before. The yellow and vapoury sunset which had wrapped up Eustacia from his parting gaze had presaged change. It was one of those not infrequent days of an English June which are as wet and boisterous as November. The cold clouds hastened on in a body, as if painted on a moving slide. Vapours from other continents arrived upon the wind, which curled and parted round him as he walked on.

At length Clym reached the margin of a fir and beech plantation that had been enclosed from heath land in the year of his birth. Here the trees, laden heavily with their new and humid leaves, were now suffering more damage than during the highest winds of winter, when the boughs are specially disencumbered to do battle with the storm. The wet young beeches were undergoing amputations, bruises, cripplings, and harsh lacerations, from which the wasting sap would bleed for many a day to come, and which would leave scars visible till the day of their burning. Each stem was wrenched at the root, where it moved like a bone in its socket, and at every onset of the gale convulsive sounds came from the branches, as if pain were felt. In a neighbouring brake a finch was trying to sing; but the wind blew under his feathers till they stood on end, twisted round his little tail, and made him give up his song.

Yet a few yards to Yeobright's left, on the open heath, how ineffectively gnashed the storm! Those gusts which tore the trees merely waved the furze and heather in a light caress. Egdon was made for such times as these.

Yeobright reached the empty house about mid-day. It was almost as lonely as that of Eustacia's grandfather, but the fact that it stood near a heath was disguised by a belt of firs which almost enclosed the premises. He journeyed on about a mile further to the village in which the owner lived, and, returning with him to the house, arrangements were completed, and the man undertook that one room at least should be ready for occupation the next day. Clym's intention was to live there alone until Eustacia should join him on their wedding-day.

Then he turned to pursue his way homeward through the drizzle that had so greatly transformed the scene. The ferns, among which he had lain in comfort yesterday, were dripping moisture from every frond, wetting his legs through as he brushed past; and the fur of the rabbits leaping before him was clotted into dark locks by the same watery surrounding.

He reached home damp and weary enough after his ten-mile walk. It had hardly been a propitious beginning, but he had chosen his course, and would show no swerving. The evening and the following morning were spent in concluding arrangements for his departure. To stay at home a minute longer than necessary after having once come to his determination would be, he felt, only to give new pain to his mother by some word, look, or deed.

He had hired a conveyance and sent off his goods by two o'clock that day. The next step was to get some furniture, which, after serving for temporary use in the cottage, would be available for the house at Budmouth when increased by goods of a better description. A mart extensive enough for the purpose existed at Anglebury, some miles beyond the spot chosen for his residence, and there he resolved to pass the coming night.

It now only remained to wish his mother good-bye. She was sitting by the window as usual when he came downstairs.

'Mother, I am going to leave you,' he said, holding out his hand.

'I thought you were, by your packing,' replied Mrs. Yeobright in a voice from which every particle of emotion was painfully excluded.

'And you will part friends with me?'

'Certainly, Clym.'

'I am going to be married on the twenty-fifth.'

'I thought you were going to be married.'

'And then—and then you must come and see us. You will understand me better after that, and our situation will not be so wretched as it is now.'

'I do not think it likely I shall come to see you.'

'Then it will not be my fault or Eustacia's, mother. Good-bye!'

He kissed her cheek, and departed in great misery, which was several hours in lessening itself to a controllable level. The position had been such that nothing more could be said without, in the first place, breaking down a barrier; and that was not to be done.

No sooner had Yeobright gone from his mother's house than her face changed its rigid aspect for one of blank despair. After a while she wept, and her tears brought some relief. During the rest of the day she did nothing but walk up and down the garden path in a state bordering on stupefaction. Night came, and with it but little rest. The next day, with an instinct to do something which should reduce prostration to mournfulness, she went to her son's room, and with her own hands arranged it in order, for an imaginary time when he should return again. She gave some attention to her flowers, but it was perfunctorily bestowed, for they no longer charmed her.

It was a great relief when, early in the afternoon, Thomasin paid her an unexpected visit. This was not the first meeting between the relatives since Thomasin's marriage; and past blunders having been in a rough way rectified, they could always greet each other with pleasure and ease.

The oblique band of sunlight which followed her through the door became the young wife well. It illuminated her as her presence illuminated the heath. In her movements, in her gaze, she reminded the beholder of the feathered creatures who lived around her home. All similes and allegories concerning her began and ended with birds. There was as much variety in her motions as in their flight. When she was musing she was a kestrel, which hangs in the air by an invisible motion of its wings. When she was in a high wind her light body was blown against trees and banks like a heron's. When she was frightened she darted noiselessly like a kingfisher. When she was serene she skimmed like a swallow, and that is how she was moving now.

'You are looking very blithe, upon my word, Tamsie,' said Mrs. Yeobright, with a sad smile. 'How is Damon?'

'He is very well.'

'Is he kind to you, Thomasin?' And Mrs. Yeobright observed her narrowly.

'Pretty fairly.'

'Is that honestly said?'

'Yes, aunt. I would tell you if he were unkind.' She added, blushing, and with hesitation, 'He—I don't know if I ought to complain to you about this, but I am not quite sure what to do. I want some money, you know, aunt—some to buy little things for myself—and he doesn't give me any. I don't like to ask him; and yet, perhaps, he doesn't give it me because he doesn't know. Ought I to mention it to him, aunt?'

'Of course you ought. Have you never said a word on the matter?'

'You see, I had some of my own,' said Thomasin evasively; 'and I have not wanted any of his until lately. I did just say something about it last week; but he seems—not to remember.'

'He must be made to remember. You are aware that I have a little box full of spade-guineas,[1] which your uncle put into my hands to divide between yourself and Clym whenever I chose. Perhaps the time has come when it should be done. They can be turned into sovereigns at any moment.'

'I think I should like to have my share—that is, if you don't mind.'

'You shall, if necessary. But it is only proper that you should first tell your husband distinctly that you are without any, and see what he will do.'

'Very well, I will. . . . Aunt, I have heard about Clym. I know you are in trouble about him, and that's why I have come.'

Mrs. Yeobright turned away, and her features worked in her attempt to conceal her feelings. Then she ceased to make any attempt, and said, weeping, 'O Thomasin, do you think he hates me? How can he bear to grieve me so, when I have lived only for him through all these years?'

'Hate you—no,' said Thomasin soothingly. 'It is only that he loves her too well. Look at it quietly—do. It is not so very bad of him. Do you know, I thought it not the worst match he could have made. Miss Vye's family is a good one on her mother's side; and her father was a romantic wanderer—a sort of Greek Ulysses.'[2]

'It is no use, Thomasin; it is no use. Your intention is good; but I will not trouble you to argue. I have gone through the whole that can be said on either side times, and many times. Clym and I have not parted in anger; we have parted in a worse way. It is not a passionate quarrel that would have broken my heart; it is the steady opposition and persistence in going wrong that he has shown. O Thomasin, he was so good as a little boy—so tender and kind!'

'He was, I know.'

'I did not think one whom I called mine would grow up to treat me like this. He spoke to me as if I opposed him to injure him. As though I could wish him ill!'

'There are worse women in the world than Eustacia Vye.'

'There are too many better; that's the agony of it. It was she, Thomasin, and she only, who led your husband to act as he did: I would swear it!'

'No,' said Thomasin eagerly. 'It was before he knew me that he thought of her, and it was nothing but a mere flirtation.'

'Very well; we will let it be so. There is little use in unravelling that now. Sons must be blind if they will. Why is it that a woman can see from a distance what a man cannot see close? Clym must do as he will—he is nothing more to me. And this is maternity—to

1. Guineas minted between 1787 and 1799, with a spade-shaped shield on the reverse.
2. Thomasin is apparently unaware that Ulysses is the Latin name for the Greek hero Odysseus, whose long wanderings form the subject of Homer's *Odyssey*.

give one's best years and best love to ensure the fate of being despised!'

'You are too unyielding. Think how many mothers there are
whose sons have brought them to public shame by real crimes before you feel so deeply a case like this.'

'Thomasin, don't lecture me—I can't have it. It is the excess
above what we expect that makes the force of the blow, and that
may not be greater in their case than in mine: they may have foreseen the worst. . . . I am wrongly made, Thomasin,' she added, with
a mournful smile. 'Some widows can guard against the wounds
their children give them by turning their hearts to another husband
and beginning life again. But I always was a poor, weak, one-idea'd
creature—I had not the compass of heart nor the enterprise for
that. Just as forlorn and stupefied as I was when my husband's
spirit flew away I have sat ever since—never attempting to mend
matters at all. I was comparatively a young woman then, and I
might have had another family by this time, and have been comforted by them for the failure of this one son.'

'It is more noble in you that you did not.'

'The more noble, the less wise.'

'Forget it, and be soothed, dear aunt. And I shall not leave you
alone for long. I shall come and see you every day.'

And for one week Thomasin literally fulfilled her word. She endeavoured to make light of the wedding; and brought news of the
preparations, and that she was invited to be present. The next week
she was rather unwell, and did not appear. Nothing had as yet been
done about the guineas, for Thomasin feared to address her husband
again on the subject, and Mrs. Yeobright had insisted upon this.

One day just before this time Wildeve was standing at the door of
the Quiet Woman. In addition to the upward path through the
heath to Rainbarrow and Mistover, there was a road which
branched from the highway a short distance below the inn, and ascended to Mistover by a circuitous and easy incline. This was the
only route on that side for vehicles to the captain's retreat. A light
cart from the nearest town descended the road, and the lad who
was driving pulled up in front of the inn for something to drink.

'You come from Mistover?' said Wildeve.

'Yes. They are taking in good things up there. Going to be a wedding.' And the driver buried his face in his mug.

Wildeve had not received an inkling of the fact before, and a sudden expression of pain overspread his face. He turned for a moment into the passage to hide it. Then he came back again.

'Do you mean Miss Vye?' he said. 'How is it—that she can be
married so soon?'

'By the will of God and a ready young man, I suppose.'

'You don't mean Mr. Yeobright?'

'Yes. He has been creeping about with her all the spring.'

'I suppose—she was immensely taken with him?'

'She is crazy about him, so their general servant of all work tells me. And that lad Charley that looks after the horse is all in a daze about it. The stun-poll[3] has got fond-like of her.'

'Is she lively—is she glad? Going to be married so soon—well!'

'It isn't so very soon.'

'No; not so very soon.'

Wildeve went indoors to the empty room, a curious heart-ache within him. He rested his elbow upon the mantelpiece and his face upon his hand. When Thomasin entered the room he did not tell her of what he had heard. The old longing for Eustacia had reappeared in his soul: and it was mainly because he had discovered that it was another man's intention to possess her.

To be yearning for the difficult, to be weary of that offered; to care for the remote, to dislike the near; it was Wildeve's nature always. This is the true mark of the man of sentiment. Though Wildeve's fevered feeling had not been elaborated to real poetical compass, it was of the standard sort. He might have been called the Rousseau of Egdon.[4]

The Morning and the Evening of a Day

VII

The wedding morning came. Nobody would have imagined from appearances that Blooms-End had any interest in Mistover that day. A solemn stillness prevailed around the house of Clym's mother, and there was no more animation indoors. Mrs. Yeobright, who had declined to attend the ceremony, sat by the breakfast-table in the old room which communicated immediately with the porch, her eyes listlessly directed towards the open door. It was the room in which, six months earlier, the merry Christmas party had met, to which Eustacia came secretly and as a stranger. The only living thing that entered now was a sparrow; and seeing no movements to cause alarm, he hopped boldly round the room, endeavoured to go out by the window, and fluttered among the pot-flowers. This roused the lonely sitter, who got up, released the bird, and went to the door. She was expecting Thomasin, who had written the night before to state that the time had come when she would wish to have the money, and that she would if possible call this day.

3. Fool, blockhead.
4. Jean-Jacques Rousseau (1712–78), French philosopher, whose emphasis on the moral power of feeling or sentiment was often interpreted as emotional self-indulgence.

Yet Thomasin occupied Mrs. Yeobright's thoughts but slightly as she looked up the valley of the heath, alive with butterflies, and with grasshoppers whose husky noises on every side formed a whispered chorus. A domestic drama, for which the preparations were now being made a mile or two off, was but little less vividly present to her eyes than if enacted before her. She tried to dismiss the vision, and walked about the garden-plot; but her eyes ever and anon sought out the direction of the parish church to which Mistover belonged, and her excited fancy clove the hills which divided the building from her eyes. The morning wore away. Eleven o'clock struck: could it be that the wedding was then in progress? It must be so. She went on imagining the scene at the church, which he had by this time approached with his bride. She pictured the little group of children by the gate as the pony-carriage drove up, in which, as Thomasin had learnt, they were going to perform the short journey. Then she saw them enter and proceed to the chancel and kneel; and the service seemed to go on.

She covered her face with her hands. 'O, it is a mistake!' she groaned. 'And he will rue it some day, and think of me!'

While she remained thus, overcome by her forebodings, the old clock indoors whizzed forth twelve strokes. Soon after, faint sounds floated to her ear from afar over the hills. The breeze came from that quarter, and it had brought with it the notes of distant bells, gaily starting off in a peal: one, two, three, four, five. The ringers at East Egdon were announcing the nuptials of Eustacia and her son.

'Then it is over,' she murmured. 'Well, well! and life too will be over soon. And why should I go on scalding my face like this? Cry about one thing in life, cry about all; one thread runs through the whole piece. And yet we say, "a time to laugh!" '[1]

Towards evening Wildeve came. Since Thomasin's marriage Mrs. Yeobright had shown towards him that grim friendliness which at last arises in all such cases of undesired affinity. The vision of what ought to have been is thrown aside in sheer weariness, and browbeaten human endeavour listlessly makes the best of the fact that is. Wildeve, to do him justice, had behaved very courteously to his wife's aunt; and it was with no surprise that she saw him enter now.

'Thomasin has not been able to come, as she promised to do,' he replied to her inquiry, which had been anxious, for she knew that her niece was badly in want of money. 'The captain came down last night and personally pressed her to join them to-day. So, not to be unpleasant, she determined to go. They fetched her in the pony-chaise, and are going to bring her back.'

---

1. According to Ecclesiastes 3, there is a time for all human purposes, including "a time to weep, and a time to laugh" (verse 4).

'Then it is done,' said Mrs. Yeobright. 'Have they gone to their new home?'

'I don't know. I have had no news from Mistover since Thomasin left to go.'

'You did not go with her?' said she, as if there might be good reasons why.

'I could not,' said Wildeve, reddening slightly. 'We could not both leave the house; it was rather a busy morning, on account of Anglebury Great Market. I believe you have something to give to Thomasin? If you like, I will take it.'

Mrs. Yeobright hesitated, and wondered if Wildeve knew what the something was. 'Did she tell you of this?' she inquired.

'Not particularly. She casually dropped a remark about having arranged to fetch some article or other.'

'It is hardly necessary to send it. She can have it whenever she chooses to come.'

'That won't be yet. In the present state of her health she must not go on walking so much as she has done.' He added, with a faint twang of sarcasm, 'What wonderful thing is it that I cannot be trusted to take?'

'Nothing worth troubling you with.'

'One would think you doubted my honesty,' he said, with a laugh, though his colour rose in a quick resentfulness frequent with him.

'You need think no such thing,' said she drily. 'It is simply that I, in common with the rest of the world, feel that there are certain things which had better be done by certain people than by others.'

'As you like, as you like,' said Wildeve laconically. 'It is not worth arguing about. Well, I think I must turn homeward again, as the inn must not be left long in charge of the lad and the maid only.'

He went his way, his farewell being scarcely so courteous as his greeting. But Mrs. Yeobright knew him thoroughly by this time, and took little notice of his manner, good or bad.

When Wildeve was gone Mrs. Yeobright stood and considered what would be the best course to adopt with regard to the guineas, which she had not liked to entrust to Wildeve. It was hardly credible that Thomasin had told him to ask for them, when the necessity for them had arisen from the difficulty of obtaining money at his hands. At the same time Thomasin really wanted them, and might be unable to come to Blooms-End for another week at least. To take or send the money to her at the inn would be impolitic, since Wildeve would pretty surely be present, or would discover the transaction; and if, as her aunt suspected, he treated her less kindly than she deserved to be treated, he might then get the whole sum out of her gentle hands. But on this particular evening Thomasin was at Mistover, and anything might be conveyed to her there without the knowledge of her husband. Upon the whole the opportunity was worth taking advantage of.

Her son, too, was there, and was now married. There could be no more proper moment to render him his share of the money than the present. And the chance that would be afforded her, by sending him this gift, of showing how far she was from bearing him ill-will, cheered the sad mother's heart.

She went upstairs and took from a locked drawer a little box, out of which she poured a hoard of broad unworn guineas that had lain there many a year. There were a hundred in all, and she divided them into two heaps, fifty in each. Tying up these in small canvas bags, she went down to the garden and called to Christian Cantle, who was loitering about in hope of a supper which was not really owed him. Mrs. Yeobright gave him the money-bags, charged him to go to Mistover, and on no account to deliver them into any one's hands save her son's and Thomasin's. On further thought she deemed it advisable to tell Christian precisely what the two bags contained, that he might be fully impressed with their importance. Christian pocketed the money-bags, promised the greatest carefulness, and set out on his way.

'You need not hurry,' said Mrs. Yeobright. 'It will be better not to get there till after dusk, and then nobody will notice you. Come back here to supper, if it is not too late.'

It was nearly nine o'clock when he began to ascend the vale towards Mistover; but the long days of summer being at their climax, the first obscurity of evening had only just begun to tan the landscape. At this point of his journey Christian heard voices, and found that they proceeded from a company of men and women who were traversing a hollow ahead of him, the tops only of their heads being visible.

He paused and thought of the money he carried. It was almost too early even for Christian seriously to fear robbery; nevertheless he took a precaution which ever since his boyhood he had adopted whenever he carried more than two or three shillings upon his person—a precaution somewhat like that of the owner of the Pitt Diamond[2] when filled with similar misgivings. He took off his boots, untied the guineas, and emptied the contents of one little bag into the right boot, and of the other into the left, spreading them as flatly as possible over the bottom of each, which was really a spacious coffer by no means limited to the size of the foot. Pulling them on again and lacing them to the very top, he proceeded on his way, more easy in his head than under his soles.

His path converged towards that of the noisy company, and on

2. Thomas Pitt (1653–1726), who acquired the diamond while in India as Governor of Madras, was said to have sent it to England hidden in the heel of his son's shoe.

coming nearer he found to his relief that they were several Egdon people whom he knew very well, while with them walked Fairway, of Blooms-End.

'What! Christian going too?' said Fairway as soon as he recognized the new-comer. 'You've got no young woman nor wife to your name to gie a gown-piece to, I'm sure.'

'What d'ye mean?' said Christian.

'Why, the raffle. The one we go to every year. Going to the raffle as well as ourselves?'

'Never knew a word o't. Is it like cudgel-playing or other sportful forms of bloodshed? I don't want to go, thank you, Mister Fairway, and no offence.'

'Christian don't know the fun o't, and 'twould be a fine sight for him,' said a buxom woman. 'There's no danger at all, Christian. Every man puts in a shilling apiece, and one wins a gown-piece for his wife or sweetheart if he's got one.'

'Well, as that's not my fortune there's no meaning in it to me. But I should like to see the fun, if there's nothing of the black art in it, and if a man may look on without cost or getting into any dangerous wrangle?'

'There will be no uproar at all,' said Timothy. 'Sure, Christian, if you'd like to come we'll see there's no harm done.'

'And no ba'dy³ gaieties, I suppose? You see, neighbours, if so, it would be setting father a bad example, as he is so light moral'd. But a gown-piece for a shilling, and no black art—'tis worth looking in to see, and it wouldn't hinder me half an hour. Yes, I'll come, if you'll step a little way towards Mistover with me afterwards, supposing night should have closed in, and nobody else is going that way?'

One or two promised; and Christian, diverging from his direct path, turned round to the right with his companions towards the Quiet Woman.

When they entered the large common room of the inn they found assembled there about ten men from among the neighbouring population, and the group was increased by the new contingent to double that number. Most of them were sitting round the room in seats divided by wooden elbows like those of crude cathedral stalls, which were carved with the initials of many an illustrious drunkard of former times who had passed his days and his nights between them, and now lay as an alcoholic cinder in the nearest churchyard. Among the cups on the long table before the sitters lay an open parcel of light drapery—the gown-piece, as it was called—which was to be raffled for. Wildeve was standing with his back to

3. Bawdy, wicked (dialect).

the fireplace, smoking a cigar; and the promoter of the raffle, a packman from a distant town, was expatiating upon the value of the fabric as material for a summer dress.

'Now, gentlemen,' he continued, as the new-comers drew up to the table, 'there's five have entered, and we want four more to make up the number. I think, by the faces of those gentlemen who have just come in, that they are shrewd enough to take advantage of this rare opportunity of beautifying their ladies at a very trifling expense.'

Fairway, Sam, and another placed their shillings on the table, and the man turned to Christian.

'No, sir,' said Christian, drawing back, with a quick gaze of misgiving. 'I am only a poor chap come to look on, an it please ye, sir. I don't so much as know how you do it. If so be I was sure of getting it I would put down the shilling; but I couldn't otherwise.'

'I think you might almost be sure,' said the pedlar. 'In fact, now I look into your face, even if I can't say you are sure to win, I can say that I never saw anything look more like winning in my life.'

'You'll anyhow have the same chance as the rest of us,' said Sam.

'And the extra luck of being the last comer,' said another.

'And I was born wi' a caul,[4] and perhaps can be no more ruined than drowned?' Christian added, beginning to give way.

Ultimately Christian laid down his shilling, the raffle began, and the dice went round. When it came to Christian's turn he took the box with a trembling hand, shook it fearfully, and threw a pair-royal.[5] Three of the others had thrown common low pairs, and all the rest mere points.

'The gentleman looked like winning, as I said,' observed the chapman blandly. 'Take it, sir; the article is yours.'

'Haw-haw-haw!' said Fairway. 'I'm damned if this isn't the quarest start that ever I knowed!'

'Mine?' asked Christian, with a vacant stare from his target eyes. 'I—I haven't got neither maid, wife, nor widder belonging to me at all, and I'm afeard it will make me laughed at to ha'e it, Master Traveller. What with being curious to join in I never thought of that! What shall I do wi' a woman's clothes in my bedroom, and not lose my decency!'

'Keep 'em, to be sure,' said Fairway, 'if it is only for luck. Perhaps 'twill tempt some woman that thy poor carcase had no power over when standing empty-handed.'

'Keep it, certainly,' said Wildeve, who had idly watched the scene from a distance.

---

4. A caul is the membrane enclosing the foetus, part of which sometimes covers a baby's head at birth; this was popularly considered a lucky omen, and a charm against death by drowning.
5. Three of a kind, i.e., three dice of the same value. For Hardy's explanation of the game, see *Letters*, III. 69–70.

The table was then cleared of the articles, and the men began to drink.

'Well, to be sure!' said Christian, half to himself. 'To think I should have been born so lucky as this, and not have found it out until now! What curious creatures these dice be—powerful rulers of us all, and yet at my command! I am sure I never need be afeard of anything after this.' He handled the dice fondly one by one. 'Why, sir,' he said in a confidential whisper to Wildeve, who was near his left hand, 'if I could only use this power that's in me of multiplying money I might do some good to a near relation of yours, seeing what I've got about me of hers—eh?' He tapped one of his money-laden boots upon the floor.

'What do you mean?' said Wildeve.

'That's a secret. Well, I must be going now.' He looked anxiously towards Fairway.

'Where are you going?' Wildeve asked.

'To Mistover Knap. I have to see Mrs. Thomasin there—that's all.'

'I am going there, too, to fetch Mrs. Wildeve. We can walk together.'

Wildeve became lost in thought; and a look of inward illumination came into his eyes. It was money for his wife that Mrs. Yeobright could not trust him with. 'Yet she could trust this fellow,' he said to himself. 'Why doesn't that which belongs to the wife belong to the husband too?'[6]

He called to the pot-boy to bring him his hat, and said, 'Now, Christian, I am ready.'

'Mr. Wildeve,' said Christian timidly, as he turned to leave the room, 'would you mind lending me them wonderful little things that carry my luck inside 'em, that I might practise a bit by myself, you know?' He looked wistfully at the dice and box lying on the mantelpiece.

'Certainly,' said Wildeve carelessly. 'They were only cut out by some lad with his knife, and are worth nothing.' And Christian went back and privately pocketed them.

Wildeve opened the door and looked out. The night was warm and cloudy. 'By Gad! 'tis dark,' he continued. 'But I suppose we shall find our way.'

'If we should lose the path it might be awkward,' said Christian. 'A lantern is the only shield that will make it safe for us.'

'Let's have a lantern by all means.' The stable-lantern was

6. Under common law, Thomasin's money does indeed belong to Wildeve; prior to the Married Women's Property Acts of 1870 and 1882, a woman's personal property, including money, passed on her marriage into her husband's absolute control and disposal.

fetched and lighted. Christian took up his gown-piece, and the two set out to ascend the hill.

Within the room the men fell into chat till their attention was for a moment drawn to the chimney-corner. This was large, and, in addition to its proper recess, contained within its jambs, like many on Egdon, a receding seat, so that a person might sit there absolutely unobserved, provided there was no fire to light him up, as was the case now and throughout the summer. From the niche a single object protruded into the light from the candles on the table. It was a clay pipe, and its colour was reddish. The men had been attracted to this object by a voice behind the pipe asking for a light.

'Upon my life, it fairly startled me when the man spoke!' said Fairway, handing a candle. 'Oh—'tis the reddleman! You've kept a quiet tongue, young man.'

'Yes, I had nothing to say,' observed Venn. In a few minutes he arose and wished the company good night.

Meanwhile Wildeve and Christian had plunged into the heath.

It was a stagnant, warm, and misty night, full of all the heavy perfumes of new vegetation not yet dried by hot sun, and among these particularly the scent of the fern. The lantern, dangling from Christian's hand, brushed the feathery fronds in passing by, disturbing moths and other winged insects, which flew out and alighted upon its horny panes.[7]

'So you have money to carry to Mrs. Wildeve?' said Christian's companion, after a silence. 'Don't you think it very odd that it shouldn't be given to me?'

'As man and wife be one flesh, 'twould have been all the same, I should think,' said Christian. 'But my strict documents[8] was, to give the money into Mrs. Wildeve's hand: and 'tis well to do things right.'

'No doubt,' said Wildeve. Any person who had known the circumstances might have perceived that Wildeve was mortified by the discovery that the matter in transit was money, and not, as he had supposed when at Blooms-End, some fancy nick-nack which only interested the two women themselves. Mrs. Yeobright's refusal implied that his honour was not considered to be of sufficiently good quality to make him a safe bearer of his wife's property.

'How very warm it is to-night, Christian!' he said, panting, when they were nearly under Rainbarrow. 'Let us sit down for a few minutes, for Heaven's sake.'

Wildeve flung himself down on the soft ferns; and Christian, placing the lantern and parcel on the ground, perched himself in a cramped position hard by, his knees almost touching his chin. He

7. Horn, cut so thin as to be semi-transparent, was used in lanterns instead of glass.
8. (Here) instructions.

presently thrust one hand into his coat-pocket and began shaking it about.

'What are you rattling in there?' said Wildeve.

'Only the dice, sir,' said Christian, quickly withdrawing his hand. 'What magical machines these little things be, Mr. Wildeve! 'Tis a game I should never get tired of. Would you mind my taking 'em out and looking at 'em for a minute, to see how they are made? I didn't like to look close before the other men, for fear they should think it bad manners in me.' Christian took them out and examined them in the hollow of his hand by the lantern light. 'That these little things should carry such luck, and such charm, and such a spell, and such power in 'em, passes all I ever heard or zeed,' he went on, with a fascinated gaze at the dice, which, as is frequently the case in country places, were made of wood, the points being burnt upon each face with the end of a wire.

'They are a great deal in a small compass, you think?'

'Yes. Do ye suppose they really be the devil's playthings, Mr. Wildeve? If so, 'tis no good sign that I be such a lucky man.'

'You ought to win some money, now that you've got them. Any woman would marry you then. Now is your time, Christian, and I would recommend you not to let it slip. Some men are born to luck, some are not. I belong to the latter class.'

'Did you ever know anybody who was born to it besides myself?'

'O yes. I once heard of an Italian, who sat down at a gaming-table with only a louis (that's a foreign sovereign) in his pocket. He played on for twenty-four hours, and won ten thousand pounds, stripping the bank he had played against. Then there was another man who had lost a thousand pounds, and went to the broker's next day to sell stock, that he might pay the debt. The man to whom he owed the money went with him in a hackney-coach; and to pass the time they tossed who should pay the fare. The ruined man won, and the other was tempted to continue the game, and they played all the way. When the coachman stopped he was told to drive home again: the whole thousand pounds had been won back by the man who was going to sell.'

'Ha—ha—splendid!' exclaimed Christian. 'Go on—go on!'

'Then there was a man of London, who was only a waiter at White's club-house.[9] He began playing first half-crown stakes, and then higher and higher, till he became very rich, got an appointment in India, and rose to be Governor of Madras.[1] His daughter married a member of parliament, and the Bishop of Carlisle stood godfather to one of the children.'

9. White's Club, one of the oldest gentleman's clubs and gambling houses in London.
1. In the 1878 edition, Wildeve names Sir Thomas Rumbold (1736–91), who became Governor of Madras in 1777; Rumbold's descendants protested that the story was untrue, and Hardy removed the name for the 1880 and later editions.

'Wonderful! wonderful!'

'And once there was a young man in America who gambled till he had lost his last dollar. He staked his watch and chain; and lost as before: staked his umbrella; lost again: staked his hat; lost again: staked his coat and stood in his shirt-sleeves; lost again. Began taking off his breeches, and then a looker-on gave him a trifle for his pluck. With this he won. Won back his coat, won back his hat, won back his umbrella, his watch, his money, and went out of the door a rich man.'

'O, 'tis too good—it takes away my breath! Mr. Wildeve, I think I will try another shilling with you, as I am one of that sort; no danger can come o't, and you can afford to lose.'

'Very well,' said Wildeve, rising. Searching about with the lantern, he found a large flat stone, which he placed between himself and Christian, and sat down again. The lantern was opened to give more light, and its rays directed upon the stone. Christian put down a shilling, Wildeve another, and each threw. Christian won. They played for two. Christian won again.

'Let us try four,' said Wildeve. They played for four. This time the stakes were won by Wildeve.

'Ah, those little accidents will, of course, sometimes happen to the luckiest man,' he observed.

'And now I have no more money!' exclaimed Christian excitedly. 'And yet, if I could go on, I should get it back again, and more. I wish this was mine.' He struck his boot upon the ground, so that the guineas chinked within.

'What! you have not put Mrs. Wildeve's money there?'

'Yes. 'Tis for safety. Is it any harm to raffle with a married lady's money when, if I win, I shall only keep my winnings, and give her her own all the same; and if t'other man wins, her money will go to the lawful owner?'

'None at all.'

Wildeve had been brooding ever since they started on the mean estimation in which he was held by his wife's friends; and it cut his heart severely. As the minutes passed he had gradually drifted into a revengeful intention without knowing the precise moment of forming it. This was to teach Mrs. Yeobright a lesson, as he considered it to be; in other words, to show her if he could, that her niece's husband was the proper guardian of her niece's money.

'Well, here goes!' said Christian, beginning to unlace one boot. 'I shall dream of it nights and nights, I suppose; but I shall always swear my flesh don't crawl when I think o't!'

He thrust his hand into the boot and withdrew one of poor Thomasin's precious guineas, piping hot. Wildeve had already placed a sovereign on the stone. The game was then resumed.

'The stakes were won by Wildeve.'

Wildeve won first, and Christian ventured another, winning himself this time. The game fluctuated, but the average was in Wildeve's favour. Both men became so absorbed in the game that they took no heed of anything but the pigmy objects immediately beneath their eyes; the flat stone, the open lantern, the dice, and the few illuminated fern-leaves which lay under the light, were the whole world to them.

At length Christian lost rapidly; and presently, to his horror, the whole fifty guineas belonging to Thomasin had been handed over to his adversary.

'I don't care—I don't care!' he moaned, and desperately set about untying his left boot to get at the other fifty. 'The devil will toss me into the flames on his three-pronged fork for this night's work, I know! But perhaps I shall win yet, and then I'll get a wife to sit up with me o' nights, and I won't be afeard, I won't! Here's another for'ee, my man!' He slapped another guinea down upon the stone, and the dice-box was rattled again.

Time passed on. Wildeve began to be as excited as Christian himself. When commencing the game his intention had been nothing further than a bitter practical joke on Mrs. Yeobright. To win the money, fairly or otherwise, and to hand it contemptuously to Thomasin in her aunt's presence, had been the dim outline of his purpose. But men are drawn from their intentions even in the course of carrying them out, and it was extremely doubtful, by the time the twentieth guinea had been reached, whether Wildeve was conscious of any other intention than that of winning for his own personal benefit. Moreover, he was now no longer gambling for his wife's money, but for Yeobright's; though of this fact Christian, in his apprehensiveness, did not inform him till afterwards.

It was nearly eleven o'clock, when, with almost a shriek, Christian placed Yeobright's last gleaming guinea upon the stone. In thirty seconds it had gone the way of its companions.

Christian turned and flung himself on the ferns in a convulsion of remorse. 'O, what shall I do with my wretched self?' he groaned. 'What shall I do? Will any good Heaven hae mercy upon my wicked soul?'

'Do? Live on just the same.'

'I won't live on just the same! I'll die! I say you are a—a——'

'A man sharper than my neighbour.'

'Yes, a man sharper than my neighbour; a regular sharper!'

'Poor chips-in-porridge,[2] you are very unmannerly.'

'I don't know about that! And I say you be unmannerly! You've got money that isn't your own. Half the guineas are poor Mr. Clym's.'

'How's that?'

'Because I had to gie fifty of 'em to him. Mrs. Yeobright said so.'

'Oh? . . . Well, 'twould have been more graceful of her to have given them to his wife Eustacia. But they are in my hands now.'

Christian pulled on his boots, and with heavy breathings, which could be heard to some distance, dragged his limbs together, arose; and tottered away out of sight. Wildeve set about shutting the lantern to return to the house, for he deemed it too late to go to Mistover to meet his wife, who was to be driven home in the captain's four-wheel. While he was closing the little horn door a figure rose from behind a neighbouring bush and came forward into the lantern light. It was the reddleman approaching.

A New Force Disturbs the Current

VIII

Wildeve stared. Venn looked coolly towards Wildeve, and, without a word being spoken, he deliberately sat himself down where Christian had been seated, thrust his hand into his pocket, drew out a sovereign, and laid it on the stone.

'You have been watching us from behind that bush?' said Wildeve.

The reddleman nodded. 'Down with your stake,' he said. 'Or haven't you pluck enough to go on?'

---

2. Proverbial expression for a person of no significance. Hardy also uses it in *Under the Greenwood Tree* (II.iv), where he added a note: "This, a local expression, must be a corruption of something less questionable."

Now, gambling is a species of amusement which is much more easily begun with full pockets than left off with the same; and though Wildeve in a cooler temper might have prudently declined this invitation, the excitement of his recent success carried him completely away. He placed one of the guineas on the slab beside the reddleman's sovereign. 'Mine is a guinea,' he said.

'A guinea that's not your own,' said Venn sarcastically.

'It is my own,' answered Wildeve haughtily. 'It is my wife's, and what is hers is mine.'

'Very well; let's make a beginning.' He shook the box, and threw eight, ten, and nine; the three casts amounted to twenty-seven.

This encouraged Wildeve. He took the box; and his three casts amounted to forty-five.

Down went another of the reddleman's sovereigns against his first one which Wildeve laid. This time Wildeve threw fifty-one points, but no pair. The reddleman looked grim, threw a raffle of aces,[1] and pocketed the stakes.

'Here you are again,' said Wildeve contemptuously. 'Double the stakes.' He laid two of Thomasin's guineas, and the reddleman his two pounds. Venn won again. New stakes were laid on the stone, and the gamblers proceeded as before.

Wildeve was a nervous and excitable man; and the game was beginning to tell upon his temper. He writhed, fumed, shifted his seat; and the beating of his heart was almost audible. Venn sat with lips impassively closed and eyes reduced to a pair of unimportant twinkles; he scarcely appeared to breathe. He might have been an Arab, or an automaton; he would have been like a red-sandstone statue but for the motion of his arm with the dice-box.

The game fluctuated, now in favour of one, now in favour of the other, without any great advantage on the side of either. Nearly twenty minutes were passed thus. The light of the candle had by this time attracted heath-flies, moths, and other winged creatures of night, which floated round the lantern, flew into the flame, or beat about the faces of the two players.

But neither of the men paid much attention to these things, their eyes being concentrated upon the little flat stone, which to them was an arena vast and important as a battle-field. By this time a change had come over the game; the reddleman won continually. At length sixty guineas—Thomasin's fifty, and ten of Clym's—had passed into his hands. Wildeve was reckless, frantic, exasperated.

' "Won back his coat," ' said Venn slily.

---

1. Three ones, or aces. A raffle, or a throw where all three dice have the same value, beats a pair; where neither is thrown, the highest total of points wins the game.

Another throw, and the money went the same way.

' "Won back his hat," ' continued Venn.

'Oh, oh!' said Wildeve.

' "Won back his watch, won back his money, and went out of the door a rich man," ' added Venn sentence by sentence, as stake after stake passed over to him.

'Five more!' shouted Wildeve, dashing down the money. 'And three casts be hanged—one shall decide.'

The red automaton opposite lapsed into silence, nodded, and followed his example. Wildeve rattled the box, and threw a pair of sixes and five points. He clapped his hands; 'I have done it this time—hurrah!'

'There are two playing, and only one has thrown,' said the reddleman, quietly bringing down the box. The eyes of each were then so intently converged upon the stone that one could fancy their beams were visible, like rays in a fog.

Venn lifted the box, and behold a triplet of sixes was disclosed.

Wildeve was full of fury. While the reddleman was grasping the stakes Wildeve seized the dice and hurled them, box and all, into the darkness, uttering a fearful imprecation. Then he arose and began stamping up and down like a madman.

'It is all over, then?' said Venn.

'No, no!' cried Wildeve. 'I mean to have another chance yet. I must!'

'But, my good man, what have you done with the dice?'

'I threw them away—it was a momentary irritation. What a fool I am! Here—come and help me to look for them—we must find them again.'

Wildeve snatched up the lantern and began anxiously prowling among the furze and fern.

'You are not likely to find them there,' said Venn, following. 'What did you do such a crazy thing as that for? Here's the box. The dice can't be far off.'

Wildeve turned the light eagerly upon the spot where Venn had found the box, and mauled the herbage right and left. In the course of a few minutes one of the dice was found. They searched on for some time, but no other was to be seen.

'Never mind,' said Wildeve; 'let's play with one.'

'Agreed,' said Venn.

Down they sat again, and recommenced with single guinea stakes; and the play went on smartly. But Fortune had unmistakably fallen in love with the reddleman to-night. He won steadily, till he was the owner of fourteen more of the gold pieces. Seventy-nine of the hundred guineas were his, Wildeve possessing only twenty-one.

The aspect of the two opponents was now singular. Apart from motions, a complete diorama[2] of the fluctuations of the game went on in their eyes. A diminutive candle-flame was mirrored in each pupil, and it would have been possible to distinguish therein between the moods of hope and the moods of abandonment, even as regards the reddleman, though his facial muscles betrayed nothing at all. Wildeve played on with the recklessness of despair.

'What's that?' he suddenly exclaimed, hearing a rustle; and they both looked up.

They were surrounded by dusky forms between four and five feet high, standing a few paces beyond the rays of the lantern. A moment's inspection revealed that the encircling figures were heath-croppers, their heads being all towards the players, at whom they gazed intently.

'Hoosh!' said Wildeve; and the whole forty or fifty animals at once turned and galloped away. Play was again resumed.

Ten minutes passed away. Then a large death's head moth[3] advanced from the obscure outer air, wheeled twice round the lantern, flew straight at the candle, and extinguished it by the force of the blow. Wildeve had just thrown, but had not lifted the box to see what he had cast; and now it was impossible.

'What the infernal!' he shrieked. 'Now, what shall we do? Perhaps I have thrown six—have you any matches?'

'None,' said Venn.

'Christian had some—I wonder where he is. Christian!'

But there was no reply to Wildeve's shout, save a mournful whining from the herons which were nesting lower down the vale. Both men looked blankly round without rising. As their eyes grew accustomed to the darkness they perceived faint greenish points of light among the grass and fern. These lights dotted the hillside like stars of a low magnitude.

'Ah—glowworms,'[4] said Wildeve. 'Wait a minute. We can continue the game.'

Venn sat still, and his companion went hither and thither till he had gathered thirteen glowworms—as many as he could find in a space of four or five minutes—upon a foxglove leaf which he pulled for the purpose. The reddleman vented a low humorous laugh when he saw his adversary return with these. 'Determined to go on, then?' he said drily.

2. The London Diorama, opened in 1823, featured huge pictures on transparent cloth, lit to suggest different effects of season and weather; subsequently the term was used for any spectacle with dramatic effects of light and sound.
3. The large hawkmoth has pale markings resembling a skull on the back of the thorax.
4. Beetles of the family Lampyridae; the wingless female emits a greenish light from its abdomen.

'I always am!' said Wildeve angrily. And shaking the glowworms from the leaf he ranged them with a trembling hand in a circle on the stone, leaving a space in the middle for the descent of the dice-box, over which the thirteen tiny lamps threw a pale phosphoric shine. The game was again renewed. It happened to be that season of the year at which glowworms put forth their greatest brilliancy, and the light they yielded was more than ample for the purpose, since it is possible on such nights to read the handwriting of a letter by the light of two or three.

The incongruity between the men's deeds and their environment was great. Amid the soft juicy vegetation of the hollow in which they sat, the motionless and the uninhabited solitude, intruded the chink of guineas, the rattle of dice, the exclamations of the reckless players.

Wildeve had lifted the box as soon as the lights were obtained, and the solitary die proclaimed that the game was still against him.

'I won't play any more: you've been tampering with the dice,' he shouted.

'How—when they were your own?' said the reddleman.

'We'll change the game: the lowest point shall win the stake—it may cut off my ill luck. Do you refuse?'

'No—go on,' said Venn.

'O, there they are again—damn them!' cried Wildeve, looking up. The heath-croppers had returned noiselessly, and were looking on with erect heads just as before, their timid eyes fixed upon the scene, as if they were wondering what mankind and candle-light could have to do in these haunts at this untoward hour.

'What a plague those creatures are—staring at me so!' he said, and flung a stone, which scattered them; when the game was continued as before.

Wildeve had now ten guineas left; and each laid five. Wildeve threw three points; Venn two, and raked in the coins. The other seized the die, and clenched his teeth upon it in sheer rage, as if he would bite it in pieces. 'Never give in—here are my last five!' he cried, throwing them down. 'Hang the glowworms—they are going out. Why don't you burn, you little fools? Stir them up with a thorn.'

He probed the glowworms with a bit of stick, and rolled them over, till the bright side of their tails was upwards.

'There's light enough. Throw on,' said Venn.

Wildeve brought down the box within the shining circle and looked eagerly. He had thrown ace. 'Well done!—I said it would turn, and it has turned.' Venn said nothing; but his hand shook slightly.

He threw ace also.

'O!' said Wildeve. 'Curse me!'

The die smacked the stone a second time. It was ace again. Venn looked gloomy, threw: the die was seen to be lying in two pieces, the cleft sides uppermost.

'I've thrown nothing at all,' he said.

'Serves me right—I split the die with my teeth. Here—take your money. Blank is less than one.'

'I don't wish it.'

'Take it, I say—you've won it!' And Wildeve threw the stakes against the reddleman's chest. Venn gathered them up, arose, and withdrew from the hollow, Wildeve sitting stupefied.

When he had come to himself he also arose, and, with the extinguished lantern in his hand, went towards the high-road. On reaching it he stood still. The silence of night pervaded the whole heath except in one direction; and that was towards Mistover. There he could hear the noise of light wheels, and presently saw two carriage-lamps descending the hill. Wildeve screened himself under a bush and waited.

The vehicle came on and passed before him. It was a hired carriage, and behind the coachman were two persons whom he knew well. There sat Eustacia and Yeobright, the arm of the latter being round her waist. They turned the sharp corner at the bottom towards the temporary home which Clym had hired and furnished, about five miles to the eastward.

Wildeve forgot the loss of the money at the sight of his lost love, whose preciousness in his eyes was increasing in geometrical progression with each new incident that reminded him of their hopeless division. Brimming with the subtilized misery that he was capable of feeling, he followed the opposite way towards the inn.

About the same moment that Wildeve stepped into the highway Venn also had reached it at a point a hundred yards further on; and he, hearing the same wheels, likewise waited till the carriage should come up. When he saw who sat therein he seemed to be disappointed. Reflecting a minute or two, during which interval the carriage rolled on, he crossed the road, and took a short cut through the furze and heath to a point where the turnpike-road bent round in ascending a hill. He was now again in front of the carriage, which presently came up at a walking pace. Venn stepped forward and showed himself.

Eustacia started when the lamp shone upon him, and Clym's arm was involuntarily withdrawn from her waist. He said, 'What, Diggory? You are having a lonely walk.'

'Yes—I beg your pardon for stopping you,' said Venn. 'But I am waiting about for Mrs. Wildeve: I have something to give her from Mrs. Yeobright. Can you tell me if she's gone home from the party yet?'

'No. But she will be leaving soon. You may possibly meet her at the corner.'

Venn made a farewell obeisance, and walked back to his former position, where the by-road from Mistover joined the highway. Here he remained fixed for nearly half an hour; and then another pair of lights came down the hill. It was the old-fashioned wheeled nondescript belonging to the captain, and Thomasin sat in it alone, driven by Charley.

The reddleman came up as they slowly turned the corner. 'I beg pardon for stopping you, Mrs. Wildeve,' he said. 'But I have something to give you privately from Mrs. Yeobright.' He handed a small parcel; it consisted of the hundred guineas he had just won, roughly twisted up in a piece of paper.

Thomasin recovered from her surprise, and took the packet. 'That's all, ma'am—I wish you goodnight,' he said, and vanished from her view.

Thus Venn, in his anxiety to rectify matters, had placed in Thomasin's hands not only the fifty guineas which rightly belonged to her, but also the fifty intended for her cousin Clym. His mistake had been based upon Wildeve's words at the opening of the game, when he indignantly denied that the guinea was not his own. It had not been comprehended by the reddleman that at half-way through the performance the game was continued with the money of another person; and it was an error which afterwards helped to cause more misfortune than treble the loss in money value could have done.

The night was now somewhat advanced; and Venn plunged deeper into the heath, till he came to a ravine where his van was standing—a spot not more than two hundred yards from the site of the gambling bout. He entered this movable home of his, lit his lantern, and, before closing his door for the night, stood reflecting on the circumstances of the preceding hours. While he stood the dawn grew visible in the north-east quarter of the heavens, which, the clouds having cleared off, was bright with a soft sheen at this midsummer time, though it was only between one and two o'clock. Venn, thoroughly weary, then shut his door and flung himself down to sleep.

Book Fourth. The Closed Door

The Rencounter by the Pool[1]

I

The July sun shone over Egdon and fired its crimson heather to scarlet. It was the one season of the year, and the one weather of the season, in which the heath was gorgeous. This flowering period represented the second or noontide division in the cycle of those superficial changes which alone were possible here; it followed the green or young-fern period, representing the morn, and preceded the brown period, when the heath-bells and ferns would wear the russet tinges of evening; to be in turn displaced by the dark hue of the winter period, representing night.

Clym and Eustacia, in their little house at Alderworth, beyond East Egdon, were living on with a monotony which was delightful to them. The heath and changes of weather were quite blotted out from their eyes for the present. They were enclosed in a sort of luminous mist, which hid from them surroundings of any inharmonious colour, and gave to all things the character of light. When it rained they were charmed, because they could remain indoors together all day with such a show of reason; when it was fine they were charmed, because they could sit together on the hills. They were like those double stars which revolve round and round each other, and from a distance appear to be one. The absolute solitude in which they lived intensified their reciprocal thoughts; yet some might have said that it had the disadvantage of consuming their mutual affections at a fearfully prodigal rate. Yeobright did not fear for his own part; but recollection of Eustacia's old speech about the evanescence of love, now apparently forgotten by her, sometimes caused him to ask himself a question; and he recoiled at the thought that the quality of finiteness was not foreign to Eden.

When three or four weeks had been passed thus, Yeobright resumed his reading in earnest. To make up for lost time he studied indefatigably, for he wished to enter his new profession with the least possible delay.

Now, Eustacia's dream had always been that, once married to Clym, she would have the power of inducing him to return to Paris. He had carefully withheld all promise to do so; but would he be proof against her coaxing and argument? She had calculated to such a degree on the probability of success that she had represented Paris, and not Budmouth, to her grandfather as in all likeli-

1. A rencounter is a meeting of hostile forces, as of a duel, battle, or collision.

hood their future home. Her hopes were bound up in this dream. In the quiet days since their marriage, when Yeobright had been poring over her lips, her eyes, and the lines of her face, she had mused and mused on the subject, even while in the act of returning his gaze; and now the sight of the books, indicating a future which was antagonistic to her dream, struck her with a positively painful jar. She was hoping for the time when, as the mistress of some pretty establishment, however small, near a Parisian Boulevard, she would be passing her days on the skirts at least of the gay world, and catching stray wafts from those town pleasures she was so well fitted to enjoy. Yet Yeobright was as firm in the contrary intention as if the tendency of marriage were rather to develop the fantasies of young philanthropy than to sweep them away.

Her anxiety reached a high pitch; but there was something in Clym's undeviating manner which made her hesitate before sounding him on the subject. At this point in their experience, however, an incident helped her. It occurred one evening about six weeks after their union, and arose entirely out of the unconscious misapplication by Venn of the fifty guineas intended for Yeobright.

A day or two after the receipt of the money Thomasin had sent a note to her aunt to thank her. She had been surprised at the largeness of the amount; but as no sum had ever been mentioned she set that down to her late uncle's generosity. She had been strictly charged by her aunt to say nothing to her husband of this gift; and Wildeve, as was natural enough, had not brought himself to mention to his wife a single particular of the midnight scene in the heath. Christian's terror, in like manner, had tied his tongue on the share he took in that proceeding; and hoping that by some means or other the money had gone to its proper destination, he simply asserted as much, without giving details.

Therefore, when a week or two had passed away, Mrs. Yeobright began to wonder why she never heard from her son of the receipt of the present; and to add gloom to her perplexity came the possibility that resentment might be the cause of his silence. She could hardly believe as much, but why did he not write? She questioned Christian, and the confusion in his answers would at once have led her to believe that something was wrong, had not one-half of his story been corroborated by Thomasin's note.

Mrs. Yeobright was in this state of uncertainty when she was informed one morning that her son's wife was visiting her grandfather at Mistover. She determined to walk up the hill, see Eustacia, and ascertain from her daughter-in-law's lips whether the family guineas, which were to Mrs. Yeobright what family jewels are to wealthier dowagers, had miscarried or not.

When Christian learnt where she was going his concern reached its height. At the moment of her departure he could prevaricate no longer, and, confessing to the gambling, told her the truth as far as he knew it—that the guineas had been won by Wildeve.

'What, is he going to keep them?' Mrs. Yeobright cried.

'I hope and trust not!' moaned Christian. 'He's a good man, and perhaps will do right things. He said you ought to have gied[2] Mr. Clym's share to Eustacia, and that's perhaps what he'll do himself.'

To Mrs. Yeobright, as soon as she could calmly reflect, there was much likelihood in this, for she could hardly believe that Wildeve would really appropriate money belonging to her son. The intermediate course of giving it to Eustacia was the sort of thing to please Wildeve's fancy. But it filled the mother with anger none the less. That Wildeve should have got command of the guineas after all, and should rearrange the disposal of them, placing Clym's share in Clym's wife's hands, because she had been his own sweetheart, and might be so still, was as irritating a pain as any that Mrs. Yeobright had ever borne.

She instantly dismissed the wretched Christian from her employ for his conduct in the affair; but, feeling quite helpless and unable to do without him, told him afterwards that he might say a little longer if he chose. Then she hastened off to Eustacia, moved by a much less promising emotion towards her daughter-in-law than she had felt half an hour earlier, when planning her journey. At that time it was to inquire in a friendly spirit if there had been any accidental loss; now it was to ask plainly if Wildeve had privately given her money which had been intended as a sacred gift to Clym.

She started at two o'clock, and her meeting with Eustacia was hastened by the appearance of the young lady beside the pool and bank which bordered her grandfather's premises, where she stood surveying the scene, and perhaps thinking of the romantic enactments it had witnessed in past days. When Mrs. Yeobright approached, Eustacia surveyed her with the calm stare of a stranger.

The mother-in-law was the first to speak. 'I was coming to see you,' she said.

'Indeed!' said Eustacia with surprise, for Mrs. Yeobright, much to the girl's mortification, had refused to be present at the wedding. 'I did not at all expect you.'

'I was coming on business only,' said the visitor, more coldly than at first. 'Will you excuse my asking this—Have you received a gift from Thomasin's husband?'[3]

'A gift?'

2. Given (dialect).
3. In the manuscript and serial versions, Mrs. Yeobright asks only if the money has been received, without mentioning Wildeve's name. The change goes some way to justify Eustacia's anger.

'I mean money!'

'What—I myself?'

'Well, I meant yourself, privately—though I was not going to put it in that way.'

'Money from Mr. Wildeve? No—never! Madam, what do you mean by that?' Eustacia fired up all too quickly, for her own consciousness of the old attachment between herself and Wildeve led her to jump to the conclusion that Mrs. Yeobright also knew of it, and might have come to accuse her of receiving dishonourable presents from him now.

'I simply ask the question,' said Mrs. Yeobright. 'I have been—'

'You ought to have better opinions of me—I feared you were against me from the first!' exclaimed Eustacia.

'No. I was simply for Clym,' replied Mrs. Yeobright, with too much emphasis in her earnestness. 'It is the instinct of every one to look after their own.'

'How can you imply that he required guarding against me?' cried Eustacia, passionate tears in her eyes. 'I have not injured him by marrying him! What sin have I done that you should think so ill of me? You had no right to speak against me to him when I have never wronged you.'

'I only did what was fair under the circumstances,' said Mrs. Yeobright more softly. 'I would rather not have gone into this question at present, but you compel me. I am not ashamed to tell you the honest truth. I was firmly convinced that he ought not to marry you—therefore I tried to dissuade him by all the means in my power. But it is done now, and I have no idea of complaining any more. I am ready to welcome you.'

'Ah, yes, it is very well to see things in that business point of view,' murmured Eustacia with a smothered fire of feeling. 'But why should you think there is anything between me and Mr. Wildeve?[4] I have a spirit as well as you. I am indignant; and so would any woman be. It was a condescension in me to be Clym's wife, and not a manœuvre, let me remind you; and therefore I will not be treated as a schemer whom it becomes necessary to bear with because she has crept into the family.'

'Oh!' said Mrs. Yeobright, vainly endeavouring to control her anger. 'I have never heard anything to show that my son's lineage is not as good as the Vyes'—perhaps better. It is amusing to hear you talk of condescension.'

'It was condescension, nevertheless,' said Eustacia vehemently. 'And if I had known then what I know now, that I should be living

---

4. This sentence too was not in the manuscript.

in this wild heath a month after my marriage, I—I should have thought twice before agreeing.'

'It would be better not to say that; it might not sound truthful. I am not aware that any deception was used on his part—I know there was not—whatever might have been the case on the other side.'

'This is too exasperating!' answered the younger woman huskily, her face crimsoning, and her eyes darting light. 'How can you dare to speak to me like that? I insist upon repeating to you that had I known that my life would from my marriage up to this time have been as it is, I should have said *No*. I don't complain. I have never uttered a sound of such a thing to him; but it is true. I hope therefore that in the future you will be silent on my eagerness. If you injure me now you injure yourself.'

'Injure you? Do you think I am an evil-disposed person?'

'You injured me before my marriage, and you have now suspected me of secretly favouring another man for money!'

'I could not help what I thought. But I have never spoken of you outside my house.'

'You spoke of me within it, to Clym, and you could not do worse.'

'I did my duty.'

'And I'll do mine.'

'A part of which will possibly be to set him against his mother. It is always so. But why should I not bear it as others have borne it before me!'

'I understand you,' said Eustacia, breathless with emotion. 'You think me capable of every bad thing. Who can be worse than a wife who encourages a lover, and poisons her husband's mind against his relative? Yet that is now the character given to me. Will you not come and drag him out of my hands?'

Mrs. Yeobright gave back heat for heat.

'Don't rage at me, madam! It ill becomes your beauty, and I am not worth the injury you may do it on my account, I assure you. I am only a poor old woman who has lost a son.'

'If you had treated me honourably you would have had him still,' Eustacia said, while scalding tears trickled from her eyes. 'You have brought yourself to folly; you have caused a division which can never he healed!'

'I have done nothing. This audacity from a young woman is more than I can bear.'

'It was asked for: you have suspected me, and you have made me speak of my husband in a way I would not have done. You will let him know that I have spoken thus, and it will cause misery between us. Will you go away from me? You are no friend!'

'I will go when I have spoken a word. If any one says I have come here to question you without good grounds for it, that person speaks untruly. If any one says that I attempted to stop your marriage by any but honest means, that person, too, does not speak the truth. I have fallen on an evil time; God has been unjust to me in letting you insult me! Probably my son's happiness does not lie on this side of the grave, for he is a foolish man who neglects the advice of his parent. You, Eustacia, stand on the edge of a precipice without knowing it. Only show my son one-half the temper you have shown me to-day—and you may before long—and you will find that though he is as gentle as a child with you now, he can be as hard as steel!'

The excited mother then withdrew, and Eustacia, panting, stood looking into the pool.

He Is Set upon by Adversities but He Sings a Song

II

The result of that unpropitious interview was that Eustacia, instead of passing the afternoon with her grandfather, hastily returned home to Clym, where she arrived three hours earlier than she had been expected.

She came indoors with her face flushed, and her eyes still showing traces of her recent excitement. Yeobright looked up astonished; he had never seen her in any way approaching to that state before. She passed him by, and would have gone upstairs unnoticed, but Clym was so concerned that he immediately followed her.

'What is the matter, Eustacia?' he said. She was standing on the hearthrug in the bedroom, looking upon the floor, her hands clasped in front of her, her bonnet yet unremoved. For a moment she did not answer; and then she replied in a low voice—

'I have seen your mother; and I will never see her again!'

A weight fell like a stone upon Clym. That same morning, when Eustacia had arranged to go and see her grandfather, Clym had expressed a wish that she would drive down to Blooms-End and inquire for her mother-in-law, or adopt any other means she might think fit to bring about a reconciliation. She had set out gaily; and he had hoped for much.

'Why is this?' he asked.

'I cannot tell—I cannot remember. I met your mother. And I will never meet her again.'

'Why?'

'What do I know about Mr. Wildeve now? I won't have wicked opinions passed on me by anybody. O! it was too humiliating to be asked if I had received any money from him, or encouraged him, or something of the sort—I don't exactly know what!'

'How could she have asked you that?'

'She did.'

'Then there must have been some meaning in it. What did my mother say besides?'

'I don't know what she said, except in so far as this, that we both said words which can never be forgiven!'

'O, there must be some misapprehension. Whose fault was it that her meaning was not made clear?'

'I would rather not say. It may have been the fault of the circumstances, which were awkward at the very least. O Clym—I cannot help expressing it—this is an unpleasant position that you have placed me in. But you must improve it—yes, say you will—for I hate it all now! Yes, take me to Paris, and go on with your old occupation, Clym! I don't mind how humbly we live there at first, if it can only be Paris, and not Egdon Heath.'

'But I have quite given up that idea,' said Yeobright, with surprise. 'Surely I never led you to expect such a thing?'

'I own it. Yet there are thoughts which cannot be kept out of mind, and that one was mine. Must I not have a voice in the matter, now I am your wife and the sharer of your doom?'

'Well, there are things which are placed beyond the pale of discussion; and I thought this was specially so, and by mutual agreement.'

'Clym, I am unhappy at what I hear,' she said in a low voice; and her eyes drooped, and she turned away.

This indication of an unexpected mine of hope in Eustacia's bosom disconcerted her husband. It was the first time that he had confronted the fact of the indirectness of a woman's movement towards her desire. But his intention was unshaken, though he loved Eustacia well. All the effect that her remark had upon him was a resolve to chain himself more closely than ever to his books, so as to be the sooner enabled to appeal to substantial results from another course in arguing against her whim.

Next day the mystery of the guineas was explained. Thomasin paid them a hurried visit, and Clym's share was delivered up to him by her own hands. Eustacia was not present at the time.

'Then this is what my mother meant,' exclaimed Clym. 'Thomasin, do you know that they have had a bitter quarrel?'

There was a little more reticence now than formerly in Thomasin's manner towards her cousin. It is the effect of marriage to engender in several directions some of the reserve it annihilates in one. 'Your mother told me,' she said quietly. 'She came back to my house after seeing Eustacia.'

'The worst thing I dreaded has come to pass. Was mother much disturbed when she came to you, Thomasin?'

'Yes.'

'Very much indeed?'

'Yes.'

Clym leant his elbow upon the post of the garden gate, and covered his eyes with his hand.

'Don't trouble about it, Clym. They may get to be friends.'

He shook his head. 'Not two people with inflammable natures like theirs. Well, what must be will be.'

'One thing is cheerful in it—the guineas are not lost.'

'I would rather have lost them twice over than have had this happen.'

Amid these jarring events Yeobright felt one thing to be indispensable—that he should speedily make some show of progress in his scholastic plans. With this view he read far into the small hours during many nights.

One morning, after a severer strain than usual, he awoke with a strange sensation in his eyes. The sun was shining directly upon the window-blind, and at his first glance thitherward a sharp pain obliged him to close his eyelids quickly. At every new attempt to look about him the same morbid sensibility to light was manifested, and excoriating tears ran down his cheeks. He was obliged to tie a bandage over his brow while dressing; and during the day it could not be abandoned. Eustacia was thoroughly alarmed. On finding that the case was no better the next morning they decided to send to Anglebury for a surgeon.

Towards evening he arrived, and pronounced the disease to be acute inflammation induced by Clym's night studies, continued in spite of a cold previously caught, which had weakened his eyes for the time.

Fretting with impatience at this interruption to a task he was so anxious to hasten, Clym was transformed into an invalid. He was shut up in a room from which all light was excluded, and his condition would have been one of absolute misery had not Eustacia read to him by the glimmer of a shaded lamp. He hoped that the worst would soon be over; but at the surgeon's third visit he learnt to his dismay that although he might venture out of doors with shaded eyes in the course of a month, all thought of pursuing his work, or of reading print of any description, would have to be given up for a long time to come.

One week and another week wore on, and nothing seemed to lighten the gloom of the young couple. Dreadful imaginings occurred to Eustacia, but she carefully refrained from uttering them to her husband. Suppose he should become blind, or, at all events, never recover sufficient strength of sight to engage in an occupation which would be congenial to her feelings, and conduce to her removal from this lonely dwelling among the hills? That dream of beautiful Paris was not likely to cohere into substance in the presence of this misfortune. As day after day passed by, and he got no better, her mind ran more and more in this mournful groove, and she would go away from him into the garden and weep despairing tears.

Yeobright thought he would send for his mother; and then he thought he would not. Knowledge of his state could only make her the more unhappy; and the seclusion of their life was such that she would hardly be likely to learn the news except through a special messenger. Endeavouring to take the trouble as philosophically as possible, he waited on till the third week had arrived, when he went into the open air for the first time since the attack. The surgeon visited him again at this stage, and Clym urged him to express a distinct opinion. The young man learnt with added surprise that the date at which he might expect to resume his labours was as uncertain as ever, his eyes being in that peculiar state which, though affording him sight enough for walking about, would not admit of their being strained upon any definite object without incurring the risk of reproducing ophthalmia[1] in its acute form.

Clym was very grave at the intelligence, but not despairing. A quiet firmness, and even cheerfulness, took possession of him. He was not to be blind; that was enough. To be doomed to behold the world through smoked glass for an indefinite period was bad enough, and fatal to any kind of advance; but Yeobright was an absolute stoic in the face of mishaps which only affected his social standing; and, apart from Eustacia, the humblest walk of life would satisfy him if it could be made to work in with some form of his culture scheme. To keep a cottage nightschool was one such form; and his affliction did not master his spirit as it might otherwise have done.

He walked through the warm sun westward into those tracts of Egdon with which he was best acquainted, being those lying nearer to his old home. He saw before him in one of the valleys the gleaming of whetted iron, and advancing, dimly perceived that the shine came from the tool of a man who was cutting furze. The worker recognized Clym, and Yeobright learnt from the voice that the speaker was Humphrey.

Humphrey expressed his sorrow at Clym's condition; and added, 'Now, if yours was low-class work like mine, you could go on with it just the same.'

---

1. A general term for an inflammation of the eye, rather than a specific complaint.

'Yes; I could,' said Yeobright musingly. 'How much do you get for cutting these faggots?'

'Half-a-crown a hundred, and in these long days I can live very well on the wages.'

During the whole of Yeobright's walk home to Alderworth he was lost in reflections which were not of an unpleasant kind. On his coming up to the house Eustacia spoke to him from the open window, and he went across to her.

'Darling,' he said, 'I am much happier. And if my mother were reconciled to me and to you I should, I think, be happy quite.'

'I fear that will never be,' she said, looking afar with her beautiful stormy eyes. 'How *can* you say "I am happier," and nothing changed?'

'It arises from my having at last discovered something I can do, and get a living at, in this time of misfortune.'

'Yes?'

'I am going to be a furze and turf cutter.'

'No, Clym!' she said, the slight hopefulness previously apparent in her face going off again, and leaving her worse than before.

'Surely I shall. Is it not very unwise in us to go on spending the little money we've got when I can keep down expenditure by an honest occupation? The outdoor exercise will do me good, and who knows but that in a few months I shall be able to go on with my reading again?'

'But my grandfather offers to assist us, if we require assistance.'

'We don't require it. If I go furze-cutting we shall be fairly well off.'

'In comparison with slaves, and the Israelites in Egypt,[2] and such people!' A bitter tear rolled down Eustacia's face, which he did not see. There had been *nonchalance* in his tone, showing her that he felt no absolute grief at a consummation which to her was a positive horror.

The very next day Yeobright went to Humphrey's cottage, and borrowed of him leggings, gloves, a whetstone, and a hook, to use till he should be able to purchase some for himself. Then he sallied forth with his new fellow-labourer and old acquaintance, and selecting a spot where the furze grew thickest he struck the first blow in his adopted calling. His sight, like the wings in 'Rasselas,'[3] though useless to him for his grand purpose, sufficed for this strait, and he found that when a little practice should have hardened his palms against blistering he would be able to work with ease.

2. Initially exiles in Egypt, the Israelites were later enslaved; see Exodus 1.8–14.
3. In Chapter VI of Samuel Johnson's didactic romance *Rasselas* (1759), an inventor tries to fly using artificial wings, only to fall into a lake; the wings, though of no use for flight, do keep him afloat in the water.

Day after day he rose with the sun, buckled on his leggings, and went off to the rendezvous with Humphrey. His custom was to work from four o'clock in the morning till noon; then, when the heat of the day was at its highest, to go home and sleep for an hour or two; afterwards coming out again and working till dusk at nine.

This man from Paris was now so disguised by his leather accoutrements, and by the goggles he was obliged to wear over his eyes, that his closest friend might have passed by without recognizing him. He was a brown spot in the midst of an expanse of olive-green gorse, and nothing more. Though frequently depressed in spirit when not actually at work, owing to thoughts of Eustacia's position and his mother's estrangement, when in the full swing of labour he was cheerfully disposed and calm.

His daily life was of a curious microscopic sort, his whole world being limited to a circuit of a few feet from his person. His familiars were creeping and winged things, and they seemed to enroll him in their band. Bees hummed around his ears with an intimate air, and tugged at the heath and furze-flowers at his side in such numbers as to weigh them down to the sod. The strange amber-coloured butterflies which Egdon produced, and which were never seen elsewhere, quivered in the breath of his lips, alighted upon his bowed back, and sported with the glittering point of his hook as he flourished it up and down. Tribes of emerald-green grasshoppers leaped over his feet, falling awkwardly on their backs, heads, or hips, like unskilful acrobats, as chance might rule; or engaged themselves in noisy flirtations under the fern-fronds with silent ones of homely hue. Huge flies, ignorant of larders and wire-netting, and quite in a savage state, buzzed about him without knowing that he was a man. In and out of the fern-dells snakes glided in their most brilliant blue and yellow guise, it being the season immediately following the shedding of their old skins, when their colours are brightest. Litters of young rabbits came out from their forms to sun themselves upon hillocks, the hot beams blazing through the delicate tissue of each thin-fleshed ear, and firing it to a blood-red transparency in which the veins could be seen. None of them feared him.

The monotony of his occupation soothed him, and was in itself a pleasure. A forced limitation of effort offered a justification of homely courses to an unambitious man, whose conscience would hardly have allowed him to remain in such obscurity while his powers were unimpeded. Hence Yeobright sometimes sang to himself, and when obliged to accompany Humphrey in search of brambles for faggot-bonds he would amuse his companion with sketches of Parisian life and character, and so while away the time.

On one of these warm afternoons Eustacia walked out alone in the direction of Yeobright's place of work. He was busily chopping away at the furze, a long row of faggots which stretched downward from his position representing the labour of the day. He did not observe her approach, and she stood close to him, and heard his undercurrent of song. It shocked her. To see him there, a poor afflicted man, earning money by the sweat of his brow, had at first moved her to tears; but to hear him sing and not at all rebel against an occupation which, however satisfactory to himself, was degrading to her, as an educated lady-wife, wounded her through. Unconscious of her presence he still went on singing:—

'Le point du jour
À nos bosquets rend toute leur parure;
  Flore est plus belle à son retour;
  L'oiseau reprend doux chant d'amour;
  Tout célébre dans la nature
    Le point du jour.

'Le point du jour
Cause parfois, cause douleur extrême;
  Que l'espace des nuits est court
  Pour le berger brûlant d'amour,
  Forcé de quitter ce qu'il aime
    Au point du jour!'[4]

It was bitterly plain to Eustacia that he did not care much about social failure; and the proud fair woman bowed her head and wept in sick despair at thought of the blasting effect upon her own life of that mood and condition in him. Then she came forward.

'I would starve rather than do it!' she exclaimed vehemently. 'And you can sing! I will go and live with my grandfather again!'

'Eustacia! I did not see you, though I noticed something moving,' he said gently. He came forward, pulled off his huge leather glove, and took her hand. 'Why do you speak in such a strange way? It is only a little old song which struck my fancy when I was in Paris, and now just applies to my life with you. Has your love for me all died, then, because my appearance is no longer that of a fine gentleman?'

'Dearest, you must not question me unpleasantly, or it may make me not love you.'

'Do you believe it possible that I would run the risk of doing that?'

4. From a French comic opera, *Gulistan* (1805), with music by Nicolas-Marie Dalayrac, and libretto by Charles-Guillaume Etienne and A.-E.-X. de la Chabeaussière. "The break of day restores all the beauty of our groves; Flora is more lovely at its return; the bird takes up a sweet song of love; everything in nature praises the break of day. The break of day sometimes brings great sorrow; how brief are the nights, for the shepherd burning with love, forced to leave the one he loves at the break of day!"

'Unconscious of her presence, he still went on singing.'

'Well, you follow out your own ideas, and won't give in to mine when I wish you to leave off this shameful labour. Is there anything you dislike in me that you act so contrarily to my wishes? I am your wife, and why will you not listen? Yes, I am your wife indeed!'

'I know what that tone means.'

'What tone?'

'The tone in which you said, "Your wife indeed." It meant, "Your wife, worse luck." '

'It is hard in you to probe me with that remark. A woman may have reason, though she is not without heart, and if I felt "worse luck," it was no ignoble feeling—it was only too natural. There, you see that at any rate I do not attempt untruths. Do you remember how, before we were married, I warned you that I had not good wifely qualities?'

'You mock me to say that now. On that point at least the only noble course would be to hold your tongue, for you are still queen of me, Eustacia, though I may no longer be king of you.'

'You are my husband. Does not that content you?'

'Not unless you are my wife without regret.'

'I cannot answer you. I remember saying that I should be a serious matter on your hands.'

'Yes, I saw that.'

'Then you were too quick to see! No true lover would have seen any such thing; you are too severe upon me, Clym—I don't like your speaking so at all.'

'Well, I married you in spite of it, and don't regret doing so. How cold you seem this afternoon! and yet I used to think there never was a warmer heart than yours.'

'Yes, I fear we are cooling—I see it as well as you,' she sighed mournfully. 'And how madly we loved two months ago! You were never tired of contemplating me, nor I of contemplating you. Who could have thought then that by this time my eyes would not seem so very bright to yours, nor your lips so very sweet to mine? Two months—is it possible? Yes, 'tis too true!'

'You sigh, dear, as if you were sorry for it; and that's a hopeful sign.'

'No. I don't sigh for that. There are other things for me to sigh for, or any other woman in my place.'

'That your chances in life are ruined by marrying in haste an unfortunate man?'

'Why will you force me, Clym, to say bitter things? I deserve pity as much as you. As much?—I think I deserve it more. For you can sing! It would be a strange hour which should catch me singing under such a cloud as this! Believe me, sweet, I could weep to a degree that would astonish and confound such an elastic mind as yours. Even had you felt careless about your own affliction, you might have refrained from singing out of sheer pity for mine. God! if I were a man in such a position I would curse rather than sing.'

Yeobright placed his hand upon her arm. 'Now, don't you suppose, my inexperienced girl, that I cannot rebel, in high Promethean fashion, against the gods and fate as well as you. I have felt more steam and smoke of that sort than you have ever heard of. But the more I see of life the more do I perceive that there is nothing particularly great in its greatest walks, and therefore nothing particularly small in mine of furze-cutting. If I feel that the greatest blessings vouchsafed to us are not very valuable, how can I feel it to be any great hardship when they are taken away? So I sing to pass the time. Have you indeed lost all tenderness for me, that you begrudge me a few cheerful moments?'

'I have still some tenderness left for you.'

'Your words have no longer their old flavour. And so love dies with good fortune!'

'I cannot listen to this, Clym—it will end bitterly,' she said in a broken voice. 'I will go home.'

She Goes out to Battle Against Depression

III

A few days later, before the month of August had expired, Eustacia and Yeobright sat together at their early dinner.

Eustacia's manner had become of late almost apathetic. There was a forlorn look about her beautiful eyes which, whether she deserved it or not, would have excited pity in the breast of any one who had known her during the full flush of her love for Clym. The feelings of husband and wife varied, in some measure, inversely with their positions. Clym, the afflicted man, was cheerful; and he even tried to comfort her, who had never felt a moment of physical suffering in her whole life.

'Come, brighten up, dearest; we shall be all right again. Some day perhaps I shall see as well as ever. And I solemnly promise that I'll leave off cutting furze as soon as I have the power to do anything better. You cannot seriously wish me to stay idling at home all day?'

'But it is so dreadful—a furze-cutter! and you a man who have lived about the world, and speak French, and German, and who are fit for what is so much better than this.'

'I suppose when you first saw me and heard about me I was wrapped in a sort of golden halo to your eyes—a man who knew glorious things, and had mixed in brilliant scenes—in short, an adorable, delightful, distracting hero?'

'Yes,' she said, sobbing.

'And now I am a poor fellow in brown leather.'

'Don't taunt me. But enough of this. I will not be depressed any more. I am going from home this afternoon, unless you greatly object. There is to be a village picnic—a gipsying, they call it—at East Egdon, and I shall go.'

'To dance?'

'Why not? You can sing.'

'Well, well, as you will. Must I come to fetch you?'

'If you return soon enough from your work. But do not inconvenience yourself about it. I know the way home, and the heath has no terror for me.'

'And can you cling to gaiety so eagerly as to walk all the way to a village festival in search of it?'

'Now, you don't like my going alone! Clym, you are not jealous?'

'No. But I would come with you if it could give you any pleasure; though, as things stand, perhaps you have too much of me already. Still, I somehow wish that you did not want to go. Yes, perhaps I am jealous; and who could be jealous with more reason than I, a half-blind man, over such a woman as you?'

'Don't think like it. Let me go, and don't take all my spirits away!'

'I would rather lose all my own, my sweet wife. Go and do whatever you like. Who can forbid your indulgence in any whim? You have all my heart yet, I believe; and because you bear with me, who am in truth a drag upon you, I owe you thanks. Yes, go alone and shine. As for me, I will stick to my doom. At that kind of meeting people would shun me. My hook and gloves are like the St. Lazarus rattle[1] of the leper, warning the world to get out of the way of a sight that would sadden them.' He kissed her, put on his leggings, and went out.

When he was gone she rested her head upon her hands and said to herself, 'Two wasted lives—his and mine. And I am come to this! Will it drive me out of my mind?'

She cast about for any possible course which offered the least improvement on the existing state of things, and could find none. She imagined how all those Budmouth ones who should learn what had become of her would say, 'Look at the girl for whom nobody was good enough!' To Eustacia the situation seemed such a mockery of her hopes that death appeared the only door of relief if the satire of Heaven should go much further.

Suddenly she aroused herself and exclaimed, 'But I'll shake it off. Yes, I *will* shake it off! No one shall know my suffering. I'll be bitterly merry, and ironically gay, and I'll laugh in derision! And I'll begin by going to this dance on the green.'

She ascended to her bedroom and dressed herself with scrupulous care. To an onlooker her beauty would have made her feelings almost seem reasonable. The gloomy corner into which accident as much as indiscretion had brought this woman might have led even a moderate partisan to feel that she had cogent reasons for asking the Supreme Power by what right a being of such exquisite finish had been placed in circumstances calculated to make of her charms a curse rather than a blessing.

1. Lazarus, the beggar covered in sores in Christ's parable about the rich and the poor (Luke 16.19–31), was adopted in the middle ages as the patron saint of lepers, who used bells or rattles to warn others to keep away.

It was five in the afternoon when she came out from the house ready for her walk. There was material enough in the picture for twenty new conquests. The rebellious sadness that was rather too apparent when she sat indoors without a bonnet was cloaked and softened by her outdoor attire, which always had a sort of nebulousness about it, devoid of harsh edges anywhere; so that her face looked from its environment as from a cloud, with no noticeable lines of demarcation between flesh and clothes. The heat of the day had scarcely declined as yet, and she went along the sunny hills at a leisurely pace, there being ample time for her idle expedition. Tall ferns buried her in their leafage whenever her path lay through them, which now formed miniature forests, though not one stem of them would remain to bud the next year.

The site chosen for the village festivity was one of the lawn-like oases which were occasionally, yet not often, met with on the plateaux of the heath district. The brakes of furze and fern terminated abruptly round the margin, and the grass was unbroken. A green cattle-track skirted the spot, without, however, emerging from the screen of fern, and this path Eustacia followed, in order to reconnoitre the group before joining it. The lusty notes of the East Egdon band had directed her unerringly, and she now beheld the musicians themselves, sitting in a blue waggon with red wheels scrubbed as bright as new, and arched with sticks, to which boughs and flowers were tied. In front of this was the grand central dance of fifteen or twenty couples, flanked by minor dances of inferior individuals whose gyrations were not always in strict keeping with the tune.

The young men wore blue and white rosettes, and with a flush on their faces footed it to the girls, who, with the excitement and the exercise, blushed deeper than the pink of their numerous ribbons. Fair ones with long curls, fair ones with short curls, fair ones with love-locks,[2] fair ones with braids, flew round and round; and a beholder might well have wondered how such a prepossessing set of young women of like size, age, and disposition, could have been collected together where there were only one or two villages to choose from. In the background was one happy man dancing by himself, with closed eyes, totally oblivious of all the rest. A fire was burning under a pollard thorn[3] a few paces off, over which three kettles hung in a row. Hard by was a table where elderly dames prepared tea, but Eustacia looked among them in vain for the cattle-dealer's wife who had suggested that she should come, and had promised to obtain a courteous welcome for her.

This unexpected absence of the only local resident whom Eusta-

2. Curls of hair, sometimes artificial, worn on the forehead.
3. A pollard is a tree which has been polled, or cut back.

cia knew considerably damaged her scheme for an afternoon of reckless gaiety. Joining in became a matter of difficulty, notwithstanding that, were she to advance, cheerful dames would come forward with cups of tea and make much of her as a stranger of superior grace and knowledge to themselves. Having watched the company through the figures of two dances, she decided to walk a little further, to a cottage where she might get some refreshment, and then return homeward in the shady time of evening.

This she did; and by the time that she retraced her steps towards the scene of the gipsying, which it was necessary to repass on her way to Alderworth, the sun was going down. The air was now so still that she could hear the band afar off, and it seemed to be playing with more spirit, if that were possible, than when she had come away. On reaching the hill the sun had quite disappeared; but this made little difference either to Eustacia or to the revellers, for a round yellow moon was rising before her, though its rays had not yet outmastered those from the west. The dance was going on just the same, but strangers had arrived and formed a ring around the figure, so that Eustacia could stand among these without a chance of being recognized.

A whole village-full of sensuous emotion, scattered abroad all the year long, surged here in a focus for an hour. The forty hearts of those waving couples were beating as they had not done since, twelve months before, they had come together in similar jollity. For the time Paganism was revived in their hearts, the pride of life[4] was all in all, and they adored none other than themselves.

How many of those impassioned but temporary embraces were destined to become perpetual was possibly the wonder of some of those who indulged in them, as well as of Eustacia who looked on. She began to envy those pirouetters, to hunger for the hope and happiness which the fascination of the dance seemed to engender within them. Desperately fond of dancing herself, one of Eustacia's expectations of Paris had been the opportunity it might afford her of indulgence in this favourite pastime. Unhappily, that expectation was now extinct within her for ever.

Whilst she abstractedly watched them spinning and fluctuating in the increasing moonlight she suddenly heard her name whispered by a voice over her shoulder. Turning in surprise, she beheld at her elbow one whose presence instantly caused her to flush to the temples.

It was Wildeve. Till this moment he had not met her eye since the morning of his marriage, when she had been loitering in the church, and had startled him by lifting her veil and coming forward

---

4. Perhaps alluding to 1 John 2.16: "For all that is in the world, the lust of the flesh, and the lust of the eyes, and the pride of life, is not of the Father, but is of the world."

to sign the register as witness. Yet why the sight of him should have instigated that sudden rush of blood she could not tell.

Before she could speak he whispered, 'Do you like dancing as much as ever?'

'I think I do,' she replied in a low voice.

'Will you dance with me?'

'It would be a great change for me; but will it not seem strange?'

'What strangeness can there be in relations dancing together?'

'Ah—yes, relations. Perhaps none.'

'Still, if you don't like to be seen, pull down your veil; though there is not much risk of being known by this light. Lots of strangers are here.'

She did as he suggested; and the act was a tacit acknowledgment that she accepted his offer.

Wildeve gave her his arm and took her down on the outside of the ring to the bottom of the dance, which they entered. In two minutes more they were involved in the figure and began working their way upwards to the top. Till they had advanced half-way thither Eustacia wished more than once that she had not yielded to his request; from the middle to the top she felt that, since she had come out to seek pleasure, she was only doing a natural thing to obtain it. Fairly launched into the ceaseless glides and whirls which their new position as top couple opened up to them, Eustacia's pulses began to move too quickly for longer rumination of any kind.

Through the length of five-and-twenty couples they threaded their giddy way, and a new vitality entered her form. The pale ray of evening lent a fascination to the experience. There is a certain degree and tone of light which tends to disturb the equilibrium of the senses, and to promote dangerously the tenderer moods; added to movement, it drives the emotions to rankness, the reason becoming sleepy and unperceiving in inverse proportion; and this light fell now upon these two from the disc of the moon. All the dancing girls felt the symptoms, but Eustacia most of all. The grass under their feet became trodden away, and the hard, beaten surface of the sod, when viewed aslant towards the moonlight, shone like a polished table. The air became quite still; the flag above the waggon which held the musicians clung to the pole, and the players appeared only in outline against the sky; except when the circular mouths of the trombone, ophicleide,[5] and French horn gleamed out like huge eyes from the shade of their figures. The pretty dresses of the maids lost their subtler day colours and showed more or less of a misty white. Eustacia floated round and round on Wildeve's arm, her face rapt and statuesque; her soul had passed

5. A deep-toned, brass instrument, part of the family of keyed bugles invented in the early nineteenth century.

away from and forgotten her features, which were left empty and quiescent, as they always are when feeling goes beyond their register.

How near she was to Wildeve! it was terrible to think of. She could feel his breathing, and he, of course, could feel hers. How badly she had treated him! yet, here they were treading one measure. The enchantment of the dance surprised her. A clear line of difference divided like a tangible fence her experience within this maze of motion from her experience without it. Her beginning to dance had been like a change of atmosphere; outside, she had been steeped in arctic frigidity by comparison with the tropical sensations here. She had entered the dance from the troubled hours of her late life as one might enter a brilliant chamber after a night walk in a wood. Wildeve by himself would have been merely an agitation; Wildeve added to the dance, and the moonlight, and the secrecy, began to be a delight. Whether his personality supplied the greater part of this sweetly compounded feeling, or whether the dance and the scene weighed the more therein, was a nice point upon which Eustacia herself was entirely in a cloud.

People began to say 'Who are they?' but no invidious inquiries were made. Had Eustacia mingled with the other girls in their ordinary daily walks the case would have been different: here she was not inconvenienced by excessive inspection, for all were wrought to their brightest grace by the occasion. Like the planet Mercury surrounded by the lustre of sunset, her permanent brilliancy passed without much notice in the temporary glory of the situation.

As for Wildeve, his feelings are easy to guess. Obstacles were a ripening sun to his love, and he was at this moment in a delirium of exquisite misery. To clasp as his for five minutes what was another man's through all the rest of the year was a kind of thing he of all men could appreciate. He had long since begun to sigh again for Eustacia; indeed, it may be asserted that signing the marriage register with Thomasin was the natural signal to his heart to return to its first quarters, and that the extra complication of Eustacia's marriage was the one addition required to make that return compulsory.

Thus, for different reasons, what was to the rest an exhilarating movement was to these two a riding upon the whirlwind. The dance had come like an irresistible attack upon whatever sense of social order there was in their minds, to drive them back into old paths which were now doubly irregular. Through three dances in succession they spun their way; and then, fatigued with the incessant motion, Eustacia turned to quit the circle in which she had already remained too long. Wildeve led her to a grassy mound a few yards distant, where she sat down, her partner standing beside her.

From the time that he addressed her at the beginning of the dance till now they had not exchanged a word.

'The dance and the walking have tired you?' he said tenderly.

'No; not greatly.'

'It is strange that we should have met here of all places, after missing each other so long.'

'We have missed because we tried to miss, I suppose.'

'Yes. But you began that proceeding—by breaking a promise.'

'It is scarcely worth while to talk of that now. We have formed other ties since then—you no less than I.'

'I am sorry to hear that your husband is ill.'

'He is not ill—only incapacitated.'

'Yes: that is what I mean. I sincerely sympathize with you in your trouble. Fate has treated you cruelly.'

She was silent awhile. 'Have you heard that he has chosen to work as a furze-cutter?' she said in a low, mournful voice.

'It has been mentioned to me,' answered Wildeve hesitatingly. 'But I hardly believed it.'

'It is true. What do you think of me as a furze-cutter's wife?'

'I think the same as ever of you, Eustacia. Nothing of that sort can degrade you: you ennoble the occupation of your husband.'

'I wish I could feel it.'

'Is there any chance of Mr. Yeobright getting better?'

'He thinks so. I doubt it.'

'I was quite surprised to hear that he had taken a cottage. I thought, in common with other people, that he would have taken you off to a home in Paris immediately after you had married him. "What a gay, bright future she has before her!" I thought. He will, I suppose, return there with you, if his sight gets strong again?'

Observing that she did not reply he regarded her more closely. She was almost weeping. Images of a future never to be enjoyed, the revived sense of her bitter disappointment, the picture of the neighbours' suspended ridicule which was raised by Wildeve's words, had been too much for proud Eustacia's equanimity.

Wildeve could hardly control his own too forward feelings when he saw her silent perturbation. But he affected not to notice this, and she soon recovered her calmness.

'You did not intend to walk home by yourself?' he asked.

'O yes,' said Eustacia. 'What could hurt me on this heath, who have nothing?'

'By diverging a little I can make my way home the same as yours. I shall be glad to keep you company as far as Throope Corner.' Seeing that Eustacia sat on in hesitation he added, 'Perhaps you think it unwise to be seen in the same road with me after the events of last summer?'

'Indeed I think no such thing,' she said haughtily. 'I shall accept whose company I choose, for all that may be said by the miserable inhabitants of Egdon.'

'Then let us walk on—if you are ready. Our nearest way is towards that holly-bush with the dark shadow that you see down there.'

Eustacia arose, and walked beside him in the direction signified, brushing her way over the damping heath and fern, and followed by the strains of the merrymakers, who still kept up the dance. The moon had now waxed bright and silvery, but the heath was proof against such illumination, and there was to be observed the striking scene of a dark, rayless tract of country under an atmosphere charged from its zenith to its extremities with whitest light. To an eye above them their two faces would have appeared amid the expanse like two pearls on a table of ebony.

On this account the irregularities of the path were not visible, and Wildeve occasionally stumbled; whilst Eustacia found it necessary to perform some graceful feats of balancing whenever a small tuft of heather or root of furze protruded itself through the grass of the narrow track and entangled her feet. At these junctures in her progress a hand was invariably stretched forward to steady her, holding her firmly until smooth ground was again reached, when the hand was again withdrawn to a respectful distance.

They performed the journey for the most part in silence, and drew near to Throope Corner, a few hundred yards from which a short path branched away to Eustacia's house. By degrees they discerned coming towards them a pair of human figures, apparently of the male sex.

When they came a little nearer Eustacia broke the silence by saying, 'One of those men is my husband. He promised to come to meet me.'

'And the other is my greatest enemy,' said Wildeve.

'It looks like Diggory Venn.'

'That is the man.'

'It is an awkward meeting,' said she; 'but such is my fortune. He knows too much about me, unless he could know more, and so prove to himself that what he now knows counts for nothing. Well, let it be: you must deliver me up to them.'

'You will think twice before you direct me to do that. Here is a man who has not forgotten an item in our meeting at Rainbarrow: he is in company with your husband. Which of them, seeing us together here, will believe that our meeting and dancing at the gipsy-party was by chance?'

'Very well,' she whispered gloomily. 'Leave me before they come up.'

Wildeve bade her a tender farewell, and plunged across the fern and furze, Eustacia slowly walking on. In two or three minutes she met her husband and his companion.

'My journey ends here for to-night, reddleman,' said Yeobright as soon as he perceived her. 'I turn back with this lady. Good night.'

'Good night, Mr. Yeobright,' said Venn. 'I hope to see you better soon.'

The moonlight shone directly upon Venn's face as he spoke, and revealed all its lines to Eustacia. He was looking suspiciously at her. That Venn's keen eye had discerned what Yeobright's feeble vision had not—a man in the act of withdrawing from Eustacia's side—was within the limits of the probable.

If Eustacia had been able to follow the reddleman she would soon have found striking confirmation of her thought. No sooner had Clym given her his arm and led her off the scene than the reddleman turned back from the beaten track toward East Egdon, whither he had been strolling merely to accompany Clym in his walk, Diggory's van being again in the neighbourhood. Stretching out his long legs he crossed the pathless portion of the heath somewhat in the direction which Wildeve had taken. Only a man accustomed to nocturnal rambles could at this hour have descended those shaggy slopes with Venn's velocity without falling headlong into a pit, or snapping off his leg by jamming his foot into some rabbit-burrow. But Venn went on without much inconvenience to himself, and the course of his scamper was towards the Quiet Woman Inn. This place he reached in about half an hour, and he was well aware that no person who had been near Throope Corner when he started could have got down here before him.

The lonely inn was not yet closed, though scarcely an individual was there, the business done being chiefly with travellers who passed the inn on long journeys, and these had now gone on their way. Venn went to the public room, called for a mug of ale, and inquired of the maid in an indifferent tone if Mr. Wildeve was at home.

Thomasin sat in an inner room and heard Venn's voice. When customers were present she seldom showed herself, owing to her inherent dislike for the business; but perceiving that no one else was there to-night she came out.

'He is not at home yet, Diggory,' she said pleasantly. 'But I expected him sooner. He has been to East Egdon to buy a horse.'

'Did he wear a light wideawake?'[6]

'Yes.'

'Then I saw him at Throope Corner, leading one home,' said Venn drily. 'A beauty, with a white face and a mane as black as

6. Felt hat with a broad brim and low crown.

night. He will soon be here, no doubt.' Rising and looking for a moment at the pure, sweet face of Thomasin, over which a shadow of sadness had passed since the time when he had last seen her, he ventured to add, 'Mr. Wildeve seems to be often away at this time.'

'O yes,' cried Thomasin in what was intended to be a tone of gaiety. 'Husbands will play the truant, you know. I wish you could tell me of some secret plan that would help me to keep him home at my will in the evenings.'

'I will consider if I know of one,' replied Venn in that same light tone which meant no lightness. And then he bowed in a manner of his own invention and moved to go. Thomasin offered him her hand; and without a sigh, though with food for many, the reddleman went out.

When Wildeve returned, a quarter of an hour later, Thomasin said simply, and in the abashed manner usual with her now, 'Where is the horse, Damon?'

'O, I have not bought it, after all. The man asks too much.'

'But somebody saw you at Throope Corner leading it home—a beauty, with a white face and a mane as black as night.'

'Ah!' said Wildeve, fixing his eyes upon her; 'who told you that?'

'Venn the reddleman.'

The expression of Wildeve's face became curiously condensed. 'That is a mistake—it must have been some one else,' he said slowly and testily, for he perceived that Venn's counter-moves had begun again.

Rough Coercion Is Employed

IV

Those words of Thomasin, which seemed so little, but meant so much, remained in the ears of Diggory Venn: 'Help me to keep him home in the evenings.'

On this occasion Venn had arrived on Egdon Heath only to cross to the other side: he had no further connection with the interests of the Yeobright family, and he had a business of his own to attend to. Yet he suddenly began to feel himself drifting into the old track of manœuvring on Thomasin's account.

He sat in his van and considered. From Thomasin's words and manner he had plainly gathered that Wildeve neglected her. For whom could he neglect her if not for Eustacia? Yet it was scarcely credible that things had come to such a head as to indicate that Eustacia systematically encouraged him. Venn resolved to reconnoitre somewhat carefully the lonely road which led along the vale from Wildeve's dwelling to Clym's house at Alderworth.

At this time, as has been seen, Wildeve was quite innocent of any predetermined act of intrigue, and except at the dance on the green he had not once met Eustacia since her marriage. But that the spirit of intrigue was in him had been shown by a recent romantic habit of his: a habit of going out after dark and strolling towards Alderworth, there looking at the moon and stars, looking at Eustacia's house, and walking back at leisure.

Accordingly, when watching on the night after the festival, the reddleman saw him ascend by the little path, lean over the front gate of Clym's garden, sigh, and turn to go back again. It was plain that Wildeve's intrigue was rather ideal than real. Venn retreated before him down the hill to a place where the path was merely a deep groove between the heather; here he mysteriously bent over the ground for a few minutes, and retired. When Wildeve came on to that spot his ankle was caught by something, and he fell headlong.

As soon as he had recovered the power of respiration he sat up and listened. There was not a sound in the gloom beyond the spiritless stir of the summer wind. Feeling about for the obstacle which had flung him down, he discovered that two tufts of heath had been tied together across the path, forming a loop, which to a traveller was certain overthrow. Wildeve pulled off the string that bound them, and went on with tolerable quickness. On reaching home he found the cord to be of a reddish colour. It was just what he had expected.

Although his weaknesses were not specially those akin to physical fear, this species of *coup-de-Jarnac*[1] from one he knew too well troubled the mind of Wildeve. But his movements were unaltered thereby. A night or two later he again went along the vale to Alderworth, taking the precaution of keeping out of any path. The sense that he was watched, that craft was employed to circumvent his errant tastes, added piquancy to a journey so entirely sentimental, so long as the danger was of no fearful sort. He imagined that Venn and Mrs. Yeobright were in league, and felt that there was a certain legitimacy in combating such a coalition.

The heath to-night appeared to be totally deserted; and Wildeve, after looking over Eustacia's garden gate for some little time, with a cigar in his mouth, was tempted by the fascination that emotional smuggling had for his nature to advance towards the window, which was not quite closed, the blind being only partly drawn down. He could see into the room, and Eustacia was sitting there alone. Wildeve contemplated her for a minute, and then retreating into the heath beat the ferns lightly, whereupon moths flew out

---

1. Entry 613 in Hardy's *Literary Notebooks* (I.63), taken from Charles Mackay's *Memoirs of Extraordinary Delusions*, explains this as "a sly & unexpected blow so called from a duel."

alarmed. Securing one, he returned to the window, and holding the moth to the chink, opened his hand. The moth made towards the candle upon Eustacia's table, hovered round it two or three times, and flew into the flame.

Eustacia started up. This had been a well-known signal in old times when Wildeve had used to come secretly wooing to Mistover. She at once knew that Wildeve was outside, but before she could consider what to do her husband came in from upstairs. Eustacia's face burnt crimson at the unexpected collision of incidents, and filled with an animation that it too frequently lacked.

'You have a very high colour, dearest,' said Yeobright, when he came close enough to see it. 'Your appearance would be no worse if it were always so.'

'I am warm,' said Eustacia. 'I think I will go into the air for a few minutes.'

'Shall I go with you?'

'O no. I am only going to the gate.'

She arose, but before she had time to get out of the room a loud rapping began upon the front door.

'I'll go—I'll go,' said Eustacia in an unusually quick tone for her; and she glanced eagerly towards the window whence the moth had flown; but nothing appeared there.

'You had better not at this time of the evening,' he said. Clym stepped before her into the passage, and Eustacia waited, her somnolent manner covering her inner heat and agitation.

She listened, and Clym opened the door. No words were uttered outside, and presently he closed it and came back, saying, 'Nobody was there. I wonder what that could have meant?'

He was left to wonder during the rest of the evening, for no explanation offered itself, and Eustacia said nothing, the additional fact that she knew of only adding more mystery to the performance.

Meanwhile a little drama had been acted outside which saved Eustacia from all possibility of compromising herself that evening at least. Whilst Wildeve had been preparing his moth-signal another person had come behind him up to the gate. This man, who carried a gun in his hand, looked on for a moment at the other's operation by the window, walked up to the house, knocked at the door, and then vanished round the corner and over the hedge.

'Damn him!' said Wildeve. 'He has been watching me again.'

As his signal had been rendered futile by this uproarious rapping Wildeve withdrew, passed out at the gate, and walked quickly down the path without thinking of anything except getting away unnoticed. Half-way down the hill the path ran near a knot of stunted hollies, which in the general darkness of the scene stood as the pupil in a black eye. When Wildeve reached this point a report startled his ear, and a few spent gunshots fell among the leaves around him.

There was no doubt that he himself was the cause of that gun's discharge; and he rushed into the clump of hollies, beating the bushes furiously with his stick; but nobody was there. This attack was a more serious matter than the last, and it was some time before Wildeve recovered his equanimity. A new and most unpleasant system of menace had begun, and the intent appeared to be to do him grievous bodily harm. Wildeve had looked upon Venn's first attempt as a species of horse-play, which the reddleman had indulged in for want of knowing better; but now the boundary-line was passed which divides the annoying from the perilous.

Had Wildeve known how thoroughly in earnest Venn had become he might have been still more alarmed. The reddleman had been almost exasperated by the sight of Wildeve outside Clym's house, and he was prepared to go to any lengths short of absolutely shooting him, to terrify the young innkeeper out of his recalcitrant impulses. The doubtful legitimacy of such rough coercion did not disturb the mind of Venn. It troubles few such minds in such cases, and sometimes this is not to be regretted. From the impeachment of Strafford[2] to Farmer Lynch's short way with the scamps of Virginia[3] there have been many triumphs of justice which are mockeries of law.

About half a mile below Clym's secluded dwelling lay a hamlet where lived one of the two constables who preserved the peace in the parish of Alderworth, and Wildeve went straight to the constable's cottage. Almost the first thing that he saw on opening the door was the constable's truncheon hanging to a nail, as if to assure him that here were the means to his purpose. On inquiry, however, of the constable's wife he learnt that the constable was not at home. Wildeve said he would wait.

The minutes ticked on, and the constable did not arrive. Wildeve cooled down from his state of high indignation to a restless dissatisfaction with himself, the scene, the constable's wife, and the whole set of circumstances. He arose and left the house. Altogether, the experience of that evening had had a cooling, not to say a chilling, effect on misdirected tenderness, and Wildeve was in no mood to ramble again to Alderworth after nightfall in hope of a stray glance from Eustacia.

2. The impeachment and execution in 1641 of Thomas Wentworth, Earl of Strafford and a valued councillor to Charles I, was based on evidence deliberately misrepresented by his and the king's political opponents.
3. Charles Lynch (1736–96), a justice of the peace in Virginia, instituted extralegal trials and the summary execution of those who remained loyal to Britain during the American Revolutionary War. Neither of the examples offered by the narrator in fact suggests "triumphs of justice."

Thus far the reddleman had been tolerably successful in his rude contrivances for keeping down Wildeve's inclination to rove in the evening. He had nipped in the bud the possible meeting between Eustacia and her old lover this very night. But he had not anticipated that the tendency of his action would be to divert Wildeve's movement rather than to stop it. The gambling with the guineas had not conduced to make him a welcome guest to Clym; but to call upon his wife's relative was natural, and he was determined to see Eustacia. It was necessary to choose some less untoward hour than ten o'clock at night. 'Since it is unsafe to go in the evening,' he said, 'I'll go by day.'

Meanwhile Venn had left the heath and gone to call upon Mrs. Yeobright, with whom he had been on friendly terms since she had learnt what a providential counter-move he had made towards the restitution of the family guineas. She wondered at the lateness of his call, but had no objection to see him.

He gave her a full account of Clym's affliction, and of the state in which he was living; then, referring to Thomasin, touched gently upon the apparent sadness of her days. 'Now, ma'am, depend upon it,' he said, 'you couldn't do a better thing for either of 'em than to make yourself at home in their houses, even if there should be a little rebuff at first.'

'Both she and my son disobeyed me in marrying; therefore I have no interest in their households. Their troubles are of their own making.' Mrs. Yeobright tried to speak severely; but the account of her son's state had moved her more than she cared to show.

'Your visits would make Wildeve walk straighter than he is inclined to do, and might prevent unhappiness down the heath.'

'What do you mean?'

'I saw something to-night out there which I didn't like at all. I wish your son's house and Mr. Wildeve's were a hundred miles apart instead of four or five.'

'Then there *was* an understanding between him and Clym's wife when he made a fool of Thomasin!'

'We'll hope there's no understanding now.'

'And our hope will probably be very vain. O Clym! O Thomasin!'

'There's no harm done yet. In fact, I've persuaded Wildeve to mind his own business.'

'How?'

'O, not by talking—by a plan of mine called the silent system.'

'I hope you'll succeed.'

'I shall if you help me by calling and making friends with your son. You'll have a chance then of using your eyes.'

'Well, since it has come to this,' said Mrs. Yeobright sadly, 'I will own to you, reddleman, that I thought of going. I should be much happier if we were reconciled. The marriage is unalterable, my life may be cut short, and I should wish to die in peace. He is my only son; and since sons are made of such stuff I am not sorry I have no other. As for Thomasin, I never expected much from her; and she has not disappointed me. But I forgave her long ago; and I forgive him now. I'll go.'

At this very time of the reddleman's conversation with Mrs. Yeobright at Blooms-End another conversation on the same subject was languidly proceeding at Alderworth.

All the day Clym had borne himself as if his mind were too full of its own matter to allow him to care about outward things, and his words now showed what had occupied his thoughts. It was just after the mysterious knocking that he began the theme. 'Since I have been away to-day, Eustacia, I have considered that something must be done to heal up this ghastly breach between my dear mother and myself. It troubles me.'

'What do you propose to do?' said Eustacia abstractedly, for she could not clear away from her the excitement caused by Wildeve's recent manœuvre for an interview.

'You seem to take a very mild interest in what I propose, little or much,' said Clym, with tolerable warmth.

'You mistake me,' she answered, reviving at his reproach. 'I am only thinking.'

'What of?'

'Partly of that moth whose skeleton is getting burnt up in the wick of the candle,' she said slowly. 'But you know I always take an interest in what you say.'

'Very well, dear. Then I think I must go and call upon her.' . . . He went on with tender feeling: 'It is a thing I am not at all too proud to do, and only a fear that I might irritate her has kept me away so long. But I must do something. It is wrong in me to allow this sort of thing to go on.'

'What have you to blame yourself about?'

'She is getting old, and her life is lonely, and I am her only son.'

'She has Thomasin.'

'Thomasin is not her daughter; and if she were that would not excuse me. But this is beside the point. I have made up my mind to go to her, and all I wish to ask you is whether you will do your best to help me—that is, forget the past; and if she shows her willingness to be reconciled, meet her half-way by welcoming her to our house, or by accepting a welcome to hers?'

At first Eustacia closed her lips as if she would rather do anything on the whole globe than what he suggested. But the lines of her mouth softened with thought, though not so far as they might have softened; and she said, 'I will put nothing in your way; but after what has passed it is asking too much that I go and make advances.'

'You never distinctly told me what did pass between you.'

'I could not do it then, nor can I now. Sometimes more bitterness is sown in five minutes than can be got rid of in a whole life; and that may be the case here.' She paused a few moments, and added, 'If you had never returned to your native place, Clym, what a blessing it would have been for you! . . . It has altered the destinies of——'

'Three people.'

'Five,' Eustacia thought; but she kept that in.

The Journey across the Heath

V

Thursday, the thirty-first of August, was one of a series of days during which snug houses were stifling, and when cool draughts were treats; when cracks appeared in clayey gardens, and were called 'earthquakes' by apprehensive children; when loose spokes were discovered in the wheels of carts and carriages; and when stinging insects haunted the air, the earth and every drop of water that was to be found.

In Mrs. Yeobright's garden large-leaved plants of a tender kind flagged by ten o'clock in the morning; rhubarb bent downward at eleven; and even stiff cabbages were limp by noon.

It was about eleven o'clock on this day that Mrs. Yeobright started across the heath towards her son's house, to do her best in getting reconciled with him and Eustacia, in conformity with her words to the reddleman. She had hoped to be well advanced in her walk before the heat of the day was at its highest, but after setting out she found that this was not to be done. The sun had branded the whole heath with his mark, even the purple heath-flowers having put on a brownness under the dry blazes of the few preceding days. Every valley was filled with air like that of a kiln, and the clean quartz sand of the winter water-courses, which formed summer paths, had undergone a species of incineration since the drought had set in.

In cool, fresh weather Mrs. Yeobright would have found no inconvenience in walking to Alderworth, but the present torrid attack made the journey a heavy undertaking for a woman past middle age; and at the end of the third mile she wished that she had hired Fairway to drive her a portion at least of the distance. But from the point at which she had arrived it was as easy to reach Clym's house as to get home again. So she went on, the air around her pulsating silently, and oppressing the earth with lassitude. She looked at the sky overhead, and saw that the sapphirine hue of the zenith in spring and early summer had been replaced by a metallic violet.

Occasionally she came to a spot where independent worlds of ephemerons[1] were passing their time in mad carousal, some in the air, some on the hot ground and vegetation, some in the tepid and stringy water of a nearly dried pool. All the shallower ponds had decreased to a vaporous mud amid which the maggoty shapes of innumerable obscure creatures could be indistinctly seen, heaving and wallowing with enjoyment. Being a woman not disinclined to philosophize she sometimes sat down under her umbrella to rest and to watch their happiness, for a certain hopefulness as to the result of her visit gave ease to her mind, and between important thoughts left it free to dwell on any infinitesimal matter which caught her eyes.

Mrs. Yeobright had never before been to her son's house, and its exact position was unknown to her. She tried one ascending path and another, and found that they led her astray. Retracing her steps she came again to an open level, where she perceived at a distance a man at work. She went towards him and inquired the way.

The labourer pointed out the direction, and added, 'Do you see that furze-cutter, ma'am, going up that footpath yond?'

Mrs. Yeobright strained her eyes, and at last said that she did perceive him.

'Well, if you follow him you can make no mistake. He's going to the same place, ma'am.'

She followed the figure indicated. He appeared of a russet hue, not more distinguishable from the scene around him than the green caterpillar from the leaf it feeds on. His progress when actually walking was more rapid than Mrs. Yeobright's; but she was enabled to keep at an equable distance from him by his habit of stopping whenever he came to a brake of brambles, where he paused awhile. On coming in her turn to each of these spots she found half a dozen long limp brambles which he had cut from the bush during his halt and laid out straight beside the path. They were evidently intended for furze-faggot bonds which he meant to collect on his return.

The silent being who thus occupied himself seemed to be of no more account in life than an insect. He appeared as a mere parasite of the heath, fretting its surface in his daily labour as a moth frets a garment, entirely engrossed with its products, having no knowledge of anything in the world but fern, furze, heath, lichens, and moss.

The furze-cutter was so absorbed in the business of his journey

1. Insects that live for only one day in their winged form.

that he never turned his head; and his leather-legged and gauntleted form at length became to her as nothing more than a moving handpost to show her the way. Suddenly she was attracted to his individuality by observing peculiarities in his walk. It was a gait she had seen somewhere before; and the gait revealed the man to her, as the gait of Ahimaaz[2] in the distant plain made him known to the watchman of the king. 'His walk is exactly as my husband's used to be,' she said; and then the thought burst upon her that the furze-cutter was her son.

She was scarcely able to familiarize herself with this strange reality. She had been told that Clym was in the habit of cutting furze, but she had supposed that he occupied himself with the labour only at odd times, by way of useful pastime; yet she now beheld him as a furze-cutter and nothing more—wearing the regulation dress of the craft, and thinking the regulation thoughts, to judge by his motions. Planning a dozen hasty schemes for at once preserving him and Eustacia from this mode of life she throbbingly followed the way, and saw him enter his own door.

At one side of Clym's house was a knoll, and on the top of the knoll a clump of fir trees so highly thrust up into the sky that their foliage from a distance appeared as a black spot in the air above the crown of the hill. On reaching this place Mrs. Yeobright felt distressingly agitated, weary, and unwell. She ascended, and sat down under their shade to recover herself, and to consider how best to break the ground with Eustacia, so as not to irritate a woman underneath whose apparent indolence lurked passions even stronger and more active than her own.

The trees beneath which she sat were singularly battered, rude, and wild, and for a few minutes Mrs. Yeobright dismissed thoughts of her own storm-broken and exhausted state to contemplate theirs. Not a bough in the nine trees which composed the group but was splintered, lopped, and distorted by the fierce weather that there held them at its mercy whenever it prevailed. Some were blasted and split as if by lightning, black stains as from fire marking their sides, while the ground at their feet was strewn with dead fir-needles and heaps of cones blown down in the gales of past years. The place was called the Devil's Bellows, and it was only necessary to come there on a March or November night to discover the forcible reasons for that name. On the present heated afternoon, when no perceptible wind was blowing, the trees kept up a perpetual moan which one could hardly believe to be caused by the air.

Here she sat for twenty minutes or more ere she could summon

2. Ahimaaz was recognized from afar by the sentries as he ran to bring news of the death of Absalom, the son of David (see 2 Samuel 18.27).

resolution to go down to the door, her courage being lowered to zero by her physical lassitude. To any other person than a mother it might have seemed a little humiliating that she, the elder of the two women, should be the first to make advances. But Mrs. Yeobright had well considered all that, and she only thought how best to make her visit appear to Eustacia not abject but wise.

From her elevated position the exhausted woman could perceive the roof of the house below, and the garden and the whole enclosure of the little domicile. And now, at the moment of rising, she saw a second man approaching the gate. His manner was peculiar, hesitating, and not that of a person come on business or by invitation. He surveyed the house with interest, and then walked round and scanned the outer boundary of the garden, as one might have done had it been the birthplace of Shakespeare, the prison of Mary Stuart, or the Château of Hougomont.[3] After passing round and again reaching the gate he went in. Mrs. Yeobright was vexed at this, having reckoned on finding her son and his wife by themselves; but a moment's thought showed her that the presence of an acquaintance would take off the awkwardness of her first appearance in the house, by confining the talk to general matters until she had begun to feel comfortable with them. She came down the hill to the gate, and looked into the hot garden.

There lay the cat asleep on the bare gravel of the path, as if beds, rugs, and carpets were unendurable. The leaves of the hollyhocks hung like half-closed umbrellas, the sap almost simmered in the stems, and foliage with a smooth surface glared like metallic mirrors. A small apple tree, of the sort called Ratheripe,[4] grew just inside the gate, the only one which throve in the garden, by reason of the lightness of the soil; and among the fallen apples on the ground beneath were wasps rolling drunk with the juice, or creeping about the little caves in each fruit which they had eaten out before stupefied by its sweetness. By the door lay Clym's furze-hook and the last handful of faggot-bonds she had seen him gather; they had plainly been thrown down there as he entered the house.

A Conjuncture, and Its Result upon the Pedestrian

VI

Wildeve, as has been stated, was determined to visit Eustacia boldly, by day, and on the easy terms of a relation, since the reddle-

3. Shakespeare was born at Stratford-upon-Avon; Mary, Queen of Scots (1542–87), was first imprisoned and later executed in Fotheringhay Castle; the house and farm at Hougoumont, part of Wellington's right flank at the Battle of Waterloo (1815), were the target of a major French assault. Hardy visited Waterloo in 1876.
4. Ratheripe is used for any fruit that ripens early in the season ("rathe" means early).

man had spied out and spoilt his walks to her by night. The spell that she had thrown over him in the moonlight dance made it impossible for a man having no strong puritanic force within him to keep away altogether. He merely calculated on meeting her and her husband in an ordinary manner, chatting a little while, and leaving again. Every outward sign was to be conventional; but the one great fact would be there to satisfy him: he would see her. He did not even desire Clym's absence, since it was just possible that Eustacia might resent any situation which could compromise her dignity as a wife, whatever the state of her heart towards him. Women were often so.

He went accordingly; and it happened that the time of his arrival coincided with that of Mrs. Yeobright's pause on the hill near the house. When he had looked round the premises in the manner she had noticed he went and knocked at the door. There was a few minutes' interval, and then the key turned in the lock, the door opened, and Eustacia herself confronted him.

Nobody could have imagined from her bearing now that here stood the woman who had joined with him in the impassioned dance of the week before, unless indeed he could have penetrated below the surface and gauged the real depth of that still stream.

'I hope you reached home safely?' said Wildeve.

'O yes,' she carelessly returned.

'And were you not tired the next day? I feared you might be.'

'I was rather. You need not speak low—nobody will overhear us. My small servant is gone on an errand to the village.'

'Then Clym is not at home?'

'Yes, he is.'

'O! I thought that perhaps you had locked the door because you were alone and were afraid of tramps.'

'No—here is my husband.'

They had been standing in the entry. Closing the front door and turning the key, as before, she threw open the door of the adjoining room and asked him to walk in. Wildeve entered, the room appearing to be empty; but as soon as he had advanced a few steps he started. On the hearthrug lay Clym asleep. Beside him were the leggings, thick boots, leather gloves, and sleeve-waistcoat in which he worked.

'You may go in; you will not disturb him,' she said, following behind. 'My reason for fastening the door is that he may not be intruded upon by any chance comer while lying here, if I should be in the garden or upstairs.'

'Why is he sleeping there?' said Wildeve in low tones.

'He is very weary. He went out at half-past four this morning, and has been working ever since. He cuts furze because it is the only thing he can do that does not put any strain upon his poor eyes.' The contrast between the sleeper's appearance and Wildeve's at this moment was painfully apparent to Eustacia, Wildeve being elegantly dressed in a new summer suit and light hat; and she continued: 'Ah! you don't know how differently he appeared when I first met him, though it is such a little while ago. His hands were as white and soft as mine; and look at them now, how rough and brown they are! His complexion is by nature fair, and that rusty look he has now, all of a colour with his leather clothes, is caused by the burning of the sun.'

'Why does he go out at all?' Wildeve whispered.

'Because he hates to be idle; though what he earns doesn't add much to our exchequer. However, he says that when people are living upon their capital they must keep down current expenses by turning a penny where they can.'

'The fates have not been kind to you, Eustacia Yeobright.'

'I have nothing to thank them for.'

'Nor has he—except for their one great gift to him.'

'What's that?'

Wildeve looked her in the eyes.

Eustacia blushed for the first time that day. 'Well, I am a questionable gift,' she said quietly. 'I thought you meant the gift of content—which he has, and I have not.'

'I can understand content in such a case—though how the outward situation can attract him puzzles me.'

'That's because you don't know him. He's an enthusiast about ideas, and careless about outward things. He often reminds me of the Apostle Paul.'[1]

'I am glad to hear that he's so grand in character as that.'

'Yes; but the worst of it is that though Paul was excellent as a man in the Bible he would hardly have done in real life.'

Their voices had instinctively dropped lower, though at first they had taken no particular care to avoid awakening Clym. 'Well, if that means that your marriage is a misfortune to you, you know who is to blame,' said Wildeve.

'The marriage is no misfortune in itself,' she retorted with some little petulance. 'It is simply the accident which has happened since that has been the cause of my ruin. I have certainly got thistles for figs[2] in a worldly sense, but how could I tell what time would bring forth?'

'Sometimes, Eustacia, I think it is a judgment upon you. You

---

1. Eustacia is perhaps thinking of Paul's view that married life was not only of less value than spiritual integrity, but also a possible barrier to it; see 1 Corinthians 8.26–35.
2. Perhaps an allusion to Matthew 7.16, where Christ explains that people are known by their deeds: "Do men gather grapes of thorns, or figs of thistles?"

rightly belonged to me, you know; and I had no idea of losing you.'

'No, it was not my fault! Two could not belong to you; and remember that, before I was aware, you turned aside to another woman. It was cruel levity in you to do that. I never dreamt of playing such a game on my side till you began it on yours.'

'I meant nothing by it,' replied Wildeve. 'It was a mere interlude. Men are given to the trick of having a passing fancy for somebody else in the midst of a permanent love, which reasserts itself afterwards just as before. On account of your rebellious manner to me I was tempted to go further than I should have done; and when you still would keep playing the same tantalizing part I went further still, and married her.' Turning and looking again at the unconscious form of Clym he murmured, 'I am afraid that you don't value your prize, Clym. . . . He ought to be happier than I in one thing at least. He may know what it is to come down in the world, and to be afflicted with a great personal calamity; but he probably doesn't know what it is to lose the woman he loved.'

'He is not ungrateful for winning her,' whispered Eustacia, 'and in that respect he is a good man. Many women would go far for such a husband. But do I desire unreasonably much in wanting what is called life—music, poetry, passion, war, and all the beating and pulsing that is going on in the great arteries of the world?[3] That was the shape of my youthful dream; but I did not get it. Yet I thought I saw the way to it in my Clym.'

'And you only married him on that account?'

'There you mistake me. I married him because I loved him, but I won't say that I didn't love him partly because I thought I saw a promise of that life in him.'

'You have dropped into your old mournful key.'

'But I am not going to be depressed,' she cried perversely. 'I began a new system by going to that dance, and I mean to stick to it. Clym can sing merrily; why should not I?'

Wildeve looked thoughtfully at her. 'It is easier to say you will sing than to do it; though if I could I would encourage you in your attempt. But as life means nothing to me, without one thing which is now impossible, you will forgive me for not being able to encourage you.'

'Damon, what is the matter with you, that you speak like that?' she asked, raising her deep shady eyes to his.

'That's a thing I shall never tell plainly; and perhaps if I try to tell you in riddles you will not care to guess them.'

Eustacia remained silent for a minute, and she said, 'We are in a

---

3. The thought and phrasing here echo the "Conclusion" to Walter Pater's *Studies in the History of the Renaissance* (1873).

strange relationship to-day. You mince matters to an uncommon nicety. You mean, Damon, that you still love me. Well, that gives me sorrow, for I am not made so entirely happy by my marriage that I am willing to spurn you for the information, as I ought to do. But we have said too much about this. Do you mean to wait until my husband is awake?'

'I thought to speak to him; but it is unnecessary. Eustacia, if I offend you by not forgetting you, you are right to mention it; but do not talk of spurning.'

She did not reply, and they stood looking musingly at Clym as he slept on in that profound sleep which is the result of physical labour carried on in circumstances that wake no nervous fear.

'God, how I envy him that sweet sleep!' said Wildeve. 'I have not slept like that since I was a boy—years and years ago.'

While they thus watched him a click at the gate was audible, and a knock came to the door. Eustacia went to a window and looked out.

Her countenance changed. First she became crimson, and then the red subsided till it even partially left her lips.

'Shall I go away?' said Wildeve, standing up.

'I hardly know.'

'Who is it?'

'Mrs. Yeobright. O, what she said to me that day! I cannot understand this visit—what does she mean? And she suspects that past time of ours.'

'I am in your hands. If you think she had better not see me here I'll go into the next room.'

'Well, yes: go.'

Wildeve at once withdrew; but before he had been half a minute in the adjoining apartment Eustacia came after him.

'No,' she said, 'we won't have any of this. If she comes in she must see you—and think if she likes there's something wrong! But how can I open the door to her, when she dislikes me—wishes to see not me, but her son? I won't open the door!'

Mrs. Yeobright knocked again more loudly.

'Her knocking will, in all likelihood, awaken him,' continued Eustacia; 'and then he will let her in himself. Ah—listen.'

They could hear Clym moving in the other room, as if disturbed by the knocking, and he uttered the word 'Mother.'

'Yes—he is awake—he will go to the door,' she said, with a breath of relief. 'Come this way. I have a bad name with her, and you must not be seen. Thus I am obliged to act by stealth, not because I do ill, but because others are pleased to say so.'

By this time she had taken him to the back door, which was open, disclosing a path leading down the garden. 'Now, one word,

Damon,' she remarked as he stepped forth. 'This is your first visit here; let it be your last. We have been hot lovers in our time, but it won't do now. Good-bye.'

'Good-bye,' said Wildeve. 'I have had all I came for, and I am satisfied.'

'What was it?'

'A sight of you. Upon my eternal honour I came for no more.'

Wildeve kissed his hand to the beautiful girl he addressed, and passed into the garden, where she watched him down the path, over the stile at the end, and into the ferns outside, which brushed his hips as he went along till he became lost in their thickets. When he had quite gone she slowly turned, and directed her attention to the interior of the house.

But it was possible that her presence might not be desired by Clym and his mother at this moment of their first meeting, or that it would be superfluous. At all events, she was in no hurry to meet Mrs. Yeobright. She resolved to wait till Clym came to look for her, and glided back into the garden. Here she idly occupied herself for a few minutes, till finding no notice was taken of her she retraced her steps through the house to the front, where she listened for voices in the parlour. But hearing none she opened the door and went in. To her astonishment Clym lay precisely as Wildeve and herself had left him, his sleep apparently unbroken. He had been disturbed and made to dream and murmur by the knocking, but he had not awakened. Eustacia hastened to the door, and in spite of her reluctance to open it to a woman who had spoken of her so bitterly, she unfastened it and looked out. Nobody was to be seen. There, by the scraper, lay Clym's hook and the handful of faggot-bonds he had brought home; in front of her were the empty path, the garden gate standing slightly ajar; and, beyond, the great valley of purple heath thrilling silently in the sun. Mrs. Yeobright was gone.

Clym's mother was at this time following a path which lay hidden from Eustacia by a shoulder of the hill. Her walk thither from the garden gate had been hasty and determined, as of a woman who was now no less anxious to escape from the scene than she had previously been to enter it. Her eyes were fixed on the ground; within her two sights were graven—that of Clym's hook and brambles at the door, and that of a woman's face at a window. Her lips trembled, becoming unnaturally thin as she murmured, ' 'Tis too much—Clym, how can he bear to do it! He is at home; and yet he lets her shut the door against me!'

In her anxiety to get out of the direct view of the house she had diverged from the straightest path homeward, and while looking about to regain it she came upon a little boy gathering whortle-berries in a hollow. The boy was Johnny Nunsuch, who had been Eustacia's stoker at the bonfire, and, with the tendency of a minute body to gravitate towards a greater, he began hovering round Mrs. Yeobright as soon as she appeared, and trotted on beside her without perceptible consciousness of his act.

Mrs. Yeobright spoke to him as one in a mesmeric sleep. ' 'Tis a long way home, my child, and we shall not get there till evening.'

'I shall,' said her small companion. 'I am going to play marnels[4] afore supper, and we go to supper at six o'clock, because father comes home. Does your father come home at six too?'

'No: he never comes; nor my son either, nor anybody.'

'What have made you so down? Have you seen a ooser?'[5]

'I have seen what's worse—a woman's face looking at me through a window-pane.'

'Is that a bad sight?'

'Yes. It is always a bad sight to see a woman looking out at a weary wayfarer and not letting her in.'

'Once when I went to Throope Great Pond to catch effets[6] I seed myself looking up at myself, and I was frightened and jumped back like anything.'

. . . 'If they had only shown signs of meeting my advances half-way how well it might have been done! But there is no chance. Shut out! She must have set him against me. Can there be beautiful bodies without hearts inside? I think so. I would not have done it against a neighbour's cat on such a fiery day as this!'[7]

'What is it you say?'

'Never again—never! Not even if they send for me!'

'You must be a very curious woman to talk like that.'

'O no, not at all,' she said, returning to the boy's prattle. 'Most people who grow up and have children talk as I do. When you grow up your mother will talk as I do too.'

'I hope she won't; because 'tis very bad to talk nonsense.'

'Yes, child; it is nonsense, I suppose. Are you not nearly spent with the heat?'

'Yes. But not so much as you be.'

'How do you know?'

---

4. Marnels, or marnulls, named after the village of Marnhull in Dorset, is a child's version of an ancient board game for two players; also known as nine men's morris.
5. Dialect name for a grotesque wooden mask, with a movable jaw, often surmounted with cow's horns.
6. Newts (dialect).
7. An echo of two scenes in *King Lear*: Lear's question about his daughters Goneril and Regan, "Is there any cause in nature that makes these hard hearts?" (III.6.35–36); and Cordelia's response to the news that her sisters had driven her father out on the heath: "Mine enemy's dog, though he had bit me, should have stood / That night against my fire" (IV.6.29–30).

'Your face is white and wet, and your head is hanging-down-like.'

'Ah, I am exhausted from inside.'

'Why do you, every time you take a step, go like this?' The child in speaking gave to his motion the jerk and limp of an invalid.

'Because I have a burden which is more than I can bear.'

The little boy remained silently pondering, and they tottered on side by side until more than a quarter of an hour had elapsed, when Mrs. Yeobright, whose weakness plainly increased, said to him, 'I must sit down here to rest.'

When she had seated herself he looked long in her face and said, 'How funny you draw your breath—like a lamb when you drive him till he's nearly done for. Do you always draw your breath like that?'

'Not always.' Her voice was now so low as to be scarcely above a whisper.

'You will go to sleep there, I suppose, won't you? You have shut your eyes already.'

'No. I shall not sleep much till—another day, and then I hope to have a long, long one—very long. Now can you tell me if Rimsmoor Pond is dry this summer?'

'Rimsmoor Pond is, but Oker's Pool isn't, because he is deep, and is never dry—'tis just over there.'

'Is the water clear?'

'Yes, middling—except where the heath-croppers walk into it.'

'Then, take this, and go as fast as you can, and dip me up the clearest you can find. I am very faint.'

She drew from the small willow reticule that she carried in her hand an old-fashioned china teacup without a handle; it was one of half a dozen of the same sort lying in the reticule, which she had preserved ever since her childhood, and had brought with her to-day as a small present for Clym and Eustacia.

The boy started on his errand, and soon came back with the water, such as it was. Mrs. Yeobright attempted to drink, but it was so warm as to give her nausea, and she threw it away. Afterwards she still remained sitting, with her eyes closed.

The boy waited, played near her, caught several of the little brown butterflies which abounded, and then said as he waited again, 'I like going on better than biding still. Will you soon start again?'

'I don't know.'

'I wish I might go on by myself,' he resumed, fearing, apparently, that he was to be pressed into some unpleasant service. 'Do you want me any more, please?'

Mrs. Yeobright made no reply.

'What shall I tell mother?' the boy continued.

'Tell her you have seen a broken-hearted woman cast off by her son.'

Before quite leaving her he threw upon her face a wistful glance, as if he had misgivings on the generosity of forsaking her thus. He gazed into her face in a vague, wondering manner, like that of one examining some strange old manuscript the key to whose characters is undiscoverable. He was not so young as to be absolutely without a sense that sympathy was demanded, he was not old enough to be free from the terror felt in childhood at beholding misery in adult quarters hitherto deemed impregnable; and whether she were in a position to cause trouble or to suffer from it, whether she and her affliction were something to pity or something to fear, it was beyond him to decide. He lowered his eyes and went on without another word. Before he had gone half a mile he had forgotten all about her, except that she was a woman who had sat down to rest.

Mrs. Yeobright's exertions, physical and emotional, had well-nigh prostrated her; but she continued to creep along in short stages with long breaks between. The sun had now got far to the west of south and stood directly in her face,[8] like some merciless incendiary, brand in hand, waiting to consume her. With the departure of the boy all visible animation disappeared from the landscape, though the intermittent husky notes of the male grasshoppers from every tuft of furze were enough to show that amid the prostration of the larger animal species an unseen insect world was busy in all the fulness of life.

In two hours she reached a slope about three-fourths the whole distance from Alderworth to her own home, where a little patch of shepherd's-thyme intruded upon the path; and she sat down upon the perfumed mat it formed there. In front of her a colony of ants had established a thoroughfare across the way, where they toiled a never-ending and heavy-laden throng. To look down upon them was like observing a city street from the top of a tower. She remembered that this bustle of ants had been in progress for years at the same spot—doubtless those of the old times were the ancestors of these which walked there now.[9] She leant back to obtain more thorough rest, and the soft eastern portion of the sky was as great a relief to her eyes as the thyme was to her head. While she looked a heron arose on that side of the sky and flew on with his face towards the sun. He had come dripping wet from some pool in the valleys, and as he flew the edges and lining of his wings, his thighs, and his breast were so caught by the bright sunbeams that he appeared as if formed of burnished silver. Up in the zenith where he

8. That Mrs. Yeobright is traveling westward makes it clear that the map Hardy prepared for the 1878 edition of the novel departs from convention by placing east rather than north at the top of the page. The change was probably made to obscure the connection between Blooms-End and Hardy's own family home at Bockhampton.
9. This is another detail picked up from J. G. Woods's *Insects at Home*.

was seemed a free and happy place, away from all contact with the earthly ball to which she was pinioned; and she wished that she could arise uncrushed from its surface and fly as he flew then.

But, being a mother, it was inevitable that she should soon cease to ruminate upon her own condition. Had the track of her next thought been marked by a streak in the air, like the path of a meteor, it would have shown a direction contrary to the heron's, and have descended to the eastward upon the roof of Clym's house.

The Tragic Meeting of Two Old Friends

VII

He in the meantime had aroused himself from sleep, sat up, and looked around. Eustacia was sitting in a chair hard by him, and though she held a book in her hand she had not looked into it for some time.

'Well, indeed!' said Clym, brushing his eyes with his hands. 'How soundly I have slept! I have had such a tremendous dream, too: one I shall never forget.'

'I thought you had been dreaming,' said she.

'Yes. It was about my mother. I dreamt that I took you to her house to make up differences, and when we got there we couldn't get in, though she kept on crying to us for help. However, dreams are dreams. What o'clock is it, Eustacia?'

'Half-past two.'

'So late, is it? I didn't mean to stay so long. By the time I have had something to eat it will be after three.'

'Ann is not come back from the village, and I thought I would let you sleep on till she returned.'

Clym went to the window and looked out. Presently he said, musingly, 'Week after week passes, and yet mother does not come. I thought I should have heard something from her long before this.'

Misgiving, regret, fear, resolution, ran their swift course of expression in Eustacia's dark eyes. She was face to face with a monstrous difficulty, and she resolved to get free of it by postponement.

'I must certainly go to Blooms-End soon,' he continued, 'and I think I had better go alone.' He picked up his leggings and gloves, threw them down again, and added, 'As dinner will be so late to-day I will not go back to the heath, but work in the garden till the evening, and then, when it will be cooler, I will walk to Blooms-End. I am quite sure that if I make a little advance mother will be willing to forget all. It will be rather late before I can get home, as I shall not be able to do the distance either way in less than an hour and a half. But you will not mind for one evening, dear? What are you thinking of to make you look so abstracted?'

'I cannot tell you,' she said heavily. 'I wish we didn't live here, Clym. The world seems all wrong in this place.'

'Well—if we make it so. I wonder if Thomasin has been to Blooms-End lately. I hope so. But probably not, as she is, I believe, expecting to be confined in a month or so. I wish I had thought of that before. Poor mother must indeed be very lonely.'

'I don't like you going to-night.'

'Why not to-night?'

'Something may be said which will terribly injure me.'

'My mother is not vindictive,' said Clym, his colour faintly rising.

'But I wish you would not go,' Eustacia repeated in a low tone. 'If you agree not to go to-night I promise to go by myself to her house to-morrow, and make it up with her, and wait till you fetch me.'

'Why do you want to do that at this particular time, when at every previous time that I have proposed it you have refused?'

'I cannot explain further than that I should like to see her alone before you go,' she answered, with an impatient move of her head, and looking at him with an anxiety more frequently seen upon those of a sanguine temperament[1] than upon such as herself.

'Well, it is very odd that just when I had decided to go myself you should want to do what I proposed long ago. If I wait for you to go to-morrow another day will be lost; and I know I shall be unable to rest another night without having been. I want to get this settled, and will. You must visit her afterwards: it will be all the same.'

'I could even go with you now?'

'You could scarcely walk there and back without a longer rest than I shall take. No, not to-night, Eustacia.'

'Let it be as you say, then,' she replied in the quiet way of one who, though willing to ward off evil consequences by a mild effort, would let events fall out as they might sooner than wrestle hard to direct them.

Clym then went into the garden; and a thoughtful languor stole over Eustacia for the remainder of the afternoon, which her husband attributed to the heat of the weather.

In the evening he set out on the journey. Although the heat of summer was yet intense the days had considerably shortened, and before he had advanced a mile on his way all the heath purples, browns, and greens had merged in a uniform dress without airiness or gradation, and broken only by touches of white where the little heaps of clean quartz sand showed the entrance to a rabbit-burrow, or where the white flints of a footpath lay like a thread over the

---

1. Since a sanguine temperament is an optimistic one, it is unclear why it should more frequently express anxiety.

slopes. In almost every one of the isolated and stunted thorns which grew here and there a night-hawk[2] revealed his presence by whirring like the clack of a mill as long as he could hold his breath, then stopping, flapping his wings, wheeling round the bush, alighting, and after a silent interval of listening beginning to whirr again. At each brushing of Clym's feet white miller-moths flew into the air just high enough to catch upon their dusty wings the mellowed light from the west, which now shone across the depressions and levels of the ground without falling thereon to light them up.

Yeobright walked on amid this quiet scene with a hope that all would soon be well. Three miles on he came to a spot where a soft perfume was wafted across his path, and he stood still for a moment to inhale the familiar scent. It was the place at which, four hours earlier, his mother had sat down exhausted on the knoll covered with shepherd's-thyme. While he stood a sound between a breathing and a moan suddenly reached his ears.

He looked to where the sound came from; but nothing appeared there save the verge of the hillock stretching against the sky in an unbroken line. He moved a few steps in that direction, and now he perceived a recumbent figure almost close at his feet.

Among the different possibilities as to the person's individuality there did not for a moment occur to Yeobright that it might be one of his own family. Sometimes furze-cutters had been known to sleep out of doors at these times, to save a long journey homeward and back again; but Clym remembered the moan and looked closer, and saw that the form was feminine; and a distress came over him like cold air from a cave. But he was not absolutely certain that the woman was his mother till he stooped and beheld her face, pallid, and with closed eyes.

His breath went, as it were, out of his body and the cry of anguish which would have escaped him died upon his lips. During the momentary interval that elapsed before he became conscious that something must be done all sense of time and place left him, and it seemed as if he and his mother were as when he was a child with her many years ago on this heath at hours similar to the present. Then he awoke to activity; and bending yet lower he found that she still breathed, and that her breath though feeble was regular, except when disturbed by an occasional gasp.

'O, what is it! Mother, are you very ill—you are not dying?' he cried, pressing his lips to her face. 'I am your Clym. How did you come here? What does it all mean?'

At that moment the chasm in their lives which his love for Eu-

---

2. The nightjar rather than the Common Nighthawk, which despite its name is very rarely seen in Britain; though the nightjar, a summer visitor, would also be uncommon as late as August 31.

stacia had caused was not remembered by Yeobright, and to him the present joined continuously with that friendly past that had been their experience before the division.

She moved her lips, appeared to know him, but could not speak; and then Clym strove to consider how best to move her, as it would be necessary to get her away from the spot before the dews were intense. He was able-bodied, and his mother was thin. He clasped his arms round her, lifted her a little, and said, 'Does that hurt you?'

She shook her head, and he lifted her up; then, at a slow pace, went onward with his load. The air was now completely cool; but whenever he passed over a sandy patch of ground uncarpeted with vegetation there was reflected from its surface into his face the heat which it had imbibed during the day. At the beginning of his undertaking he had thought but little of the distance which yet would have to be traversed before Blooms-End could be reached; but though he had slept that afternoon he soon began to feel the weight of his burden. Thus he proceeded, like Æneas with his father;[3] the bats circling round his head, nightjars flapping their wings within a yard of his face, and not a human being within call.

While he was yet nearly a mile from the house his mother exhibited signs of restlessness under the constraint of being borne along, as if his arms were irksome to her. He lowered her upon his knees and looked around. The point they had now reached, though far from any road, was not more than a mile from the Blooms-End cottages occupied by Fairway, Sam, Humphrey, and the Cantles. Moreover, fifty yards off stood a hut, built of clods and covered with thin turves, but now entirely disused. The simple outline of the lonely shed was visible, and thither he determined to direct his steps. As soon as he arrived he laid her down carefully by the entrance, and then ran and cut with his pocket-knife an armful of the dryest fern. Spreading this within the shed, which was entirely open on one side, he placed his mother thereon: then he ran with all his might towards the dwelling of Fairway.

Nearly a quarter of an hour had passed, disturbed only by the broken breathing of the sufferer, when moving figures began to animate the line between heath and sky. In a few moments Clym arrived with Fairway, Humphrey, and Susan Nunsuch; Olly Dowden, who had chanced to be at Fairway's, Christian and Grandfer Cantle following helter-skelter behind. They had brought a lantern and matches, water, a pillow, and a few other articles which had oc-

3. After the fall of Troy, Aeneas carried his father, Anchises, from the burning city (Virgil, *Aeneid*, Book 2).

curred to their minds in the hurry of the moment. Sam had been despatched back again for brandy, and a boy brought Fairway's pony, upon which he rode off to the nearest medical man, with directions to call at Wildeve's on his way, and inform Thomasin that her aunt was unwell.

Sam and the brandy soon arrived, and it was administered by the light of the lantern; after which she became sufficiently conscious to signify by signs that something was wrong with her foot. Olly Dowden at length understood her meaning, and examined the foot indicated. It was swollen and red. Even as they watched the red began to assume a more livid colour, in the midst of which appeared a scarlet speck, smaller than a pea, and it was found to consist of a drop of blood, which rose above the smooth flesh of her ankle in a hemisphere.

'I know what it is,' cried Sam. 'She has been stung by an adder!'

'Yes,' said Clym instantly. 'I remember when I was a child seeing just such a bite. O, my poor mother!'

'It was my father who was bit,' said Sam. 'And there's only one way to cure it. You must rub the place with the fat of other adders, and the only way to get that is by frying them. That's what they did for him.'

' 'Tis an old remedy,' said Clym distrustfully, 'and I have doubts about it. But we can do nothing else till the doctor comes.'

''Tis a sure cure,' said Olly Dowden, with emphasis. 'I've used it when I used to go out nursing.'

'Then we must pray for daylight, to catch them,' said Clym gloomily.

'I will see what I can do,' said Sam.

He took a green hazel which he had used as a walking-stick, split it at the end, inserted a small pebble, and with the lantern in his hand went out into the heath. Clym had by this time lit a small fire, and despatched Susan Nunsuch for a frying-pan. Before she had returned Sam came in with three adders, one briskly coiling and uncoiling in the cleft of the stick, and the other two hanging dead across it.

'I have only been able to get one alive and fresh as he ought to be,' said Sam. 'These limp ones are two I killed to-day at work; but as they don't die till the sun goes down they can't be very stale meat.'

The live adder regarded the assembled group with a sinister look in its small black eye, and the beautiful brown and jet pattern on its back seemed to intensify with indignation. Mrs. Yeobright saw the creature, and the creature saw her: she quivered throughout, and averted her eyes.

'Look at that,' murmured Christian Cantle. 'Neighbours, how do

'Something was wrong with her foot.'

we know but that something of the old serpent in God's garden,[4] that gied the apple to the young woman with no clothes, lives on in adders and snakes still? Look at his eye—for all the world like a villainous sort of black currant. 'Tis to be hoped he can't ill-wish us! There's folks in heath who've been overlooked[5] already. I will never kill another adder as long as I live.'

'Well, 'tis right to be afeard of things, if folks can't help it,' said Grandfer Cantle. ' 'Twould have saved me many a brave danger in my time.'

'I fancy I heard something outside the shed,' said Christian. 'I wish troubles would come in the day-time, for then a man could show his courage, and hardly beg for mercy of the most broomstick old woman he should see, if he was a brave man, and able to run out of her sight!'

'Even such an ignorant fellow as I should know better than do that,' said Sam.

'Well, there's calamities where we least expect it, whether or no. Neighbours, if Mrs. Yeobright were to die, d'ye think we should be took up and tried for the manslaughter of a woman?'

'No, they couldn't bring it in as that,' said Sam, 'unless they could prove we had been poachers at some time of our lives. But she'll fetch round.'

'Now, if I had been stung by ten adders I should hardly have lost

4. Eden.
5. Looked on with the evil eye; betwitched.

a day's work for't,' said Grandfer Cantle. 'Such is my spirit when I am on my mettle. But perhaps 'tis natural in a man trained for war. Yes, I've gone through a good deal; but nothing ever came amiss to me after I joined the Locals in four.' He shook his head and smiled at a mental picture of himself in uniform. 'I was always first in the most galliantest scrapes in my younger days!'

'I suppose that was because they always used to put the biggest fool afore,' said Fairway from the fire, beside which he knelt, blowing it with his breath.

'D'ye think so, Timothy?' said Grandfer Cantle, coming forward to Fairway's side with sudden depression in his face. 'Then a man may feel for years that he is good solid company, and be wrong about himself after all?'

'Never mind that question, Grandfer. Stir your stumps and get some more sticks. 'Tis very nonsense of an old man to prattle so when life and death's in mangling.'[6]

'Yes, yes,' said Grandfer Cantle, with melancholy conviction. 'Well, this is a bad night altogether for them that have done well in their time; and if I were ever such a dab at the hautboy[7] or tenor-viol, I shouldn't have the heart to play tunes upon 'em now.'

Susan now arrived with the frying-pan, when the live adder was killed and the heads of the three taken off. The remainders, being cut into lengths and split open, were tossed into the pan, which began hissing and crackling over the fire. Soon a rill of clear oil trickled from the carcases, whereupon Clym dipped the corner of his handkerchief into the liquid and anointed the wound.

Eustacia Hears of Good Fortune and Beholds Evil

VIII

In the meantime Eustacia, left alone in her cottage at Alderworth, had become considerably depressed by the posture of affairs. The consequences which might result from Clym's discovery that his mother had been turned from his door that day were likely to be disagreeable, and this was a quality in events which she hated as much as the dreadful.

To be left to pass the evening by herself was irksome to her at any time, and this evening it was more irksome than usual by reason of the excitements of the past hours. The two visits had stirred her into restlessness. She was not wrought to any great pitch of uneasiness by the probability of appearing in an ill light in the discussion

---

6. In the balance, at stake.
7. A dab, or dab hand, is an expert; the hautboy is an oboe, the tenor-viol a stringed instrument, often with frets, held between the knees like a cello.

between Clym and his mother, but she was wrought to vexation; and her slumbering activities were quickened to the extent of wishing that she had opened the door. She had certainly believed that Clym was awake, and the excuse would be an honest one as far as it went; but nothing could save her from censure in refusing to answer at the first knock. Yet, instead of blaming herself for the issue she laid the fault upon the shoulders of some indistinct, colossal Prince of the World,[1] who had framed her situation and ruled her lot.

At this time of the year it was pleasanter to walk by night than by day, and when Clym had been absent about an hour she suddenly resolved to go out in the direction of Blooms-End, on the chance of meeting him on his return. When she reached the garden gate she heard wheels approaching, and looking round beheld her grandfather coming up in his car.

'I can't stay a minute, thank ye,' he answered to her greeting. 'I am driving to East Egdon; but I came round here just to tell you the news. Perhaps you have heard—about Mr. Wildeve's fortune?'

'No,' said Eustacia blankly.

'Well, he has come into a fortune of eleven thousand pounds— uncle died in Canada, just after hearing that all his family, whom he was sending home, had gone to the bottom in the *Cassiopeia*; so Wildeve has come into everything, without in the least expecting it.'

Eustacia stood motionless awhile. 'How long has he known of this?' she asked.

'Well, it was known to him this morning early, for I knew it at ten o'clock, when Charley came back. Now, he is what I call a lucky man. What a fool you were, Eustacia!'

'In what way?' she said, lifting her eyes in apparent calmness.

'Why, in not sticking to him when you had him.'

'Had him, indeed!'

'I did not know there had ever been anything between you till lately; and, faith, I should have been hot and strong against it if I had known; but since it seems that there was some sniffing between ye, why the deuce didn't you stick to him?'

Eustacia made no reply, but she looked as if she could say as much upon that subject as he if she chose.

'And how is your poor purblind[2] husband?' continued the old man. 'Not a bad fellow either, as far as he goes.'

'He is quite well.'

'It is a good thing for his cousin what-d'ye-call-her? By George,

---

1. Jesus thus describes the devil at John 12.31. In the manuscript Eustacia refers more vaguely to "Zeus, or colossal Ozymandias"; she is imagining a malevolent Fate, rather than invoking Christian theology.
2. In its older sense, completely blind, but used here in its later sense to mean partly blind.

you ought to have been in that galley, my girl! Now I must drive on. Do you want any assistance? What's mine is yours, you know.'

'Thank you, grandfather, we are not in want at present,' she said coldly. 'Clym cuts furze, but he does it mostly as a useful pastime, because he can do nothing else.'

'He is paid for his pastime, isn't he? Three shillings a hundred, I heard.'

'Clym has money,' she said, colouring; 'but he likes to earn a little.'

'Very well; good night.' And the captain drove on.

When her grandfather was gone Eustacia went on her way mechanically; but her thoughts were no longer concerning her mother-in-law and Clym. Wildeve, notwithstanding his complaints against his fate, had been seized upon by destiny and placed in the sunshine once more. Eleven thousand pounds! From every Egdon point of view he was a rich man. In Eustacia's eyes, too, it was an ample sum—one sufficient to supply those wants of hers which had been stigmatized by Clym in his more austere moods as vain and luxurious. Though she was no lover of money she loved what money could bring; and the new accessories she imagined around him clothed Wildeve with a great deal of interest. She recollected now how quietly well-dressed he had been that morning: he had probably put on his newest suit, regardless of damage by briars and thorns. And then she thought of his manner towards herself.

'O I see it, I see it,' she said. 'How much he wishes he had me now, that he might give me all I desire!'

In recalling the details of his glances and words—at the time scarcely regarded—it became plain to her how greatly they had been dictated by his knowledge of this new event. 'Had he been a man to bear a jilt ill-will he would have told me of his good fortune in crowing tones; instead of doing that he mentioned not a word, in deference to my misfortunes, and merely implied that he loved me still, as one superior to him.'

Wildeve's silence that day on what had happened to him was just the kind of behaviour calculated to make an impression on such a woman. Those delicate touches of good taste were, in fact, one of the strong points in his demeanour towards the other sex. The peculiarity of Wildeve was that, while at one time passionate, upbraiding, and resentful towards a woman, at another he would treat her with such unparalleled grace as to make previous neglect appear as no discourtesy, injury as no insult, interference as a delicate attention, and the ruin of her honour as excess of chivalry. This man, whose admiration to-day Eustacia had disregarded, whose good wishes she had scarcely taken the trouble to accept, whom she had shown out of the house by the back door, was the possessor of eleven thousand pounds—a man of fair professional education, and one who had served his articles[3] with a civil engineer.

So intent was Eustacia upon Wildeve's fortunes that she forgot how much closer to her own course were those of Clym; and instead of walking on to meet him at once she sat down upon a stone. She was disturbed in her reverie by a voice behind, and turning her head beheld the old lover and fortunate inheritor of wealth immediately beside her.

She remained sitting, though the fluctuation in her look might have told any man who knew her so well as Wildeve that she was thinking of him.

'How did you come here?' she said in her clear low tone. 'I thought you were at home.'

'I went on to the village after leaving your garden; and now I have come back again: that's all. Which way are you walking, may I ask?'

She waved her hand in the direction of Blooms-End. 'I am going to meet my husband. I think I may possibly have got into trouble whilst you were with me to-day.'

'How could that be?'

'By not letting in Mrs. Yeobright.'

'I hope that visit of mine did you no harm.'

'None. It was not your fault,' she said quietly.

By this time she had risen; and they involuntarily sauntered on together, without speaking, for two or three minutes; when Eustacia broke silence by saying, 'I assume I must congratulate you.'

'On what? O yes; on my eleven thousand pounds, you mean. Well, since I didn't get something else, I must be content with getting that.'

'You seem very indifferent about it. Why didn't you tell me to-day when you came?' she said in the tone of a neglected person. 'I heard of it quite by accident.'

'I did mean to tell you,' said Wildeve. 'But I—well, I will speak frankly—I did not like to mention it when I saw, Eustacia, that your star was not high. The sight of a man lying wearied out with hard work, as your husband lay, made me feel that to brag of my own fortune to you would be greatly out of place. Yet, as you stood there beside him, I could not help feeling too that in many respects he was a richer man than I.'

At this Eustacia said, with slumbering mischievousness, 'What, would you exchange with him—your fortune for me?'

'I certainly would,' said Wildeve.

'As we are imagining what is impossible and absurd, suppose we change the subject?'

3. Completed his training.

'Very well; and I will tell you of my plans for the future, if you care to hear them. I shall permanently invest nine thousand pounds, keep one thousand as ready money, and with the remaining thousand travel for a year or so.'

'Travel? What a bright idea! Where will you go to?'

'From here to Paris, where I shall pass the winter and spring. Then I shall go to Italy, Greece, Egypt, and Palestine, before the hot weather comes on. In the summer I shall go to America; and then, by a plan not yet settled, I shall go to Australia and round to India. By that time I shall have begun to have had enough of it. Then I shall probably come back to Paris again, and there I shall stay as long as I can afford to.'

'Back to Paris again,' she murmured in a voice that was nearly a sigh. She had not once told Wildeve of the Parisian desires which Clym's description had sown in her; yet here was he involuntarily in a position to gratify them. 'You think a good deal of Paris?' she added.

'Yes. In my opinion it is the central beauty-spot of the world.'

'And in mine! And Thomasin will go with you?'

'Yes, if she cares to. She may prefer to stay at home.'

'So you will be going about, and I shall be staying here!'

'I suppose you will. But we know whose fault that is.'

'I am not blaming you,' she said quickly.

'Oh, I thought you were. If ever you *should* be inclined to blame me, think of a certain evening by Rainbarrow, when you promised to meet me and did not. You sent me a letter; and my heart ached to read that as I hope yours never will. That was one point of divergence. I then did something in haste. . . But she is a good woman, and I will say no more.'

'I know that the blame was on my side that time,' said Eustacia. 'But it had not always been so. However, it is my misfortune to be too sudden in feeling. O Damon, don't reproach me any more—I can't bear that.'

They went on silently for a distance of two or three miles, when Eustacia said suddenly, 'Haven't you come out of your way, Mr. Wildeve?'

'My way is anywhere to-night. I will go with you as far as the hill on which we can see Blooms-End, as it is getting late for you to be alone.'

'Don't trouble. I am not obliged to be out at all. I think I would rather you did not accompany me further. This sort of thing would have an odd look if known.'

'Very well, I will leave you.' He took her hand unexpectedly, and kissed it—for the first time since her marriage.[4] 'What light is that on the hill?' he added, as it were to hide the caress.

---

4. This sentence was added in 1895, as was the end of the following sentence (from "he added").

She looked, and saw a flickering firelight proceeding from the open side of a hovel a little way before them. The hovel, which she had hitherto always found empty, seemed to be inhabited now.

'Since you have come so far,' said Eustacia, 'will you see me safely past that hut? I thought I should have met Clym somewhere about here, but as he doesn't appear I will hasten on and get to Blooms-End before he leaves.'

They advanced to the turf-shed, and when they got near it the firelight and the lantern inside showed distinctly enough the form of a woman reclining on a bed of fern, a group of heath men and women standing around her. Eustacia did not recognize Mrs. Yeobright in the reclining figure, nor Clym as one of the standers-by till she came close. Then she quickly pressed her hand upon Wildeve's arm and signified to him to come back from the open side of the shed into the shadow.

'It is my husband and his mother,' she whispered in an agitated voice. 'What can it mean? Will you step forward and tell me?'

Wildeve left her side and went to the back wall of the hut. Presently Eustacia perceived that he was beckoning to her, and she advanced and joined him.

'It is a serious case,' said Wildeve.

From their position they could hear what was proceeding inside.

'I cannot think where she could have been going,' said Clym to some one. 'She had evidently walked a long way, but even when she was able to speak just now she would not tell me where. What do you really think of her?'

'There is a great deal to fear,' was gravely answered, in a voice which Eustacia recognized as that of the only surgeon in the district. 'She has suffered somewhat from the bite of the adder; but it is exhaustion which has overpowered her. My impression is that her walk must have been exceptionally long.'

'I used to tell her not to overwalk herself this weather,' said Clym, with distress. 'Do you think we did well in using the adder's fat?'

'Well, it is a very ancient remedy—the old remedy of the viper-catchers, I believe,' replied the doctor. 'It is mentioned as an infallible ointment by Hoffman, Mead, and I think the Abbé Fontana.[5] Undoubtedly it was as good a thing as you could do; though I question if some other oils would not have been equally efficacious.'

'Come here, come here!' was then rapidly said in anxious female tones; and Clym and the doctor could be heard rushing forward from the back part of the shed to where Mrs. Yeobright lay.

'O, what is it?' whispered Eustacia.

5. Friedrich Hoffman (1660–1742), Richard Mead (1673–1754), and Felice Fontana (1730–1805), were all experts on medical matters; Mead's *A Mechanical Account of Poisons* (1702) deals extensively with adder bites.

' 'Twas Thomasin who spoke,' said Wildeve. 'Then they have fetched her. I wonder if I had better go in—yet it might do harm.'

For a long time there was utter silence among the group within; and it was broken at last by Clym saying, in an agonized voice, 'O doctor, what does it mean?'

The doctor did not reply at once; ultimately he said, 'She is sinking fast. Her heart was previously affected, and physical exhaustion has dealt the finishing blow.'

Then there was a weeping of women, then waiting, then hushed exclamations, then a strange gasping sound, then a painful stillness.

'It is all over,' said the doctor.

Further back in the hut the cotters whispered, 'Mrs. Yeobright is dead.'

Almost at the same moment the two watchers observed the form of a small old-fashioned child entering at the open side of the shed. Susan Nunsuch, whose boy it was, went forward to the opening and silently beckoned to him to go back.

'I've got something to tell 'ee, mother,' he cried in a shrill tone. 'That woman asleep there walked along with me to-day; and she said I was to say that I had seed her, and she was a broken-hearted woman and cast off by her son, and then I came on home.'

A confused sob as from a man was heard within, upon which Eustacia gasped faintly, 'That's Clym—I must go to him—yet dare I do it? No: come away!'

When they had withdrawn from the neighbourhood of the shed she said huskily, 'I am to blame for this. There is evil in store for me.'

'Was she not admitted to your house after all?' Wildeve inquired.

'No; and that's where it all lies! O, what shall I do! I shall not intrude upon them: I shall go straight home. Damon, good-bye! I cannot speak to you any more now.'

They parted company; and when Eustacia had reached the next hill she looked back. A melancholy procession was wending its way by the light of the lantern from the hut towards Blooms-End. Wildeve was nowhere to be seen.

Book Fifth. The Discovery

'Wherefore Is Light Given to Him That Is in Misery'[1]

I

One evening, about three weeks after the funeral of Mrs. Yeobright, when the silver face of the moon sent a bundle of beams directly upon the floor of Clym's house at Alderworth, a woman came forth from within. She reclined over the garden gate as if to refresh herself awhile. The pale lunar touches which make beauties of hags lent divinity to this face, already beautiful.

She had not long been there when a man came up the road and with some hesitation said to her, 'How is he to-night, ma'am, if you please?'

'He is better, though still very unwell, Humphrey,' replied Eustacia.

'Is he light-headed, ma'am?'

'No. He is quite sensible now.'

'Do he rave about his mother just the same, poor fellow?' continued Humphrey.

'Just as much, though not quite so wildly,' she said in a low voice.

'It was very unfortunate, ma'am, that the boy Johnny should ever ha' told him his mother's dying words, about her being broken-hearted and cast off by her son. 'Twas enough to upset any man alive.'

Eustacia made no reply beyond that of a slight catch in her breath, as of one who fain would speak but could not; and Humphrey, declining her invitation to come in, went away.

Eustacia turned, entered the house, and ascended to the front bedroom, where a shaded light was burning. In the bed lay Clym, pale, haggard, wide awake, tossing to one side and to the other, his eyes lit by a hot light, as if the fire in their pupils were burning up their substance.

'Is it you, Eustacia?' he said as she sat down.

'Yes, Clym. I have been down to the gate. The moon is shining beautifully, and there is not a leaf stirring.'

'Shining, is it? What's the moon to a man like me? Let it shine— let anything be, so that I never see another day! . . Eustacia, I don't know where to look: my thoughts go through me like swords. O, if any man wants to make himself immortal by painting a picture of wretchedness, let him come here!'

'Why do you say so?'

---

1. Quoting Job 3.20; the passage goes on to express Job's wish for death.

'I cannot help feeling that I did my best to kill her.'

'No, Clym.'

'Yes, it was so; it is useless to excuse me! My conduct to her was too hideous—I made no advances; and she could not bring herself to forgive me. Now she is dead! If I had only shown myself willing to make it up with her sooner, and we had been friends, and then she had died, it wouldn't be so hard to bear. But I never went near her house, so she never came near mine, and didn't know how welcome she would have been—that's what troubles me. She did not know I was going to her house that very night, for she was too insensible to understand me. If she had only come to see me! I longed that she would. But it was not to be.'

There escaped from Eustacia one of those shivering sighs which used to shake her like a pestilent blast. She had not yet told.

But Yeobright was too deeply absorbed in the ramblings incidental to his remorseful state to notice her. During his illness he had been continually talking thus. Despair had been added to his original grief by the unfortunate disclosure of the boy who had received the last words of Mrs. Yeobright—words too bitterly uttered in an hour of misapprehension. Then his distress had overwhelmed him, and he longed for death as a field labourer longs for the shade. It was the pitiful sight of a man standing in the very focus of sorrow. He continually bewailed his tardy journey to his mother's house, because it was an error which could never be rectified, and insisted that he must have been horribly perverted by some fiend not to have thought before that it was his duty to go to her, since she did not come to him. He would ask Eustacia to agree with him in his self-condemnation; and when she, seared inwardly by a secret she dared not tell, declared that she could not give an opinion, he would say, 'That's because you didn't know my mother's nature. She was always ready to forgive if asked to do so; but I seemed to her to be as an obstinate child, and that made her unyielding. Yet not unyielding: she was proud and reserved, no more. . . . Yes, I can understand why she held out against me so long. She was waiting for me. I dare say she said a hundred times in her sorrow, "What a return he makes for all the sacrifices I have made for him!" I never went to her! When I set out to visit her it was too late. To think of that is nearly intolerable!'

Sometimes his condition had been one of utter remorse, unsoftened by a single tear of pure sorrow: and then he writhed as he lay, fevered far more by thought than by physical ills. 'If I could only get one assurance that she did not die in a belief that I was resentful,' he said one day when in this mood, 'it would be better to think of than a hope of heaven. But that I cannot do.'

'You give yourself up too much to this wearying despair,' said Eustacia. 'Other men's mothers have died.'

'That doesn't make the loss of mine less. Yet it is less the loss than the circumstances of the loss. I sinned against her, and on that account there is no light for me.'

'She sinned against you, I think.'

'No: she did not. I committed the guilt; and may the whole burden be upon my head!'

'I think you might consider twice before you say that,' Eustacia replied. 'Single men have, no doubt, a right to curse themselves as much as they please; but men with wives involve two in the doom they pray down.'

'I am in too sorry a state to understand what you are refining on,' said the wretched man. 'Day and night shout at me, "You have helped to kill her." But in loathing myself I may, I own, be unjust to you, my poor wife. Forgive me for it, Eustacia, for I scarcely know what I do.'[2]

Eustacia was always anxious to avoid the sight of her husband in such a state as this, which had become as dreadful to her as the trial scene was to Judas Iscariot.[3] It brought before her eyes the spectre of a worn-out woman knocking at a door which she would not open; and she shrank from contemplating it. Yet it was better for Yeobright himself when he spoke openly of his sharp regret, for in silence he endured infinitely more, and would sometimes remain so long in a tense, brooding mood, consuming himself by the gnawing of his thought, that it was imperatively necessary to make him talk aloud, that his grief might in some degree expend itself in the effort.

Eustacia had not been long indoors after her look at the moonlight when a soft footstep came up to the house, and Thomasin was announced by the woman downstairs.

'Ah, Thomasin! Thank you for coming to-night,' said Clym when she entered the room. 'Here am I, you see. Such a wretched spectacle am I, that I shrink from being seen by a single friend, and almost from you.'

'You must not shrink from me, dear Clym,' said Thomasin earnestly, in that sweet voice of hers which came to a sufferer like fresh air into a Black Hole.[4] 'Nothing in you can ever shock me or drive me away. I have been here before, but you don't remember it.'

---

2. Clym's words echo those of Christ on the cross: "Father, forgive them; for they know not what they do" (Luke 23.34).

3. Judas betrayed Christ, but later repented and hanged himself; see Matthew 27.3–6.

4. In 1756, after the fall of Calcutta to Indian forces, 146 Europeans were confined overnight in a small, airless room ("the Black Hole of Calcutta"); only 23 survived.

'Yes, I do; I am not delirious, Thomasin, nor have I been so at all. Don't you believe that if they say so. I am only in great misery at what I have done: and that, with the weakness, makes me seem mad. But it has not upset my reason. Do you think I should remember all about my mother's death if I were out of my mind? No such good luck. Two months and a half, Thomasin, the last of her life, did my poor mother live alone, distracted and mourning because of me; yet she was unvisited by me, though I was living only six miles off. Two months and a half—seventy-five days did the sun rise and set upon her in that deserted state which a dog didn't deserve! Poor people who had nothing in common with her would have cared for her, and visited her had they known her sickness and loneliness; but I, who should have been all to her, stayed away like a cur. If there is any justice in God let Him kill me now. He has nearly blinded me, but that is not enough. If He would only strike me with more pain I would believe in Him for ever!'

'Hush, hush! O, pray, Clym, don't, don't say it!' implored Thomasin, affrighted into sobs and tears; while Eustacia, at the other side of the room, though her pale face remained calm, writhed in her chair. Clym went on without heeding his cousin.

'But I am not worth receiving further proof even of Heaven's reprobation. Do you think, Thomasin, that she knew me—that she did not die in that horrid mistaken notion about my not forgiving her, which I can't tell you how she acquired? If you could only assure me of that! Do you think so, Eustacia? Do speak to me.'

'I think I can assure you that she knew better at last,' said Thomasin. The pallid Eustacia said nothing.

'Why didn't she come to my house? I would have taken her in and showed her how I loved her in spite of all. But she never came; and I didn't go to her, and she died on the heath like an animal kicked out, nobody to help her till it was too late. If you could have seen her, Thomasin, as I saw her—a poor dying woman, lying in the dark upon the bare ground, moaning, nobody near, believing she was utterly deserted by all the world, it would have moved you to anguish, it would have moved a brute. And this poor woman my mother! No wonder she said to the child, "You have seen a broken-hearted woman." What a state she must have been brought to, to say that! and who can have done it but I? It is too dreadful to think of, and I wish I could be punished more heavily than I am. How long was I what they called out of my senses?'

'A week, I think.'

'And then I became calm.'

'Yes, for four days.'

'And now I have left off being calm.'

'But try to be quiet: please do, and you will soon be strong. If you could remove that impression from your mind——'

'Yes, yes,' he said impatiently. 'But I don't want to get strong. What's the use of my getting well? It would be better for me if I die, and it would certainly be better for Eustacia. Is Eustacia there?'

'Yes.'

'It would be better for you, Eustacia, if I were to die?'

'Don't press such a question, dear Clym.'

'Well, it really is but a shadowy supposition; for unfortunately I am going to live. I feel myself getting better. Thomasin, how long are you going to stay at the inn, now that all this money has come to your husband?'

'Another month or two, probably; until my illness[5] is over. We cannot get off till then. I think it will be a month or more.'

'Yes, yes. Of course. Ah, Cousin Tamsie, you will get over your trouble—one little month will take you through it, and bring something to console you; but I shall never get over mine, and no consolation will come!'

'Clym, you are unjust to yourself. Depend upon it, aunt thought kindly of you. I know that, if she had lived, you would have been reconciled with her.'

'But she didn't come to see me, though I asked her, before I married, if she would come. Had she come, or had I gone there, she would never have died saying, "I am a broken-hearted woman, cast off by my son." My door has always been open to her—a welcome here has always awaited her. But that she never came to see.'

'You had better not talk any more now, Clym,' said Eustacia faintly from the other part of the room, for the scene was growing intolerable to her.

'Let me talk to you instead for the little time I shall be here,' Thomasin said soothingly. 'Consider what a one-sided way you have of looking at the matter, Clym. When she said that to the little boy you had not found her and taken her into your arms; and it might have been uttered in a moment of bitterness. It was rather like aunt to say things in haste. She sometimes used to speak so to me. Though she did not come I am convinced that she thought of coming to see you. Do you suppose a man's mother could live two or three months without one forgiving thought? She forgave me; and why should she not have forgiven you?'

'You laboured to win her round; I did nothing. I, who was going to teach people the higher secrets of happiness, did not know how

5. Her pregnancy.

to keep out of that gross misery which the most untaught are wise enough to avoid.'

'How did you get here to-night, Thomasin?' said Eustacia.

'Damon set me down at the end of the lane. He has driven into East Egdon on business, and he will come and pick me up by-and-by.'

Accordingly they soon after heard the noise of wheels. Wildeve had come, and was waiting outside with his horse and gig.

'Send out and tell him I will be down in two minutes,' said Thomasin.

'I will run down myself,' said Eustacia.

She went down. Wildeve had alighted, and was standing before the horse's head when Eustacia opened the door. He did not turn for a moment, thinking the comer Thomasin. Then he looked, started ever so little, and said one word: 'Well?'

'I have not yet told him,' she replied in a whisper.

'Then don't do so till he is well—it will be fatal. You are ill yourself.'

'I am wretched. . . . O Damon,' she said, bursting into tears, 'I—I can't tell you how unhappy I am! I can hardly bear this. I can tell nobody of my trouble—nobody knows of it but you.'

'Poor girl!' said Wildeve, visibly affected at her distress, and at last led on so far as to take her hand. 'It is hard, when you have done nothing to deserve it, that you should have got involved in such a web as this. You were not made for these sad scenes. I am to blame most. If I could only have saved you from it all!'

'But, Damon, please pray tell me what I must do? To sit by him hour after hour, and hear him reproach himself as being the cause of her death, and to know that I am the sinner if any human being is at all, drives me into cold despair. I don't know what to do. Should I tell him or should I not tell him? I always am asking myself that. O, I want to tell him; and yet I am afraid. If he finds it out he must surely kill me, for nothing else will be in proportion to his feelings now. "Beware the fury of a patient man"[6] sounds day by day in my ears as I watch him.'

'Well, wait till he is better, and trust to chance. And when you tell, you must only tell part—for his own sake.'

'Which part should I keep back?'

Wildeve paused. 'That I was in the house at the time,' he said in a low tone.

'Yes; it must be concealed, seeing what has been whispered. How much easier are hasty actions than speeches that will excuse them!'

6. Quoting John Dryden, *Absalom and Achitophel* (1681), I.1005; the line comes from a speech lamenting the disloyalty of a son, though this irony is presumably lost on Eustacia.

'If he were only to die——' Wildeve murmured.

'Do not think of it! I would not buy hope of immunity by so cowardly a desire even if I hated him. Now I am going up to him again. Thomasin bade me tell you she would be down in a few minutes. Good-bye.'

She returned, and Thomasin soon appeared. When she was seated in the gig with her husband, and the horse was turning to go off, Wildeve lifted his eyes to the bedroom windows. Looking from one of them he could discern a pale, tragic face watching him drive away. It was Eustacia's.

A *Lurid Light Breaks in upon a Darkened Understanding*

II

Clym's grief became mitigated by wearing itself out. His strength returned, and a month after the visit of Thomasin he might have been seen walking about the garden. Endurance and despair, equanimity and gloom, the tints of health and the pallor of death, mingled weirdly in his face. He was now unnaturally silent upon all of the past that related to his mother; and though Eustacia knew that he was thinking of it none the less, she was only too glad to escape the topic ever to bring it up anew. When his mind had been weaker his heart had led him to speak out; but reason having now somewhat recovered itself he sank into taciturnity.

One evening when he was thus standing in the garden, abstractedly spudding up[1] a weed with his stick, a bony figure turned the corner of the house and came up to him.

'Christian, isn't it?' said Clym. 'I am glad you have found me out. I shall soon want you to go to Blooms-End and assist me in putting the house in order. I suppose it is all locked up as I left it?'

'Yes, Mister Clym.'

'Have you dug up the potatoes and other roots?'

'Yes, without a drop o' rain, thank God. But I was coming to tell 'ee of something else which is quite different from what we have lately had in the family. I am sent by the rich gentleman at the Woman, that we used to call the landlord, to tell 'ee that Mrs. Wildeve is doing well of a girl, which was born punctually at one o'clock at noon, or a few minutes more or less; and 'tis said that expecting of this increase is what have kept 'em there since they came into their money.'

'And she is getting on well, you say?'

'Yes, sir. Only Mr. Wildeve is twanky[2] because 'tisn't a boy—that's

---

1. Digging up.
2. Peevish, complaining (dialect).

what they say in the kitchen, but I was not supposed to notice that.'

'Christian, now listen to me.'

'Yes, sure, Mr. Yeobright.'

'Did you see my mother the day before she died?'

'No, I did not.'

Yeobright's face expressed disappointment.

'But I zeed her the morning of the same day she died.'

Clym's look lighted up. 'That's nearer still to my meaning,' he said.

'Yes, I know 'twas the same day; for she said, "I be going to see him, Christian; so I shall not want any vegetables brought in for dinner." '

'See whom?'

'See you. She was going to your house, you understand.'

Yeobright regarded Christian with intense surprise. 'Why did you never mention this?' he said. 'Are you sure it was my house she was coming to?'

'O yes. I didn't mention it because I've never zeed you lately. And as she didn't get there it was all nought, and nothing to tell.'

'And I have been wondering why she should have walked in the heath on that hot day! Well, did she say what she was coming for? It is a thing, Christian, I am very anxious to know.'

'Yes, Mister Clym. She didn't say it to me, though I think she did to one here and there.'

'Do you know one person to whom she spoke of it?'

'There is one man, please, sir, but I hope you won't mention my name to him, as I have seen him in strange places, particular in dreams. One night last summer he glared at me like Famine and Sword,[3] and it made me feel so low that I didn't comb out my few hairs for two days. He was standing, as it might be, Mister Yeobright, in the middle of the path to Mistover, and your mother came up, looking as pale——'

'Yes, when was that?'

'Last summer, in my dream.'

'Pooh! Who's the man?'

'Diggory, the reddleman. He called upon her and sat with her the evening before she set out to see you. I hadn't gone home from work when he came up to the gate.'

'I must see Venn—I wish I had known it before,' said Clym anxiously. 'I wonder why he has not come to tell me?'

'He went out of Egdon Heath the next day, so would not be likely to know you wanted him.'

---

3. Famine and sword are mentioned together at Isaiah 51.19 and a number of times in Jeremiah (e.g., 11.22, 14.12, 42.16), though Christian may be recalling a representation of the Four Horsemen of the Apocalypse, who have the power to kill with the sword, or with hunger; see Revelation 6.1–8.

'Christian,' said Clym, 'you must go and find Venn. I am otherwise engaged, or I would go myself. Find him at once, and tell him
I want to speak to him.'

'I am a good hand at hunting up folk by day,' said Christian, looking dubiously round at the declining light; 'but as to night-time,
never is such a bad hand as I, Mister Yeobright.'

'Search the heath when you will, so that you bring him soon.
Bring him to-morrow, if you can.'

Christian then departed. The morrow came, but no Venn. In the
evening Christian arrived, looking very weary. He had been searching all day, and had heard nothing of the reddleman.

'Inquire as much as you can to-morrow without neglecting your
work,' said Yeobright. 'Don't come again till you have found him.'

The next day Yeobright set out for the old house at Blooms-End,
which, with the garden, was now his own. His severe illness had
hindered all preparations for his removal thither; but it had become
necessary that he should go and overlook its contents, as administrator to his mother's little property; for which purpose he decided
to pass the next night on the premises.

He journeyed onward, not quickly or decisively, but in the slow
walk of one who has been awakened from a stupefying sleep. It was
early afternoon when he reached the valley. The expression of the
place, the tone of the hour, were precisely those of many such occasions in days gone by; and these antecedent similarities fostered
the illusion that she, who was there no longer, would come out to
welcome him. The garden gate was locked and the shutters were
closed, just as he himself had left them on the evening after the funeral. He unlocked the gate, and found that a spider had already
constructed a large web, tying the door to the lintel, on the supposition that it was never to be opened again. When he had entered
the house and flung back the shutters he set about his task of over-
hauling the cupboards and closets, burning papers, and considering
how best to arrange the place for Eustacia's reception, until such
time as he might be in a position to carry out his long-delayed
scheme, should that time ever arrive.

As he surveyed the rooms he felt strongly disinclined for the alterations which would have to be made in the time-honoured fur-
nishing of his parents and grandparents, to suit Eustacia's modern
ideas. The gaunt oak-cased clock, with the picture of the Ascension[4] on the door-panel and the Miraculous Draught of Fishes[5] on
the base; his grandmother's corner cupboard with the glass door,

---

4. The Ascension of Christ into Heaven is described several times in the Bible, most fully
at Acts 1.9–11.
5. See Luke 5.1–11, or John 21.4–14, where the story is connected with Christ's third appearance to his disciples after the resurrection.

through which the spotted china was visible; the dumb-waiter;[6] the wooden tea-trays; the hanging fountain[7] with the brass tap—whither would these venerable articles have to be banished?

He noticed that the flowers in the window had died for want of water, and he placed them out upon the ledge, that they might be taken away. While thus engaged he heard footsteps on the gravel without, and somebody knocked at the door.

Yeobright opened it, and Venn was standing before him.

'Good morning,' said the reddleman. 'Is Mrs. Yeobright at home?'

Yeobright looked upon the ground. 'Then you have not seen Christian or any of the Egdon folks?' he said.

'No. I have only just returned after a long stay away. I called here the day before I left.'

'And you have heard nothing?'

'Nothing.'

'My mother is—dead.'

'Dead!' said Venn mechanically.

'Her home now is where I shouldn't mind having mine.'

Venn regarded him, and then said, 'If I didn't see your face I could never believe your words. Have you been ill?'

'I had an illness.'

'Well, the change! When I parted from her a month ago everything seemed to say that she was going to begin a new life.'

'And what seemed came true.'

'You say right, no doubt. Trouble has taught you a deeper vein of talk than mine. All I meant was regarding her life here. She has died too soon.'

'Perhaps through my living too long. I have had a bitter experience on that score this last month, Diggory. But come in; I have been wanting to see you.'

He conducted the reddleman into the large room where the dancing had taken place the previous Christmas; and they sat down in the settle together. 'There's the cold fireplace, you see,' said Clym. 'When that half-burnt log and those cinders were alight she was alive! Little has been changed here yet. I can do nothing. My life creeps like a snail.'

'How came she to die?' said Venn.

Yeobright gave him some particulars of her illness and death, and continued: 'After this no kind of pain will ever seem more than an indisposition to me.—I began saying that I wanted to ask you something, but I stray from subjects like a drunken man. I am anxious to know what my mother said to you when she last saw you. You talked with her a long time, I think?'

6. Movable table, usually with revolving shelves, for use in a dining room.
7. Container hung up indoors to provide a supply of fresh water.

'I talked with her more than half an hour.'

'About me?'

'Yes. And it must have been on account of what we said that she was on the heath. Without question she was coming to see you.'

'But why should she come to see me if she felt so bitterly against me? There's the mystery.'

'Yet I know she quite forgave 'ee.'

'But, Diggory—would a woman, who had quite forgiven her son, say, when she felt herself ill on the way to his house, that she was broken-hearted because of his ill-usage? Never!'

'What I know is that she didn't blame you at all. She blamed herself for what had happened, and only herself. I had it from her own lips.'

'You had it from her lips that I had *not* ill-treated her; and at the same time another had it from her lips that I *had* ill-treated her? My mother was no impulsive woman who changed her opinion every hour without reason. How can it be, Venn, that she should have told such different stories in close succession?'

'I cannot say. It is certainly odd, when she had forgiven you, and had forgiven your wife, and was going to see ye on purpose to make friends.'

'If there was one thing wanting to bewilder me it was this incomprehensible thing! . . . Diggory, if we, who remain alive, were only allowed to hold conversation with the dead—just once, a bare minute, even through a screen of iron bars, as with persons in prison—what we might learn! How many who now ride smiling would hide their heads! And this mystery—I should then be at the bottom of it at once. But the grave has for ever shut her in; and how shall it be found out now?'

No reply was returned by his companion, since none could be given; and when Venn left, a few minutes later, Clym had passed from the dulness of sorrow to the fluctuation of carking[8] incertitude.

He continued in the same state all the afternoon. A bed was made up for him in the same house by a neighbour, that he might not have to return again the next day; and when he retired to rest in the deserted place it was only to remain awake hour after hour thinking the same thoughts. How to discover a solution to this riddle of death seemed a query of more importance than highest problems of the living. There was housed in his memory a vivid picture of the face of a little boy as he entered the hovel where Clym's mother lay. The round eyes, eager gaze, the piping voice which enunciated the words, had operated like stilettos on his brain.

8. Troubling, burdensome.

A visit to the boy suggested itself as a means of gleaning new particulars; though it might be quite unproductive. To probe a child's
mind after the lapse of six weeks, not for facts which the child had
seen and understood, but to get at those which were in their nature
beyond him, did not promise much; yet when every obvious channel is blocked we grope towards the small and obscure. There was
nothing else left to do; after that he would allow the enigma to drop
into the abyss of undiscoverable things.

It was about daybreak when he had reached this decision, and he
at once arose. He locked up the house and went out into the green
patch which merged in heather further on. In front of the white
garden-palings the path branched into three like a broad-arrow.
The road to the right led to the Quiet Woman and its neighbourhood; the middle track led to Mistover Knap; the left-hand track
led over the hill to another part of Mistover, where the child lived.
On inclining into the latter path Yeobright felt a creeping chilliness,
familiar enough to most people, and probably caused by the un-
sunned morning air. In after days he thought of it as a thing of singular significance.

When Yeobright reached the cottage of Susan Nunsuch, the
mother of the boy he sought, he found that the inmates were not
yet astir. But in upland hamlets the transition from a-bed to abroad
is surprisingly swift and easy. There no dense partition of yawns
and toilets divides humanity by night from humanity by day. Yeobright tapped at the upper window-sill, which he could reach with
his walking-stick; and in three or four minutes the woman came
down.

It was not till this moment that Clym recollected her to be the
person who had behaved so barbarously to Eustacia. It partly explained the insuavity with which the woman greeted him. Moreover, the boy had been ailing again; and Susan now, as ever since
the night when he had been pressed into Eustacia's service at the
bonfire, attributed his indispositions to Eustacia's influence as a
witch. It was one of those sentiments which lurk like moles underneath the visible surface of manners, and may have been kept alive
by Eustacia's entreaty to the captain, at the time that he had intended to prosecute Susan for the pricking in church, to let the
matter drop; which he accordingly had done.

Yeobright overcame his repugnance, for Susan had at least borne
his mother no ill-will. He asked kindly for the boy; but her manner
did not improve.

'I wish to see him,' continued Yeobright, with some hesitation; 'to
ask him if he remembers anything more of his walk with my mother
than what he has previously told.'

She regarded him in a peculiar and criticizing manner. To anybody but a half-blind man it would have said, 'You want another of the knocks which have already laid you so low.'

She called the boy downstairs, asked Clym to sit down on a stool, and continued, 'Now, Johnny, tell Mr. Yeobright anything you can call to mind.'

'You have not forgotten how you walked with the poor lady on that hot day?' said Clym.

'No,' said the boy.

'And what she said to you?'

The boy repeated the exact words he had used on entering the hut. Yeobright rested his elbow on the table and shaded his face with his hand; and the mother looked as if she wondered how a man could want more of what had stung him so deeply.

'She was going to Alderworth when you first met her?'

'No; she was coming away.'

'That can't be.'

'Yes; she walked along with me. I was coming away, too.'

'Then where did you first see her?'

'At your house.'

'Attend, and speak the truth!' said Clym sternly.

'Yes, sir; at your house was where I seed her first.'

Clym started up, and Susan smiled in an expectant way which did not embellish her face; it seemed to mean, 'Something sinister is coming!'

'What did she do at my house?'

'She went and sat under the trees at the Devil's Bellows.'

'Good God! this is all news to me!'

'You never told me this before?' said Susan.

'No, mother; because I didn't like to tell 'ee I had been so far. I was picking black-hearts,[9] and went further than I meant.'

'What did she do then?' said Yeobright.

'Looked at a man who came up and went into your house.'

'That was myself—a furze-cutter, with brambles in his hand.'

'No; 'twas not you. 'Twas a gentleman. You had gone in afore.'

'Who was he?'

'I don't know.'

'Now tell me what happened next.'

'The poor lady went and knocked at your door, and the lady with black hair looked out of the side-window at her.'

The boy's mother turned to Clym and said, 'This is something you didn't expect?'

Yeobright took no more notice of her than if he had been of stone. 'Go on, go on,' he said hoarsely to the boy.

9. Whortleberries.

'And when she saw the young lady look out of the window the old lady knocked again; and when nobody came she took up the furze-hook and looked at it, and put it down again, and then she looked at the faggot-bonds; and then she went away, and walked across to me, and blowed her breath very hard, like this. We walked on together, she and I, and I talked to her and she talked to me a bit, but not much, because she couldn't blow her breath.'

'O!' murmured Clym, in a low tone, and bowed his head. 'Let's have more,' he said.

'She couldn't talk much, and she couldn't walk; and her face was, O so queer!'

'How was her face?'

'Like yours is now.'

The woman looked at Yeobright, and beheld him colourless, in a cold sweat. 'Isn't there meaning in it?' she said stealthily. 'What do you think of her now?'

'Silence!' said Clym fiercely. And, turning to the boy, 'And then you left her to die?'

'No,' said the woman, quickly and and agrily. 'He did not leave her to die! She sent him away. Whoever says he forsook her says what's not true.'

'Trouble no more about that,' answered Clym, with a quivering mouth. 'What he did is a trifle in comparison with what he saw. Door kept shut, did you say? Kept shut, she looking out of window? Good heart of God!—what does it mean?'

The child shrank away from the gaze of his questioner.

'He said so,' answered the mother, 'and Johnny's a God-fearing boy and tells no lies.'

' "Cast off by my son!" No, by my best life, dear mother, it is not so! But by your son's, your son's—May all murderesses get the torment they deserve!'

With these words Yeobright went forth from the little dwelling. The pupils of his eyes, fixed steadfastly on blankness, were vaguely lit with an icy shine; his mouth had passed into the phase more or less imaginatively rendered in studies of Oedipus.[1] The strangest deeds were possible to his mood. But they were not possible to his situation. Instead of there being before him the pale face of Eustacia, and a masculine shape unknown, there was only the imperturbable countenance of the heath, which, having defied the cataclysmal onsets of centuries, reduced to insignificance by its seamed and antique features the wildest turmoil of a single man.

1. Oedipus killed his father, King Laius of Thebes, and married his mother, Jocasta, not knowing that he was their son; when he discovered the truth, he blinded himself. Prior to the 1895 edition, the comparison was with Laocoön, priest of Apollo at Troy, who was killed in a struggle with serpents; the change emphasizes Clym's intense relationship with his mother.

Eustacia Dresses Herself on a Black Morning

III

A consciousness of a vast impassivity in all which lay around him took possession even of Yeobright in his wild walk towards Alderworth. He had once before felt in his own person this overpowering of the fervid by the inanimate; but then it had tended to enervate a passion far sweeter than that which at present pervaded him. It was once when he stood parting from Eustacia in the moist still levels beyond the hills.

But dismissing all this he went onward home, and came to the front of his house. The blinds of Eustacia's bedroom were still closely drawn, for she was no early riser. All the life visible was in the shape of a solitary thrush cracking a small snail upon the door-stone for his breakfast, and his tapping seemed a loud noise in the general silence which prevailed; but on going to the door Clym found it unfastened, the young girl who attended upon Eustacia being astir in the back part of the premises. Yeobright entered and went straight to his wife's room.

The noise of his arrival must have aroused her, for when he opened the door she was standing before the looking-glass in her night-dress, the ends of her hair gathered into one hand, with which she was coiling the whole mass round her head, previous to beginning toilette operations. She was not a woman given to speaking first at a meeting, and she allowed Clym to walk across in silence, without turning her head. He came behind her, and she saw his face in the glass. It was ashy, haggard, and terrible. Instead of starting towards him in sorrowful surprise, as even Eustacia, undemonstrative wife as she was, would have done in days before she burdened herself with a secret, she remained motionless, looking at him in the glass. And while she looked the carmine flush with which warmth and sound sleep had suffused her cheeks and neck, dissolved from view, and the death-like pallor in his face flew across into hers. He was close enough to see this, and the sight instigated his tongue.

'You know what is the matter,' he said huskily. 'I see it in your face.'

Her hand relinquished the rope of hair and dropped to her side, and the pile of tresses, no longer supported, fell from the crown of her head about her shoulders and over the white night-gown. She made no reply.

'Speak to me,' said Yeobright peremptorily.

The blanching process did not cease in her, and her lips now became as white as her face. She turned to him and said, 'Yes, Clym,

I'll speak to you. Why do you return so early? Can I do anything for you?'

'Yes, you can listen to me. It seems that my wife is not very well?'

'Why?'

'Your face, my dear; your face. Or perhaps it is the pale morning light which takes your colour away? Now I am going to reveal a secret to you. Ha-ha!'

'O, that is ghastly!'

'What?'

'Your laugh.'

'There's reason for ghastliness. Eustacia; you have held my happiness in the hollow of your hand, and like a devil you have dashed it down!'

She started back from the dressing-table, retreated a few steps from him, and looked him in the face. 'Ah! you think to frighten me,' she said, with a slight laugh. 'Is it worth while? I am undefended, and alone.'

'How extraordinary!'

'What do you mean?'

'As there is ample time I will tell you, though you know well enough. I mean that it is extraordinary that you should be alone in my absence. Tell me, now, where is he who was with you on the afternoon of the thirty-first of August? Under the bed? Up the chimney?'

A shudder overcame her and shook the light fabric of her nightdress throughout. 'I do not remember dates so exactly,' she said. 'I cannot recollect that anybody was with me besides yourself.'

'The day I mean,' said Yeobright, his voice growing louder and harsher, 'was the day you shut the door against my mother and killed her. O, it is too much—too bad!' He leant over the footpiece of the bedstead for a few moments, with his back towards her; then rising again: 'Tell me, tell me! tell me—do you hear?' he cried, rushing up to her and seizing her by the loose folds of her sleeve.

The superstratum of timidity which often overlies those who are daring and defiant at heart had been passed through, and the mettlesome substance of the woman was reached. The red blood inundated her face, previously so pale.

'What are you going to do?' she said in a low voice, regarding him with a proud smile. 'You will not alarm me by holding on so; but it would be a pity to tear my sleeve.'

Instead of letting go he drew her closer to him. 'Tell me the particulars of—my mother's death,' he said in a hard, panting whisper; 'or—I'll—I'll——'

'Clym,' she answered slowly, 'do you think you dare do anything to me that I dare not bear? But before you strike me listen. You will get nothing from me by a blow, even though it should kill me, as it probably will. But perhaps you do not wish me to speak—killing may be all you mean?'

'Kill you! Do you expect it?'

'I do.'

'Why?'

'No less degree of rage against me will match your previous grief for her.'

'Phew—I shall not kill you,' he said contemptuously, as if under a sudden change of purpose. 'I did think of it; but—I shall not. That would be making a martyr of you, and sending you to where she is; and I would keep you away from her till the universe come to an end, if I could.'

'I almost wish you would kill me,' said she with gloomy bitterness. 'It is with no strong desire, I assure you, that I play the part I have lately played on earth. You are no blessing, my husband.'

'You shut the door—you looked out of the window upon her—you had a man in the house with you—you sent her away to die. The inhumanity—the treachery—I will not touch you—stand away from me—and confess every word!'

'Never! I'll hold my tongue like the very death that I don't mind meeting, even though I can clear myself of half you believe by speaking. Yes. I will! Who of any dignity would take the trouble to clear cobwebs from a wild man's mind after such language as this? No; let him go on, and think his narrow thoughts, and run his head into the mire. I have other cares.'

' 'Tis too much—but I must spare you.'

'Poor charity.'

'By my wretched soul you sting me, Eustacia! I can keep it up, and hotly too. Now, then, madam, tell me his name!'

'Never, I am resolved.'

'How often does he write to you? Where does he put his letters—when does he meet you? Ah, his letters! Do you tell me his name?'

'I do not.'

'Then I'll find it myself.' His eye had fallen upon a small desk that stood near, on which she was accustomed to write her letters. He went to it. It was locked.

'Unlock this!'

'You have no right to say it. That's mine.'

Without another word he seized the desk and dashed it to the floor. The hinge burst open, and a number of letters tumbled out.

'Stay!' said Eustacia, stepping before him with more excitement than she had hitherto shown.

'Come, come! stand away! I must see them.'

She looked at the letters as they lay, checked her feeling, and moved indifferently aside; when he gathered them up, and examined them.

By no stretch of meaning could any but a harmless construction be placed upon a single one of the letters themselves. The solitary exception was an empty envelope directed to her, and the handwriting was Wildeve's. Yeobright held it up. Eustacia was doggedly silent.

'Can you read, madam?[1] Look at this envelope. Doubtless we shall find more soon, and what was inside them. I shall no doubt be gratified by learning in good time what a well-finished and full-blown adept in a certain trade my lady is.'

'Do you say it to me—do you?' she gasped.

He searched further, but found nothing more. 'What was in this letter?' he said.

'Ask the writer. Am I your hound that you should talk to me in this way?'

'Do you brave me? do you stand me out, mistress? Answer. Don't look at me with those eyes as if you would bewitch me again! Sooner than that I die. You refuse to answer?'

'I wouldn't tell you after this, if I were as innocent as the sweetest babe in heaven!'

'Which you are not.'

'Certainly I am not absolutely,' she replied. 'I have not done what you suppose; but if to have done no harm at all is the only innocence recognized, I am beyond forgiveness. But I require no help from your conscience.'

'You can resist, and resist again! Instead of hating you I could, I think, mourn for and pity you, if you were contrite, and would confess all. Forgive you I never can. I don't speak of your lover—I will give you the benefit of the doubt in that matter, for it only affects me personally. But the other: had you half-killed *me*, had it been that you wilfully took the sight away from these feeble eyes of mine, I could have forgiven you. But *that's* too much for nature!'

'Say no more. I will do without your pity. But I would have saved you from uttering what you will regret.'

'I am going away now. I shall leave you.'

'You need not go, as I am going myself. You will keep just as far away from me by staying here.'

'Call her to mind—think of her—what goodness there was in her: it showed in every line of her face! Most women, even when but slightly annoyed, show a flicker of evil in some curl of the mouth or some corner of the cheek; but as for her, never in her an-

---

1. Compare Brachiano's "Can you read Mistresse?" in John Webster's play *The White Devil* (c. 1608), IV.2.81: one of a number of striking echoes between the two scenes. Hardy was reading Webster in the summer of 1876.

griest moments was there anything malicious in her look. She was angered quickly, but she forgave just as readily, and underneath her pride there was the meekness of a child. What came of it?—what cared you? You hated her just as she was learning to love you. O! couldn't you see what was best for you, but must bring a curse upon me, and agony and death upon her, by doing that cruel deed! What was the fellow's name who was keeping you company and causing you to add cruelty to her to your wrong to me? Was it Wildeve? Was it poor Thomasin's husband? Heaven, what wickedness! Lost your voice, have you? It is natural after detection of that most noble trick. . . . Eustacia, didn't any tender thought of your own mother lead you to think of being gentle to mine at such a time of weariness? Did not one grain of pity enter your heart as she turned away? Think what a vast opportunity was then lost of beginning a forgiving and honest course. Why did not you kick him out, and let her in, and say, I'll be an honest wife and a noble woman from this hour? Had I told you to go and quench eternally our last flickering chance of happiness here you could have done no worse. Well, she's asleep now; and have you a hundred gallants,[2] neither they nor you can insult her any more.'

'You exaggerate fearfully,' she said in a faint, weary voice; 'but I cannot enter into my defence—it is not worth doing. You are nothing to me in future, and the past side of the story may as well remain untold. I have lost all through you, but I have not complained. Your blunders and misfortunes may have been a sorrow to you, but they have been a wrong to me. All persons of refinement have been scared away from me since I sank into the mire of marriage. Is this your cherishing—to put me into a hut like this, and keep me like the wife of a hind?[3] You deceived me—not by words, but by appearances, which are less seen through than words. But the place will serve as well as any other—as somewhere to pass from—into my grave.' Her words were smothered in her throat, and her head drooped down.

'I don't know what you mean by that. Am I the cause of your sin?' (Eustacia made a trembling motion towards him.) 'What, you can begin to shed tears and offer me your hand? Good God! can you? No, not I. I'll not commit the fault of taking that.' (The hand she had offered dropped nervelessly, but the tears continued flowing.) 'Well, yes, I'll take it, if only for the sake of my own foolish kisses that were wasted there before I knew what I cherished. How bewitched I was! How could there be any good in a woman that everybody spoke ill of?'

2. Lovers.
3. Laborer.

'O, O, O!' she cried, breaking down at last; and, shaking with sobs which choked her, she sank upon her knees. 'O, will you have done! O, you are too relentless—there's a limit to the cruelty of savages! I have held out long—but you crush me down. I beg for mercy—I cannot bear this any longer—it is inhuman to go further with this! If I had—killed your—mother with my own hand—I should not deserve such a scourging to the bone as this. O, O! God have mercy upon a miserable woman! . . . You have beaten me in this game—I beg you to stay your hand in pity! . . . I confess that I—wilfully did not undo the door the first time she knocked—but—I—should have unfastened it the second—if I had not thought you had gone to do it yourself. When I found you had not I opened it, but she was gone. That's the extent of my crime—towards *her*. Best natures commit bad faults sometimes, don't they?—I think they do. Now I will leave you—for ever and ever!'

'Tell all, and I *will* pity you. Was the man in the house with you Wildeve?'

'I cannot tell,' she said desperately through her sobbing. 'Don't insist further—I cannot tell. I am going from this house. We cannot both stay here.'

'You need not go: I will go. You can stay here.'

'No, I will dress, and then I will go.'

'Where?'

'Where I came from, or *else*where.'

She hastily dressed herself, Yeobright moodily walking up and down the room the whole of the time. At last all her things were on. Her little hands quivered so violently as she held them to her chin to fasten her bonnet that she could not tie the strings, and after a few moments she relinquished the attempt. Seeing this he moved forward and said, 'Let me tie them.'

She assented in silence, and lifted her chin. For once at least in her life she was totally oblivious of the charm of her attitude. But he was not, and he turned his eyes aside, that he might not be tempted to softness.

The strings were tied; she turned from him. 'Do you still prefer going away yourself to my leaving you?' he inquired again.

'I do.'

'Very well—let it be. And when you will confess to the man I may pity you.'

She flung her shawl about her and went downstairs, leaving him standing in the room.

Eustacia had not long been gone when there came a knock at the door of the bedroom; and Yeobright said, 'Well?'

It was the servant; and she replied, 'Somebody from Mrs.

Wildeve's have called to tell 'ee that the mis'ess and the baby are getting on wonderful well, and the baby's name is to be Eustacia Clementine.' And the girl retired.

'What a mockery!' said Clym. 'This unhappy marriage of mine to be perpetuated in that child's name!'

The Ministrations of a Half-Forgotten One

IV

Eustacia's journey was at first as vague in direction as that of this-tledown on the wind. She did not know what to do. She wished it had been night instead of morning, that she might at least have borne her misery without the possibility of being seen. Tracing mile after mile along between the dying ferns and the wet white spiders' webs, she at length turned her steps towards her grandfather's house. She found the front door closed and locked. Mechanically she went round to the end where the stable was, and on looking in at the stable-door she saw Charley standing within.

'Captain Vye is not at home?' she said.

'No, ma'am,' said the lad in a flutter of feeling; 'he's gone to Weatherbury, and won't be home till night. And the servant is gone home for a holiday. So the house is locked up.'

Eustacia's face was not visible to Charley as she stood at the doorway, her back being to the sky, and the stable but indifferently lighted; but the wildness of her manner arrested his attention. She turned and walked away across the enclosure to the gate, and was hidden by the bank.

When she had disappeared Charley, with misgiving in his eyes, slowly came from the stable-door, and going to another point in the bank he looked over. Eustacia was leaning against it on the outside, her face covered with her hands, and her head pressing the dewy heather which bearded the bank's outer side. She appeared to be utterly indifferent to the circumstance that her bonnet, hair, and garments were becoming wet and disarranged by the moisture of her cold, harsh pillow. Clearly something was wrong.

Charley had always regarded Eustacia as Eustacia had regarded Clym when she first beheld him—as a romantic and sweet vision, scarcely incarnate. He had been so shut off from her by the dignity of her look and the pride of her speech, except at that one blissful interval when he was allowed to hold her hand, that he had hardly deemed her a woman, wingless and earthly, subject to household conditions and domestic jars. The inner details of her life he had only conjectured. She had been a lovely wonder, predestined to an orbit in which the whole of his own was but a point; and this sight of her leaning like a helpless, despairing creature against a wild wet bank, filled him with an amazed horror. He could no longer remain where he was. Leaping over, he came up, touched her with his finger, and said tenderly, 'You are poorly, ma'am. What can I do?'

Eustacia started up, and said, 'Ah, Charley—you have followed me. You did not think when I left home in the summer that I should come back like this!'

'I did not, dear ma'am. Can I help you now?'

'I am afraid not. I wish I could get into the house. I feel giddy—that's all.'

'Lean on my arm, ma'am, till we get to the porch; and I will try to open the door.'

He supported her to the porch, and there depositing her on a seat hastened to the back, climbed to a window by the help of a ladder, and descending inside opened the door. Next he assisted her into the room, where there was an old-fashioned horsehair settee as large as a donkey-waggon. She lay down here, and Charley covered her with a cloak he found in the hall.

'Shall I get you something to eat and drink?' he said.

'If you please, Charley. But I suppose there is no fire?'

'I can light it, ma'am.'

He vanished, and she heard a splitting of wood and a blowing of bellows; and presently he returned, saying, 'I have lighted a fire in the kitchen, and now I'll light one here.'

He lit the fire, Eustacia dreamily observing him from her couch. When it was blazing up he said, 'Shall I wheel you round in front of it, ma'am, as the morning is chilly?'

'Yes, if you like.'

'Shall I go and bring the victuals now?'

'Yes, do,' she murmured languidly.

When he had gone, and the dull sounds occasionally reached her ears of his movements in the kitchen, she forgot where she was, and had for a moment to consider by an effort what the sounds meant. After an interval which seemed short to her whose thoughts were elsewhere, he came in with a tray on which steamed tea and toast, though it was nearly lunch-time.

'Place it on the table,' she said. 'I shall be ready soon.'

He did so, and retired to the door: when, however, he perceived that she did not move he came back a few steps.

'Let me hold it to you, if you don't wish to get up,' said Charley. He brought the tray to the front of the couch, where he knelt down, adding, 'I will hold it for you.'

Eustacia sat up and poured out a cup of tea. 'You are very kind to me, Charley,' she murmured as she sipped.

'Well, I ought to be,' said he diffidently, taking great trouble not

'He brought the tray to the front of the couch.'

to rest his eyes upon her, though this was their only natural position, Eustacia being immediately before him. 'You have been kind to me.'

'How have I?' said Eustacia.

'You let me hold your hand when you were a maiden at home.'

'Ah, so I did. Why did I do that? My mind is lost—it had to do with the mumming, had it not?'

'Yes, you wanted to go in my place.'

'I remember. I do indeed remember—too well!'

She again became utterly downcast; and Charley, seeing that she was not going to eat or drink any more, took away the tray.

Afterwards he occasionally came in to see if the fire was burning, to ask her if she wanted anything, to tell her that the wind had shifted from south to west, to ask her if she would like him to gather her some blackberries; to all which inquiries she replied in the negative or with indifference.

She remained on the settee some time longer, when she aroused herself and went upstairs. The room in which she had formerly slept still remained much as she had left it, and the recollection that this forced upon her of her own greatly changed and infinitely worsened situation again set on her face the undetermined and formless misery which it had worn on her first arrival. She peeped into her grandfather's room, through which the fresh autumn air was blowing from the open window. Her eye was arrested by what was a familiar sight enough, though it broke upon her now with a new significance.

It was a brace of pistols, hanging near the head of her grandfather's bed, which he always kept there loaded, as a precaution against possible burglars, the house being very lonely. Eustacia regarded them long, as if they were the page of a book in which she read a new and a strange matter.[1] Quickly, like one afraid of herself, she returned downstairs and stood in deep thought.

'If I could only do it!' she said. 'It would be doing much good to myself and all connected with me, and no harm to a single one.'

The idea seemed to gather force within her, and she remained in a fixed attitude nearly ten minutes, when a certain finality was expressed in her gaze, and no longer the blankness of indecision.

She turned and went up the second time—softly and stealthily now—and entered her grandfather's room, her eyes at once seeking the head of the bed. The pistols were gone.

The instant quashing of her purpose by their absence affected her brain as a sudden vacuum affects the body: she nearly fainted. Who had done this? There was only one person on the premises besides herself. Eustacia involuntarily turned to the open window which overlooked the garden as far as the bank that bounded it. On the summit of the latter stood Charley, sufficiently elevated by its height to see into the room. His gaze was directed eagerly and solicitously upon her.

She went downstairs to the door and beckoned to him.

'You have taken them away?'

'Yes, ma'am.'

'Why did you do it?'

'I saw you looking at them too long.'

'What has that to do with it?'

---

1. An echo of Lady Macbeth's remark to her husband: "Your face, my thane, is as a book where men / May read strange matters" (*Macbeth*, I.5.61–62).

'You have been heart-broken all the morning, as if you did not want to live.'

'Well?'

'And I could not bear to leave them in your way. There was meaning in your look at them.'

'Where are they now?'

'Locked up.'

'Where?'

'In the stable.'

'Give them to me.'

'No, ma'am.'

'You refuse?'

'I do. I care too much for you to give 'em up.'

She turned aside, her face for the first time softening from the stony immobility of the earlier day, and the corners of her mouth resuming something of that delicacy of cut which was always lost in her moments of despair. At last she confronted him again.

'Why should I not die if I wish?' she said tremulously. 'I have made a bad bargain with life, and I am weary of it—weary. And now you have hindered my escape. O, why did you, Charley! What makes death painful except the thought of others' grief?—and that is absent in my case, for not a sigh would follow me!'

'Ah, it is trouble that has done this! I wish in my very soul that he who brought it about might die and rot, even if 'tis transportation[2] to say it!'

'Charley, no more of that. What do you mean to do about this you have seen?'

'Keep it close as night, if you promise not to think of it again.'

'You need not fear. The moment has passed. I promise.' She then went away, entered the house, and lay down.

Later in the afternoon her grandfather returned. He was about to question her categorically; but on looking at her he withheld his words.

'Yes, it is too bad to talk of,' she slowly returned in answer to his glance. 'Can my old room be got ready for me to-night, grandfather? I shall want to occupy it again.'

He did not ask what it all meant, or why she had left her husband, but ordered the room to be prepared.

---

2. To the colonies, especially Australia, as a punishment for crime.

An Old Move Inadvertently Repeated

V

Charley's attentions to his former mistress were unbounded. The only solace to his own trouble lay in his attempts to relieve hers. Hour after hour he considered her wants: he thought of her presence there with a sort of gratitude, and, while uttering imprecations on the cause of her unhappiness, in some measure blessed the result. Perhaps she would always remain there, he thought, and then he would be as happy as he had been before. His dread was lest she should think fit to return to Alderworth, and in that dread his eyes, with all the inquisitiveness of affection, frequently sought her face when she was not observing him, as he would have watched the head of a stockdove[1] to learn if it contemplated flight. Having once really succoured her, and possibly preserved her from the rashest of acts, he mentally assumed in addition a guardian's responsibility for her welfare.

For this reason he busily endeavoured to provide her with pleasant distractions, bringing home curious objects which he found in the heath, such as white trumpet-shaped mosses, red-headed lichens, stone arrow-heads used by the old tribes on Egdon, and faceted crystals from the hollows of flints. These he deposited on the premises in such positions that she should see them as if by accident.

A week passed, Eustacia never going out of the house. Then she walked into the enclosed plot and looked through her grandfather's spy-glass, as she had been in the habit of doing before her marriage. One day she saw, at a place where the high-road crossed the distant valley, a heavily laden waggon passing along. It was piled with household furniture. She looked again and again, and recognized it to be her own. In the evening her grandfather came indoors with a rumour that Yeobright had removed that day from Alderworth to the old house at Blooms-End.

On another occasion when reconnoitring thus she beheld two female figures walking in the vale. The day was fine and clear; and the persons not being more than half a mile off she could see their every detail with the telescope. The woman walking in front carried a white bundle in her arms, from one end of which hung a long appendage of drapery; and when the walkers turned, so that the sun fell more directly upon them, Eustacia could see that the object was a baby. She called Charley, and asked him if he knew who they were, though she well guessed.

'Mrs. Wildeve and the nurse-girl,' said Charley.

1. Wild pigeon, commonly found in woods and parklands.

'The nurse is carrying the baby?' said Eustacia.

'No, 'tis Mrs. Wildeve carrying that,' he answered, 'and the nurse walks behind carrying nothing.'

The lad was in good spirits that day, for the fifth of November had again come round, and he was planning yet another scheme to divert her from her too absorbing thoughts. For two successive years his mistress had seemed to take pleasure in lighting a bonfire on the bank overlooking the valley; but this year she had apparently quite forgotten the day and the customary deed. He was careful not to remind her, and went on with his secret preparations for a cheerful surprise, the more zealously that he had been absent last time and unable to assist. At every vacant minute he hastened to gather furze-stumps, thorn-tree roots, and other solid materials from the adjacent slopes, hiding them from cursory view.

The evening came, and Eustacia was still seemingly unconscious of the anniversary. She had gone indoors after her survey through the glass, and had not been visible since. As soon as it was quite dark Charley began to build the bonfire, choosing precisely that spot on the bank which Eustacia had chosen at previous times.

When all the surrounding bonfires had burst into existence Charley kindled his, and arranged its fuel so that it should not require tending for some time. He then went back to the house, and lingered round the door and windows till she should by some means or other learn of his achievement and come out to witness it. But the shutters were closed, the door remained shut, and no heed whatever seemed to be taken of his performance. Not liking to call her he went back and replenished the fire, continuing to do this for more than half an hour. It was not till his stock of fuel had greatly diminished that he went to the back door and sent in to beg that Mrs. Yeobright would open the window-shutters and see the sight outside.

Eustacia, who had been sitting listlessly in the parlour, started up at the intelligence and flung open the shutters. Facing her on the bank blazed the fire, which at once sent a ruddy glare into the room where she was, and overpowered the candles.

'Well done, Charley!' said Captain Vye from the chimney-corner. 'But I hope it is not my wood that he's burning. . . . Ah, it was this time last year that I met with that man Venn, bringing home Thomasin Yeobright—to be sure it was! Well, who would have thought that girl's troubles would have ended so well? What a snipe[2] you were in that matter, Eustacia! Has your husband written to you yet?'

'No,' said Eustacia, looking vaguely through the window at the

2. Contemptuous or dismissive term.

fire, which just then so much engaged her mind that she did not resent her grandfather's blunt opinion. She could see Charley's form
on the bank, shovelling and stirring the fire; and there flashed upon
her imagination some other form which that fire might call up.

She left the room, put on her garden-bonnet and cloak, and went
out. Reaching the bank she looked over with a wild curiosity and
misgiving, when Charley said to her, with a pleased sense of himself, 'I made it o' purpose for you, ma'am.'

'Thank you,' she said hastily. 'But I wish you to put it out now.'

'It will soon burn down,' said Charley, rather disappointed. 'Is it
not a pity to knock it out?'

'I don't know,' she musingly answered.

They stood in silence, broken only by the crackling of the flames,
till Charley, perceiving that she did not want to talk to him, moved
reluctantly away.

Eustacia remained within the bank looking at the fire, intending
to go indoors, yet lingering still. Had she not by her situation been
inclined to hold in indifference all things honoured of the gods and
of men she would probably have come away. But her state was so
hopeless that she could play with it. To have lost is less disturbing
than to wonder if we may possibly have won: and Eustacia could
now, like other people at such a stage, take a standing-point outside
herself, observe herself as a disinterested spectator, and think what
a sport for Heaven[3] this woman Eustacia was.

While she stood she heard a sound. It was the splash of a stone
in the pond.

Had Eustacia received the stone full in the bosom her heart
could not have given a more decided thump. She had thought of
the possibility of such a signal in answer to that which had been
unwittingly given by Charley; but she had not expected it yet. How
prompt Wildeve was! Yet how could he think her capable of deliberately wishing to renew their assignations now? An impulse to leave
the spot, a desire to stay, struggled within her; and the desire held
its own. More than that it did not do, for she refrained even from
ascending the bank and looking over. She remained motionless, not
disturbing a muscle of her face or raising her eyes; for were she to
turn up her face the fire on the bank would shine upon it, and
Wildeve might be looking down.

There was a second splash into the pond.

Why did he stay so long without advancing and looking over? Curiosity had its way: she ascended one or two of the earth-steps in
the bank and glanced out.

---

3. An anticipation of the more notorious comment in the last paragraph of *Tess of the
d'Urbervilles*: "the President of the Immortals . . . had ended his sport with Tess."

Wildeve was before her. He had come forward after throwing the last pebble, and the fire now shone into each of their faces from the bank stretching breast-high between them.

'I did not light it!' cried Eustacia quickly. 'It was lit without my knowledge. Don't, don't come over to me!'

'Why have you been living here all these days without telling me? You have left your home. I fear I am something to blame in this?'

'I did not let in his mother; that's how it is!'

'You do not deserve what you have got, Eustacia; you are in great misery; I see it in your eyes, your mouth, and all over you. My poor, poor girl!' He stepped over the bank. 'You are beyond everything unhappy!'

'No, no; not exactly——'

'It has been pushed too far—it is killing you: I do think it!'

Her usually quiet breathing had grown quicker with his words. 'I—I——' she began, and then burst into quivering sobs, shaken to the very heart by the unexpected voice of pity—a sentiment whose existence in relation to herself she had almost forgotten.

This outbreak of weeping took Eustacia herself so much by surprise that she could not leave off, and she turned aside from him in some shame, though turning hid nothing from him. She sobbed on desperately; then the outpour lessened, and she became quieter. Wildeve had resisted the impulse to clasp her,[4] and stood without speaking.

'Are you not ashamed of me, who used never to be a crying animal?' she asked in a weak whisper as she wiped her eyes. 'Why didn't you go away? I wish you had not seen quite all that; it reveals too much by half.'

'You might have wished it, because it makes me as sad as you,' he said with emotion and deference. 'As for revealing—the word is impossible between us two.'

'I did not send for you—don't forget it, Damon; I am in pain, but I did not send for you! As a wife, at least, I've been straight.'[5]

'Never mind—I came. O, Eustacia, forgive me for the harm I have done you in these two past years! I see more and more that I have been your ruin.'

'Not you. This place I live in.'

'Ah, your generosity may naturally make you say that. But I am the culprit. I should either have done more or nothing at all.'

'In what way?'

'I ought never to have hunted you out; or, having done it, I ought

---

4. This impulse is mentioned for the first time in the 1895 edition, when the episode was revised to show the continuing intensity of the relationship between Wildeve and Eustacia.

5. This sentence was added in 1895.

to have persisted in retaining you. But of course I have no right to talk of that now. I will only ask this: can I do anything for you? Is there anything on the face of the earth that a man can do to make you happier than you are at present? If there is, I will do it. You may command me, Eustacia, to the limit of my influence; and don't forget that I am richer now. Surely something can be done to save you from this! Such a rare plant in such a wild place it grieves me to see. Do you want anything bought? Do you want to go anywhere? Do you want to escape the place altogether? Only say it, and I'll do anything to put an end to those tears, which but for me would never have been at all.'

'We are each married to another person,' she said faintly; 'and assistance from you would have an evil sound—after—after——'

'Well, there's no preventing slanderers from having their fill at any time; but you need not be afraid. Whatever I may feel I promise you on my word of honour never to speak to you about—or act upon—until you say I may. I know my duty to Thomasin quite as well as I know my duty to you as a woman unfairly treated.[6] What shall I assist you in?'

'In getting away from here.'

'Where do you wish to go to?'

'I have a place in my mind. If you could help me as far as Budmouth I can do all the rest. Steamers sail from there across the Channel, and so I can get to Paris, where I want to be. Yes,' she pleaded earnestly, 'help me to get to Budmouth harbour without my grandfather's or my husband's knowledge, and I can do all the rest.'

'Will it be safe to leave you there alone?'

'Yes, yes. I know Budmouth well.'

'Shall I go with you? I am rich now.'

She was silent.

'Say yes, sweet!'

She was silent still.

'Well, let me know when you wish to go. We shall be at our present house till December; after that we remove to Casterbridge. Command me in anything till that time.'

'I will think of this,' she said hurriedly. 'Whether I can honestly make use of you as a friend, or must close with you as a lover[7]— that is what I must ask myself. If I wish to go and decide to accept your company I will signal to you some evening at eight o'clock punctually, and this will mean that you are to be ready with a horse and trap at twelve o'clock the same night to drive me to Budmouth harbour in time for the morning boat.'

6. In the editions before 1895 Wildeve added a promise: "I will assist you without prejudice to her."
7. The possibility of accepting Wildeve as a lover was added in 1895.

'I will look out every night at eight, and no signal shall escape me.'

'Now please go away. If I decide on this escape I can only meet you once more unless—I cannot go without you.[8] Go—I cannot bear it longer. Go—go!'

Wildeve slowly went up the steps and descended into the darkness on the other side; and as he walked he glanced back, till the bank blotted out her form from his further view.

Thomasin Argues with Her Cousin, and He Writes a Letter

VI

Yeobright was at this time at Blooms-End, hoping that Eustacia would return to him. The removal of furniture had been accomplished only that day, though Clym had lived in the old house for more than a week. He had spent the time in working about the premises, sweeping leaves from the garden-paths, cutting dead stalks from the flower-beds, and nailing up creepers which had been displaced by the autumn winds. He took no particular pleasure in these deeds, but they formed a screen between himself and despair. Moreover, it had become a religion with him to preserve in good condition all that had lapsed from his mother's hands to his own.

During these operations he was constantly on the watch for Eustacia. That there should be no mistake about her knowing where to find him he had ordered a notice-board to be affixed to the garden gate at Alderworth, signifying in white letters whither he had removed. When a leaf floated to the earth he turned his head, thinking it might be her footfall. A bird searching for worms in the mould of the flower-beds sounded like her hand on the latch of the gate; and at dusk, when soft, strange ventriloquisms came from holes in the ground, hollow stalks, curled dead leaves, and other crannies wherein breezes, worms, and insects can work their will, he fancied that they were Eustacia, standing without and breathing wishes of reconciliation.

Up to this hour he had persevered in his resolve not to invite her back. At the same time the severity with which he had treated her lulled the sharpness of his regret for his mother, and awoke some of his old solicitude for his mother's supplanter. Harsh feelings produce harsh usage, and this by reaction quenches the sentiments that gave it birth. The more he reflected the more he softened. But to look upon his wife as innocence in distress was impossible,

---

8. Added in 1895; in earlier editions, Eustacia tells Wildeve that if she accepts his help to leave, she will not see him again.

though he could ask himself whether he had given her quite time enough—if he had not come a little too suddenly upon her on that sombre morning.

Now that the first flush of his anger had paled he was disinclined to ascribe to her more than an indiscreet friendship with Wildeve, for there had not appeared in her manner the signs of dishonour. And this once admitted, an absolutely dark interpretation of her act towards his mother was no longer forced upon him.

On the evening of the fifth November his thoughts of Eustacia were intense. Echoes from those past times when they had exchanged tender words all the day long came like the diffused murmur of a seashore left miles behind. 'Surely,' he said, 'she might have brought herself to communicate with me before now, and confess honestly what Wildeve was to her.'

Instead of remaining at home that night he determined to go and see Thomasin and her husband. If he found opportunity he would allude to the cause of the separation between Eustacia and himself, keeping silence, however, on the fact that there was a third person in his house when his mother was turned away. If it proved that Wildeve was innocently there he would doubtless openly mention it. If he were there with unjust intentions Wildeve, being a man of quick feeling, might possibly say something to reveal the extent to which Eustacia was compromised.

But on reaching his cousin's house he found that only Thomasin was at home, Wildeve being at that time on his way towards the bonfire innocently lit by Charley at Mistover. Thomasin then, as always, was glad to see Clym, and took him to inspect the sleeping baby, carefully screening the candlelight from the infant's eyes with her hand.

'Tamsin, have you heard that Eustacia is not with me now?' he said when they had sat down again.

'No,' said Thomasin, alarmed.

'And not that I have left Alderworth?'

'No. I never hear tidings from Alderworth unless you bring them. What is the matter?'

Clym in a disturbed voice related to her his visit to Susan Nunsuch's boy, the revelation he had made, and what had resulted from his charging Eustacia with having wilfully and heartlessly done the deed. He suppressed all mention of Wildeve's presence with her.

'All this, and I not knowing it!' murmured Thomasin in an awestruck tone. 'Terrible! What could have made her—— O, Eustacia! And when you found it out you went in hot haste to her? Were you too cruel?—or is she really so wicked as she seems?'

'Can a man be too cruel to his mother's enemy?'

'I can fancy so.'

'Very well, then—I'll admit that he can. But now what is to be done?'

'Make it up again—if a quarrel so deadly can ever be made up. I almost wish you had not told me. But do try to be reconciled. There are ways, after all, if you both wish to.'

'I don't know that we do both wish to make it up,' said Clym. 'If she had wished it, would she not have sent to me by this time?'

'You seem to wish to, and yet you have not sent to her.'

'True; but I have been tossed to and fro in doubt if I ought, after such strong provocation. To see me now, Thomasin, gives you no idea of what I have been; of what depths I have descended to in these few last days. O, it was a bitter shame to shut out my mother like that! Can I ever forget it, or even agree to see her again?'

'She might not have known that anything serious would come of it, and perhaps she did not mean to keep aunt out altogether.'

'She says herself that she did not. But the fact remains that keep her out she did.'

'Believe her sorry, and send for her.'

'How if she will not come?'

'It will prove her guilty, by showing that it is her habit to nourish enmity. But I do not think that for a moment.'

'I will do this. I will wait for a day or two longer—not longer than two days certainly; and if she does not send to me in that time I will indeed send to her. I thought to have seen Wildeve here to-night. Is he from home?'

Thomasin blushed a little. 'No,' she said. 'He is merely gone out for a walk.'

'Why didn't he take you with him? The evening is fine. You want fresh air as well as he.'

'O, I don't care for going anywhere; besides, there is baby.'

'Yes, yes. Well, I have been thinking whether I should not consult your husband about this as well as you,' said Clym steadily.

'I fancy I would not,' she quickly answered. 'It can do no good.'

Her cousin looked her in the face. No doubt Thomasin was ignorant that her husband had any share in the events of that tragic afternoon; but her countenance seemed to signify that she concealed some suspicion or thought of the reputed tender relations between Wildeve and Eustacia in days gone by.

Clym, however, could make nothing of it, and he rose to depart, more in doubt than when he came.

'You will write to her in a day or two?' said the young woman earnestly. 'I do so hope the wretched separation may come to an end.'

'I will,' said Clym; 'I don't rejoice in my present state at all.'

288 The Return of the Native

And he left her and climbed over the hill to Blooms-End. Before going to bed he sat down and wrote the following letter:—

> 'MY DEAR EUSTACIA,—I must obey my heart without consulting my reason too closely. Will you come back to me? Do so, and the past shall never be mentioned. I was too severe; but O, Eustacia, the provocation! You don't know, you never will know, what those words of anger cost me which you drew down upon yourself. All that an honest man can promise you I promise now, which is that from me you shall never suffer anything on this score again. After all the vows we have made, Eustacia, I think we had better pass the remainder of our lives in trying to keep them. Come to me, then, even if you reproach me. I have thought of your sufferings that morning on which I parted from you; I know they were genuine, and they are as much as you ought to bear. Our love must still continue. Such hearts as ours would never have been given us but to be concerned with each other. I could not ask you back at first, Eustacia, for I was unable to persuade myself that he who was with you was not there as a lover. But if you will come and explain distracting appearances I do not question that you can show your honesty to me. Why have you not come before? Do you think I will not listen to you? Surely not, when you remember the kisses and vows we exchanged under the summer moon. Return then, and you shall be warmly welcomed. I can no longer think of you to your prejudice—I am but too much absorbed in justifying you.—Your husband as ever,
>
> CLYM.'

'There,' he said, as he laid it in his desk, 'that's a good thing done. If she does not come before to-morrow night I will send it to her.'

Meanwhile, at the house he had just left Thomasin sat sighing uneasily. Fidelity to her husband had that evening induced her to conceal all suspicion that Wildeve's interest in Eustacia had not ended with his marriage. But she knew nothing positive; and though Clym was her well-beloved cousin there was one nearer to her still.

When, a little later, Wildeve returned from his walk to Mistover, Thomasin said, 'Damon, where have you been? I was getting quite frightened, and thought you had fallen into the river. I dislike being in the house by myself.'

'Frightened?' he said, touching her cheek as if she were some domestic animal. 'Why, I thought nothing could frighten you. It is that you are getting proud, I am sure, and don't like living here since we have risen above our business. Well, it is a tedious matter, this getting a new house; but I couldn't have set about it sooner, unless our ten thousand pounds had been a hundred thousand, when we could have afforded to despise caution.'

'No—I don't mind waiting—I would rather stay here twelve months longer than run any risk with baby. But I don't like your vanishing so in the evenings. There's something on your mind—I know there is, Damon. You go about so gloomily, and look at the heath as if it were somebody's gaol instead of a nice wild place to walk in.'

He looked towards her with pitying surprise. 'What, do you like Egdon Heath?' he said.

'I like what I was born near to; I admire its grim old face.'

'Pooh, my dear. You don't know what you like.'

'I am sure I do. There's only one thing unpleasant about Egdon.'

'What's that?'

'You never take me with you when you walk there. Why do you wander so much in it yourself if you so dislike it?'

The inquiry, though a simple one, was plainly disconcerting, and he sat down before replying. 'I don't think you often see me there. Give an instance.'

'I will,' she answered triumphantly. 'When you went out this evening I thought that as baby was asleep I would see where you were going to so mysteriously without telling me. So I ran out and followed behind you. You stopped at the place where the road forks, looked round at the bonfires, and then said, "Damn it, I'll go!" And you went quickly up the left-hand road. Then I stood and watched you.'

Wildeve frowned, afterwards saying, with a forced smile, 'Well, what wonderful discovery did you make?'

'There—now you are angry, and we won't talk of this any more.' She went across to him, sat on a footstool, and looked up in his face.

'Nonsense!' he said; 'that's how you always back out. We will go on with it now we have begun. What did you next see? I particularly want to know.'

'Don't be like that, Damon!' she murmured. 'I didn't see anything. You vanished out of sight, and then I looked round at the bonfires and came in.'

'Perhaps this is not the only time you have dogged my steps. Are you trying to find out something bad about me?'

'Not at all! I have never done such a thing before, and I shouldn't have done it now if words had not sometimes been dropped about you.'

'What *do* you mean?' he impatiently asked.

'They say—they say you used to go to Alderworth in the evenings, and it puts into my mind what I have heard about——'

Wildeve turned angrily and stood up in front of her. 'Now,' he said, flourishing his hand in the air, 'just out with it, madam! I demand to know what remarks you have heard.'

'Well, I heard that you used to be very fond of Eustacia—nothing more than that, though dropped in a bit-by-bit way. You ought not to be angry!'

He observed that her eyes were brimming with tears. 'Well,' he said, 'there is nothing new in that, and of course I don't mean to be rough towards you, so you need not cry. Now, don't let us speak of the subject any more.'

And no more was said, Thomasin being glad enough of a reason for not mentioning Clym's visit to her that evening, and his story.

The Night of the Sixth of November

VII

Having resolved on flight Eustacia at times seemed anxious that something should happen to thwart her own intention. The only event that could really change her position was the appearance of Clym. The glory which had encircled him as her lover was departed now; yet some good simple quality of his would occasionally return to her memory and stir a momentary throb of hope that he would again present himself before her. But calmly considered it was not likely that such a severance as now existed would ever close up: she would have to live on as a painful object, isolated, and out of place. She had used to think of the heath alone as an uncongenial spot to be in; she felt it now of the whole world.

Towards evening on the sixth her determination to go away again revived. About four o'clock she packed up anew the few small articles she had brought in her flight from Alderworth, and also some belonging to her which had been left here: the whole formed a bundle not too large to be carried in her hand for a distance of a mile or two. The scene without grew darker; mud-coloured clouds bellied downwards from the sky like vast hammocks slung across it, and with the increase of night a stormy wind arose; but as yet there was no rain.

Eustacia could not rest indoors, having nothing more to do, and she wandered to and fro on the hill, not far from the house she was soon to leave. In these desultory ramblings she passed the cottage of Susan Nunsuch, a little lower down than her grandfather's. The door was ajar, and a riband of bright firelight fell over the ground without. As Eustacia crossed the firebeams she appeared for an instant as distinct as a figure in a phantasmagoria[1]—a creature of light surrounded by an area of darkness: the moment passed, and she was absorbed in night again.

A woman who was sitting inside the cottage had seen and recog-

1. Exhibition of optical illusions produced with the aid of a magic lantern.

nized her in that momentary irradiation. This was Susan herself, occupied in preparing a posset[2] for her little boy, who, often ailing, was now seriously unwell. Susan dropped the spoon, shook her fist at the vanished figure, and then proceeded with her work in a musing, absent way.

At eight o'clock, the hour at which Eustacia had promised to signal to Wildeve if ever she signalled at all, she looked around the premises to learn if the coast was clear, went to the furze-rick, and pulled thence a long-stemmed bough of that fuel. This she carried to the corner of the bank, and, glancing behind to see if the shutters were all closed, she struck a light, and kindled the furze. When it was thoroughly ablaze Eustacia took it by the stem and waved it in the air above her head till it had burned itself out.

She was gratified, if gratification were possible to such a mood, by seeing a similar light in the vicinity of Wildeve's residence a minute or two later. Having agreed to keep watch at this hour every night, in case she should require assistance, this promptness proved how strictly he had held to his word. Four hours after the present time, that is, at midnight, he was to be ready to drive her to Budmouth, as prearranged.

Eustacia returned to the house. Supper having been got over she retired early, and sat in her bedroom waiting for the time to go by. The night being dark and threatening Captain Vye had not strolled out to gossip in any cottage or to call at the inn, as was sometimes his custom on these long autumn nights; and he sat sipping grog alone downstairs. About ten o'clock there was a knock at the door. When the servant opened it the rays of the candle fell upon the form of Fairway.

'I was a-forced to go to Lower Mistover to-night,' he said; 'and Mr. Yeobright asked me to leave this here on my way; but, faith, I put it in the lining of my hat, and thought no more about it till I got back and was hasping[3] my gate before going to bed. So I have run back with it at once.'

He handed in a letter and went his way. The girl brought it to the captain, who found that it was directed to Eustacia. He turned it over and over, and fancied that the writing was her husband's, though he could not be sure. However, he decided to let her have it at once if possible, and took it upstairs for that purpose; but on reaching the door of her room and looking in at the keyhole he found there was no light within, the fact being that Eustacia, without undressing, had flung herself upon the bed, to rest and gather a little strength for her coming journey. Her grandfather concluded

2. Soothing drink of hot milk mixed with spirits or ale, usually flavored with spices.
3. Fastening (especially with a latch).

from what he saw that he ought not to disturb her; and descending again to the parlour he placed the letter on the mantelpiece to give it to her in the morning.

At eleven o'clock he went to bed himself, smoked for some time in his bedroom, put out his light at half-past eleven, and then, as was his invariable custom, pulled up the blind before getting into bed, that he might see which way the wind blew on opening his eyes in the morning, his bedroom window commanding a view of the flagstaff and vane. Just as he had lain down he was surprised to observe the white pole of the staff flash into existence like a streak of phosphorus drawn downwards across the shade of night without. Only one explanation met this—a light had been suddenly thrown upon the pole from the direction of the house. As everybody had retired to rest the old man felt it necessary to get out of bed, open the window softly, and look to the right and left. Eustacia's bedroom was lighted up, and it was the shine from her window which had lighted the pole. Wondering what had aroused her he remained undecided at the window, and was thinking of fetching the letter to slip it under her door, when he heard a slight brushing of garments on the partition dividing his room from the passage.

The captain concluded that Eustacia, feeling wakeful, had gone for a book, and would have dismissed the matter as unimportant if he had not also heard her distinctly weeping as she passed.

'She is thinking of that husband of hers,' he said to himself. 'Ah, the silly goose! she had no business to marry him. I wonder if that letter is really his?'

He arose, threw his boat-cloak round him, opened the door, and said, 'Eustacia!' There was no answer. 'Eustacia!' he repeated louder, 'there is a letter on the mantelpiece for you.'

But no response was made to this statement save an imaginary one from the wind, which seemed to gnaw at the corners of the house, and the stroke of a few drops of rain upon the windows.

He went on to the landing, and stood waiting nearly five minutes. Still she did not return. He went back for a light, and prepared to follow her; but first he looked into her bedroom. There, on the outside of the quilt, was the impression of her form, showing that the bed had not been opened; and, what was more significant, she had not taken her candlestick downstairs. He was now thoroughly alarmed; and hastily putting on his clothes he descended to the front door, which he himself had bolted and locked. It was now unfastened. There was no longer any doubt that Eustacia had left the house at this midnight hour; and whither could she have gone? To follow her was almost impossible. Had the dwelling stood in an ordinary road, two persons setting out, one in each direction, might have made sure of overtaking her; but it was a hopeless task to seek for anybody on a heath in the dark, the practicable directions for flight across it from any point being as numerous as the meridians radiating from the pole. Perplexed what to do he looked into the parlour, and was vexed to find that the letter still lay there untouched.

At half-past eleven, finding that the house was silent, Eustacia had lighted her candle, put on some warm outer wrappings, taken her bag in her hand, and, extinguishing the light again, descended the staircase. When she got into the outer air she found that it had begun to rain, and as she stood pausing at the door it increased, threatening to come on heavily. But having committed herself to this line of action there was no retreating for bad weather. Even the receipt of Clym's letter would not have stopped her now.[4] The gloom of the night was funereal; all nature seemed clothed in crape. The spiky points of the fir trees behind the house rose into the sky like the turrets and pinnacles of an abbey. Nothing below the horizon was visible save a light which was still burning in the cottage of Susan Nunsuch.

Eustacia opened her umbrella and went out from the enclosure by the steps over the bank, after which she was beyond all danger of being perceived. Skirting the pool she followed the path towards Rainbarrow, occasionally stumbling over twisted furze-roots, tufts of rushes, or oozing lumps of fleshy fungi, which at this season lay scattered about the heath like the rotten liver and lungs of some colossal animal. The moon and stars were closed up by cloud and rain to the degree of extinction. It was a night which led the traveller's thoughts instinctively to dwell on noctural scenes of disaster in the chronicles of the world, on all that is terrible and dark in history and legend—the last plague of Egypt, the destruction of Sennacherib's host, the agony in Gethsemane.[5]

Eustacia at length reached Rainbarrow, and stood still there to think. Never was harmony more perfect than that between the chaos of her mind and the chaos of the world without. A sudden recollection had flashed on her this moment: she had not money enough for undertaking a long journey. Amid the fluctuating sentiments of the day her unpractical mind had not dwelt on the necessity of being well-provided, and now that she thoroughly realized the conditions she sighed bitterly and ceased to stand erect, gradually crouching down under the umbrella as if she were drawn into the Barrow by a hand from beneath. Could it be that she was to re-

4. This sentence was added in the 1912 edition.
5. God's killing of the firstborn child of every Egyptian family, to ensure that the Israelites would be allowed to leave Egypt (Exodus 12.29–30); the slaughter of 185,000 Assyrians, as a punishment for King Sennacherib's blasphemy (2 Kings 19.35); and Christ's vigil in the Garden of Gethsemane on the night of his arrest (Matthew 26.36–56).

main a captive still? Money: she had never felt its value before. Even to efface herself from the country means were required. To ask Wildeve for pecuniary aid without allowing him to accompany her was impossible to a woman with a shadow of pride left in her: to fly as his mistress—and she knew that he loved her—was of the nature of humiliation.[6]

Any one who had stood by now would have pitied her, not so much on account of her exposure to weather, and isolation from all of humanity except the mouldered remains inside the tumulus; but for that other form of misery which was denoted by the slightly rocking movement that her feelings imparted to her person. Extreme unhappiness weighed visibly upon her. Between the drippings of the rain from her umbrella to her mantle, from her mantle to the heather, from the heather to the earth, very similar sounds could be heard coming from her lips; and the tearfulness of the outer scene was repeated upon her face. The wings of her soul were broken by the cruel obstructiveness of all about her; and even had she seen herself in a promising way of getting to Budmouth, entering a steamer, and sailing to some opposite port, she would have been but little more buoyant, so fearfully malignant were other things. She uttered words aloud. When a woman in such a situation, neither old, deaf, crazed, nor whimsical, takes upon herself to sob and soliloquize aloud there is something grievous the matter.

'Can I go, can I go?' she moaned. 'He's not *great* enough for me to give myself to—he does not suffice for my desire![7] . . . If he had been a Saul or a Bonaparte—ah! But to break my marriage vow for him—it is too poor a luxury! . . . And I have no money to go alone! And if I could, what comfort to me? I must drag on next year, as I have dragged on this year, and the year after that as before. How I have tried and tried to be a splendid woman, and how destiny has been against me! . . . I do not deserve my lot!' she cried in a frenzy of bitter revolt. 'O, the cruelty of putting me into this ill-conceived world! I was capable of much; but I have been injured and blighted and crushed by things beyond my control! O, how hard it is of Heaven to devise such tortures for me, who have done no harm to Heaven at all!'

The distant light which Eustacia had cursorily observed in leaving the house came, as she had divined, from the cottage-window of Susan Nunsuch. What Eustacia did not divine was the occupation of

---

6. Eustacia's realization here, that if she accepted Wildeve's financial help she would feel bound to accept him as a lover, was added in the 1895 edition.
7. This sentence and the two following were added in 1895.

the woman within at that moment. Susan's sight of her passing figure earlier in the evening, not five minutes after the sick boy's exclamation, 'Mother, I do feel so bad!' persuaded the matron that an evil influence was certainly exercised by Eustacia's propinquity.

On this account Susan did not go to bed as soon as the evening's work was over, as she would have done at ordinary times. To counteract the malign spell which she imagined poor Eustacia to be working, the boy's mother busied herself with a ghastly invention of superstition, calculated to bring powerlessness, atrophy, and annihilation on any human being against whom it was directed. It was a practice well known on Egdon at that date, and one that is not quite extinct at the present day.

She passed with her candle into an inner room, where, among other utensils, were two large brown pans, containing together perhaps a hundredweight of liquid honey, the produce of the bees during the foregoing summer. On a shelf over the pans was a smooth and solid yellow mass of a hemispherical form, consisting of beeswax from the same take of honey. Susan took down the lump, and, cutting off several thin slices, heaped them in an iron ladle, with which she returned to the living-room, and placed the vessel in the hot ashes of the fireplace. As soon as the wax had softened to the plasticity of dough she kneaded the pieces together. And now her face became more intent. She began moulding the wax; and it was evident from her manner of manipulation that she was endeavouring to give it some preconceived form. The form was human.

By warming and kneading, cutting and twisting, dismembering and re-joining the incipient image she had in about a quarter of an hour produced a shape which tolerably well resembled a woman, and was about six inches high. She laid it on the table to get cold and hard. Meanwhile she took the candle and went upstairs to where the little boy was lying.

'Did you notice, my dear, what Mrs. Eustacia wore this afternoon besides the dark dress?'

'A red ribbon round her neck.'

'Anything else?'

'No—except sandal-shoes.'

'A red ribbon and sandal-shoes,' she said to herself.

Mrs. Nunsuch went and searched till she found a fragment of the narrowest red ribbon, which she took downstairs and tied round the neck of the image. Then fetching ink and a quill from the rickety bureau by the window, she blackened the feet of the image to the extent presumably covered by shoes; and on the instep of each foot marked cross-lines in the shape taken by the sandal-strings of those days. Finally she tied a bit of black thread round the upper part of the head, in faint resemblance to a snood[8] worn for confining the hair.

Susan held the object at arm's length and contemplated it with a satisfaction in which there was no smile. To anybody acquainted with the inhabitants of Egdon Heath the image would have suggested Eustacia Yeobright.

From her work-basket in the window-seat the woman took a paper of pins, of the old long and yellow sort, whose heads were disposed to come off at their first usage. These she began to thrust into the image in all directions, with apparently excruciating energy. Probably as many as fifty were thus inserted, some into the head of the wax model, some into the shoulders, some into the trunk, some upwards through the soles of the feet, till the figure was completely permeated with pins.

She turned to the fire. It had been of turf; and though the high heap of ashes which turf fires produce was somewhat dark and dead on the outside, upon raking it abroad with the shovel the inside of the mass showed a glow of red heat. She took a few pieces of fresh turf from the chimney-corner and built them together over the glow, upon which the fire brightened. Seizing with the tongs the image that she had made of Eustacia, she held it in the heat, and watched it as it began to waste slowly away. And while she stood thus engaged there came from between her lips a murmur of words.

It was a strange jargon—the Lord's Prayer repeated backwards—the incantation usual in proceedings for obtaining unhallowed assistance against an enemy. Susan uttered the lugubrious discourse three times slowly, and when it was completed the image had considerably diminished. As the wax dropped into the fire a long flame arose from the spot, and curling its tongue round the figure eat still further into its substance. A pin occasionally dropped with the wax, and the embers heated it red as it lay.

Rain, Darkness, and Anxious Wanderers

VIII

While the effigy of Eustacia was melting to nothing, and the fair woman herself was standing on Rainbarrow, her soul in an abyss of desolation seldom plumbed by one so young, Yeobright sat lonely at Blooms-End. He had fulfilled his word to Thomasin by sending off Fairway with the letter to his wife, and now waited with increased impatience for some sound or signal of her return. Were Eustacia still at Mistover the very least he expected was that she would send

8. Hair-band or ribbon.

him back a reply to-night by the same hand; though, to leave all to her inclination, he had cautioned Fairway not to ask for an answer. If one were handed to him he was to bring it immediately; if not, he was to go straight home without troubling to come round to Blooms-End again that night.

But secretly Clym had a more pleasing hope. Eustacia might possibly decline to use her pen—it was rather her way to work silently—and surprise him by appearing at his door. How fully her mind was made up to do otherwise he did not know.[1]

To Clym's regret it began to rain and blow hard as the evening advanced. The wind rasped and scraped at the corners of the house, and filliped the eavesdroppings[2] like peas against the panes. He walked restlessly about the untenanted rooms, stopping strange noises in windows and doors by jamming splinters of wood into the casements and crevices, and pressing together the lead-work of the quarries[3] where it had become loosened from the glass. It was one of those nights when cracks in the walls of old churches widen, when ancient stains on the ceilings of decayed manor-houses are renewed and enlarged from the size of a man's hand to an area of many feet. The little gate in the palings before his dwelling continually opened and clicked together again, but when he looked out eagerly nobody was there; it was as if invisible shapes of the dead were passing in on their way to visit him.

Between ten and eleven o'clock, finding that neither Fairway nor anybody else came to him, he retired to rest, and despite his anxieties soon fell asleep. His sleep, however, was not very sound, by reason of the expectancy he had given way to, and he was easily awakened by a knocking which began at the door about an hour after. Clym arose and looked out of the window. Rain was still falling heavily, the whole expanse of heath before him emitting a subdued hiss under the downpour. It was too dark to see anything at all.

'Who's there?' he cried.

Light footsteps shifted their position in the porch, and he could just distinguish in a plaintive female voice the words, 'O Clym, come down and let me in!'

He flushed hot with agitation. 'Surely it is Eustacia!' he murmured. If so, she had indeed come to him unawares.

He hastily got a light, dressed himself, and went down. On his flinging open the door the rays of the candle fell upon a woman closely wrapped up, who at once came forward.

'Thomasin!' he exclaimed in an indescribable tone of disappoint-

---

1. This sentence was added in 1912.
2. To fillip is to flick or flip, usually with the fingers; eavesdroppings are drops of water from the eaves.
3. Small, diamond-shaped panes of glass.

ment. 'It is Thomasin, and on such a night as this! O, where is Eustacia?'

Thomasin it was, wet, frightened, and panting.

'Eustacia? I don't know, Clym; but I can think,' she said with much perturbation. 'Let me come in and rest—I will explain this. There is a great trouble brewing—my husband and Eustacia!'

'What, what?'

'I think my husband is going to leave me or do something dreadful—I don't know what—Clym, will you go and see? I have nobody to help me but you! Eustacia has not yet come home?'

'No.'

She went on breathlessly: 'Then they are going to run off together! He came indoors to-night about eight o'clock and said in an off-hand way, "Tamsie, I have just found that I must go a journey." "When?" I said. "To-night," he said. "Where?" I asked him. "I cannot tell you at present," he said; "I shall be back again to-morrow." He then went and busied himself in looking up his things, and took no notice of me at all. I expected to see him start, but he did not, and then it came to be ten o'clock, when he said, "You had better go to bed." I didn't know what to do, and I went to bed. I believe he thought I fell asleep, for half an hour after that he came up and unlocked the oak chest we keep money in when we have much in the house and took out a roll of something which I believe was banknotes, though I was not aware that he had 'em there. These he must have got from the bank when he went there the other day. What does he want bank-notes for, if he is only going off for a day? When he had gone down I thought of Eustacia, and how he had met her the night before—I know he did meet her, Clym, for I followed him part of the way; but I did not like to tell you when you called, and so make you think ill of him, as I did not think it was so serious. Then I could not stay in bed: I got up and dressed myself, and when I heard him out in the stable I thought I would come and tell you. So I came downstairs without any noise and slipped out.'

'Then he was not absolutely gone when you left?'

'No. Will you, dear Cousin Clym, go and try to persuade him not to go? He takes no notice of what I say, and puts me off with the story of his going on a journey, and will be home to-morrow, and all that; but I don't believe it. I think you could influence him.'

'I'll go,' said Clym. 'O, Eustacia!'

Thomasin carried in her arms a large bundle; and having by this time seated herself she began to unroll it, when a baby appeared as the kernel to the husks—dry, warm, and unconscious of travel or rough weather. Thomasin briefly kissed the baby, and then found time to begin crying as she said, 'I brought baby, for I was afraid what might happen to her. I suppose it will be her death, but I couldn't leave her with Rachel!'

Clym hastily put together the logs on the hearth, raked abroad the embers, which were scarcely yet extinct, and blew up a flame with the bellows.

'Dry yourself,' he said. 'I'll go and get some more wood.'

'No, no—don't stay for that. I'll make up the fire. Will you go at once—please will you?'

Yeobright ran upstairs to finish dressing himself. While he was gone another rapping came to the door. This time there was no delusion that it might be Eustacia's: the footsteps just preceding it had been heavy and slow. Yeobright, thinking it might possibly be Fairway with a note in answer, descended again and opened the door.

'Captain Vye?' he said to a dripping figure.

'Is my grand-daughter here?' said the captain.

'No.'

'Then where is she?'

'I don't know.'

'But you ought to know—you are her husband.'

'Only in name apparently,' said Clym with rising excitement. 'I believe she means to elope to-night with Wildeve. I am just going to look to it.'

'Well, she has left my house; she left about half an hour ago. Who's sitting there?'

'My cousin Thomasin.'

The captain bowed in a preoccupied way to her. 'I only hope it is no worse than an elopement,' he said.

'Worse? What's worse than the worst a wife can do?'

'Well, I have been told a strange tale. Before starting in search of her I called up Charley, my stable-lad. I missed my pistols the other day.'

'Pistols?'

'He said at the time that he took them down to clean. He has now owned that he took them because he saw Eustacia looking curiously at them; and she afterwards owned to him that she was thinking of taking her life, but bound him to secrecy, and promised never to think of such a thing again. I hardly suppose she will ever have bravado enough to use one of them; but it shows what has been lurking in her mind; and people who think of that sort of thing once think of it again.'

'Where are the pistols?'

'Safely locked up. O no, she won't touch them again. But there are more ways of letting out life than through a bullet-hole. What did you quarrel about so bitterly with her to drive her to all this?

You must have treated her badly indeed. Well, I was always against the marriage, and I was right.'

'Are you going with me?' said Yeobright, paying no attention to the captain's latter remark. 'If so I can tell you what we quarrelled about as we walk along.'

'Where to?'

'To Wildeve's—that was her destination, depend upon it.'

Thomasin here broke in, still weeping: 'He said he was only going on a sudden short journey; but if so why did he want so much money? O, Clym, what do you think will happen? I am afraid that you, my poor baby, will soon have no father left to you!'

'I am off now,' said Yeobright, stepping into the porch.

'I would fain go with 'ee,' said the old man doubtfully. 'But I begin to be afraid that my legs will hardly carry me there such a night as this. I am not so young as I was. If they are interrupted in their flight she will be sure to come back to me, and I ought to be at the house to receive her. But be it as 'twill I can't walk to the Quiet Woman, and that's an end on't. I'll go straight home.'

'It will perhaps be best,' said Clym. 'Thomasin, dry yourself, and be as comfortable as you can.'

With this he closed the door upon her, and left the house in company with Captain Vye, who parted from him outside the gate, taking the middle path, which led to Mistover. Clym crossed by the right-hand track towards the inn.

Thomasin, being left alone, took off some of her wet garments, carried the baby upstairs to Clym's bed, and then came down to the sitting-room again, where she made a larger fire, and began drying herself. The fire soon flared up the chimney, giving the room an appearance of comfort that was doubled by contrast with the drumming of the storm without, which snapped at the window-panes and breathed into the chimney strange low utterances that seemed to be the prologue to some tragedy.

But the least part of Thomasin was in the house, for her heart being at ease about the little girl upstairs she was mentally following Clym on his journey. Having indulged in this imaginary peregrination for some considerable interval, she became impressed with a sense of the intolerable slowness of time. But she sat on. The moment then came when she could scarcely sit longer; and it was like a satire on her patience to remember that Clym could hardly have reached the inn as yet. At last she went to the baby's bedside. The child was sleeping soundly; but her imagination of possibly disastrous events at her home, the predominance within her of the unseen over the seen, agitated her beyond endurance. She could not refrain from going down and opening the door. The rain still continued, the candlelight falling upon the nearest drops and making

glistening darts of them as they descended across the throng of invisible ones behind. To plunge into that medium was to plunge into
water slightly diluted with air. But the difficulty of returning to her
house at this moment made her all the more desirous of doing so:
anything was better than suspense. 'I have come here well enough,'
she said, 'and why shouldn't I go back again? It is a mistake for me
to be away.'

She hastily fetched the infant, wrapped it up, cloaked herself as
before, and shovelling the ashes over the fire, to prevent accidents,
went into the open air. Pausing first to put the door-key in its old
place behind the shutter, she resolutely turned her face to the con-
fronting pile of firmamental darkness beyond the palings, and
stepped into its midst. But Thomasin's imagination being so actively engaged elsewhere, the night and the weather had for her no
terror beyond that of their actual discomfort and difficulty.

She was soon ascending Blooms-End valley and traversing the
undulations on the side of the hill. The noise of the wind over the
heath was shrill, and as if it whistled for joy at finding a night so
congenial as this. Sometimes the path led her to hollows between
thickets of tall and dripping bracken, dead, though not yet prostrate, which enclosed her like a pool. When they were more than
usually tall she lifted the baby to the top of her head, that it might
be out of the reach of their drenching fronds. On higher ground,
where the wind was brisk and sustained, the rain flew in a level
flight without sensible descent, so that it was beyond all power to
imagine the remoteness of the point at which it left the bosoms of
the clouds. Here self-defence was impossible, and individual drops
stuck into her like the arrows into Saint Sebastian.[4] She was enabled to avoid puddles by the nebulous paleness which signified
their presence, though beside anything less dark than the heath
they themselves would have appeared as blackness.

Yet in spite of all this Thomasin was not sorry that she had
started. To her there were not, as to Eustacia, demons in the air,
and malice in every bush and bough. The drops which lashed her
face were not scorpions, but prosy rain; Egdon in the mass was no
monster whatever, but impersonal open ground. Her fears of the
place were rational, her dislikes of its worst moods reasonable. At
this time it was in her view a windy, wet place, in which a person
might experience much discomfort, lose the path without care, and
possibly catch cold.

If the path is well known the difficulty at such times of keeping
therein is not altogether great, from its familiar feel to the feet; but
once lost it is irrecoverable. Owing to her baby, who somewhat im-

4. Roman who suffered martyrdom around 288; he frequently appears in Renaissance art
   as a beautiful youth pierced full of arrows.

peded Thomasin's view forward and distracted her mind, she did at last lose the track. This mishap occurred when she was descending an open slope about two-thirds home. Instead of attempting, by wandering hither and thither, the hopeless task of finding such a mere thread, she went straight on, trusting for guidance to her general knowledge of the contours, which was scarcely surpassed by Clym's or by that of the heath-croppers themselves.

At length Thomasin reached a hollow and began to discern through the rain a faint blotted radiance, which presently assumed the oblong form of an open door. She knew that no house stood hereabouts, and was soon aware of the nature of the door by its height above the ground.

'Why, it is Diggory Venn's van, surely!' she said.

A certain secluded spot near Rainbarrow was, she knew, often Venn's chosen centre when staying in this neighbourhood; and she guessed at once that she had stumbled upon this mysterious retreat. The question arose in her mind whether or not she should ask him to guide her into the path. In her anxiety to reach home she decided that she would appeal to him, notwithstanding the strangeness of appearing before his eyes at this place and season. But when, in pursuance of this resolve, Thomasin reached the van and looked in she found it to be untenanted; though there was no doubt that it was the reddleman's. The fire was burning in the stove, the lantern hung from the nail. Round the doorway the floor was merely sprinkled with rain, and not saturated, which told her that the door had not long been opened.

While she stood uncertainly looking in Thomasin heard a footstep advancing from the darkness behind her; and turning, beheld the well-known form in corduroy, lurid from head to foot, the lantern beams falling upon him through an intervening gauze of raindrops.

'I thought you went down the slope,' he said, without noticing her face. 'How do you come back here again?'

'Diggory?' said Thomasin faintly.

'Who are you?' said Venn, still unperceiving. 'And why were you crying so just now?'

'O, Diggory! don't you know me?' said she. 'But of course you don't, wrapped up like this. What do you mean? I have not been crying here, and I have not been here before.'

Venn then came nearer till he could see the illuminated side of her form.

'Mrs. Wildeve!' he exclaimed, starting. 'What a time for us to meet! And the baby too! What dreadful thing can have brought you out on such a night as this?'

She could not immediately answer; and without asking her permission he hopped into his van, took her by the arm, and drew her up after him.

'What is it?' he continued when they stood within.

'I have lost my way coming from Blooms-End, and I am in a great hurry to get home. Please show me as quickly as you can! It is so silly of me not to know Egdon better, and I cannot think how I came to lose the path. Show me quickly, Diggory, please.'

'Yes, of course. I will go with 'ee. But you came to me before this, Mrs. Wildeve?'

'I only came this minute.'

'That's strange. I was lying down here asleep about five minutes ago, with the door shut to keep out the weather, when the brushing of a woman's clothes over the heath-bushes just outside woke me up (for I don't sleep heavy), and at the same time I heard a sobbing or crying from the same woman. I opened my door and held out my lantern, and just as far as the light would reach I saw a woman: she turned her head when the light sheened on her, and then hurried on downhill. I hung up the lantern, and was curious enough to pull on my things and dog her a few steps, but I could see nothing of her any more. That was where I had been when you came up; and when I saw you I thought you were the same one.'

'Perhaps it was one of the heath-folk going home?'

'No, it couldn't be. 'Tis too late. The noise of her gown over the he'th was of a whistling sort that nothing but silk will make.'

'It wasn't I, then. My dress is not silk, you see. . . . Are we anywhere in a line between Mistover and the inn?'

'Well, yes; not far out.'

'Ah, I wonder if it was she! Diggory, I must go at once!'

She jumped down from the van before he was aware, when Venn unhooked the lantern and leaped down after her. 'I'll take the baby, ma'am,' he said. 'You must be tired out by the weight.'

Thomasin hesitated a moment, and then delivered the baby into Venn's hands. 'Don't squeeze her, Diggory,' she said, 'or hurt her little arm; and keep the cloak close over her like this, so that the rain may not drop in her face.'

'I will,' said Venn earnestly. 'As if I could hurt anything belonging to you!'

'I only meant accidentally,' said Thomasin.

'The baby is dry enough, but you are pretty wet,' said the reddleman when, in closing the door of his cart to padlock it, he noticed on the floor a ring of water-drops where her cloak had hung from her.

Thomasin followed him as he wound right and left to avoid the larger bushes, stopping occasionally and covering the lantern, while he looked over his shoulder to gain some idea of the position of

' 'Tis not from the window. That's a gig-lamp, to the best of my belief.'

Rainbarrow above them, which it was necessary to keep directly be-hind their backs to preserve a proper course.

'You are sure the rain does not fall upon baby?'

'Quite sure. May I ask how old he is, ma'am?'

'He!' said Thomasin reproachfully. 'Anybody can see better than that in a moment. She is nearly two months old. How far is it now to the inn?'

'A little over a quarter of a mile.'

'Will you walk a little faster?'

'I was afraid you could not keep up.'

'I am very anxious to get there. Ah, there is a light from the win-dow!'

' 'Tis not from the window. That's a gig-lamp,[5] to the best of my belief.'

'O!' said Thomasin in despair. 'I wish I had been there sooner—give me the baby, Diggory—you can go back now.'

'I must go all the way,' said Venn. 'There is a quag[6] between us and that light, and you will walk into it up to your neck unless I take you round.'

'But the light is at the inn, and there is no quag in front of that.'

'No, the light is below the inn some two or three hundred yards.'

'Never mind,' said Thomasin hurriedly. 'Go towards the light, and not towards the inn.'

5. A gig is a light, two-wheeled carriage.
6. Marsh or bog.

'Yes,' answered Venn, swerving round in obedience; and, after a pause, 'I wish you would tell me what this great trouble is. I think you have proved that I can be trusted.'

'There are some things that cannot be—cannot be told to——' And then her heart rose into her throat, and she could say no more.

Sights and Sounds Draw the Wanderers Together

IX

Having seen Eustacia's signal from the hill at eight o'clock, Wildeve immediately prepared to assist her in her flight, and, as he hoped, accompany her.[1] He was somewhat perturbed, and his manner of informing Thomasin that he was going on a journey was in itself sufficient to rouse her suspicions. When she had gone to bed he collected the few articles he would require, and went upstairs to the money-chest, whence he took a tolerably bountiful sum in notes, which had been advanced to him on the property he was so soon to have in possession, to defray expenses incidental to the removal.

He then went to the stable and coach-house to assure himself that the horse, gig, and harness were in a fit condition for a long drive. Nearly half an hour was spent thus, and on returning to the house Wildeve had no thought of Thomasin being anywhere but in bed. He had told the stable-lad not to stay up, leading the boy to understand that his departure would be at three or four in the morning; for this, though an exceptional hour, was less strange than midnight, the time actually agreed on, the packet from Bud-mouth sailing between one and two.

At last all was quiet, and he had nothing to do but to wait. By no effort could he shake off the oppression of spirits which he had experienced ever since his last meeting with Eustacia, but he hoped there was that in his situation which money could cure. He had persuaded himself that to act not ungenerously towards his gentle wife by settling on her the half of his property, and with chivalrous devotion towards another and greater woman by sharing her fate, was possible. And though he meant to adhere to Eustacia's instructions to the letter, to deposit her where she wished and to leave her, should that be her will, the spell that she had cast over him intensified, and his heart was beating fast in the anticipated futility of such commands in the face of a mutual wish that they should throw in their lot together.

He would not allow himself to dwell long upon these conjectures, maxims, and hopes, and at twenty minutes to twelve he again

1. The last six words of this sentence were added in 1895; this and other changes in the chapter emphasize Wildeve's hope that he and Eustacia will leave Egdon together.

went softly to the stable, harnessed the horse, and lit the lamps; whence, taking the horse by the head, he led him with the covered car out of the yard to a spot by the roadside some quarter of a mile below the inn.

Here Wildeve waited, slightly sheltered from the driving rain by a high bank that had been cast up at this place. Along the surface of the road where lit by the lamps the loosened gravel and small stones scudded and clicked together before the wind, which, leaving them in heaps, plunged into the heath and boomed across the bushes into darkness. Only one sound rose above this din of weather, and that was the roaring of a ten-hatch weir[2] to the southward, from a river in the meads which formed the boundary of the heath in this direction.

He lingered on in perfect stillness till he began to fancy that the midnight hour must have struck. A very strong doubt had arisen in his mind if Eustacia would venture down the hill in such weather; yet knowing her nature he felt that she might. 'Poor thing! 'tis like her ill-luck,' he murmured.

At length he turned to the lamp and looked at his watch. To his surprise it was nearly a quarter past midnight. He now wished that he had driven up the circuitous road to Mistover, a plan not adopted because of the enormous length of the route in proportion to that of the pedestrian's path down the open hillside, and the consequent increase of labour for the horse.

At this moment a footstep approached; but the light of the lamps being in a different direction the comer was not visible. The step paused, then came on again.

'Eustacia?' said Wildeve.

The person came forward, and the light fell upon the form of Clym, glistening with wet, whom Wildeve immediately recognized; but Wildeve, who stood behind the lamp, was not at once recognized by Yeobright.

He stopped as if in doubt whether this waiting vehicle could have anything to do with the flight of his wife or not. The sight of Yeobright at once banished Wildeve's sober feelings, who saw him again as the deadly rival from whom Eustacia was to be kept at all hazards. Hence Wildeve did not speak, in the hope that Clym would pass by without particular inquiry.

While they both hung thus in hesitation a dull sound became audible above the storm and wind. Its origin was unmistakable—it was the fall[3] of a body into the stream in the adjoining mead, apparently at a point near the weir.

---

2. A weir is a dam to regulate the flow of water in a stream; a hatch is a floodgate.
3. The manuscript shows that Hardy first wrote, and then crossed out, "plunge," which perhaps more strongly suggests intention; all editions have "fall," though "plunge" is used again later in the chapter.

Both started. 'Good God! can it be she?' said Clym.

'Why should it be she?' said Wildeve, in his alarm forgetting that he had hitherto screened himself.

'Ah!—that's you, you traitor, is it?' cried Yeobright. 'Why should it be she? Because last week she would have put an end to her life if she had been able. She ought to have been watched! Take one of the lamps and come with me.'

Yeobright seized the one on his side and hastened on; Wildeve did not wait to unfasten the other, but followed at once along the meadow-track to the weir, a little in the rear of Clym.

Shadwater Weir had at its foot a large circular pool, fifty feet in diameter, into which the water flowed through ten huge hatches, raised and lowered by a winch and cogs in the ordinary manner. The sides of the pool were of masonry, to prevent the water from washing away the bank; but the force of the stream in winter was sometimes such as to undermine the retaining wall and precipitate it into the hole. Clym reached the hatches, the framework of which was shaken to its foundations by the velocity of the current. Nothing but the froth of the waves could be discerned in the pool below. He got upon the plank bridge over the race, and holding to the rail, that the wind might not blow him off, crossed to the other side of the river. There he leant over the wall and lowered the lamp, only to behold the vortex formed at the curl of the returning current.

Wildeve meanwhile had arrived on the former side, and the light from Yeobright's lamp shed a flecked and agitated radiance across the weir-pool, revealing to the ex-engineer the tumbling courses of the currents from the hatches above. Across this gashed and puckered mirror a dark body was slowly borne by one of the backward currents.

'O, my darling!' exclaimed Wildeve in an agonized voice; and, without showing sufficient presence of mind even to throw off his great-coat, he leaped into the boiling caldron.

Yeobright could now also discern the floating body, though but indistinctly; and imagining from Wildeve's plunge that there was life to be saved he was about to leap after. Bethinking himself of a wiser plan he placed the lamp against a post to make it stand upright, and running round to the lower part of the pool, where there was no wall, he sprang in and boldly waded upwards towards the deeper portion. Here he was taken off his legs, and in swimming was carried round into the centre of the basin, where he perceived Wildeve struggling.

While these hasty actions were in progress here, Venn and Thomasin had been toiling through the lower corner of the heath in the direction of the light. They had not been near enough to the river to hear the plunge, but they saw the removal of the carriage-lamp, and watched its motion into the mead. As soon as they reached the car and horse Venn guessed that something new was amiss, and hastened to follow in the course of the moving light. Venn walked faster than Thomasin, and came to the weir alone.

The lamp placed against the post by Clym still shone across the water, and the reddleman observed something floating motionless. Being encumbered with the infant he ran back to meet Thomasin.

'Take the baby, please, Mrs. Wildeve,' he said hastily. 'Run home with her, call the stable-lad, and make him send down to me any men who may be living near. Somebody has fallen into the weir.'

Thomasin took the child and ran. When she came to the covered car the horse, though fresh from the stable, was standing perfectly still, as if conscious of misfortune. She saw for the first time whose it was. She nearly fainted, and would have been unable to proceed another step but that the necessity of preserving the little girl from harm nerved her to an amazing self-control. In this agony of suspense she entered the house, put the baby in a place of safety, woke the lad and the female domestic, and ran out to give the alarm at the nearest cottage.

Diggory, having returned to the brink of the pool, observed that the small upper hatches or floats were withdrawn. He found one of these lying upon the grass, and taking it under one arm, and with his lantern in his hand, entered at the bottom of the pool as Clym had done. As soon as he began to be in deep water he flung himself across the hatch; thus supported he was able to keep afloat as long as he chose, holding the lantern aloft with his disengaged hand. Propelled by his feet he steered round and round the pool, ascending each time by one of the back streams and descending in the middle of the current.

At first he could see nothing. Then amidst the glistening of the whirlpools and the white clots of foam he distinguished a woman's bonnet floating alone. His search was now under the left wall, when something came to the surface almost close beside him. It was not, as he had expected, a woman, but a man. The reddleman put the ring of the lantern between his teeth, seized the floating man by the collar, and, holding on to the hatch with his remaining arm, struck out into the strongest race, by which the unconscious man, the hatch, and himself were carried down the stream. As soon as Venn found his feet dragging over the pebbles of the shallower part below he secured his footing and waded towards the brink. There, where the water stood at about the height of his waist, he flung away the hatch, and attempted to drag forth the man. This was a matter of great difficulty, and he found as the reason that the legs of the unfortunate stranger were tightly embraced by the arms of another man, who had hitherto been entirely beneath the surface.

At this moment his heart bounded to hear footsteps running towards him, and two men, roused by Thomasin, appeared at the
brink above. They ran to where Venn was, and helped him in lifting
out the apparently drowned persons, separating them, and laying
them out upon the grass. Venn turned the light upon their faces.
The one who had been uppermost was Yeobright; he who had been
completely submerged was Wildeve.

'Now we must search the hole again,' said Venn. 'A woman is in
there somewhere. Get a pole.'

One of the men went to the foot-bridge and tore off the handrail.
The reddleman and the two others then entered the water together
from below as before, and with their united force probed the pool
forwards to where it sloped down to its central depth. Venn was not
mistaken in supposing that any person who had sunk for the last
time would be washed down to this point, for when they had examined to about halfway across something impeded their thrust.

'Pull it forward,' said Venn, and they raked it in with the pole till
it was close to their feet.

Venn vanished under the stream, and came up with an armful of
wet drapery enclosing a woman's cold form, which was all that remained of the desperate Eustacia.

When they reached the bank there stood Thomasin, in a stress of
grief, bending over the two unconscious ones who already lay there.
The horse and car were brought to the nearest point in the road,
and it was the work of a few minutes only to place the three in the

'All that remained of the desperate and unfortunate Eustacia.'

vehicle. Venn led on the horse, supporting Thomasin upon his arm, and the two men followed, till they reached the inn.

The woman who had been shaken out of her sleep by Thomasin had hastily dressed herself and lighted a fire, the other servant being left to snore on in peace at the back of the house. The insensible forms of Eustacia, Clym, and Wildeve were then brought in and laid on the carpet, with their feet to the fire, when such restorative processes as could be thought of were adopted at once, the stableman being in the meantime sent for a doctor. But there seemed to be not a whiff of life left in either of the bodies. Then Thomasin, whose stupor of grief had been thrust off awhile by frantic action, applied a bottle of hartshorn[4] to Clym's nostrils, having tried it in vain upon the other two. He sighed.

'Clym's alive!' she exclaimed.

He soon breathed distinctly, and again and again did she attempt to revive her husband by the same means; but Wildeve gave no sign. There was too much reason to think that he and Eustacia both were for ever beyond the reach of stimulating perfumes. Their exertions did not relax till the doctor arrived, when, one by one, the senseless three were taken upstairs and put into warm beds.

Venn soon felt himself relieved from further attendance, and went to the door, scarcely able yet to realize the strange catastrophe that had befallen the family in which he took so great an interest. Thomasin surely would be broken down by the sudden and overwhelming nature of this event. No firm and sensible Mrs. Yeobright lived now to support the gentle girl through the ordeal; and, whatever an unimpassioned spectator might think of her loss of such a husband as Wildeve, there could be no doubt that for the moment she was distracted and horrified by the blow. As for himself, not being privileged to go to her and comfort her, he saw no reason for waiting longer in a house where he remained only as a stranger.

He returned across the heath to his van. The fire was not yet out, and everything remained as he had left it. Venn now bethought himself of his clothes, which were saturated with water to the weight of lead. He changed them, spread them before the fire, and lay down to sleep. But it was more than he could do to rest here while excited by a vivid imagination of the turmoil they were in at the house he had quitted, and, blaming himself for coming away, he dressed in another suit, locked up the door, and again hastened across to the inn. Rain was still falling heavily when he entered the kitchen. A bright fire was shining from the hearth, and two women were bustling about, one of whom was Olly Dowden.

---

4. Smelling salts; the horns or antlers of a hart were ground to provide the ammonia on which the salts are based.

'Well, how is it going on now?' said Venn in a whisper.

'Mr. Yeobright is better; but Mrs. Yeobright and Mr. Wildeve are dead and cold. The doctor says they were quite gone before they were out of the water.'

'Ah! I thought as much when I hauled 'em up. And Mrs. Wildeve?'

'She is as well as can be expected. The doctor had her put between blankets, for she was almost as wet as they that had been in the river, poor young thing. You don't seem very dry, reddleman.'

'O, 'tis not much. I have changed my things. This is only a little dampness I've got coming through the rain again.'

'Stand by the fire. Mis'ess says you be to have whatever you want, and she was sorry when she was told that you'd gone away.'

Venn drew near to the fireplace, and looked into the flames in an absent mood. The steam came from his leggings and ascended the chimney with the smoke, while he thought of those who were upstairs. Two were corpses, one had barely escaped the jaws of death, another was sick and a widow. The last occasion on which he had lingered by that fireplace was when the raffle was in progress; when Wildeve was alive and well; Thomasin active and smiling in the next room; Yeobright and Eustacia just made husband and wife, and Mrs. Yeobright living at Blooms-End. It had seemed at that time that the then position of affairs was good for at least twenty years to come. Yet, of all the circle, he himself was the only one whose situation had not materially changed.

While he ruminated a footstep descended the stairs. It was the nurse, who brought in her hand a rolled mass of wet paper. The woman was so engrossed with her occupation that she hardly saw Venn. She took from a cupboard some pieces of twine, which she strained across the fireplace, tying the end of each piece to the fire-dog,[5] previously pulled forward for the purpose, and, unrolling the wet papers, she began pinning them one by one to the strings in a manner of clothes on a line.

'What be they?' said Venn.

'Poor master's bank-notes,' she answered. 'They were found in his pocket when they undressed him.'

'Then he was not coming back again for some time?' said Venn.

'That we shall never know,' said she.

Venn was loth to depart, for all on earth that interested him lay under this roof. As nobody in the house had any more sleep that night, except the two who slept for ever, there was no reason why he should not remain. So he retired into the niche of the fireplace where he had used to sit, and there he continued, watching the

5. Andiron: metal stand used to support burning wood on a hearth.

steam from the double row of bank-notes as they waved backwards and forwards in the draught of the chimney till their flaccidity was changed to dry crispness throughout. Then the woman came and unpinned them, and, folding them together, carried the handful upstairs. Presently the doctor appeared from above with the look of a man who could do no more, and, pulling on his gloves, went out of the house, the trotting of his horse soon dying away upon the road.

At four o'clock there was a gentle knock at the door. It was from Charley, who had been sent by Captain Vye to inquire if anything had been heard of Eustacia. The girl who admitted him looked in his face as if she did not know what answer to return, and showed him in to where Venn was seated, saying to the reddleman, 'Will you tell him, please?'

Venn told. Charley's only utterance was a feeble, indistinct sound. He stood quite still; then he burst out spasmodically, 'I shall see her once more?'

'I dare say you may see her,' said Diggory gravely. 'But hadn't you better run and tell Captain Vye?'

'Yes, yes. Only I do hope I shall see her just once again.'

'You shall,' said a low voice behind; and starting round they beheld by the dim light a thin, pallid, almost spectral form, wrapped in a blanket, and looking like Lazarus[6] coming from the tomb.

It was Yeobright. Neither Venn nor Charley spoke, and Clym continued: 'You shall see her. There will be time enough to tell the captain when it gets daylight. You would like to see her too—would you not, Diggory? She looks very beautiful now.'

Venn assented by rising to his feet, and with Charley he followed Clym to the foot of the staircase, where he took off his boots; Charley did the same. They followed Yeobright upstairs to the landing, where there was a candle burning, which Yeobright took in his hand, and with it led the way into an adjoining room. Here he went to the bedside and folded back the sheet.

They stood silently looking upon Eustacia, who, as she lay there still in death, eclipsed all her living phases. Pallor did not include all the quality of her complexion, which seemed more than whiteness; it was almost light. The expression of her finely carved mouth was pleasant, as if a sense of dignity had just compelled her to leave off speaking. Eternal rigidity had seized upon it in a momentary transition between fervour and resignation. Her black hair was looser now than either of them had ever seen it before, and surrounded her brow like a forest. The stateliness of look which had been almost too marked for a dweller in a country domicile had at last found an artistically happy background.

6. The story of Christ raising Lazarus from the dead is told in John 11.1–46.

Nobody spoke, till at length Clym covered her and turned aside. 'Now come here,' he said.

They went to a recess in the same room, and there, on a smaller bed, lay another figure—Wildeve. Less repose was visible in his face than in Eustacia's, but the same luminous youthfulness overspread it, and the least sympathetic observer would have felt at sight of him now that he was born for a higher destiny than this. The only sign upon him of his recent struggle for life was in his finger-tips, which were worn and scarified in his dying endeavours to obtain a hold on the face of the weir-wall.

Yeobright's manner had been so quiet, he had uttered so few syllables since his reappearance, that Venn imagined him resigned. It was only when they had left the room and stood upon the landing that the true state of his mind was apparent. Here he said, with a wild smile, inclining his head towards the chamber in which Eustacia lay, 'She is the second woman I have killed this year. I was a great cause of my mother's death; and I am the chief cause of hers.'

'How?' said Venn.

'I spoke cruel words to her, and she left my house. I did not invite her back till it was too late. It is I who ought to have drowned myself. It would have been a charity to the living had the river overwhelmed me and borne her up. But I cannot die. Those who ought to have lived lie dead; and here am I alive!'

'But you can't charge yourself with crimes in that way,' said Venn. 'You may as well say that the parents be the cause of a murder by the child, for without the parents the child would never have been begot.'

'Yes, Venn, that is very true; but you don't know all the circumstances. If it had pleased God to put an end to me it would have been a good thing for all. But I am getting used to the horror of my existence. They say that a time comes when men laugh at misery through long acquaintance with it. Surely that time will soon come to me!'

'Your aim has always been good,' said Venn. 'Why should you say such desperate things?'

'No, they are not desperate. They are only hopeless; and my great regret is that for what I have done no man or law can punish me!'

Book Sixth. Aftercourses

The Inevitable Movement Onward

I

The story of the deaths of Eustacia and Wildeve was told through-out Egdon, and far beyond, for many weeks and months. All the known incidents of their love were enlarged, distorted, touched up, and modified, till the original reality bore but a slight resemblance to the counterfeit presentation by surrounding tongues. Yet, upon the whole, neither the man nor the woman lost dignity by sudden death. Misfortune had struck them gracefully, cutting off their erratic histories with a catastrophic dash, instead of, as with many, attenuating each life to an uninteresting meagreness, through long years of wrinkles, neglect, and decay.

On those most nearly concerned the effect was somewhat different. Strangers who had heard of many such cases now merely heard of one more; but immediately where a blow falls no previous imaginings amount to appreciable preparation for it. The very suddenness of her bereavement dulled, to some extent, Thomasin's feelings; yet, irrationally enough, a consciousness that the husband she had lost ought to have been a better man did not lessen her mourning at all. On the contrary, this fact seemed at first to set off the dead husband in his young wife's eyes, and to be the necessary cloud to the rainbow.

But the horrors of the unknown had passed. Vague misgivings about her future as a deserted wife were at an end. The worst had once been matter of trembling conjecture; it was now matter of reason only, a limited badness. Her chief interest, the little Eustacia, still remained. There was humility in her grief, no defiance in her attitude; and when this is the case a shaken spirit is apt to be stilled.

Could Thomasin's mournfulness now and Eustacia's serenity during life have been reduced to common measure, they would have touched the same mark nearly. But Thomasin's former brightness made shadow of that which in a sombre atmosphere was light itself.

The spring came and calmed her; the summer came and soothed her; the autumn arrived, and she began to be comforted, for her little girl was strong and happy, growing in size and knowledge every day. Outward events flattered Thomasin not a little. Wildeve had died intestate, and she and the child were his only relatives. When administration had been granted, all the debts paid, and the residue of her husband's uncle's property had come into her hands, it was found that the sum waiting to be invested for her own and the child's benefit was little less than ten thousand pounds.[1]

Where should she live? The obvious place was Blooms-End. The old rooms, it is true, were not much higher than the between-decks of a frigate,[2] necessitating a sinking in the floor under the new clock-case she brought from the inn, and the removal of the handsome brass knobs on its head, before there was height for it to stand; but, such as the rooms were, there were plenty of them, and the place was endeared to her by every early recollection. Clym very gladly admitted her as a tenant, confining his own existence to two rooms at the top of the back staircase, where he lived on quietly, shut off from Thomasin and the three servants she had thought fit to indulge in now that she was a mistress of money, going his own ways, and thinking his own thoughts.

His sorrows had made some change in his outward appearance; and yet the alteration was chiefly within. It might have been said that he had a wrinkled mind. He had no enemies, and he could get nobody to reproach him, which was why he so bitterly reproached himself.

He did sometimes think he had been ill-used by fortune, so far as to say that to be born is a palpable dilemma, and that instead of men aiming to advance in life with glory they should calculate how to retreat out of it without shame. But that he and his had been sarcastically and pitilessly handled in having such irons thrust into their souls[3] he did not maintain long. It is usually so, except with the sternest of men. Human beings, in their generous endeavour to construct a hypothesis that shall not degrade a First Cause, have always hesitated to conceive a dominant power of lower moral quality than their own; and, even while they sit down and weep by the waters of Babylon,[4] invent excuses for the oppression which prompts their tears.

Thus, though words of solace were vainly uttered in his presence, he found relief in a direction of his own choosing when left to himself. For a man of his habits the house and the hundred and twenty pounds a year which he had inherited from his mother were enough to supply all worldly needs. Resources do not depend upon gross amounts, but upon the proportion of spendings to takings.

He frequently walked the heath alone, when the past seized upon

---

1. Under the law of the time, when a husband died intestate, his widow never recovered more than half his property, with the remainder going to his children or other near relatives, or, if he had none, to the Crown.
2. A frigate was significantly smaller than a man-of-war.
3. The expression, used to describe the pangs of bitterness or grief, comes from the version of Psalm 105.18 used in the Prayer Book, which mistranslates the Hebrew words meaning to place someone in irons, i.e., in fetters or chains.
4. Quoting Psalm 137.1, expressing the anguish of the Jews in exile: "By the rivers of Babylon, there we sat down, yea, we wept, when we remembered Zion."

him with its shadowy hand, and held him there to listen to its tale. His imagination would then people the spot with its ancient inhabitants: forgotten Celtic tribes trod their tracks about him, and he could almost live among them, look in their faces, and see them standing beside the barrows which swelled around, untouched and perfect as at the time of their erection. Those of the dyed barbarians who had chosen the cultivable tracts were, in comparison with those who had left their marks here, as writers on paper beside writers on parchment. Their records had perished long ago by the plough, while the works of these remained. Yet they all had lived and died unconscious of the different fates awaiting their relics. It reminded him that unforeseen factors operate in the evolution of immortality.

Winter again came around, with its winds, frosts, tame robins, and sparkling starlight. The year previous Thomasin had hardly been conscious of the season's advance; this year she laid her heart open to external influences of every kind. The life of this sweet cousin, her baby, and her servants, came to Clym's senses only in the form of sounds through a wood partition as he sat over books of exceptionally large type; but his ear became at last so accustomed to these slight noises from the other part of the house that he almost could witness the scenes they signified. A faint beat of half-seconds conjured up Thomasin rocking the cradle, a wavering hum meant that she was singing the baby to sleep, a crunching of sand as between millstones raised the picture of Humphrey's, Fairway's, or Sam's heavy feet crossing the stone floor of the kitchen; a light boyish step, and a gay tune in a high key, betokened a visit from Grandfer Cantle; a sudden break-off in the Grandfer's utterances implied the application to his lips of a mug of small beer; a bustling and slamming of doors meant starting to go to market; for Thomasin, in spite of her added scope for gentility, led a ludicrously narrow life, to the end that she might save every possible pound for her little daughter.

One summer day Clym was in the garden, immediately outside the parlour-window, which was as usual open. He was looking at the pot-flowers on the sill; they had been revived and restored by Thomasin to the state in which his mother had left them. He heard a slight scream from Thomasin, who was sitting inside the room.

'O, how you frightened me!' she said to some one who had entered. 'I thought you were the ghost of yourself.'

Clym was curious enough to advance a little further and look in at the window. To his astonishment there stood within the room Diggory Venn, no longer a reddleman, but exhibiting the strangely altered hues of an ordinary Christian countenance, white shirt-front, light flowered waistcoat, blue-spotted neckerchief, and bottle-green coat. Nothing in this appearance was at all singular but the fact of its great difference from what he had formerly been. Red, and all approach to red, was carefully excluded from every article of clothes upon him; for what is there that persons just out of harness dread so much as reminders of the trade which has enriched them?

Yeobright went round to the door and entered.

'I was so alarmed!' said Thomasin, smiling from one to the other. 'I couldn't believe that he had got white of his own accord! It seemed supernatural.'

'I gave up dealing in reddle last Christmas,' said Venn. 'It was a profitable trade, and I found that by that time I had made enough to take the dairy of fifty cows that my father had in his lifetime. I always thought of getting to that place again if I changed at all; and now I am there.'

'How did you manage to become white, Diggory?' Thomasin asked.

'I turned so by degrees, ma'am.'

'You look much better than ever you did before.'

Venn appeared confused; and Thomasin, seeing how inadvertently she had spoken to a man who might possibly have tender feelings for her still, blushed a little. Clym saw nothing of this, and added good-humouredly—

'What shall we have to frighten Thomasin's baby with, now you have become a human being again?'

'Sit down, Diggory,' said Thomasin, 'and stay to tea.'

Venn moved as if he would retire to the kitchen, when Thomasin said with pleasant pertness as she went on with some sewing. 'Of course you must sit down here. And where does your fifty-cow dairy lie, Mr. Venn?'

'At Stickleford—about two miles to the right of Alderworth, ma'am, where the meads begin. I have thought that if Mr. Yeobright would like to pay me a visit sometimes he shouldn't stay away for want of asking. I'll not bide to tea this afternoon, thank'ee, for I've got something on hand that must be settled. 'Tis Maypole-day tomorrow, and the Shadwater folk have clubbed with a few of your neighbours here to have a pole just outside your palings in the heath, as it is a nice green place.' Venn waved his elbow towards the patch in front of the house. 'I have been talking to Fairway about it,' he continued, 'and I said to him that before we put up the pole it would be as well to ask Mrs. Wildeve.'

'I can say nothing against it,' she answered. 'Our property does not reach an inch further than the white palings.'

'But you might not like to see a lot of folk going crazy round a stick, under your very nose?'

'I shall have no objection at all.'

Venn soon after went away, and in the evening Yeobright strolled as far as Fairway's cottage. It was a lovely May sunset, and the birch trees which grew on this margin of the vast Egdon wilderness had put on their new leaves, delicate as butterflies' wings, and diaphanous as amber. Beside Fairway's dwelling was an open space recessed from the road, and here were now collected all the young people from within a radius of a couple of miles. The pole lay with one end supported on a trestle, and women were engaged in wreathing it from the top downwards with wild-flowers. The instincts of merry England lingered on here with exceptional vitality, and the symbolic customs which tradition has attached to each season of the year were yet a reality on Egdon. Indeed, the impulses of all such outlandish hamlets are pagan still: in these spots homage to nature, self-adoration, frantic gaieties, fragments of Teutonic rites[5] to divinities whose names are forgotten, seem in some way or other to have survived mediæval doctrine.

Yeobright did not interrupt the preparations, and went home again. The next morning, when Thomasin withdrew the curtains of her bedroom window, there stood the Maypole in the middle of the green, its top cutting into the sky. It had sprung up in the night, or rather early morning, like Jack's bean-stalk.[6] She opened the casement to get a better view of the garlands and posies that adorned it. The sweet perfume of the flowers had already spread into the surrounding air, which, being free from every taint, conducted to her lips a full measure of the fragrance received from the spire of blossom in its midst. At the top of the pole were crossed hoops decked with small flowers; beneath these came a milk-white zone of May-bloom; then a zone of bluebells, then of cowslips, then of lilacs, then of ragged-robins,[7] daffodils, and so on, till the lowest stage was reached. Thomasin noticed all these, and was delighted that the May-revel was to be so near.

When afternoon came people began to gather on the green, and Yeobright was interested enough to look out upon them from the open window of his room. Soon after this Thomasin walked out from the door immediately below and turned her eyes up to her cousin's face. She was dressed more gaily than Yeobright had ever seen her dress since the time of Wildeve's death, eighteen months before; since the day of her marriage even she had not exhibited herself to such advantage.

---

5. Victorian folklorists speculated on the Germanic origin of many popular English customs; the Folklore Society, founded in London in 1878, the year of this novel, included several of Hardy's friends among its members.
6. In the nursery tale, as told by (among others) Andrew Lang in *The Red Fairy Book* (1890), magic beans thrown into the garden grow overnight into a giant beanstalk.
7. A plant of the pink family, found in damp meadows.

'How pretty you look to-day, Thomasin!' he said. 'Is it because of the Maypole?'

'Not altogether.' And then she blushed and dropped her eyes, which he did not specially observe, though her manner seemed to him to be rather peculiar, considering that she was only addressing himself. Could it be possible that she had put on her summer clothes to please him?

He recalled her conduct towards him throughout the last few weeks, when they had often been working together in the garden, just as they had formerly done when they were boy and girl under his mother's eye. What if her interest in him were not so entirely that of a relative as it had formerly been? To Yeobright any possibility of this sort was a serious matter; and he almost felt troubled at the thought of it. Every pulse of loverlike feeling which had not been stilled during Eustacia's lifetime had gone into the grave with her. His passion for her had occurred too far on in his manhood to leave fuel enough on hand for another fire of that sort, as may happen with more boyish loves. Even supposing him capable of loving again, that love would be a plant of slow and laboured growth, and in the end only small and sickly, like an autumn-hatched bird.

He was so distressed by this new complexity that when the enthusiastic brass band arrived and struck up, which it did about five o'clock, with apparently wind enough among its members to blow down his house, he withdrew from his rooms by the back door, went down the garden, through the gate in the hedge, and away out of sight. He could not bear to remain in the presence of enjoyment to-day, though he had tried hard.

Nothing was seen of him for four hours. When he came back by the same path it was dusk, and the dews were coating every green thing. The boisterous music had ceased; but, entering the premises as he did from behind, he could not see if the May party had all gone till he had passed through Thomasin's division of the house to the front door. Thomasin was standing within the porch alone.

She looked at him reproachfully. 'You went away just when it began, Clym,' she said.

'Yes. I felt I could not join in. You went out with them, of course?'

'No, I did not.'

'You appeared to be dressed on purpose.'

'Yes, but I could not go out alone; so many people were there. One is there now.'

Yeobright strained his eyes across the dark-green patch beyond the paling, and near the black form of the Maypole he discerned a shadowy figure, sauntering idly up and down. 'Who is it?' he said.

'Mr. Venn,' said Thomasin.

'You might have asked him to come in, I think, Tamsie. He has been very kind to you first and last.'

'I will now,' she said; and, acting on the impulse, went through the wicket to where Venn stood under the Maypole.

'It is Mr. Venn, I think?' she inquired.

Venn started as if he had not seen her—artful man that he was—and said, 'Yes.'

'Will you come in?'

'I am afraid that I——'

'I have seen you dancing this evening, and you had the very best of the girls for your partners. Is it that you won't come in because you wish to stand here, and think over the past hours of enjoyment?'

'Well, that's partly it,' said Mr. Venn, with ostentatious sentiment. 'But the main reason why I am biding here like this is that I want to wait till the moon rises.'

'To see how pretty the Maypole looks in the moonlight?'

'No. To look for a glove that was dropped by one of the maidens.'

Thomasin was speechless with surprise. That a man who had to walk some four or five miles to his home should wait here for such a reason pointed to only one conclusion: the man must be amazingly interested in that glove's owner.

'Were you dancing with her, Diggory?' she asked, in a voice which revealed that he had made himself considerably more interesting to her by this disclosure.

'No,' he sighed.

'And you will not come in, then?'

'Not to-night, thank you, ma'am.'

'Shall I lend you a lantern to look for the young person's glove, Mr. Venn?'

'O no; it is not necessary, Mrs. Wildeve, thank you. The moon will rise in a few minutes.'

Thomasin went back to the porch. 'Is he coming in?' said Clym, who had been waiting where she had left him.

'He would rather not to-night,' she said, and then passed by him into the house; whereupon Clym too retired to his own rooms.

When Clym was gone Thomasin crept upstairs in the dark, and, just listening by the cot, to assure herself that the child was asleep, she went to the window, gently lifted the corner of the white curtain, and looked out. Venn was still there. She watched the growth of the faint radiance appearing in the sky by the eastern hill, till presently the edge of the moon burst upwards and flooded the valley with light. Diggory's form was now distinct on the green; he was moving about in a bowed attitude, evidently scanning the grass for the precious missing article, walking in zigzags right and left till he should have passed over every foot of the ground.

'How very ridiculous!' Thomasin murmured to herself, in a tone which was intended to be satirical. 'To think that a man should be so silly as to go mooning about like that for a girl's glove! A respectable dairyman, too, and a man of money as he is now. What a pity!'

At last Venn appeared to find it; whereupon he stood up and raised it to his lips. Then placing it in his breast-pocket—the nearest receptable to a man's heart permitted by modern raiment—he ascended the valley in a mathematically direct line towards his distant home in the meadows.

Thomasin Walks in a Green Place by the Roman Road

II

Clym saw little of Thomasin for several days after this; and when they met she was more silent than usual. At length he asked her what she was thinking of so intently.

'I am thoroughly perplexed,' she said candidly. 'I cannot for my life think who it is that Diggory Venn is so much in love with. None of the girls at the Maypole were good enough for him, and yet she must have been there.'

Clym tried to imagine Venn's choice for a moment; but ceasing to be interested in the question he went on again with his gardening.

No clearing up of the mystery was granted her for some time. But one afternoon Thomasin was upstairs getting ready for a walk, when she had occasion to come to the landing and call 'Rachel.' Rachel was a girl about thirteen, who carried the baby out for airings; and she came upstairs at the call.

'Have you seen one of my last new gloves about the house, Rachel?' inquired Thomasin. 'It is the fellow to this one.'

Rachel did not reply.

'Why don't you answer?' said her mistress.

'I think it is lost, ma'am.'

'Lost? Who lost it? I have never worn them but once.'

Rachel appeared as one dreadfully troubled, and at last began to cry. 'Please, ma'am, on the day of the Maypole I had none to wear, and I seed yours on the table, and I thought I would borrow 'em. I did not mean to hurt 'em at all, but one of them got lost. Somebody gave me some money to buy another pair for you, but I have not been able to go anywhere to get 'em.'

'Who's somebody?'

'Mr. Venn.'

'Did he know it was my glove?'

'Yes. I told him.'

Thomasin was so surprised by the explanation that she quite forgot to lecture the girl, who glided silently away. Thomasin did not move further than to turn her eyes upon the grass-plat where the Maypole had stood. She remained thinking, then said to herself that she would not go out that afternoon, but would work hard at the baby's unfinished lovely plaid frock, cut on the cross[1] in the newest fashion. How she managed to work hard, and yet do no more than she had done at the end of two hours, would have been a mystery to any one not aware that the recent incident was of a kind likely to divert her industry from a manual to a mental channel.

Next day she went her ways as usual, and continued her custom of walking in the heath with no other companion than little Eustacia, now of the age when it is a matter of doubt with such characters whether they are intended to walk through the world on their hands or on their feet; so that they get into painful complications by trying both. It was very pleasant to Thomasin, when she had carried the child to some lonely place, to give her a little private practice on the green turf and shepherd's-thyme, which formed a soft mat to fall headlong upon when equilibrium was lost.

Once, when engaged in this system of training, and stooping to remove bits of stick, fern-stalks, and other such fragments from the child's path, that the journey might not be brought to an untimely end by some insuperable barrier a quarter of an inch high, she was alarmed by discovering that a man on horseback was almost close beside her, the soft natural carpet having muffled the horse's tread. The rider, who was Venn, waved his hat in the air and bowed gallantly.

'Diggory, give me my glove,' said Thomasin, whose manner it was under any circumstances to plunge into the midst of a subject which engrossed her.

Venn immediately dismounted, put his hand in his breast-pocket, and handed the glove.

'Thank you. It was very good of you to take care of it.'

'It is very good of you to say so.'

'O no. I was quite glad to find you had it. Everybody gets so indifferent that I was surprised to know you thought of me.'

'If you had remembered what I was once you wouldn't have been surprised.'

'Ah, no,' she said quickly. 'But men of your character are mostly so independent.'

---

1. Diagonally, across the pattern or weave, rather than in line with it.

'What is my character?' he asked.

'I don't exactly know,' said Thomasin simply, 'except it is to cover up your feelings under a practical manner, and only to show them when you are alone.'

'Ah, how do you know that?' said Venn strategically.

'Because,' said she, stopping to put the little girl, who had managed to get herself upside down, right end up again, 'because I do.'

'You mustn't judge by folks in general,' said Venn. 'Still I don't know much what feelings are now-a-days. I have got so mixed up with business of one sort and t'other that my soft sentiments are gone off in vapour like. Yes, I am given up body and soul to the making of money. Money is all my dream.'

'O Diggory, how wicked!' said Thomasin reproachfully, and looking at him in exact balance between taking his words seriously and judging them as said to tease her.

'Yes, 'tis rather a rum course,' said Venn, in the bland tone of one comfortably resigned to sins he could no longer overcome.

'You, who used to be so nice!'

'Well, that's an argument I rather like, because what a man has once been he may be again.' Thomasin blushed. 'Except that it is rather harder now,' Venn continued.

'Why?' she asked.

'Because you be richer than you were at that time.'

'O no—not much. I have made it nearly all over to the baby, as it was my duty to do, except just enough to live on.'

'I am rather glad of that,' said Venn softly, and regarding her from the corner of his eye, 'for it makes it easier for us to be friendly.'

Thomasin blushed again, and, when a few more words had been said of a not unpleasing kind, Venn mounted his horse and rode on.

This conversation had passed in a hollow of the heath near the old Roman road, a place much frequented by Thomasin. And it might have been observed that she did not in future walk that way less often from having met Venn there now. Whether or not Venn abstained from riding thither because he had met Thomasin in the same place might easily have been guessed from her proceedings about two months later in the same year.

The Serious Discourse of Clym with His Cousin

III

Throughout this period Yeobright had more or less pondered on his duty to his cousin Thomasin. He could not help feeling that it would be a pitiful waste of sweet material if the tender-natured thing should be doomed from this early stage of her life onwards to dribble away her winsome qualities on lonely gorse and fern. But he felt this as an economist merely, and not as a lover. His passion for Eustacia had been a sort of conserve[1] of his whole life, and he had nothing more of that supreme quality left to bestow. So far the obvious thing was not to entertain any idea of marriage with Thomasin, even to oblige her.

But this was not all. Years ago there had been in his mother's mind a great fancy about Thomasin and himself. It had not positively amounted to a desire, but it had always been a favourite dream. That they should be man and wife in good time, if the happiness of neither were endangered thereby, was the fancy in question. So that what course save one was there now left for any son who reverenced his mother's memory as Yeobright did? It is an unfortunate fact that any particular whim of parents, which might have been dispersed by half an hour's conversation during their lives, becomes sublimated by their deaths into a fiat[2] the most absolute, with such results to conscientious children as those parents, had they lived, would have been the first to decry.

Had only Yeobright's own future been involved he would have proposed to Thomasin with a ready heart. He had nothing to lose by carrying out a dead mother's hope. But he dreaded to contemplate Thomasin wedded to the mere corpse of a lover that he now felt himself to be. He had but three activities alive in him. One was his almost daily walk to the little graveyard wherein his mother lay; another, his just as frequent visits by night to the more distant enclosure which numbered his Eustacia among its dead; the third was self-preparation for a vocation which alone seemed likely to satisfy his cravings—that of an itinerant preacher of the eleventh commandment.[3] It was difficult to believe that Thomasin would be cheered by a husband with such tendencies as these.

Yet he resolved to ask her, and let her decide for herself. It was even with a pleasant sense of doing his duty that he went downstairs to her one evening for this purpose, when the sun was printing on the valley the same long shadow of the housetop that he had seen lying there times out of number while his mother lived.

Thomasin was not in her room, and he found her in the front garden. 'I have long been wanting, Thomasin,' he began, 'to say something about a matter that concerns both our futures.'

'And you are going to say it now?' she remarked quickly, colouring as she met his gaze. 'Do stop a minute, Clym, and let me speak first, for, oddly enough, I have been wanting to say something to you.'

1. A concentration or distillation of the essential elements, leaving the remainder as a residue.
2. Command (literally, the Latin for "Let it be done").
3. Jesus told his disciples, "A new commandment I give unto you, that ye love one another" (John 13.34).

'By all means say on, Tamsie.'

'I suppose nobody can overhear us?' she went on, casting her eyes around and lowering her voice. 'Well, first you will promise me this—that you won't be angry and call me anything harsh if you disagree with what I propose?'

Yeobright promised, and she continued. 'What I want is your advice, for you are my relation—I mean, a sort of guardian to me—aren't you, Clym?'

'Well, yes, I suppose I am; a sort of guardian. In fact, I am, of course,' he said, altogether perplexed as to her drift.

'I am thinking of marrying,' she then observed blandly. 'But I shall not marry unless you assure me that you approve of such a step. Why don't you speak?'

'I was taken rather by surprise. But, nevertheless, I am very glad to hear such news. I shall approve, of course, dear Tamsie. Who can it be? I am quite at a loss to guess. No, I am not—'tis the old doctor!—not that I mean to call him old, for he is not very old after all. Ah—I noticed when he attended you last time!'

'No, no,' she said hastily. ' 'Tis Mr. Venn.'

Clym's face suddenly became grave.

'There, now, you don't like him, and I wish I hadn't mentioned him!' she exclaimed almost petulantly. 'And I shouldn't have done it, either, only he keeps on bothering me so till I don't know what to do!'

Clym looked at the heath. 'I like Venn well enough,' he answered at last. 'He is a very honest and at the same time astute man. He is clever too, as is proved by his having got you to favour him. But really, Thomasin, he is not quite——'

'Gentleman enough for me? That is just what I feel. I am sorry now that I asked you, and I won't think any more of him. At the same time I must marry him if I marry anybody—that I *will* say!'

'I don't see that,' said Clym, carefully concealing every clue to his own interrupted intention, which she plainly had not guessed. 'You might marry a professional man, or somebody of that sort, by going into the town to live and forming acquaintances there.'

'I am not fit for town life—so very rural and silly as I always have been. Do not you yourself notice my countrified ways?'

'Well, when I came home from Paris I did, a little; but I don't now.'

'That's because you have got countrified too. O, I couldn't live in a street for the world! Egdon is a ridiculous old place; but I have got used to it, and I couldn't be happy anywhere else at all.'

'Neither could I,' said Clym.

'Then how could you say that I should marry some town man? I am sure, say what you will, that I must marry Diggory, if I marry at all. He has been kinder to me than anybody else, and has helped me in many ways that I don't know of!' Thomasin almost pouted now.

'Yes, he has,' said Clym in a neutral tone. 'Well, I wish with all my heart that I could say, marry him. But I cannot forget what my mother thought on that matter, and it goes rather against me not to respect her opinion. There is too much reason why we should do the little we can to respect it now.'

'Very well, then,' sighed Thomasin. 'I will say no more.'

'But you are not bound to obey my wishes. I merely say what I think.'

'O no—I don't want to be rebellious in that way,' she said sadly. 'I had no business to think of him—I ought to have thought of my family. What dreadfully bad impulses there are in me!' Her lip trembled, and she turned away to hide a tear.

Clym, though vexed at what seemed her unaccountable taste, was in a measure relieved to find that at any rate the marriage question in relation to himself was shelved. Through several succeeding days he saw her at different times from the window of his room moping disconsolately about the garden. He was half angry with her for choosing Venn; then he was grieved at having put himself in the way of Venn's happiness, who was, after all, as honest and persevering a young fellow as any on Egdon, since he had turned over a new leaf. In short, Clym did not know what to do.

When next they met she said abruptly, 'He is much more respectable now than he was then!'

'Who? O yes—Diggory Venn.'

'Aunt only objected because he was a reddleman.'

'Well, Thomasin, perhaps I don't know all the particulars of my mother's wish. So you had better use your own discretion.'

'You will always feel that I slighted your mother's memory.'

'No, I will not. I shall think you are convinced that, had she seen Diggory in his present position, she would have considered him a fitting husband for you. Now, that's my real feeling. Don't consult me any more, but do as you like, Thomasin. I shall be content.'

It is to be supposed that Thomasin was convinced; for a few days after this, when Clym strayed into a part of the heath that he had not lately visited, Humphrey, who was at work there, said to him, 'I am glad to see that Mrs. Wildeve and Venn have made it up again, seemingly.'

'Have they?' said Clym abstractedly.

'Yes; and he do contrive to stumble upon her whenever she walks out on fine days with the chiel.[4] But, Mr. Yeobright, I can't help

4. Child (dialect).

feeling that your cousin ought to have married you. 'Tis a pity to make two chimley-corners[5] where there need be only one. You could get her away from him now, 'tis my belief, if you were only to set about it.'

'How can I have the conscience to marry after having driven two women to their deaths? Don't think such a thing, Humphrey. After my experience I should consider it too much of a burlesque to go to church and take a wife. In the words of Job, "I have made a covenant with mine eyes; why then should I think upon a maid?" '[6]

'No, Mr. Clym, don't fancy that about driving two women to their deaths. You shouldn't say it.'

'Well, we'll leave that out,' said Yeobright. 'But anyhow God has set a mark upon me which wouldn't look well in a love-making scene. I have two ideas in my head, and no others. I am going to keep a night-school; and I am going to turn preacher. What have you got to say to that, Humphrey?'

'I'll come and hear 'ee with all my heart.'

'Thanks. 'Tis all I wish.'

As Clym descended into the valley Thomasin came down by the other path, and met him at the gate. 'What do you think I have to tell you, Clym?' she said, looking archly over her shoulder at him.

'I can guess,' he replied.

She scrutinized his face. 'Yes, you guess right. It is going to be after all. He thinks I may as well make up my mind, and I have got to think so too. It is to be on the twenty-fifth of next month, if you don't object.'

'Do what you think right, dear. I am only too glad that you see your way clear to happiness again. My sex owes you every amends for the treatment you received in days gone by.'[7]

---

5. Chimney-corners (dialect).
6. Quoting Job 31.1. Though Clym is expressing his resolve not to marry, the quoted words are part of Job's declaration of his own guiltlessness.
7. Hardy added a footnote here for the 1912 edition: "The writer may state here that the original conception of the story did not design a marriage between Thomasin and Venn. He was to have retained his isolated and weird character to the last, and to have disappeared mysteriously from the heath, nobody knowing whither—Thomasin remaining a widow. But certain circumstances of serial publication led to a change of intent.

    Readers can therefore choose between the endings, and those with an austere artistic code can assume the more consistent conclusion to be the true one."

    Hardy's note is somewhat misleading, since as early as February 1878, when only one installment of the novel had been published, Hardy told his illustrator, Arthur Hopkins, that Thomasin was to marry Venn. There is no record of editorial interference.

Cheerfulness Again Asserts Itself at Blooms-End, and
Clym Finds His Vocation

IV

Anybody who had passed through Blooms-End about eleven o'clock
on the morning fixed for the wedding would have found that, while
Yeobright's house was comparatively quiet, sounds denoting great
activity came from the dwelling of his nearest neighbour, Timothy
Fairway. It was chiefly a noise of feet, briskly crunching hither and
thither over the sanded floor within. One man only was visible outside, and he seemed to be later at an appointment than he had intended to be, for he hastened up to the door, lifted the latch, and
walked in without ceremony.

The scene within was not quite the customary one. Standing
about the room was the little knot of men who formed the chief
part of the Egdon coterie, there being present Fairway himself,
Grandfer Cantle, Humphrey, Christian, and one or two turf-
cutters. It was a warm day, and the men were as a matter of course
in their shirt-sleeves, except Christian, who had always a nervous
fear of parting with a scrap of his clothing when in anybody's house
but his own. Across the stout oak table in the middle of the room
was thrown a mass of striped linen, which Grandfer Cantle held
down on one side, and Humphrey on the other, while Fairway
rubbed its surface with a yellow lump, his face being damp and
creased with the effort of the labour.

'Waxing a bed-tick,[1] souls?' said the new-comer.

'Yes, Sam,' said Grandfer Cantle, as a man too busy to waste
words. 'Shall I stretch this corner a shade tighter, Timothy?'

Fairway replied, and the waxing went on with unabated vigour.
' 'Tis going to be a good bed, by the look o't,' continued Sam, after
an interval of silence. 'Who may it be for?'

' 'Tis a present for the new folks that's going to set up house-
keeping,' said Christian, who stood helpless and overcome by the
majesty of the proceedings.

'Ah, to be sure; and a valuable one, 'a b'lieve.'

'Beds be dear to fokes that don't keep geese, bain't they, Mister
Fairway?' said Christian, as to an omniscient being.

'Yes,' said the furze-dealer, standing up, giving his forehead a
thorough mopping, and handing the beeswax to Humphrey, who
succeeded at the rubbing forthwith. 'Not that this couple be in
want of one, but 'twas well to show 'em a bit of friendliness at this

---

1. The inside of the cover of a feather mattress was waxed to provide an adhesive surface,
   so that the feathers would remain more evenly spread.

great racketing vagary[2] of their lives. I set up both my own daughters in one when they was married, and there have been feathers enough for another in the house the last twelve months. Now then, neighbours, I think we have laid on enough wax. Grandfer Cantle, you turn the tick the right way outwards, and then I'll begin to shake in the feathers.'

When the bed was in proper trim Fairway and Christian brought forward vast paper bags, stuffed to the full, but light as balloons, and began to turn the contents of each into the receptacle just prepared. As bag after bag was emptied, airy tufts of down and feathers floated about the room in increasing quantity till, through a mishap of Christian's, who shook the contents of one bag outside the tick, the atmosphere of the room became dense with gigantic flakes, which descended upon the workers like a windless snow-storm.

'I never saw such a clumsy chap as you, Christian,' said Grandfer Cantle severely. 'You might have been the son of a man that's never been outside Blooms-End in his life for all the wit you have. Really all the soldiering and smartness in the world in the father seems to count for nothing in forming the nater of the son. As far as that chiel Christian is concerned I might as well have stayed at home and seed nothing, like all the rest of ye here. Though, as far as myself is concerned, a dashing spirit has counted for sommat, to be sure!'

'Don't ye let me down so, father; I feel no bigger than a ninepin after it. I've made but a bruckle hit,[3] I'm afeard.'

'Come, come. Never pitch yerself in such a low key as that, Christian; you should try more,' said Fairway.

'Yes, you should try more,' echoed the Grandfer with insistence, as if he had been the first to make the suggestion. 'In common conscience every man ought either to marry or go for a soldier. 'Tis a scandal to the nation to do neither one nor t'other. I did both, thank God! Neither to raise men nor to lay 'em low—that shows a poor do-nothing spirit indeed.'

'I never had the nerve to stand fire,' faltered Christian. 'But as to marrying, I own I've asked here and there, though without much fruit from it. Yes, there's some house or other that might have had a man for a master—such as he is—that's now ruled by a woman alone. Still it might have been awkward if I had found her; for, d'ye see, neighbours, there'd have been nobody left at home to keep down father's spirits to the decent pitch that becomes a old man.'

'And you've your work cut out to do that, my son,' said Grandfer Cantle smartly. 'I wish that the dread of infirmities was not so strong

2. Exciting juncture or turning point (to racket is to take part in a noisy celebration; a vagary is a whim, or an eccentric course of action).
3. Mistake (dialect).

in me!—I'd start the very first thing to-morrow to see the world over again! But seventy-one, though nothing at home, is a high figure for a rover. . . . Ay, seventy-one last Candlemas-day.[4] Gad, I'd sooner have it in guineas than in years!' And the old man sighed.

'Don't you be mournful, Grandfer,' said Fairway. 'Empty some more feathers into the bed-tick, and keep up yer heart. Though rather lean in the stalks you be a green-leaved old man still. There's time enough left to ye yet to fill whole chronicles.'

'Begad, I'll go to 'em, Timothy—to the married pair!' said Grandfer Cantle in an encouraged voice, and starting round briskly. 'I'll go to 'em to-night and sing a wedding-song, hey? 'Tis like me to do so, you know; and they'd see it as such. My "Down in Cupid's Gardens"[5] was well liked in four; still, I've got others as good, and even better. What do you say to my

> "She cal´-led to´ her love´
> From the lat´-tice a-bove,
> 'O, come in´ from the fog´-gy fog´-gy dew´.'" [6]

'Twould please 'em well at such a time! Really, now I come to think of it, I haven't turned my tongue in my head to the shape of a real good song since Old Midsummer night, when we had the "Barley Mow"[7] at the Woman; and 'tis a pity to neglect your strong point where there's few that have the compass for such things!'

'So 'tis, so 'tis,' said Fairway. 'Now gie the bed a shake down. We've put in seventy pound of best feathers, and I think that's as many as the tick will fairly hold. A bit and a drap wouldn't be amiss now, I reckon. Christian, maul down[8] the victuals from corner-cupboard if canst reach, man, and I'll draw a drap o' sommat to wet it with.'

They sat down to a lunch in the midst of their work, feathers around, above, and below them; the original owners of which occasionally came to the open door and cackled begrudgingly at sight of such a quantity of their old clothes.

'Upon my soul I shall be chokt,' said Fairway when, having extracted a feather from his mouth, he found several others floating on the mug as it was handed round.

'I've swallered several; and one had a tolerable quill,' said Sam placidly from the corner.

'Hullo—what's that—wheels I hear coming?' Grandfer Cantle ex-

---

4. February 2; so named because it marks the Feast of the Purification of Mary, when candles are blessed during the ceremonies.
5. Popular song in which a sailor finds a lover while looking for flowers; Cupid's Gardens was an eighteenth-century pleasure garden in London.
6. From "The Foggy, Foggy Dew," a popular ballad about seduction, but hardly a fit song for a wedding.
7. A popular drinking song (a mow is a pile of hay or straw).
8. Lift down (dialect).

claimed, jumping up and hastening to the door. 'Why, 'tis they back again: I didn't expect 'em yet this half-hour. To be sure, how quick marrying can be done when you are in the mind for't!'

'O yes, it can soon be *done*,' said Fairway, as if something should be added to make the statement complete.

He arose and followed the Grandfer, and the rest also went to the door. In a moment an open fly[9] was driven past, in which sat Venn and Mrs. Venn, Yeobright, and a grand relative of Venn's who had come from Budmouth for the occasion. The fly had been hired at the nearest town, regardless of distance and cost, there being nothing on Egdon Heath, in Venn's opinion, dignified enough for such an event when such a woman as Thomasin was the bride; and the church was too remote for a walking bridal-party.

As the fly passed the group which had run out from the home-stead they shouted 'Hurrah!' and waved their hands; feathers and down floating from their hair, their sleeves, and the folds of their garments at every motion, and Grandfer Cantle's seals dancing merrily in the sunlight as he twirled himself about. The driver of the fly turned a supercilious gaze upon them; he even treated the wedded pair themselves with something like condescension; for in what other state than heathen could people, rich or poor, exist who were doomed to abide in such a world's end as Egdon? Thomasin showed no such superiority to the group at the door, fluttering her hand as quickly as a bird's wing towards them, and asking Diggory, with tears in her eyes, if they ought not to alight and speak to these kind neighbours. Venn, however, suggested that, as they were all coming to the house in the evening, this was hardly necessary.

After this excitement the saluting party returned to their occupation, and the stuffing and sewing was soon afterwards finished, when Fairway harnessed a horse, wrapped up the cumbrous present, and drove off with it in the cart to Venn's house at Stickleford.

Yeobright, having filled the office at the wedding-service which naturally fell to his hands, and afterwards returned to the house with the husband and wife, was indisposed to take part in the feasting and dancing that wound up the evening. Thomasin was disappointed.

'I wish I could be there without dashing your spirits,' he said. 'But I might be too much like the skull at the banquet.'[1]

'No, no.'

'Well, dear, apart from that, if you would excuse me, I should be glad. I know it seems unkind; but, dear Thomasin, I fear I should not be happy in the company—there, that's the truth of it. I shall

9. Carriage drawn by one horse; usually covered.
1. As a *memento mori*, or reminder of mortality.

always be coming to see you at your new home, you know, so that my absence now will not matter.'

'Then I give in. Do whatever will be most comfortable to yourself.'

Clym retired to his lodging at the housetop much relieved, and occupied himself during the afternoon in noting down the heads of a sermon, with which he intended to initiate all that really seemed practicable of the scheme that had originally brought him hither, and that he had so long kept in view under various modifications, and through evil and good report.[2] He had tested and weighed his convictions again and again, and saw no reason to alter them, though he had considerably lessened his plan. His eyesight, by long humouring in his native air, had grown stronger, but not sufficiently strong to warrant his attempting his extensive educational project. Yet he did not repine: there was still more than enough of an unambitious sort to tax all his energies and occupy all his hours.

Evening drew on, and sounds of life and movement in the lower part of the domicile became more pronounced, the gate in the palings clicking incessantly. The party was to be an early one, and all the guests were assembled long before it was dark. Yeobright went down the back staircase and into the heath by another path than that in front, intending to walk in the open air till the party was over, when he would return to wish Thomasin and her husband good-bye as they departed. His steps were insensibly bent towards Mistover by the path that he had followed on that terrible morning when he learnt the strange news from Susan's boy.

He did not turn aside to the cottage, but pushed on to an eminence, whence he could see over the whole quarter that had once been Eustacia's home. While he stood observing the darkening scene somebody came up. Clym, seeing him but dimly, would have let him pass by silently, had not the pedestrian, who was Charley, recognized the young man and spoken to him.

'Charley, I have not seen you for a length of time,' said Yeobright. 'Do you often walk this way?'

'No,' the lad replied. 'I don't often come outside the bank.'

'You were not at the Maypole.'

'No,' said Charley, in the same listless tone. 'I don't care for that sort of thing now.'

'You rather liked Miss Eustacia, didn't you?' Yeobright gently asked. Eustacia had frequently told him of Charley's romantic attachment.

'Yes, very much. Ah, I wish——'

2. Christians at Corinth were urged to remain patient through "evil report and good report" (2 Corinthians 6.8).

'Yes?'

'I wish, Mr. Yeobright, you could give me something to keep that once belonged to her—if you don't mind.'

'I shall be very happy to. It will give me very great pleasure, Charley. Let me think what I have of hers that you would like. But come with me to the house, and I'll see.'

They walked towards Blooms-End together. When they reached the front it was dark, and the shutters were closed, so that nothing of the interior could be seen.

'Come round this way,' said Clym. 'My entrance is at the back for the present.'

The two went round and ascended the crooked stair in darkness till Clym's sitting-room on the upper floor was reached, where he lit a candle, Charley entering gently behind. Yeobright searched his desk, and taking out a sheet of tissue-paper unfolded from it two or three undulating locks of raven hair, which fell over the paper like black streams. From these he selected one, wrapped it up, and gave it to the lad, whose eyes had filled with tears. He kissed the packet, put it in his pocket, and said in a voice of emotion, 'O, Mr. Clym, how good you are to me!'

'I will go a little way with you,' said Clym. And amid the noise of merriment from below they descended. Their path to the front led them close to a little side-window, whence the rays of candles streamed across the shrubs. The window, being screened from general observation by the bushes, had been left unblinded, so that a person in this private nook could see all that was going on within the room which contained the wedding-guests, except in so far as vision was hindered by the green antiquity of the panes.

'Charley, what are they doing?' said Clym. 'My sight is weaker again to-night, and the glass of this window is not good.'

Charley wiped his own eyes, which were rather blurred with moisture, and stepped closer to the casement. 'Mr. Venn is asking Christian Cantle to sing,' he replied; 'and Christian is moving about in his chair as if he were much frightened at the question, and his father has struck up a stave instead of him.'

'Yes, I can hear the old man's voice,' said Clym. 'So there's to be no dancing, I suppose. And is Thomasin in the room? I see something moving in front of the candles that resembles her shape, I think.'

'Yes. She do seem happy. She is red in the face, and laughing at something Fairway has said to her. O my!'

'What noise was that?' said Clym.

'Mr. Venn is so tall that he has knocked his head against the beam in gieing a skip as he passed under. Mrs. Venn has run up quite frightened and now she's put her hand to his head to feel if there's a lump. And now they be all laughing again as if nothing had happened.'

'Do any of them seem to care about my not being there?' Clym asked.

'No, not a bit in the world. Now they are all holding up their glasses and drinking somebody's health.'

'I wonder if it is mine?'

'No, 'tis Mr. and Mrs. Venn's, because he is making a hearty sort of speech. There—now Mrs. Venn has got up, and is going away to put on her things, I think.'

'Well, they haven't concerned themselves about me, and it is quite right they should not. It is all as it should be, and Thomasin at least is happy. We will not stay any longer now, as they will soon be coming out to go home.'

He accompanied the lad into the heath on his way home, and, returning alone to the house a quarter of an hour later, found Venn and Thomasin ready to start, all the guests having departed in his absence. The wedded pair took their seats in the four-wheeled dogcart which Venn's head milker and handy man had driven from Stickleford to fetch them in; little Eustacia and the nurse were packed securely upon the open flap behind; and the milker, on an ancient overstepping pony, whose shoes clashed like cymbals at every tread, rode in the rear, in the manner of a body-servant of the last century.

'Now we leave you in absolute possession of your own house again,' said Thomasin as she bent down to wish her cousin goodnight. 'It will be rather lonely for you, Clym, after the hubbub we have been making.'

'O, that's no inconvenience,' said Clym, smiling rather sadly. And then the party drove off and vanished in the night-shades, and Yeobright entered the house. The ticking of the clock was the only sound that greeted him, for not a soul remained; Christian, who acted as cook, valet, and gardener to Clym, sleeping at his father's house. Yeobright sat down in one of the vacant chairs, and remained in thought a long time. His mother's old chair was opposite; it had been sat in that evening by those who had scarcely remembered that it ever was hers. But to Clym she was almost a presence there, now as always. Whatever she was in other people's memories, in his she was the sublime saint whose radiance even his tenderness for Eustacia could not obscure. But his heart was heavy; that mother had *not* crowned him in the day of his espousals and in the day of the gladness of his heart.[3] And events had borne out the

3. Alluding to the Song of Solomon 3.11: "behold king Solomon with the crown wherewith his mother crowned him in the day of his espousals, and in the day of the gladness of his heart."

accuracy of her judgment, and proved the devotedness of her care. He should have heeded her for Eustacia's sake even more than for his own. 'It was all my fault,' he whispered. 'O, my mother, my mother! would to God that I could live my life again, and endure for you what you endured for me!'

On the Sunday after this wedding an unusual sight was to be seen on Rainbarrow. From a distance there simply appeared to be a motionless figure standing on the top of the tumulus, just as Eustacia had stood on that lonely summit some two years and a half before. But now it was fine warm weather, with only a summer breeze blowing, and early afternoon instead of dull twilight. Those who ascended to the immediate neighbourhood of the Barrow perceived that the erect form in the centre, piercing the sky, was not really alone. Round him upon the slopes of the Barrow a number of heathmen and women were reclining or sitting at their ease. They listened to the words of the man in their midst, who was preaching, while they abstractedly pulled heather, stripped ferns, or tossed pebbles down the slope. This was the first of a series of moral lectures or Sermons on the Mount,[4] which were to be delivered from the same place every Sunday afternoon as long as the fine weather lasted.

The commanding elevation of Rainbarrow had been chosen for two reasons: first, that it occupied a central position among the remote cottages around; secondly, that the preacher thereon could be seen from all adjacent points as soon as he arrived at his post, the view of him being thus a convenient signal to those stragglers who wished to draw near. The speaker was bareheaded, and the breeze at each waft gently lifted and lowered his hair, somewhat too thin for a man of his years, these still numbering less than thirty-three.[5] He wore a shade over his eyes, and his face was pensive and lined; but, though these bodily features were marked with decay there was no defect in the tones of his voice, which were rich, musical, and stirring. He stated that his discourses to people were to be sometimes secular, and sometimes religious, but never dogmatic; and that his texts would be taken from all kinds of books. This afternoon the words were as follows:—

' "And the king rose up to meet her, and bowed himself unto her, and sat down on his throne, and caused a seat to be set for the king's mother; and she sat on his right hand. Then she said, I desire one small petition of thee; I pray thee say me not nay.

---

4. The Sermon on the Mount includes key elements of Christ's ethical teaching; see Matthew 5–7.
5. Traditionally the age at which Christ died; in the editions before 1895, Clym is said to be less than thirty.

And the king said unto her, Ask on, my mother: for I will not say thee nay." '6

Yeobright had, in fact, found his vocation in the career of an itinerant open-air preacher and lecturer on morally unimpeachable subjects; and from this day he laboured incessantly in that office, speaking not only in simple language on Rainbarrow and in the hamlets round, but in a more cultivated strain elsewhere—from the steps and porticoes of town-halls, from market-crosses, from conduits, on esplanades and on wharves, from the parapets of bridges, in barns and outhouses, and all other such places in the neighbouring Wessex towns and villages. He left alone creeds and systems of philosophy, finding enough and more than enough to occupy his tongue in the opinions and actions common to all good men. Some believed him, and some believed not; some said that his words were commonplace, others complained of his want of theological doctrine; while others again remarked that it was well enough for a man to take to preaching who could not see to do anything else. But everywhere he was kindly received, for the story of his life had become generally known.

THE END

6. Clym quotes 1 Kings 2.19–20. Taken in context, however, the passage is not an illustration of filial duty. Solomon's mother asks him to arrange the marriage of his half-brother Adonijah; suspecting a plot, Solomon instead has Adonijah put to death.

BACKGROUNDS AND CONTEXTS

From *The Life and Death of the Mayor of Casterbridge*, by Thomas Hardy (London: The Macmillan Co. Ltd., 1912), pp. 388–89. Reprinted by permission of the Trustees of the Hardy Estate and Macmillan London and Bassingstoke and the Macmillan Company of Canada Ltd.

Map of the
WESSEX
of the
Novels and Poems

Scale of Miles

Septentrio

Occidens   Oriens

Meridies

Lumsdon Christminster

R. Thames

NORTH

The Brown House Alfredston

Cresscombe

Marygreen

MID

Marlbury
Downs

WESSEX

Castle
Royal

Gaymead

Aldbrickham

Kennetbridge

ESSEX

Inkpen Beacon

Great
ain

Stonehenge

Stoke Barehills

Quartershot

Weydon
Priors

Icenway
House

UPPER

Melchester

Wingreen
hase

The Slopes

Chaseborough

Cross

Knollingwood Hall

ord

Lornton
Inn

om

Warborne

EX

Chene
Manor

th

Havenpool

Hebury

gate

Knollsea

Fernel Hall

Wintoncester

WESSEX

Deansleigh
Park

Southampton

The Great

Bramshurst

Forest

Portsmouth

Solentsea

Sandbourne

The
Island

he Channel

Emery Walker, sc.

Glossary of Dialect Words

'a	I, or he
ath'art, athwart	across
ba'dy	bawdy, indecent
bagnet	bayonet
baint	are not
ballet	ballad, song
banging	fine, first-rate
basinet	light helmet
becall	abuse
bedazed	mild form of damned
Be Gad	By God (mild oath)
besom	broom made of twigs, usually heather
billets	logs cut for fuel
black-hearts	whortleberries
bruckle hit	mistake, poor effort
by now	just now
carking	troubling, burdensome
cellaret	small cabinet used to hold (wine) bottles
chiel	child
cleft-wood	split pieces of timber
cotter	person occupying a farm cottage
dab	expert, adept
dandy	fine, smart
diment	diamond
dog-days	periods of very hot weather
drap	drop
effets, efts	newts
faggot	bundle of sticks or furze
fess	proud, vigorous
fokes	folk
gallicrow	scarecrow
gie, gied	give, gave
gipsyings	outdoor dances or festivities
guisers	mummers
harrowing	vexing
hartshorn	smelling salts
hasping	shutting or fastening (as of a door)
hautboy	oboe
heling	pouring (as of a drink)
hind	laborer
huffle	blow, gust (as of winds)

hussy	woman of low morals
jown, jowned	mild oath (as in "jown it," "be jowned")
kex	dry, hollow stems
Lammas-tide	Lammas Day, 1 August (a time for harvest celebrations)
linhay	shed, lean-to building
mandy	saucy, impertinent
mangling	going on; in the balance (usually as "in mangling")
maning	meaning
maphrotight	hermaphrodite
martel	mortal, person
maul down	lift or get down
mid	might
mollyhorning	idling, wasting time
mommet	scarecrow, effigy
mossel	bit, morsel
nammet time	lunchtime
nater	nature
nobbling	hanging around, idling
nonce	once (usually as in "for the nonce": for this one time)
nunnywatch	state of confusion
ooser	mask, or person wearing a mask
ophicleide	obsolete form of bugle
outstep	out of the way
overlook	look upon someone with the evil eye, bewitch
pattens	overshoes
pixy-led	lost, bewildered
plashed	trimmed, cut
playward	playful, lighthearted
posset	drink of heated milk, usually with spirits
quarries	small panes of leaded glass
racket	party
rames	skeleton
Rathe-ripe	early ripening variety of apple
rozum	work away vigorously (as with a bow on a violin)
scammish	awkward, clumsy
scroff	leftovers, bits and pieces
serpent	large wooden wind instrument
set-to	state of affairs
settle	wooden bench, usually with a high back
slack-twisted	spineless, ineffectual
slittering	carefree
sniffing	courting (derogatory)

snipe	dismissive term, usually suggesting a person of low morals or class
sommat	something
spatterdashes	leggings
speäker	stake, long pole used to carry bundles
spudding	digging up
stave	snatch or verse of song
stock	high, stiff neckband
strawmote	stalk of grass or straw
stunpoll	fool
taties	potatoes
tide-times	times of religious festivals, such as Christmas
tilt	canvas canopy, usually over a cart or wagon
to-year	this year
twanky	moody, irritated
up-sides (with)	equal (to)
vell	trace (literally, skin or hide)
vlankers	sparks, flakes of fire
weasand	wind-pipe
withywind	bindweed
zany	fool, eccentric
zeed, zid	saw, observed

Composition

SIMON GATRELL

The Textual History of *The Return of the Native*†

On 26 January 1876 Hardy sent the last episode of *The Hand of Ethelberta* to the *Cornhill Magazine*; by the middle of March he had finished with the proofs both for the last episodes and for the novel's appearance in three volumes. The first that can be discovered of his next novel, eventually to be called *The Return of the Native*, is in a letter from Hardy to George Smith of Smith and Elder, the publishers of *Cornhill*, dated 5 February 1877:

> I have sent the MS. of my new story—as far as written—to Mr Stephen. If you could bestow a spare half hour upon it, & tell me if you think it a kind of story likely to create a demand in the market, I should owe you many thanks.[1]

There is little indirect evidence to assist speculation concerning the time at which Hardy began work upon the story. *The Hand of Ethelberta* had brought him a considerable amount of money, perhaps around £1,500, and he can have felt no urgency of financial pressure to begin writing again; at the end of May 1876 he and his wife began a month's holiday on the Continent.

Lennart Björk, in the introductory essay to his edition of Hardy's literary notes, suggests that in 1876 Hardy deliberately took time from writing to broaden his general education—"a year's sabbatical," as Björk calls it. He shows that the probability is that Hardy and his wife began the systematic annotation and collection of earlier notes that constitutes the volume known as "Literary Notes I" in the first half of 1876.

† This essay appears for the first time in this Norton Critical Edition, and draws on work done in introductions to the Garland edition of the manuscripts of *The Return of the Native*, and to the World's Classics edition of the novel, and in two monographs, Simon Gatrell, *Hardy the Creator: A Textual Biography* (1988) and Simon Gatrell, *Thomas Hardy's Vision of Wessex* (2003).
1. *Letters*, I.47.

This dating is, above all, supported by the obvious enthusiasm
for the whole project reflected in the great number of entries
with material published in 1876, particularly in the late spring
of that year: of the total 2641 entries about 850 are extracted
from publications dated 1876, and a substantial number
is based on sources printed in the three months between
18 March and 17 June.[2]

It seems probable that the enthusiasm was not dissipated before
the autumn of the year at least.

It was on 3 July that the Hardys moved house to Sturminster
Newton, where *The Return of the Native* was written; Hardy, as is
well known, called this their happiest time together, but when exactly the need to begin writing again set him to thinking about
Egdon Heath and its inhabitants is impossible to tell. Most commentators on the origins of the novel have pointed to Hardy's
Christmas visit with his wife to his family home at Bockhampton—
on the edge of the area that he transformed as the environment of
his story—suggesting that it provided the necessary stimulus. It does
seem likely, however, that he began some form of work on the novel
well before the end of the year, since he felt confident enough of the
general design and the detailed progress of its opening to submit it
to Leslie Stephen at the beginning of February 1877.

There is no record of a response to Hardy's letter, but only eight
days later he wrote to John Blackwood of *Blackwood's Magazine*:

> I wish to ask you if you would at any time inform me when a
> vacancy for a serial story is about to occur in the magazine. . . .
> I may add that I have recently begun a story dealing with re-
> mote country life, somewhat of the nature of "Far from the
> Madding Crowd", though I have not yet written enough to be
> worth sending. I should be obliged by your letting me know be-
> fore I make any other arrangements for it, if that class of story
> & scenery is what you would care to introduce into the maga-
> zine.[3]

He was clearly keeping his options open: perhaps his experience
with Stephen as editor led him to suspect that he might not be
happy with the new story as it was developing; perhaps he thought
that the reputation of *Blackwood's* for publishing weird and strange
stories might make it a more likely home for the tale.

Blackwood's response was friendly but neutral; on 22 February
he wrote hoping that Hardy would be in touch again when his work
was further advanced, but unsure of possible space in the magazine. It seems likely that as a response to this mild encouragement

---

2. Lennart A. Björk, ed., *The Literary Notebooks of Thomas Hardy*, I.xxxvii–viii.
3. *Letters*, I.47.

Hardy asked Smith, Elder to return the manuscript of the new story "as soon as you conveniently can: I cannot well get on for want of it, as I have no exact copy."[4] This may have been true, though it is also possible that he had made a fair copy for Stephen and Smith, which he now wanted to send off to Blackwood. This was on 1 March. There is no further evidence concerning the novel until 11 April, when Hardy sent fifteen chapters to Blackwood; whether these fifteen chapters were substantially the same as those seen by Stephen and Smith is utterly uncertain. We do not know whether Smith or Stephen replied to the submission of the manuscript in such a way as to encourage Hardy to rewrite it before sending it anywhere else; we do not know how much of the manuscript Stephen and Smith saw; and we do not know when Smith, Elder returned the manuscript to Hardy. The month's gap between requesting its return and sending it to Blackwood may have been no more than a calculated pause in which Blackwood might think Hardy was writing an amount sufficient to send him, or he might in reality have been rethinking the first third of the story.

Hardy followed the parcel of manuscript with a letter on the following day, which includes the following interesting and characteristic paragraph:

> I will just add that, should there accidentally occur any word or reflection not in harmony with the general tone of the magazine, you would be quite at liberty to strike it out if you chose. I always mention this to my editors, as it simplifies matters. I do not, however, think you will meet with any such passage, as you will perceive that the story deals with a world almost isolated from civilization—moreover before beginning it I had resolved to write with a partial view to Blackwood.[5]

As Frank Pinion has pointed out,[6] the reaction of John Blackwood to the story as far as it had gone is the first indication we have of Hardy's plot this early in its development. Hardy wanted his novel out in three volumes by the beginning of May 1878; Blackwood had warned him in February that he had "several arrangements more or less complete for works (also more or less complete)," and these arrangements were now more firm. Nevertheless he read the manuscript and offered, in a letter dated 24 April, the criticism that Hardy had invited, details of which will be taken up later:

> My dear Sir
>   My engagements for Serial Stories in the Magazine are still so numerous and now binding that I cannot hold out any hope

4. *Letters*, I.48.
5. *Letters*, I.49.
6. "*The Return of the Native* in the Making," *Times Literary Supplement*, 21 August 1970.

of being able to accept a Tale from you this year. In these circumstances I would have returned the M.S. you were so good as to send me had I not heartily joined in your wish that I should read it. This I have done. It is excessively clever. Nothing can be more graphic than the description of that awful Egdon Heath. One feels the very atmosphere of it and cannot but sympathise with all who wish to get away from it be they good or bad.

The natives and their conversations have a wonderfully real life like look but are they not more curious than interesting?

The doubt that occurs to me is whether you are right to occupy so large a portion at the beginning of your story without a thread of light to throw an interest round the rugged figures you so vividly paint.

There is hardly anything like what is called Novel interest until the connection between the villainous Toogoon and that she devil Avice appears and they are run to ground by the indefatigable riddleman.

I venture to make this suggestion because I care about your writings and publishing in Numbers. I fear the first two might fail to catch popular interest.

Avice is a remarkable character and might have been educated in Paris.

The second section of what you sent me ends at a very exciting point and I shall look forward with much interest to the rest of the Tale on publication.

The M.S. is returned along with this and you should have heard from me sooner had I not been very busy.[7]

Hardy wrote back on 26 April with his thanks for the analysis, adding "You may be sure that I shall avail myself of your valuable hints as far as I can apply them to the remainder of the story."[8] This implies that he intended to keep the opening as it was, but we can tell from the surviving manuscript that the beginning has also been changed quite substantially. Following this disappointment, it seems that Hardy offered the story to Stephen, who replied on 28 May:

My dear Mr Hardy,

You seemed to be anxious when you last wrote for a speedy decision as to your story. I think, therefore, that I ought to tell you that I could probably make up my mind pretty clearly within the next 2 or 3 weeks. I should still prefer, indeed, both on your account & my own to wait a little longer; but, as matters stand, delay is not likely to make so much difference as before.

7. Blackwood Letterbook: National Library of Scotland AccMS 5643 D10, f48.
8. *Letters*, I.49.

At any rate I should be glad to know when I am likely to
hear from you & I should also be glad if—when you send me
the story—you will give me as full details as you can of its intended development.[9]

It is to be supposed that Hardy sent some of the manuscript to
Stephen, though it is not certain whether it was in the same state
as when Blackwood had seen it six weeks earlier. The only account
we have of the sequel is that which Hardy wrote for F. W. Maitland's *Life and Letters of Leslie Stephen*:

. . . though [Stephen] liked the opening, he feared that relations between Eustacia, Wildeve, and Thomasin might develop
into something "dangerous" for a family magazine, and he refused to have anything to do with it unless he could see the
whole. This I never sent him; and the matter fell through.[1]

This was written nearly thirty years after the event and presumably
relies upon a letter from Stephen that Hardy subsequently destroyed; he uses the names the characters were to be given later,
and it is possible that other details have been modified. The central
point, Stephen's desire to see the whole before deciding, is, however, almost certainly accurate. It seems likely that financial considerations pushed Hardy into wanting his partly written novel
placed as a serial as soon as possible, and so he could not wait
for Stephen's approval. Stephen's letter may have come on 14 or
15 June, as on 16 June Hardy wrote to George Bentley, the editor
of *Temple Bar*, to ask whether they had a vacancy for a serial such
as he was at that moment writing; it is not impossible that he also
sent similar letters to the editors of other magazines at this time,
which have not survived. At any rate, Bentley must have refused,
and nine days later Chatto and Windus, the proprietors of *Belgravia*
and *The Gentleman's Magazine*, responded to a letter from Hardy:

As we already have another serial story for one of the magazines under consideration, before making you an offer we
should be glad to be favoured with a sight of a considerable
portion of your MS. We should not put you to this trouble if
you would give us some idea of the price you have set upon the
magazine rights of your story as the sum at our disposal for
this purpose is in some degree limited.[2]

By now it is to be supposed that Hardy was fairly desperate to secure a berth for his novel, and he closed with them; he had clearly
priced himself right, for on 28 June Chatto and Windus wrote:

9. Dorset County Museum.
1. F. W. Maitland, *Life and Letters of Leslie Stephen* (London, 1907), pp. 276–7.
2. Chatto and Windus Letter Book: Reading University Library MS 2444/9 f. 109.

> We shall have much pleasure in accepting the serial rights of
> publication of your new novel upon the terms you mention viz
> twenty pounds per month. We ought to have the opening
> chapters early in November and we should like to know your
> title as soon as convenient to you in order that we may effec-
> tually announce it in advance.[3]

There is no further evidence of correspondence with Hardy about
the serialization in Chatto and Windus's letter books, so the next
surviving strand in the history of *The Return of the Native* is
Hardy's letter to them of 28 August:

> I send to-day to the Editor of Belgravia Parts 1 & 2 (Jan &
> Feb) of my new story, called "The return of the native"—a title
> which I hope you will like. I forward the MS. thus early that
> there may be full time for early proofs.[4]

Hardy was anxious about early proofs so that he could send them in
good time to Harpers in New York, who were to publish the story in
Harper's New Monthly Magazine. Though the original agreement
with Harpers was to pay £3 per page of the magazine, "not to exceed £360 for serial and book-form," eventually Hardy was paid a
total of £472 by October 1878. The American publisher recouped
some of this by leasing the book rights to Henry Holt for ten per-
cent of the retail price of $1 a copy.[5]

The last datable stage in the production of the manuscript is
logged in the *Life*:

> . . . his main occupation at Riverside Villa . . . was writing *The
> Return of the Native*. The only note [Hardy] makes of its
> progress is that, on November 8, parts 3, 4 and 5 of the story
> were posted to Messrs Chatto and Windus for publication in
> (of all places) *Belgravia*—a monthly magazine then running.[6]

When did Hardy submit the remainder of the manuscript to Chatto
and Windus? Evidence in the manuscript itself has a bearing on
this question. The last occurrence of a name that belongs to the
early conception of the novel is "Avice" on f. 206, early in the sixth
part; there is a change in the paper stock at f. 211; many of the
latest-written leaves in the first five parts are on the verso of false
starts for other leaves that use the same early paper stock, and it
seems likely that Hardy was using up the last remaining serviceable
leaves before beginning a fresh purchase of paper.

It is tempting then to think that, not wishing to risk further re-

3. Ibid., f. 114.
4. *Letters*, I.50.
5. Harper Memorandum Book IV f. 125.
6. *Life and Work of Thomas Hardy*, p. 120.

jection, Hardy stopped writing the novel at the end of July, having
reached just beyond the end of what was to become part five, and
spent the time between then and the beginning of November
rewriting what already existed, the remainder of the novel being in
rough draft or note form of the kind we find in the manuscript of
"Wessex Folk" (Berg Collection, New York Public Library). If this
were so, then *The Return of the Native* would offer an early parallel
for the more completely documented progress of *Tess of the
d'Urbervilles*, in which the latter half of the story has little in it that
might upset a magazine editor. The last part of this manuscript also
has only minor reworkings and alterations (minor in degree of variation, though occasionally extensive in length).

Supposing this hypothesis accurate, then there is equally tenuous circumstantial evidence to suggest that Hardy may have finished with the manuscript of *The Return of the Native* by the time
he and his wife moved from Sturminster Newton to Upper Tooting
on 22 March 1878. On 14 January 1878 Francis Hueffer wrote to
ask Hardy for a story to appear in the *New Quarterly Magazine*, saying that he needed it by 10 March at the latest. Hardy was unable
to meet that date; though he wrote to Hueffer on 4 June to say that
he was sending the manuscript then. The story was "An Indiscretion in the Life of an Heiress," and though it derives directly from
what remained unpillaged of his first, unpublished novel, the task
of adaptation must have taken some time. It seems possible, then,
that the work on the end of *The Return of the Native* meant that he
could not do the story by March, but that once the trials of the
move were over it was feasible to get down to the *Quarterly* piece,
since the novel was also out of the way.

All this, however, is speculation; what we know for certain is that
Hardy had clear in his mind the end of the novel by 8 February, for
on that day he wrote to Arthur Hopkins, the illustrator of the story
in *Belgravia*, with an outline of the plot that included this detail:
"Thomasin, as you have divined, is the *good* heroine, & she ultimately marries the reddleman, & lives happily."[7]

The first person to analyze this manuscript (which is now in the
library of the National University of Ireland in Dublin) was John
Paterson in his *The Making of "The Return of the Native"* (University of California Press, 1960). Of particular importance is the second chapter, entitled "Genesis," in which Paterson explores what
he calls the ur-novel. The manuscript is on the whole closer to fair-
copy than most of those Hardy sent to the printer, even in the early
leaves; but it still contains many deleted (but still legible) and

7. *Letters*, I.53.

rewritten passages, and (as has been noted) Hardy's economical use of paper ensured that pages on which he had made false starts were inverted and reused. From this material Paterson developed ideas of where Hardy started from when he began work on the novel's manuscript, and where he went. The evidence is, of course, incomplete. Many of the early leaves of the manuscript can be shown, by analysis of the paper, of Hardy's numeration systems, and of aspects of the text—proper names in particular—to be replacements rather than original; some cancelations Hardy made so effectively that recovery is impossible. But even so Paterson does not consider all of the evidence that does survive. It seems possible that he worked primarily from a microfilm of the manuscript—at any rate a comparison of the transcriptions quoted in the "Genesis" chapter with the manuscript itself shows occasional error, oversight and inability to read canceled material quite legible in the original document. To give one example, he must have been unable to read an important canceled passage on the verso of f. 21 of the manuscript, for he does not mention it. It runs:

> They may call him Conjuror Toogood, & white witch, & what not, but we all know that what the man really is is a herbalist, & to gie him his due he's very deep-knowing in some most racking complaints.

Paterson does point out at the beginning of "Genesis" (p. 8) that Wildeve's name at first was Toogood; but the significance of this passage, once it is deciphered, for understanding Hardy's initial conception of the character is obvious, and I will return to it later.

The other significant limitation of Paterson's book is that in his anxiety to tell a striking story he radically overinterprets his material. The patchy nature of the available evidence means that a certain amount of inference or outright guesswork is necessary if any scholar is to produce a coherent impression of Hardy's earliest ideas, and the surviving details themselves will have to bear a larger burden of interpretation than literary criticism in general is comfortable with. It is also true that *The Making of "The Return of the Native"* was a pioneering book, written at a time when Hardy's value as an artist on the critical stock exchange was pretty low, and Paterson may well have felt he had to emphasize the more dramatic aspects of his discoveries in order to sell his work to his editors. But even when such allowances are made, the case is spoiled.

The primary example is Paterson's analysis of Hardy's original conception of Eustacia Vye. It begins on p. 18: "in the opinion of the peasant chorus, 'Avice Vye [was] a *witch*' (fol. 31)," and continues in phrases like "The diabolism basic to Eustacia's original conception" (p. 19), "the spirit of the satanic adventuress" (p. 21) or

"Eustacia's original demonism" (p. 24). If Paterson's original source on fol. 31 of the manuscript is consulted, there are altogether four lines of canceled material:

> What? inquired Timothy Fairway.
> A witch, said the woman firmly. Young Avice Vye is a witch, as her mother was afore her.
> "That's new to me I own," said Fairway.

Possibly Paterson was unable to read all of this; but it suggests that since Fairway, the primary spokesman of the Egdon workfolk, has never heard it said that Avice Vye was a witch, it may be only one woman who believes she is. The immediately anterior female speaker is Susan Nunsuch, and it seems likely that she it is who makes the assertion. Later on Susan pricks Eustacia in church as a witch, and toward the end of the novel we see her practising counter-witchcraft herself; so it seems reasonable to see her as obsessed by an idea that was not shared by most people on Egdon. On a leaf fair-copied by Hardy's wife Emma (f. 54), in which the Egdon folk discuss Avice, Fairway talks of "that lonesome dark eyed creature up there—ever I should call a fine young woman such a name." It is just about plausible that the name Fairway apologized for was "creature," but more meaningful sense is made if it is suggested that Emma had accidentally omitted words that Hardy later added, which change the speech to: "that lonesome dark eyed creature up there that some say is a witch—ever I should call a fine young woman such a name." Again Fairway evidently doesn't subscribe to the view, though we can imagine that perhaps Christian Cantle does, along with Susan Nunsuch. There is no evidence that the narrator does.

The unfortunate effect of Paterson's overinterpretation of the very scanty evidence is to obscure the fact that there is indeed a substantial difference between Hardy's earlier manuscript version of Avice and his later one of Eustacia, and further that Paterson identifies most of the evidence for this distinction. Take, for instance, this observation from p. 18 of his book:

> In the final form of this chapter [Eustacia] yields passively to the bramble that has caught in her skirt and, instead of hastening along, stands perfectly still in a mood of "desponding reverie" before slowly unwinding herself. This image of a rich and sensuous womanhood was antedated, however, by another image altogether, an image more evocative of the demon than the woman. Instead of surrendering herself to the bramble, Eustacia was to have "*uttered hot words of passion* [?]." And her mood was identified not as "desponding reverie" but as "*anger, which there found a temporary leak*" (fol. 62).

The passage referred to is rather complicated. Originally it read:

> A bramble caught hold of her skirt, and checked her progress
> for an instant, it tore nothing and it injured nothing yet the
> woman uttered hot words of passion as she loosened it and
> passed on. The immediate cause was quite insufficient for the
> mood, and it was plain that she had previously been charged
> brim-full with anger, which here found a temporary leak.

At first revision it became

> A bramble caught hold of her skirt, and checked her progress
> for an instant; it tore nothing of her dress—and it injured
> nothing yet the woman uttered hot words of passion and
> sounds worthy of Tisiphone as she loosened it from her robe
> and passed on. The immediate cause was quite insufficient for
> the mood, and it was plain that she had previously been
> charged brim-full with anger, which here found a temporary
> leak.

Then it was

> A bramble caught hold of her skirt, and checked her progress
> for an instant. Instead of putting it off and hastening along she
> yielded herself up to the pull, and stood passively still. When
> she began to extricate herself it was by turning round and
> round on her axis, and so unwinding the prickly switch. It was
> plain that she was in an idle mood.

And finally the last sentence was altered to "She was in a desponding reverie." This sequence is characteristic of many of the changes
made in the process of transforming Avice into Eustacia. It begins
with pure passion and anger, which is then qualified by an interesting classical reference;[8] then comes the significant change—from
activity to passivity, from energy to idleness; and finally the further element of thoughtful sadness is added. Avice's heated anger,

---

8. Tisiphone was one of the furies, the snake-haired women recognized as the persecutors
of men and women who broke "natural laws," and especially of Orestes, who kills his
mother Clytemnestra for the murder of his father Agamemnon. One might see a connection here with Clym's sense that he has killed his mother, and that he is persecuted
by his feelings for Eustacia; and indeed take the connection further by adding that at
Athena's behest the furies turned into the kindhearted Eumenides, offering the loving-
kindness of Clym's later years. It is also the case that Tisiphone is recorded as having
fallen in love with Cithaeron, whom she subsequently killed through a bite from one of
the snakes on her head. Eustacia does not kill Clym, of course, but she does destroy part
of him. And in yet another relevance the furies were held to live in Tartarus, the lowest
region of the classical underworld; in the "Queen of Night" chapter Hardy's narrator
says of Eustacia: "A true Tartarean dignity sat upon her brow, and not factitiously, or
with marks of constraint, for it had grown in her with years." (It might be added that
Hardy seems, inaccurately, to have understood Tartarus as a synonym for Hades.) He
also calls night on the heath a "Tartarean situation" for two unaccompanied women.
However, he later chose to remove the allusion to Tisiphone.

though worthy of one of the avenging Furies, is not reasonably described as demonic or thought of as a defining characteristic of a witch.

To give another example, Paterson points (p. 20) to two changes on f. 73. In the first the shape of her eyes allowed Avice to "watch without seeming to watch," while it enables Eustacia to "indulge in reverie without seeming to do so"; certainly the former version has somewhat sinister overtones quite lacking in the latter, which picks up Eustacia's tendency to introspection noted in the extended revision given above. The second instance has the speculative color of Avice's soul as "lurid red," but Eustacia's as "flame-like"; the adjective "lurid" does have overtones not appropriate for the final version of the heroine—but, like the deceptive eyelids, is hardly evidence of satanism.[9]

Hardy hung on to the name Avice much longer than any other original name in the novel, and much longer than most of the names he changed in any of his novels; and, if my hypothesis about the process of composition of the novel is correct, then it was not until he was forced to recognize from editors' responses to the first part of the manuscript the problems he would have in getting his story published as it stood, that he felt compelled to remake the character of his heroine.

It was not just the incendiary and unscrupulous temperament of Avice that Hardy felt he had to revise, and Paterson is more accurate in representing some of Hardy's plot changes, the most important of which involves Thomasin Brittan (as she was) and her relationship with the conjuror Toogood. Even here there are occa-

9. There are more examples in this famous seventh chapter of the first book, entitled "Queen of Night," in which the narrator lets loose in heightened fashion his understanding of his heroine. The chapter is made up of leaves representing two stages of development, since some have Avice and others Eustacia as the heroine's original name. On f. 74 the heroine is at first sometimes given over to "angry despair," then to "gloomy despair," and finally to "sudden fits of gloom"; these were defined by the narrator at first as "one of the phases of the night-side of passion which she knew too well," but it became, for Eustacia, "sentiment" rather than "passion." A list of Avice's attributes, "imperiousness, jealousy, wrath and courage," became "imperiousness, love, wrath and fervour." Then on f. 75 we were told that Avice had "fiery gloom" within her, but this became "gloomy and stifled warmth." On f. 78, where Avice's sense of the transience of love "bred actions of reckless and unscrupulous compass" designed to snatch even an hour's passion, Eustacia's similar perception "tended to breed actions of reckless unconventionality" to the same end; the difference between "bred" and "tended to breed" indicates sensitively the difference between the active Avice and the passive Eustacia, and while both are reckless, the difference between unscrupulous and unconventional marks a radical distinction. On f. 79, the last earlier leaf in the chapter, where Avice was a woman, Eustacia is a girl; where Avice looked to defects in the beehives, Eustacia did nothing so rural; while Avice hummed "Saturday-night and fair-day songs," Eustacia hummed "the Saturday-night ballads of the country people"—the narrator thus dissociating her from the Egdon workfolk.

But the first versions at all these places are just hints at Hardy's first ideas about Avice, slender survivals from an abandoned conception amid the romantic portrait the manuscript chapter offers.

sional errors in detail,[1] but they do not affect his essential perception that in the narrative as Hardy first wrote it Thomasin and Toogood spent a week away from Egdon together, then returned as man and wife, and continued living that way for a while, until some now irrecoverable incident made it clear to Thomasin that Toogood had tricked her, and she was not legally married to him. The surviving evidence is slender but convincing, and it is particularly so in that the crucial details are spread throughout the first quarter of the manuscript (roughly the amount that Hardy sent to Blackwood). It is not often in Hardy's printers' manuscripts that a central but discarded element in the plot survived for so long before he changed his mind, and when Paterson concludes his exposition by writing that this "revision of the novel must have been inspired by an editorial directive" it is only his certainty that might cause dissent. It does seem most likely that, having heard from Blackwood, Leslie Stephen, and George Bentley, Hardy recognized that his original conception would not fly in the magazine world. This would account well for the relatively large number of second-fair-copy leaves, among which are scattered those that survive from his first fair-copy inscription and bear the canceled remains of the early plot.

The implications of this fundamental difference from the novel as we have it now are considerable. This is how the story might once have run: Egdon is described, with more emphasis than at present on its dark power over the light and time, and less historical information or philosophical speculation. Avice, who lives with her father in a humble way on the heath, has drunk from it "all that was dark in its tone" (f. 75). Thomasin and Toogood are living together in a cottage, observed by Avice (without telescope, but with powerful imaginative vision) from Blackbarrow (Venn does not yet appear). She gives way to the bonfirers, who eventually go down to the pub for a drink and then across to the cottage to give the newly arrived couple a song in celebration of their marriage a week earlier. The sexually voracious Avice is furious, has been furious for a week, that Toogood has abandoned her to marry her friend Thomasin, and plots revenge, summoning the wizard with her bonfire.[2] When they meet Toogood tells Avice that he has tricked Thomasin, since he knew the only way Thomasin would agree to have sex with him would be if he married her; she represented a challenge. Willy Orchard overhears some of this. Avice is still furi-

---

1. See pp. 10–17. The misreading of " 'ee" as "us" in the quoted cancellation on p. 14 invalidates the point Paterson wishes to make; he misinterprets other passages on pp. 12 and 13.
2. A canceled sentence on f. 78 reads: "She was, in short, a perfect locust in regard to love." On f. 207, when Clym heard that Avice had been pierced by a needle, he exclaimed " 'Tis Tamsin's friend!"

ous, but admires the unscrupulousness of the man. He makes advances, she plays hard to get, he taunts her with how he has stolen her friend away from her. They part, both unsatisfied.

Willy stumbles on Diggory Venn the reddleman, camped in a gravel pit, and relates what he has heard. Venn had once wanted to court Thomasin, but she had turned him down because she couldn't think of loving him. He still loves her, however, and with thoughts of protecting her plays the spy on Avice and Toogood. In a few days he catches their assignation on Blackbarrow, where, among other things, he gathers that Thomasin has been deceived by a fake marriage ceremony. The sexual sparring between the two continues, each exercising some power over the other. Diggory decides his best bet is to show Avice that he knows the truth, and to try to persuade her to leave the heath for the glories of Budmouth. In this he fails, and it seems possible that as a consequence he writes a note to Thomasin, or in some other way demonstrates to her that she is not truly married to Toogood. Thomasin at once leaves Toogood's house and goes back to her mother.

After this, there are in the manuscript many pages of late fair-copy, and it is impossible even to speculate about an earlier version. The next incident certainly to befall Avice is that she overhears the information that Thomasin's brother Clym is coming home from Budmouth. She hasn't seen him for several years, and is intrigued by the news, especially since her name and his have been linked together by the men she was listening to. One evening soon after, loitering in the vicinity of the Brittans' house, she hears a man's voice in conversation with Thomasin; she has to assure herself that "the man was not Toogood," so evidently she does not know that Thomasin has left her supposed husband; she knows the voice must therefore be Clym's, and falls in love with its sound, and what it implies of comfort, luxury. She becomes one of the mummers (a rather more likely escapade for Avice than Eustacia) and while in disguise manages to get to see and talk with Clym.

From here onward, and probably before this, the effect of a second kind of change begins to be felt in leaves that survive from the earlier version. The gradual change from Avice to Eustacia in temperament is significant, but it is augmented by a change in her social position. Paterson does not make enough, perhaps, of the contrast in this respect between Hardy's first ideas and what was sent to the printer. Originally the story was to be one in which all were nearly equal in class and in class pretensions: all were equal before the heath, one might say. Avice was distinguished by her temperament, Clym by his education, Toogood by his skills; but Avice's father was merely the dialect speaker Jonathan Vye, whose wife had been thought a witch by Susan Nunsuch, while Mrs. Brittan was merely a well-known neighbor of no particular pretension, and her son had only been able to get a post in a jeweler's shop in Budmouth through the intervention of a friendly parson—they were slightly better off than some on the heath, that is all; Diggory Venn used to be a haulier.[3] There is little left in the surviving leaves of Toogood, but the cancelled passage already mentioned (above p. 350) shows that some people at least on Egdon thought of him as a wizard, and in revision, as a first step toward elevating him, Hardy gave Timothy Fairway the responsibility for an alternative account of him as a herbalist. On f. 23 Fairway speaks of "the quak and Mis'ess Tamsin," which may represent a further stage in the evolution of Toogood, here into a charlatan pseudo-doctor like Vilbert in *Jude the Obscure*. Paterson apparently saw none of this, and he did not know of John Blackwood's description of him as "villainous" (which might well apply to Vilbert also).

All these characters were spoken to and about as familiar equals by Fairway and Humphrey and Sam, and even Christian Cantle; but it is a pattern of revision observable in many of Hardy's novels, that the central characters, at first part of the general social fabric of the novel, are subsequently pushed out of the matrix and become social leaders, relegating less important characters to roles that permit some critics to call them a "rustic chorus." Following this process of gentrification, Eustacia is a Budmouth exotic with a now-dead musician-father, forced to live on Egdon with her grandfather, the naval Lieutenant (later Captain) Drew; Clym works in Paris; Wildeve has been an engineer, is an innkeeper, who inherits money; Mrs Yeobright is a curate's daughter, whose standing "can only be expressed by the word genteel"; Diggory Venn was a dairy farmer before taking up the reddle trade. As to why Hardy did this, the best guess is that he was motivated partly by his own aesthetic sense and partly by the comments of editors and reviewers. His initial narrative impulse derived from the people he had grown up among, but he recognized, and others told him, that to attract a sufficient audience from the predominantly urban and upper-middle-class readership of fiction, he would have to bring his major characters closer to something they could understand and identify with.

It was probably the same motive that led him to remove a proportion of the dialect vocabulary across the board, even from speakers like Grandfer Cantle. Thomasin changes least in this respect, but even she originally peppered her letter to Diggory with dialect expressions; she also becomes Clym's cousin rather than his sis-

3. On p. 9 Paterson misreads a cancelation on f. 89. Instead of "The reddleman who was Christian Cantle's nephew . . .", it runs "The reddleman whom Christian Candle's nephew . . .": so Hardy never intended a relationship between Venn and the Cantles (originally Candles).

ter—an alteration made so that Eustacia can be propelled toward Clym more urgently by the thought that Thomasin (still unmarried to Wildeve and living with her aunt) really must be attracted to him. There are two hints, one on the verso of f. 187, the other on f. 196, of a further development in her part in the narrative. The latter had originally: "On the Sunday morning following the week of Thomasin's marriage . . .", which becomes "On the Sunday morning following the week of Thomasin's refusal to marry . . .", which in turn reverts to the first version. The leaf (which was originally numbered something else now indecipherable) is from the early stage of the novel, and it is possible that the first "marriage" referred to a remarriage with Toogood, the second to her marriage to Wildeve, but that sandwiched between them was a plot-strand in which Thomasin refused to marry Toogood when he offered to put things right. The false start on the back of f. 187 was numbered 96, and is a fragment of discussion between Toogood and Avice:

> he tells me nothing—least of all about you.
> He is no friend of mine. However perhaps you could hardly have heard yet in any circumstances, so few people know. This is the matter: my marriage with Tamsin will not take place.
> No immediate word came from Avice.

Putting the two together, it is feasible that Hardy may at one time have thought to take Thomasin further, perhaps in company with an illegitimate child, along the road later followed by Tess Durbeyfield, before either self-censorship or the words of magazine editors turned her back.[4]

It is interesting to note that there is evidence of such censorship in smaller details also—for instance on f. 32, during the impromptu dance ("the demoniac measure") through the ashes of the bonfire, the "chief noises" were originally "women's shrill curses, men's laughter . . ." but Hardy thought better (or worse) of allowing women to curse, even when dragged around by laughing men through hot ashes, and altered "curses" to "cries." Whether he made the change because tender sensibilities (of editor or reader) might be shocked, or because he didn't wish to give such an audience more chance to look on the rural working class with disdain, is unclear. Later on (ff. 148–9), he decides not to let Avice/Eustacia swear even when she is pretending to be a man.

---

4. There is a third corroborative detail. On f. 204 Clym and his mother are talking; then "No more was said on the subject till dinner-time." The end of this sentence was first changed to "till dinner-time, Thomasin being absent," and then to "till the end of dinner." The reader knows that Thomasin is absent in the final version of the novel, being married, so the statement of her absence would be redundant. If, however, she had decided not to marry, then she would be expected to be at home, and the reader would need to know she wasn't there.

In the second half of the novel, written on the second stock of paper, there is, as Paterson suggests, less of consuming interest. There are, though, alterations to the dicing episode and its aftermath, not all of which Paterson takes into his account (pp. 90–100). On the day of Clym and Eustacia's wedding, after Christian Cantle has won his raffle, and before Damon Wildeve and he set out together for Mistover (where Christian is to deliver money from Mrs. Yeobright to Thomasin), Hardy has to add on the verso of the previous leaf Christian's request for the dice to take with him, and a few lines later has similarly to add Diggory Venn's presence as a silent witness of the whole incident. When to this is added the facts that the page that concludes the gambling with Diggory's inadvertent misdistribution of the guineas is numbered 265a, and that the leaf that begins the following chapter, though now 266, was originally numbered in the 250s, and moreover has been cut down to two-thirds of a page, then it seems quite likely that initially Hardy had Wildeve gain control of the money in some other way not now retrievable. It seems probable, from the alteration on f. 268 of "the unconscious misappropriation by Thomasin of the fifty guineas" to "the unconscious misapplication by Venn of the fifty guineas", that Venn was not initially involved in the episode at all.

In another revision indicated by altered numeration, f. 273 was originally 269; this four-leaf displacement continues until f. 289, which was f. 285. This implies that the quarrel between Eustacia and Mrs. Yeobright, now on ff. 267–272, was also substantially rewritten, and indeed the canceled chapter title on the partial leaf f. 25?/266, "A little fire kindles a great flame," doesn't seem quite suited to the new version. Paterson's hypothesis that originally Mrs. Yeobright had brought up against Eustacia her affair with Damon, but that on reflection Hardy thought it better not to insist on sexual irregularities, is plausible and well argued, though again he is over-certain of its correctness.

It seems clear that Diggory Venn's "rough coercion" of Wildeve was an afterthought. The passage canceled at the foot of f. 295 is repeated almost verbatim on the penultimate page of Chapter IV of the fourth book "Rough coercion is employed" (f. 301); the motivation, in a conversation with Thomasin, for Venn's unconventional shepherding of Wildeve, had to be added to the text on the verso of f. 294; and on f. 302 a reference to "Wildeve's recent manoeuvre"—his moth-signal—had to be added.

Otis Wheeler's essay "Four Versions of *The Return of the Native*" was in fact published a few months before Paterson's book, in *Nineteenth-Century Fiction* for June 1959 (pp. 27–44). Wheeler didn't look at the manuscript, but collated most of the printed embodiments of the text that Hardy altered, and all that he altered significantly. Wheeler's first section outlines the major differences he found between the serial issue in *Belgravia* and the Wessex edition, summarizing his enterprise somewhat surprisingly as tracing "the steps by which this pallid beginning becomes the novel that many critics regard as Hardy's masterpiece" (p. 29). In this area Wheeler's account is briefer and clearer than Paterson's in his later chapters, though it cannot possess the cumulative effect of Paterson's more detailed study; both reach similar conclusions. Wheeler outlines the most substantial changes that Hardy made to the narrative: the rendering more plausible Eustacia's hostility to Clym's mother through alteration to the gambling scene, and the clarification of the sexual nature of the early relationship between Damon and Eustacia, including the consequent alterations to their motivation at the end of the novel; he mentions but does not thoroughly investigate the topographical alterations; he discusses the changes that elevate socially many of the characters, though he treats them individually rather than part of a pattern; and he indicates patterns in stylistic and dialectal revision. As a final point, he suggests that Hardy weakened the novel by adding "Even the receipt of Clym's letter would not have stopped her now" to the narrator's account of Eustacia's departure to meet Wildeve at the end of the novel. Wheeler writes

> There is little point in Hardy building suspense about whether Clym will write a letter, and then injecting the element of chance in Fairway's forgetting to deliver it early enough for Eustacia to receive it, if the letter could have had no effect on her anyway.

But what Wheeler does not consider is that if Fairway had delivered the letter in time, it might have influenced Eustacia; it is only once she has left the house and finds the weather to be atrocious that Hardy has the narrator say that reading Clym's letter would not have stopped her.

I have been particularly interested in exploring how and why Hardy altered the environment of the novel. Everybody who has read *The Return of the Native* is aware of the potent force Hardy gives to the heath, or that Hardy drew from it. The natures of both Clym and Avice/Eustacia are formed in intimate relation with the heath, Avice more clearly than Eustacia. It was, when Hardy first imagined it for the novel, as he had experienced it as a young child—vast, of uncertain boundaries, wild, untameable—and it remains that; but gradually imposed upon it (rather the way that

superior social status is imposed upon the major characters) is an
environment of a different scale, limited in scope by measured distances, by the association of fictional locations with places in
Dorset, by maps, and by other novels and stories, in particular "The
Withered Arm."

By 1878, when *The Return of the Native* first reached the public,
Hardy had firmly established Wessex as the name for the fictional
county in which the action of *The Hand of Ethelberta* takes place
(his first use of the name was in chapter 50 of *Far from the
Madding Crowd* in 1874); but in this, the next following novel,
Wessex has at first a tenuous presence. Egdon is within Wessex—
there are three references to the surrounding county[5]—but at the
same time it is in many ways dissociated from Wessex, an isolated
enclave of uncultivatable wilderness amid profitable farmland, on
which people eke a living from what is naturally present. Only two
place-names recur from earlier novels; one is Budmouth, that had
been a fashionable seaside resort in *Under the Greenwood Tree* and
Far from the Madding Crowd (it is worth noting that Hardy vacil-
lated between calling the place Budmouth and Cresmouth—a
name that appears nowhere else in his writing); it is between
twenty and thirty miles from Egdon. The other surviving link to earlier novels is an anecdotal connection to the occasion in *Far from
the Madding Crowd* for the first appearance of Wessex, when Timothy Fairway remembers his wife as a young woman running "for
smocks and gown-pieces at Greenhill Fair." When the heath-
dwellers need urban services, they go to Southerton, but Hardy offers no indication where the town lies in relation to Egdon, and we
only ever hear reports of visits there. It is another name that occurs
nowhere else in Hardy's work. At one time in the composition of
the manuscript Hardy thought to have Clym go ten miles off the
heath to Casterbridge (another location in *Under the Greenwood
Tree* and *Far from the Madding Crowd*), but he deleted the reference.

It is perhaps surprising, given the heroic, mythic qualities Hardy
ascribes to Egdon, that for the novel's first edition he prepared a
map of the district. He wrote to Smith, Elder, the publishers of the
first edition:

> I enclose for your inspection a Sketch of the supposed scene in
> which "The Return of the Native" is laid—copied from the one
> I used in writing the story—& my suggestion is that we place

5. We learn that reddlemen are dying out in Wessex because railway transport is making
   them redundant (there being no sheep on Egdon they have never been required there),
   that Grandfer Cantle belonged to the South Wessex Militia during the Napoleonic wars
   (an enterprise that took him off the heath), and that people in Wessex towns and villages
   neighboring the heath were sympathetic to Clym at the end of the novel.

an engraving of it as frontispiece to the first volume. . . . I am of opinion that it would be a desirable novelty, likely to increase a reader's interest.[6]

The publishers evidently agreed, though this map has its curiosities, and might have increased "a reader's interest" by inviting him to puzzle out the exact relationship between the map and the descriptions of distances and directions in the narrative. Not the least of the curiosities is that there is no conventional compass to make it clear where north lies. Nor is a scale provided, perhaps for the good reason that the map is evidently not drawn to scale.

Hardy promoted the map because the geography of *The Return of the Native* is limited; but even so by no means all the places mentioned in the text appear in the map. There are the locations on the heath, some, but not all, marked on the map. Other important places, in particular Budmouth, lie beyond the scope of Hardy's cartography.[7] Like many of Hardy's early descriptions of places, the map is intended to conceal as much as it is to reveal, and it was presumably for this reason that it was not reprinted when Hardy came to collect *The Return of the Native* for the Osgood, McIlvaine edition of his novels in 1895.

Egdon in 1878 was a balancing act between poetry and prose—or, perhaps, between metaphor and geography. In 1895 Hardy tipped the scales toward geography. He was faced by a difficult problem: Wessex had taken on a life over which he only had partial control. Everyone who cared to know was aware that most of Hardy's places were based closely on locations in Dorset and neighboring counties, and people were beginning to make specific identifications in published commentaries. Even so, he might have retained the anonymity of Egdon and its immediate environment, he might, in particular, have kept Southerton, and let the speculators speculate over it. Such a gesture would have been (for himself, if for no one else) a powerful assertion of the novel's environmental distinctness among his works. But in the intervening years he had written other accounts of Egdon, of which this from the story "The Withered Arm" is the most significant:

> Though the date was comparatively recent, Egdon was much less fragmentary in character than now. The attempts—successful and otherwise—at cultivation on the lower slopes, which intrude and break up the original heath into small detached heaths, had not been carried far: Enclosure Acts had

---

6. *Letters*, I.61.
7. For details of the problems involved in relating the map to the accounts of the heath in the first edition see under *The Return of the Native* on the Wessex website *www. english.uga.edu/Wessex*

not taken effect, and the banks and fences which now exclude the cattle of those villagers who formerly enjoyed rights of commonage thereon, and the carts of those who had turbary privileges which kept them in firing all the year round, were not erected. Gertrude therefore rode along with no other obstacles than the prickly furze-bushes, the mats of heather, the white water-courses, and the natural steeps and declivities of the ground.

Here Hardy, one might say, demystifies Egdon. The version of the heath in the first edition of *The Return of the Native* would hardly have admitted of such explanation, and it is a measure of Hardy's changing attitude to the relationship between Wessex and Dorset that he chooses to give such historical instruction, cementing the identity between dream and reality. It is thus not particularly surprising that when he was faced with revising the novel, history and geography won out over poetry and metaphor. Southerton became Dorchester and Anglebury and Weatherbury; descriptions, distances, and directions were altered to conform as closely as possible to what a visitor to Dorset might find. Or at least in 1895 some were. It is a striking feature of the alteration to the shape of Egdon for this first collected edition that Hardy made remarkably few changes in the part of the text that was contained in the second volume and the early part of the third volume of the first edition. It is, for instance, almost astonishing that he made no change to this from the second volume of the first edition: "Longer coffins were never made in the whole county of Wessex"—"Wessex" had to wait until 1912 to become "South Wessex." It seems as if Hardy were not paying very close attention to what he was doing for a few days. He revised *The Return of the Native* during July, when he and his wife were in London for the season, and there were plenty of distractions. It is also possible that as he pinned down Egdon more and more firmly to the map, he conceived a distaste for the enterprise, and only pulled himself together when the end was in sight. There are, at any rate, correspondingly more revisions in that part of the novel for the Wessex edition in 1912.[8]

The text embodied in this edition has come a long way from Hardy's earliest conception, and it represents the final stage of development. I should have liked to read what Hardy might have made in a completed account of the relationships among Avice,

8. The preface to the novel that Hardy wrote in 1895 gives notice of the new relationship of his creation with reality: "Under the general name of 'Egdon Heath', which has been given to the sombre scene of the story, are united or typified heaths of various real names, to the number of at least a dozen; these being virtually one in character and aspect, though their original unity, or partial unity, is now somewhat disguised by intrusive strips and slices brought under the plough with varying degrees of success, or planted to woodland."

Toogood, Clym, Diggory, and Thomasin, and I prefer to think of Egdon as Hardy originally conceived of it. But the final version has its virtues also; the novel takes its place as a substantial element in the larger narrative that Wessex has become, and Eustacia and Wildeve contemplating an elopement to the Continent together seem more at home in this environment.

ANDREW NASH

The Return of the Native and Belgravia†

Like most of Hardy's novels, *The Return of the Native* has a complicated textual history. There are four substantially different versions of the work: the serial version, and the book editions published respectively in 1878, 1895 and 1912. The serial version was issued in the United Kingdom in *Belgravia* from January to December 1878 and in America in *Harper's New Monthly Magazine* from February 1878 to January 1879. A slightly altered version was published in three-volumes by Smith, Elder in November 1878, after which rights in the work passed to Kegan Paul in December 1879, who issued a one-volume edition at six shillings the following month, and then to Sampson, Low & Co who published a further edition in 1884. A considerably revised version of the work was published together with a preface in 1895 by Osgood, McIlvaine as part of the first collected edition of Hardy's works (entitled the "Wessex Novels"). Finally, a further phase of revision was undertaken and a postscript added to the preface in 1912 when Macmillan issued a new collected edition entitled "The Wessex Edition".[1]

Accounts of these texts and of the publishing history of the work have been numerous and have become more comprehensive as relevant publishers' archives have been made available. Most recently, Simon Gatrell has reviewed the scholarship and written extensively on the composition of the novel, showing in the process how Hardy's dealings with editors and publishers affected the way he wrote and revised his text.[2] Further evidence regarding the serialisation of the novel, however, can be found in the archive of the

† This is a revised version of an essay originally published as "The Serialization and Publication of *The Return of the Native*: A New Thomas Hardy Letter," in *The Library: The Transactions of the Bibliographical Society* 2.1 (2001): 53–59. Reprinted by permission of the author.

1. For further introductory details of the textual history see Richard Little Purdy, *Thomas Hardy: A Bibliographical Study* (Oxford, 1954, repr. 1968, 2002), pp. 24–7.

2. See Simon Gatrell (ed.), *The Return of the Native: A Facsimile of the manuscript with related materials* (New York and London: Garland Publishing, 1986); Simon Gatrell, *Hardy the Creator: A Textual Biography* (Oxford, 1988), pp. 29–51, as well as the essay by Gatrell written for this edition.

publishing firm of Chatto & Windus, which contains a letter by
Hardy that is not included in the seven-volume *Collected Letters*.
Dated 27 June 1877, the letter concerns the negotiation for the
publication of *The Return of the Native* in *Belgravia*, the monthly
magazine owned by the firm.[3]

As Gatrell has made clear, it seems probable that Hardy began
The Return of the Native towards the end of 1876 and had written a
substantial part of it (a different version of what came to form the
first two books of the published version) by February the following
year, which he submitted to both Leslie Stephen (editor of the *Cornhill Magazine*) and William Blackwood (editor of *Blackwood's Magazine*). After receiving their criticisms in April he set about revising
and rewriting the work, and on 16 June 1887 made another unsuccessful approach to George Bentley, editor of *Temple Bar*.[4] It is clear
from the published letters that he did not send Bentley any portion
of the story and no record exists of him having received any response. It is likely that he was sent one of the pre-printed *Temple
Bar* rejection slips that survive in the archive of Richard Bentley &
Son.

Following the rejection by Bentley, Hardy wrote almost immediately to Chatto & Windus enquiring about terms for a serial. The
Chatto & Windus archive, held on deposit in Reading University
Library, has an uninterrupted sequence of outgoing letter books
dating from the 1860s when the business was in the hands of John
Camden Hotten.[5] Unfortunately, most of the firm's incoming letters were destroyed in 1915, apparently sent for salvage during the
war, but a number remain, either among the collection of author
contracts or pasted into the outgoing letter books. Hardy's initial
letter of approach has not survived but it is possible to date it to
shortly before 25 June because on that day a reply was sent to the
author (signed as from the firm but in Andrew Chatto's hand) explaining the situation regarding their magazines:

> As we already have another serial story for one of our maga-
> zines under consideration, before making you an offer we
> should be glad to be favoured with a sight of a considerable
> portion of your MS. We should not put you to this trouble if
> you would give us some idea of the price you have set upon the
> magazine right of your story as the sum at our disposal for this
> purpose is in some degree limited.[6]

3. For permission to reproduce the letter I gratefully acknowledge the Miss E. A. Dugdale
   Will Trust, copyright holders of Hardy's unpublished writings.
4. *Letters*, I.51.
5. Andrew Chatto bought the business from Hotten's widow when Hotten died in 1873.
   W. E. Windus was a sleeping partner.
6. Chatto & Windus to Thomas Hardy, 25 June 1877, Letter Book 10, p. 109. The firm
   published two magazines at the time: *Belgravia* and the *Gentleman's Magazine*. For a

The serial story already under consideration was George Whyte-Melville's *Roy's Wife* (1878), which was serialised in the *Gentleman's Magazine*, the other periodical owned by Chatto & Windus at this time. Hardy's letter of reply to Chatto, which is filed in one of the boxes of author-contracts, contains his response to the options laid before him. It was not unusual for Chatto & Windus to preserve letters in this way when a separate, formal contract had not been drawn up. Hardy's address is die-stamped and at the head of the letter is a MS insertion, in the hand of Percy Spalding (Chatto's partner from 1876), noting a reference and date for the reply sent by the firm.

> Sturminster Newton
> Blandford
> June 27. 1877
>
> Dear Sirs,
>
> I should have great pleasure in sending you as much of the MS. as you would require to base an opinion upon, were a sufficient quantity written. But this is far from being the case; & I had hoped to take a few weeks holiday before settling down to the bulk of the story. So that if I were to wait till it should be far enough advanced for such a purpose there would be hardly time for me to enter into an arrangement elsewhere (if our negociations fail) by the date at which I should like to begin publishing.
>
> I think therefore that, to expedite the matter, it will be best for me to suggest terms. My chief difficulty in doing this lies in the fact that on all previous occasions the magazine right & that for the volumes have been thrown into one sum, so that I have not a clear idea of the proportion the magazine payment should bear to the total value of the book.
>
> However, I am willing to dispose of the serial right to you at the rate of twenty pounds per monthly part of 23 or 24 pages in the magazine. Or should you prefer to purchase the right both to the magazine form & to the 3-volume form of the story, I will dispose of this for nine hundred pounds. The quantity of the whole will be about equal to 12 monthly parts in the magazine: the right to any cheaper edition of the story to remain in my hands.
>
> Trusting that one or the other of these proposals will meet your views,
>
> I am, dear Sirs,
> Yours faithfully
> Thomas Hardy.

---

short period in 1879 they also published the *New Quarterly Magazine*, dividing the profits with the magazine's editor, Francis Hueffer, who had earlier solicited from Hardy a short story 'An Indiscretion'.

Chatto wrote immediately to accept the first part of Hardy's proposal:

> We shall have much pleasure in accepting the serial right of
> publication of your new novel upon the terms you mention viz.
> twenty pounds per month. We ought to have the opening
> chapters early in November and we should like to know the ti-
> tle as soon as convenient to you in order that we may effec-
> tively announce it in advance.[7]

Hardy sent copy for the first two instalments on 28 August and in
one of only two references he makes to the novel in the *Life of
Thomas Hardy* recorded that "on November 8, parts 3, 4, and 5 of
the story were posted to Messrs Chatto and Windus for publication
in (of all places) *Belgravia*—a monthly magazine then running."[8]

The parenthetical statement says a lot about the reputation that
Belgravia held as a literary magazine. It had been founded in November 1866 by the publisher John Maxwell, ostensibly to provide
a vehicle for the fiction of Mary Elizabeth Braddon, author of the
notorious *Lady Audley's Secret*. Maxwell and Braddon had been living together since 1861 and their first illegitimate child was born in
1862. Braddon edited *Belgravia* until the copyright was sold to
Chatto & Windus in 1876 and during the period of her control the
magazine developed a rather low-brow reputation, closely associated with the sensationalism of her own fiction and the scandal of
her private life. Biographies of Hardy have continued to fall into error, however, by assuming that Braddon actually played a role in the
acceptance of *The Return of the Native* for publication in the magazine. Both Paul Turner and Michael Millgate are wrong in stating
that *Belgravia* was edited by Braddon at this time.[9] Her control of
the magazine ceased when it was acquired by Chatto & Windus in
March 1876; during the period of his ownership Andrew Chatto
himself acted as editor of the magazine.[1] This simple fact makes redundant Martin Seymour-Smith's speculations that Braddon would
probably have been pleased when she received the manuscript from

7. Chatto & Windus to Thomas Hardy, 28 June 1877, Letter Book 10, p. 114.
8. *Life*, p. 120.
9. Michael Millgate, *Thomas Hardy: A Biography* (Oxford & New York, 1982), p. 188; Paul
   Turner *The Life of Thomas Hardy: A Critical Biography* (Oxford, 1988), p. 59. Braddon is
   also cited as editor in the notes to *Letters*, I. 51n. Millgate has removed the error in the
   revised edition of his biography, *Thomas Hardy: A Biography Revisited* (Oxford: OUP,
   2004).
1. The contract between John Maxwell and Chatto & Windus is dated 17 March 1876 and
   records that Chatto agreed to pay £6,757:16:9 for the copyright of the magazine and annual together with all the stock of the numbers and volumes, woodcuts, stereos and
   electros from and after 10 April 1876. There were other sundry payments for drawings
   and engravings already ordered and payments to authors already being made for serials
   currently running in the magazine. Andrew Chatto did not employ an editor, just as he
   did not employ a reader to comment on the very large number of manuscripts that
   passed through the hands of his firm. Instead, he and Percy Spalding read and judged all

Hardy because of its affinities to her own work.[2] Braddon simply had no part in the negotiations.

Sales of *Belgravia* declined during the period in which it was owned by Chatto & Windus, 12,000 copies were printed of the April 1876 number (the first under Chatto's ownership) but within four months the print-run had dropped to 10,000. Over the course of 1878 and the serialisation of *The Return of the Native*, 9,750 copies were printed each month. Such a figure would seem to suggest that Hardy's novel did not greatly affect the sales of the magazine; by June 1879, however, the print-run had dropped further to 8,000 copies and over the next ten years sales fell drastically. When Chatto & Windus sold the magazine to F. V. White in September 1889 the print-run had slumped to 3,250 copies per month. It is possible to suggest, therefore, that, along with other factors, the appearance of Hardy's novel temporarily kept up demand for a magazine that was in a state of irreparable decline. Among the other material that appeared in the magazine during the course of the serialisation of *The Return of the Native* were short stories by Mark Twain, Wilkie Collins and Bret Harte, as well as the completion of James Payn's serial *By Proxy* and the whole of Collin's short serial *The Haunted Hotel*.

A significant fact arising from the negotiation between author and publisher is that Andrew Chatto accepted the work without seeing any of the manuscript.[3] This was not an unusual practice so far as serials in *Belgravia* were concerned. Agreements with authors were often made in advance without submission of any material if the author was sufficiently well known. Thus despite his statement in a footnote to the 1912 edition of the book that "certain circumstances of serial publication led to a change of intent" regarding the ending of the story, Hardy probably did not specifically tailor his work to meet the demands of *Belgravia* and certainly was not required to do so.[4] The fact that he did not send any portion of the work to either Bentley or Chatto—and in the case of the latter made clear that he could not—suggests that "the change of intent" had probably already been made, that he was no longer trying to get publishers interested in the fifteen chapters he had sent Stephen and Blackwood; he was very probably acting on the suggestions the latter had made, and which he had assured him he would consider.[5]

---

the unpublished manuscripts themselves. My identification of Chatto as editor confirms the suggestions to this effect made both by Gatrell (*The Return of the Native: a facsimile of the manuscript*, xix, n.14), and by P. D. Edwards in his introduction to *Indexes to Fiction in Belgravia*, Victorian Fiction Research Guides XIV, (Queensland, 1989), p. 4.

2. Martin Seymour-Smith: *Hardy* (London, 1994), p. 228.
3. This point is speculated by Purdy and Millgate in the corrigenda to *Letters*, VII.171.
4. Wessex Edition (London: Macmillan, 1912), 473.
5. This point is argued convincingly by Gatrell, *Hardy the Creator*, pp. 33 foll.

The rewriting was therefore likely to be as much a response to their criticisms as it was an anticipation of the new audience in *Belgravia*.

A further significant point from the correspondence is that Chatto placed the initial question of terms entirely within Hardy's hands, who himself suggested the payment of £240. Despite his professed ignorance over the proportionate value of magazine rights to the total value of the book, Hardy in fact suggested a sum that was pretty much in line with the payments made to other novelists publishing in *Belgravia*. When *The Return of the Native* began its run in January 1878 it joined Eliza Lynn Linton's *The World Well Lost*, for which Chatto had paid £250 for ten instalments, i.e. £5 more per instalment than Hardy received. The same rate was paid to Wilkie Collins for his novel *The Haunted Hotel*, which commenced serialisation in June 1878. It is possible to speculate that if Hardy had proposed £25 he may well have received it. His payment of £20 put his work in line with that of James Payn who received £200 for ten instalments of his novel *By Proxy*, serialised from May 1877.

It is unlikely that Chatto would have even contemplated taking up Hardy's alternative offer of serial and three-volume rights for £900, and he does not mention it in his reply to the author. That Hardy proposed such a sum provides an insight, however, into the sense the author had of the commercial standing his work occupied at this time. *The Return of the Native* was written at a pivotal moment in Hardy's career as a professional author. Buoyed up by the success they had had with *Far from the Madding Crowd* (1874), the firm of Smith, Elder had paid Hardy £700 for serial and three-volume rights in *The Hand of Ethelberta* (1875). The comparative failure of that novel had played no small part, however, in Leslie Stephen's decision to reject *The Return*, and was not likely to have increased the commercial viability of his future work. Hardy's offer of £900 was thus optimistic in the extreme, and not likely to interest a firm like Chatto & Windus who were not in the practice of making such payments for works of fiction.

Some indication of the extravagance of Hardy's proposal can be seen from a comparison with the payments made for the works by Linton, Payn and Collins mentioned above, where in each case Chatto had also purchased the rights to publication in book form. Payn and Linton both disposed of the entire copyright in their works, Payn receiving an extra £200 on top of his serial payment of £200 and Linton £300, making her total payment £550.[6] The

---

6. Contract between Chatto & Windus and James Payn, dated 21 July 1876; Andrew Chatto to Eliza Lynn Linton, 3 January 1877, Letter Book 9, p. 861.

agreement with Collins was more complicated. He was to be paid an additional £400 for a seven-year lease on the book rights of both *The Haunted Hotel* and his story *My Lady's Money*, which had appeared in the Christmas number of *The Illustrated London News*.[7] Collins' reputation was in decline by 1878 but as a popular author the comparison with Hardy's offer of £900 for serial and three-volume rights alone is instructive. Collins' payment of £650 for what was only a two-volume collection of two different works—far less marketable than a three-volume novel—reserved for Collins the right of authorising translations of both works and of printing in the United States and on the continent, but it gave Chatto a lease over cheap reprints of the work, the rights to which Hardy had wanted to retain on his own novel. It was largely through the issue of cheap reprints of popular works, priced first at 6s and later at 3s/6d or 2s, that Andrew Chatto had built his publishing business, cornering a major niche in the market for fiction and helping to hasten the decline of the three-decker.[8] It was therefore unlikely that he would have been interested in paying a large sum for *The Return of the Native* unless he could have the option of adding it to his burgeoning "Piccadilly Library", which already contained Hardy's own *Under the Greenwood Tree*, purchased by Chatto from Tinsley in January 1877.

From Hardy's point of view, the proposal of £900 illustrates the mixture of experience and naivety that he brought to the economics of publishing at this stage of his career. He clearly felt that his status as a newly-successful author warranted pushing hard for a healthy increase on the payment received for his previous work. At the same time, his approach to Chatto shows how his bargaining power was hampered by a professed ignorance over the proportionate value of magazine and book rights. What is perhaps most interesting about the approach to Chatto is Hardy's firm desire to retain control over the rights to cheap reprints of his novel. He had clearly already begun to regret having sold outright the copyright of *Under the Greenwood Tree* to Tinsley in 1871, for a mere £30. This remained the only work over which he had relinquished control; a situation that led to a certain amount of contractual difficulty when he put together the collected editions of his works in 1895 and 1912. In view of the alterations to the texts that he made for these collected editions it is clear that Hardy valued enormously the means of retaining authorial control over his work, and from the correspondence with Chatto it is possible to speculate that even at this early stage of his career this prospect was uppermost in his mind.

7. Contract between Chatto & Windus and Wilkie Collins, dated 20 February 1878.
8. See Simon Eliot, "The Three-Decker Novel and Its First Cheap Reprint 1862–94", *The Library*, 6th Series, VII, 1 (March, 1985), pp. 38–53.

Less than a fortnight after Hardy sent the first two instalments of the story, Andrew Chatto set about arranging illustrations. He first approached Frank Dicksee, whom he mistakenly thought had composed the illustrations for *Far from the Madding Crowd* and *The Hand of Ethelberta*.[9] Once his error was pointed out to him he turned to Arthur Hopkins, younger brother of Gerard Manley Hopkins, a regular worker for *Belgravia* who was in the process of illustrating James Payn's serial *By Proxy*. As was his custom, Hopkins corresponded with Hardy during the course of serialisation.

The Return of the Native was eventually issued in three-volume form by Smith, Elder, but it appears that negotiations over the terms of publication were not finalised until September 1878, only three months before the work completed its run in *Belgravia*. George Smith wrote to Hardy on 19 September 1878 proposing to pay £200 for the three-volume rights in the novel and Hardy later recorded in his *Life* that on 30 September he wrote agreeing to the terms.[1] The Smith, Elder Publications Book records that Hardy was duly paid this sum on 26 November 1878 for the rights to an edition of 1,000 copies. The contract had an additional clause stating that in the event of there being demand for a further edition the author was to be paid £75 for every 250 copies printed.[2] No such edition was required, however.

The payment by Smith, Elder meant that the amount Hardy received for serial and three-volume rights in the work was £440, a considerable regression from the £700 he had been paid for similar rights in *The Hand of Ethelberta* and less than half the £900 he had proposed to Chatto. The whole story illustrates the topsy-turvy nature of the profession of authorship in the late-Victorian period. Just over a year later Hardy was paid £1,300 by the American firm of Harper for the right to serialise *A Laodicean* in the first numbers of their European edition of *Harper's New Monthly Magazine*. That kind of sum was well beyond the scope of a magazine like *Belgravia* and the contrast points to the extraordinary extremes of a market that, as the publishing history of *The Return of the Native* makes clear, Hardy was still trying to master.

9. Chatto & Windus to Frank Dicksee, 6 September 1877, Letter Book 10, p. 156. Francis Bernard Dicksee, later Sir (1853–1928), son of Thomas Francis Dicksee (1819–1895). Although the younger Dicksee would have been only in his mid-twenties when approached by Chatto he was already an active painter and illustrator.
1. Millgate, *Thomas Hardy: A Biography*, p. 197; *Life*, p. 125.
2. In tracing this record of payment I am grateful to Virginia Murray of John Murray Publishers, who hold some of the records of the firm of Smith, Elder.

PHILLIP MALLETT

The Serialization of *The Return of the Native*

For the *Belgravia* publication of *The Return of the Native*, Hardy wrote summaries of the action to come at the start of each Book of the novel; these were marked "omit in vols" or "mag[azine] only," and were presumably intended to assist serial readers who had to wait a further four or eight weeks for the conclusion of each Book, as well as to whet their appetites for later episodes: hence, no doubt, the liberal use of words such as entanglement, impossible, accident, precipitates, unexpected, irretrievable, critical, conjuncture, consequences, awakening, hasty, catastrophe—all of which draw attention to the complexities of the plot. The summaries were replaced with Book titles—"The Three Women," etc.—in the first volume edition.

The Book summaries are given below, followed by the dates of publication of each instalment:

Book First (January):
Depicts the scenes which result from an entanglement in the hopes of four persons inhabiting one of the innermost recesses of Wessex. By reason of the interdependence, a happy consummation to all concerned is impossible as matters stand; but an easing of the situation is begun by the arrival of a new character from a distant city, who has for a long time been talked of.

Book Second (April):
The cause that no persuasion or strategy could advance is unconsciously helped on, in a social sense, by the accident of the stranger's arrival; this event, by giving a new bias to emotions in one quarter precipitates affairs in another with unexpected rapidity.

Book Third (June):
The man and his scheme are fully described; and he begins his work. But a rencounter leads to emotions which hamper his plans, and cause a sharp divergence of opinion, ultimately committing him to an irretrievable step which a few months earlier he did not dream of.

Book Fourth (August):
The old affection between mother and son re-asserts itself, and relenting steps are taken. A critical conjuncture supervenes, truly the turning point in the lives of all concerned. Eustacia has the move and she makes it; but not till the sun has set does she suspect the consequences involved in her choice of courses.

Book Fifth (October):

Contains the material effects of the foregoing misadventure, namely; contrition in one quarter; in another an awakening to harrowing discoveries; hasty action thereupon; and what ensued before milder intentions could take effect.

Book Sixth (December):

Shortly relates the gradual righting of affairs after the foregoing catastrophe, and how there resulted another general gathering at Blooms-End, with which, and other particulars, the story closes.

The installments, of roughly equal length, appeared as follows: January, Book I, ch. 1–4; February, Book I, ch. 5–7; March, Book I, ch. 8–11; April, Book II, ch. 1–5; May, Book II, ch. 6–8; June, Book III, ch. 1–4; July, Book III, ch. 5–8; August, Book IV, ch. 1–4; September, Book IV, ch. 5–8; October, Book V, ch. 1–4; November, Book V, ch. 5–8; December, Book V, ch. 9, Book VI, ch. 1–4.

Hardy's 1912 Note to Book VI, Chapter III

For the 1912 Wessex Edition of *The Return of the Native*, Hardy added a note at the end of Chapter III, Book Sixth of the novel:

> The writer may state here that the original conception of the novel did not design a marriage between Thomasin and Venn. He was to have retained his isolated and weird character to the last, and to have disappeared mysteriously from the heath, nobody knowing whither—Thomasin remaining a widow. But certain circumstances of serial publication led to a change of intent.
>
> Readers can therefore choose between the endings, and those with an austere artistic code can assume the more consistent conclusion to be the true one.

This note has understandably puzzled many readers, and for a number of reasons. First, it is not clear what "circumstances of serial publication" Hardy had in mind. Andrew Chatto, who acted as both publisher and editor of the *Belgravia*, had agreed terms for *The Return* without even asking to see a sample of the manuscript; his readers, accustomed to the novels of Mrs. Braddon, were not especially timid, and he himself was not—as Leslie Stephen had been at the *Cornhill*—a man who felt the need to keep his authors under tight rein. It seems unlikely, then, that Hardy was under immediate editorial pressure to provide a regulation happy ending. In any case, more than three decades had passed since the novel was first published; if at the time of writing it Hardy had felt himself limited by the "circumstances of serial publication," they had long since ceased to apply. He had extensively revised other novels, yet he had never taken the opportunity to bring out an edition of *The Return* governed by an "austere artistic code," if by that is meant the more tragic ending, nor was he ever to do so.

Hardy's phrasing gives rise to another question. Most readers have assumed that the bleaker conclusion—Thomasin left a widow, the reddleman vanished—would be "the more consistent," and more in keeping with Hardy's ambition to write tragic fiction, but the note does not say so: it merely invites the reader to choose. The first chapter of Book Sixth is entitled "The Inevitable Movement Onward," and it might reasonably be argued that Thomasin's desire to remarry, and Diggory Venn's to become her husband, are indeed "inevitable": an instance on a domestic scale of what the second chapter of the novel describes as "the instinctive and resistant act of man"—to light a fire, to find means of comfort, and to rebel against "foul times, cold darkness, misery and death." From another angle, the Maypole celebrations and wedding preparations of Book Sixth, the one marked by flowers, music, and dancing, the other by a feather-storm, might be construed as a toned-down version of the Satyr play, the burlesque comedy performed at the end of the Greek tragic trilogy, and to that extent formally consistent with classical ideas of tragedy. Either position offers reasons to find the existing ending "consistent."

Hardy's reference to "the original conception" of the novel is also puzzling. It has been taken to mean that the more consoling ending was decided upon at a late stage, but this is by no means certain. In February 1878 Hardy wrote to his illustrator, Arthur Hopkins, outlining the plot and explaining that "Thomasin . . . ultimately marries the reddleman." Michael Millgate takes this letter as "an interesting indication that the conclusion of the novel was not recast at the last moment" (*Letters*, I.53). In one sense this must be right: since Book Sixth was not to appear until December, the material for it need not have reached the printers much before August, and it is clearly not the case that Chatto somehow caught sight of another and more "austere" version of the denouement, now lost, and wrote to Hardy demanding that he provide a happy ending instead. But this in itself is not enough to prove that the novel was conceived with something like the present Book Sixth in mind. Hardy had offered it, without success, to at least three magazines before it was accepted by the *Belgravia*, and these initial rejections may have led him not merely to revise what he had already written—roughly, the material that now comprises the first two Books—but to anticipate future objections by reshaping the conclusion into a form more likely to meet the expectations of his readers.

It is, then, impossible to be sure when Hardy determined on the present ending: it might have been while he was still seeking a publisher; it might have been close to the time of his letter to Hopkins. We do know, however, that he had been at work on *The Return* since late 1876, and by November 1877 had sent in five of the twelve scheduled installments, leaving seven more to write. In March 1878 he and Emma were to move from Sturminster to London, and it seems likely that he would have wanted to finish it before moving house. This would have been feasible, but difficult, and it would be understandable if as he reached the conclusion he was ready to settle for a more conventional ending. It is at least possible that the "circumstances of serial publication" that Hardy refers to were not those of editorial interference but merely his desire to get the novel out of the way, and in the agreed number of installments, so that he could use his time in London to begin research for *The Trumpet-Major*.

But Hardy (like other authors) cannot always be taken as a reliable guide to his own intentions, and it is also possible that the note records what he had come to think by 1912, rather than what he had thought in 1878. The convention of the omniscient narrator had allowed mid-Victorian novelists to assume an air of authority in their fiction, and many chose to do so—Trollope, for example, or George Eliot. Others opted to employ multiple narrators (Emily Brontë in *Wuthering Heights*, Wilkie Collins in *The Moonstone*), unreliable narrators (Thackeray in *Vanity Fair*), or even, as with Charlotte Brontë in *Villette*, an unreliable first-person narrator together with an ambiguous ending. Hardy's own fiction frequently undermines the authority of the narrative point of view: hence the use of such locutions as "an observer might have thought . . . ," "it might have been noticed that . . . ." The effect of Hardy's note is to call into question both the writer's authority, and by implication the very idea of authority. In the General Preface he wrote at the same time Hardy insists that his novels and poems contain no positive views on "the Whence and Wherefore of things" and make no attempt to explain a universe of which, as he and many of his contemporaries had come to feel, "there exists no comprehension . . . anywhere." Whatever its occasion, the 1912 note may be taken as a further instance of Hardy's typically post-Darwinian interest in the nondetermined, the essential chanciness of what happens to happen. *The Return of the Native*, like other Hardy novels, is haunted by the sense that what is, or has been, might equally have been otherwise.

Hardy's Nonfictional Writings

From Hardy's Letters†

To George Smith[1]
[February 5, 1877]

Can you, or your clerk, give me any idea of the time when the new edition[2] is to appear?

I will take this opportunity of mentioning that I have sent the MS. of my new story—as far as written—to Mr Stephen. If you could bestow a spare half hour upon it, & tell me if you think it a kind of story likely to create a demand in the market I should owe you many thanks.

To John Blackwood[3]
[February 13, 1877]

I have frequently wished for an opportunity of communicating with you otherwise than as a stranger, but as there seems no probability of any such event just yet I write without an introduction.

I wish to ask you if you would at any time inform me when a vacancy for a serial story is about to occur in the magazine. It would give me great pleasure to be a contributor, apart from the fact that an occasional change of quarters brings new readers; & if I have

---

† The selections that follow give some idea of Hardy's dealings with *The Return of the Native*, first in finding a publisher for it, then in seeing it through the press in various editions, and as the basis for dramatic performance. Letters are given here without address or signature, and with dates standardized—Hardy himself used varying forms—in square brackets.

1. George Smith (1824–1901), founder of the publishing house Smith, Elder & Co., and publisher of the *Cornhill Magazine*. Hardy wrote later that Leslie Stephen, editor of the *Cornhill*, "feared that relations between Eustacia, Wildeve, and Thomasin might develop into something 'dangerous' for a family magazine," and their negotiations fell through.

2. The one-volume edition of *The Hand of Ethelberta*, published in May 1877.

3. John Blackwood (1818–1879), publisher, and editor of *Blackwood's Magazine*. By the 1870s *Blackwood's* was losing ground to the *Cornhill*, but remained one of the most respected of nineteenth-century periodicals: long-lived, politically conservative, and paternalistic in its dealing with its authors.

anything ready on such an occasion, & likely to suit, I would offer you the MS. I may add that I have recently begun a story dealing with remote country life, somewhat of the nature of "Far from the Madding Crowd", though I have not yet written enough to be worth sending. I should be obliged by your letting me know before I make any other arrangements for it, if that class of story & scenery is what you would care to introduce into the magazine.

To Smith, Elder & Co.
[March 1, 1877]

Will you be good enough to return to me the manuscript of the new story, as soon as you conveniently can: I cannot well get on for want of it, as I have no exact copy.

To John Blackwood
[April 12, 1877]

I have great pleasure in sending you the first 15 chapters of my new story—posted last night.

It occurred to me that it would be better thus to put the MS. into your hands, that you might look through it as far as written, than to attempt to give you an outline of the story by letter. Its length, as nearly as I can judge, will be about three times that of the portion sent—that is, it will contain matter enough for 10 or 12 parts in a magazine.

Should you think the story to be of a kind which will suit readers of your magazine I will give you any further particulars. The only point at all conditional in my offer of the MS. to you as editor, would have reference to the time at which, in the event of your liking it, the first part could appear, my wish being, if possible, to get the book issued complete not later than 1st May 1878.

I will just add that, should there accidentally occur any word or reflection not in harmony with the magazine, you would be quite at liberty to strike it out if you chose. I always mention this to my editors, as it simplifies matters. I do not, however, think you will meet with any such passage, as you will perceive that the story deals with a world almost isolated from civilization—moreover from beginning it I had resolved to write with a partial view to *Blackwood*.

I shall be greatly pleased if you think well of the story—partly from a personal wish to appear in your pages, & partly, as before stated, that by changing into another periodical occasionally one acquires new readers for the book when it appears in volumes. Even should you not be disposed to accept it I trust you will not re-

frain from making any remarks upon it that you may think fit, in
the shape of criticism—from which, I am sure, I shall profit.

To John Blackwood
[April 26, 1877]

I am exceedingly obliged for the trouble you have taken in reading the MS., & giving your criticism when the time at which I
wished to appear in print made me useless to you. You may be sure
that I shall avail myself of your valuable hints as far as I can apply
them to the remainder of the story.[4]

To George Bentley[5]
[June 16, 1877]

I have frequently been attracted by the prominence that is given
to the serial stories that appear in "Temple Bar"; & at length I am
induced to ask you if you would like to include one of mine among
them—a story of country life, somewhat of the nature of "Far from
the Madding Crowd".

Should you be of opinion that such a story would be likely to
please readers of the magazine, would you be good enough to inform me in what month the next vacancy for a serial will occur. It
would give me great pleasure to arrange with you for filling it, if
time & circumstances could be made to suit.

To Chatto & Windus[6]
[August 28, 1877]

I send to-day to the Editor of Belgravia Parts 1 & 2 (Jan & Feb)
of my new story, called "The return of the native"—a title which I

4. Blackwood found the rustics "more curious than interesting," and worried that there was
too much scene-setting and not enough of "what is called Novel interest" in the early
chapters.
5. George Bentley (1828–95), of Richard Bentley and Son, leading producers of multivol-
ume fiction in the mid-nineteenth century. Contributors to *Temple Bar* included Mary
Braddon, Wilkie Collins, and R. L. Stevenson; like *Belgravia* (see note below), it had a
bohemian reputation.
6. The publishing house founded in 1855 by John Hampden Cotten (1832–73) was sold
after his death to Andrew Chatto and W. E. Windus. Among their ventures was *Belgravia: an Illustrated Magazine*, founded in 1866 by the publisher John Maxwell, and edited (though she preferred the term "conducted") by the novelist Mary Elizabeth
Braddon (1835–1915), author of the sensational best seller *Lady Audley's Secret* (1861),
and also, notoriously, Maxwell's mistress. Though the couple were married in 1874, after the death of Maxwell's wife in a Dublin mental institution, this only emphasized the
adulterous nature of their relationship until then, and the illegitimacy of their five children. The *Belgravia* was sold to Chatto and Windus in 1876, before Hardy sent them
The Return of the Native, but did not shake off its association with scandal. Hardy wrote
later that he "always liked Miss Braddon." An earlier letter from Hardy to Chatto & Windus is included in the essay by Andrew Nash in this volume.

hope you will like. I forward the MS. thus early that there may be full time for early proofs.

I informed Messrs Harper & Brothers—the publishers of Harpers' Magazine—in which the story is also to appear—that they might have electros of the illustrations. They say that they will communicate with you.

With regard to the illustrations I may state that, should the artist be willing to receive a rough sketch of any unusual objects which come into the story, I shall be happy to furnish them. I have occasionally provided such sketches to the artists who illustrated my previous stories, with good results.

To Arthur Hopkins[7]
[February 8, 1878]

I am glad to receive a letter from you, for it is more satisfactory when artist & author are in correspondence. I liked your first drawing much: the third I have not yet seen, but I daresay that it is a good one, from your description. Strangely enough I myself thought that Thomasin in the apple-loft would be the best illustration for the fourth number. It is rather ungenerous to criticise; but since you invite me to do so I will say that I think Eustacia should have been represented as more youthful in face, supple in figure, &, in general, with a little more roundness & softness than you have given her. * * *

Perhaps it is well for me to give you the following idea of the story as a guide—Thomasin, as you have divined, is the *good* heroine, & she ultimately marries the reddleman, & lives happily. Eustacia is the wayward & erring heroine—She marries Yeobright, the son of Mrs Yeobright, is unhappy, & dies. The order of importance of the characters is as follows.

1 Clym Yeobright
2 Eustacia
3 Thomasin & the reddleman
4 Wildeve
5 Mrs Yeobright

Should you, at any time after choosing a subject for illustration, be in doubt about any of the accessories to the scene, &c. I shall have great pleasure in sending a rough sketch, done to the best of my power. I mention this because the scenes are somewhat outlandish, & may be unduly troublesome to you.

---

7. Arthur Hopkins (1848–1930), younger brother of the poet Gerard Manley Hopkins, had already worked as an illustrator for several periodicals, including the *Cornhill*.

To Arthur Hopkins
[February 20, 1878]

I think you have chosen well for the May illustration—certainly
the incident after the mumming, with the mummers looking on,
will be better than the mumming performance itself. Eustacia in
boy's clothes, though pleasant enough to the imagination, would
perhaps be unsafe as a picture. The sketch of a mummer's dress
which I sent was merely intended to show the general system on
which they used to decorate themselves: the surcoat or tunic was
formed of a white smockfrock rather shorter than usual, tied in
round the waist by a strap—this was almost invariably the groundwork of the costume: thus.[8] * * *

The sword was wood, of course, & the *staff*, which was never dis-
pensed with, consisted of a straight stick the size of a broom handle, 5 or 6 feet long, with small sticks inserted cross wise at the
upper end: from the end of these small sticks paper tassels dangled.
This was held erect in the left hand while the sword was bran-
dished in the right. Father Christmas was a conventional figure—
an old man with a hump-back, & a great club.

I should prefer to leave Clym's face entirely to you. A thoughtful
young man of 25 is all that can be shown, as the particulars of his
appearance given in the story are too minute to be represented in a
drawing.

A mummer or two in the picture would make it very interesting—but do not be at all hampered by my suggestions for I may attach an undue importance to the mummers.[9]

To Arthur Hopkins
[August 3, 1878]

Allow me to congratulate you on your success this month with
the illustration to The Return of the Native. I think Eustacia is
charming—she is certainly just what I imagined her to be, & the rebelliousness of her nature is precisely caught in your drawing. The
grouping of the three figures is also excellent.

---

8. Hardy's letter includes small sketches illustrating a laborer wearing a smock frock, first
untied, then tied at the waist, and then decorated with ribbons; an explanation that the
mummers' helmets, made of pasteboard, resembled "those articles called 'tea cosys'
which people use now a days for keeping the tea-pot warm"; and a sketch of a staff, as
described in the text. The letter is given in facsimile in Richard Little Purdy *Thomas
Hardy: A Bibliographical Study*, ed. Charles P. C. Pettit (London: The British Library),
p. 24.
9. Hopkins accepted Hardy's suggestion.

To Chatto & Windus
[September 21, 1878]

It would be convenient for me to publish the library edition of the *Return of the Native* as is usually done, that is, somewhat before its conclusion in the magazine, & I have thought that it might appear a month before the last number without prejudice to *Belgravia*.[1] Will you kindly say if this meets your approbation. * * *

To the Revd. Thomas Perkins[2]
[April 20, 1900]

My sincere thanks for the photographs, which interest me, & are excellent. That you may be less troubled as to localities I send a copy of the last edn of the R. of N.—in which are some corrections & a preface—which please do not trouble to return.

Although "Blooms End" embodies vague recollections of Bhompston Farm House[3] it was not intended to be an exact description; & the position was a little shifted, if I remember. I do not know if Bhompston has white palings now towards the heath as it had formerly—if not the chief feature of my description wd be gone. "The Quiet Woman" too is much changed from what it was when a public-house, & quite open to the heath * * *

P.S.   On looking into the book I find that "Alderworth"—the fictitious name of Clym's cottage—is a cottage I once drove near to, but shd have some trouble in finding now. It is in the *parish* of Affpuddle—on Affpuddle Heath I think—but some couple of miles from the village & church of Affpuddle—called "East Egdon"—But all these particulars are "a vain shadow"—not worth preserving!

To Sir George Douglas[4]
[November 20, 1901]

A few days ago I went more into the middle of "Egdon Heath" than is the part where you were able to visit; the district I called "East Egdon" (where Clym lived with Eustacia when his mother

---

1. The three-volume edition was published on November 4, 1878; the last installment in *Belgravia* appeared in the December issue. Hardy wrote on November 8 to Smith, Elder, thanking them for sending copies of the novel, and adding: "The appearance of the book is good, the new brown of the covers having a pleasing effect." On December 8 he wrote again, enclosing "a few sentences from reviews, which would be effective as advertisements."
2. Thomas Perkins (1842–1907), the rector of Turnworth in Dorset, and the author in 1901 of an illustrated article on "Thomas Hardy's Country."
3. Bhompston is a mile or so from Hardy's birthplace at Higher Bockhampton.
4. Sir George Douglas (1856–1935), Scottish landowner, author, and, from 1881, a friend of Hardy's.

came.) The Government have obtained possession, or use, of it, for camping purposes; & there are stones stuck about marked "W.D."[5] A strange vicissitude for a spot which, until now, has lain untouched since man appeared on the earth!

To Clement Shorter[6]
[June 4, 1908]

The bound MS. of *Tess* arrived this morning, so that they now all have come back. I am much obliged, & will send the MS. of the *Native* as I promised to do, as soon as I can get it dispatched to Dorchester Head Office for registry.

I have not written anything in it as you suggested, since I merely agreed in a mercenary spirit to do what you proposed—let you keep one MS. in consideration of your binding the others, & it would be affectation now to invent the fiction of a gift. I am quite content with the bargain, for all the MSS. would have remained in a state of wastepaper if you had not thought of doing this.

To Sir Frederick Macmillan[7]
[January 17, 1911]

The map of Wessex in the novels was first published in 1895, & is an extension of an idea I first used in The Return of the Native (1st edn 1878) to which was prefixed a map of Egdon Heath, the scene of the story.

As to the map being an authorized picture of where the localities really are, it is not precisely so, for though I certainly drew it, it was rather unwillingly done, owing to the constant inquiries of readers for the actual places. But I stated, I think, in one of the Prefaces at the time it was published, that the scenes of the stories were not guaranteed to be solidly standing where shown on the map, but were only suggested more or less by places that stood there, & fully existed nowhere but in the novels themselves.[8]

---

5. War Department; the war against South Africa (1899–1902) was still at its height.
6. Clement Shorter (1857–1926), journalist and editor, notably of the *Illustrated London News*. Shorter arranged for the binding of Hardy's manuscripts; in return, Hardy gave him that of *The Return of the Native* (now, by Shorter's bequest, in the library of University College, Dublin).
7. Frederick Macmillan (1851–1936), publisher, and personal friend; in 1902 Hardy transferred all his British rights to Macmillan & Co.
8. The map appeared in the Osgood, McIlvaine edition of the novels (1895–6); none of the Prefaces makes the point Hardy insists upon here.

To Florence Dugdale[9]
[April 22, 1912]

I am now on p. 140 of *The Woodlanders* (in *copy* I mean, not in proofs, of course). That is vol. vi. Some of the later ones will be shorter. I read ten hours yesterday—finishing the *proofs* of the *Native* (wh. I have thus got rid of).[1] I got to like the character of Clym before I had done with him. I think he is the nicest of all my heroes, and *not a bit* like me.

On taking up the Woodlanders & reading it after many years I think I like it, *as a story*, the best of all. Perhaps that is owing to the locality and scenery of the action, a part I am very fond of. It seems a more quaint and fresh story than the "Native" * * *

To Harold Child[2]
[November 11, 1920]

The Dorchester Dramatic Society is going to perform The Return of the Native next week. The dramatization is entirely the work of our respected Alderman, Mr Tilley—to whom I have given no assistance whatever, beyond letting him have the complete words of the old mumming play from which speeches are quoted in the novel.[3] How it will turn out I haven't an idea. They have got me to promise to go to the dress rehearsal, so I suppose I must. My wife takes a great deal of interest in the performance, & sends you her views * * *

To Florence Henniker[4]
[December 22, 1920]

Our Christmas threatens to be quite an old fashioned one. For some reason best known to themselves the Dorchester Mummers & carolsingers are coming here on Christmas night, & we have to entertain them after their performance. I wish you could see the mumming: it is an exact representation of the Dorset mumming of 100 years ago, as described in "The Return of the Native". (By the

9. Florence Dugdale (1879–1937); she and Hardy were married in February 1914.
1. Hardy was revising proofs for the 1912 Wessex edition, in which *The Return of the Native* was volume four.
2. Harold Child (1869–1945), drama critic; author of *Thomas Hardy* (1916), a critical study.
3. Hardy had hunted out a text of the mumming play two years earlier, in preparation for a "short entertainment" in Dorchester; this was later abandoned, following the signing of the armistice on November 11, 1918. For Hardy's text of the mumming play, see Peter Robson, "Thomas Hardy's Play of Saint George," *Lore and Language*, 17.1–2 (1999), pp. 257–271.
4. Florence Henniker (1855–1923), the most significant of a number of friends Hardy made among married, literary women in his later years.

way, the Company is going to London on Jan. 27 next week, & will perform the dramatization *including* the mumming before the Dorset Men in L. at the Guildhall School of Music, wherever that may be—so that you *could* see it if you wished.)

To Sir Frederick Macmillan
[May 17, 1923]

I have received the enclosed inquiry from the Société des Films Albatros, about their producing The Return of the Native. I don't remember that the novel has been used in this way as yet, but I know nothing of the Company. If you should have heard of them, and think them worth answering, would you kindly do so? The only consideration is of course a commercial one (there being nothing literary in films), and any good it may do in making the book known to readers, etc.[5]

To G. Herbert Thring[6]
[March 16, 1925]

The Return of the Native
Please let the lawyers do whatever they can in respect of the rendering of the above in Czecho-slovakian, at a 10 per cent fee. I have not parted with any rights over there, though strictly, I believe translators may appropriate freely any book that has been out more than ten years. But publishers like to have a sort of authorization.

From The Life and Work of Thomas Hardy†

[1874]
However, that he did not care much for a reputation as novelist in lieu of being able to follow the pursuit of poetry—now for ever

---

5. The Société des Films Albatros agreed a fee of £250 for the film rights to the novel, though it seems not to have been produced.
6. G. H. Thring was secretary to the Society of Authors. *The Return of the Native* had already been translated into Hungarian and French; a braille edition, for the use of the blind, appeared in 1919.
† Much of the last decade of Hardy's life was taken up with the preparation of the two volumes that appeared after his death as *The Early Life of Thomas Hardy 1840–91* (1928) and *The Later Years of Thomas Hardy* (1930), reissued in a one-volume edition in 1962 as *The Life of Thomas Hardy 1840–1928*. The title page states that the work was "compiled largely from contemporary notes, letters, diaries, and biographical memoranda, as well as from oral information in conversations extending over many years by Florence Emily Hardy," but although Florence continued to be listed as the author, it has long been known that the work is essentially a third-person autobiography, crafted by Hardy himself, before being typed up by Florence. The edition by Michael Millgate, *The Life and Work of Thomas Hardy, by Thomas Hardy* (London: Macmillan, 1984), seeks to recover the work as it stood at the time of Hardy's death, and to identify later additions,

hindered, as it seemed—becomes obvious from a remark written to Mr Stephen[1] about this time:

> The truth is that I am willing, and indeed anxious, to give up any points which may be desirable in a story when read as a whole, for the sake of others which shall please those who read it in numbers. Perhaps I may have higher aims some day, and be a great stickler for the proper artistic balance of the completed work, but for the present circumstances lead me to wish to be considered merely a good hand at a serial.

[1875]

One reflection about himself at this date sometimes made Hardy uneasy. He perceived that he was "up against" the position of having to carry on his life not as an emotion, but as a scientific game; that he was committed by circumstances to novel-writing as a regular trade, as much as he had formerly been to architecture; and that hence he would, he deemed, have to look for material in manners— in ordinary social and fashionable life as other novelists did. Yet he took no interest in manners, but in the substance of life only. So far what he had written had not been novels at all, as usually understood—that is pictures of modern customs and observances—and might not long sustain the interest of the circulating-library subscriber who cared mainly for these things. On the other hand, to go about to dinners and clubs and crushes as a business was not much to his mind. Yet that was necessary meat and drink to the popular author. * * * He mentioned this doubt of himself one day to Miss Thackeray,[2] who confirmed his gloomy misgivings by saying with surprise: "Certainly, a novelist must necessarily like society!"

[1875]

[F]inding himself committed to prose, he renewed his consideration of a prose style, as is evident from the following note:

> "Read again Addison, Macaulay, Newman, Sterne, De Foe, Lamb, Gibbon, Burke, Times Leaders, &c. in a study of style. Am more and more confirmed in an idea I have long held, as a

---

omissions, amendments, etc. At first glance the *Life* appears a casual and old-fashioned compilation, in the Victorian "life and letters" mode, but Hardy clearly took pains to provide a number of key statements about his work both as novelist and poet. Those of most interest to a reader of *The Return of the Native* are included here, along with the few direct references to the novel. Ellipses (. . .) are Hardy's; dates in square brackets have been added by the editor of this edition.

1. Leslie Stephen (1832–1904) was the editor of the *Cornhill Magazine*, which published Hardy's *Far from the Madding Crowd* and *The Hand of Ethelberta*; he declined *The Return of the Native*, fearing that it might not be suitable for a family magazine, but the two men remained on friendly terms.

2. Anne Thackeray Ritchie (1837–1919), daughter of the novelist William Makepeace Thackeray, and an entertaining novelist, memoirist, and essayist in her own right.

matter of commonsense, long before I thought of any old aphorism bearing on the subject: 'Ars est celare artem'[3] The whole secret of a living style and the difference between it and a dead style, lies in not having too much style—being—in fact, a little careless, or rather seeming to be, here and there. It brings wonderful life into the writing. * * * Otherwise your style is like worn half-pence—all the fresh images rounded off by rubbing, and no crispness or movement at all.

"It is, of course, simply a carrying into prose the knowledge I have acquired in poetry—that inexact rhymes and rhythms are now and then more pleasing than correct ones."

[1876]

"June 26. If it be possible to compress into a sentence all that a man learns between 20 & 40, it is that all things merge in one another—good into evil, generosity into justice, religion into politics, the year into the ages, the world into the universe. With this in view the evolution of species seems but a minute process in the same movement."

[1876]

" 'All is vanity', saith the Preacher.[4] But if all were only vanity, who would mind? Alas, it is too often worse than vanity; agony, darkness, death also."

"A man would never laugh were he not to forget his situation, or were he not one who has never learnt it. After risibility from comedy how often does the thoughtful mind reproach itself for forgetting the truth! Laughter always means blindness—either from defect, choice, or accident."

[1877]

"So, then, if Nature's defects must be looked in the face and transcribed, whence arises the *art* in poetry and novel-writing? which must certainly show art, or it becomes merely mechanical reporting. I think the art lies in making these defects the basis of a hitherto unperceived beauty, by irradiating them with 'the light that never was'[5] on their surface, but is seen to be latent in them with the spiritual eye."

---

3. "The art lies in concealing the art" (a familiar Latin tag, though of unknown origin).
4. See Ecclesiastes 1.2.
5. Quoting William Wordsworth, "Elegiac Stanzas, Suggested by a Picture of Peele Castle" (1807): "The light that never was, on sea or land, / The consecration, and the Poet's dream" (lines 15–16).

[1877]

"An object or mark raised or made by man on a scene is worth ten times any such formed by unconscious Nature. Hence clouds, mists, and mountains are unimportant beside the wear on a threshold, or the print of a hand."

[1877]

But his main occupation at Riverside Villa * * * was writing *The Return of the Native*. The only note he makes of its progress is that, on November 8, parts 3, 4, and 5 of the story were posted to Messrs Chatto and Windus for publication in (of all places) *Belgravia*[6]—a monthly magazine then running. Strangely enough, the rich alluvial district of Sturminster Newton in which the author was now living was not used by him at this time as a setting for the story he was constructing there, but the heath country twenty miles off. It may be mentioned here that the name "Eustacia" which he gave to his heroine was that of the wife of the owner of the manor of Ower-Moigne in the reign of Henry IV, which parish includes part of the "Egdon" Heath of the story * * * and that "Clement", the name of the hero, was suggested by its being borne by one of his supposed ancestors, Clement le Hardy, of Jersey, whose family migrated from that isle to the west of England at the beginning of the sixteenth century.

[1878]

"March 18. End of the Sturminster Newton idyll . . ." (The following is written in later)[7] "Our happiest time."

It was also a poetical time. Several poems in *Moments of Vision* contain memories of it, such as "Overlooking the River Stour", "The Musical Box", and "On Sturminster Foot-Bridge".

[1878]

"April—Note. A Plot, or Tragedy, should arise from the gradual closing in of a situation that comes of ordinary human passions, prejudices, and ambitions, by reason of the characters taking no trouble to ward off the disastrous events produced by the said passions, prejudices, and ambitions."

[1878]

"April 22.—The method of Boldini,[8] the painter of 'The Morning Walk' in the French Gallery two or three years ago (a young lady be-

6. For *Belgravia: an Illustrated Magazine*, see the note to Hardy's letter of August 28 1877 to Chatto and Windus on p. 377.
7. The parenthesis is Hardy's.
8. Giovanni Boldini (1842–1931), an Italian artist living in Paris, working mainly in a tepid academic style; his *The Morning Walk*, now in a private collection, is reproduced by J. B. Bullen in his *The Expressive Eye: Fiction and Perception in the Works of Thomas Hardy* (Oxford: Clarendon Press, 1986).

side an ugly blank wall on an ugly highway)—of Hobbema,[9] in his
view of a road with formal lopped trees and flat tame scenery—is
that of infusing emotion into the baldest external objects either by
the presence of a human figure among them, or by mark of some
human connection with them.

"This accords with my feeling about, say, Heidelberg and Baden
versus Scheveningen—as I wrote at the beginning of 'The Return of
the Native'—that the beauty of association is entirely superior to
the beauty of aspect, and a beloved relative's old battered tankard
to the finest Greek vase. Paradoxically put, it is to see the beauty in
ugliness."

[1878]

"September 30.—Returned and called on G[eorge] Smith.[1]
Agreed to his terms for publishing 'The Return of the Native'."

Shortly after he wrote to Messrs Smith and Elder:

> I enclose a sketch-map of the supposed scene in which 'The
> Return of the Native' is laid, copied from the one I used in
> writing the story; and my suggestion is that we place an en-
> graving of it as frontispiece to the first volume. Unity of place
> is so seldom preserved in novels that a map of the scene of the
> action is as a rule quite impracticable. But since the present
> story affords an opportunity of doing so I am of opinion that it
> would be a desirable novelty.[2]

The publishers fell in with the idea and the map was made. It
was adopted afterwards by R[obert] L[ouis] Stevenson in *Treasure
Island*.

[1878]

The Return of the Native was published by Messrs Smith and Elder in November, *The Times'* remark upon the book being that the
reader found himself taken further from the madding crowd than
ever. Old Mrs Procter's[3] amusing criticism in a letter was: "Poor
Eustacia. I so fully understand her longing for the Beautiful. I love

9. Meyndert Hobbema (1638–1709), Dutch landscape painter; the painting to which
Hardy refers, *The Avenue, Middelharnis*, in the National Gallery in London, is also reproduced in Bullen, *The Expressive Eye*.
1. George Smith, of Smith, Elder & Co., publishers of the three-volume edition of the
novel.
2. In the original letter, dated "Oct. 1. 1878", this sentence continues: " . . . likely to increase a reader's interest. I may add that a critic once remarked to me that nothing could
give such reality to a tale as a map of this sort: & I myself have often thought the same
thing." The critic was John Hutton, brother of Richard Holt Hutton, editor of the *Spectator*, whose review of the novel is included in this edition.
3. Anne Procter, née Skepper (1799–1888), widow of the poet B. W. Procter ("Barry Corn-
wall"), a well-known and well-liked literary hostess. The parenthesis identifying Mrs.
Procter's "stupid woman" as Thomasin is Hardy's.

the Common; but still one may wish for something else. I rejoice that Venn * * * is happy. A man is never cured when he loves a stupid woman [Thomasin]. Beauty fades, and intelligence and wit grow irritating; but your dear Dulness is always the same."

[1878]
"November 28. Woke before it was light. Felt that I had not enough staying power to hold my own in the world."

[1881]
"Style—consider the Wordsworthian dictum (the more perfectly the natural object is reproduced, the more truly poetic the picture). This reproduction is achieved by seeing into the *heart of a thing* (as rain, wind, for instance,) and is realism, in fact, though through being pursued by means of the imagination it is confounded with invention, which is pursued by the same means."

[1882]
"June 3rd . . . As, in looking at a carpet, by following one colour a certain pattern is suggested, by following another colour, another; so in life the seer should watch that pattern among general things which his idiosyncrasy moves him to observe, and describe that alone. This is, quite accurately, a going to Nature; yet the result is no photograph, but purely the product of the writer's own mind."

[1885]
"April 19th. The business of the poet and novelist is to show the sorriness underlying the grandest things, and the grandeur underlying the sorriest things."

[1885]
"Tragedy. It may be put thus in brief: a tragedy exhibits a state of things in the life of an individual which unavoidably causes some natural aim or desire of his to end in a catastrophe when carried out."

[1886]
"Jan 3. My art is to intensify the expression of things, as is done by Crivelli, Bellini,[4] &c. so that the heart and inner meaning is made vividly visible."

---

4. The work of both Carlo Crivelli (c. 1430–95), and Giovanni Bellini (c. 1430–1516), Venetian painters of the early Renaissance, was regarded as hard, primitive, or even grotesque, yet also admired as concentrated and expressive.

[1887]

"After looking at the landscape by Bonington[5] in our drawing-room * * * I feel that Nature is played out as a Beauty, but not as a Mystery. I don't want to see landscapes, i.e., scenic paintings of them, because I don't want to see the original realities—as optical effects, that is. I want to see the deeper reality underlying the scenic, the expression of what are sometimes called abstract imaginings.

"The 'simply natural' is interesting no longer. The much-decried, mad, late-Turner[6] rendering is now necessary to create my interest. The exact truth as to material fact ceases to be of importance in art—it is a student's style—the style of a period when the mind is serene and unawakened to the tragical mysteries of life; when it does not bring anything to the object that coalesces with and translates the qualities that are already there,—half-hidden, it may be— and the two united are depicted as the All."

[1888]

"Thought of the determination to enjoy. We see it in all of nature, from the leaf on the tree to the titled lady at the ball. . . . It is achieved, of a sort, under superhuman difficulties. Like pent-up water it will find a chink of possibility somewhere. Even the most oppressed of men and animals find it, so that out of a thousand there is hardly one who has not a sun of some sort for his soul."

"August 5. To find beauty in ugliness is the province of the poet."

[1888]

"If you look beneath the surface of any farce you see a tragedy; and, on the contrary, if you blind yourself to the deeper issues of a tragedy you see a farce."

[1889]

"April 7. A woeful fact—that the human race is too extremely developed for its corporeal conditions, the nerves being evolved to an activity abnormal in such an environment. Even the higher animals are in excess in this respect. It may be questioned if Nature, or what we call Nature, so far back as when she crossed the line from invertebrates to vertebrates, did not exceed her mission. This planet cannot supply the materials for happiness to higher existences. Other planets may, though one can hardly see how."

5. Richard Parkes Bonington (1802–28), English artist, best known for his restrained depictions of landscape; the work owned by the Hardys, *Landscape of Down and Stream*, is now lost.
6. The later paintings of J. M. W. Turner (1775–1851) are now much admired, but in the 1840s and 1850s attracted abuse and mockery for the extreme freedom with which he rendered effects of light and color.

[1890]

"August 5.—Reflections on Art. Art is a changing of the actual proportions and order of things, so as to bring out more forcibly than might otherwise be done that feature in them which appeals most strongly to the idiosyncrasy of the artist. * * *

"Art is a disproportioning—(i.e., distorting, throwing out of proportion) of realities, to show more clearly the features that matter in those realities, which, if merely copied or reported inventorially, might possibly be observed, but would more probably be overlooked. Hence 'realism' is not Art."

[1890]

"Dec. 18. Mr E. Clodd[7] this morning gives an excellently neat answer to my question why the superstitions of a remote Asiatic and a Dorset labourer are the same;—'The attitude of man,' he says, 'at corresponding levels of culture, before like phenomena, is pretty much the same, your Dorset peasant representing the persistence of the barbaric idea which confuses persons and things, and founds wide generalizations on the slenderest analogies.'

"(This 'barbaric idea which confuses persons and things' is, by the way, also common to the highest imaginative genius—that of the poet)."

[1892]

"Among the many stories of spell-working that I have been told the following is one of how it was done by two girls about 1830. They killed a pigeon, stuck its heart full of pins, made a tripod of three knitting-needles, and suspended the heart over them on a lamp, murmuring an incantation while it roasted, and using the name of the young man in whom one or both were interested. The said young man felt racking pains about the region of the heart, and suspecting something went to the constable. The girls were sent to prison."

[1892]

"Oct. 24. The best tragedy—highest tragedy in short—is that of the WORTHY encompassed by the INEVITABLE. The tragedies of immoral and worthless people are not of the best."

[1893]

"Feb. 23. A story must be exceptional enough to justify its telling. We tale-tellers are all Ancient Mariners,[8] and none of us is war-

---

7. Edward Clodd (1840–1930), banker, rationalist, and folklorist, who became one of Hardy's closest friends.
8. In Samuel Taylor Coleridge's poem, "The Rime of the Ancient Mariner" (1798), the

ranted in stopping Wedding Guests (in other words, the hurrying public) unless he has something more to relate than the ordinary experience of every average man and woman.

"The whole secret of fiction and the drama—in the constructional part—lies in the adjustment of things unusual to things eternal and universal. The writer who knows exactly how exceptional, and how non-exceptional, his events should be made, possesses the key to the art."

[1895]

"Tragedy may be created by an opposing environment either of things inherent in the universe, or of human institutions. If the former be the means exhibited and deplored, the writer is regarded as impious; if the latter, as subversive and dangerous; when all the while he may never have questioned the necessity or urged the non-necessity of either . . ."

[1896]

"Poetry. Perhaps I can express more fully in verse ideas and emotions which run counter to the inert crystallized opinion—hard as a rock—which the vast body of men have vested interests in supporting. To cry out in a passionate poem that (for instance) the Supreme Mover or Movers, the Prime Force or Forces, must be either limited in power, unknowing, or cruel—which is obvious enough, and has been for centuries—will cause them merely a shake of the head; but to put it in argumentative prose will make them sneer, or foam, and set all the literary contortionists jumping upon me, a harmless agnostic, as if I were a clamorous atheist, which in their crass illiteracy they seem to think is the same thing. . . . If Galileo[9] had said in verse that the world moved, the Inquisition might have left him alone."

[1897]

The change,[1] after all, was not so great as it seemed. It was not as if he had been a writer of novels proper, and as more specifically understood, that is, stories of modern artificial life and manners showing a certain smartness of treatment. He had mostly aimed, and mostly succeeded, to keep his narratives close to natural life, and as near to poetry in their subject as the conditions would allow,

---

Mariner compels a reluctant Wedding Guest to listen to the tale of the curse laid upon him for shooting an albatross.

9. In 1633 Galileo Galilei (1564–1642) was sentenced to life imprisonment for holding that the earth revolves around the sun. The Catholic Church conceded in 1992 that the theological advisers at the original trial might have been in error.

1. From prose to verse: Hardy's last novel, *The Well-Beloved*, was published in 1897, and his first volume of poems, *Wessex Poems*, in 1898.

and had often regretted that those conditions would not let him keep them nearer still.

[1920]

A friend of mine[2] writes objecting to what he calls my "philosophy" (though I have no philosophy—merely what I have often explained to be only a confused heap of impressions, like those of a bewildered child at a conjuring show). He says he has never been able to conceive a Cause of Things that could be less in any respect than the thing caused. This apparent impossibility to him, and to so many, has long ago been proved non-existent by philosophers, and is very likely owing to his running his head against a *Single* Cause, and perceiving no possible other. But if he would discern that what we call the First Cause should be called First Causes, his difficulty would be lessened. Assume a thousand unconscious causes—lumped together in poetry as one Cause, or God—and bear in mind that a coloured liquid can be produced by the mixture of colourless ones, a noise by the juxtaposition of silences, etc., etc., and you see that the assumption that intelligent beings arise from the combined action of unintelligent causes is sufficiently probable for imaginative writing, and I have never attempted scientific. It is my misfortune that people *will* treat all my mood-dictated writing as a single scientific theory.

Two Letters on Dialect in the Novel

Hardy's letter to the Athenaeum†

[Sir,—] A somewhat vexed question is reopened in your criticism of my story, *The Return of the Native*; namely, the representation in writing of the speech of the peasantry when that writing is intended to show mainly the character of the speakers, and only to give a general idea of their linguistic peculiarities.

An author may be said to fairly convey the spirit of intelligent peasant talk if he retains the idiom, compass, and characteristic expressions, although he may not encumber the page with obsolete pronunciations of the purely English words, and with mispronunciations of those derived from Latin and Greek. In the printing of

2. Alfred Noyes (1880–1958), poet, and in 1927 a convert to the Catholic Church. For Hardy's reply, insisting that the "Cause of Things . . . is neither moral nor immoral, but *un*moral," see *Letters*, VI.53–5.
† Several reviewers of *The Return of the Native* criticized the dialogue of the rustic characters, including the *Athenaeum*, which complained that "the talk seems pitched throughout in too high a key to suit the talkers." The first of the two pieces given here is Hardy's reply, in the following edition of the *Athenaeum*, on 30 November 1878.

standard speech hardly any phonetic principle at all is observed; and if a writer attempts to exhibit on paper the precise accents of a rustic speaker he disturbs the proper balance of a true representation by unduly insisting on the grotesque element; thus directing attention to a point of inferior interest, and diverting if from the speaker's meaning, which is by far the chief concern where the aim is to depict the men and their natures rather than their dialect forms.

Hardy's letter to the Spectator†

Sir,—In your last week's article on the *Papers of the Manchester Literary Club*, there seems a slight error, which, though possibly accidental, calls for a word of correction from myself. In treating of dialect in novels, I am instanced by the writer as one of two popular novelists "whose thorough knowledge of the dialectal peculiarities of certain districts has tempted them to write whole conversations which are, to the ordinary reader, nothing but a series of linguistic puzzles". So much has my practice been the reverse of this (as a glance at my novels will show), that I have been reproved for too freely translating dialect-English into readable English, by those of your contemporaries who attach more importance to the publication of local niceties of speech than I do. The rule of scrupulously preserving the local idiom, together with the words which have no synonym among those in general use, while printing in the ordinary way most of those local expressions which are but a modified articulation of words in use elsewhere, is the rule I generally follow; and it is, I believe, generally recognised as the best, where every such rule must of necessity be a compromise, more or less unsatisfactory to lovers of form. It must, of course, be always a matter for regret that, in order to be understood, writers should be obliged thus slightingly to treat varieties of English which are intrinsically as genuine, grammatical, and worthy of the royal title as is the all-prevailing competitor which bears it;[1] whose only fault was that they happened not to be central, and therefore were worsted in the struggle for existence, when a uniform tongue became a necessity among the advanced classes of the population.

---

† In October 1881, in an unsigned review in the *Spectator*, Hardy was criticized, as was the Scottish novelist George Macdonald, for excessive use of dialect; the second piece here is his reply to that criticism, in a letter to the *Spectator* (15 October 1881).

1. The use of the term "Queen's English" to designate approved or standard forms of speech seems to date from 1869. Hardy repeated elsewhere that the Dorset dialect was "a tongue, and not a corruption"; see for example his Preface to *Select Poems of William Barnes* (1908), reprinted in *Thomas Hardy's Public Voice: The Essays, Speeches, and Miscellaneous Prose*, ed. Michael Millgate (Oxford: Clarendon Press, 2001), pp. 291–97.

From The Profitable Reading of Fiction†

If it be true, as is frequently asserted, that young people nowadays go to novels for their sentiments, their religion, and their morals, the question as to the wisdom or folly of those young people hangs upon their methods of acquisition in each case. A deduction from what these works exemplify by action that bears evidence of being a counterpart of life, has a distinct educational value; but an imitation of what may be called the philosophy of the personages—the doctrines of the actors, as shown in their conversation—may lead to surprising results. They should be informed that a writer whose story is not a tract in disguise has as his main object that of characterizing the people of his little world. A philosophy that appears between the inverted commas of a dialogue may, with propriety, be as full of holes as a sieve if the person or persons who advance it gain any reality of humanity thereby. * * *

It may seem something of a paradox to assert that the novels which most conduce to moral profit are likely to be among those written without a moral purpose. But the truth of the statement may be realized if we consider that the didactic novel is so generally devoid of *vraisemblance*[1] as to teach nothing but the impossibility of tampering with natural truth to advance dogmatic opinion. Those, on the other hand, which impress the reader with the inevitableness of character and environment in working out destiny, whether that destiny be just or unjust, enviable or cruel, must have a sound effect, if not what is called a good effect, upon a healthy mind.

Of the effects of such sincere presentation on weak minds, when the courses of the characters are not exemplary, and the rewards and punishments ill adjusted to deserts, it is not our duty to consider too closely. A novel which does moral injury to a dozen imbeciles, and has bracing results upon a thousand intellects of normal vigor, can justify its existence; and probably a novel was never written by the purest-minded author for which there could not be found some moral invalid or other whom it was capable of harming.

From Candour in English Fiction‡

By a sincere school of Fiction we may understand a Fiction that expresses truly the views of life prevalent in its time, by means of a

† From Hardy's essay "The Profitable Reading of Fiction," first published in *Forum* (March 1888, pp. 57–70); reprinted in full in *Thomas Hardy's Personal Writings*, ed. Harold Orel (London: Macmillan, 1967), pp. 110–25, and in Millgate, *Hardy's Public Voice*, pp. 75–88.
1. Verisimilitude, likeness to reality.
‡ From Hardy's contribution to a symposium, "Candour in English Fiction," in the *New*

selected chain of action best suited for their exhibition. What are
the prevalent views of life just now is a question upon which it is
not necessary to enter further than to suggest that the most natural
method of presenting them, the method most in accordance with
the views themselves, seems to be by a procedure mainly impassive
in its tone and tragic in its developments.

Things move in cycles; dormant principles renew themselves,
and exhausted principles are thrust by. There is a revival of the
artistic instincts towards great dramatic motives—setting forth that
"collision between the individual and the general"[1] formerly worked
out with such force by the Periclean and Elizabethan dramatists, to
name no other. More than this, the periodicity which marks the
course of taste in civilised countries does not take the form of a
true cycle of repetition, but what Comte, in speaking of general
progress happily characterises as a "looped orbit:"[2] not a movement
of revolution but—to use the current word—evolution. Hence, in
perceiving now that taste is arriving anew at the point of high
tragedy, writers are conscious that its revived presentation demands
enrichment by further truths—in other words, original treatment:
treatment which seeks to show Nature's unconsciousness not of essential laws, but of those laws framed merely as social expedients
by humanity, without a basis in the heart of things; treatment
which expresses the triumph of the crowd over the hero, of the
commonplace majority over the exceptional few.

But originality makes scores of failures for one final success, precisely because its essence is to acknowledge no immediate precursor or guide. It is probably to these inevitable conditions of further
acquisition that may be attributed some developments of natural-
ism in French novelists of the present day, and certain crude results
from meritorious attempts in the same direction by intellectual ad-
venturers here and there among our own authors.

Anyhow, conscientious fiction alone it is which can excite a reflective and abiding interest in the minds of thoughtful readers of
mature age, who are weary of puerile inventions and famishing for
accuracy; who consider that in representations of the world, the
passions ought to be proportioned as the world itself. This is the interest which was excited in the minds of the Athenians by their im-

---

Review (January 1890, pp. 15–21); at the time, Hardy was struggling to shape *Tess
of the d'Urbervilles* into a form acceptable to publishers. The full text is given in
Orel *Hardy's Personal Writings*, pp. 125–33, and in Millgate, *Hardy's Public Voice*,
pp. 95–102.

1. Unidentified; perhaps an example of Hardy's willingness to put quotation marks around
words that are not strictly quoted.
2. See *Literary Notebooks*, I.76, where Hardy summarizes from Auguste Comte's *Cours de
philosophie positive* (1830–42), describing social progress as "like a 'looped orbit', sometimes apparently backwards, but really always forwards."

mortal tragedies, and in the minds of Londoners at the first performance of the finer plays of three hundred years ago. They reflected life, revealed life, criticised life. Life being a physiological
fact, its honest portrayal must be largely concerned with, for one
thing, the relations of the sexes, and the substitution for such catastrophes as favour the false colouring best expressed by the regulation finish that "they married and were happy ever after", of
catastrophes based upon sexual relationship as it is. To this expansion English society opposes a well-nigh insuperable bar.

The popular vehicles for the introduction of a novel to the public
have grown to be, from one cause and another, the magazine and
the circulating library; and the object of the magazine and the circulating library is not upward advance but lateral advance; to suit
themselves to what is called household reading, which means, or is
made to mean, the reading either of the majority in a household or
of the household collectively. The number of adults, even in a large
household, being normally two, and these being the members
which, as a rule, have least time on their hands to bestow on current literature, the taste of the majority can hardly be, and seldom
is, tempered by the right judgement which desires fidelity. However,
the immature members of a household often keep an open mind,
and they might, and no doubt would, take sincere fiction with the
rest but for another condition, almost generally co-existent: which
is that adults who would desire true views for their own reading insist, for a plausible but questionable reason, upon false views for
the reading of their young people.

As a consequence, the magazine in particular and the circulating
library in general do not foster the growth of the novel which reflects and reveals life. They directly tend to exterminate it by mo-
nopolising all literary space. * * * That the magazine and the
library have arrogated to themselves the dispensation of fiction is
not the fault of the authors, but of circumstances over which they,
as representatives of Grub Street,[3] have no control.

What this practically amounts to is that the patrons of literature—no longer Peers with a taste—acting under the censorship of
prudery, rigorously exclude from the pages they regulate subjects
that have been made, by general approval of the best judges, the
bases of the finest imaginative compositions since literature rose to
the dignity of an art. The crash of broken commandments is as necessary an accompaniment to the catastrophe of a tragedy as the
noise of drum and cymbals to a triumphal march. But the crash of
broken commandments shall not be heard; or, if at all, but gently,
like the roaring of Bottom—gently as any sucking dove, or as 'twere

3. The literary world, usually in a derogatory context.

any nightingale, lest we should fright the ladies out of their wits.[4] More precisely, an arbitrary proclamation has gone forth that certain picked commandments of the ten shall be preserved intact—to wit, the first, third, and seventh; that the ninth shall be infringed but gingerly; the sixth only as much as necessary; and the remainder alone as much as you please, in a genteel manner.[5]

From General Preface to the Novels and Poems†

It has sometimes been conceived of novels that evolve their action on a circumscribed scene—as do many (though not all) of these—that they cannot be so inclusive in their exhibition of human nature as novels wherein the scenes cover large extents of country, in which events figure amid towns and cities, even wander over the four quarters of the globe. I am not concerned to argue this point further than to suggest that the conception is an untrue one in respect of the elementary passions. But I would state that the geographical limits of the stage here trodden were not absolutely forced on the writer by circumstances; he forced them upon himself by judgement. I considered that our magnificent heritage from the Greeks in dramatic literature found sufficient room for its action in an extent of country not much larger than the half-dozen counties here reunited under the old name of Wessex, that the domestic emotions have throbbed in Wessex nooks with as much intensity as in the palaces of Europe, and that, anyhow, there was quite enough human nature in Wessex for one man's literary purpose. So far was I possessed by this idea that I kept within the frontiers when it would have been easier to overleap them and give more cosmopolitan features to the narrative.

Thus, though the people in most of the novels (and in much of the shorter verse) are dwellers in a province bounded on the north by the Thames, on the south by the English Channel, on the east by a line running from Hayling Island to Windsor Forest, and on the west by the Cornish coast, they were meant to be typically and essentially those of any and every place where

Thought's the slave of life, and life's time's fool[1]

---

4. Alluding to Shakespeare's *A Midsummer Night's Dream*, I.2.74–8.
5. See Exodus 20.1–17; in the order cited here, the commandments against idolatry, blasphemy and adultery; against bearing false witness; and against murder.
† The Preface, dated October 1911, appeared in Volume I of the Wessex Edition of 1912. It begins by distinguishing the novels as "Novels of Character and Environment," "Romances and Intrigues," and "Novels of Ingenuity." *The Return of the Native* is assigned to the first group.
1. From Hotspur's dying speech; see Shakespeare's *Henry IV, Part I*, V.4.80.

—beings in whose hearts and minds that which is apparently local should be really universal.

But whatever the success of this intention, and the value of these novels as delineations of humanity, they have at least a humble supplementary quality of which I may be justified in reminding the reader, though it is one that was quite unintentional and unforeseen. At the dates represented in the various narrations things were like that in Wessex; the inhabitants lived in certain ways, engaged in certain occupations, kept alive certain customs, just as they are shown doing in these pages. And in particularizing such I have often been reminded of Boswell's remarks on the trouble to which he was put and the pilgrimages he was obliged to make to authenticate some detail, though the labour was one which could bring him no praise.[2] Unlike his achievement, however, on which an error would as he says have brought discredit, if these country customs and vocations, obsolete and obsolescent, had been detailed wrongly, nobody would have discovered such errors to the end of Time. Yet I have instituted enquiries to correct tricks of memory, and striven against temptations to exaggerate, in order to preserve for my own satisfaction a fairly true record of a vanishing life.

It is advisable to state here, in response to inquiries from readers interested in landscape, prehistoric antiquities, and especially old English architecture, that the description of these backgrounds has been done from the real—that is to say, has something real for its basis, however illusively treated. * * *

One word on what has been called the present writer's philosophy of life. * * * Positive views on the Whence and Wherefore of things have never been advanced by this pen as a consistent philosophy. Nor is it likely, indeed, that imaginative writings extending over more than forty years would exhibit a coherent scientific theory of the universe even if it had been attempted—of that universe concerning which Spencer owns to the "paralyzing thought" that possibly there exists no comprehension of it anywhere.[3] But such objectless consistency never has been attempted, and the sentiments in the following pages have been stated truly to be mere impressions of the moment, and not convictions or arguments.

That these impressions have been condemned as "pessimistic"— as if that were a very wicked adjective—shows a curious muddle-mindedness. It must be obvious that there is a higher characteristic of philosophy than pessimism, or than meliorism, or even than the optimism of these critics—which is truth. Existence is either or-

---

2. James Boswell (1740–95) makes these remarks in the Advertisement to the first edition of his *The Life of Samuel Johnson* (1791).
3. The words may not be an exact quotation, but Herbert Spencer (1820–1903) does reach this conclusion in the section on "The Unknowable" in his *First Principles* (1862).

dered in a certain way, or it is not so ordered, and conjectures which harmonize best with experience are removed above all comparison with other conjectures which do not so harmonize. So that to say one view is worse than other views without proving it erroneous implies the possibility of a false view being better or more expedient than a true view; and no pragmatic proppings can make that *idolum specus*[4] stand on its feet, for it postulates a prescience denied to humanity.

And there is another consideration. Differing natures find their tongue in the presence of differing spectacles. Some natures become vocal at tragedy, some are made vocal by comedy, and it seems to me that to whichever of these aspects of life a writer's instinct for expression the more readily responds, to that he should allow it to respond. That before a contrasting side of things he remains undemonstrative need not be assumed to mean that he remains unperceiving.

---

4. Literally, "an idol of the cave"; used by Francis Bacon, Viscount St. Alban (1561–1626), in his *Novum Organum* to denote the confusion of an image of reality with the thing itself. Hardy Notebooks include this entry: "Bacon's striking image of the *Idola*, the 'shams' men fall down & worship" (*Literary Notebooks*, II.18).

CRITICISM

Contemporary Reception

Despite his professed indifference to the opinions of the critics, Hardy pasted a number of reviews of *The Return of the Native* into a scrapbook, which is now among the Hardy materials in the Dorset County Museum. These were from

Evening Standard, May 2 1878
Athenaeum, November 23 1878
The Observer, January 5 1879
The Daily Telegraph, December 3 1878
The Times, December 5 1878
Graphic, December 7 1878
Spectator, February 8 1879
London, November 23 1878
Liverpool Weekly Albion, January 10 1880
The Examiner, November 30 1878
Vanity Fair, November 30 1878
Saturday Review, January 4 1879
Academy, November 30 1878
Liverpool Mercury, December 16 1879
John Bull, November 30 1878

There were a number of other notices—for example, in the *Contemporary Review* and the *British Quarterly*, which Hardy either missed or chose not to collect, but they add little that was not said equally well elsewhere. Nor did the American reviewers, though the New York *Eclectic*, in March 1879, was unusually eloquent in its denunciation of Eustacia: "never, perhaps, at least in fiction, has beauty lent a certain baleful charm to a more thoroughly selfish, cruel, unprincipled, and despicable woman."

Some of the reviews were very slight, though even the briefest could carry a sting. The entry in the *Evening Standard* (written before serial publication of the novel had reached the halfway stage) reads in its entirety as follows:

> In *Belgravia* the distinguishing feature is still Mr Hardy's novel of "The Return of the Native". It possesses all his great power

of developing a plot of absorbing interest from what seems a restrictive basis, his concentrated power of expression, his massive style, and also his tedious love of tiresome commonplace characters.

The apparent contradiction, between interest in the plot and lack of interest in the characters who feature in it, was echoed in *The Times*, which was unsure whether to welcome or deplore the unfamiliar setting—unfamiliar, that is, to London reviewers and the London middle and upper class: "We are transported . . . into another world; and the fact is that we feel rather abroad there, and can scarcely get up a satisfactory interest in people whose history and habits are so entirely foreign to our own. Yet the story is a striking one, and well worth reading." The note of metropolitan disdain was sounded most clearly in the *Saturday Review*, which dismissed Eustacia as a "wayward and impulsive woman, essentially commonplace in her feelings and wishes," Clym as "a moonstruck dreamer," and Wildeve as "an underbred country clodhopper." Perhaps anticipating some such response, Hardy had gradually raised the social standing of his main characters as he worked on the novel: Eustacia's grandfather becomes a former Royal Navy Captain, Wildeve a one-time engineer, Clym the manager of a business rather than a jeweler's assistant, and so on. But evidently he had not done enough, and the critics who had rebuked him for writing about London life in his previous novel, *The Hand of Ethelberta*, on the grounds that he was too much an outsider to understand it, now complained that his world was too "foreign."

Such views reflect a tension in the way Victorian reviewers approached the novel. Typically they demanded "realism": a term variously defined, but essentially connoting plausible characters, a recognizable setting, and clearly motivated lines of action. But at the same time they sought agreeable characters, where possible a happy ending, and in any event a morally reassuring distribution of rewards and punishments. Hardy was widely supposed to have come closest to meeting these criteria in *Far from the Madding Crowd*, and readers and reviewers alike were prone to grumble when later novels took a different track. The *Graphic*, however, was more sympathetic: "To show to those who have eyes to see that this rural life, placid and somewhat humdrum as it may well look, viewed from afar off, contains within itself all the materials for tragedy, has been a chief aim of Mr Hardy in all his stories, and in none of them is this aim more marked than in the book before us." Hardy might have had these words in mind in 1887, when in the opening chapter of *The Woodlanders* he insisted that "sequestered spots, outside the gates of the world," no less than elsewhere, could

provide the arena for "dramas of a grandeur and unity truly Sopho-
clean." Hardy's fiction, like that of George Eliot and Elizabeth
Gaskell, was a further step toward the democratization of sympathy
that Wordsworth and Coleridge had hoped to foster in the *Lyrical
Ballads* (1798); but it was an achievement the reviewers were slow
to recognize.

The *Graphic* also admired the presentation of Eustacia, noting
that Hardy was "never happier than when revelling in emotional
subtleties." The *Observer* was similarly appreciative: "the whole
outcome of her flirtation, her passion, and her ill-balanced nature
is worked up with genuine dramatic force, allied to no small
amount of psychological discernment." So too the reviewer in *Vanity Fair*, for whom Eustacia was "one of the completest and best
studies of woman [sic] in literature." This praise was however severely qualified: Hardy "rarely gets at our emotions; he delights us,
but does not move us greatly." The same point was made by W. E.
Henley, writing in the *Academy*, who found Hardy's "sympathy with
his personages . . . rather intellectual than emotional," and more
sweepingly in *London*: "His sympathy is after all an intellectual and
not an emotional sympathy; you never cry over him and you never
laugh. . . . He regards his world from above; his men and women
are seen in bird's-eye view; and it is not as human beings but as
studies that they interest you." Similar comments were to be made
later about other Hardy novels; the exception was *Tess of the
d'Urbervilles* (1891), where he was criticized instead for being too
obviously and too deeply engaged with his central character.

To the reviewer in *John Bull*, *The Return of the Native* was the
kind of novel "only a very clever man could have written; but then
the cleverness is somewhat too obviously brought to our notice."
Cleverness, if not quite a vice, was at any rate less English than
French—a number of reviewers made comparisons with Balzac,
Flaubert, or Victor Hugo—as was the somber tone of the novel.
Hardy, complained the *London* reviewer, was like Balzac "a lover of
futile tragedy. . . . Is not life wretched enough as it is; and must an
author to be impressive invent accidents to make it still more so?"
The *Saturday Review* lamented Hardy's refusal to concede that "the
primary object of a story is to amuse"; for all its power, *The Return
of the Native* was not amusing. It was instead, thought Henley, in
words that summed up this line of criticism, "all very mournful,
and very cruel, and very French."

Three other aspects of the novel received a good deal of critical
notice. Most reviewers admired Hardy's powers of description, particularly in the opening chapter, but occasionally wondered if they
were not over-employed; the *Daily Telegraph* unkindly suggested
that the passages of "word-painting"—the painting analogy recurs

in a number of reviews—could usefully have been presented in a different type-face, to allow the reader to skip over them. Hardy's prose style too came in for some rough handling. To the *Saturday Review* it gave "the idea of a literary gymnast who is always striving after sensation in the form of some *tour de force*," the *Athenaeum* complained of "forced allusions and images," and *London* of what it saw as Hardy's tendency to spoil his effects by "the introduction of exaggerated circumstances, of an offensive personality, of an inopportune conceit." As Lennart Björk's edition of Hardy's *Literary Notebooks* makes clear, Hardy had undertaken an intensive course of reading in the year or so before beginning *The Return of the Native*; the results, to the reviewers at least, were all too often evident in the novel.

The rustic characters also attracted comment. Though sometimes applauded, they too came in for criticism, particularly in the *Athenaeum*: "People talk as no people ever talked before, or perhaps we should rather say as no people ever talk now. The language of his peasants may be Elizabethan, but it can hardly be Victorian." Hardy was sufficiently provoked to write to the *Athenaeum*, defending his handling of dialect, and his letter is given elsewhere in this edition. It was not enough, however, to dissuade Richard Hutton, in the *Spectator*, from raising the issue again. This was perhaps the most thoughtful review the novel was to receive, though Hutton objected to what he took to be its pessimism, arguing that Hardy's work "gives us the measure of human miserableness rather than grief." This review too is included here.

The reviews, then, were mixed, but not wholly unfavorable. Even where Hardy was criticized, he was for the most part being taken seriously, as a deliberate and significant artist, of unmistakable originality. To *Vanity Fair*, *The Return of the Native* was "one of the most remarkable books of the last twenty years. . . . Mr Hardy can be measured by the stature and power of no one else. He stands alone, imitating none, imitable by none." Even the most self-doubting of novelists might have settled for that.

Unsigned Review, *The Athenaeum*, 23 November 1878

Where are we to turn for a novelist? Mr Black[1] having commanded success, appears to be in some little danger of allowing his past performances to remain his chief title to deserving it; and now Mr

---

1. William Black (1841–1898) was admired as a novelist in the 1870s, in particular for his portraits of young women and powers of description; a number of Hardy's reviewers refer to his work.

Hardy, who at one time seemed as promising as any of the younger generation of story-tellers, has published a book distinctly inferior to anything of his which we have yet read. It is not that the story is ill-conceived—on the contrary, there are the elements of a good novel in it; but there is just that fault which would appear in the pictures of a person who has a keen eye for the picturesque without having learnt to draw. One sees what he means, and is all the more disappointed at the clumsy way in which the meaning is expressed. People talk as no people ever talked before, or perhaps we should rather say as no people ever talk now. The language of his peasants may be Elizabethan, but it can hardly be Victorian. Such phrases as "being a man of the mournfullest make, I was scared a little", or "he always had his great indignation ready against anything under-hand", are surprising in the mouth of the modern rustic. Indeed, the talk seems pitched throughout in too high a key to suit the talkers. A curious feature in the book is the low social position of the characters. The upper rank is represented by a young man who is assistant to a Paris jeweller, an innkeeper who has served his apprenticeship to a civil engineer, the daughter of a bandsman, and two or three of the small farmer class. These people all speak in a manner suggestive of high cultivation, and some of them intrigue almost like dwellers in Mayfair,[2] while they live on nearly equal terms with the furze-cutting rustics who form a chorus reminding one of "On ne badine pas avec l'amour."[3] All this is mingled with a great deal of description, showing a keen observation of natural things, though disfigured at times by forced allusions and images. The sound of reeds in a wind is likened to "sounds as of a congregation praying humbly".[4] A girl's recollections "stand like gilded uncials upon the dark tablet of her present surroundings".[5] The general plot of the story turns on the old theme of a man who is in love with two women, and a woman who is in love with two men; the man and the woman being both selfish and sensual. We use the last word in its more extended sense; for there is nothing in the book to provoke a comparison with the vagaries of some recent novelists, mostly of the gentler sex. But one cannot help seeing that the two persons in question know no other law than the gratification of their own passion, although this is not carried to the point which would place the book on the "Index"[6] of respectable house-

2. A fashionable part of London.
3. French: literally, "One does not joke about love."
4. Hardy had planned to use something like this image as early as 1871: "In Church. The sibilants in the responses of the congregation, who bend their heads like pine-trees in a wind." See *The Personal Notebooks of Thomas Hardy*, ed. Richard H. Taylor (London, 1979), p. 9.
5. Hardy seems to have taken this to heart: "uncials" becomes "letters" in later editions.
6. I.e., an Index of Prohibited Books, like those issued by the Catholic Church.

holds. At the same time it is clear that Eustacia Vye belongs essentially to the class of which Madame Bovary is the type[7]; and it is impossible not to regret, since this is a type which English opinion will not allow a novelist to depict in its completeness, that Mr Hardy should have wasted his powers in giving what after all is an imperfect and to some extent misleading account of it.

W. E. Henley,[8] *The Academy*, 30 November 1878

In Mr Hardy's work there is a certain Hugoesque[9] quality of insincerity; but there is withal so much to admire and be grateful for that it takes high rank among the good romantic work of the generation, and perhaps this quality of insincerity itself is more apparent than real. * * * Mr Hardy has such a right and masterful faculty of analysis; he perceives and apprehends his characters so completely; he has such a strong and poetic feeling for scenery; such a clear and vivid habit of description; he phrases so adequately and so lucidly, that, carried away by the consideration of these qualities, one fails to remember that his dialogue is only here and there dramatic in the highest sense; that there is much of what looks like affectation in his work; that his sympathy with his personages is rather intellectual than emotional; that he rarely makes you laugh and never makes you cry, and that his books are interesting and valuable as the outcome of a certain mind rather than as pictures of society or studies in human nature; that his tragedy is arbitrary and accidental rather than heroic and inevitable; and that, rare artist as he is, there is something wanting in his personality, and he is not quite a great man. In *The Return of the Native* * * * these defects and these merits are exampled pretty strongly, and the general impression it produces is the one I have tried to set down. The story is a sad one; but the sadness is unnecessary and uncalled for. A chapter of accidents makes the hero seem to cast off his mother, who thereupon dies; a second chapter of accidents sends the heroine to her death by drowning. And the hero, burdened by a double remorse, is left to live on, and to take what is substantially the place in the world he had desired ere destruction came upon him. It is all very cruel, and very mournful, and very French; and to those who have

---

7. *Madame Bovary* (1857), Gustave Flaubert's novel of small-town adultery, was both criticized and admired for its realism. The reviewer's comments here about "English opinion" anticipate Hardy's 1890 essay, "Candour in English Fiction" (see pp. 394–5 in this edition).

8. William Ernest Henley (1849–1903), critic, editor, dramatist, poet, and militant Tory. As editor of the *National Observer*, Henley first published the seduction scene in *Tess of the d'Urbervilles*, omitted when the novel appeared as a serial in the *Graphic*.

9. Victor-Marie Hugo (1802–85), French poet, dramatist, and novelist. English critics often objected that he sacrificed realism in the search for symbolic effects.

the weakness of liking to be pleasantly interested in a book it is also very disagreeable. Perhaps, too, it is false art; but of that, believing Mr Hardy to have a very complete theory about his books, I will not speak. To me, however, nearly all that is best in the novel is analytic and descriptive. I know of nothing in later English so striking and on the whole so sound as several pictures of Egdon Heath, or the introductory analysis in the character of Eustacia [Vye]. In these Mr Hardy is seen at his best and strongest. Acute, prescient, imaginative, insatiably observant, and at the same time so rigidly and so finely artistic that there is scarce a point in the whole that can be fairly questioned, he seems to me to paint the woman and the place as no other living writer could have done. Whether he makes the best use of them afterwards need not be here discussed. Nearly all the characters are, it should be added, of value and interest; Mrs Yeobright, I think being particularly to be commended. But so far as its dramatics are concerned *The Return of the Native* appears to be rather well meant than happily done. Such a speech as this, for instance, is admirable: "Well, then I spoke to her in my well-known merry way, and she said, 'O that what's shaped so venerable should talk like a fool!'—that's what she said to me. I don't care for her, be jowned if I do, and so I told her. 'Be jowned if I care for 'ee,' I said. I had her there—hey?"* * * And there are things as good as these of frequent occurrence; but they do not constitute what may be called the body of the comic dialogue, and the impression that it produces is, as a consequence, unsatisfactory. To turn to the tragic part is, I think, to have yet more room for sorrow; in one scene— the scene where Clym is informed of the way of his mother's death—Mr Hardy rises to the situation, and does nobly; but elsewhere he is only excessively clever, and earnest, and disappointing. But, in spite of these shortcomings, the novel is so clever and so strong that it excites both interest and admiration, and takes a first place among the novels of the season. Mr Hardy has, I ought to note, been at the pains of making a map of his locality, which should be consulted attentively, as it is of considerable use.

Unsigned Review, *The Saturday Review*, 4 January 1879

[T]here is a rising school of novelists, of which Mr Hardy is one of the ablest members, who seem to construct their fictions for themselves rather than for other people. It would be scarcely fair to say that they are dull; and they give us the fullest persuasion of a latent power which would enable them, as our ideas go, to write infinitely more agreeably if it pleased them. In one respect they resemble those fashionable and self-opinionated artists who embody their personal conceptions of art in forms that scandalize traditional opinions. In another respect, as we are glad to think, they differ from them very widely. For, whatever may be our estimate of their manner in the main, there is no denying the care they bestow upon their workmanship, and this is a thing to be grateful for in these days of slovenly writing. After all, however, we are brought round to the point we started from. We maintain that the primary object of a story is to amuse, and in the attempt to amuse us Mr Hardy, in our opinion, breaks down.* * * [H]is *Far from the Madding Crowd* was launched under favourable circumstances in a leading magazine, and—with reason—it won him a host of admirers. There may have been too much of the recurrence of marked mannerisms in it, with a good deal of what was hardly to be distinguished from affectation. But its characters were made living and breathing realities; there was a powerful love tale ingeniously worked out; the author showed a most intimate knowledge of the rural scenes he sympathetically described; and, above all, as is almost invariably his habit, he was quaintly humorous in the talk which he put into the mouths of his rustics. In this *Return of the Native* he has been less happy. The faults of *Far from the Madding Crowd* are exaggerated, and in the rugged and studied simplicity of its subject the story strikes us as intensely artificial. We are in England all the time, but in a world of which we seem to be absolutely ignorant; even a vague uncertainty hangs over the chronology. Every one of the people we meet is worked in as more or less of "a character"; and such coincidence of "originals", under conditions more or less fantastic, must inevitably be repugnant to our sense of the probable. Originality may very easily be overdone, especially when it is often more apparent than genuine. We need not say that Mr Hardy's descriptions are always vivid and often most picturesque. But he weakens rather than increases their force by going out of his way for eccentric forms of expression which are far less suggestive of his meaning than the everyday words he carefully avoids. His similes and metaphors are often strained and far-fetched; and his style gives one the idea of a literary gymnast who is always striving after sensation in the form of some *tour de force*. In his very names he is unreal and unlifelike; so much so that we doubt whether nine out of ten of them are to be met with in the pages of the London Directory. It is true that they may possibly be local for all we know to the contrary; and, if so, we may praise them as being in happy harmony with the theatrically local colouring of his fiction.

At the same time, having decided to write a story which should be out of the common, Mr Hardy has shown both discretion and

self-knowledge in the choice of its scene. It gives him ample opportunity for the display of his peculiar gifts and for the gratification of
his very pronounced inclinations, Egdon Heath is one of the
wildest spots in all England, and is situated among some of the
most sequestered of parishes. The people seem to know nothing of
high-roads or stage-coaches; there is nothing of a market-town in
the immediate vicinity where the men might brush up their bucoli-
cal brains by weekly gossip on a market-day; there is not a good-
sized village, and hardly even a hamlet. The inhabitants live chiefly
in lonely dwellings, where the snow heaps itself round the doors in
the dreary winter-time, and where they lie listening in their tem-
pestuous weather to the melancholy howling of the winds. The very
public-house stands by itself, and bears the quaint sign of "The
Quiet Woman", who is a lady carrying her head under her arm. So
that naturally we have the unadorned simplicity of nature in every
shape. There must have been landed proprietors, we presume, and
yet we hear nothing of a squire; while there is only incidental notice of a parson when some of the natives are joined together in
matrimony. The people above the class of labourers or paupers are
still in very humble stations, and for the most part extremely eccentric in their habits. There is a veteran captain of the merchant service who has come to moorings in his old age in a solitary cottage
in the middle of these desolate wastes, which give every convenient
facility for assignations to his beautiful granddaughter, who is one
of a pair of heroines. There is a Mrs Yeobright, who is tolerably
well-to-do and the mother of "the Native" whose return is chroni-
cled; and there is the innkeeper, Mr Wildeve, who is comparatively
rich, and who figures relatively as a man of the world and a gay and
fascinating Lothario.[1] It is of these somewhat unpromising materials that Mr Hardy has undertaken to weave his romance, and he
has so far overcome the initial difficulties by making his hero, "the
Native", with his leading heroine, superior by their natures to their
situation and surroundings. * * * [W]e are given to understand
that had their circumstances been different, or if fortune and ambition had served them better, they might have played a very different part in the grand drama of the world:

> Eustacia Vye was the raw material of a divinity. On Olympus
> she would have done well with a little preparation. She had the
> passions and instincts which make a model goddess—that is,
> those which make not quite a model woman. Had it been pos-
> sible for the earth and mankind to be entirely in her grasp for
> a while, had she handled the distaff, the spindle, and the

1. Term for a libertine, after the character in Nicholas Rowe's blank-verse tragedy *The Fair
Penitent* (1703).

shears at her own free will, few in the world would have noticed the change of government.

Again, "in Clym Yeobright's face could be dimly seen the typical
countenance of the future. Should there be a divine period to art
hereafter, its Phidias may produce such faces." Those natures of
élite tend towards each other instinctively. And when the lovers
have one of their meetings, after three short months of acquaintance, "they remained long without a single utterance, for no language could reach the level of their condition. Words were as the
rusty implements of a barbarous bygone epoch, and only occasionally to be tolerated." The harmony of ill-tutored minds so highly
pitched could hardly fail in a sensational novel to end in discord
and tragedy. Clym prevails on Eustacia to marry him; he loses
money and health, and sees his dreams of good fortune gradually
dissipated, while the brooding shadows of despondency fall thickly
on his domestic horizon. For Eustacia is equally disenchanted of
her expectations. She had given admiring devotion to her husband,
contrasting him with the boors about him; she had recognized the
superiority of his manners, acquirements, and intellect; but she
had looked, above all, to being introduced by him to the wonders of
the world, and to the dazzling delights of Parisian society. For before Clym is presented to us as "the Native" returning to his native
wilds he had been serving an apprenticeship as a shopman[2] in
Paris. But when Eustacia sees herself shut up with him in a lonely
cottage on that Egdon Heath of which she has grown so heartily
sick; when she sees him labouring to keep their bodies and souls
together by cutting furze and sods like a common day labourer;
when she sees him covering up his expressive eyes with spectacles;
and, in short, when she is settling down to the monotony of penury,
feeling at the same time that she might have done far better for
herself, then she decides to take leave of the world. With "her soul
in an abyss of desolation seldom plumbed by one so young", she
quits her home to strike across the moors, "occasionally stumbling
over twisted furze-roots, tufts of rushes, or oozing lumps of fleshy
fungi, which at this season lay scattered about the heath like the
rotting liver and lungs of some colossal animal", and seeks a refuge
from her troubles in a deed of desperation. She and her husband,
and her admirer, Damon Wildeve, all have a meeting at last in the
gloomy waters; and the crowning horror of a succession of sombre
descriptions is in the search for senseless bodies in Shadwater
Weir. Unfortunately, our sympathies have never been strongly en-
listed in any of the three. Even the style of Eustacia's beauty is so

2. Hardy progressively raised Clym's status from "assistant" in a shop to "Manager to a diamond merchant."

vaguely and transcendentally described that it neither wins our hearts nor takes our fancy. For the rest she is a wayward and impulsive woman, essentially commonplace in her feelings and wishes, who compromises herself by vulgar indiscretions. Thus she bribes a country lad to help her by permitting him to hold her hand for fifteen minutes, although she knows that he exacts those terms because he has fallen hopelessly in love with her. Damon Wildeve, the innkeeper, although in a measure idealized in a doubtful atmosphere of romance, is in reality an underbred country clodhopper who plumes himself on his substance and gentility, and an education superior to that of his neighbours; while Clym Yeobright is a moon-struck dreamer, who seems singularly out of place among the eminently practical population of Egdon.

Still, we would not be misunderstood, nor would we wish to do Mr Hardy injustice. We think he has been injudicious in his invention of characters, and that he has deliberately prepared disappointment for us in his method of treatment, if he aimed at making his story in any way realistic. But, as usual, there are dialogues of true and quaint humour, which have never been rivalled by any writer of the present day, and which remind one of Dogberry and Verges;[3] and there are many *tableaux* of wild and powerful picturesqueness. Take, for example, the opening scene, where the whole of the barren country on a dreary November night is kindling to the blaze of roaring bonfires; when we are introduced to the old-fashioned parishioners of Egdon, crowding round the pyramid of furze, thirty feet in circumference, that crowns the summit of the tumulus of Blackbarrow; and there, in his description of the excited little mob, we have some of Mr Hardy's most distinctive touches:

> All was unstable: quivering as leaves, evanescent as lightning. Shadowy eye-sockets, deep as those of a death's head, suddenly turned into pits of lustre; a lantern jaw was cavernous, then it was shining; wrinkles were emphasized to ravines, or obliterated entirely by a changed ray. Nostrils were dark wells; sinews in old necks were grotesque mouldings; things with no particular polish in them were glazed; bright objects—such as the tip of a furze-hook one of the men carried—were as glass; eye-balls glowed like little lanterns. Those whom Nature had depicted as merely quaint became grotesque, the grotesque became preternatural—for all was in extremity.

Or again, when the fair and stately Eustacia Vye steals through the darkness of the night into the glowing reflection of the balefire to keep an appointment with Wildeve, who was then paying his court to her; or when Wildeve, in his wretchedness and recklessness,

3. The bumbling constables in Shakespeare's play *Much Ado about Nothing.*

later in the story, sits down to gamble by lantern-light on the lonely moors with an enemy and rival, who has thrown himself into the game with all the rancour of inveterate hatred. They are scared by spectral shadows falling across the stone table and the dice, which turn out to come from a gang of moorland ponies. When the lantern is extinguished by a great death's-head moth, they replace it with the handful of glow-worms that they gather, and the wild game goes on, in its alternations of triumph and despair, till Wildeve loses his last sovereign. This scene has striking vividness and power. There can be no doubt that Mr Hardy has no ordinary talent; and we regret the more that he should not condescend to human frivolity, and exert his unquestionable powers in trying to be more natural and entertaining. We dare say the effort would soon come easily to him, and then our gratitude might give him less stinted praise.

Unsigned Review, *The Spectator*, 8 February 1879[4]

The Return of the Native is a story of singular power and interest— very original, very gloomy, very great in some respects, though these respects are not the highest—and from beginning to end in the highest degree vivid. But there is one great defect in almost all of Mr Hardy's books, which reappears here, that the strange figures of his Wessex peasantry, though full of picturesque and humorous elements, are never so presented that the reader is able to accept them as true pictures of rustic life even on these wild moors; and in *The Return of the Native* there is one other great defect peculiar to itself, that the book, which is meant to be tragic in its gloom, and would assuredly be tragic but for a tendency, which we attribute to the sombre fatalism of the author, to lower appreciably below the truth the whole tone and significance of human destiny, treats tragedy itself as hardly more than a deeper tinge of the common leaden-colour of the human lot, and so makes it seem less than tragedy—dreariness, rather than tragedy—by making human passion in general commonplace and poor. These are the two leading defects of a book of brilliant talent, even of high genius here and there, especially in the touches which describe the life and spirit of the great heath; and also of very considerable power of plot.

We will try and make clear what we mean in relation to both points, and yet illustrate at the same time the great ability of the

---

4. Unsigned, but almost certainly by Richard Holt Hutton (1826–97), theologian and man of letters, editor and joint proprietor of the *Spectator* from 1861 until his death, and author of some 1500 reviews of contemporary fiction.

story. Mr Hardy makes the talk of his Wessex peasants, as we have said, most amusing and original; but he constantly slips in touches that show him to be painting something compounded of his knowledge of the most original rustics of the class, and of the kind of reflections on them which he himself would probably indulge in. * * * And this is the general fault in the rustic elements of his books. We almost always find ideas and words more or less belonging to the stratum of comparative culture, blending with the ideas and words of rough and superstitious ignorance; and the mingling of the two bewilders and confuses the reader of his books, till he finds it impossible to determine what odd *tertium quid*[5] it is that Mr Hardy has created in his imagination, which is neither rustic nor critic, but something halfway between the two. * * *

To illustrate our second criticism, that Mr Hardy's gloomy fatalism lowers the effect of his tragedy, by lowering almost all of the passion and sentiment of the book to something rather near the same dead-level of dreary light, or not much more than dreary shade, it is necessary to quote some passages illustrative of Mr Hardy's general creed;

> In Clym Yeobright's face could be dimly seen the typical countenance of the future. Should there be a divine period to art hereafter, its Phidias may produce such faces. The view of life as a thing to be put up with, replacing that zest for existence which was so intense in early civilizations, must ultimately enter so thoroughly into the constitution of the advanced races, that its facial expression will become accepted as a new artistic departure. People already feel that a man who lives without disturbing a curve of feature, or setting a mark of mental concern anywhere upon himself, is too removed from perceptiveness to be a modern type. Physically beautiful men—the glory of the race when it was young—are almost an anachronism now; and we may wonder whether, at some time or other, physically beautiful women may not be an anachronism likewise. The truth seems to be that a long line of disillusive centuries has permanently displaced the Hellenic idea of life, or whatever it may be called. What the Greeks only suspected we know well; what their Aeschylus imagined our nursery children feel. That old-fashioned revelling in the general situation grows less and less possible as we uncover the defects of natural laws, and the quandary that man is in by their operation.[6]

5. Literally, "third thing": neither one thing nor the other.
6. The review goes on to quote the paragraph beginning: "He did sometimes think he had been ill-used by fortune," in the opening chapter of "Book Sixth: Aftercourses."

All this pessimism, of which Mr Hardy speaks with the calm confidence of one who has found Schopenhauer[7] far superior to all the prophets and seers, tells upon his picture of human character and destiny. His coldly passionate heroine, Eustacia Vye, never reproaches herself for a moment with the inconstancy and poverty of her own affections. On the contrary, she has no feeling that anything which happens within her, has relation to right and wrong at all, or that such a thing as responsibility exists. This state of feeling lowers sensibly the glow of her love, when she is in love, and makes her even in its highest moments forecast clearly its rapid decay; and then again, when the decay comes, and she has lost the love which made her so happy, she is not remorseful, but only dull, in its loss. Hence, in her case, we never really reach the point of tragedy at all. Tragedy is almost impossible to people who feel and act as if they were puppets of a sort of fate. Tragedy gives us the measure of human greatness, and elevates us by giving it in the very moment when we sound the depth of human suffering. Mr Hardy's tragedy seems carefully limited to gloom. It gives us the measure of human miserableness, rather than of human grief—of the incapacity of man to be great in suffering, or in anything else, rather than of his greatness in suffering. The death of Mrs Yeobright—the mother of the hero—is gloom in its deepest intensity; and even her son's excruciating self-reproaches, though they at least have plenty of remorse in them, are too little softened by religious feeling or anything else to express anything but misery. Mr Hardy refuses to give us what, even without any higher worlds of feeling, would have raised this alienation of son and mother into tragedy—the mutual recognition of mother and son, and the recognition of their misunderstanding, before her death. The hero's agony is pure, unalloyed misery, not grief of the deepest and noblest type, which can see a hope in the future and repent the errors of the past. And so it is with the other features of the tale. Eustacia's inability to tell whether she really loves her husband or not, whether she really loves Wildeve or not, and Wildeve's inability to tell whether he really loves his wife or not—whether his passion for Eustacia is nothing but jealousy of another man—and the death which overtakes them both when on a doubtful errand, concerning which neither of them is quite certain whether it is to be innocent or not—all these are characteristics of a peculiar imaginative mood—a mood in which there seems to be no room for freedom, no great heights, no great depths in human life, only the ups and downs of a dark necessity, in which men play the parts of mere offsprings of the physical universe, and are governed by forces and tides no less inscrutable.

7. Arthur Schopenhauer (1788–1860), philosopher; Hardy owned a copy of his *The World as Will and Idea* (1819, but not available in English until 1883), and in 1891 made notes on his *Studies in Pessimism*.

Unsigned Review, *Harper's New Monthly Magazine*,[8] March 1879

Mr Hardy's *Return of the Native* is a descriptive and emotional novel of more than average artistic merit, which is chiefly displayed by a succession of powerful scenes and skillful or striking contrasts. His descriptions of the scene of the story, Egdon Heath, as night and mist are settling on its barren ruggedness, and the surrounding gloom is made to seem blacker and more impenetrable by the huge fires of furze which its denizens have lighted on its central barrow, have many of the features of Rembrandt's paintings of fire-light, camp-light, and torch-light scenes, and, like them, the deep shadows of these artificial lights operate to invest a grim and commonplace reality with a romance that is fruitful of shuddering fancies and creeping half-fears. In this production, as in his *Far from the Madding Crowd*, Mr Hardy introduces a large body of actors belonging to the class of English peasantry, and their manners, customs, humors, amusements, superstitions, and dialect colloquies are reproduced with picturesque effect. Nearly all the characters belong to these primitive people, one of the exceptions being the admirably painted heroine Eustacia Vye, an exotic from a more advanced state of society, who has been planted on this unattractive wild and among its simple folk by circumstances which she could not control, and against which she unceasingly rebels, and whose nature is a singular compound of contradictions—of fierceness and gentleness, resolution and vacillation, love and inconstancy, coldness and passion, strength and weakness. The other exception is one of her lovers, Wildeve, another waif from the outside world, who is a bundle of petty attractions and foibles, sufficient, however, to find grace in her eyes. The subordinate figures, especially those of Mrs Yeobright, Diggory Venn, and "Charley", are scarcely less engaging than the central ones. The story is powerfully scenic rather than dramatic. While many of its scenes might be represented upon the stage singly with great effectiveness, they are not knit closely enough together by the tie of a controlling interest, they contribute too slightly to the progress of the plot, and the influence which they exert upon the catastrophe is too remote or inconsiderable to render the story, as a whole, capable of successful dramatization or representation. Nevertheless, it is delightful reading.

---

8. Harper & Brothers had published the serial version of *The Return of the Native* in America; they also held the American rights for volume publication, but relinquished these to Henry Holt, to Hardy's regret.

Modern Criticism

D. H. LAWRENCE

Study of Thomas Hardy†

This is supposed to be a book about the people in Thomas Hardy's novels. But if one wrote everything they give rise to it would fill the Judgement Book.

One thing about them is that none of the heroes and heroines care very much for money, or immediate self-preservation, and all of them are struggling hard to come into being. What exactly the struggle into being consists in, is the question. But most obviously, from the Wessex novels, the first and chiefest factor is the struggle into love and the struggle with love: by love, meaning the love of a man for a woman and a woman for a man. The via media to being, for man or woman, is love, and love alone. Having achieved and accomplished love, then the man passes into the unknown. He has become himself, his tale is told. Of anything that is complete there is no more tale to tell. The tale is about becoming complete, or about the failure to become complete.

It is urged against Thomas Hardy's characters that they do unreasonable things—quite, quite unreasonable things. They are always going off unexpectedly and doing something that nobody would do. That is quite true, and the charge is amusing. These people of Wessex are always bursting suddenly out of bud and taking a wild flight into flower, always shooting suddenly out of a tight convention, a tight, hide-bound cabbage state into something quite

† D. H. Lawrence (1885–1930) conceived the *Study of Thomas Hardy* in July 1914, and wrote and then re-wrote it during the early months of the Great War, though it was not published till after his death. In part an argument with himself, as Lawrence pondered issues he was to explore further in *The Rainbow* and *Women in Love*, the *Study* is also an account of the way Hardy imagines the self in relation to what Lawrence elsewhere calls "the circumambient universe," and of Hardy as a tragic and religious writer. Chapter III, reproduced here, was first published separately in 1932; the *Study* as a whole was first published in 1936 in Lawrence's *Phoenix*. The text used here, including the sometimes erratic punctuation, is that established by Bruce Steele in his edition of *The Study of Thomas Hardy and Other Essays* (Cambridge: Cambridge University Press, 1985) and is reprinted with the permission of Cambridge University Press. Notes are by the editor of this Norton Critical Edition.

madly personal. It would be amusing to count the number of special marriage licenses taken out in Hardy's books. Nowhere, except perhaps in Jude, is there the slightest development of personal action in the characters: it is all explosive. Jude, however, does see more or less what he is doing, and act from choice. He is more consecutive. The rest explode out of the convention. They are people each with a real, vital, potential self, even the apparently wishy-washy heroines of the earlier books, and this self suddenly bursts the shell of manner and convention and commonplace opinion, and acts independently, absurdly, without mental knowledge or acquiescence.

And from such an outburst the tragedy usually develops. For there does exist, after all, the great self-preservation scheme, and in it we must all live. How to live in it after bursting out of it was the problem these Wessex people found themselves faced with. And they never solved the problem, none of them except the comically-, insufficiently-, treated Ethelberta.

This because they must subscribe to the system in themselves. From the more immediate claims of self-preservation they could free themselves: from money, from ambition for social success. None of the heroes or heroines of Hardy cared much for these things. But there is the greater idea of self-preservation, which is formulated in the State, in the whole modelling of the community. And from this idea, the heroes and heroines of Wessex, like the heroes and heroines of almost anywhere else, could not free themselves. In the long run, the State, the Community, the established form of life remained, remained intact and impregnable, the individual, trying to break forth from it, died of fear, of exhaustion, or of exposure to attacks from all sides, like men who have left the walled city to live outside in the precarious open.

This is the tragedy of Hardy, always the same: the tragedy of those who, more or less pioneers, have died in the wilderness, whither they had escaped for free action, after having left the walled security, and the comparative imprisonment, of the established convention. This is the theme of novel after novel: remain quite within the convention, and you are good, safe, and happy in the long run, though you never have the vivid pang of sympathy on your side: or, on the other hand, be passionate, individual, wilful, you will find the security of the convention a walled prison, you will escape, and you will die, either of your own lack of strength to bear the isolation and the exposure, or by direct revenge from the community, or from both. This is the tragedy, and only this: it is nothing more metaphysical than the division of a man against himself in such a way: first, that he is a member of the community, and must, upon his honour, in no way move to disintegrate the community, either in its moral or its practical form; second, that the convention of the community is a prison to his natural, individual desire, a desire that compels him, whether he feel justified or not, to break the bounds of the community, lands him outside the pale, there to stand alone, and say: "I was right, my desire was real and inevitable; if I was to be myself I must fulfil it, convention or no convention", or else, there to stand alone, doubting, and saying: "Was I right, was I wrong? If I was wrong, oh, let me die!"—in which case he courts death.

The growth and the development of this tragedy, the deeper and deeper realisation of this division and this problem, the coming towards some conclusion, is the one theme of the Wessex novels.

And therefore the books must be taken chronologically, to reveal the development and to advance towards the conclusion. * * *

6. *The Return of the Native.*

This is the first tragic and important novel. Eustacia, dark, wild, passionate, quite conscious of her desires and inheriting no tradition which would make her ashamed of them, since she is of a novelistic Italian birth, loves first, the unstable Wildeve, who does not satisfy her, then casts him aside for the newly returned Clym, whom she marries. What does she want? She does not know, but it is evidently some form of self-realisation; she wants to be herself, to attain herself. But she does not know how, by what means, so romantic imagination says Paris and the beau monde.[1] As if that would stay her unsatisfaction.

Clym has found out the vanity of Paris and the beau monde. What then does he want? He does not know, his imagination tells him he wants to serve the moral system of the community, since the material system is despicable. He wants to teach little Egdon boys in school. There is [as] much vanity in this, easily, as in Eustacia's Paris. For what is the moral system but the ratified form of the material system? What is Clym's altruism but a deep very subtle cowardice, that makes him shirk his own being whilst apparently acting nobly; which makes him choose to improve mankind rather than to struggle at the quick of himself into being. He is not able to undertake his own soul, so he will take a commission for society to enlighten the souls of others. It is a subtle equivocation. Thus both Eustacia and he side-track from themselves, and each leaves the other unconvinced, unsatisfied, unrealised. Eustacia because she moves outside the convention, must die, Clym because he identified himself with the community, is transferred from Paris to

1. The fashionable world.

preaching. He had never become an integral man, because when faced with the demand to produce himself, he remained under cover of the community and excused by his altruism.

His remorse over his mother is adulterated with sentiment, it is exaggerated by the push of tradition behind it. Even in this he does not ring true. He is always according to pattern, producing his feelings more or less on demand, according to the accepted standard. Practically never is he able to act or even feel in his original self: he is always according to the convention. His punishment is his final loss of all his original self: he is left preaching, out of sheer emptiness.

Thomasin and Venn have nothing in them turbulent enough to push them to the bounds of the convention. There is always room for them inside. They are genuine people, and they get the prize within the walls.

Wildeve, shifty and unhappy, attracted always from outside and never driven from within, can neither stand with or without the established system. He cares nothing for it, because he is unstable, has no positive being. He is an eternal assumption.

The other victim, Clym's mother, is the crashing-down of one of the old, rigid pillars of the system. The pressure on her is too great. She is weakened from the inside also, for her nature is non-conventional; it cannot own the bounds.

So, in this book, all the exceptional people, those with strong feelings and unusual characters, are reduced, only those remain who are steady and genuine, if commonplace. Let a man will for himself, and he is destroyed. He must will according to the established system.

The real sense of tragedy is got from the setting. What is the great, tragic power in the book?—it is Egdon Heath. And who are the real spirits of the Heath?—first Eustacia, then Clym's mother, then Wildeve. The natives have little or nothing in common with the place.

What is the real stuff of tragedy in the book? It is the Heath. It is the primitive, primal earth, where the instinctive life heaves up. There, in the deep, rude stirring of the instincts, there was the reality that worked the tragedy. Close to the body of things, there can be heard the stir that makes us and destroys us. The [earth] heaved with raw instinct, Egdon whose dark soil was strong and crude and organic as the body of a beast. Out of the body of this crude earth are born Eustacia, Wildeve, Mistress Yeobright, Clym, and all the others. They are one year's accidental crop. What matter if some are drowned or dead, and others preaching or married: what matter, any more than the withering heath, the reddening berries, the seedy furze, and the dead fern of one autumn of Egdon. The Heath persists. Its body is strong and fecund, it will bear many more crops beside this. Here is the sombre, latent power that will go on producing, no matter what happen to the product. Here is the deep, black source from whence all these little contents of lives are drawn. And the contents of the small lives are spilled and wasted. There is savage satisfaction in it: for so much more remains to come, such a black, powerful fecundity is working there that what does it matter!

Three people die and are taken back into the Heath, they mingle their strong earth again with its powerful soil, having been broken off at their stem. It is very good. Not Egdon is futile, sending forth life on the powerful heave of passion. It cannot be futile, for it is eternal. What is futile is the purpose of man.

Man has a purpose which he has divorced from the passionate purpose that issued him out of the earth, into being. The Heath threw forth its shaggy heather and furze and fern, clean into being. It threw forth Eustacia and Wildeve and Mistress Yeobright and Clym, but to what purpose? Eustacia thought she wanted the hats and bonnets of Paris. Perhaps she was right. The heavy, strong soil of Egdon, breeding original native beings, is under Paris as well as under Wessex, and Eustacia sought herself in the gay city. She thought life there, in Paris, would be tropical, and all her energy and passion out of Egdon would there come into handsome flower. And if Paris real had been Paris as she imagined it, no doubt she was right, and her instinct was soundly expressed. But Paris real was not Eustacia's imagined Paris. Where was her imagined Paris, the place where her powerful nature could come to blossom? Beside some strong-passioned, unconfined man, her mate.

Which mate Clym might have been. He was born out of passionate Egdon to live as a passionate being whose strong feelings moved him ever further into being. But quite early his life became narrowed down to a small purpose: he must of necessity go into business, and submit his whole being, body and soul as well as mind, to the business and to the greater system it represented. His feelings, that should have produced the man, were suppressed and contained, he worked according to a system imposed from without. The dark struggle of Egdon, a struggle into being as the furze struggles into flower, went on in him, but could not burst the enclosure of the idea, the system which contained him. Impotent to *be*, he must transform himself, and live in an abstraction, in a generalisation, he must identify himself with the system. He must live as Man or Humanity, or as the Community, or as Society, or as Civilisation. "An inner strenuousness was preying on his outer symmetry, and they rated his look as singular——His countenance was overlaid with legible meanings. Without being thought-worn, he yet had certain marks derived from a perception of his surroundings, such as are not unfrequently found on men at the end of the four or five years of endeavour which follow the close of placid pupilage. He already showed that thought is a disease of the flesh, and indirectly bore evidence that ideal physical beauty is incompatible with emotional development and a full recognition of the coil of things. Mental luminousness must be fed with the oil of life, even if there is already a physical seed for it; and the pitiful sight of two demands on one supply was just showing itself here."[2]

But did the face of Clym show that thought is a disease of flesh, or merely that in his case a dis-ease, an un-ease of flesh produced thought. One does not catch thought like a fever: one produces it. If it be in any way a disease of flesh, it is rather the rash that indicates the disease, than the disease itself. The "inner strenuousness" of Clym's nature was not fighting against his physical symmetry, but against the limits imposed on his physical movement. By nature, as a passionate, violent product of Egdon, he should have loved and suffered in flesh and in soul from love, long before this age. He should have lived and moved and had his being, whereas he had only his business, and afterwards his inactivity. His years of pupilage were past, "he was one of whom something original was expected", yet he continued in pupilage. For he produced nothing original in being or act, and certainly no original thought. None of his ideas were original. Even he himself was not original. He was over-taught, had become an echo. His life had been arrested, and his activity turned into repetition. [Far] from being emotionally developed, he was emotionally undeveloped, almost entirely. Only his mental faculties were developed. And his emotions were obliged to work according to the label he put upon them: a ready-made label.

Yet he remained for all that an original, the force of life was in him, however much he frustrated and suppressed its natural movement. "As is usual with bright natures, the deity that lies ignominiously chained within an ephemeral human carcase shone out of him like a ray."[3] But was the deity chained within his ephemeral human carcase, or within his limited human consciousness? Was it his blood, which rose dark and potent out of Egdon, which hampered and confined the deity, or was it his mind, that house built of extraneous knowledge and guarded by his will, which formed the prison.

He came back to Egdon—what for? To re-unite himself with the strong, free flow of life that rose out of Egdon as from a source? No—"to preach to the Egdon eremites that they might rise to a

2. Quoting from Book II, Chapter VI.
3. Quoting from Book II, Chapter VI.

serene comprehensiveness without going through the process of enriching themselves."[4] As if the Egdon eremites had not already far more serene comprehensiveness than ever he had himself, rooted as they were in the soil of all things, and living from the root. What did it matter how they enriched themselves, so long as [they] kept this strong, deep root in the primal soil, so long as their instincts moved out to action and to expression. The system was big enough for them, and had not power over their instincts. They should have taught him rather than he them.

And Egdon made him marry Eustacia. Here was action and life, here was a move into being on his part. But as soon as he got her, she became an idea to him, she had to fit in his system of ideas. According to his way of living, he knew her already, she was labelled and classed and fixed down. He had got into this way of living, and he could not get out of it. He had identified himself with the system, and he could not extricate himself. He did not know that Eustacia had her being beyond him. He did not know that she existed untouched by his system and his mind, where no system had sway and where no consciousness had risen to the surface. He did not know that she was Egdon, the powerful, eternal origin seething with production. He thought he knew. Egdon to him was the tract of common land, producing familiar rough herbage, and having some few unenlightened inhabitants. So he skated over heaven and hell, and having made a map of the surface, thought he knew all. But underneath and among his mapped world, the eternal powerful fecundity worked on heedless of him and his arrogance. His preaching, his superficiality made no difference. What did it matter if he had calculated a moral chart from the surface of life? Could that affect life, any more than a chart of the heavens affects the stars, affects the whole stellar universe which exists beyond out knowledge? Could the sound of his words affect the working of the body of Egdon, where in the unfathomable womb was begot and conceived all that would ever come forth. Did not his own heart beat far removed and immune from his thinking and talking. Had he been able to put even his own heart's mysterious resonance upon his map, from which he charted the course of lives in his moral system? And how much more completely, then, had he left out in utter ignorance, the dark, powerful source whence all things rise into being, whence they will always continue to rise, to struggle forward to further being. A little of the static surface he could see, and map out. Then he thought his map was the thing itself. How blind he was, how utterly blind to the tremendous movement carrying and producing the surface. He did not know that the greater

4. Quoting from Book III, Chapter II.

part of every life is underground, like roots in the dark in contact with the beyond. He preached thinking lives could be moved like hen-houses from here to there. His blindness indeed brought on the calamity. But what matter if Eustacia or Wildeve or Mrs. Yeobright died: what matter if he himself became a mere rattle of repetitive words—what did it matter? It was regrettable, no more. Egdon, the primal impulsive body would go on producing all that was to be produced, eternally, though the will of man should destroy the blossom yet in bud, over and over again. At last he must learn what it is to be at one, in his mind and will, with the primal impulses that rise in him. Till then let him perish or preach. The great reality on which the little tragedies enact themselves cannot be detracted from. The will and words which militate against it are the only vanity.

This is a constant revelation in Hardy's novels: that there exists a great background, vital and vivid, which matters more than the people who move upon it. Against the background of dark, passionate Egdon, of the leafy, sappy passion and sentiment of the woodlands, of the unfathomed stars, is drawn the lesser scheme of lives: *The Return of the Native*, *The Woodlanders*, or *Two on a Tower*. Upon the vast, incomprehensible pattern of some primal morality greater than ever the human mind can grasp, is drawn the little, pathetic pattern of man's moral life and struggle, pathetic almost ridiculous. The little fold of law and order, the little walled city within which man has to defend himself from the waste enormity of nature becomes always too small, and the pioneers venturing out with the code of the walled city upon them, die [confined] in the bonds of that code, free and yet unfree, preaching the walled city and looking to the waste.

This is the wonder of Hardy's novels, and gives them their beauty. The vast, unexplored morality of life itself, what we call the immorality of nature, surrounds us in its eternal incomprehensibility, and in its midst goes on the little human morality play, with its queer frame of morality and its mechanised movement; seriously, portentously, till some one of the protagonists chance to look out of the charmed circle, weary of the stage, to look into the wilderness raging round. Then he is lost, his little drama falls to pieces, or becomes mere repetition, but the stupendous theatre outside goes on enacting its own incomprehensible drama, untouched. There is this quality in almost all Hardy's work, and this is the magnificent irony it all contains, the challenge, the contempt. Not the deliberate ironies, little tales of widows or widowers, contain the irony of human life as we live it in our self-aggrandised gravity, but the big novels, *The Return of the Native*, and the others.

And this is the quality Hardy shares with the great writers,

Shakespeare or Sophocles or Tolstoi, this setting behind the small action of his protagonists the terrific action of unfathomed nature, setting a smaller system of morality, the one grasped and formulated by the human consciousness within the vast, uncomprehended and incomprehensible morality of nature or of life itself, surpassing human consciousness. The difference is, that whereas in Shakespeare or Sophocles the greater, uncomprehended morality, or fate, is actively transgressed and gives active punishment, in Hardy and Tolstoi the lesser, human morality, the mechanical system is actively transgressed, and holds, and punishes the protagonist, whilst the greater morality is only passively, negatively transgressed, it is represented merely as being present in background, in scenery, not taking any active part, having no direct connection with the protagonist. Oedipus, Hamlet, Macbeth set themselves up against, or find themselves set up against the unfathomed moral forces of nature, and out of this unfathomed force comes their death. Whereas Anna Karenin, Eustacia, Tess, Sue, and Jude find themselves up against the established system of human government and morality, they cannot detach themselves, and are brought down. Their real tragedy is that they are unfaithful to the greater unwritten morality, which would have bidden Anna Karenin be patient and wait until she, by virtue of greater right, could take what she needed from society; would have bidden Vronsky detach himself from the system, become an individual, creating a new colony of morality with Anna; would have bidden Eustacia fight Clym for his own soul, and Tess take and claim her Angel, since she had the greater light; would have bidden Jude and Sue endure for very honour's sake, since one must bide by the best that one has known, and not succumb to the lesser good.

Had Oedipus, Hamlet, Macbeth been weaker, less full of real, potent life, they would have made no tragedy: they would have comprehended and contrived some arrangement of their affairs, sheltering in the human morality from the great stress and attack of the unknown morality. But, being as they are, men to the fullest capacity, when they [find] themselves daggers drawn with the very forces of life itself, they can only fight till they themselves are killed, since the morality of life, the greater morality, is eternally unalterable and invincible. It can be dodged for some time, but not opposed. On the other hand, Anna, Eustacia, Tess or Sue—what was there in their position that was necessarily tragic? Necessarily painful it was, but they were not at war with God, only with Society. Yet they were all cowed by the mere judgement of man upon them, and all the while by their own souls they were right. And the judgement of men killed them, not the judgement of their own souls, or the judgement of Eternal God.

Which is the weakness of modern tragedy, where transgression against the social code is made to bring destruction, as though the social code worked our irrevocable fate. Like Clym, the map appears to us more real than the land. Short sighted almost to blindness, we [pore] over the chart, map out journeys, and confirm them: and we cannot see life giving us the lie the whole time.

DONALD DAVIDSON

The Traditional Basis of Thomas Hardy's Fiction†

* * *

There was a real intellectual distance between Hardy and the critics—indeed, between Hardy and almost three generations of critics. The critics had not so much underrated—or overrated—Hardy as missed him, in somewhat the same way as, in our opinion, Dr. Johnson missed John Donne. When we look over the impressive list of those who have made literary pronouncements in Hardy's time and ours, they do not seem to be the kind of people who would have affinity with Hardy. From George Meredith, his first literary adviser, up to T. S. Eliot, one can hardly think of a critic whose view of Hardy's work, however well-intentioned, would not be so external as to set up a gross incongruity like what we find in Marxian criticisms of Shakespeare.

Possibly the critics have been most in error in not realizing the comparative isolation of Hardy in modern literary history. Misled by the superficial resemblance between his work and the product current in their day, they have invariably attempted to treat him as a current author—or at least as a queer blend of tendencies receding and tendencies coming on. They have been further misled by Hardy's own attempt (not always happy) to shape his work into a marketable form or to bring it up to what he conceived to be a good current literary standard. For Hardy seems to have had little idea of being an innovator or an iconoclast. He sought to please and entertain, and perhaps to instruct, and he must have been amazed to find himself now acclaimed, now condemned, as heretic.

The appearance of Thomas Hardy among the temporal phenomena of the England of 1870 to 1928—that is the amazing, the confusing thing. I believe we ought to begin consideration by admitting that though Hardy was *in* that time, and was affected by its thought

† From "The Traditional Basis of Thomas Hardy's Fiction," *Southern Review* 6 (Summer, 1940): 163–78. Reprinted by permission of Louisiana State University Press. Notes are by the editor of this Norton Critical Edition.

and art, he was not really *of* that time whenever he was his essential self. It is not enough to say that Hardy is "old-fashioned" or "quaint." Certainly he did not try consciously to be old-fashioned. Although there are archaisms of language in his poetry and prose, and much general display of the antique in subject matter, there is nowhere in Hardy the affectation of archaism (found in such ironic romanticists as Cabell)[1] or the deliberate exploitation of archaism (found in a great many of the literary specialties offered in America). The old-fashioned quality in Hardy is not in the obvious places, but lies deeper. It is in the habit of Hardy's mind rather than in "folk-lore" or the phenomena of language and style.

Hardy wrote, or tried to write, more or less as a modern—modern, for him, being late nineteenth century. But he thought, or artistically conceived, like a man of another century—indeed, of a century that we should be hard put to name. It might be better to say that he wrote like a creator of tales and poems who is a little embarrassed at having to adapt the creation of tales and poems to the conditions of a written, or printed, literature, and yet tries to do his faithful best under the regrettable circumstances. He is not in any sense a "folk author," and yet he does approach his tale-telling and poem-making as if three centuries of Renaissance effort had worked only upon the outward form of tale and poem without changing its essential character. He wrote as a ballad-maker would write if a ballad-maker were to have to write novels; or as a bardic or epic poet would write if faced with the necessity of performing in the quasi-lyrical but non-singable strains of the nineteenth century and later.

Hardy is the only specimen of his genus in modern English literature, and I do not know how to account for him. He has no immediate predecessors; and though he has some imitators, no real followers as yet. For his habit of mind has seemingly disappeared in England, and threatens to disappear in America; and without the habit of mind to begin with no real following can be done. I am almost ready to characterize Hardy (if he must be "placed") as an American whose ancestors failed to migrate at the proper time and who accordingly found himself stranded, a couple of centuries later, in the wrong literary climate. In this connection it is amusing to remember that Hardy has been charged with borrowing a description from Augustus Baldwin Longstreet's *Georgia Scenes* for use in *The Trumpet Major*.[2] The truth is that his general affiliation

---

1. James Branch Cabell (1879–1958), novelist, from Richmond, Virginia; best known for his ironic fantasy *Jürgen* (1919).
2. Augustus Longstreet (1790–1870), American writer and humorist. The drilling scene in Chapter XXIII of *The Trumpet-Major* (1880) derived indirectly from Longstreet's *Georgia Scenes* (1835).

with the frontier humorists of the Old Southwest is a good deal more discernible than his affiliation with Victorian romantic-realists or with French Naturalists. It is an organic affiliation, not a literary attachment, because the Southwestern humorists drew their art, such as it was, from the same kind of source that Hardy used, and wrote (when they had to write) under the same embarrassment. If Hardy's distant seventeenth-century progenitor had migrated to America at the time of the Monmouth Rebellion[3]—as some of his progenitor's relatives and many of his neighbors did, in all haste, migrate, then Thomas Hardy might easily have been a frontier humorist of the Longstreet school. And then he would never have been accused of pessimism, though he might, to be sure, have caused eyebrows to lift in Boston.

*   *   *

Hardy was born early enough—and far enough away from looming Arnoldian or Marxian influences—to receive a conception of art as something homely, natural, functional, and in short traditional. He grew up in a Dorset where fiction was a tale told or sung; and where the art of music, always important to him, was primarily for worship or merriment. The Hardys, up through the time of Thomas Hardy's father, were "church-players" of the type of the Mellstock Choir—performers on the violin, cello, and bass who adhered to a traditional psalmody and instrumental performance (of which echoes are preserved here today in the music of the "shape note" singers of the South). Thomas Hardy, as a child, was "extraordinarily sensitive to music." He danced to "the endless jigs, horn-pipes, reels, waltzes, and country-dances" that his own father played and, without knowing why, was contradictorily moved to tears by some of the tunes. Later he himself could "twiddle from notation some hundreds of jigs and country-dances that he found in his father's and grandfather's old books"—he was an "oldtime fiddler." Young Thomas played the fiddle at weddings and in farmer's parlors. On one occasion he bowed away for a solid three-quarters of an hour while twelve tireless couples danced to a single favorite tune. At one notable harvest-home he heard the maids sing ballads. Among these Hardy remembered particularly "The Outlandish Knight"—a Dorset version of the ballad recorded by Child[4] as "Lady Isabel and the Elf Knight."

And of course he must have heard, in time, many another ballad, if we may make a justifiable inference from the snatches of balladry in the novels and tales, and if Dorset was the kind of countryside

---

3. The supporters of James, Duke of Monmouth (1649–1685), many of them from the southwestern counties of England, faced severe penalties, including execution and transportation, following his unsuccessful rebellion against James II in 1685.
4. The American scholar Francis J. Child (1825–96) collected and published five volumes of *English and Scottish Popular Ballads* (1882–98).

we are led to think it to be. Mrs. Hardy would have us believe that upon the extension of the railway to Dorset in the middle nineteenth century "the orally transmitted ballads were slain at a stroke by the London comic songs," but she underestimates the vitality of folk art. As late as 1922, one R. Thurston Hopkins published a book entitled *Thomas Hardy's Dorset*, in which he tells how he found a singing blacksmith at Lyme Regis, in Devon. Hopkins gives the blacksmith's song, but evidently does not know enough of balladry to recognize it. It is a perfectly good version of the ballad known as "Mollie Vaughn" or "Mollie Bond."

For what it may be worth I note that Hardy first conceived *The Dynasts* as a ballad, or group of ballads. In May, 1875, he wrote in his journal:

> Mem: A Ballad of the Hundred Days. Then another of Moscow. Others of earlier campaigns—forming altogether an Iliad of Europe from 1789 to 1815.

This, Mrs. Hardy says, is the first mention in Hardy's memoranda of the conception later to take shape in the epic drama. Again, on March 27, 1881, Hardy referred to his scheme: "A Homeric Ballad, in which Napoleon is a sort of Achilles, to be written."

To evidence of this kind I should naturally add the following facts: that Hardy wrote a number of ballads, like "The Bride-Night Fire," and ballad-like poems; that his poems like his novels are full of references to old singers, tunes, and dances, and that many of the poems proceed from the same sources as his novels; that he is fond of inserting in his journals, among philosophizings and other memoranda, summaries of anecdotes or stories he has heard. Of the latter sort is the following entry:

> Conjurer Mynterne when consulted by Patt P. (a strapping handsome young woman), told her that her husband would die on a certain day, and showed her the funeral in a glass of water. . . . She used to impress all this on her inoffensive husband, and assure him that he would go to hell if he made the conjurer a liar. He didn't, but died on the day foretold.

Such notations should not be unduly emphasized. Yet they appear in his journal with such frequency that we are justified in assuming Hardy's special interest in such material. On the other hand, in the record of Hardy's life thus far available to us, there is little evidence to indicate that, in devising the greater stories, he had some specific literary model before him, or was trying out some theory of fiction, or had, at the beginning of his conception, a particular philosophical or social thesis. Critics may show that such and such a literary induence reached him, or that a theory or philosophy ultimately engaged his mind; but I cannot believe that such elements controlled the original conception or determined the essential character of the greater novels and stories. The poetry offers a somewhat different field of critical speculation, which I do not propose to enter, but it seems worth while to argue that his characteristic habit of mind, early established and naturally developed, has much to do with certain peculiarities of his fiction.

My thesis is that the characteristic Hardy novel is conceived as a *told* (or *sung*) story, or at least not as a literary story; that it is an extension, in the form of a modern prose fiction, of a traditional ballad or an oral tale—a tale of the kind which Hardy reproduces with great skill in *A Few Crusted Characters* and less successfully in *A Group of Noble Dames*; but, furthermore, that this habit of mind is a rather unconscious element in Hardy's art. The conscious side of his art manifests itself in two ways: first, he "works up" his core of traditional, or nonliterary narrative into a literary form; but, second, at the same time he labors to establish, in his "Wessex," the kind of artistic climate and environment which will enable him to handle his traditional story with conviction—a world in which typical ballad heroes and heroines can flourish with a thoroughly rationalized "mythology" to sustain them. The novels that support this thesis are the great Hardy novels: *Under the Greenwood Tree, Far from the Madding Crowd, The Mayor of Casterbridge, The Return of the Native, The Woodlanders,* and *Tess of the D'Urbervilles*—in other words, the Wessex novels proper. *Jude the Obscure* and *The Trumpet Major* can be included, with some reservations, in the same list. The novels that do not support this thesis are commonly held to be, by comparison with those named above, of inferior quality: *The Hand of Ethelberta* and *A Laodicean,* for example. These are Hardy's attempt to be a fully modern—and literary—novelist.

The fictions that result from Hardy's habit of mind resemble traditional, or nonliterary, types of narrative in many ways. They are always conceived of as stories primarily, with the narrative always of foremost interest. They have the rounded, often intricate plot and the balance and antithesis of characters associated with traditional fiction from ancient times. It is natural, of course, that they should in such respects resemble classic drama. But that does not mean that Hardy thought in terms of dramatic composition. His studies in Greek (like his experience in architecture) simply reinforced an original tendency. The interspersed descriptive elements—always important, but not overwhelmingly important, in a Hardy novel—do not encumber the narrative, as they invariably do in the works of novelists who conceive their task in wholly literary terms; but they blend rather quickly into the narrative. Action, not description, is always foremost; the event dominates, rather than motive, or psy-

chology, or comment. There is no loose episodic structure. Hardy
does not write the chronicle novel or the biographical novel. Nor
does he build up circumstantial detail like a Zola or a Flaubert.

Hardy has an evident fondness for what we might call the "country
story"—the kind of story *told* by the passengers in the van in *A Few
Crusted Characters*; or *sung* in ballads of the type attributed by scholars to the seventeenth and eighteenth century and sometimes called
"vulgar" ballads to distinguish them from the supposedly more genuine "popular" ballads of an earlier day. In *Under the Greenwood
Tree*, the coquettish behavior of Fancy Day is a delicate feminine parallel to the difficulties of Tony Kytes, the Arch-deceiver, related in *A
Few Crusted Characters*. The coy maiden, after involvement with the
solid farmer Shiner and the excellent Vicar, rejects them both at last
for the brisk young country lad, Dick Dewy. Gabriel Oak, in *Far from
the Madding Crowd*, is the "faithful lover" of many a ballad, who has
many of the elements of a masculine "patient Griselda"; he endures a
kind of "testing" not irretrievably remote from the testings that ladies
put upon their lovers in romances and ballads; and he is also obviously the excellent lover of "low degree" who aims his affections high
and is finally rewarded. Fanny Robin, of the same novel, is a typical
deserted maiden, lacking nothing but a turtledove on her tombstone;
or perhaps she is the more luridly forsaken girl found in "Mary of the
Wild Moor." Her lover, Sergeant Troy, is the soldier (or sailor) of any
number of later ballads. And it is worth remarking, in this connection, that Hardy's fondness for soldiers has everywhere in it the echo
of many ballads about the military composed in the half-century or
more preceding his birth and even in his own time. It flavors strongly,
that is, of such pieces as "Polly Oliver," "Bold Dighton," "High Germany," and "Bloody Waterloo."[5]

The Return of the Native gives us far more complexity, but many
of its focal incidents are of the stuff in which tale-tellers and
ballad-makers delight. Mrs. Yeobright is bitten by a snake; Eustacia
and Wildeve are drowned in one pool, to make a simultaneous romantic death, and we almost expect to learn that they were buried
in the old churchyard and presently sprouted—a rose from her
breast, a briar from his. We should not forget that Eustacia disguises herself in man's clothing (as heroines of traditional stories
have long done) for the mummers' play.

*   *   *

The high degree of coincidence in the typical Hardy narrative
has been noted by all observers, often unfavorably. Mr. Samuel
Chew[6] explains it as partly a result of the influence of the "sensa-

5. Popular ballads of the eighteenth and nineteenth centuries, sung in America as well as
in Britain.
6. See Samuel Chew, *Thomas Hardy: Poet and Novelist* (1921).

tion novelists," and partly as a deliberate emphasis on "the persistence of the unforeseen"[7]—hence a grim, if exaggerated, evidence of the sardonic humor of the purblind Doomsters. Let us pay this view all respect, and still remember that such conscious and artful emphasis may be only a rationalization of unconscious habit. The logic of the traditional story is not the logic of modern literary fiction. The traditional story admits, and even cherishes, the improbable and unpredictable. The miraculous, or nearly miraculous, is what makes a story a story, in the old way. Unless a story has some strange and unusual features it will hardly be told and will not be remembered. Most of the anecdotes that Hardy records in his journal savor of the odd and unusual. And occasionally he speaks directly to the point, as in the following passages:

> The writer's problem is, how to strike the balance between the uncommon and the ordinary, so as on the one hand to give interest, on the other to give reality.
>
> In working out this problem, human nature must never be abnormal, which is introducing incredibility. The uncommonness must be in the events, not in the characters . . . (July, 1881).
>
> A story must be exceptional enough to justify its telling. We tale-tellers are all Ancient Mariners, and none of us is warranted in stopping Wedding Guests (in other words, the hurrying public) unless he has something more unusual to relate than the ordinary experience of every average man and woman.

Thus coincidence in Hardy's narratives represents a conviction about the nature of story as such. Hardy's world is of course not the world of the most antique ballads and folk tales—where devils, demons, fairies, and mermaids intervene in human affairs, and ghosts, witches, and revenants are commonplace. It is a world like that of later balladry and folk tale, from which old beliefs have receded, leaving a residue of the merely strange. Improbability and accident have replaced the miraculous. The process is illustrated in the ballad "Mollie Vaughn" (sometimes Van, Bond, or Baun), in which the speaker, warning young men not to go shooting after sundown, tells how Mollie was shot by her lover. I quote from an American version recorded by Louise Pound:

> Jim Random was out hunting, a-hunting in the dark;
> He shot at his true love and missed not his mark.
> With a white apron pinned around her he took her for a swan,
> He shot her and killed her, and it was Mollie Bond.

In many versions, even the American ones, Mollie's ghost appears in court and testifies, in her lover's behalf, that the shooting

---

7. See the final sentence of *The Mayor of Casterbridge*.

was indeed accidental. But the ballad very likely preserves echoes, misunderstood by a later generation, of an actual swan maiden and her lover. This particular ballad is certainly unusual in admitting the presence of a ghost in a court of law. But at least the apparition is a ghost, not a swan maiden, and so we get the event rationalized in terms of an unlikely but not impossible accident: he saw the apron and "took her for a swan."

Hardy's coincidences may be explained as a similar kind of substitution. He felt that the unlikely (or quasi-miraculous) element belonged in any proper story—especially a Wessex story; but he would go only so far as the late ballads and country tales went, in substituting improbabilities for supernaturalisms. Never does he concoct a pseudo-folk tale like Stephen V. Benét's "The Devil and Daniel Webster."[8] Superstitions are used in the background of his narrative; coincidence, in the actual mechanics. Tess hears the legend of the D'Urberville phantom coach, but does not actually see it, though the moment is appropriate for its appearance. In *The Return of the Native* Susan Nonesuch pricks Eustacia Vye for a witch and later makes a waxen image of her, just before her drowning; but coincidence, not superstition, dominates the action. Henchard visits the conjurer just before his great speculation in grain, but only out of habit and in half-belief; and it is coincidence that makes Farfrae a winner just at the moment when Henchard is a loser. The supernatural, in Hardy, is allowed in the narrative, but in a subordinate position; the quasi-miraculous takes its place in the main position.

If we use a similar approach to the problem of Hardy's pessimism, it is easy to see why he was irritated by insensitive and obtuse critics. Are the ballad stories of "Edward," "Little Musgrave," and "Johnnie Armstrong" pessimistic? Were their unknown authors convinced of the fatal indifference of the Universe toward human beings? Should we, reading such stories, take the next step in the context of modern critical realism and advocate psychoanalysis for Edward's mother and social security for Johnnie Armstrong? In formal doctrine Hardy professed himself to be an "evolutionary meliorist," or almost a conventional modern. But that had nothing to do with the stories that started up in his head. The charge of pessimism has about the same relevance as the charge of indelicacy which Hardy encountered when he first began to publish. An age of polite literature, which had lost touch with the oral arts—except so far as they might survive in chit-chat, gossip, and risqué stories— could not believe that an author who embodied in his serious stories the typical seductions, rapes, murders, and lusty lovemakings

8. Stephen Vincent Benet (1898–1943), American poet and novelist.

of the old tradition intended anything but a breach of decorum. Even today, I suppose, a group gathered for tea might be a little astonished if a respectable old gentleman in spats suddenly began to warble the outrageous ballad of Little Musgrave. But Hardy did not know he was being rough, and had no more notion than a ballad-maker of turning out a story to be either pessimistic or optimistic.

To be sure, Hardy is a little to blame, since he does moralize at times. But the passage about the President of the Immortals in *Tess* and about the persistence of the unforeseen in *The Mayor of Casterbridge* probably came to him like such ballad tags as "Better they'd never been born" or "Young men, take warning from me." He had a mistaken idea, too, that he could argue and philosophize with impunity in verse, whereas he might have to go carefully, say, in an essay or speech. "Perhaps I can express more fully in verse," he wrote in 1896, "ideas and emotions which run counter to the inert crystallized opinion . . . which the vast body of men have vested interests in supporting. . . . If Galileo had said in verse that the world moved, the Inquisition might have let him alone." The good and innocent Hardy could somehow not easily learn that a bard was no longer a bard but a social critic.

The most striking feature of Hardy's habit of mind, as traditional narrator, is in his creation of characters. The characters of the Wessex novels, with certain important exceptions, are fixed or "nondeveloping" characters. Their fortunes may change, but they do not change with their fortunes. Once fully established as characters, they move unchanged through the narrative and at the end are what they were at the beginning. They have the changelessness of the figures of traditional narrative from epic, saga, and romance to broadside balladry and its prose parallels. In this respect they differ fundamentally from the typical characters of modern literary fiction. Our story-writers have learned how to exploit the possibilities of the changing, or changeful, or "developing" character. The theory of progress has seemed to influence them to apply an analogical generalization to the heroes of their stories: to wit, the only good hero in a serious novel is one that *changes* in some important respect during the course of the narrative; and the essence of the story is the change. This has become almost an aesthetic axiom. It is assumed that a story has no merit unless it is based on a changing character. If the modern author uses the changeless character, it is only in a minor rôle, or as a foil; or he may appear as a caricature.

But we have forgotten a truth that Hardy must have known from the time when, as a child, he heard at the harvest home the ballad of the outlandish knight. The changeless character has as much aesthetic richness as the changeful character. Traditional narrative of every sort is built upon the changeless character. It is a defect in modern fiction that the value of the changeless character is apparently not even suspected. But since the human desire for the changeless character is after all insatiable, we do have our changeless characters—in the comic strips, the movies, the detective story. Perhaps all is not well with a literary art that leaves the rôle of Achilles to be filled by Pop-Eye.

At any rate Hardy made extensive use of the changeless character. The habit of his mind probably forbade him to do otherwise; or at least he could not with complete success build his stories upon the changeful character. And so his novels of manners and genteel society are failures. At the same time, Hardy was no untutored child of the folk but a great author who learned by trial and error how to utilize self-consciously the rich material which by unselfconscious habit crowded his mind. He was thinking of his problem, I believe, when he wrote: "The uncommonness must be in the events, not in the characters." He did not make the mistake of exploiting his material for its mere picturesqueness—its *special* quality. He did not write dialect poems like William Barnes or romantic reconstructions like Blackmore's *Lorna Doone*.[9]

What Hardy did is, in its astonishing completeness and verity, a rebuke to superficial quasi-regionalists and to all who attempt to exploit "folk material" with the shallow assumption that the "folkishness" of the material is alone enough to dignify it. Hardy rationalizes the changeless characters by creating in highest circumstantiality not only the local environment in which they move, but the entire social order—the tradition itself, and the basis of the tradition—which will accommodate them. The basis of the tradition is a natural environment—a nature not very much despoiled or exploited, a town life neither wholly antique nor wholly modern, and the whole removed a little in time from the strictly contemporary, but not so far removed as to seem like a historical reconstruction. The antiquities, the local color, the folk customs are not decorative or merely picturesque; they are organic with the total scheme. They are no less essential and no more decorative than the occupations, ambitions, and interrelationships of the changeless characters. He accepts the assumptions of the society that he depicts, and neither apologizes for it nor condescends to it. The stories are stories of human beings, not of peasants or moordwellers as such.

The scheme is somewhat more complex than it might appear to

9. William Barnes (1801–86), Dorset dialect poet and philologist; Richard Blackmore's novel of the West Country, *Lorna Doone* (1869), is set at the time of the Monmouth rebellion.

be. The changeless characters of the Wessex world are of both minor and major order; and they are generally set in juxtaposition
with one or two characters of a more changeful or modern type.
The interplay between the two kinds of characters is the focus of
the struggle that makes the story. Hardy is almost the only modern
novelist who makes serious use of this conflict and at the same
time preserves full and equal respect for both sets of characters.
His great art lies in not setting up too great or obvious a distance
between his changeless and his changeful characters. The difference between Hardy and other novelists will be clear if I cite a typical example. Ellen Glasgow's *Barren Ground*,[1] a novel which seems
to copy Hardy at certain points, reduces all the thoroughly rustic
characters to a condition either of amusing oddity or of gross inep-
titude; and the excellent Dorinda, who makes such an obviously admirable change from rustic backwardness to rural progressivism, is
at all times infinitely above all the rest.

Nature, itself unchangeable and inscrutable, is the norm, the
basis of Wessex life. Those who accept nature as unchangeable
and passively accommodate themselves to nature in the ordered
ritual of their lives, not rebelling against it or attempting rash
Promethean manipulations—these are the changeless characters.

Nearest to nature, and therefore most changeless, are the rustics
(all crusted characters) who throng Hardy's pages. In the rural
comedies, like *Under the Greenwood Tree* and *Far from the Madding Crowd*, they dominate the scene. Only the vicar, in *Under the
Greenwood Tree*, with his newfangled church organ, and perhaps in
a slight way Sergeant Troy, in the other novel, foreshadow the kind
of disturbance set up by the changeful character. But these novels
are essentially comedy, joyful and almost idyllic. In Hardy, tragedy
does not arrive until changeless and changeful are engaged in bitter
conflict.

Such a conflict is found in *The Return of the Native*. Here the
rustics are Timothy Fairway, Grandfer Cantle, Christian Cantle,
Susan Nonesuch and her son Johnny, and the mummers. It would
be wrong to regard these persons as curiosities, or as interesting literary fossils planted in the environment for the verisimilitude that
they give. They not only take part in the series of festivals that provide a symbolic chronological pattern for the novel; but they also
participate in the critical action itself, as agents of destiny. Timothy
carries the letter which was so fatally not delivered at last. Johnny
Nonesuch is liaison agent between Eustacia and Wildeve. Christian
Cantle carries the guineas, and gambles them away. Susan None-

1. Ellen Glasgow (1874–1945), novelist, from Richmond, Virginia; *Barren Ground*, her
best known work, was published in 1925.

such and her son intervene actively in the lives of both Eustacia and Clym. Their part is organic, not decorative; they are much more than the "Greek chorus" that they have been called. They are, in fact, the basic pattern to which other characters conform or from which they differ. Diggory Venn and Thomasin, at a slightly higher level, conform more or less; they are changeless characters who venture near the danger line of changefulness but do not pass over it. Eustacia and Clym have passed over the line, though not beyond the possibility of retraction. They are changeful characters, strongly touched by Promethean influences—as Wildeve, in a vulgar way, is also touched. Modernism has worked on Eustacia to lure her away from Egdon Heath; but Clym, who has already lived in Paris, has reached a second stage of revulsion against modernism. Yet when this native returns he brings with him a characteristically modern program of education and evangelism. Eustacia and Clym, as changeful characters, do not diverge extravagantly from the changeless pattern, but their rebellion is great enough to render their life-courses inconstant and tragic.

Hardy has taken some pains to mark the essential nature of Clym's character. The motto for the chapter that describes Clym is: "My mind to me a kingdom is." Clym is a Renaissance, or nontraditional, man. His face, already marked with disillusionment, foreshadows "the typical countenance of the future." Jude, another changeful character, is like Clym in some ways. He too is a rebel against nature, whose rebellion is also idealistic; but it leads him away from Wessex. His story might have been entitled: "The Migration of the Native." In Jude's life the changeless and the changeful are further represented in Arabella and Sue; Arabella, the changeless but too gross; Sue Bridehead, the changeful but too refined. In *Tess* there are two changeful and ruin-wreaking characters. In Alec Stoke-D'Urberville the changeful character takes on a vulgar form. He is an imposter, who has appropriated an old country name and bought his way into Wessex; and the Stoke-D'Urberville establishment, with its preposterous chicken culture, is a fake rural establishment. Angel Clare, on the other hand, is a rarefied form of alien. He is willing, condescendingly, to accept Wessex, and dairy farming, and Tess, provided he can possess all this in an abstractly "pure," or respectable form. The tragedy arrives when he cannot adjust (the sociological term is necessary) his delicate sensibility to a gross, but, in the natural order, an understandable biological fact. It is the changeful modern character in Angel that cannot abide Tess's delinquency. The changeless characters might have found fault, but would not have been shocked, would not have sulked, would have not been too slow to pardon. A similar opposition appears in *The Woodlanders*, where changefulness appears in Fitzpiers and Mrs. Charmond; changelessness in Giles Winterborne and Marty South.

Perhaps these are dangerous simplifications. I do not offer them as definitive explanations of Hardy's fictions, but rather as possibilities not yet explored. Hardy's habit of mind, and his method of using his habit of mind in fiction, seem to me the least discussed of the aspects of his work. I have found no other approach that does not seem to impose a critical explanation from without, with an arbitrariness that often seems to do violence to the art work itself.

There is surely no other example in modern English fiction of an author who, while reaching the highest levels of sophisticated artistic performance, comes bringing his tradition with him, not only the mechanics of the tradition but the inner conception that is often lacking. The admonitions we hear so often nowadays about the relation of the artist and his tradition seem dry and academic when we look closely at Hardy's actual performance. He seems to illustrate what we might think the ideal way of realizing and activating a tradition, for he did, without admonition, what the admonishers are always claiming ought to be done; and yet for that particular achievement he got no thanks, or even a notice. The achievement is the more extraordinary when we consider that he worked (if I read his career rightly) against the dominant pattern of his day. He did what the modern critic (despite his concern about tradition) is always implying to be impossible. That is, Hardy accepted the assumptions of a society which in England was already being condemned to death, and he wrote in terms of those assumptions, almost as if Wessex, and perhaps Wessex only, would understand. From his work I get few of the meanings, pessimistic or otherwise, that are commonly ascribed to him. His purpose seems to have been to tell about human life in the terms that would present it as most recognizably, and validly, and completely human. That he succeeded best when he wrote of rural Wessex is significant. He probably had strong convictions on one point—convictions that had little to do with his official inquiries into Darwinism and the nature of Deity.

JOHN PATERSON

The Return of the Native as Antichristian Document†

In such spots as Egdon, Hardy was to report, where festive May-pole-days could still be faithfully observed, "homage to nature, self-

† From *Nineteenth-Century Fiction* 14.2 (1959): 11–27. Reprinted by permission of the University of California Press. Page references have been changed to correspond to this Norton Critical Edition.

adoration, frantic gaieties, fragments of Teutonic rites to divinities whose names are forgotten, seem in some way or other to have survived mediaeval doctrine."[1] An examination of the manuscript reveals that this handsome celebration of the natural life originally was placed in opposition not to "mediaeval *doctrine*" but, more explicitly and more dramatically, to "mediaeval *Christianity*."[2] In the final terms of the novel, again, the highly charged dancing at East Egdon was to be defined as a recrudescence of paganism: "For the time Paganism was revived in their hearts, the pride of life was all in all, and they adored none other than themselves" (p. 218). In the original terms of the manuscript, the dancing was defined not only as a reaffirmation of the pagan but also, and more specifically, as a rejection of the Christian: "*Christianity was eclipsed in their hearts*, Paganism was revived, the pride of life was all in all, they adored themselves & [sic] *their own natural instincts*."[3]

In the novel in its present form, Eustacia Vye stands of course outside the conventional categories of good and evil: her "high gods" are William the Conqueror, Strafford, and Napoleon; she prefers Saul or Sisera to Jacob or David; she sides with the Philistines and admires Pontius Pilate (p. 65). In the text of the manuscript, however, the implications of her perverse and impious loyalties were fully articulated: "*Her chief priest was Byron: her antichrist a well-meaning preacher at Budmouth, of the name of Slatters.*"[4] Indeed, where she now aspires to look "with indifference upon the cruel satires that *Fate* loves to indulge in" (p. 176), she earlier aspired to look "with indifference upon the cruel satires that *God* loves to indulge in."[5]

Of course, not all traces of antichristian sentiment were stricken from the record. At the conclusion of the novel, Hardy could still permit himself the nearly bitter reflection that "human beings, in their generous endeavour to construct a hypothesis that shall not degrade a First Cause, have always hesitated to conceive a dominant power of lower moral quality than their own . . ." (p. 315). As the revisions would testify, however, the virulent censorship current in 1878 more generally had the effect of driving underground what evidently threatened to materialize as an open denigration of Christianity. It compelled Hardy to suppress the repudiation of the Christian implicit in the novel's celebration of the pagan. The revi-

---

1. Thomas Hardy, *The Return of the Native*, p. 318.
2. The change was made on f.407 of the holograph manuscript now in the possession of the University College Library, Dublin.
3. F.287. The reference to the eclipse of Christianity appeared in the text of the serial edition of 1878 (*Belgravia, An Illustrated London Magazine*, XXXVI, 244), but was omitted in the text of the first edition (Vol. 2, p. 280) published in the same year.
4. F.78v. This reference appeared in the serial edition but was expunged from the text of the first (cf. *Belgravia*, XXXIV, 506, and the first edition, Vol. I, p. 155).
5. Cf. *Belgravia*, XXXVI, 4 and the first edition, Vol. 2, p. 161.

sions draw attention, then, to a subversive content no longer visible to the naked eye. Indeed, they positively invite a reexamination of *The Return of the Native* as an anticlerical tract.

The antichristian bias of the novel is first of all apparent in its celebration of Eustacia Vye. For as a symbolic character, Eustacia belongs to a world that has not yet been touched by the spectral hand of Christianity: she reincarnates on the withered parish of Egdon Heath the larger and braver vision of the ancient Greeks. Her dignity is described, for example, as "Tartarean" (p. 62); she strikes with ease "the note of Artemis, Athena, or Hera" (p. 62); she is said to descend from Homeric kings, "from Alcinous' line, her father hailing from Phaeacia's isle" (p. 63). Elsewhere, she can be chastised by Clym as a rebel in the Promethean tradition: " 'Now don't you suppose . . . that I cannot rebel, in high Promethean fashion, against the gods and fate as well as you' " (p. 214). And persistently associated with fire as she is—the color of her soul is fancied, for example, as "flame-like" (p. 61), and the pool in which she dies is defined as a "boiling caldron" (p. 307)—she everywhere evokes the image of the Promethean heroine. In its central action in the suffering and death of Eustacia Vye, in other words, *The Return of the Native* dramatizes the tragic humiliation, in the diminished world of the modern consciousness, of an heroic, prechristian understanding of life.

Up to a certain point, of course, the diminished landscape of modern times, the Egdon Heath against which she struggles in vain, is ascribed not to the Christian but to the scientific dispensation. Hardy philosophizes at one point:

> The truth seems to be that a long line of disillusive centuries has permanently displaced the Hellenic idea of life. . . . That old-fashioned revelling in the general situation grows less and less possible as we uncover the defects of natural laws, and see the quandary that man is in by their operation (p. 143).

In this perspective Eustacia Vye, as the anachronistic survival of "the Hellenic idea of life," stands opposed to Clym Yeobright, who, having read aright the grim Darwinian message of the heath and having assimilated at Paris the "ethical systems popular at the time" (p. 147), is prepared to abjure Prometheanism and to accept the modern, or antiheroic, idea of life. Beyond this point, however, it becomes increasingly clear that the deterioration of the heroic Greek consciousness is ascribed less to the scientific revelation, less to the discovery of "the defects of natural laws," than to the establishment of a Christian order and belief.

In the first place, as the interchangeability in Hardy's mind of "God" and "Fate" and as the heroine's contempt for Slatters, "the well-meaning preacher at Budmouth," would intimate, Eustacia's quarrel is ultimately more with the Christian way of life than with the objective structure of the universe. If she is no longer free to despise poor Slatters, she can still, after all, hum Saturday night ballads on the Sabbath (p. 65) and openly declare her aversion for English Sundays (p. 169). And it is surely significant that of all the parts in the mummers' play, she should draw precisely that of the antichrist, the Turkish Knight, who must, with ritual inexorability, suffer defeat and death at the hands of the Christian champion.[6] In the last analysis, however, nothing more sharply defines Eustacia's antichristian implications than her persistent identification as a black witch, that immemorial antagonist of the Christian faith.[7] Early defined by the peasant chorus as " 'the lonesome dark-eyed creature up there that some say is a witch' " (p. 47), she is perse-cuted by Susan Nunsuch for allegedly "bewitching" her children (p. 151) and denounced by Clym for having, "like a devil," destroyed his happiness (p. 270): " 'Don't look at me with those eyes,' " he declaims, " 'as if you would bewitch me again!' " (p. 272).

That this identification is fundamental to her conception would be verified by the fact that whole scenes are conditioned and even dominated by the formidable image it evokes. The crooked sixpence with which she bribes Johnny Nunsuch to tend her bonfire—" 'Stay a little longer and I will give you a crooked sixpence' " (p. 55)—is represented in folk-tradition as a charm against witchcraft[8] and in the particular context of the novel identifies her as a member of that dark sorority. Still more convincingly, when she summons to her bonfire the dim, half-realized figure of Damon Wildeve, she recreates the presence of the wicked enchantress presiding over unholy fires and evoking out of darkness or out of nothingness shapes and images that are the stuff of no human reality. Thus when her lover does materialize—and the term is used carefully—it is as a form which, if it does not quite suggest the monstrous, does not quite suggest the human either: "Thereupon the contour of a man became dimly visible against the low-reaching sky over the val-ley, beyond the outer margin of the pool. He came round it and leapt upon the bank beside her" (p. 56). And the scene that follows is rendered in terms that unmistakably suggest a sinister supernat-ural: Eustacia gazes upon Wildeve as Milton's Satan must have gazed upon the horrid crew called up from the baleful lake, "as

6. The mummers' play may be thought, in fact, to reenact in miniature the central action of the novel: i.e., the defeat of the pagan and the triumph of the Christian.
7. The argument that Eustacia was originally conceived by Hardy as a witch was developed in John Paterson's later study, *The Making of "The Return of the Native"* (Berkeley: University of California Press, 1960) [*Editor*].
8. Ruth A. Firor, *Folkways in Thomas Hardy* (Philadelphia: University of Pennsylvania Press, 1931), p. 91.

upon some wondrous thing she had created out of chaos" (p. 57). Moreover, in exulting over him, she employs a heightened language that leaves no doubt as to the demoniacal nature of her summons: I " 'thought,' " she tells him, " 'I would get a little excitement by calling you up and triumphing over you as the Witch of Endor called up Samuel. I determined you should come; and you have come! I have shown my power . . .' " (pp. 59–60). Even at the very close of the novel, in fact, when the episode is repeated and a fire is once again seen on Mistover Knap, Hardy evokes the same imagery of magic: "there flashed upon [Eustacia's] imagination some other form which that fire might call up" (p. 282).

Eustacia's status as witch or demon would be supported by the fact that Damon Wildeve, the slave and image of her own invention, is composed of exactly the same stuff. Frequently seen and satirized as "the Rousseau of Egdon" (p. 183), as the type of the decrepit and disreputable romantic, he is just as frequently seen and celebrated as the dreamer of a purely human and, to that extent, unchristian consummation, and hence, like Eustacia herself, he justifies comparison with the darker powers. Suddenly accosted by the reddleman, for example, he starts "like Satan at the touch of Ithuriel's spear" (p. 132). And in the tradition of the revolted angel, he is said to have known better days, to have fallen from high places. " 'He was brought up to better things than keeping the Quiet Woman,' " the peasant chorus observes, in a homely recapitulation of the Satan-story. " 'An engineer—that's what the man was, as we know; but he threw away his chance, and so 'a took a public-house to live. His learning was no use to him at all' " (p. 23). At one point, indeed, Wildeve, beholding innocence and wounded by a remorse for which there is no cure, evokes the pathos of Satan at the gates of Eden: " 'God, how I envy him that sweet sleep!' " he mourns, observing Clym Yeobright at rest. " 'I have not slept like that since I was a boy—years and years ago' " (p. 237).

However, as the name "Damon Wildeve," with its evocation of "daimons" and nocturnal orgies would imply, Hardy evidently conceived him as—with Eustacia's "witch"—the agent of powers and energies older even than Satan, as the agent of mysterious powers and energies that once haunted the primeval landscape in the shapes of ogres and goblins and demons until the blight of Christianity drove them to the darkness of cave and fen and forest and at last, except on barbaric Egdon, out of the human imagination altogether. In our first glimpse of him, when he is approached by an indignant Mrs. Yeobright, he assumes, as in his materialization before Eustacia's bonfire, nothing more distinct than a shadowy shape or form: "a vast shadow, in which could be dimly traced portions of a masculine contour, blotted half the ceiling" (p. 40). He assumes, in fact, something of the laborious formlessness of a Caliban: "the back and shoulders of a man came between Mrs. Yeobright's eyes and the fire. Wildeve, whose form it was, immediately turned, arose, and advanced to meet his visitors" (p. 40). The demonism inherent in the character-image of Damon Wildeve would confirm, then, the demonism inherent in the character-image of Eustacia Vye. As the virtual author of a subhuman, if not superhuman, lover, as the practitioner of a black witchcraft, and, above all, as the avatar of the heroic Greek sense of life, Eustacia suggests nothing so much as a pagan exile in a Christian province.

The antichristian sentiment implicit in her pre-Christianity is dramatized, finally, by her opposition to Clym Yeobright, who is actuated in the last analysis less by scientific consciousness than by Christian conscience. Hardy preferred of course to see his hero as the very emanation of the pagan heath: "He was permeated with its scenes, with its substance, and with its odours" (p. 148). He preferred, too, to see him, in his role of meliorist, in his role of schoolmaster to the proletariat of Egdon, as, with Eustacia Vye, a Promethean figure: "As is usual with bright natures, the deity that lies ignominiously chained within an ephemeral human carcase shone out of him like a ray" (p. 120). At the very last, however, Clym has as little in common with the barbaric heath as any character in the novel, and although he does occasionally appear in the image of Prometheus, it is more generally, as his chastisement of Eustacia should indicate, as the reformed Promethean: " 'I have felt more steam and smoke of that sort than you have ever heard of' " (p. 214). His characteristic note is everywhere, in fact, the note of Christian self-renunciation. The scientific humanism he is alleged to have imbibed in the schools of Paris only thinly disguises the Christian martyr.

For if Clym consistently deceives himself and even the author, who will later regard him as quite the nicest of all his heroes,[9] he does not succeed in deceiving his women, whose instinct in this case turns out to be nearly infallible. Thus the skeptical Mrs. Yeobright very correctly understands him as a missionary in disguise: " 'It is right,' " she concedes at one point, " 'that there should be schoolmasters, and missionaries, and all such men . . .' " (p. 152). And Eustacia, not far behind in insight, associates him half-satirically with the Apostle Paul: " '. . . but the worst of it is that though Paul was excellent as a man in the Bible he would hardly have done in real life' " (p. 235). It becomes a question, in fact, whether Clym even deceives the author who can interpret him, both before and after his tragedy, in terms of Christian metaphors

9. Mrs. Hardy, *The Later Years of Thomas Hardy* (New York, 1930), p. 151.

and images or, put otherwise, as an inverted Christian. He is, Hardy remarks, "a John the Baptist who took ennoblement rather than repentance for his text" (p. 147). In his mission to the unwashed denizens of the heath, he is seen as "preaching to the Egdon cremites" (p. 148). And in defending his mission against the more secular intelligence of his mother, he is moved to invoke the aid of St. Paul himself: " 'I get up every morning,' " he tells her, " 'and see the whole creation groaning and travailing in pain, as St. Paul says, and yet there am I, trafficking in glittering splendours with wealthy women and titled libertines . . .' " (p. 150).

Certainly, if Clym has earlier flirted, as the humanitarian reformer, with a dangerous Prometheanism, he is, following the deaths of his wife and mother, the very much chastened, the very much frightened, Christian. Like the Sue Bridehead of a later novel, he is converted by tragedy, by his encounter with evil, back to the faith of his fathers. " 'If there is any justice in God,' " he declaims out of a new sense of Christian guilt and remorse, " 'let Him kill me now. . . . If He would only strike me with more pain I would believe in Him for ever!' " (p. 258). And having, at the close of the book, "found his vocation in the career of an itinerant open-air preacher and lecturer on morally unimpeachable subjects" (p. 336), the pseudo-Promethean stands revealed in his true colours as the scripture-quoting Christian: "But his heart was heavy; that mother had *not* crowned him in the day of his espousals and in the day of the gladness of his heart" (p. 334). Indeed, preaching a series of what are called Sermons on the Mount to a captive audience of supernaturally quiescent heath-folk, Clym emerges at the end in the guise of a Christ-figure.

Where Clym was concerned, of course, Hardy's critical faculties would appear to have been temporarily suspended. There are distinct occasions, however, when perhaps unconsciously and certainly in spite of himself, Hardy exposed his hero to the cruelest and most damaging ironies. These occasions are nowhere more in evidence than when Clym's theoretical intelligence is juxtaposed with the practical and instinctive intelligence of the still-unchristened peasant community from which he has, to his considerable sorrow, been separated. There is an irony, retroactive in effect, in the comment evoked by the first news of his coming: " 'Wonderful clever, 'a believe,' " Grandfer Cantle crows ecstatically, " '—ah, I should like to have all that's under that young man's hair' " (p. 20). There is an even more specific and more trenchant irony, however—and one more clearly at Clym's expense—in the peasants' response to his program for their intellectual, if not moral, improvement. " 'He'll never carry it out in the world,' " says Timothy Fairway prophetically from the vantage-point of a superior wisdom, a wisdom as old as the heath. " 'In a few weeks he'll learn to see things otherwise.' " " ' 'Tis goodhearted of the young man,' " says another member of the peasant family with a condescension that events will justify. " 'But, for my part,' " and with this the chapter is brought to an ironic period, " 'I think he had better mind his business' " (p. 147).

Clym nowhere suffers more from the exposures of irony than in the terminal chapters of the novel where his repudiation of life in a spirit of Christian self-renunciation contrasts dramatically not only with the life-renewing rites of Maypole-day but also with the life-renewing rites of Thomasin's marriage to the reddleman. Whether Hardy intended it or not—and it is hard to believe that he did not—Clym's theatrical conversion is reduced by the "savage" rites of spring and marriage, to ludicrous terms. Thus at the same time that he is distressed by the inconvenience of Thomasin's loving him, she has already set her cap for the less ethereal person of Diggory Venn and just when he is at the point, "with a pleasant sense of doing his duty" (p. 324), of offering his hand in marriage, she asks him, as the head of the family, to bless her union with another (p. 325). The irony at Clym's expense becomes positively unmistakable in the penultimate scene of the novel when Charley describes for the benefit of the hero (significantly still blind) the joyous wedding-festivities of which they have chosen to be the unobserved and pathetic spectators:

> "Do any of them seem to care about my not being there?" Clym asked.
> "No, not a bit in the world. Now they are all holding up their glasses and drinking somebody's health."
> "I wonder if it is mine?"
> "No, 'tis Mr. and Mrs. Venn's, because he is making a hearty sort of speech . . ." (p. 334).

In the context of *The Return of the Native*, then, Clym Yeobright not only functions as a figure of Christian piety but becomes, as such, the victim of a number of highly damaging ironies. Moreover, insofar as he serves as Eustacia's foil and antagonist, this Christian hero underlines the antichristian sentiment explicit in her denigrations of Christian mediocrity but more generally implicit in her metaphorical identifications as witch and as Greek heroine. In the death of Eustacia Vye, in other words, and in the Christian apotheosis of Clym Yeobright, *The Return of the Native* commemorates, in an elegiac if not tragic mood, the defeat of pagan consciousness and the triumph of Christian conscience.

The completeness with which the novel exploits the pagan-Christian antithesis only becomes fully apparent with an examination of the subsidiary figures of the reddleman and the peasant

chorus. Diggory Venn in his role of reddleman, for example, suggests nothing so much as a creature—goblin, elf, or demon—out of
Celtic mythology. Like so many sprites of popular superstition, he
makes his habitation, temporarily at least, in "a pit under the hill"
(p. 67). He appears and disappears throughout the novel, as
Wildeve for one has good reason to know, with an uncanny rapidity
that suggests the possession of magical powers: "On [Wildeve's]
reaching the top a shape grew up from the earth immediately behind him" (p. 132). Apparently beyond good and evil, he intervenes
in, and disrupts, the normal course of human affairs with results
that cannot clearly be established as either for better or for worse.
And, in the best tradition of folk romance, his psychology is frequently enigmatical. It is, of course, perfectly accordant with this
essential conception of the reddleman as a nature-spirit that he
should be seen as standing, with Eustacia Vye the black witch and
Damon Wildeve her succubus, outside the pale of Christian salva-
tion. The whole race of reddlemen are imagined as "criminals for
whose misdeeds other men had wrongfully suffered," as criminals
who had escaped the law but who "had not escaped their own consciences, and had taken to the trade as a lifelong penance" (p. 72).
They persistently evoke, certainly, an image calculated to horrify
the pious imagination, the image of the outcast from the Christian
community: they are of the race of "Mephistophelian visitants"
(p. 71); they are stamped by reddle "as with the mark of Cain"
(p. 71); and like the heath itself (p. 10), they are designated, in the
figure of Diggory Venn, as "Ishmaelitish" (p. 129).

The antichristian implications of Diggory's reddlemanship are
perhaps most clearly dramatized, however, by the specifically Christian implications of the transformation which Hardy reluctantly
permitted him at the close of the novel.[1] For his generally middle-
class rehabilitation turns out to be, in part at least, a Christian rehabilitation, a species of Christian conversion. Certainly, it is more
than adventitious that Diggory should give up the reddle trade and,
presumably, the illegitimate powers and privileges that go along
with it, at—of all times of the year—*Christmas:* " 'I gave up dealing
in reddle,' " he declares to Thomasin's comic astonishment, " 'last
Christmas' " (p. 317). And it is surely more than adventitious that
when the red dye does fade from his complexion, it is to disclose
not only the lineaments of the respectable dairy farmer but also
"the strangely altered hues of an ordinary *Christian* countenance"
(p. 316). As the unreconstructed reddleman, that is to say, Diggory
is evidently designed to honor the stoic and realistic values of a pre-

1. See Hardy's celebrated footnote on p. 473 of the British Wessex Edition. It is evident
   that he consented to Diggory's transformation as Thomasin's Christian bridegroom only
   under editorial pressure.

Christian way of life and, tacitly at least, to criticize the nicer, less permissive values that come in with Christianity. Indeed, insofar as he was, according to Hardy's original prospectus, not to have joined Thomasin in Christian marriage, but "to have retained his isolated and weird character to the last, and to have disappeared mysteriously from the heath, nobody knowing whither" (p. 327), he may very well have been intended to symbolize at the very end the humiliating and tragic defeat, with the institution of Christian discipline, of that elusive and nearly demoniacal spirit of fen and forest that has found its last resting place in savage Egdon.

For the antichristian tendency of the novel, however, the peasant community with its hearty celebration of the natural life and its instinctive distrust of the church is in the last analysis mainly responsible. For where Eustacia and Wildeve and Diggory Venn are identified in symbolic terms with prechristian beliefs and values, the humble members of the peasant society are so identified in relatively realistic terms. Their performances derive, that is to say, from levels of thinking and feeling older than, and happily oblivious to, the innovations of Christianity. In their first appearance in the novel, for example, they are seen as the builders of bonfires that have their antecedents in a barbaric past: "such blazes as this the heathmen were now enjoying are rather the lineal descendants from jumbled Druidical rites and Saxon ceremonies than the invention of popular feeling about Gunpowder Plot" (p. 18). The lighting of the fires represents, in fact, something more, even, than the reincarnated spirit of pagan idolatry. It is positively a gesture of impious defiance in the teeth of whatever powers there be: "to light a fire," Hardy observes,

> is the instinctive and resistant act of man when, at the winter ingress, the curfew is sounded throughout Nature. It indicates a spontaneous, Promethean rebelliousness against the fiat that this recurrent season shall bring foul times, cold darkness, misery and death . . . (p. 18).

Not surprisingly under these profane circumstances, the citizens of the heath tend in the presence of the bonfire to lose all distinctive moral identity:

> the permanent moral expression of each face it was impossible to discover, for as the nimble flames towered, nodded, and swooped through the surrounding air, the blots of shade and flakes of light upon the countenance of the group changed shape and position endlessly (pp. 18–19).

Throughout the novel, however, the members of this natural community participate without knowing it in ritual acts of a pagan or pre-Christian origin. In their next major appearance on the occasion of Mrs. Yeobright's Christmas party, they reenact the ancient folkplay, the St. George play, whose Christian veneer scarcely conceals its pre-Christian character as fertility rite celebrating the death of the year and its resurrection in the spring. Hardy is in fact at pains to verify the authenticity of the performance: "Like Balaam and other unwilling prophets," he reports,

> the agents seem moved by an inner compulsion to say and do their allotted parts whether they will or no. This unweeting manner of performance is the true ring by which, in this refurbishing age, a fossilized survival may be known from a spurious reproduction (p. 107).

At the conclusion of the novel, furthermore, the renewal of life following the deaths of Eustacia and Wildeve is symbolized in the ancient rite of Maypole-day with its celebration of a vitality older and stronger than all that Christianity could bring to bear against it: "The instincts of merry England," Hardy notes with approval,

> lingered on here with exceptional vitality, and the symbolic customs which tradition has attached to each season of the year were yet a reality on Egdon. Indeed, the impulses of all such outlandish hamlets are pagan still: in these spots homage to nature, self-adoration, frantic gaieties, fragments of Teutonic rites to divinities whose names are forgotten, seem in some way or other to have survived mediaeval doctrine (p. 318).

Even on occasions less ceremonial than the mumming and the Maypoling, however, the denizens of the heath are actuated by emotions that antedate, and comment ironically upon, the sober authority of the Christian tradition. From the beginning of the novel to the end, they are ready at the slightest provocation to break into song and dance whose fervor and violence bodes ill for the cause of Christian piety. Thus they conclude their commemoration of November 5 by whirling about their Promethean bonfire in a mad measure, a species of witches' dance, that is, in fact, specifically described as demoniacal:

> . . . in half a minute all that could be seen on Rainbarrow was a whirling of dark shapes amid a boiling confusion of sparks, which leapt around the dancers as high as their waists. The chief noises were women's shrill cries, men's laughter, Susan's stays and pattens, Olly Dowden's "heu-heu-heu!" and the strumming of the wind upon the furze-bushes, which formed a kind of tune to the *demoniac* measure they trod (p. 31).

And it is surely more than apt coincidence that the physically-abandoned dance which delays the appearance of the mummers at the Christmas party should be called the "Devil's Dream":

> The air was now that one without any particular beginning, middle, or end, which perhaps . . . best conveys the idea of the interminable—the celebrated "Devil's Dream." The fury of personal movement that was kindled by the fury of the notes could be approximately imagined . . . from the occasional kicks of toes and heels against the door, whenever the whirl round had been of more than customary velocity (p. 115).

Indeed, it becomes clear that in its sheer physicality, in its unabashed celebration of the human body and its dangerous sexual energies, dancing as it is practiced on Egdon constitutes a clear and present danger to Christian law and order. "A whole village-full of sensuous emotion, scattered abroad all the year long," it is said of the revels at East Egdon, "surged here in a focus for an hour. . . . For the time Paganism was revived in their hearts, the pride of life was all in all, and they adored none other than themselves" (p. 218).

The fact that by "mediaeval doctrine" Hardy had meant "mediaeval Christianity" and that against "Paganism was revived" he had set "Christianity was eclipsed" bears witness that Egdon's celebration of pagan vitality was specifically opposed in his imagination to the prohibitions and restrictions authorized by the Christian tradition. That this was indeed the case would be verified by his comic exploitation of the peasants' informal, not to say tenuous, relations with the local church. To begin with, their attendance at the Christian service would seem at best to be casual and intermittent. "In name they were parishioners," Hardy notes with evident satisfaction,

> but virtually they belonged to no parish at all. . . . Rain, snow, ice, mud everywhere around, they did not care to trudge two or three miles to sit wet-footed and splashed to the nape of their necks among those who . . . lived close to the church, and entered it clean and dry (p. 106).

Quite as pagan as the great heath whose stubbornly skeptical and pragmatic values they would appear to have inherited, they are utterly unresponsive to such consolations as the church has to offer. " 'I ha'n't been there to-year,' " Grandfer Cantle boasts; " 'and now the winter is a-coming on I won't say I shall.' " " 'I ha'n't been these three years,' " Humphrey reflects, " 'for I'm so dead sleepy of a Sunday; and 'tis so terrible far to get there; and when you do get there 'tis such a mortal poor chance that you'll be chose for up above, when so many bain't, that I bide at home and don't go at all' " (pp. 21–22).

Certainly, when they do go to church, it is in no spirit of Christian piety. It is rather to witness an unscheduled dramatic exhibition, Mrs. Yeobright rising to forbid Thomasin's banns and Susan Nunsuch plunging the knitting needle into the arm of a "witch." Or to listen to a musical performance more likely to arouse the spirit of the Devil than the spirit of the Lord: " ' 'Twas the Hundred-and-thirty-third to "Lydia," ' " says Timothy Fairway in his lusty account of the musical prowess of Thomasin's father;

> "and when they'd come to 'Ran down his beard and o'er his robes its costly moisture shed,' neighbour Yeobright, who had just warmed to his work, drove his bow into them strings that glorious grand that he e'en a'most sawed the bass-viol into two pieces. Every winder in church rattled as if 'twere a thunderstorm." (p. 45).

It becomes apparent, in fact, that their response to the service is not far removed from a primitive fetishism. When Mrs. Yeobright forbids the banns, for example, no aspect of the episode surprises Timothy Fairway more than that the parson should have exposed himself as a human being of flesh and blood: " ' "I'll speak to you after the service," said the parson, in quite a homely way—yes, turning all at once into a common man no holier than you or I' " (p. 22). On the occasion of Yeobright's memorable performance on the bass-viol, he registers the same astonished response: " 'Old Pa'son Williams lifted his hands in his great holy surplice as natural as if he'd been in common clothes . . .' " (pp. 46–47). And Christian Cantle can pause in his account of Eustacia's pricking-in-church to report the same stirring phenomenon: " 'O, and what d'ye think I found out, Mrs. Yeobright? The pa'son wears a suit of clothes under his surplice!—I could see his black sleeve when he held up his arm' " (p. 152).

Nothing in the novel, of course, is more significant of the low ebb of Christian worship on Egdon Heath, of its powerlessness in the face of the primitive and unconscious impulses of its citizens, than the machinations of Susan Nunsuch. At the conclusion of the novel, burning Eustacia Vye in effigy, she repeats the Lord's Prayer backwards and repudiates, in effect, two thousand years of Christian piety. Even more dramatically, she has earlier plunged a knitting needle into the arm of the local "witch" and has reduced at once to a comic shambles the conventional rites of the Christian service. It should not be difficult after this to assess the function in the novel of the peasant chorus. It is not only to celebrate a pagan health and sanity but, less directly, to expose Christianity to a comic, and even satirical, light. Certainly, there is more than a trace of irony in Humphrey's bland comment, following the news of Eustacia's pricking-in-church, " ' 'Tis a very strange thing that whenever one of Egdon folk goes to church some rum job or other is sure to be doing' " (p. 152).

Nowhere in the novel, however, is Hardy's denigration of Christianity more open than in the ludicrous figure of Christian Cantle. For Christian constitutes, as his name would suggest, the caricature of the Christian man. This is first of all apparent in his being placed in opposition to the secular figure of the reddleman, who incarnates, as a nature-spirit, the subdued and skeptical paganism of Egdon Heath itself. Thus when Diggory hails from the darkness the group gathered about the bonfire, the terrified Christian recites a scriptural counterspell and therewith not only emphasizes the secular heresy for which the reddleman stands but also parodies the pietistic response to that heresy: " 'Matthew, Mark, Luke, and John, bless the bed that I lie on; four angels guard—' " (p. 31).[2] Furthermore, when the reddleman does appear, Christian further defines himself and his subject with, " 'If he had a handkerchief over his head he'd look for all the world like the Devil in the picture of the Temptation' " (p. 32).

Christian functions most clearly as a satire on Christianity, however, in his relationship to the pagan community of peasants and, specifically, in his separation from that community. Up to a certain point, of course, his Christianity is, like that of his country brethren, rooted in primitive superstition: it exists for him as a source of counterspells with which to deal with the aboriginal ghosts and ogres and demons which constantly possess his fearful imagination. And to this extent, he tends to join the inhabitants of the heath in exposing Christianity to ridicule. In his characteristic role, however, Christian is dissociated altogether from the peasant community with its profane celebration of the joys and virtues of the natural life, and in this role he becomes preeminently the caricature of conventional piety. His dissociation as Christian from their paganism is, in fact, specifically dramatized on the occasion of their "demoniac" demonstration about the reckless flames. For Christian alone stands apart and establishes thereby, as the pious terms of his reproaches should indicate, not only the submerged antichristianity of the infamous dance but also the comic demoralization of the God-fearing man in the presence of so much pagan energy: "Christian alone stood aloof, uneasily rocking himself as he murmured, 'They ought not to do it—how the vlankers do fly! 'tis tempting the Wicked one, 'tis' " (p. 31). This opposition is indeed explored elsewhere to reveal still further the disadvantages of a Christian education. Thus Christian's physical decrepitude and sex-

2. In fact, Hardy has Timothy Fairway interrupt Christian's prayer with an unceremonious " 'Hold your tongue.' " It is not difficult to imagine the author's vicarious pleasure in this sharp repudiation of Christian's piety.

ual impotence—he is the man no woman will marry (p. 26)—are in dramatic contrast to the life-worshipping vitality of Grandfer and Timothy and the rest of that lusty crew. And where he lives in constant terror of the sights and sounds of the savage heath, they, complete pagans that they are, feel perfectly at home in this grimmest of all possible worlds. The comic Christian Cantle-pagan chorus antithesis joins, then, with the "tragic" Clym-Eustacia antithesis to compose a critical and sometimes satirical examination of the Christian idea of life.

"A hymn rolls from a church-window," Hardy was to note in 1883, "and the uncompromising No-God-ist or Unconscious God-ist takes up the refrain."[3] Caught in the conflict between reason and emotion, this imaginary figure might just as well have been Thomas Hardy himself. As a young man intended for the clergy, he had lost his faith in the decade of Darwin, Colenso, and the *Essays and Reviews*. But, long after he could no longer avail himself of the consolations of religion, he remained, perhaps inevitably, a man of strong religious needs and feelings. To consider *The Return of the Native* as purely and simply a diatribe against Christianity may very well be, then, to dishonor the complexity of the novel as a dramatic representation of Hardy's mixed feelings. In his portrait of Christian Cantle there is pathos, after all, as well as satire. And if Clym Yeobright is exposed to the irreverent ironies of a skeptical author, so, too, for that matter, are Wildeve and Eustacia, his pagan antagonists. There is in fact a singular appropriateness in the novel's ending, in the Christian and middle-class marriage of Thomasin and Diggory, that far transcends motives of editorial necessity or convenience. Interpreted as it is in a spirit of high comedy, this domestic anticlimax passes an ironical comment on, and in effect reconciles us to, the splendid but wasteful deaths of Wildeve and Eustacia. In the end, then, the novel is as much a dramatic exploration and exposition of the pagan-Christian polarity as an unqualified denunciation of the Christian outlook.

Once this is granted, however, one has still to contend with the bitterness of the unfrocked priest who can love and loathe at once the thing of which he has been deprived. Certainly, if the dramatic balance of the novel is tipped at all, there is little doubt that it is, as this study may have shown, to the disadvantage of the Christian point of view and to the substantial advantage of the pagan. Hardy would be able in the novels of the 1890's, in *Tess* and in *Jude*, to record in more specific terms his quarrel with the Christian order of things. But it is doubtful that, with all his later opportunities for open denunciation, he ever directed a more forceful and more ef-

3. Mrs. Hardy, *The Early Life*, p. 211.

fective attack upon the lost faith of his youth than in this earlier
novel. The textual alterations that substituted "doctrine" for "Christianity" and "Fate" for "God" are the very real symptoms, then, of a
motive every bit as diabolical as that which governed Eustacia, the
reddleman and the deceptively-innocent association of peasants:
they disguise the subversive, anti-christian argument which would
seem to have been a main motive and organizing force of *The Return of the Native* and which, although it could not openly be asserted, was, and is still, everywhere active beneath its unassuming
surface.

RICHARD SWIGG

Thomas Hardy and the Problem of the 'Middle Distance'†

It is not difficult to see a confusion of purpose in the art of Hardy's
novels, but less easy to describe the source of the unease. We may
put aside the philosophic defences by which Hardy seems to be explaining (and misrepresenting) his art, but then we must contend
with the nature of the impulses, the strange energies, the tender-
nesses—all that sensitive knowledge, in fact, which the 'philosophy'
is trying to defend. Through this inner knowledge there seems to
run a basic misgiving on Hardy's part, a sense of bemusement,
something vulnerable in him which winces and falters. It is a hesi-
tancy in the art which denies adequate voice to the latent urgings
of the novels and which gives them the shape of an imprecise meta-
physic or an approximate 'impression'.

Hardy, however, in letting the approximations remain, seems
quite knowingly to tolerate this restricting of his art.[1] But, as a passage from *Jude the Obscure* reveals, there is consistency in his self-
limiting. Somewhat like his own Jude he stands at bay behind an
intervening filter or 'philosophy', partly sheltered from the harsh
sun of contingency:

---

† From *Lawrence, Hardy, and American Literature* (Oxford: Oxford UP, 1972), pp. 3–13.
Reprinted by permission of the author.
1. See Hardy's note on an article about him in *The Fortnightly Magazine*, April 1917: 'Like
so many critics, Mr. Courtney treats my works of art as if they were a scientific system of
philosophy, although I have repeatedly stated in prefaces and elsewhere that the views in
them are *seemings*, provisional impressions only, used for artistic purposes because they
represent approximately the impressions of the age, and are plausible, till somebody produces better theories of the universe' (*The Life of Thomas Hardy, 1840–1928*, by Florence Emily Hardy (1962), p. 375). See also a letter, December 1920: '. . . I have no
philosophy—merely what I have often explained to be only a confused heap of impressions, like those of a bewildered child at a conjuring show . . .' (Ibid., p. 410).

He pulled his straw hat over his face, and peered through the interstices of the plaiting at the white brightness, vaguely reflecting. Growing up brought responsibilities, he found. Events did not rhyme quite as he had thought. Nature's logic was too horrid for him to care for. That mercy towards one set of creatures was cruelty towards another sickened his sense of harmony. As you got older, and felt yourself to be at the centre of your time, and not at a point in its circumference, as you had felt when you were little, you were seized with a sort of shuddering, he perceived. All around you there seemed to be something glaring, garish, rattling, and the noises and glares hit upon the little cell called your life, and shook it, and warped it.[2]

As the 'little cell' shrinks back from the glare of full consciousness, one touches with it the erratic stamina at the heart of the novels—the unreliable energies, the fitful determination, which are ultimately disappointing when they fail to carry Hardy's intuitiveness all the way into firm, mature realization. One touches with Jude the diffident imagination of the earlier novelist, the man who noted in his diary the month that he published *The Return of the Native*: 'Woke before it was light. Felt that I had not enough staying power to hold my own in the world' (28 November 1878; *Life*, p. 124).

I

In contrast, *The Return of the Native* itself does possess a 'staying power' of a circumscribed but decisive kind. By the creation of Egdon Heath, Hardy propounds a mental defensiveness of a quality to be found nowhere else in the novels, for here a stern, undaunted face is turned against the mysterious illogicalities of life. The Heath is as much an outer mental barrier as it is a place, a strange 'philosophic' safeguard for that life and knowledge which is content to stay within the boundary of its attitudes. This 'great inviolate place', 'slighted and enduring'—and doggedly insensitive to the pains of human history—is like the haggard rind grown round the inner, sensitive organism. It is the stubborn, long-distance vision which protects the small satisfactions to be found within the casing, the microscopic joys or contentment of the insects' consciousness—as with the ants toiling and bustling in their Heath thoroughfare, the stupefied wasps creeping or rolling inside the fallen apples, the maggots wallowing in the dried ponds, and the butterfly-acrobats sporting round Clym Yeobright's furze-book. At this minute level the imagination is stable, free, uninhibited.

2. *Jude the Obscure*, Part First, Chapter 2. Page references to *The Return of the Native*, given in the text, have been changed to correspond to this edition.

But if this sensuous vision is touched by Hardy's defensive consciousness, a blight seems to occur. It is as if all the inner succulence, all the vivid strangeness, become one, in tragic withering,
with the outer mental shell, Egdon. When the Heath speaks
through the 'mummied heath-bells of the past summer, originally
tender and purple, now washed colourless by Michaelmas rains,
and dried to dead skins by October suns,' its November winds create a note akin to 'the ruins of human song . . . a worn whisper, dry
and papery.' Human aspirations in the novel press for some realization beyond the small satisfactions, beyond the Egdon limits, but
this would take Hardy out and into the blinding light of original,
perplexing consciousness. The creative energy in him hesitates, and
so, like the heath-bells, the aspirations lose their succulence and
integrity, passing into dead forms, into dull, inferior motives.

This is the fate of Eustacia and Mrs. Yeobright, who are ultimately assigned a withered expression for their unspecified yearnings. Both women are intuitive in generalized vision as they look
beyond the encompassing Heath, and both lack the finer featuring,
the more conscious rendering, to champion and give exact shape to
their vague desires. Hardy says of Eustacia (p. 63), 'There was no
middle distance in her perspective.' What *we* might say is that he
cannot let her progress from her unconscious desire close at hand
to the uncertainly-perceived finer form in the far distance, because
there is a connecting step missing in his consciousness. At the
point in Hardy's thinking where he falters over the problem of conscious shape (and so has to betray the imagination in him), there
the bright, fluid vision of Eustacia's dreams must dry and dull.
Thus, after hearing Clym's voice on the night of his arrival on the
Heath, Eustacia dreams of herself (p. 104) dancing as in Paradise
with a man in silver armour, both moving in brilliance and harmony
against the background of the Heath. After the dancers have dived
into one of the Heath pools and come out 'into an iridescent hollow, arched with rainbows', the silver knight begins to remove his
casque to kiss her. But the features are not to be seen, the shape
cannot be stabilized: 'At that moment there was a cracking noise,
and his figure fell into fragments like a pack of cards.' Daylight has
arrived while Eustacia is dreaming, and a maidservant has opened
the window-shutter. But the imaginative brilliance again appears
(p. 169) in Eustacia's fascination with Clym's talk of the Louvre
and of the room filled with glittering treasure: ' ". . . a perfect blaze
of splendour. The rays bristle and dart from the encrustations of
gilding to the magnificent inlaid coffers . . . till there is a perfect
network of light which quite dazzles the eye." ' And Clym, as the
native returned from Paris and the diamond trade, is in Eustacia's
eyes the human featuring of these alien riches: ' "Clym, the

eclipsed moonlight shines upon your face with a strange foreign colour, and shows its shape as if it were cut out in gold." '

Eustacia's paradisal yearnings are akin to Mrs. Yeobright's less romantic but equally far-gazing intuitive sight. Meditatively flying beyond the limits of her own body, the older woman also lacks a middle distance: 'Communities were seen by her as from a distance . . . vast masses of beings, jostling, zigzagging, and processioning in definite directions, but whose features are indistinguishable by the very comprehensiveness of the view.' Her undetailed grasp of mankind in its general, overall shiftings is comparable to Eustacia's dream of free movement and brilliant imaginative treasure, and makes Mrs. Yeobright one of those blind, female seers who 'can watch a world which they never saw, and estimate forces of which they have only heard.' Like Eustacia, she seeks some unembodied larger liberty beyond the hemmings-in of the unthinking Heath routine, and so she must instinctively turn from the sight of the busy ants working across their age-old little track on the Heath, to see (p. 241) a heron flying 'with his face towards the sun'. It is her equivalent of Eustacia's anonymous knight: 'He had come dripping wet from some pool in the valleys, and as he flew the edges and lining of his wings, his thighs, and his breast were so caught by the bright sunbeams that he appeared as if formed of burnished silver.'

Amongst these fluid cravings as they pursue conscious identity or form, one finds the real inner plan of the novel lying dormant or imperfectly construed. At moments Hardy can suggest, almost with the general comprehensiveness of his Mrs. Yeobright, the clear path of aspiration—most notably when he pictures Eustacia (p. 15) standing anonymous and alone on Rainbarrow:

> Above the plain rose the hill, above the hill rose the barrow, and above the barrow rose the figure. Above the figure was nothing that could be mapped elsewhere than on a celestial globe.

Significantly it is here, where the imagination needs it—above the 'homogeneous' organism of earth merging with the human figure, above the featureless and unparticularized—that Hardy places the man from heaven in Eustacia's dream, the 'high thinking' Clym Yeobright, heard only as a voice when he first comes back and seen for a moment as the worn, mentally-ridden 'countenance of the future'. His is the face or the human identity in which the anonymous desires of the women locate themselves, but when those desires are directly particularized in relation to Clym, when Hardy interprets them through Clym's mind, the precious metal becomes selfish currency. The aspiring for an enrichment to the spirit, as suggested by the glistening values of the silver knight, the Louvre treasure, and the burnished heron, is translated through the strain upon Clym as the desire for social gain—Eustacia seen as hopelessly romantic in pursuit of a Paris of fashion and pleasure; Mrs. Yeobright seen as more staid in her desire for Clym's enhancement in status and affluence in business. On this level Hardy makes the conflict one of social versus nonsocial purposes, with Clym shared out and broken between the claims of his two loves; but on the level of imagination, the problem is more radical.

What one sees in Clym's breakdown is Hardy's failure to sustain him as the enactor of *any* desires. Hardy can carry the striving dreams no further in Clym, and they must end as shrivelled ideas, taking on the brown gaunt look which both the Heath and Clym come to have. So although Clym is blinded and burnt out by the women's overpowering wishes, the burden he really carries is the strain of the novel's consciousness. His 'culture scheme' displays the impasse in which he and the women are fixed. He comes back to teach the ordinary Egdon people 'that they might rise to a serene comprehensiveness without going through the process of enriching themselves.' But there is no intermediate stage, no middle distance, no method of translating desires into accurate reality, which Clym can give to the women, let alone to his pupils. In terms of the plot-conflict, Mrs. Yeobright and Eustacia are disappointed in Clym as a teacher because their social ambitions have been betrayed; but in terms of imagination his 'culture scheme' betrays them because it has no means of giving stability to their deeper, spiritual ambitions. Therefore Clym must be an implausible figure of consciousness. If the two women are the question of the novel, Clym is the wavering answer.

There is no adequate reply to the aspirings but Hardy fashions a semblance of one when he characterizes the desires inside a simple moral picture. At the same time he leaves himself free not to have to confirm the accuracy of the picture. When the unfulfilled ambitions are seen through the eyes of the ordinary Heath people, when they are interpreted through the obviously approximate 'impression' of custom, humour, ignorance, and superstition, then the vital desires of the aspirers can be evaluated and given the appearance of being more manageable than they really are—all without Hardy's having to take explicit responsibility for the crude moral shaping and identification which he uses.

Thus the actors, Egdon people and aspirers, are assigned their parts in a primitive drama in which, as with the defiant bonfires at the beginning of the novel and the mummers' play later, the small community defeats evil menaces from the outer darkness: so on Rainbarrow the Devil is tempted into the small area of firelight, and at Christmas St. George is victorious over the Saracen. Yet though this primitive, superstitious morality allows Hardy to simplify the issues, he does not give complete, creative assent to the work of the morality's agents, Venn and Susan Nunsuch. These covert protectors of the innocent in the little commonwealth remain suspiciously like the devils and witches they actively war upon—Venn, the faithful defender of Thomasin's honour, the constant knight, appears on Rainbarrow like a red demon summoned up by the wild dance of the community; Susan Nunsuch, the proclaimer of Eustacia as a witch, remains the superstitious victimizer, not the victim.

But although Hardy will not support these agents when they carry the moral verdict beyond the narrow system of values and strike out in real violence, with Susan's knife attack on Eustacia in the church and Venn's gun assault on Wildeve, he will happily establish the simple moral arena from which they are only extending its judgements. There, with sanction, it seems, Eustacia and Wildeve in their passion can be more clearly seen as threats to the peace of Thomasin and Clym. Once brought within the bounds of the moral ordering, their identity becomes that of intruders, controlled by their traditionally doomed roles in a predictable folk play. The desires which create the silver knight of Eustacia's dream cannot be met by the ultimately disappointing higher consciousness of Clym but they can be replied to by the crude moral consciousness. Therefore, Eustacia in pursuit of Clym as the knight of her romantic dream, intrudes into the Christmas mumming as the Turkish knight, slays the Valiant Soldier, and is finally killed after a 'gradual sinking to earth' by St. George. In the same way, Wildeve intrudes on Christian Cantle's mission with Mrs. Yeobright's guineas, and the small circle of heath where they gamble by lantern-light becomes another morality arena, inside which Christian cries out against the dice as 'the devil's play-things' and fears damnation: ' "The devil will toss me into the flames." ' This Valiant Soldier is easily cleared of his money, but as he falls, Venn appears as another St. George to win back the guineas from the Devil in a burst of intense play.

Hardy almost admits that the moral ordering is a travesty of passion, a device which whittles energy down to the size of caricature. His imagination cannot help suggesting this of the gambling fury— 'their eyes being concentrated upon the little flat stone, which to them was an arena vast and important as a battle-field.' Nevertheless, Hardy retreats to this small-scale simplicity in order to make acceptable those events which are really caused by the failure of consciousness in his aspirers, as one sees with the death of Mrs. Yeobright. After being excluded from her son's house because Eustacia feared Wildeve's discovery there, Mrs. Yeobright dies from an adder's bite and from fatigued despair on the Heath. But one feels that the character is overwhelmed by a lack of 'staying power', by Hardy's withdrawal of energy from a cause that cannot hold its own in the merciless glare of the sun—the blinding light which parches the imagination dry. Brought to the ground from her spiritual and social aloofness, she reaches the level of the creeping things previously unconsidered in her vision and the level of the morality at which her decline can be more easily interpreted.

At the gathering in the turf-hut (pp. 246–48) where they attempt to revive her, the morality arena again appears—at first in Christian Cantle's remark on the snake, like the ' "old serpent in God's garden, that gied the apple to the young woman with no clothes" ', and later when the indictment of unseen evil reaches out beyond the small group round Mrs. Yeobright in the flickering light of the hut and implicates Eustacia and Wildeve, standing in the shadows. It is from these simple terms of moral reference, by which the fierce glare which *really* kills Mrs. Yeobright is lit more manageably, that Clym ultimately takes his consciousness. He is worn by remorse and his discovery of Eustacia's part in the affair, yielding up his high thinking to accept in exhaustion the superstitious, conforming judgements of the ignorant: ' "How bewitched I was! How could there be any good in a woman that everybody spoke ill of?" ' He hesitates in regret after he has driven Eustacia away, but the primitive judgement remains in force, to be finally executed by her drowning.

Nevertheless, the double-sided method of presenting her death—Eustacia pulled under, exhausted and protesting against fate, while at the same moment Susan Nunsuch works vindictive magic against her—suggests more openly than in the death of Mrs. Yeobright that Hardy is leaving in doubt the justice of his moral explanation. On one side Eustacia complains (p. 294) of her unfair treatment by life, her lack of fulfilment and Wildeve's inadequacy as a passionate equal: ' "He's not *great* enough for me to give myself to—he does not suffice for my desire! . . . I was capable of much; but I have been injured and blighted and crushed by things beyond my control!" ' With her one looks up towards that blank in development which Hardy cannot bridge with his unstable, unenriched Clym. But against her, in the sinking vision, where Eustacia can be viewed as too self-willed, proud, and socially ambitious, she is scaled down to the terms of the reductive morality, made the size of the little wax image that Susan moulds, stabs, and finally melts in the fire. In spacing out the complaints Hardy is free to endorse neither Eustacia's protest against the incomprehensible nor the vengeful retort of the primitive morality. When he creates (pp. 293–94) the impression that Eustacia is inevitably engulfed by the Heath, so that she 'ceased to stand erect, gradually crouching down under the umbrella as if she were drawn into the Barrow by a hand from beneath', the moral, fatalistic effect is kept deliberately approximate—a 'seeming' which speaks only vaguely for what Hardy cannot define: the real inevitability of her fall. Eustacia must die because he cannot develop her beyond his own gaunt mental consciousness, and so she must be absorbed by Egdon, the grim expression of that consciousness.

There is a similar wavering effect in the account of Clym's fall. He comes (p. 166) at the moment of the moon's eclipse as the lover and as the 'high thinking' and mentally straining progressive. His spiritual eye travels at long distance over the lunar shape as if it were an image of an unreachable world where personal development can freely take place, unhindered by society's crass demand for status and ambition. What the silver knight and the heron are to the women, so the moon is to Clym. Yet the bright, ghastly geography of 'the silvery globe'—'the Bay of Rainbows, the sombre Sea of Crises, the Ocean of Storms, the Lake of Dreams, the vast Walled Plains, and the wondrous Ring Mountains'—is the very picture of his own ravaged consciousness, stretched to its uttermost limit. One reaches with Clym the bounds of the novel's own consciousness, for the 'far-removed landscape' of the moon, with its wild, barren deserts, is really the 'gaunt waste in Thule' which is Egdon, the outermost mental crust in which the unresolved strivings take on their final, rigid moulding. At the exact moment that Clym's limits as a developing individual are fixed, a 'tawny stain' begins to grow on the moon's edge, and the cloaked figure of Eustacia arrives to eclipse her lover's mind by a sensual darkening. So stamina falters, Clym the silver knight begins to collapse, while in the moral framework the Valiant Soldier is overwhelmed by the Turkish knight in her powerful egotism. In the same way Hardy allows a possible shift of interpretation when he recounts Eustacia's meeting (p. 79) with Wildeve on the Heath, watched from his hiding-place by Venn: 'They were as two horns which the sluggish heath had put forth from its crown, like a mollusc, and had now again drawn in.' They can be seen as abortive creations, hesitantly venturing beyond the protective shell of Egdon, but unable to survive as stable, larger figures in an atmosphere where there is no further consciousness to support them, no 'intervening . . . ether'[3] through which to pass to fulfilment. Or Eustacia and Wildeve can be viewed through the judging eyes of Venn who is disguised as part of the Heath and who submerges them within it by his moral vision, as he recalls the adventured aberrations.

3. Yeobright's preaching 'was not unlike arguing to ancient Chaldeans that in ascending from earth to the pure empyrean it was not necessary to pass first into the intervening heaven of ether' (p. 148).

The aspirers who seek paradisal harmony cannot escape from Hardy's 'tragical' stoicism and his perplexed stubbornness, his view of life's illogicalities and discords. It is only underneath that attitude, underneath the hard Egdon shell, that life begins to make strange sense and harmony, amongst the beautiful, blind movements of the purely instinctive life. But harmony can only be found at this level if the upper layer of stoicism is forgotten, if the crude moral picturing is abandoned, and if the human spirit submits to an intense restriction. So, in the gambling scene, the human intensity of the play tightens the moral consciousness of the scene to the point where it disappears, snuffed out by the moth in its blind flight into the lantern flame, and is replaced, almost immediately and unthinkingly, by the light from the glow-worms, the insect consciousness.

But Hardy's suggestion of a *quid pro quo* interchange between man and the small life of the Heath is not presented in all its astonishing variety until the description of Clym's new life as the temporarily blinded furze-cutter, 'not more distinguishable from the scene around him than the green caterpillar from the leaf it feeds on.' Here, through Clym's mindless absorption, is the sensitive inner landscape of Egdon with its strange lustres and movements, like a minute paradise, a non-human community, the only *real* place on earth where concern for social aggrandizement does not exist. Perhaps its strangest aspect arises from the inclusion of the human figure and hence the normalizing of the alien vision round him, so that the scene is more extraordinary in proportion to the unself-remarking manner:

> His daily life was of a curious microscopic sort, his whole world being limited to a circuit of a few feet from his person. His familiars were creeping and winged things, and they seemed to enroll him in their band. Bees hummed around his ears with an intimate air, and tugged at the heath and the furze-flowers at his side in such numbers as to weigh them down to the sod. The strange amber-coloured butterflies which Egdon produced, and which were never seen elsewhere, quivered in the breath of his lips, alighted upon his bowed back, and sported with the glittering point of his hook as he flourished it up and down. Tribes of emerald-green grasshoppers leaped over his feet, falling awkwardly on their backs, heads, or hips, like unskilful acrobats, as chance might rule; or engaged themselves in noisy flirtations under the fern-fronds with silent ones of homely hue. Huge flies, ignorant of larders and wire-netting, and quite in a savage state, buzzed about him without knowing that he was a man. In and out of the fern-dells snakes glided in their most brilliant blue and yellow

guise, it being the season immediately following the shedding of their old skins, when their colours are brightest. Litters of young rabbits came out from their forms to sun themselves upon hillocks, the hot beams blazing through the delicate tissue of each thin-fleshed ear, and firing it to a blood-red transparency in which the veins could be seen. None of them feared him.   (p. 211)

But the unendangered, unknowing freedom of this vision, in all its curious features and relaxed knowledge, retains a tinge of the fantastic because while the human mind is being assimilated and consoled Hardy is still aware in Mrs. Yeobright of a responsibility to higher consciousness. One senses that the 'intimate air' of Clym's 'familiars' is due to Hardy's normalizing and presenting as acceptable Clym's new mindless identity in defence against the larger view in Mrs. Yeobright which (p. 232), in disappointment, makes her 'scarcely able to familiarize herself with this strange reality.' Even though the playfulness of the microscopic world is expanded in acuteness and precise delicacy against Mrs. Yeobright's long-range generalizing vision (and social scheming), something of Hardy's own dissatisfaction with Clym as a failed human being remains in the women's disappointment and the tragic sympathy allowed them. Their disillusion, although partly accounted for by their social hopes, persists as an implicit charge of failure from which Hardy will not defend Clym. To live on, Clym must be less than a human being in his restriction; so latterly his life 'creeps like a snail'. Burnt out as a lover but dutifully he offers himself as a husband to Thomasin, and lastly becomes a preacher on 'morally unimpeachable subjects'. But 'Some believed him, and some believed not', and Hardy, as throughout the novel, refuses to confirm the truth of his moral ordering and its spokesmen.

MICHAEL WHEELER

The Defects of the Real†

*   *   *

The publication of *The Return of the Native* in 1878 is generally regarded as a turning point in Hardy's career as a novelist. The 'cleverness' of the work seems to suggest a new ambition in Hardy, and an awareness of an intelligent readership for whom he could write.[1]

---

† From *The Art of Allusion in Victorian Fiction* (London: Macmillan, 1979), Chapter 9, pp. 137–50. Reprinted by permission of the author.
1. Hardy busily collected literary fragments and quotations (his 'Literary Notes') in the year preceding the writing of the *Return*, clearly preparing himself for a major literary work.

(At least two of his contemporary reviewers complained that in striving to be clever he had failed to entertain his readers.) Modern critics have argued that his many allusions to classical literature, contemporary poetry, and other kinds of adopted texts are symptomatic of tendencies towards self-advertisement in his fiction and the attempted aggrandisement of characters who actually live in an unheroic age. There is sense in this argument, although many of the allusions which have been criticised seem designed to undermine the status of the characters rather than to elevate it. For example, some of the Promethean references suggest that Clym Yeobright is a pathetically limited product of the nineteenth century rather than a would-be superman who never quite convinces. Louis Crompton writes: 'Hardy's use of heroic archetypes is partly serious and partly ironic, his characters appearing at one moment comparable to their heroic models, at other times ludicrously smaller and weaker.'[2] Where Crompton finds liveliness in these constant variations, and richness in the novel's modal syncretism (romance, high tragedy and modern realistic fiction), other readers have found confusion and clutter. One particular parallel text, however, Keats's *Endymion*, is more important in relation to the *Return* than are the majority of isolated allusions in the novel. *Tess of the d'Urbervilles* (1891) is less cluttered than the *Return*. Hardy's deletions in the manuscript and early editions suggest that he may have recognised the dangers of incorporating too many unconnected references to a number of adopted texts in this later novel, and that even references to his most important adopted text, Ovid's *Metamorphoses*, could have been distracting. Yet allusion underlines a central theme in both novels: the vain pursuit of the ideal in a world in which 'the defects of natural laws' operate upon the 'defects of the real' (*Return*, III. 1; *Tess*, 36).

II

The Return of the Native first appeared as a serial in the monthly *Belgravia* magazine between January and December 1878. The first number has no motto under the title heading, whereas each of the three volumes which make up the first book edition, published in November 1878, has an unascribed title-page motto from Keats's *Endymion*:

See Robert Gittings, *The Older Hardy* (London, 1978), pp. 2–6, and *The Literary Notes of Thomas Hardy*, edited by Lennart A. Björk, Gothenburg Studies in English, 29, 2 vols (Gothenburg, 1974), I, xviii–xix, xxxv.

2. Louis Crompton, 'The Sunburnt God: Ritual and Tragic Myth in *The Return of the Native*', *Boston University Studies in English*, 4 (1960), 229–40 (p. 232).

'To sorrow
I bade good morrow,
And thought to leave her far away behind;
But cheerly, cheerly,
She loves me dearly;
She is so constant to me, and so kind.
I would deceive her,
And so leave her,
But ah! she is so constant and so kind.'

It is impossible to tell whether Hardy had the motto in mind before January 1878, but decided not to use it in the serial, or whether he chose it later for the first edition of November. The first explanation is tenable, since title-page mottoes which are to be borne in mind throughout a reading of a volume or an entire novel are less effective in a monthly serial version. Even if the second explanation were correct, however, and Hardy first thought of adding the motto not long before November, the allusion could have the effect of alerting the reader who recognises it to the most important parallel text in the *Return*: the text which can be 'read' alongside the novel. Another initial difficulty concerns the context of the motto in the poem (IV.173–81); the fifth stanza of the Indian Maid's 'roundelay', which she sings 'beneath the midmost forest tree'. Sometimes quoted out of context, the song is one of several atypical passages in the fourth book in which Keats breaks away from the rhyming couplet form of the rest of the poem. The stanza may have been chosen by Hardy merely as a convenient way of striking the key-note of a novel in which Sorrow is 'constant' to its central characters. Indeed, the fact that the motto is unascribed could be said to support this view. The contiguity of numerous themes and motifs in the novel and the poem suggests, however, that the motto could not just as well have been chosen from another source which touched on a similar theme.

Hardy's portrayal of Eustacia Vye in the famous 'Queen of Night' chapter in the first book is an extreme example of overstatement, where he piles reference upon reference and association upon association: Olympus, the Fates, the Sphinx, Paganism, *Athalie*, Artemis, Athena, Hera, Hades, Tartarus, Alcinous, Phaeacia, Heaven, Delphi, Héloïse, and Cleopatra (I.7). Most of these references could have been omitted without undermining their main function: to emphasise Eustacia's pride and ambition, and her frustration at being an earth-bound prisoner in Egdon. Read with *Endymion* in mind, however, certain passages share common associations. The tension between mortality and divinity which Endymion knows in his love for both Cynthia, the moon-goddess, and the Indian Maid is paralleled in the opening sentences of the chapter: 'Eustacia Vye was the raw material of a divinity. On Olympus she would have done well with a little preparation. She had the passions and instincts which make a model goddess, that is, those which make not quite a model woman' (I.7). (The word 'model', incorporated in the first and later editions, with its hint of artificiality and self-consciousness, is an improvement on 'faultless' in the manuscript[3] and the *Belgravia*[4].) Among the list of mythological allusions, the reference to the Greek Artemis, generally recognised as being identical to the Roman Diana, whose other name was Cynthia, makes the parallel between Eustacia and Cynthia more explicit: 'The new moon behind her head, an old helmet upon it, a diadem of accidental dewdrops round her brow, would have been adjuncts sufficient to strike the note of Artemis, Athena, or Hera respectively, with as close an approximation to the antique as that which passes muster on many respected canvases.' Her colouring is that of the Indian Maid, the 'stranger of dark tresses' (IV.462), and, like Cynthia's (I.591f), her face is described in relation to the sky and clouds: 'To see her hair was to fancy that a whole winter did not contain darkness enough to form its shadow: it closed over her forehead like nightfall extinguishing the western glow. . . . Across the upper part of her head she wore a thin fillet of black velvet, restraining the luxuriance of her shady hair, in a way which added much to this class of majesty by irregularly clouding her forehead.'

The shading of Eustacia's face is a recurring motif in the novel, usually associated with the moon. Clym and Eustacia first speak to each other in the moonlight after the mummers' play, when Eustacia's face is veiled with ribbons (II.6). She pushes up her veil when she signs the register at Wildeve's wedding (II.8) and later veils herself when she joins the country dance with him, by moonlight (IV.3). This veiling motif is most skilfully developed during the eclipse sequence, when Clym is enchanted by Eustacia. With sickening dramatic irony, Clym's mother has already warned him that he is 'blinded' and that it was a 'bad day' for him when he 'first set eyes on' Eustacia (III.3). The following evening he walks on to Rainbarrow and lies down, his face towards the moon: 'His eye travelled over the length and breadth of that distant country . . . till he almost felt himself to be voyaging bodily through its wild scenes' (III.4). The eclipsed moon is reminiscent of Eustacia's face, covered with a veil or clouded by her black hair: 'While he watched the far-removed landscape a tawny stain grew into being on the lower verge: the eclipse had begun. This marked a preconcerted moment:

3. *The Return of the Native*, University College, Dublin MS 11, f. 72a.
4. *Belgravia*, 34 (January–February 1878), 502.

for the remote celestial phenomenon had been pressed into sublunary service as a lover's signal. Yeobright's mind flew back to earth
at the sight; he arose, shook himself, and listened.' Having greeted
Eustacia as a lover, he examines her face as he has examined that
of the moon: 'Let me look right into your moonlit face, and dwell
on every line and curve in it! Only a few hair-breadths make the difference between this face and faces I have seen many times before
I knew you; yet what a difference—the difference between everything and nothing at all.' The fragility of this vision of beauty is un-
derlined by frequent references to sight and blindness. As the
eclipse comes to an end Eustacia laments that their 'time is slipping, slipping, slipping', and they have to part. In the final paragraph of the chapter the moon/Eustacia analogy is made explicit.
Clym knows that his love for his mother and his love for Eustacia
are incompatible. 'Thus as his sight grew accustomed to the first
blinding halo kindled about him by love and beauty, Yeobright began to perceive what a strait he was in.'

As he scrutinises the moon and Eustacia's face, Clym is a latter-
day Endymion, seeing his Cynthia in all her splendour for the first
time:

> Methought I lay
> Watching the zenith . . .
> Spreading imaginary pinions wide.
> When, presently, the stars began to glide,
> And faint away, before my eager view.
> At which I sighed that I could not pursue,
> And dropped my vision to the horizon's verge—
> And lo! from opening clouds, I saw emerge
> The loveliest moon, that ever silver'd o'er
> A shell for Neptune's goblet. She did soar
> So passionately bright, my dazzled soul
> Commingling with her argent spheres did roll. . . .
>
> To commune with those orbs, once more I raised
> My sight right upward; but it was quite dazed
> By a bright something, sailing down apace,
> Making me quickly veil my eyes and face.   (I.578–603)

Endymion's dazzling by the vision of Cynthia is as sudden as his
later enchantment by her mortal emanation, the Indian Maid
(IV.85f). On Rainbarrow, Eustacia verges on apotheosis, beautiful
in Clym's dazzled eyes and craving for higher things than Egdon
can offer. At once a would-be Cynthia and an Indian Maid, she is a
'model goddess' and 'not quite a model woman'.

When Eustacia insists on hearing about Paris, during the conversation on the barrow, the reluctant Clym chooses to describe a 'sunny room in the Louvre' which he considers a fitting place for her to live in—the Galerie d'Apollon:

> Its windows are mainly east; and in the early morning, when the sun is bright, the whole apartment is in a perfect blaze of splendour. The rays bristle and dart from the encrustations of gilding to the magnificent inlaid coffers, from the coffers to the gold and silver plate, from the plate to the jewels and precious stones, from these to the enamels, till there is a perfect network of light which quite dazzles the eye. (III.4)

Cynthia commands Endymion to 'Descend/ . . . Into the sparry hollows of the world' (II.202–4). Fearfully he moves into the underworld:

> Dark, nor light,
> The region; nor bright, nor sombre wholly,
> But mingled up; a gleaming melancholy;
> A dusky empire and its diadems;
> One faint eternal eventide of gems.
> Aye, millions sparkled on a vein of gold,
> Along whose track the prince quick footsteps told,
> With all its lines abrupt and angular. . . .
> Chilly and numb
> His bosom grew when first he far away
> Descried an orbèd diamond, set to fray
> Old darkness from his throne.   (II.221–46)

He then moves into 'a marble gallery, passing through / A mimic temple', sees 'a fair shrine' and, 'just beyond, on light tiptoe divine, / A quivered Dian', before which he veils his 'eye' (II.256–63). In this alien place he finds that 'thoughts of self' come on, 'how crude and sore / The journey homeward to habitual self' (275–6). Back on his native heath, as his 'habitual self', Clym is uneasy about recalling his Paris experiences, knowing that what was alien to him is apparently Eustacia's idea of the perfect home. (When Hardy decided to make Clym give up the Paris diamond business, rather than humble shopkeeping as he first planned, he gave himself more scope to emphasise the disparity between Clym's and the 'luxurious' Eustacia's world-views.) His sight deteriorates after his marriage to Eustacia and, like Endymion, he can cry: 'Before mine eyes thick films and shadows float' (II. 323).

In the chapter which follows the eclipse episode, the jealous Mrs Yeobright's 'sharp words' foil Clym's attempt to bring her and Eustacia together. Instead, he goes to meet his lover alone on the heath:

He was in a nest of vivid green. The ferny vegetation round him, though so abundant, was quite uniform: it was a grove of machine-made foliage, a world of green triangles with saw-edges, and not a single flower. The air was warm with a vaporous warmth, and the stillness was unbroken. Lizards, grass-hoppers, and ants were the only living things to be beheld. The scene seemed to belong to the ancient world of the carboniferous period, when the forms of plants were few, and of the fern kind; when there was neither bud nor blossom, nothing but a monotonous extent of leafage, amid which no bird sang. (III.5)

Isolated, and temporarily enclosed by these older and lower forms of plant and animal life, Clym is associated with the 'wretched wight' of Keats's 'La Belle Dame Sans Merci', in the unmarked quotation at the end of the paragraph:

> Oh, what can ail thee, knight-at-arms,
> Alone and palely loitering?
> The sedge has withered from the lake,
> And no birds sing! (1–4)

In this variation on the theme of the *femme fatale* and her victim, Hardy moves his protagonists from the Latmos of Rainbarrow to the 'elfin grot' (29) of the 'nest of vivid green' on the heath. As on the barrow, Eustacia regrets that 'the actual moment of a thing is so soon gone' and that her 'bliss . . . has been too intense and consuming'. Further echoes of Keats's poetry confirm this sense of the transitoriness of their love. They walk through the ferns together to 'the nether margin of the heath, where it became marshy, and merged in moorland'. The landscape is first reminiscent of 'Autumn':

The sun, resting on the horizon line, streamed across the ground from between copper-coloured and lilac clouds, stretched out in flats beneath a sky of pale soft green . . . groups of wailing gnats shone out, rising upwards and dancing about like sparks of fire. (III.5)	While barrèd clouds bloom the soft-dying day, And touch the stubble-plains with rosy hue. Then in a wailful choir the small gnats mourn Among the river sallows, borne aloft Or sinking as the light wind lives or dies . . . (25–9)

When Eustacia leaves Clym, having agreed that they will be married in a fortnight's time, she moves through the landscape of 'La Belle Dame':

> Clym watched her as she retired towards the sun. The lumi-
> nous rays wrapped her up with her increasing distance, and
> the rustle of her dress over the sprouting sedge and grass died
> away. As he watched, the dead flat of the scenery overpowered
> him, though he was fully alive to the beauty of that untar-
> nished early summer green which was worn for the nonce by
> the poorest blade. (III.5)

Symbolic of Clym's and Eustacia's love, the greenness of the foliage
is temporary, 'worn for the nonce'. The 'sedge' will 'wither' by late
autumn, when the 'squirrel's granary is full, / And the harvest's
done' (7–8). Clym can now concentrate on his most immediate
problems: 'Eustacia was now no longer the goddess but the woman
to him, a being to fight for, support, help, be maligned for.' She is
still, however, as elusively ethereal as La Belle Dame. Torn between
the enchantment of the beautiful goddess-Eustacia and the practical problems posed by the woman-Eustacia, his comparative security already seems undermined. The last bald statement of the
chapter in which the lovers decide to marry makes the point less
powerfully than the parallels with Keats's studies of anguished love
for immortal beauties: 'Whether Eustacia was to add one other to
the list of those who love too hotly to love long and well, the forthcoming event was certainly a ready way of proving' (III.5).

Hardy is often at his best when he places his people in an environment to which they respond imaginatively. In the two chapters
discussed above, that environment is associated with Keatsian landscapes in which human responses to elusive beauties are pathetically vulnerable. In both chapters, theme and scene become
indistinguishable. Hardy's response to Keats, shared by the reader
who recognises the parallels or what appear to be unmarked quotations, seems less a reading than a rewriting.

By the end of the subsequent (fourth) book, Clym has several
reasons for keeping his eyes to the ground, rather than scrutinising
the moon and Eustacia's face. His vision has deteriorated, ostensibly through excessive reading, forcing him to work at furze-cutting:
'His daily life was of a curious microscopic sort, his whole world being limited to a circuit of a few feet from his person' (IV.2). Eustacia's resentment causes a rift to develop between the couple which
widens after the death of Clym's mother. Book Fifth, which is to
end with the drownings in the weir, opens with a chapter motto:
'WHEREFORE IS LIGHT GIVEN TO HIM THAT IS IN MISERY.' Job 'cursed
his day':

> Let the day perish wherein I was born . . .
> Let that day be darkness . . .

> Wherefore is light given to him that is in
> misery, and life unto the bitter in soul;
>   Which long for death, but it cometh
> not . . . ?

(Job 3.3–4, 20–21)

The narrative opens with Clym and Eustacia responding to the moon in quite different ways. One moonlit evening, about three weeks after Mrs. Yeobright's funeral, Eustacia 'reclined over the garden gate as if to refresh herself awhile. The pale lunar touches which make beauties of hags lent divinity to this face, already beautiful' (V.1). Back in the house the 'pale, haggard' Clym lies in the front bedroom where a shaded light is burning. (He now more closely resembles the 'knight-at-arms' of 'La Belle Dame': 'Alone and palely loitering . . . / So haggard and so woe-begone' (2,6).) When Eustacia tells him that 'the moon is shining beautifully' his reply is Job-like: 'Shining, is it? What's the moon to a man like me? Let it shine—let anything be, so that I never see another day.' Now that Cynthia's spell is broken, the estrangement of the couple is inevitable.

When the catastrophe comes, Eustacia herself cannot see the moon. Setting out in the rain to meet Wildeve she is no longer the sure-footed lover who used to hurry to trysts on the heath: 'Skirting the pool she followed the path towards Rainbarrow, occasionally stumbling over twisted furze-roots, tufts of rushes, or oozing lumps of fleshy fungi, which at this season lay scattered about the heath like the rotten liver and lungs of some colossal animal. The moon and stars were closed up by cloud and rain to the degree of extinction' (V.7). The landscape seems as grotesque as the waste land through which Browning's Roland rides on his way to the Dark Tower. The manuscript (f.376) and *Belgravia* version of the second sentence quoted, amended for the first edition, lays more emphasis on the state of the heavens, but with an exactness which Hardy may have thought too ponderous: 'The moon and stars were closed up by cloud and rain, the density amounting to a lunar and sidereal extinction' (*Belgravia*, vol. 37, p. 14). Endymion's sense of foreboding, both in the underworld and after he has met the Indian Maid, has a special resonance when Wildeve and Eustacia drown in Shadwater Weir. His 'journey homeward to habitual self' is like a 'mad pursuing of the fog-born elf', whose 'flitting lantern . . . / Cheats us into a swamp' (II.277–9). He sits with the Maid 'waiting for some destruction' (IV.330) and later says to her: 'We might embrace and die—voluptuous thought' (IV.759). Whereas Endymion's fears prove unfounded when the Indian Maid is apotheosised as Cynthia and carries him off, 'spiritualized', to 'range/ These forests'

(IV.993–4), Eustacia dies in the pool and Clym survives only as a 'thin, pallid' Lazarus (V.9). Eustacia breaks the bonds of mortality only in death: 'They stood silently looking upon Eustacia, who, as she lay there still in death, eclipsed all her living phases. Pallor did not include all the quality of her complexion, which seemed more than whiteness; it was *almost* light' (V.9; my emphasis). This Indian Maid never becomes a Cynthia.

Although Hardy's 'original conception of the story did not design a marriage between Thomasin and Venn' (Note to VI.3), his changes being dictated by 'certain circumstances of serial publication', he handled Venn's courtship in such a way as to heighten the pathos of Clym's early love for his goddess-Eustacia and her own frustration as a mere mortal living on Edgon Heath. After the Maypole dancing on the green in front of Blooms-End, Venn tells Thomasin that he is waiting till the moon rises (VI.1). The subsequent scene parodies Clym's courtship of Eustacia at the time of the eclipse. As Venn looks for her glove, Thomasin watches him with eyes at once more acute and less visionary than her cousin's:

> Venn was still there. She watched the growth of the faint radiance appearing in the sky by the eastern hill, till presently the edge of the moon burst upwards and flooded the valley with light. Diggory's form was now distinct on the green; he was moving about in a bowed attitude, evidently scanning the grass for the precious missing article, walking in zigzags right and left till he should have passed over every foot of the ground.
>
> 'How very ridiculous!' Thomasin murmured to herself, in a tone which was intended to be satirical. 'To think that a man should be so silly as to go mooning about like that for a girl's glove! A respectable dairyman, too, and a man of money as he is now. What a pity!'

Unwittingly, Venn mimics Clym's stooping movements with his furze-hook. His 'mooning' is a pale imitation of Clym's lunar enchantment. That Thomasin's attitude is a healthy sign for a no-nonsense marriage only adds to one's sense of loss. Through the scene Hardy develops what formerly he had only stated in passing, when Thomasin set out on the night of the drownings: 'To her there were not, as to Eustacia, demons in the air, and malice in every bush and bough. The drops which lashed her face were not scorpions, but prosy rain; Egdon in the mass was no monster whatever, but impersonal open ground' (V.8). Eustacia's sublime conception of a grand passion leads to the weir, whereas Thomasin's commonsensical outlook leads to an Egdon wedding.

The triumph of normality over the sublime and the ideal conforms to the pattern of undermining which can be traced in the de-

velopment of the novel's main themes. The *Return* can be read as
an 'Antichristian Document', or as an early study of the 'Ache of
Modernism', in which traditional values and beliefs are exposed as
naive optimism in a hostile, godless universe.[5] Burkean sublimity
gives way to prosiness,[6] and classical concepts of the heroic are
shown to be 'displaced' in the modern age. Indeed, all Hardy's classical allusions should be read in the light of the paragraph which
he inserts in his commentary on Clym at the beginning of the third
book:

> The truth seems to be that a long line of disillusive centuries
> has permanently displaced the Hellenic idea of life, or what-
> ever it may be called. What the Greeks only suspected we
> know well; what their Aeschylus imagined our nursery children
> feel. That old-fashioned revelling in the general situation
> grows less and less possible as we uncover the defects of natu-
> ral laws, and see the quandary that man is in by their opera-
> tion. (III.1)

Printed in the first edition, this is a shortened version of the paragraph in the manuscript (f.194) which appeared in the *Belgravia*:

> It has been said that the capacity to enjoy is at bottom iden-
> tical with the capacity to produce; and the civilised world's
> lack of power to prolong in new combinations of art the old
> special beauties of men and gods, would imply that its sympa-
> thies lie secretly in other directions, despite any transient fash-
> ion. We have lost the true Hellenic eye, for this requires
> behind it the Hellenic idea of life; and a long line of disillusive
> centuries has permanently displaced that. The solecisms of an-
> cient thought are the grammar of modern. What the Greeks
> only suspected we know well. . . . (*Belgravia*, vol. 35, p. 480)

(The *Belgravia* version also has 'cosmic' for 'natural' laws.) This earlier version specifically draws attention to the role of the modern
artist, whereas the area of reference in the first and later editions is
more general. In a novel in which the hero is dazzled and almost
blinded, the phrase 'Hellenic eye' suggests limitations in both its
creator and his creatures. (Hardy may have deleted the passage because it seemed pretentious and over explicit.) In the *Return*, the
'physical beauty' to which he refers in the previous paragraph is
transient, perceived by eyes which become dim. The *Endymion* parallels in the novel mark a shift from visionary Romanticism (itself

5. See John Paterson, 'The *Return of the Native* as Antichristian Document', *Nineteenth-
Century Fiction*, 14 (1959–60), 111–27; David J. de Laura, ' "The Ache of Modernism"
in Hardy's Later Novels', *ELH*, 34 (1967), 380–99.
6. See S. F. Johnson, 'Hardy and Burke's "Sublime" ', in *Style in Prose Fiction: English
Institute Essays 1956*, edited by Harold C. Martin (New York and London, 1959),
pp. 55–86.

fragile in those hurried last lines in which Endymion is 'spiritualized') to a bleak vision of the 'defects of natural [or 'cosmic'] laws'.
Those who stand upright on Egdon will be knocked down. Aspirations beyond the most subservient stance in relation to the heath
will be ruthlessly crushed. A 'long line of disillusive centuries' belies
the possibility of escape through apotheosis.

Hardy's handling of all the Keatsian parallels discussed above
cannot be neatly classified as either the reworking of private literary
sources or the establishment of a relationship between his novel
and (public) adopted texts through allusion. *Endymion* is one of
those intermediate works to which I referred in Chapter 2, being
neither arcane nor familiar. Without the motto, even those Victorian readers of the *Return* who knew the poem would probably not
have noticed parallels. Only the motto can be categorised as an unmistakable allusion, but its lack of ascription and its special independent nature (as a passage which is better known than the poem
in which it is embedded) make its putative function as an indicator
of a parallel text questionable. What I have called the unmarked
quotations from 'La Belle Dame' and 'Autumn' ('no bird sang',
'sedge' and 'wailing gnats') are extremely flimsy and could easily be
missed. Indeed, it could be argued that they are not unmarked quotations at all, but merely echoes, fragments of sources which Hardy
was consciously or unconsciously reworking or developing as he
wrote. If the motto had been ascribed, the parallel *Endymion* passages more clearly indicated through allusion, and the echoes of
'La Belle Dame' and 'Autumn' made marked quotations, one could
confidently assert that Hardy as narrator used quotations from
Keats in order to focus the reader's attention on the demythologis-
ing of Romantic literary tradition, idealising and visionary, which is
one of the novel's major concerns. As it is, his highly illuminating
use of Keatsian themes must have been missed by many of the
novel's admirers.

ROSEMARIE MORGAN

Conflicting Courses in *The Return of the Native*†

At around the time Hardy was putting a coordinating finish on the
Wessex novels, two contemporary critics, the Folletts, while com-
mending the "half-inaudible discord" of his endings—that they
leave a taste that is "bitter-sweet, like that of life"—considered his

---

† This essay appears for the first time in this Norton Critical Edition. Page references are
   to this Norton Critical Edition.

greatest literary quality to be his scientific detachment. They held *The Return of the Native* to be exemplary. The internal setting of the novel, Egdon Heath, manifests, in a unique way, a "microcosm of personality" which in turn sets the stage "for the interplay of almost cosmic forces."[1] Thinking, at this time, along similar lines, but with the characters on stage to the fore, the *Spectator* praises Hardy for producing a "great art" that is "representative of life, not critical of it": *The Return of the Native* stands as Hardy's most complete "representation of life" because of its "intuitive sympathy with humanity in all its moods."[2]

Egdon itself is a "mood." Noted for its function as a central character in the novel, it personifies the mood of immanent nature, or perhaps more accurately, the moods of immanence. Gustav Holst, captivated by *The Return of the Native*, walked the Dorset heathlands just before Hardy died to soak up yet more atmosphere for his symphony. Capturing Egdon's mood and a sense of immanence in the symphonic "Egdon Heath," he moves with power and subtlety from the *adagio* of the quiet emergency of the novel's opening scenes through the *poco allegro* of nether regions alternately light and dark, restless and sudden, gloomy and glad, to an *andante maestoso* that aptly conveys that sensation so palpably felt in the novel of threshold, of all things verging on the brink: the brink of somewhere or something unknowable—forever poised.

In the case of Eustacia, who features centrally in this article, poise is the nature of her being. If Egdon is immanence personified, Eustacia is poise. Physically, she is statuesque, intellectually she is ready and expectant, emotionally and sexually she is strongly contained, repressed by a killingly monotonous existence to which she responds almost gravitationally (walking the earth by night and day), weighed down from first to last by the heavy forces of oppression, and always watching and waiting.

With the benefit of hindsight, backtracking through Hardy's earlier novels, we can detect precursors to Eustacia's characterization. In *A Pair of Blue Eyes*, for example, Elfride also seeks free expression to her sexual passions, but is crushed in the course of exploration. Bathsheba in *Far from the Madding Crowd* experiences a greater freedom, but insufficiently: denied the means of exploration necessary to the growth of self-knowledge, she is frustrated by inexperience and undermined by the censorious forces ranged against her.

The world of freedom and action Hardy's heroines project for themselves disintegrates as rapidly as the man-made world superimposes upon them its own curbing shape: with sexual awakening,

1. Follett, Helen Thomas, and Wilson Follett, *Thomas Hardy, Some Modern Novelists: Appreciations and Estimates* (New York: Holt, 1918), pp. 127–50.
2. *Spectator*, CIX 7 Sept. 1912, pp. 335–37.

every exploratory move toward self-discovery, self-realization, and
sexual understanding meets with obstruction in a male-dominated
world determined to highrank the more controllable, docile, meek,
compliant woman over the independent, daring, assertive, self-
determining, and dynamic. There are few areas of female exploration, whether occupational, sexual, or simply developmental, that
do not eventually conflict with the dominant male's will to dispos-
sess the autonomous woman of identity, self-purpose, and power.
From Henry Knight's nullification of Elfride's desires and needs to
Sue Bridehead's rebellion against the tyranny of man-made institutions, the Hardy heroine struggles toward but never encounters the
kind of liberated world projected by John Stuart Mill in which

> each individual will prove his or her own capacities in the only
> way in which capacities can be proved—by trial; and the world
> will have the benefit of the best faculties of all its inhabitants.[3]

In the Wessex microcosm, the world cannot have the benefit of the
best faculties of its inhabitants because half of it, the female half, is
denied the right to prove them.

While he was writing *The Return of the Native* in the mid- to late
1870s Hardy would have had just such issues in mind, for he was
reading the work of an emancipated woman he admired greatly,
George Sand. Not only openly defiant and unconventional, Sand
was to Hardy one of the "Immortals" of literature, and as he read
her novel, *Mauprat*, he took careful notes on a passage discussing a
typically male view of women:

> Men imagine that a woman has no individual existence, and
> that she ought always to be absorbed in them; and yet they
> love no woman deeply, unless she elevates herself, by her char-
> acter, above the weakness and inertia of her sex.[4]

And how to achieve this in a world in which she cannot prove her
own capacities?

Leaving the pages of *Mauprat* for his own novel, Hardy turns to
Eustacia and to a husband who most certainly feels she "ought always to be absorbed" in him. She hopes to "elevate herself," to assert her "individual existence" by escaping Egdon to live in the city,
to participate in "what is called life—music, poetry, passion, war
and all the beating and pulsing that is going on in the great arteries
of the world" (*RN*, 236), but although he may love her deeply Clym
loves himself a good deal more. In the face of her hopes and what
are to her deeply cherished dreams, he can only respond by either

3. See Gertrude Himmelfarb, *On Liberty and Liberalism* (New York: Knopf, 1974), p. 173.
4. See *The Literary Notebooks of Thomas Hardy*, 2 vols., ed. Lennart Björk (London:
Macmillan, 1985), I.49 (entry 483), and Björk's note, I.300.

teasing or belittling. Why, he banters, the Galerie d'Apollon "would make a fitting place for you to live in," and "the Little Trianon would suit us beautifully to live in, and you might walk in the gardens in the moonlight" (*RN*, 169). More characteristically, in total self-absorption, he regales her with tales of "Parisian life and character" and, to her torment, sings songs from Paris as he works on the heath, seemingly oblivious to her "sick despair," "the blasting effect upon her own life of that mood and condition in him" (*RN*, 212). With no songs and no stories of her own Eustacia can only turn away and weep.

It is part of Hardy's method in *The Return of the Native* to expose the anger and frustration suffered by the intelligent mind and the energetic body restricted to an unvarying, isolated existence. Thomasin's domestic world, with all its conventional trappings, throws Eustacia's into relief by contrast; the estranged solitary woman belongs to no circumscribed world, least of all Thomasin's, in the sense of settling in it, becoming habituated to it or wishing to remain in it. Where Thomasin fulfills reader expectations of the submissive, forbearing, dutiful wife, Eustacia does not. Indeed, in contemporary terms her nonconformity goes beyond the bounds of acceptability, and Hardy took great pains, particularly at the draft stages of the novel, to tone down his original conception of her: women with latent hermaphrodite, let alone "witch" qualities, did not, as perhaps they do today, command understanding, and certainly did not command respect. They were in a sense beyond recognition.

Eustacia's rebelliousness remained an area of deep concern to Hardy's editors and thus, also, to himself.[5] On the other hand, her fantasies are not so different from our own:

> To be loved to madness—such was her great desire. Love was to her the one cordial which could drive away the eating loneliness of her days. And she seemed to long for the abstraction called passionate love more than for any particular lover. (*RN*, 64)

The man-made marriage laws which call for obedience and duty in the new bride evidently exclude women such as the independently minded, anarchic Eustacia. Yet she must have had many counterparts in the nonfictional world of contemporary readers, albeit con-

---

5. Vigilant of prevailing codes of decorum Hardy wrote to his illustrator Arthur Hopkins in February 1878: "I think you have chosen well for the May illustration—certainly the incident after the mumming, with the mummers looking on, will be better than the mumming performance itself. Eustacia in boy's clothes, though pleasant enough to the imagination, would perhaps be unsafe as a picture." *Collected Letters of Thomas Hardy*, ed. R. L. Purdy and Michael Millgate (Oxford: Clarendon Press, 1978–88), I.54; hereafter abbreviated as *Letters*.

cealed in many cases beneath tight-lacing and the appearance of conformity.

Hardy, as is commonly known, was irritated by romantic plots with happy endings. The conventional Victorian denouement, getting-married-and-living-happily-ever-after, imposed a perniciously false coloration on life—both within the novel and beyond, in the ideology of the culture. Predictably, given the rejection of editors when he submitted *The Return of the Native* for serial publication,[6] he feigned an appearance of decorum, revising the last chapters to provide a conventional marriage for Thomasin; but Eustacia, wild and nonconformist, would flee her ties and remain unclaimed at the last.[7] Evidently, Thomasin, the conventionally "*good*" heroine, was dispensable, in terms of sacrificing her to market needs and those prevailing ideologies that dictated what was "good" for women and what "good" women did.[8]

Eustacia's tense and frustrated sexuality is also far removed from Bathsheba's self-delighting, auto-erotic passions, but it is no less expressive, no less palpable, no less physical. In his customary style Hardy turns to the natural-object metaphor in order to embed in his text the sexual nature of his heroine. Take for example the hermaphroditic image of the mollusc that "couples" the lovers Eustacia and Wildeve as they roam in the twilight of the heath:

> Their black figures sank and disappeared from against the sky. They were as two horns which the sluggish heath had put forth from its crown, like a mollusc, and had now again drawn in. (*RN*, 79)

"Horny" is very much a modern term but there is no doubt that Hardy is conjuring an image here pointing to the sexual arousal of

6. Leslie Stephen, editor of the *Cornhill*, took one look at the opening chapters and declared it too dangerous for a family magazine, but eventually *Belgravia* agreed to publish it.

7. In 1912 Hardy added the following footnote:

> The writer may state here that the original conception of the story did not design a marriage between Thomasin and Venn. He was to have retained his isolated and weird character to the last, and to have disappeared mysteriously from the heath, nobody knowing whither—Thomasin remaining a widow. But certain circumstances of serial publication led to a change of intent.
>
> Readers can therefore choose between the endings, and those with an austere artistic code can assume the more consistent conclusion to be the true one (Book Sixth: Aftercourses: Chapter III).

8. Hardy writes to his illustrator, Arthur Hopkins, in February 1878: "Perhaps it is well for me to give you the following idea of the story as a guide—Thomasin, as you have divined, is the *good* heroine, & she ultimately marries the reddleman, & lives happily. Eustacia is the wayward & erring heroine—She marries Yeobright, the son of Mrs Yeobright, is unhappy, & dies" (*Letters*, I. 52). In a note to this letter, Michael Millgate regards it as "an interesting indication that the conclusion of the novel was not recast at the last minute." Given that the first parts of Hardy's manuscript were sent to *Belgravia* in August 1877, and that he had spent the months between August and February 1878 at work on it, this seems a doubtful assertion.

both the male and the female. The metonym "horns" serves aptly to convey twinned erectile protuberances and therefore heightened sexual appetites in *both* his lovers.

This concept of mutuality goes further still. Imaginatively reinforcing the latent "force" of Eustacia's nature by rendering her combative, her mouth "cut as the point of a spear," Hardy complements her latent warrior quality by endowing Clym with attributes that are passive and soft. For Clym, "the beauty here visible" is meditative, not quite "thought-worn," and born of "placid pupilage" (*RN*, 120). By contrast, this woman of "Tartarean dignity," this "Artemis," this "Athena," this "Hera" (*RN*, 62), is constantly restless, perpetually on the move, endlessly roaming. Her confined and confining world so maddeningly deprives her of sensory experience that she is driven to pull the thick skeins of her hair through the gorse, the prickly tufts of "Ulex Europeaeus," just to gain the sensation of torn roots and stimulating entanglement. And her need to ache and suffer in love expresses her deprivation at an even deeper level. "Algolagnia" means to take pleasure in pain. Eustacia resorts to that measure. "Give us back our suffering," cries her peer in life, Florence Nightingale, "for out of nothing comes nothing. But out of suffering may come the cure. Better have pain than paralysis."[9] These could be Eustacia's own words.

Hardy refers to her "hypochondriasis,"[1] and closely details her chronic condition, her deep "depression of spirits." Finding a partial relief in walking (walking is still recommended today for depression), her mood swings, despondency, and "languid calmness, artificially maintained" intensify the "eating loneliness" of her days.[2] She feels, like most chronically depressed people, that nothing is worthwhile—a feeling that ultimately overwhelms her at the last when struggling with the unbearable upheaval of her marriage. In the "chaos of her mind" she finally collapses to a "rocking movement," as if in a catatonic state, "the wings of her soul . . . broken."[3]

---

9. Florence Nightingale's words in *Cassandra*, 1852; quoted by Elaine Showalter in *A Literature of Their Own: British Women Novelists from Brontë to Lessing* (London: Virago, 1978), p. 27.
1. *Hypochondriasis*: "a generic term for a range of neurotic psychological disorders such as mild depression, low spirits, irritability, and vague and apparently baseless dissatisfaction with one's lot." See *The Return of the Native*, edited by Tony Slade (Harmondsworth: Penguin, 1999), Note 8, 406.
2. See Book I, chapters VI–VII.
3. See Book V, chapter VII. Helen Small asks why Eustacia's story does not offer "a model for thinking . . . about how one acquires a vision of community, or about individual moral agency" ("Chances Are: Henry Buckle, Thomas Hardy, and the Individual at Risk," in *Literature, Science, Psychoanalysis, 1830–1970*, eds. Helen Small and Trudi Tate [Oxford: Oxford UP, 2003], p. 79). The query stems from a seeming ignorance of the fact that Eustacia is wholly hermetic; neither she nor her author regards her[self] as a member of the "community." Moreover if she exhibits "egoism," as Small also claims, the text provides substantial psychological, causal evidence for this; it is hardly "anachronistic," as Small argues.

Eustacia's personal battle then is not only with her environment, the monotony of her lonely, isolated days in an Egdon community that excludes her at every point (why isn't she invited to his homecoming party? Clym demands of his mother)—but also with clinical depression. She longs for remission from the inutile, enervating life, the enforced seclusion of her days. To Wildeve she protests:

> I should hate it all to be smooth. Indeed, I think I like you to desert me a little once now and then. Love is the dismallest thing where the lover is quite honest. O, it is a shame to say so; but it is true! . . . My low spirits begin at the very idea. Don't you offer me tame love, or away you go! (*RN*, 76)

Wildeve bores her. But she tactfully expresses her dissatisfaction in terms of needing more challenging company and not as his deficiency—his dull, doggedly persistent and possibly unimaginative lovemaking. That she craves sensation, stimulation, is made palpably felt at several textual thresholds where her "spirits *begin*" with the "Ah!" "Ah!" of her articulations with Wildeve, (*RN*, 76), and the "O!" "O!" "O!" of those with Clym (*RN*, 177). She craves sensation and predictably cannot conceive of adequate objects for her desire. How could she imagine adequacy? She has been starved of "all the beating and pulsing that is going on in the great arteries of the world."

Yet Eustacia is not merely "romantical nonsensical" as her grandfather would have it. She is empowered not only with a deep imagination—"Seeing nothing of human life now, she imagined all the more of what she had seen" (*RN*, 63)—and a quite startling maturity (for a nineteen-year-old) in her understanding of human emotions. To the soft, passive, and romantically inclined Clym she advises that "nothing can ensure the continuance of love":

> You have seen more than I, and have been into cities and among people that I have only heard of, and have lived more years than I; but yet I am older at this than you. I loved another man once, and now I love you." (*RN*, 168)

Her candor is engaging (Tess, later, is unable to say these words). But her fundamental acceptance of serial monogamy—there was one, now there is another—as also of nonexclusive love, scarcely equips her for the commonplace world to which Clym subscribes and to which he would have her conform.

The narrator stresses her alienation still further. Her "celestial imperiousness, love, wrath and fervour" are "somewhat thrown away on netherward Egdon" (*RN*, 62), whereas on Olympus "she would have done well with a little preparation. She had the passions and instincts which make a model goddess, that is, those which make not quite a model woman" (*RN*, 60). The "model woman" in this instance is of course the "good" little Thomasin—submissive not imperious, docile not fervent, amiable not angry, sexually demure not outspoken and passionate. Evidently the "model goddess" belongs in a different world. But,

> Had it been possible for the earth and mankind to be entirely in her grasp for a while . . . few in the world would have noticed the change of government. There would have been the same inequality of lot, the same heaping up of favours here, of contumely there, the same generosity before justice, the same perpetual dilemmas, the same captious alternation of caresses and blows that we endure now. (*RN*, 61)

Is this an observation on the world and humanity or upon Eustacia? Given the weight of the paragraph it would appear to be the former. And, of course, the world is not Olympus: it is not polytheistic or filled with joyous Hellenism, let alone sexually emancipated men and women. According to Hellenic mythological tradition, the balance of power between the sexes is equally distributed: the strong, the powerful, the brave and heroic count among their number as many females as males.

That Hardy does not attempt to reconcile Eustacia, as an Olympian, with the everyday world, that her "passions and instincts" remain unrealized as well as unrealizable on netherward Egdon, brings me to what I consider a central motif in this novel: the opposition of the inner Victorian world of the novel and the Hellenic spirit embodied by both Eustacia and the Egdon paradigm.[4]

The disjunction is powerfully evoked by the personification that is Egdon in contrast with the life of the inhabitants. Egdon's highest elevation, which takes the form of Rainbarrow, is shaped from an imaginative amalgam of three Barrows, unified and centralized within the landscape, which are in actuality spatially separated and peripheral to the heath. Why is this particular construct significant? Because geographical heights lend themselves to ideological emblems: temples in Greece, castles in Europe, flags of glory universally. Such elevations are mimicked in architectural forms—the spires of churches, the domes of courthouses, and the towers of cathedrals.

"Almost crystallized to natural products by long continuance," Rainbarrow projects the brow of Egdon "above its natural level" (*RN*, 11, 15), and while the world sleeps

---

4. See also David de Laura, "The 'Ache of Modernism' in Hardy's Later Novels," *English Literary History*, vol. 34, Sept. 1967, pp. 388–89.

the heath appeared slowly to wake and listen. Every night its Titanic form seemed to await something; but it had waited thus, unmoved, during so many centuries, through the crises of so many things, that it could only be imagined to await one more crisis—the final overthrow. (*RN*, 9)

"Overthrow" is the talk of the natives. The temporal setting is mid-century, the time of great upheavals in Europe. Eustacia's Paris, "the centre and vortex of the fashionable world" (*RN*, 97), is still in the throes of social and political turbulence. Granfer Cantle talks of the Napoleonic wars. Other locals discuss the matrimonial troubles of Wildeve and Thomasin. All is on the brink.[5]

The ideological clash between Hellenistic polytheism, Greek joyousness, the pursuit of happiness on the one hand and Judaeo-Christian monotheism, self-salvation and the worship of godliness on the other, may be emblematized by the dramatic entity that is the Atlantean brow of Rainbarrow, in the first instance, and the "Hades" of netherward Egdon in the second. Eustacia crowns the former as the "perfect finish" to its "architectural" mass (*RN*, 15); Venn, the Mephisophelean devil—manifestly, Gide's devil, who appears in guises of plausibility—embodies the puritanical conscience and prurient censor of the Judaeo-Christian world.

Where Gabriel Oak, in his espials in *Far from the Madding Crowd*, squats in shadows or peers through crevices, Diggory Venn creeps along "as though he burrowed underground." In his creeping and crawling spying activities (the embodiment of the Victorian censor) Venn reveals a malevolent underside, revealed, in the text, in gradual stages. At one point, for example, he decides to accelerate his harassment of Eustacia; he will openly attack "her position as Thomasin's rival" (*RN*, 80). Just as Gabriel Oak shames Bathsheba by telling her what he has seen of her in a private moment, so Venn will shame Eustacia (albeit without the benign intent of Oak, who wishes to return Bathsbeba's lost hat). And as if to reinforce the intensity of the inflicted shame, Venn decides to call on her before she is out of bed. She is thus stripped of dignity as well as being mortified by his self-avowed espials of her activity on the heath with Wildeve. And if this were not enough, he refers to her, face-to-face, as "some person [Wildeve] has picked up with, and meets on the heath." At this point of overweening cruelty her lips tremble and "the gasp could no longer be kept down" (*RN*, 83). But Hardy's strongest act of antagonism here is to have Venn turn up on Eustacia's doorstep, not only at an indecent hour, but on a Sunday.

5. Interestingly, Hardy's "original conception of the story" was also overthrown; see Note 7 above.

Clearly this is the day of choice for a little demonic intervention.[6]

Perpetually meddling (m/reddleman), Venn does not operate as a benign regulating force on Egdon. His role, albeit deeply embedded in the narrative proper, mirrors that of the Grundyan watchdog of the earlier novels who proffers judgment on Hardy's sexually hungry girls. And in common with the earlier Grundyan observer he infiltrates the consciousness of certain characters, who in turn voice those moralistic concerns that Leslie Stephen, Hardy's former editor at the *Cornhill*, had wished there were more of. For the implied censor (a feature of most contemporary narrative proscriptions on women) redeemed many an authorial indiscretion if applied judiciously to a nonconforming, that is a sexy or "wayward" female characterization. Thus, Venn not only openly personifies the moral-watchdog at its worst—the book-burning, witch-hunting kind—but also exhibits demonic interference of the sort designed to harm rather than heal. Although the allusion may pass over the heads of lay readers, the fact that Venn conceals himself with turves in order to spy on Eustacia and Wildeve clearly aligns him with the devil—traditionally held to mine under the earth just as Venn burrows underground.

At a less esoteric level of discourse Venn enters the scene not simply as demonic but as one of those "criminals for whose misdeeds other men had wrongfully suffered" (*RN*, 72), as "the formulated threat of Wessex mothers" to miscreant children (*RN*, 72), as an interfering busybody whose actions are of "doubtful legitimacy," as a "new and most unpleasant form of menace" (*RN*, 227); and, of course, it is his meddling with Clym's inheritance that starts off the series of mishaps culminating in Mrs. Yeobright's death. And all in the name of Christian righteousness and the Mosaic law. Thus, in Venn's persecution of Eustacia, the thematic line that traces the clash between Hellenism and Hebraism comes full circle.

Venn's attempts to displace the rare, splendid woman—"How I have tried and tried to be a splendid woman" (*RN*, 294)—are paralleled in Clym's displacing of her in marriage. By this I mean his constant undermining of her hopes and dreams, his total theft of her future, indeed even of her life. Her phasing into invisibility as he grows increasingly blind grounds the ordeal in harsh physical fact: it is the invisibility (to him) of her pain, frustration, and desire that drives her out of her mind.

The primal scene that prefigures this dark outcome is that of the

---

6. Fundamentally a symbolic, allegorical figure, Venn trades on stamping indelible markers on sexually active creatures, essentially to stain the impregnated female; likewise he preys on the sexually active woman, Eustacia, tormented as she is with sexual hunger. He appears to be the precursor to the sexual predator of modern times.

lunar eclipse which, significantly, dims the radiant upper atmosphere as Clym and Eustacia meet early on as lovers, on the heath at
night. Of more obvious signification is the one and only sign that
swings on the heath: the inn sign of the "Quiet Woman" (*RN*, 39)—
"Quiet" because she is headless. This has extratextual indications.
Unlike the "*good*" little Thomasin, the "Quiet Woman" has no epis-
tolary provenance. Yet the words resonate further. They find their
parallel in women's "headless" legal, social, and sexual status in the
real world, in their lack of equal rights in a man-made constitution
in which there was no need to display the sign of the "Quiet
Woman": their nullified existence as a legal entity remained in force
for several more decades after the publication of *The Return of the
Native*.

Clym is no allegorical figure, as is Venn. He is not so much the
personification of social evils as simply an unseeing native of the
land. Even so, he is one of Hardy's more sympathetically drawn
male characters. There are not many who, in wielding power and
authority, do not trivialize and debase the woman they love—or, inversely, etherealize and rarefy her, which is simply another way of
depersonalizing her. Clym does endeavor to meet Eustacia on her
own ground. He is, Hardy says, "before his time," "mentally in a
provincial future" (*RN*, 147), and this shows in his earlier days with
Eustacia, before his vision leaves him. Take for example her radical
argument against monogamy; he neither belittles nor negates her at
any point. Her views are highly unconventional for the Victorian
mid-century, yet unlike Venn (and his peers in the real world), who
mentally categorizes Eustacia as a hussy, Clym listens to her attentively without sneers or condescension. Or so we might infer from
the self-assurance of her manner and her candor in speaking of her
past love. She even succeeds, in the moment, in deflecting him
from talk of marriage: "Shall I claim you some day?" he asks, then
tactfully adds (no doubt reading her unspoken response intuitively),
"—I don't mean at once."

> "I must think," Eustacia murmured. "At present speak of
> Paris to me. Is there any place like it on earth?"
> "It is very beautiful. But will you be mine?"
> "I will be nobody else's in the world—does that satisfy you?"
> "Yes, for the present." (*RN*, 168)

Eustacia is struggling for reassurance that Paris is a possibility. She
would of course be aware that a maid taken in marriage as man's
property not only marries the man but also his way of life. Her
stratagem then is to divert him back to Paris at every available opportunity. And this is where it becomes sadly evident that Clym is
not after all reading her closely. " 'Now tell me of the Tuileries, and

the Louvre,' she continued evasively." " 'I hate talking of Paris!' " he rejoins, rather too vehemently, and then instantly backtracks as if to blot out his falsehood: "Well, I remember one sunny room . . ." (*RN*, 168–69).

Clym *loves* talking about Paris! From the first moment of their meeting to their last conversations together, he constantly talks and even sings about Paris. And his vivid evocations betray this. He is though discomposed by the fact that both his loved women, his mother and his future bride, appear to know what is best for him. " 'How extraordinary that you and my mother should be of one mind about this!' said Yeobright. 'I have vowed not to go back, Eustacia.' " (*RN*, 169) Clym's male pride, his innate perversity, and his stubbornness are vexed. He is at the same time disturbed by Eustacia's yearning to live in Paris—a city surely redolent to her mind of revolutionary zeal and women on the barricades—for he remains, it seems, ignorant of her attraction to rebels and warriors. Unsettled by thoughts that it is perhaps Paris and not himself she desires, he taxes her with loving him "rather as a visitant from a gay world to which she rightly belonged than as a man with a purpose opposed to that recent past which so interested her" (*RN*, 171). She *has* tried to reassure him:

> "Don't mistake me Clym: though I should like Paris, I love you for yourself alone. To be your wife and live in Paris would be heaven to me; but I would rather live with you in a hermitage here than not be yours at all. It is gain to me either way, and very great gain. There's my candid confession." (*RN*, 170)

These are fatal words. Yet they are not dishonest. Clym, after all, exudes worldly wisdom, glamor, and sophistication, and there is no way that Eustacia could conceive of his eventual degeneration (even in a hermitage) to an insect-like creature laboring on the heath alongside the local furze-gatherers and heathcroppers. Moreover, with his emphasis on aristocratic Paris and high society—the Little Trianon, the Galerie d'Apollon, the Grand Palace—instead of revolutionary Paris, where her true interest would lie, she is very uneasy. Somewhere along the line she has been misunderstood. Despite the empathy of her listener she has, in some subtle way, been restated. The glamor, the glitter, the formality of landscaped gardens certainly have their appeal but they have in a mistaken way reshaped her dreams, her sense of self. This is *not* her Paris: not the world she can picture herself in. Now she is trapped in an unfamiliar identity, and in the confusion she falls back upon a culturally approved language, expressing culturally approved attitudes that completely misrepresent her. She has stalled an imminent clash of wills, only to find herself precipitated into a deeper conflict as Clym takes her "candid confession" at face value. She is, he now allows himself to believe, the dutiful, submissive woman she should be! Metaphorically patting her on the head he declares that she has "[s]poken like a woman." And in so saying, in reverting to that authoritarian manner of mixing approval with condescension, he shifts the relationship on to a different level. Not only is there now a disparity in their hopes and dreams, but there is also an imbalance of power.

Eustacia is caught in a double-bind. Suffering a check on her thoughts and emotions, her utterances are now shaped to a false representation of her true feelings. What she cannot speak of "like a woman," and what the narrator has to tell on her behalf, is that "Fidelity in love for fidelity's sake had less attraction for her than . . . fidelity because of love's grip" (*RN*, 64). She has already startled Clym with her thoughts on the non-exclusivity of love; she has frankly admitted that a cosmopolitan life would be ideal; but she has not been able to say that she has "got beyond the vision of some marriage of inexpressible glory," that the marriage tie is not for her (*RN*, 65–6). It is something of a paradox that Clym returns from a Paris in which a rebel woman such as George Sand can find a self-expressive niche, but a like-minded woman on a smaller scale, on Egdon, is wholly blocked by his patriarchal attitudes.

When Clym misreads Eustacia's languid manner as passivity he no doubt believes she is behaving "like a woman." His modernism, his enlightenment, remains in this respect more theoretical than actual. Had he been less inclined to seek (and find in Eustacia) a "model woman," he would have discovered a radical, a potential woman on-the-barricades of stimulating intellectual proportions and of social equality with himself. As it is, he turns his back on the real Eustacia, just as he turns his back on Paris and ultimately on his own mother, to "make a globe to suit [him]," and to play chieftain to what he calls "the lowest class" (*RN*, 165). As the narrator makes clear, his aims, his very thinking, are wholly unrealistic.

Egocentricity and introspection, "parasite thought," devour the vision that had once urged him to strive at "high thinking" and to become "acquainted with ethical systems popular at the time" (*RN*, 147). Even his philanthropic outlook is self-regarding (notice the self-referential "I"s in the following discourse on aims and ambitions: where is Eustacia in this picture?):

> "I no longer adhere to my intention of giving with my own mouth rudimentary education to the lowest class. I can do better. . . . I shall ultimately, I hope, be at the head of one of the best schools in the county." (*RN*, 165)

And later: "I shall do a great deal of good to my fellow-creatures" (*RN*, 173).

Despite the "waggery of fate" (*RN*, 144) which has endowed Clym with a highly privileged start in life, enabling him to "prove his . . . own capacities" in the world, indeed in the great capitals of London and Paris, and with all the social and economic freedom Eustacia has been denied, all is wasted. He sees his scope as large, as no doubt he should given his privileged background, but his visionary powers are small (one could even say, nonexistent, in physical terms). His mother and his young bride both perceive this and tell it. But they are to be "quiet"! He owns the right to choose his own way of life; this is his male birthright, and exercise this right he will.

Eustacia's dreams (as also in the physical sense, her night dreams) are by contrast either fragmented or truncated. They could scarcely be anything else. Sensitively acknowledging the extent to which her cut-off life has molded the deeps of her unconscious, Hardy depicts even her paradisal dream as truncated, in terms of both form and content. There is first of all some indication that this is a dream of such splendor as to outmatch all visionary, rapturous dreams. But nothing more than pieces of it can be assembled, notably its final disintegrating moments. It is as if Hardy would stress her dislocation from her Olympian (Atlantean) heights: are her origins, her place of belonging, her destiny, too remote, too atavistic perhaps? There is the armored figure who features centrally and ecstatically in the dream, but just as the dreamer feels he and she have reached the point of touching he splinters before her eyes.

In a sense the dream of harmonious relations, as projected on to the timeless and enduring Egdon, armored by a world of nature in which all elements act in reciprocity, mutually touching, in equilibrium, is the same dream. Is Eustacia dreaming Egdon? Or is Egdon perhaps dreaming Eustacia? Either way, is the stark and terrible shattering before her very eyes a prefiguration of her own assimilation back to the heath by drowning in its own waters?

These are but speculations merely. Back in the world of the novel Eustacia has clearly been rudely "awakened" from what she calls her "youthful dream"—the music, the pulsing, the passion—by marrying Clym. Denied all that *he* has been so freely offered and so freely squanders, she suffers bitterly at the sight of him toiling on the surface of the heath, singing mindlessly in defeat, a figure

> not more distinguishable from the scene around him than the green caterpillar from the leaf it feeds on . . . of no more account in life than an insect . . . a mere parasite of the heath. (*RN*, 231)

Drawing emotional relief from his own "curious microscopic" activities (*RN*, 211), Clym crawls on the surface of the earth like an imbecile impervious to the continuing damage to his sight. To Eustacia's attempts to steer him toward a different kind of life he says simply that he needs to keep himself occupied: "You cannot seriously wish me to stay idling at home all day?" (*RN*, 215). What then of Eustacia, condemned to idleness day after day after day?

Eustacia's displacement is now fully compounded. The rare woman with her affinity for heights has no means of elevating herself at any point. As befits her Olympian status and in common with her Wessex predecessor, King Lear, her decline into delirium calls up fury in the natural world; as she wanders in misery and desolation through the raging storm, it is "as if she were drawn into the Barrow by a hand from beneath" (*RN*, 293):

> Between the drippings of the rain from her umbrella to her mantle, from her mantle to the heather, from the heather to the earth, very similar sounds could be heard coming from her lips; and the tearfulness of the outer scene was repeated upon her face. The wings of her soul were broken . . . (*RN*, 294)

Lashed earthward by streaming torrential rain that gathers up her tears in its coursing, her life spirals down.

"Here was action and life," writes D. H. Lawrence, "here was a move into being on [Clym's] part":

> But as soon as he got her, she became an idea to him, she had to fit in his system of ideas. According to his way of loving, he knew her already, she was labelled and classed and fixed down.[7]

This then is a world in which, to misquote John Stuart Mill, women's capacities cannot be proved by trial—and it is clearly the loser.

As he lived out his days at Sturminster composing *The Return of the Native*, reading George Sand and in 1876 confronted by the shock of her death, it must have struck Hardy that this was indeed a world unfriendly to women. For he would almost certainly have read Victor Hugo's obituary of her, in the *Saturday Review*, and as he reflected upon the hostile response this drew from his compatriots he must have felt deeply the injustice of their attack. The *Saturday Review* first quotes Hugo:

> In this country, whose law is to complete the French Revolution, and begin that of the equality of the sexes, being a part of the equality of men, a great woman was needed. It was necessary to prove that a woman could have all the manly gifts without losing any of her angelic qualities; be strong without ceasing to be tender. George Sand proved it. . . . Whenever

7. D. H. Lawrence, *Lawrence on Hardy and Painting*, ed. J.V. Davies (London: Heinemann, 1973), pp. 19–20.

one of these powerful human creatures dies we hear, as it were, an immense noise of wings. Something is going; something is coming. The earth, like heaven, has its eclipses, but here, as above, the reapparition follows the appearance. The torch which was in the form of a man or a woman, and which is extinguished under that form, reappears under that of an idea. This torch is flaming higher than ever, it will constitute afterwards a part of civilization, and enter into the vast enlightenment of humanity.[8]

How interesting to find Hugo's imagery infiltrating *The Return of the Native*: the splendid woman, strong without ceasing to be tender, the apparition in human form that reappears as an idea, the Promethean flame, the winging bird—even heavenly eclipses. But the *Saturday* now launches into a bitter attack on rebellious, mutinous women, and working up to a full discrediting of Sand it concludes that if women are getting "tired of what they call the tame and monotonous existence," and "demand the active life and personal freedom . . . allowed to men," they should know that

it is the harmonious co-operation of the two distinct influences of manly force and womanly tenderness and spirituality, and not the confounding of them in one common form, which keeps society sound and strong.[9]

The *Return of the Native* has the last word. With the Egdon paradigm offering an embodiment of reciprocal female and male characteristics and an "intuitive sympathy with humanity in all its moods," the overriding motif is of the "compounding," not "confounding" of diverse sexual attributes "in one common form." This compound would indeed "keep society sound and strong."

PAMELA DALZIEL

Anxieties of Representation: The Serial Illustrations to Hardy's *The Return of the Native*†

*   *   *

The sensation and sentiment generally associated with *Belgravia* were of course present in *The Return of the Native*, particularly in

8. "An Emancipated Woman," *The Saturday Review*, June 17, 1876, vol. 40, p. 771.
9. *Saturday Review*, ibid.
† From *Nineteenth-Century Literature* 51 (1996): 84–110. Reprinted by permission of the University of California Press. Page references in this essay to illustrations in *The Return of the Native* are to this Norton Critical Edition.

those concluding sections that Hardy seems to have written only after he knew where the novel would first appear. So far as the already existing chapters were concerned, however, the surviving manuscript reveals that Hardy was primarily concerned to deemphasize the primitive wildness and classlessness of the heath as he had originally portrayed it and thus to render characters, situations, and events more acceptable to a predominantly middle-class serial-reading public.[1] Originally, for example, Thomasin spent a week away with Wildeve before learning that they were not legally married, but in the manuscript as revised—and in the serial—her reputation is not placed under so dark a cloud. Such anticipatory bowdlerization suggests that Hardy * * * was concerned not to risk a late rejection by Chatto and Windus, who evidently saw nothing of the manuscript before receiving the first two installments, posted on 28 August 1877 (*Letters*, I.50). With an eye to the placement of his future work, Hardy in any case was eager to demonstrate his professional competence, what he called when writing *Far from the Madding Crowd* his being "considered a good hand at a serial" (*Life*, p. 102), and to prove that he could recast *The Return of the Native* within the limits of the conventionally acceptable without losing the interest of the reading public. If the self-conscious deliberateness with which he approached this task was reflected above all in the writing and revision done prior to submission of copy, it was more immediately visible in specific aspects of the *Belgravia* version: in the neatness with which the division into "books" was integrated into the rhythm of serialization, each "book" except the sixth starting at the beginning of a new installment; in the provision (unique in Hardy's work) of a series of curiously abstract and resolutely unsensational headnotes to those "books";[2] and, above all, in the active interest he took in the illustrations to the serial provided by Arthur Hopkins, *Belgravia*'s regular illustrator at this period.

Perhaps best known today as the younger brother of Gerard Manley Hopkins, Arthur Hopkins (1848–1930) was in his day a successful painter and illustrator. Though still a relative newcomer at the time when Chatto and Windus first commissioned work from him in 1877, he had already established a reputation through his contributions to such leading periodicals as the *Cornhill, Good*

---

1. See John Paterson, *The Making of "The Return of the Native"* (Berkeley and Los Angeles: Univ. of California Press, 1960), pp. 8–47; and Simon Gatrell, *Hardy the Creator: A Textual Biography* (Oxford: Clarendon Press, 1988), pp. 29–43.
2. The headnote to Book First reads: "Depicts the scenes which result from an antagonism between the hopes of four persons inhabiting one of the innermost recesses of Wessex. By reason of this strife of wishes, a happy consummation to all concerned is impossible, as matters stand; but an easing of the situation is begun by the inevitable decadence of a too capricious love, and rumours of a new arrival" (*The Return of the Native*, *Belgravia*, 34–37 [1878], 34: 257; subsequent references to this edition of the novel appear in the text and specify only the volume and page numbers).

Words, the *Graphic*, and the *Illustrated London News*. The assignment of Hopkins to *The Return of the Native* had a particular appropriateness in that he had a distinct predilection for depicting scenes of rural life. At times, it is true, this had led to somewhat incongruous results: several of Hopkins's drawings for Eliza Lynn Linton's *The Atonement of Leam Dundas* (*Cornhill*, 1875–76), for example, focus on rural laborers who in fact are either absent altogether from the novel or present only in non-speaking roles. But there was nothing inappropriate about Hopkins's choice of several rural laborers standing around a bonfire as the subject of the full-page illustration preceding the first (January 1878) installment of *The Return of the Native* (see p. 25). Given Hardy's repeated insistence when trying to sell the novel that it was a country story along the lines of the popular *Far from the Madding Crowd*, it is not surprising that he should later have told Hopkins in an 8 February 1878 letter that he "liked [the] first drawing much" (*Letters*, I.52).

Hardy would also have had ample grounds for liking Hopkins's depiction of the rural laborers themselves, conforming as it does to central aspects of his own representation. In both verbal and visual texts, for example, laborers such as Humphrey and Sam are virtually interchangeable. Indeed, Hardy himself confuses the two characters: at one point Humphrey says to Sam, "They would, Humphrey" (35: 232), and Hardy's subsequent revision for the 1878 Smith, Elder three-volume edition ("'They would,' said Humphrey") serves only to emphasize the absence of individuation—a somewhat troubling absence in view of Hardy's later essay "The Dorsetshire Labourer", with its criticism of the general failure to recognize laborers as individuals.[3] Throughout Hardy's text Humphrey and Sam are defined exclusively by their respective occupations, Sam in fact remaining unnamed for some time and identified in dialogue only as "the turf-cutter" (34: 274ff). So, too, Hopkins's Humphrey and Sam—the figures on the far right—with their similar features, height, and build are essentially interchangeable,[4] differentiated solely by the signs of their occupation: Humphrey's furze-cutter leggings and Sam's turf-cutter spade.

In both texts the laborers who do emerge as individuals are primarily distinctive because comic. At the center of Hopkins's drawing is the posturing Grandfer Cantle; to the left is Christian with—to quote Hardy's narrator—"a great quantity of wrist and ankle beyond his clothes" (34: 274). Yet as Hardy, following Shakespeare, injects into the laborers' foolishness a certain amount of

3. See "The Dorsetshire Labourer", *Longman's Magazine*, 2 (1883), pp. 252–69.
4. Significantly, Hopkins has made Sam the speaker of the caption's question rather than Humphrey as specified in Hardy's text (34: 274).

wisdom, so Hopkins tempers his comedy with a suggestion of seri-
ousness: after all, the reading of Hopkins's Grandfer Cantle as a
posturing egotist depends as much on the knowledge of the narrative context as on the visual representation itself, which could
equally be interpreted as a depiction of an elderly man listening attentively with his hands placed behind him for physical support.
The caption chosen for the illustration by the editors of the novel's
American serialization sounded just such a serious note: "THE
PERMANENT MORAL EXPRESSION IN EACH FACE IT WAS
IMPOSSIBLE TO DISCOVER."[5]

The American caption is taken from a passage in which the laborers are described as the inheritors of "Druidical rites and Saxon
ceremonies", embodying "Promethean rebelliousness" in their instinctive act of lighting bonfires at the onset of winter (34: 268).
Linked with the Pagan and mythological, these heathdwellers seem
even in the revised text of the serial to suggest mysteriousness and
uncontrollability and, like Egdon itself, an element of threat. It is
no mere coincidence that throughout Hardy's text the disruptions
of the status quo are frequently associated with folk tradition: Eustacia's bonfires, the mumming, the East Egdon gypsying, Susan
Nunsuch's wax figure, and so forth. Nor is it insignificant that at
the conclusion of the novel only the laborers, along with Egdon,
survive essentially unchanged, while those who held themselves
most aloof from the community—Mrs. Yeobright, Eustacia, and
Wildeve—are dead.

No suggestion of this aspect of Hardy's representation of the laborers can be found in Hopkins's illustration, however. For Hopkins, as for many Victorian artists,[6] depicting the rural laborer was
primarily a way of introducing a picturesque element.[7] While later
Return of the Native illustrators chose to accentuate the subversive
potential of Hardy's text—representing the bonfire scene, for example, as the site of the release of carnivalesque energy[8]—Hopkins

5. *Harper's New Monthly Magazine*, 56 (1878), p. 416. The illustrations were evidently sent
   as electrotype plates, hence without captions (see *Letters*, I.51). Only the first four illustrations were published in *Harper's*, the difficulty of receiving the plates in time (the second and third illustrations appeared a month late) apparently having led to a decision to
   abandon them altogether.
6. See Julian Treuherz, *Hard Times: Social Realism in Victorian Art* (London: Lund
   Humphries, in association with Manchester City Art Galleries, 1987), pp. 9–10, 36.
7. See Hopkins's illustrations for *The Prescotts of Pamphillon* (*Good Words*, 1873), *White-
   ladies* (*Good Words*, 1875), *The Atonement of Leam Dundas* (*Cornhill*, 1875–76), and
   Queen of the Meadow (*Belgravia*, 1879). Hopkins's first Royal Academy painting, exhibited in 1877, was *The Plough* (unlocated); a later painting, *The Apple Loft* (unlocated),
   was perhaps inspired by the *Belgravia* illustration of Thomasin in the apple loft (see
   J. A. Reid, "Arthur Hopkins, R.W.S.", *Art Journal*, n.s. 38 [1899], p. 194).
8. Most notable is Clare Leighton's striking woodcut for the 1929 Harper and Brothers
   edition: dramatic contrasts of light and dark, a defiantly militant Grandfer Cantle, and
   the spectral, mummylike faces of the laborers create a sinister, hellish vision. Cf. Agnes
   Miller Parker's woodcut for the 1942 Heritage Press (New York) edition, in which

tended to avoid the threatening in any form, creating a falsely smooth surface to Hardy's frequently ruptured text. Hardy did not object to this visual bowdlerization and even praised this particular instance, which is by no means surprising in light of the unpublishability of his first and now lost "socialistic, not to say revolutionary" novel, *The Poor Man and the Lady* (*Life*, p. 63), and the withholding of public applause from his most recent novel, *The Hand of Ethelberta*, arguably subversive in its challenging of existing class assumptions.[9] It doubtless assuaged Hardy's anxieties over his new novel to find the serial's visual text mirroring the verbal only to a point short of creating an image potentially threatening to the presumed political and moral conservatism of its readers. That Hardy was willing to bowdlerize even what one critic has called the already "pallid" text of the serial[1] is suggested by the omission from the three-volume first edition of the novel—the form in which it was distributed for review—of the opening exchange between the Egdonites, which included the serial's only approximation to criticism of rural laboring conditions: "All the parishes used to be let cut furze and turf anywhere about, but they've took the right to it away from us now" (34: 266).

Although Hardy's liking for Hopkins's first illustration did not extend to the second, his response can again be linked in part to his concern for the novel's success. Hopkins's February drawing depicts Eustacia on the heath (see p. 51), an appropriate enough illustrative subject for an installment concluding with the "Queen of Night" chapter. But if it was an appropriate subject, it was not an easy one. Hopkins's challenge was to portray "the raw material of a divinity" with "deep Pagan eyes, full of nocturnal mysteries", a mouth "formed less to speak than to quiver, less to quiver than to kiss", and a profile suggesting both Marie Antoinette and Lord Byron but resembling neither (34: 502–3, 493).[2] The inherent difficulty of such a subject was compounded by the need to represent an "erring" heroine: as the narrator puts it, Eustacia possessed "the passions and instincts which make a faultless goddess, that is, those which make not quite a faultless woman" (34: 502). Hopkins, who subsequently confessed to Hardy his own lack of sympathy for Eustacia,[3] chose to focus not on the faultless goddess but on the

Grandfer Cantle, forked stick in hand, dances demoniacally about twisted roots and an apparently all-consuming flame, though the smiling faces of the laborers prevent the image as a whole from becoming unduly threatening.

9. See Peter Widdowson, *Hardy in History: A Study in Literary Sociology* (London: Routledge, 1989), pp. 155–97.
1. See Otis B. Wheeler, "Four Versions of *The Return of the Native*", *Nineteenth-Century Fiction*, 14 (1959), p. 29.
2. Revised in the 1878 Smith, Elder edition to Marie Antoinette and Mrs. Siddons, and the 1895 Osgood, McIlvaine edition to Sappho and Mrs. Siddons.
3. See Hopkins's letter of 5 February 1878 (Dorset County Museum).

less than ideal woman. Dark, heavyset, and stiff, Hopkins's Eustacia is clearly dissociated from conventional Victorian constructions of virtuous femininity and, indeed, aligned with the "masculine". She holds in her hands a phallic telescope, suggestive of both aggressive sexuality and the male worlds of exploration, seafaring, and military service; she is neither occupied with a domestic task nor located within a domestic space but set in the midst of the heath's wildness, flanked on one side by waist-high brambles and on the other by two free-ranging unbroken ponies, symbolic of her lack of control and her animal passion.[4]

In representing Eustacia thus, Hopkins was not willfully contradicting Hardy's text but was privileging selected aspects of it. After all, Hardy's narrator does frequently define Eustacia in terms of masculine images. Initially, for example, she is not even identified as a woman but seen rising from the barrow "like a spike from a helmet", suggesting "the person of one of the Celts who built the barrow", the "last . . . of his race" (34: 264–65). Her "high gods", William the Conqueror, Strafford, and Napoleon, are all powerful males (34: 506); she practices a kind of strategic generalship very different from those "small arts called womanish" (34: 508); and, as the narrative progresses, her behavior—from donning the mummer's costume to responding with "daring and defian[ce]" to Clym's accusations—is both implicitly and explicitly defined as unwomanly (35: 265–6; 36: 500). "Tall and straight in build", "full-limbed and somewhat heavy" (34: 491, 502), she does not even possess a conventionally feminine figure.

Eustacia's figure is also described, however, as one that "might have stood for that of either of the higher female deities" (34: 503), and throughout Hardy's text, though most notably in the "Queen of Night" chapter, her alignment with the "masculine" is modified by the use of equally extravagant female images. Hardy probably did not envision Eustacia as masculine per se but as distinct from the conventional middle-class "womanly" norm, in much the same way as Burne-Jones's statuesque goddesses are. What is in any case certain is that Hardy was disappointed with the *Belgravia* illustration—so much so that he wrote to Hopkins, apparently for the first time, and enclosed a sketch of Eustacia as he imagined her. Unfortunately, neither letter nor enclosure has survived, but Hopkins's reply of 5 February 1878 claims that Hardy's "little sketch does not differ very much from the face I drew, except in the chin", asks for more particular criticism, and attempts to lay as much blame as

4. For a somewhat different reading of this illustration, see Arlene M. Jackson, *Illustration and the Novels of Thomas Hardy* (Totowa, N.J.: Rowman and Littlefield, 1981), pp. 89–90.

possible on the poor engraving.[5] "It is rather ungenerous to criticise," responded Hardy on 8 February, "but since you invite me to do so I will say that I think Eustacia should have been represented as more youthful in face, supple in figure, &, in general, with a little more roundness & softness than have been given her" (*Letters*, I. 52). Evidently Hardy wished her to be more "feminine" as stereotypically defined, hence both more acceptable to a middle-class audience and more desirable. Hardy's criticism probably had a personal component: as one contemporary reviewer observed, Eustacia was "obviously Mr Hardy's favourite",[6] and Hardy was no doubt dismayed to find his "Queen of Night" rendered so unattractively. Her casually drawn profile in fact differs little from the profiles of Humphrey and Sam in the January illustration, and Hopkins's specific reference to Eustacia's chin further suggests that Hardy, well aware of the extent to which he was exploiting local topography and even local personalities,[7] may have been concerned by the coincidence between the Punch-like prominence of the heroine's nose and chin as initially represented and the similarly "Roman" features so strikingly possessed by his own mother. But in engaging in correspondence with Hopkins, Hardy's principal concern was evidently to ensure that the illustrations to the new novel, especially as it passed through these early installments, were such as to stimulate the interest of potential readers or, at the very least, not actively to discourage such interest at a first glance.

In his 5 February letter Hopkins, referring to his having just begun work on a drawing of Thomasin for the April installment, confessed: "Up to this time I must own my sympathy has been with her—& perhaps she will have the benefit." Hardy doubtless hoped that she would; on 8 February he concurred, or affected to concur, with Hopkins's choice of subject matter ("Strangely enough I myself thought that Thomasin in the apple-loft would be the best illustration for the fourth number") and provided "as a guide" for this and subsequent drawings some particulars of characterization and plot:

---

5. Dorset County Museum. The noticeable line through the center of the illustration indicates that the woodblock was cut in two—as were all the *Return of the Native* woodblocks, though the other join lines are less pronounced—to enable simultaneous engraving by different artists. The half containing Eustacia's distorted left hand was almost certainly the work of one of Joseph Swain's assistants (see Rodney K. Engen, *Dictionary of Victorian Wood Engravers* (Cambridge: Chadwyck-Healey, 1985), p. 252).

6. *The Examiner*, 30 November 1878, p. 1525.

7. The three-volume first edition omitted the serial illustrations but introduced as a frontispiece a "SKETCH MAP OF THE SCENE OF THE STORY" that would have been quite recognizable to anyone familiar with the countryside just east of Dorchester; for a discussion of the relationship between fact and fiction in the novel, see Michael Millgate, *Thomas Hardy: A Biography* (Oxford: Oxford Univ. Press, 1982), pp. 199–202.

> Thomasin, as you have divined, is the *good* heroine, & she ulti-
> mately marries the reddleman, & lives happily. Eustacia is the
> wayward & erring heroine—She marries Yeobright, the son of
> Mrs Yeobright, is unhappy, & dies. The order of importance of
> the characters is as follows.
>   1 Clym Yeobright
>   2 Eustacia
>   3 Thomasin & the reddleman
>   4 Wildeve
>   5 Mrs Yeobright. (*Letters*, I.52–53)

That Hardy was willing to define his two heroines in such conventionally schematic terms provides further evidence of his recognition of the assumed expectations of the serial-reading public. That
he was not willing, however, to allow the "wayward & erring heroine" to be represented as inherently unattractive and "unfemi-
nine"—the usual signifiers of female unorthodoxy—demonstrates
his awareness of the need to temper conforming to the expectations
of his readers with stimulation of sexual fascination and narrative
desire.

Both requirements were sufficiently achieved in the illustration
of Thomasin in the apple loft (see p. 99). Hopkins, doubtless influenced by the criticism he had just received, created for the April installment a Thomasin possessed of precisely the youthfulness,
suppleness, roundness, and softness that Hardy had missed in the
February Eustacia. In fact Hopkins's Thomasin seems at this point
to be the opposite of his Eustacia in almost every respect. She is visually marked as the "*good* heroine" by not only her "feminine" figure but also her gentle, sensitive expression and even her apparent
blondness—in spite of the fact that she is said to have chestnut
brown hair (see 34: 285; 35: 234, 23). Unlike Eustacia, Thomasin
is represented in the midst of a domestic task: kneeling (an appro-
priately submissive and pious posture), she holds in her hands not
a "masculine" instrument but the rounded forms of apples, em-
blematic (especially as held before her apron) rather of harvest and
of female fecundity than of the reputation of fallenness with which
she is currently threatened in the narrative.

In thus representing Thomasin, Hopkins was no more contradicting Hardy's text than he was in his earlier depiction of a "masculinized" Eustacia. Thomasin is initially evoked in conventional
"womanly" terms: she is said to have "a fair, sweet, and honest" face
and to be loyal, "pliable", "pleasing and innocent" (34: 285; 35:
234; 34: 500). It is simply that Hopkins's Thomasin embodies—as
his Eustacia had—only one aspect of Hardy's representation. In the
April illustration Thomasin's attitude appears to be one of sorrowful acceptance as she laments (in the words of the caption), "I wish

all good women were as good as I!"; in Hardy's text, on the other hand, it is with frustrated defiance that she "vehemently" exclaims, "Why don't people judge me by my acts? Now look at me as I kneel here, picking up these apples—do I look like a lost woman? . . . I wish all good women were as good as I!" (35: 235; ellipsis in original). The element of subversiveness textually present in Thomasin's questioning of her having been defined by the social code as in some sense fallen is thus obscured by the visual depiction of her as the conventional passive female. Nor does Hopkins subsequently respond to other textual glimpses of a more complex and potentially subversive Thomasin, survivals from earlier stages of the narrative—abandoned in response to editorial objections either encountered or anticipated—in which, for instance, Thomasin rebelled against convention by refusing to marry Wildeve after discovering his true nature.[8] But Hopkins's interpretation had effectively been authorized by Hardy's own reductive categorization of Thomasin as the "*good* heroine", and Hardy, anxiously conscious of market considerations, was no doubt relieved to find her so safely represented. Throughout most of the narrative Thomasin does in any case embody an ideal of Victorian "womanliness",[9] exemplarily enacting conventional female roles:[1] as "daughter" and "sister" (literally, as niece to Mrs. Yeobright and cousin to Clym) she is dutiful, marrying to preserve the family honor;[2] as wife to Wildeve she is loyal, even in the face of his neglect; and as mother she is selfless and protective.

If Hopkins's conventional representation of Thomasin was acceptable to Hardy, as the apparent absence of correspondence about the matter tends to suggest, the issue of Eustacia's representation was still unresolved. Responding to Hardy's original criticism of the February illustration, Hopkins had written "I will endeavour to improve on Eustacia next time she makes her appearance", but he then went on to acknowledge that this would not happen in the May illustration of the Yeobright Christmas party: "I avoided introducing Eustacia as in consequence of her disguise I believed it would be unwise."[3] Hopkins may simply have been avoiding a difficult subject: to render Eustacia in male dress as the altogether more feminine figure for which Hardy had asked would have re-

---

8. See Simon Gatrell, "Notes of Significant Revisions to the Text", in *The Return of the Native*, ed. Gatrell (Oxford: Oxford Univ. Press, 1990), p. 458.
9. Rosemarie Morgan situates Thomasin as "model woman" in *Women and Sexuality in the Novels of Thomas Hardy* (London: Routledge, 1988), pp. 59, 62.
1. See, e.g., George Elgar Hicks's triptych *Woman's Mission* (1863), the three parts of which are subtitled "Guide to Childhood" (Dunedin Public Art Gallery), "Companion of Manhood" (Tate Gallery), and "Comfort of Old Age" (Dunedin).
2. Significantly, Thomasin is most concerned about the male's (Clym's) sense of disgrace (see 35: 236–37, 274–75).
3. 19 February 1878 (Dorset County Museum).

quired a great deal of ingenuity. On the other hand it is certainly in keeping with Hopkins's persistent suppression of the potentially subversive that he chose not to represent Eustacia's cross-dressing. Hardy acknowledged the wisdom of the omission in a 20 February letter to Hopkins—"Eustacia in boy's clothes, though pleasant enough to the imagination, would perhaps be unsafe as a picture" (*Letters*, I.54)—but his substitution of the anxiety-ridden "unsafe" for Hopkins's temperate "unwise" is again suggestive of the nature of his concerns.

There was nothing even remotely "unsafe" about Eustacia's reappearance in the June illustration of the scene at Captain Vye's well, despite the mildly sensational caption: "Tie a rope round him; it is dangerous." Hopkins chose to represent Eustacia at one of the rare moments when she conforms to stereotypical "womanly" behavior, expressing her concern for Clym in "a soft and anxious voice" (35: 493). His intention was perhaps to create a context in which he could reconcile himself to Hardy's insistence upon Eustacia's greater "femininity", but in this case he avoided the issue, relegating Eustacia to a small window in the background and adhering to the letter rather than the spirit of Hardy's criticism: the June Eustacia is indeed more youthful than the February, but her body is mostly in shadow or actually out of sight; her face, foreshortened (hence literally more rounded) by the angle at which she leans forward, is almost without distinguishing features; and her short forehead curls give her a distinctly boyish look.

Although there is no evidence that Hardy complained about the June illustration, Hopkins must have been well aware of the author's continuing dissatisfaction, and in the August issue of *Belgravia* a completely reconceptualized Eustacia was prominently introduced (see p. 213). No trace of the "masculinized" Eustacia survived, and while the new Eustacia's pouting expression clearly disqualifies her as an embodiment of ideal Victorian womanhood, she is unambiguously aligned with the "feminine", not least in the conventional shapeliness of her figure. Hardy was delighted: "Allow me to congratulate you on your success this month . . .", he wrote on 3 August; "I think Eustacia is charming—she is certainly just what I imagined her to be, & the rebelliousness of her nature is precisely caught in your drawing" (*Letters*, I.59). Hopkins had at last succeeded—with considerable nudging from Hardy—in depicting a Eustacia sufficiently attractive and even fashionable to appeal to a contemporary middle-class reading public without threatening its sense of established constructions of femininity.

But if Hopkins was willing to sacrifice his original conception of Eustacia to gain Hardy's approval, he was also prepared to depart from the details of Hardy's text in order to create an effective image. The triangular grouping of the figures—praised by Hardy in his 3 August letter and strikingly reflective of Eustacia's feeling that Clym has sunk beneath her, almost to the level of a common laborer—depends entirely on Hopkins's unauthorized inclusion of Humphrey. The effectiveness of the illustration also owes much to Hopkins's independent use of detail: while Clym becomes a part of the heath, immersed past his knees in the furze, Eustacia stands as apart from it as possible, her parasol untouched by the furze and even her shoes uninfringed upon by the grass. It is almost as if she were standing in a different landscape. Only the phallic shape of the hated furze held by Clym cuts across her, suggesting his sexual desire, though his inability to fulfill that desire is in turn suggested by the abrupt cutting off of the knife in his right hand. As he unconsciously points toward her with the furze, she consciously points away from him with her parasol, held across her body in a sexually defensive position.

If Hopkins's visualization of this scene, despite its departures from the literal details of the narrative, seems to work with rather than against Hardy's text, the same cannot be said of his representation of Eustacia for the October installment (see p. 277). Hardy's letter praising the August illustration would have arrived at about the time Hopkins was beginning work on the October drawing and may have influenced the choice and treatment of his subject matter. It is certainly striking that for an installment that included such dramatic if potentially indecorous scenes as Clym's discovery of the circumstances of his mother's death and his subsequent confrontation with Eustacia,[4] Hopkins chose as his subject Eustacia's being ministered to by the faithful Charley at her grandfather's house. Hopkins's Eustacia is not, however, the Eustacia of Hardy's text at this point in the narrative—an embodiment of "undetermined and formless misery", too distressed to notice her "wetted and disarranged" hair and garments, and too weak to walk unassisted (36: 506, 505). Rather, with her expressive eyes, her melancholy expression, and a languorous posture displaying to full advantage her immaculate dress and "perfect" figure, she is an object of desire not just for Charley, the humble adorer who kneels at her feet not daring to touch so much as her shadow, but also for *Belgravia*'s readers, fashion-conscious females equally with gazing males.

Hardy seems to have offered no comment on this unabashed departure from the details of his text, doubtless recognizing that an

4. The latter in particular has proved to be a popular subject with subsequent illustrators of the novel; see, e.g., the editions illustrated by A. Burnham Shute (New York: American Publishers, [c. 1892]), Clare Leighton, Agnes Miller Parker, Nora Lavrin (Ljubljana: Mladinska Knjiga, 1967), and Roy Anderson (Franklin Center: Franklin Library, 1978). William Dean Howells's chapter on Hardy in *Heroines in Fiction*, 2 vols. (New York: Harper and Brothers, 1901), II, opp. p. 186, also includes an illustration of this scene.

alluring Eustacia, however textually inauthentic, was likely to maintain and even incite readerly interest. In any case, it would have been difficult for him to criticize what was clearly another attempt to respond to his own earlier request, endorsed by praise of the August illustration, for an unquestionably "feminine" Eustacia who would nonetheless be dissociated from the conventional "womanly" norm. Certainly the October illustration sustains the opposition between "bad" and "good" heroines that from the beginning Hardy had wanted the illustrations to stress, Eustacia's carefully posed beauty and desirability providing an obvious foil to Thomasin's "natural" prettiness and, indeed, to those maternal—rather than sexual—qualities that Hopkins had previously attributed to Thomasin and would again emphasize in his next (November) drawing, where, oblivious to the storm, to Venn, and to her own physical progress, she has eyes only for her child.

For the final (December) installment Hopkins chose to illustrate, in the words of the caption, "All that remained of the desperate and unfortunate Eustacia" as she is dragged from the river by Venn (see p. 309). His intention was presumably to create a somewhat sensational drawing in keeping with the melodramatic action at this point in Hardy's text—in keeping also with the hitherto largely unfulfilled expectations of *Belgravia* readers accustomed to illustrations of deathbeds, corpses, heroines in peril, and disasters generally.[5] Conceivably Hopkins, in a final gesture of independence, wished to reassert his original reading of Eustacia, both by emphasizing the manner of her death—drowning being the conventional, if statistically exceptional, fate of the Victorian fallen woman[6]—and by rendering her as undesirable as possible, with a grotesquely clawlike hand (reminiscent of the distorted left hand of the initial February illustration) and impossibly contorted upper body. Certainly Hopkins's misshapen corpse has no part in the erotics of death evoked by the narrator's lingering description of a Eustacia who, with her translucent skin, finely carved mouth, and abundant loose hair, "eclipsed all her living phases" (37: 232). It was too late for Hardy to protest; in any case, he was well aware that the conventions already reflected in his own plot demanded the foregrounding of the "wayward & erring" heroine's inevitable punishment.

Hardy's apparent silence with respect to Hopkins's representations of the central male characters of *The Return of the Native* also attests to his acceptance of the conditions and constraints of suc-

5. See, e.g., *Belgravia*, 29 (1876), opp. pp. 85 and 265; 30 (1876), frontispiece; and 31 (1876–77), opp. p. 176 (note that illustrations sometimes were bound at different places in different copies of the periodical).
6. See Lynda Nead, *Myths of Sexuality: Representations of Women in Victorian Britain* (Oxford: Basil Blackwell, 1988).

cessful serial publication. In these illustrations Hopkins again privileges the conventional while occluding the potentially subversive or disturbing. The first drawing of Clym (for the May installment) succeeds well enough in capturing the conflict between beauty and thought said to be embodied in his countenance (see p. 122, and 35: 258); it also manages to represent him as "manly" in spite of that (associatively "feminine") beauty.[7] Tall and broad-shouldered, Hopkins's Clym visually conforms to conventional expectations of the masculine, as indeed he does in the following month's illustration of the gathering at the well, where he is depicted as a "heroic rescuer"—even if of nothing more valuable or romantic than a water bucket. Hardy's text, however, increasingly seems to question hegemonic constructions of middle-class masculinity, as when Mrs. Yeobright orthodoxly condemns as "unmanly" Clym's lack of social and economic ambition while Clym himself rejects as "effeminate" that past career in Paris that his mother would have him emulate (see 35: 487, 484).[8] As the issue of Clym's masculinity becomes still more complex—his passion for Eustacia, for example, aligning him with the "manly" sexual desire that "unmans" in its negation of the rational (35: 508; 36: 3)[9]—Hopkins avoids direct representation of Clym. After the June installment Clym figures only twice more in the illustrations: in August, where he is effectively disguised as a furze-cutter, his face obscured by dark glasses and an untrimmed moustache, his form no longer distinguished by superior height and graceful strength; and in September, where he is seen only from the back as he stands beside his dying mother. Thus Hopkins leaves entirely unrepresented the highly problematic Clym of the final books—the Clym who confronts Eustacia with the violence of his own pain; who withdraws from the community, consumed with remorse; and who delivers new sermons on the mount that, however, seem so different in spirit and purpose from Christ's.

Wildeve, for his part, scarcely figures in Hopkins's drawings at

7. Agnes Miller Parker chooses to represent Clym as an effeminate intellectual contrasted with the virile Wildeve. That Hardy himself was well satisfied with Hopkins's representation of Clym is suggested by the choice of the May illustration as a frontispiece to the 1880 Kegan Paul one-volume edition of the novel.

8. Hardy later strengthened this point by upgrading Clym's experience as a jeweler's assistant (in *Belgravia*) to that of jeweler's manager (in the 1878 Smith, Elder edition) and of diamond merchant's manager (in the 1895 Osgood, McIlvaine edition). For an analysis of the complexities and contradictions inherent in the formulation of alternative masculinities during the decades immediately preceding Hardy's literary career, see Herbert Sussman, *Victorian Masculinities: Manhood and Masculine Poetics in Early Victorian Literature and Art* (Cambridge: Cambridge Univ. Press, 1995).

9. Cf. Elizabeth Langland's reading of Jude's susceptibility to sexual desire in relation to cultural paradigms of masculinity ("Becoming a Man in *Jude the Obscure*", in *The Sense of Sex: Feminist Perspectives on Hardy*, ed. Margaret R. Higonnet [Urbana and Chicago: Univ. of Illinois Press, 1993], pp. 32–48). Whereas Langland, following critics such as Nead (p. 6), defines this susceptibility as an "important evidence of manliness" (p. 36), Sussman maintains that "the defining quality of bourgeois masculinity [is] the control of sexual energy" (p. 203).

all: he appears only once, his face almost entirely obscured by a hat, in the July illustration of his nocturnal dice game with Christian. Having encountered substantial opposition from Hardy to his rendering of the "bad" heroine, Hopkins was perhaps reluctant to risk a similar response to the "bad" hero. Or he may simply have felt that Wildeve, faintly pathetic both as villain and as victim, was a difficult and potentially dangerous pictorial subject.

Hopkins was more at ease with Venn, linked with Thomasin from the first and capable of being depicted, like her, as unambiguously "good"—even if at the expense of Hardy's more complex representations. Venn was the chosen subject of the third (March) drawing (see p. 73), following the illustration of Eustacia on the heath and preceding that of Thomasin in the apple loft. Seated in a distinctly domesticated van, his sacks of reddle sharing space with hanging kitchen utensils and a steaming kettle atop the stove, Venn is pictured rereading—so the caption states—"an old love letter". In what sense Thomasin's letter of rejection could be so described is not readily apparent, but the purpose of the caption—to elicit sympathy for Venn—is obvious enough. Sympathy is in fact the dominant note of the drawing, pained sensitivity being writ large upon his face, as it would be upon Thomasin's in the following month's illustration, and Hopkins's Venn is in all his appearances the embodiment of selfless love, Thomasin's devoted guide and protector. In the November illustration, for example, he literally leads her through the storm, at the same time looking down at the child in his arms with what might conventionally be described as "maternal" affection.

Hopkins's Venn does figure in Hardy's text. Even the homelike van of the March illustration is based on a passage that begins with an account of Venn darning a stocking, and Venn displays throughout the novel a "feminine" delicacy and selflessness, refusing to subject Thomasin to the appropriative "male gaze" as she lies sleeping, and sacrificing his own happiness to hers in helping to bring about the marriage with Wildeve (see 35:2; 34:286; 35:270). When Venn describes such sacrifice as only doing what "a man ought" (35: 270), he aligns himself not only with the characteristically Hardyan construction of masculinity as embodied in such figures as Gabriel Oak and Giles Winterborne—similarly defined by such "womanly" virtues as patience, modesty, and self-abnegating devotion[1]—but also with ideals of manliness derived from contemporary concepts of chivalry.[2] In these respects, indeed, Venn serves more

1. See Linda M. Shires, "Narrative, Gender, and Power in *Far from the Madding Crowd*", in *Sense of Sex*, pp. 49–65.
2. See Mark Girouard, *The Return to Camelot: Chivalry and the English Gentleman* (New Haven: Yale Univ. Press, 1981).

directly and complexly as a foil to Clym, a failed aspirant in these directions, than criticism has generally recognized.

Totally absent from Hopkins's illustrations, on the other hand, is the "other" Venn of Hardy's text, the luridly colored reddleman who haunts the heath, frightens Johnny Nunsuch, and causes even Timothy Fairway to think of "the devil or the red ghost" (34: 280). It is clear, however, that this Venn had always figured importantly in Hardy's own conception of the character, and in subsequent revisions to the novel he sought to emphasize—or perhaps reassert—the threatening aspects of the reddleman's omnipresence by adding allusions to the devil, Mephistopheles, and Ishmael,[3] and finally by inserting into the 1912 Wessex Edition the famous footnote appended to Thomasin's announcement of her engagement:

> The writer may state here that the original conception of the story did not design a marriage between Thomasin and Venn. He was to have retained his isolated and weird character to the last, and to have disappeared mysteriously from the heath, nobody knowing whither—Thomasin remaining a widow. But certain circumstances of serial publication led to a change of intent.
>
> Readers can therefore choose between the endings, and those with an austere artistic code can assume the more consistent conclusion to be the true one.

Hopkins, of course, had not been privy to this insight—he had in fact been assured from the first that Venn and Thomasin would finally and "happily" marry—and he can scarcely be blamed for failing to reflect, in this and other instances, character traits that the author had chosen to de-emphasize not just for purposes of illustration but for the entire process of serialization. At the same time, the shadowy presence within the serial of a more threatening Venn and a more radical Thomasin—as well as of complex issues of gender definition glanced at rather than articulated or resolved—attests to the tension, present in so many of Hardy's texts, between his pragmatic need not to transgress overtly the limits of the conventionally acceptable and his personal desire to do just that.

In the absence of the alternative ending said to have been originally conceived, the Wessex Edition footnote in fact denies the reader any genuine choice.[4] What the footnote, written so late in Hardy's career, does importantly register, however, is precisely

3. These revisions first appeared in, respectively, the 1878 Smith, Elder edition, the 1880 Kegan Paul edition, and the 1895 Osgood, McIlvaine edition; see Gatrell, "Notes", pp. 447, 451–52, and 456.

4. See Michael Millgate, *Thomas Hardy: His Career as a Novelist* (London: Macmillan, 1971), p. 141. Millgate sees the footnote as unhelpfully "intrusive" in its disturbance of an actual ending that "seems entirely consistent" with the novel as it stands in its Wessex Edition version (Millgate, pp. 141–42).

Hardy's own continuing disturbance—the degree to which he was still troubled by the textual concessions he had made in advance of the serialization of *The Return of the Native* and, indeed, by the interpretational compromises implicit in his dealings with Hopkins during the serial's progress. But in 1877–78 the professional and economic necessities of his situation had seemed to offer no practical alternative. It can be said that the selectivity and obliquity of Hopkins's illustrations, compounded by occasional lapses in skill on his own or the engravers' part, resulted in a distorted reading of Hardy's text, especially through Hopkins's persistent avoidance of its more passionate and subversive aspects. But the thrust of the distortions and visual silences was consistently in the direction of representing the novel as substantially more conventional than it essentially was—hence of enhancing its acceptance by the *Belgravia* subscribers and the serial-reading public generally—and Hardy's failure to protest his illustrator's late departures from his text can thus perhaps be read as a belated recognition that Hopkins's sense of the expectations and likely responses of the magazine's readers was superior to his own. Hardy's toleration, in fact, of what now seem for the most part simplistic, insensitive, or "unrepresentative" representations of his work was clearly related to his anxiety about the novel's success and based on his perception that the very conventionality of the illustrations could be a valuable ally in the struggle—so frequent in his career—to render publishable a text that pushed persistently against the limits of the then acceptable.

GILLIAN BEER

Can the Native Return?†

My title is a question: 'Can the Native Return?' It may put you in mind of Hardy, and *The Return of the Native* will indeed be a crucial instance in the later part of my argument, forming the centre of a triptych of examples: 'triptych' here not in the devotional sense, but in the original meaning of a set of three writing-tablets hinged together. But I want briefly to set Hardy's theme in a longer literary perspective and then to demonstrate how for the Victorians the idea of the native's return held particularly disturbing cultural possibilities. For one thing, this was a community that set store by em-

† From *Open Fields: Science in Cultural Encounter* (Oxford: Clarendon Press, 1996), pp. 31–54. Reprinted by permission of the University of London. Page references to *The Return of the Native* have been changed to correspond to this edition.

igration as a solution to social problems: the economically enforced journeying of the poor and the disadvantaged did not expect them back. Self-betterment required, in the fullest sense of the word, *displacement*. Novelists understood the dilemma. Elizabeth Gaskell's *Mary Barton* rescues some of the characters at the end of the book for a new life in Canada, thus producing a happy ending which need not pretend that the situation in England has changed for the better. Dickens's *Great Expectations*, in the histories equally of Magwitch and of Pip, probes the nightmares of return.

There were other issues at stake as well. I shall refer to two important and symptomatic non-fictional controversies that raise these further questions. Both illustrate the particular problems of communal self-valuing active for the Victorians in the idea of the return of the native. The cases, to which I shall come a little later in my argument, are those of Jemmy Button and of Sir John Franklin.

December is a good month to talk about natives' return. The uneasy if pleasurable approach of Christmas with its necessary choice of where to be, how long to stay, or whom to ask, brings into sharp focus *place* as the nexus of kinship and the past. Return is not a matter of memory only, it is *going* somewhere. Indeed the return of the native has as often been an occasion of confusion, bloodshed and dismay as of rejoicing—in literature at least, let us say. From Ulysses and Agamemnon to Pinter's *Homecoming* and Dürrenmatt's *The Visit*, return has unsettled rather than stabilized. The idea of the native's return seems to offer comfort and completion, but it also harbours a confounding paradox. That the native can return seems plain enough, but can he or she return *as a native*?

The act of return includes recognition and estrangement. Hardy in *The Return of the Native* suggests that 'any native home for the holidays' is a kind of toy person, going to church to see and be seen: 'Thus the congregation on Christmas morning is mostly a Tussaud collection of celebrities who have been born in the neighbourhood' (p. 105). Instead of a now-active person, they present a waxwork display, a mere simulacrum of identity. The safest way. Christmas visits, after all, also imply a promise to go away again. Mrs. Yeobright is delighted to have her son home for Christmas. Her alarm begins when he shows no sign of leaving afterwards.

Let me start the argument, though, nearer the literary beginnings of our culture. When Ovid pictured the golden age at the beginning of *Metamorphoses* it was of a time when no one travelled, when people were not conscious of boundaries as bounds to be crossed, when all were at one with the place where they were born and satisfied by the beneficent harvests it provided. Ovid's image of change is the shift from vertical to horizontal. The trees, upright in the woods, are cut and lowered, shaped into boats. Fruitful stasis becomes driven movement. That shift of axes begins the history of the world. In its wake comes trade, conflict, invasion, mingling, and travel.

Happiness may take the form of believing that return is possible while freely delaying the journey. Though return to his homeland is Ulysses' overriding desire, the pleasures of the *Odyssey* depend, for the hero as much as the reader, upon the hindrances and delays of that return. But Ulysses does at last get back to his native land, reclaim his wife, and rule again. Penelope's constant unpicking of her weaving during his absence expresses a magical staying of the processes of onward time. Each day simply begins again the business of the previous one, until the completion of her husband's return is achieved. Decay is held off. By repetition and unravelling, strength and youth are sustained and time is impacted.

The insatiable zeal for travel becomes the expression of life itself. Tennyson in the mid-nineteenth century emended Homer's happy close to show instead Ulysses impatient and alienated in a native land where he is no longer *known*, since the meaning of his life has been in his adventures elsewhere:

> It little profits that an idle king,
> By this still hearth, among these barren crags,
> Matched with an aged wife, I mete and dole
> Unequal laws unto a savage race,
> That hoard, and sleep, and feed, and know not me.
>
> I cannot rest from travel . . .

'Unequal laws unto a savage race': it seems as though he feels himself to have returned into an earlier cultural phase.

Doubts about the satisfactoriness of return did not begin with Tennyson's *Ulysses*. It was a persistent topic in eighteenth-century literature: Defoe's *Captain Singleton* and *Robinson Crusoe* and Johnson's *Rasselas* work out counter-possibilities. Captain Singleton has never known a mother and has no idea what 'home' might mean until he forms a friendship with the Quaker, William. Friendship for him gives a possible meaning to the word. At the end of *Rasselas* the return to the happy valley is an image of satiety. (Hardy's mother gave him this masterpiece of disappointment to read when he was 8.)

Gulliver's Travels most fully works through the problems embedded in the idea of the native's return. At the end of *Gulliver's Travels* Gulliver returns, and in a passage less often noted than his account of how he felt about his family, he raises general issues of power and predation. He takes a final leave of his courteous readers, having justified his behaviour against charges that as a traveller he did not pursue with sufficient zeal the enlargement of his Majesty's dominions by his discoveries.

> To say the truth, I had conceived a few scruples with relation to the distributive justice of princes upon these occasions. For instance, a crew of pirates are driven by a storm they know not whither, at length a boy discovers land from the topmast, they go on shore to rob and plunder, they see a harmless people, are entertained with kindness, they give the country a new name, they take formal possession of it for the king, they set up a rotten plank or a stone for a memorial, they murder two or three dozen of the natives, bring away a couple more by force as a sample, return home, and get their pardon. Here commences a new dominion acquired with a title *by divine right*.[1]

In contrast, Gulliver will 'return to enjoy my own speculations in my little garden at Redriff'. That sounds very much like the conclusion of *Candide*, cultivating his garden some thirty years later. But Gulliver is not so much cultivating his garden as his speculations. And these are burdened with his alienation from his native land and its inhabitants. Among the rational horses, the Houyhnhnms, he was seen as a member of the race of filthy Yahoos, albeit a Yahoo of unusually docile and teachable propensities: Gulliver steels himself, like an anti-narcissus, to survey his body in the looking glass: 'to behold my figure often in a glass, and thus if possible habituate myself by time to tolerate the sight of a human creature'. By such forced recognition he intends to begin the process of reconcilement that may, one day, make of him again a native in his own land.

To him, human beings now are animals, according with the stereotypes by which human beings describe the 'brutes': merely stinking and irrational. But worse, puffed up with human pride. He has earlier within one sentence described the invaders, or explorers, as an 'execrable crew of butchers employed in so pious an expedition', and as 'a modern colony sent to convert and civilize an idolatrous and barbarous people'. In a dizzying series of ironies, the 'barbarous people' become his own family and even himself, stubbornly and self-woundingly gazing into his looking glass. His 'old habits' now are not those of the clan but those learnt on his journeys: 'And although it be hard for a man late in life to remove old habits, I am not altogether out of hopes in some time to suffer a neighbour Yahoo in my company without the apprehensions I am yet under of his teeth or his claws'.

In this collapsing pyramid of superiorities Gulliver is left with no-

---

1. Jonathan Swift, *Gulliver's Travels, and Other Writings*, ed. Louis Landa (Oxford, 1976), p. 237. Subsequent references are to pp. 237–38 of this edition.

body with whom to identify. He enacts dualism, split between the body of a Yahoo, the mind of a Houyhnhnm—or so he hopes. He is as proud as the rest of the human race he spurns, even while he claims his alienation from it as a sign of virtue.

Swift here savagely decomposes the trope of the return of the native. At one, and at home at last, Gulliver is more profoundly divided than ever, retching with the stench of other human beings, autocratic, imposing, incapable of any healing dialogue with the natives among whom it is now his lot to live.

He just permits his wife 'to sit at dinner with me, at the farthest end of a long table, and to answer (but with the utmost brevity) the few questions I ask her'. The subjugated and silenced wife, held far off, is not put in direct parallel with the harmless people plundered by the representatives of a so-called higher civilization that I have quoted from the previous page. But the potential for such a comparison lies only just beneath the surface of the language. Gulliver thinks of himself as the man elevated by travel and by his discourse with the superior Houyhnhnms. He thinks of himself as an educator. But he is, demeaningly, also the token savage, the sample, educated as far as may be into the image of Houyhnhnm civilization but never accepted by them as one of their own. I shall offer another example of that token figure later in this argument in the person of the Fuegian, Jemmy Button. Gulliver has been undermined for life in his native land by the education he has received among the horses. The last irony (though in Swift we can never be sure that we have quite reached the ultimate irony) is that Houyhnhnm civilization configures many of the claimed or acclaimed values of Western civilization.

Swift's scarifying version of the native's return puts into jeopardy two comforting words: return and native. Their ambiguities increasingly haunt nineteenth-century fiction, politics, and philosophy. (And I shall not even begin to talk about Nietzsche nor, directly, Freud, whose concept of *The Return of the Repressed* Perry Meisel well elaborates in his study of Hardy.)

Patriotism—the ideology of the native land—begins when alternatives to the native land can be imagined; it brings with it all the rending ills of war and imperialism as well as the apparent blessings of pastoralism and return. The native land is the land of nativity, simply 'the place where I was born'. Knowing it again is a source of intense pleasure. The congruity between being born and a parcel of land makes of the native land a magic place in which identity, body, culture and location are condensed: 'I am native here, And to the manner born'.

Being born needs a mother. The identification between the native land and the figure of the mother (the motherland, the mother-tongue) produces another set of profound associations, played out in a variety of ways by writers of all ideological casts, and, in Hardy's novel, with extraordinary passion.

Re-cognition: knowing again; knowing anew. That is the perfected dream of return: the simple exoticism of the familiar. One of the most famous of Romantic fables of return is the parable contained within the body of Novalis's *Die Lehrlinge zu Sais*. The parable describes a perfect circle, though the circle is also a spiral of understanding. The hero sets out, leaving his familiar loved one at home. He travels to the ends of the earth. The Goddess unveils herself in his sight. Her face is the face of the loved one left behind. He comes back to his native place, seeing it and its inhabitants for the first time, bathed in the light of recognition. Or, the tale of the Swaffham pedlar, alluded to in Hardy's novel. In that folk tale the Norfolk pedlar goes to London Bridge on the impulse of a dream telling him to seek his fortune in London. There he meets another dreamer who has dreamt about a hidden treasure buried in a Swaffham garden. The pedlar completes the circle, goes home, and finds the treasure in his own yard: the treasure includes knowing the place where you began.

That backward return is possible only if the place itself is seen as unchanging. It merges, therefore, into a dream of nostalgia. The native place becomes the past; its recovery gainsays the ineluctable onward movement of time.

Hardy's novel *The Return of the Native* opens not with people but a place, and that place as unchanging as it is possible to conceive: 'The untameable, Ishmaelitish thing that Egdon now was it always had been. Civilization was its enemy; and ever since the beginning of vegetation its soil had worn the same antique brown dress, the natural and invariable garment of the particular formation' (p. 10). This landscape is savage (in the sense of uncultivated), undeveloped, and unchanged since 'the beginning of vegetation'. In natural-historical, and in anthropomorphic terms ('antique brown dress'), it represents the unaltered conditions of the world.

Hardy moves the return of the native from the end of his story to relatively near its beginning, commented on and foreseen from the point of view of the inhabitants. That return becomes the generative act of his fiction. Instead of long-delayed homecoming providing the uneasy calm of closure, as in the eighteenth-century examples I have mentioned, it here sets off the range of interlocking consequences that make the fiction.

Hardy achieves some of his most disturbing effects by extending the emphasis on the dubieties of *return* into the cultural duplicities lodged in the word *native*. These duplicities may seem to us to have been particularly sanguine and unsurveyed in the Victorian period, but, as one reads further into the period, one discovers that they also provided the matter of much contemporary debate. Edward Said's *Orientalism* has tellingly argued that, so far as the construction of knowledge goes, the difficulty for the traveller is that he or she never really leaves home however long the journey. The assumptions of the home culture and language (in Said's argument European culture and language) imbue what can be seen, and precondition what can be valued. But these assumptions are also always contested, I would argue, within the current language of the tribe: for the Victorians here, within the English language, its relations to other tongues then much under debate, and its wide range of discursive dissonances and consonances particularly active—and quite peculiarly active in the language of Hardy's fiction.

But let me first examine a less considered example than anything Hardy could write. To be a native-born Englishman is a state of privilege; to be a native elsewhere is to be a savage. We can hear the play across these two radically opposed senses of the word in R. M. Ballantyne's *The Coral Island* (1858). Newly shipwrecked on their island, the boys settle in comfortably, but 'we did not quite like the idea of settling down here for the rest of our lives, far away from our friends and our native land . . . Then there was a little uncertainty still as to there being natives on the island. But as day after day passed, and neither savages nor ships appeared . . . we set diligently to work at our homestead'.[2] Natives *on* the island, not natives *of* the island, one notes. The phrase 'native intruders' is often bandied about at that period (and indeed long after) with no recognition of its contradictoriness. The natives, rather than the boys, are figured as intruders, and the term native is replaced with its pseudosynonym savages in the next sentence. Peterkin, in a rehearsal of Gulliver's satiric terms, here nonchalantly used, though not quite without narrative irony, fantasizes their future: 'We'll take possession in the name of the king; we'll go and enter the service of its black inhabitants. Of course we'll rise, *naturally*, to the top of affairs. White men always do in savage countries'[3] (emphasis added). The boys will discover that things are not quite so simple, one should note in fairness to Ballantyne. But the word 'naturally' neatly loads the whole weight of a culture behind an assumption.

It is not necessary to suppose that Hardy is commenting directly on colonialism in his title to perceive that Clym's status as native draws both on the idea of the civilized Englishman and (as the book

2. R. M. Ballantyne, *Coral Island: A Tale of the Pacific Ocean* (London, 1858), p. 47.
3. *Coral Island*, p. 21.

goes on) on the idea of cultural regression to the savage state. Clym is shown to be in a more advanced stage of development than his neighbours who stayed at home. He is the man educated beyond his original condition, educated for an as yet non-existent future: 'in Clym Yeobright's face could be dimly seen the typical countenance of the future' (p. 143).

Country-dwellers and exotic islanders alike were seen in much mid- and later nineteenth-century anthropological writing (witness Lubbock, Tylor, Spencer) as existing in an earlier phase of cultural development than that reached by cosmopolitan European man. And here I want to draw into my discussion the first of my three examples, a symptomatic mid-nineteenth-century controversy about natives and return. Hardy may have known it. Whether he did or not does not particularly matter for my argument. The case sheds light on the uneasiness in earlier Victorian writing about 'unspoilt' communities and individual development, an uneasiness that certainly *did* tell in Hardy's work. It sheds light too on the problems of telling a story in a language that does not fit its protagonist.

Captain Fitzroy, later to be the captain of the *Beagle* when Darwin was on board as ship's naturalist, first touched land at Tierra del Fuego in 1830. Fitzroy was an earnest Christian. On the first voyage he kidnapped some Fuegians, or as he might prefer to put it, gave them the opportunity of a Western education. When Fitzroy's crew left, they took away with them a small group—in Swift's term, 'a sample'—of people from the tribe, to whom they subsequently gave grotesque jokey names (not content with renaming the land as Gulliver describes, they renamed individuals): Fuegia Basket, York Minster, Boat Memory (who died of smallpox). Among this small band was Jemmy Button, so-called because he had been exchanged for a mother-of-pearl button.[4] Jemmy Button had a considerable social success in England and became obsessive about cleanliness and clothing. Together with Fuegia Basket (who had originally been taken hostage by Fitzroy when some of her tribe, in Fitzroy's words, 'approached with the dextrous cunning peculiar to savages', ii.5) he made an apparently smooth transition to English life. Button and Fuegia Basket were even introduced to Queen Adelaide, who gave Fuegia one of her own bonnets, and were taught English and given some education (ii. 12). Fitzroy felt responsible for the Fuegians (as well he might) and for returning them home: Button, in particular, was to return as a missionary to his tribe. So when Darwin set off on the voyage of the *Beagle*, on board were Button, York Minster, and Fuegia Basket dressed in Western habits.

4. Robert Fitzroy and Charles Darwin, *Narratives of the Surveying Voyages of His Majesty's Ships Adventure and Beagle*, 3 vols. (vols. 1 and 2 by Fitzroy, vol. 3 by Darwin), (London, 1839), i.444. Subsequent references given in the text.

In 1833 the *Beagle* crew landed the Fuegians near where they had taken them and said farewell. A year later they returned to see how things were going. Darwin and Fitzroy both gave accounts of the reunion. Darwin wrote: 'It was quite painful to behold him [Button]; thin, pale, and without a remnant of clothes, excepting a bit of blanket round his waist, his hair hanging over his shoulders; and so ashamed of himself he turned his back to the ship as the canoe approached.' (Embarrassment at the jarring of two cultures and perhaps resentment might seem to us now quite as probable reasons for his action as shame: 'shame' being itself a term symptomatic of Victorian preoccupations.) Darwin continues: 'When he left us he was very fat, and so particular about his clothes, that he was always afraid of even dirtying his shoes, scarcely ever without his gloves and his hair neatly cut.' (Again, the stresses of someone afraid even to dirty shoes meant functionally for walking might lend itself to counter-analysis.) But things improve and 'lastly we found out in the evening (by her arrival) that he had got a young and very nice looking squaw. This he would not at first own to; and we were rather surprised to find he had not the least wish to return to England.' Darwin accounts for Button's reluctance romantically; English honour is thus satisfied.

After that Button was lost sight of. He was said in the English accounts to have 'disappeared', though to himself and his group he had, rather, re-appeared. He had 'gone native' (though whether someone not a native-born Englishman could 'go native' I'm not sure), or he had re-assimilated. Sent back as an educator, his triumph proved to be his capacity to merge again with his home community and to shed alien habits, though Fitzroy and Darwin feared (and in a curious way, perhaps half-hoped) that he had lost his own language. Unlike Gulliver returning from among the Houyhnhnms, Jemmy Button had not been unfitted for life at home by contact with what the European narrators saw as a higher culture.

There is a further stage to Victorian interpretation of this story. Some fifteen years later Jemmy was sighted again. In 1861 W. Parker Snow published an essay in the *Transactions of the Ethnological Society* (vol. i), in which he recounts his rediscovery of Jemmy Button. Snow apologizes persistently for his own tendency to empathize with the Fuegian community, demurs politely at the more rancorous accounts by earlier travellers of the inhabitants' morals, and gives a touching vignette of Jemmy Button's mixed reactions to their arrival.

Snow is dutifully shocked to see how little of Button's English education remains: 'Yet that same poor creature had been the petted idol of friends here at home, had been presented to royalty, and finally sent back to Fuego as a passably finished man!'[5] ('A passably finished man' is a powerfully ambiguous phrase.) Jemmy has retained some English and taught it to his group: 'It was marvellously strange that he not only retained some knowledge of the English language, but had actually taught a portion of it to his own relations. Unfortunately what they best understood was some of our worst words, though they certainly attached no wrong meaning to what was said.' Jemmy Button's appearance has returned or (as the Victorians might say) *reverted* to that of his tribe. Haunting the controversy is a debate about nature and nurture, about education and adaptation, that still has not died away.

Snow is caught across two responses: he feels that he should be shocked by this sloughing off of 'civilization'; he is delighted by Button's renewed harmony with his tribe. He is inclined to see this as a tribute to human adaptability rather than as demonstrating that other peoples cannot be educated. Like the other commentators, he does not remark their assumption that Western education is to be taken as the only model for development, though A. R. Wallace did so in *Island Life* some years later. Fitzroy, fifteen years before Snow, claimed that Jemmy's 'family were becoming considerably more humanized than any savages we had seen in Tierra del Fuego' (ii. 326). Snow notices, in a glancing and unanalysed aside, that Button's tribe alone was 'treacherous' towards their English visitors. He does not parallel this phenomenon with the treachery they have experienced in the taking away of their people. But he does record the fears of Button's youngest wife, and he does make clear his profound disapproval of removing people from their own culture, whether by force or cajolery. He only half-conceals his deep disquiet about 'what was done and is still being done regarding his people'.

Snow believes his own culture to lay too much sole stress on the development of *mind*: 'The actual difference between a savage and a civilized man is simply in the degree of cultivation given to the mind. In all other respects the savage at home is identical with the savage abroad.'[6] The ravages of *mind*, we may recollect, mar Clym Yeobright's beauty: 'The face was well shaped . . . But the mind within was beginning to use it as a mere waste tablet whereon to trace its idiosyncracies as they developed themselves. The beauty here visible would in no long time be ruthlessly overrun by its parasite, thought . . .' (p. 120).

5. W. Parker Snow, 'A Few Remarks on the Wild Tribes of Tierra del Fuego from Personal Observation,' *Transactions of the Ethnological Society of London*, NS vol. 1 (London, 1861), p. 265.
6. Snow, 'A Few Remarks,' p. 265.

Throughout Snow's essay the tone is one of mortified puzzlement. Fitzroy, Darwin, and Snow each write and rewrite extensive interpretations of the episode. They were worried and baffled by it. Snow was the most imaginative interpreter, but it is still the failure of interpretation that is the most revealing aspect of the affair. Snow cannot feel what he is supposed to feel; he does not see what he is expected to find; he presents himself therefore as a partial failure—but that self-presentation allows him mordantly to represent the treacheries and blindnesses of his own community. Snow's writing works as James Clifford in *Writing Culture* argues that good ethnography must do: 'Ethnographic truths are thus inherently *partial*—committed and incomplete . . . But once accepted and built into ethnographic art, a rigorous sense of partiality can be a source of representational tact.'[7]

So the tale of Jemmy Button is also a tale of Victorian interpretation and counter-interpretation. It seems to be the tale of a native's successful return to his people, coming back as a potential educator, settling in as an ordinary member of the tribe. But we cannot be sure; the mediation of the experience is so inadequate that we never can retrieve Button's experience. Not being able to retrieve it becomes *our* experience, an experience that includes bafflement and remorse. Nor do we inhabit the right language for retrieval: even my necessary mis-calling of him Jemmy Button makes that clear. Who is the native speaker here? And in what language can the tale be told? The poor fit between the language of interpretation and of experience tells its own story.

The Victorian justification for such acts as the taking away of Jemmy Button and his companions was partly religious but partly to be found in the belief in 'survivals'. Remote tribes and, sometimes, country people, were believed to represent intact much earlier phases in the cultural development of humankind. By studying such people the remote past could be revisited. As Edward Clodd, anthropologist and folklorist, put it to Hardy: 'your Dorset peasants represent the persistence of the same barbaric idea which confuses persons and things.' History was still active in the present time, not in the mutated form of continuity and gradual irreversible change, but *unchanged* in its early lineaments. The pockets of inhabitants in isolated places preserved intact earlier forms and traditions. Some of the connections to Hardy's thinking and to his creative building of story now begin to become clearer.

Critics have from time to time objected to the role of the country people in *The Return*, seeing them either as Shakespearean loons or as a somewhat mannered rustic Greek chorus. They are, rather

7. James Clifford and George E. Marcus, *Writing Culture: The Poetics and Politics of Ethnography* (Berkeley, 1986), p. 7.

(or also), in Hardy's writing, the surviving and continuing representatives of earlier human life.

Hardy describes the songs, the customs, the superstitions, the speech-styles of these country-dwellers, sometimes in set-pieces as in the mumming episode. He devotes entire scenes to the lighting of the bonfires on November 5th and to the malignant custom of pinsticking employed against Eustacia, who is believed to be a witch in some groups of the country community. The melting of Eustacia's image—so shortly followed by her death from drowning—unsteadies the knowing outsider's assumption that magic is malicious but ineffective. Here, as so often, Hardy establishes contiguous routes to the overdetermined event: through coincidence and witchcraft, or, at the same time, through psychological motive and independent event. Neither form of explanation drives out the other. They appear as parallel languages rather than as opposed interpretations. Present and past belief systems coexist. They do not follow an ordered succession.

In this arrangement, Hardy was pursuing a path rather different from that set out by most of the anthropologists and sociologists of the period: for example, Comte and Spencer (whom Hardy named among his chief intellectual influences) insist on fixed successive phases of culture. Tylor[8] had suggested that the vestiges of earlier belief undermined modern civilizations, and he instanced law, with its rule of primogeniture, and poetry as examples of 'survivals' within current belief-systems. Hardy himself riposted to Clodd's remark that 'the barbaric idea which confuses persons and things', in Clodd's phrase, is 'common to the highest imaginative genius, that of the poet'.

Strikingly, Hardy introduces early in the book the figure of Christian Cantle, an intersex or hermaphroditic figure. The scene in which his predicament is discussed is often read as an embarrassing Victorian comic set-piece. But it can be read along a different grain, taking us with extraordinary rapidity into the value-systems of the local community. The anthropologist Clifford Geertz has recently argued in *Local Knowledge* that attitudes to intersex people offer a means of analysing the central characteristics of diverse cultures. Geertz argues that because intersex or hermaphroditic people challenge sexual divisions in their physical make-up, and thereby gender attributions, their treatment rapidly uncovers the specifying values of particular groups. As Geertz remarks in 'Common Sense as a Cultural System': 'Common sense is not what the mind cleared of cant spontaneously apprehends; it is what the mind filled with presuppositions . . . concludes.'[9] Christian reacts

8. Edward Tylor, *Primitive Culture*, 2 vols. (London, 1871).
9. Clifford Geertz, *Local Knowledge: Further Essays in Interpretive Anthropology* (New York, 1983), p. 84.

with quaking dismay to the talk about the man whom no woman at all would marry and reveals himself as such another one, as he calls himself, a 'maphrotight'. ' "Why did ye reveal yer misfortune, Christian?" " 'Twas to be if 'twas, I suppose" ' (p. 26).

The reactions to Christian within the immediate group are low-key and humane, though edged with joking condescension. Fairway is forthright: 'Wethers must live their time as well as other sheep, poor soul' (p. 27). In this early scene Hardy pinpoints the matter-of-fact tolerance in the heath community which sees ghosts and hermaphrodites equally as unusual phenomena but native to the place, and therefore to be accepted.

The recording of customs, the allusive speech-patterns, the philological self-awareness of Hardy's composition owe much, as Hardy acknowledged, to the inspiration of his friend William Barnes, poet, folklorist, and philologist. Barnes is often referred to as a local dialect poet, one wholly centred in Dorset; but this is to misunderstand how the relations between local and total were working in Victorian culture. Victorian philology and etymology were preoccupied with the relations between English and other languages within the Indo-Germanic group. The question of common roots between remote tongues was much under discussion. The discursive array within English was being linked to issues of class, of national autonomy, of cultural progression. Barnes tracked between the local and the total. We can see this movement even in a list of some of his books' titles: *A Philological Grammar, grounded upon English, and Formed From a Comparison of More than Sixty Languages* (London, 1854); *Notes on Ancient Britain and the Britons* (1858); *Tiw; or, a View of the Roots and Stems of the English as a Teutonic Language* (1862); *Poems of Rural Life, in the Dorset Dialect*, first, second, and third collections, in the 1850s and 1860s; *Early England and the Saxon English* (1869); *A glossary of the Dorset Dialect with a grammar of its word shapening and wording* (1886). Barnes delves into remote history; he considers the relationships of English to other languages, present and past; he investigates the customs of present day country people; he elaborates that which is particular to Dorset in a way that makes it an element in an expansive and systematic enquiry.

The expansion depends upon particularity, but Barnes and Hardy share a swerve or vacillation between experience-near and experience-far language (to use Geertz's terms again). Indeed Hardy has sometimes been criticized for what commentators see as his intrusive allusions to other cultural spheres. His vocabulary ricochets across registers, between language close as touch and removed as latinate legal documents. As readers, we are shifted unendingly between microscopic and telescopic, between very old dialect words and very up-to-date references, particularly in relation to Eustacia. So within the individual observer or reader the phases of past cultural development are enacted synchronically through the language of the novel.

At the end of the description of the 'mummied heathbells of last summer' the paragraph opens: ' "The spirit moved them." A meaning of the phrase forced itself upon the attention; and an emotional listener's fetichistic mood might have ended in one of more advanced quality' (p. 50). The allusion is to Tylor's work on the sequence of psychological phases in the past of humankind, but Hardy here invokes the belief also in recapitulation within the individual of the past of human development. He shows the repeated enactment of cultural phases within the present of the reader. Though not, let it be noted, within the native inhabitants of the hearthland, other than Clym. Such enactment of earlier phases, after all, assumes (within the Victorian pattern of development) that the reader has come to the highest and last phase of the sequence.

And here I come to the third of my instances, the third writing-tablet of the triptych. One of the strangest and most original of the vacillations between near and far within the book is the recurrent invocation of Arctic scenery and of the idea of the migrating bird, creature of multiple homelands, returning as a native to our land, received as native at the other end of the world as well. This invocation of movement and of temperature-extremes forms unfamiliar sensory experience in the reader and also taps into another troubled Victorian expedition. At the book's opening, Hardy proposes a future for tourism. The extreme and barren Northern lands, Greenland, Thule, and the unmitigated flatness of Flemish landscape, rather than the South, will be the magnet for future human travel, he suggests. Egdon is as unchanging as the Arctic, a basic and ultimate natural world which ignores and outscales humankind. It is also a place much frequented and visited by other species. At the beginning of chapter 10 Hardy details the rare birds of the heath: bustards, marsh-harriers, even a cream-coloured courser, an 'African truant', a bird so rare that 'not more than a dozen have ever been seen in England' (and of course shot down as soon as sighted). Egdon Heath puts a possible traveller (the reader) 'in direct communication with regions unknown to man'. The passage ends with an ordinary mallard who becomes a fabled bird:

> A traveller who should walk and observe any of these visitants . . . could feel himself to be in direct communication with regions unknown to man. Here in front of him was a wild mallard—just arrived from the home of the north wind. The creature brought with him an amplitude of Northern knowledge. Glacial catastrophes, snow-storm episodes, glittering au-

roral effects, Polaris in the zenith, Franklin underfoot,—the
category of his commonplaces was wonderful. (p. 80).

The allusion to 'Franklin underfoot' gives access to an unsettling
episode of Victorian life, an episode that brought into lurid focus
the question of the phases of cultural development. Hardy would
have been a boy of about 13 at the height of the controversy in
around 1854–5. The senior explorer Sir John Franklin's last Arctic
expedition, seeking a Northwest Passage, disappeared in July 1846
and was never found again. A number of following expeditions were
sent to rescue them but without success. A reward was offered. And
in 1854 Dr John Rae, Chief Factor of the Hudson's Bay company,
reported that he had discovered the fate of the explorers. According
to his Eskimo informants, they were all dead, and had been driven
to cannibalism before they died.

Dickens, among others, was outraged. *Household Words* carried
the debate between Dickens and Rae: Dickens accused Rae of
trusting the words of savages and Rae replied that these people
were native to the region, understood the exigencies of starvation,
and were credible witnesses. Rae attacked Dickens's view of the Eskimos 'who seem to be looked upon by those who know them not,
as little better than brutes'. He scornfully quotes Dickens's words
opposing the summoning of Eskimo witness: 'It may be, (Rae comments) I have only the words of "babbling and false savages who
are, without exception, in heart, covetous, treacherous, and cruel"
in support of what I say.' Rae then offers a number of anecdotes to
illustrate the courage and high-mindedness of his informants.
Dickens made the expedition the basis for his play with Wilkie
Collins, *The Frozen Deep*, leaving out any reference at all to cannibalism.

Hardy's fugitive allusion to 'Franklin underfoot' here would dis-
turbingly remind the Victorian reader of the return of repressed
forms of behaviour under the durance of extreme conditions. Modern man, the well-trained English gentleman, goes to his death responding to the primal drives of hunger and thirst in 'an amplitude
of Northern knowledge'. Like Jemmy Button's, though for different
reasons, Franklin's account of his experience is missing.

Franklin did not return home; he and his companions, Rae asserted, had instead returned to the bedrock of human survival behaviour. The issue is still debated 150 years on.[1] Rae's argument was
subtle: even cannibalism may be ordered into moral scrupulousness,
and indeed is so by the Eskimos who are driven to practise it; there-

---

1. See Owen Beattie and John Geiger, *Frozen in Time* (London, 1987). For the Dickens-
Rae controversy see Ian R. Stone, " 'The Contents of the Kettles': Charles Dickens, John
Rae and Cannibalism on the 1845 Franklin Expedition," *The Dickensian*, 83 (Spring,
1987), pp. 7–15.

fore we should believe their witness *because* they occasionally practise cannibalism themselves and understand the conditions that enforce such behaviour. As we might expect, this argument about Eskimo testimony cut little ice in England. Correspondents in *The Times* were simply aghast. For most of his contemporaries, the English gentleman Franklin had come unbearably close to Frankenstein's monster, who vanishes into the Arctic wastes at the end of Mary Shelley's book—close in more than name. Denial was the only possible response.

But Hardy stirred that memory to different purposes. The dangerous realm in which the English explorers lived and died with so much suffering is the familiar domain of the mallard. The mallard is the wild duck whom we take for granted as a familiar native of the English countryside. The blurring between rural England and the Arctic in the book's allusive system disequilibriates any easy developmental assumptions the reader may bring to the work—and implicitly disturbs Clym's initial enterprise of educating the natives. *Migration* in this work represents the only resilient form of escape and survival: moving seasonally to keep in temper with a supportive environment. In Victorian anthropology the two great categories were the 'settled' and the 'nomadic' tribes. Out of the 'settled' came civilization. But here Hardy suggests a third possibility: the native inhabitants are constantly on the move within the confines, or within the range, of the heath. And where in that case (to turn to my last question) is the reader stationed in the life of the writing? How are we made native to the place as well as swerving back upon it? What migratory track are *we* to follow?

Throughout the book Hardy makes us aware of the native inhabitants' power of making sensory discriminations lost to the town-dweller, what he calls 'acoustic pictures' (p. 78): 'they could hear where the tracts of heather began and ended; where the furze was growing stalky and tall; where it had recently been cut; in what direction the fir-clump lay, and how near was the pit in which the hollies grew; for these differing features had their voices no less than their shapes and colours' (p. 78). He makes the ear attentive to the particular character of the heath, and builds a landscape derived not from eye alone but from all the senses, and above all from sound and touch: 'What was heard *there* could be heard nowhere else' (p. 49).

The most intimate expression of physical familiarity between the heath and its denizens is the natives' power of crossing and recrossing it in darkness.

> The whole secret of following these incipient paths, where there was not light enough in the atmosphere to show a turnpike-road, lay in the development of the sense of touch in the

feet, which comes with years of night-rambling in little-
trodden spots. To a walker practised in such places a difference between impact on maiden herbage, and on the crippled
stalks of a slight footway, is perceptible through the thickest
boot or shoe. (p. 52)

The ear makes acoustic pictures; the foot distinguishes intensities
of impact. Scene after scene in this book takes place at night when
sound and touch are essential to navigation: Eustacia measures
Wildeve's attachment to her by the distance travelled: 'three miles
in the dark for me. Have I not shown my power?' (p. 60).

By such means as repeated sensory description, and particularly
by awakening the senses usually muffled in reading process, such
as touch and to some degree hearing, the novel suggests a kinship
of fugitive recall between narrative and characters. That is, the
work enters a claim to be at home on the heath on behalf of writer,
and reader. Yet at the same time we are to be detached from the
heath, observing, surveying. We are to become natives and yet we
are still to sustain our outsider's gaze. A degree of empathy and detachment together is produced that goes beyond the chosen methods of anthropology and is perhaps attainable only in the thickness
of language of a fiction.

Making the reader a native is brought about by invoking sound,
touch, smell, temperature, body-weight, occasionally taste. And by
rendering morally equivocal the primary public sense of observation: sight. In this book the virtuous reddleman is a voyeur and
Clym is at his most fulfilled when he loses his sight and merges
with the heath. The writing intermittently invokes the presence of
that feasible but absent observer with whose eye Hardy so often
sets the scene. This perspectival eye creates a riddling and erratic
distance, calling into question the relationship between sight,
truth, and interpretation.

The reader's own act of reading is a sighted act, an act, moreover,
that establishes interpretative distance and cultural privilege; our
position as observer is reinforced by the repeated interposition of
possible watchers, viewers, observers, even quasi-anthropologists,
in Hardy's scene-setting. Eustacia, native to Budmouth and child of
a foreign, seagoing father, is the most frequent intercessionary figure for the reader, standing in for us, becoming, scribally, identified
with the shifting positions of the writing more than any other character. Intermittently we enter the sensory state of being a native.
The paradox remains that we do so by means of the process of reading, itself an outcome of an education most of these native inhabitants do not share. The book emphasizes this difference through its
allusions across a wealth of reference to be gained solely by means

of reading. Obliteration comes to Clym willy-nilly when his eyes fail. He works as a furze-cutter in a congruity of response to the heath that has the quality of bliss as well as of privation. So Clym, the educator and educated, loses for a time the power of reading and writing. But the reader continues to read.

Can other states of consciousness be revived by the act of reading? What, from reading-experience, can we learn about this way of life? And what, within the fiction, can Clym teach to this community? What indeed does Clym believe that he can accomplish by his return? What does he plan to teach? The properties of modern civilization? Discontent? Mathematics? Other languages? Or simply the process of inscription itself—reading and writing—by whose means in his own modern world experience principally survives? The content of his syllabus is never made clear. Yeobright figures himself initially as donor and teacher of new forms of knowledge. He is not an antiquarian, interested in legends and customs in order to preserve them. To that degree he remains a native, taking for granted what would be precious to one from further off.

The mummers, we are told, are part of an unrevived tradition, not of modern folklorism: 'This unweeting manner of performance is the true ring by which, in this refurbishing age, a fossilized survival may be known from a spurious reproduction' (p. 107). Hardy sets the geological authenticity of 'fossilised survival' over against the hotelier's 'refurbishing'. Its value (the 'true ring' of silver as opposed to base metal) is in its unchanged 'survival' from distant oral culture. The word 'unweeting', for unknowing or unconscious, itself summons up a backward trajectory that reaches across lost centuries: archaic words are still current in dialect. 'Unweeting' is used already as archaism in Edmund Spenser's *Faerie Queene* at the end of the sixteenth century. That is, the world is itself a 'survival', vouching for the authenticity of unchanged language, undislodged communities.

In such tradition the originating symbolic systems have vanished within a surplus of decoration. All the energy goes into the decoration, not the meaning now. The girls so ornately decorate their chosen men that, what with added scallops and ribbons, it is impossible to tell the Moslem from the Christian characters. The unsymbolic state of the performance is important here. It has become part of quite another ritual—of courtship—not of allusion to the crusades. Hardy is affirming an observation of the mythographer and comparative philologist Max Müller: originating meaning becomes lost and the metaphor employed to describe it takes over a substantive role.

Hardy seems to suggest here, rather, that the originating meaning is not so much lost as sunk beneath observation, imbuing the local culture, as the reddleman is imbued with a red that makes him seem, variously and at once, devil, outcast, and workaday familiar. The reddleman's ambiguities of appearance scare the children and the timid, and he does not quite fit into any of the social categories of the group. He is more symbolic, carrying a freight of diverse significations, than is the mumming play now. He is also, with the hindsight of narrative, shown to be the end of an economic phase, a dodo (as he is called), though not yet an extinct species.

Moreover, the reddleman is a wanderer who roams the heath like an unhived bee (p. 74) or like an Arab (p. 71). Hardy suggests that no clear distinction is to be made between the settled and the nomadic in a community which is so scattered. The settled–nomadic distinction fundamental to the work of many nineteenth-century anthropologists and ethnologists, such as James Prichard, is here replaced by the ideas of 'traversing' and 'migration'. A different psychic and social pattern is suggested. The wild ponies, or heath-croppers, express the endlessly *traversing* spirit of the group. But people in the book walk for a purpose, to destinations, however wayward may seem their route: and all those destinations are within the circumference of the heath. To be forced beyond its range is, for most of these people, a disaster of the kind that Hardy described in 'The Dorsetshire Labourer' and explored in *Tess of the D'Urbervilles*. The birds' free migratory movement becomes heavy-laden when translated into human social and economic terms: the enforced travel of the poor is oppression.

At the end of the book we come back to an image of stasis that we have known at the beginning when Eustacia appeared at the top of the hill like a spike on a helmet. At the end Clym replaces Eustacia as 'the motionless figure standing on the top of the tumulus'. He is preaching, on this last page of the novel, on a text obsessively concerned with the loss of the mother and the desire to re-instate her: 'This afternoon the words were as follows:—"And the king rose up to meet her, and bowed himself unto her, and sat down on his throne, and caused a seat to be set for the king's mother; and she sat on his right hand. Then she said, I desire one small petition of thee; I pray thee say me not nay. And the king said unto her, ask on, my mother: for I will not say thee nay" ' (p. 336).

In a book composed of passional triangles, by far the most intense (alternately drenching and arid in emotion) is that between Mrs Yeobright, Clym Yeobright, and Eustacia—mother, son, and wife. I argued earlier that the return of the native figures a return to nativity—to the place of birth, and, further, to the mother who gave birth in that place. Re-entering the mother's womb is impossible; entering the mother sexually is insufficient as well as destructive. Clym is debarred. The impossibility of return, back through childhood, into the womb, is dramatized in the form of the Oedipus story. And that myth is referred to at the moment that Clym discovers that his mother has visited them and was not received by Eustacia. A parallel springs up in the language between Clym's blindness and the self-blinding of Oedipus. And again the imagery of ice enters; here the relentless unchangingness of the landscape dwarfs human emotion:

> The pupils of his eyes, fixed steadfastly on blankness, were vaguely lit with an icy shine; his mouth had passed into the phase more or less imaginatively rendered in studies of Oedipus. The strangest deeds were possible to his mood. But they were not possible to his situation. Instead of there being before him the pale face of Eustacia and a masculine shape unknown, there was only the imperturbable countenance of the heath, which, having defied the cataclysmic onsets of centuries, reduced to insignificance by its seamed and antique features the wildest turmoil of a single man. (p. 268)

In this setting the primary Oedipal obsession is linked with the absolute unchangingness of the surroundings, surroundings as unaltered and as absolute as the Arctic, and as mindless of human kind. Clym's zeal as educator is worsted: if there is movement, recursiveness, not progress, is the tide that prevails.

The conflicts between Clym's urge towards the future and his foiled desire to return across time, between the endless re-enactment of remorse and the prim commentary on his calling, make for a grating humour in this last scene. Clym's listeners 'abstractedly pulled heather, stripped ferns, or tossed pebbles down the slope'. 'Yeobright had, in fact, found his vocation in the career of an itinerant open-air preacher and lecturer on morally unimpeachable subjects . . . speaking not only in simple language on Rainbarrow and in the hamlets round, but in a more cultivated strain elsewhere.' Clym, the returning native, resolves into an itinerant. Yet he is still in command of language, now turning it towards the bedrock of human experience, turning away from 'mind': 'He left alone creeds and systems of philosophy, finding enough and more than enough to occupy his tongue in the opinions and actions common to all good men.' The last irony, shifting between benign and rancorous even while you look, is that this unhoused preacher is 'everywhere kindly received, for the story of his life had become generally known'. He is received as the wanderer and the outcast, instead of as the educator.

In our century, where a characterizing ghastly movement has been that forced on people driven out of their homes as refugees by oppression, war, and famine, and the answering movement has been that of people driven by the longing to re-possess the homeland they have lost, the idea of the return of the native has become laden with kinds of tragedy pitched beyond Hardy's compass in this book. The return Hardy envisages at the end of the novel is, for Clym, one of depletion and loss; but it is also represented as a return from the casuistries of the intellect to a common tongue, a bedrock of concern with the ordinary and profound dilemmas in which people find themselves. A paradox remains within Hardy's writing: such a return can only be enacted by means of the casuistries of the intellect. The formidable range of discourses that Hardy fugitively seizes upon, the haunting immediacy with which he gives the reader bodily access to the heath-dwellers' world relies on written language, in Hardy's work extraordinarily diversified. Communality depends on records, inscribing the traces of an oral culture. Clym wanders within the span of the heath while the reddleman settles down to be a dairy-farmer again. They change places: one ceasing to be a nomad, the other becoming it. Yet this exchange will not satisfy. The final image rankles. Clym, a barren man, is welcomed for his life-story. Like Christian Cantle, he is accepted now as an oddity, outside the line of descent; a tribute (in both senses: palliative offering as well as praise) to the community he had meant to educate.

So, can the native return? For the Victorians, it seems, only at the price of returning to an earlier cultural stage in their development pattern. In Hardy's imagination, as in that of other Victorian writers, return is not possible for the native without the idea of retrogression. The reader, however, enacts all the diverse phases of cultural experience within the span of Hardy's language, not in sequence only but alongside and in contestation with each other. In this way, the novel itself suggests quite another kind of 'survival', and even a different ethnographic pattern.

JENNIFER GRIBBLE

The Quiet Women of Egdon Heath†

Revising *The Return of the Native* for the 1912 Macmillan Wessex edition, Hardy adds this couplet to Damon Wildeve's inn sign at 'The Quiet Woman':

---

† From *Essays in Criticism* 46.3 (1996): 234–57. Reprinted by permission of Oxford University Press.

SINCE THE WOMAN'S QUIET
LET NO MAN BREED A RIOT

The earlier description of the sign as 'the figure of a matron carrying her head under her arm' is further reinforced by the adjective
'gruesome'. A footnote in the 1912 revision goes on to explain that
'the inn which really bore this sign and legend stood some miles to
the north-west of the present scene'.[1] It may be, as Simon Gatrell
suggests, that these alterations were mostly directed towards ensur-
ing that literary pilgrims in search of Egdon Heath could track it
through 'observable geographic spaces'.[2] It seems likely, however,
that re-reading his novel more than thirty years after its first appearance in the 1878 numbers of *Belgravia*, Hardy perceived how
the sardonic rhyme would underline the novel's thinking about the
silence and the silencing of its quiet and unquiet women. On the
face of it, the apparently neat fit between the sign's folk wisdom
and the plot of the novel might seem to justify those readers who
see Hardy as constrained by his culture's sterotypes of women,[3] or
by negative 'neutralizing structures' forced on him by his particular
ideological moment.[4] Clym Yeobright, believing that he has 'driven
two women to their deaths' (p. 327) himself survives peaceably
enough, indeed, to discourse in fable form on his mother's terminal
silencing: 'ask on, my mother: for I will not say thee nay' (p. 336).

It turns out to be a sign that points in more than one direction:
first inward, towards the inn, that traditional refuge from the female and the domestic, which nevertheless offers its comforts with
the sign of the woman. Convivial talk on Egdon, we note, will drift
as like as not into the pleasures and pains of conjugal life, a subject
for anecdote and wonder. The sign points backwards too, to the
oral culture within which Hardy's narrative will place itself, as well
as outwards to continuing questions about gender stereotyping; the
image of the silenced woman conflates both scold and temptress.
Uncoupled from the traditional headship of the male, her disrup-
tive potentiality put to rest, she obligingly carries her own severed
head. To the pictured narrative, the couplet adds its own riddling
wit. 'Breed' indicates at one and the same time procreative needs
and the subversiveness of sexual interdependence. The riotousness
of man seems to take its cue from the unruliness of woman, but
whether as cause or consequence, who can say?

The equivocations of Hardy's sign graphically represent his inter-

1. *The Return of the Native*, p. 40. Page references have been changed to correspond to
   this edition.
2. Introduction to *The Return of the Native*, (Oxford, 1990), p. xiv.
3. Patricia Stubbs, quoted in Peter Widdowson, *Hardy in History: A Study in Literary Sociology*, (1989), p. 215.
4. Ibid., p. 217.

est in the teasing qualities of narrative—of how much will always fall away into silence or hint at what remains inexpressible or defy political readings, of what its apparent repetitions across time might have to say to its contemporary readership. In exploring sexual disgrace and the female unruliness which are the two sides of the quiet woman sign, Hardy returns with a narrative purpose often denied this novel, to 'the customs of the country', its rituals and ballads and village anecdotes. 'Trouble' is dramatized as energy—sexual energy most notably, as part of that beat of time through song and season that celebrates continuity and renewal on Egdon Heath.

It must be said that Clym's wife and mother are among Hardy's least quiet women. Mrs Yeobright, 'a matron with a tang in her tongue',[5] takes her outspokenness into the very church, rising to forbid the banns between Wildeve and her niece Tamsin. Eustacia Vye's challenges to contemporary decorum include speaking as a man while 'figuring in breeches' (p. 129). But the reader's imagination is equally held by their silencing: 'a woman's face looking at me through a window-pane' (p. 239) sends Mrs Yeobright to her death; Clym's last glimpse of Eustacia leaving their home dissolves into her death mask, 'caught in a momentary transition between fervour and resignation' (p. 312). Some of the novel's most crucial developments depend on withheld speech; the 'oral tradition' on which it draws disseminates inarticulate meanings; ancient rituals communicate tacitly, and the heath itself emerges from silence into 'wild rhetoric', endowed with the voices of pain and of jubilee.

Hardy's sense of narrative as a series of historical appropriations or palimpsests is apparent from the outset. The mind that attempts to encompass Egdon Heath in Chapter 1 is keenly aware of its own particular historical moment. What gives the writing its inflections of unease, its questionings, conjectures, and vatic pronouncements, is the struggling of 'a mind adrift on change' (p. 11) to find its ballast in a sense of the enduring. The very particularity and contemporaneity of its unfolding story ('a Saturday afternoon in November was approaching the time of twilight, and the vast tract of unenclosed wild known as Egdon Heath embrowned itself moment by moment') (p. 8) calls up long historical and geographical perspectives—from Domesday to Roman settlement to the last geographical 'change', and from one horizon of the visible world and its firmament to the other. The Janus face of Egdon is scrutinized for signs of significance; 'a face on which time makes very little impression', it is map, calendar, horoscope and narrative. 'Its true tale'

---

5. Hardy, 'The Dorsetshire Labourer', *Longman's Magazine*, July 1883, in Harold Orel ed., *Thomas Hardy's Personal Writings*, (Kansas and London, 1967), p. 187, describing the vociferous self-assertion of the rural woman.

heralds a vast shift in which the new Vale of Tempe may be 'a gaunt waste in Thule' en route to some yet-to-be revealed millenarian crisis of 'final overthrow' (p. 9). The 'smiling champaigns' of romantic pastoral are dismissed as 'beauty of the accepted kind'. The lyrical pulse in the writing reaches after more enduring comforts: 'the sea changed, the river, the village, and the people changed, yet Egdon remained' (p. 11).

Hardy needs no new historicist to instruct him that the time, place, physical laws and conditions and social customs and beliefs of the teller will help to shape the story told since that is the burden of this opening. It is far from being just 'a long descriptive essay on an empty landscape'.[6] The whole novel, indeed, is charged with the recognition that we have no moment other than our own through which to grasp that story. This perception is struggled with, and flowers, most poignantly, in the 'Poems of 1912–13': if landscape is the indifferent record of aeons of story, it must also bear witness to the transitory story 'that we two passed'.[7] The return of the literary consciousness to its native heath is clearly Hardy's drama as well as Clym Yeobright's. The vatic mood of this opening suggests that its strains are in part those of Hardy's historical moment, as the wisdom of Wordsworth's Nature confronts the impassive indifference of Darwin's. We might speculate, with Raymond Williams, that a countryman's sense of the natural world and a writer's sense of it as a source of metaphor are at odds.[8] The equivocations of the furze-cutter, reading the heath, are expressed in the question of whether to work on, or finish his faggot and go home. For the 'more thinking among mankind' (p. 10) whether 'thoroughgoing ascetic' or tourist of the aesthetic, it is imagination that is engaged and rebuffed.

What happens as the novel gets under way is a different kind of writing, in which the heath provides not metaphor, but process. If Egdon begins as a landscape on which time makes but little impression, it comes most memorably alive not as brooding presence but as a living record of immediate sensation. The effects of its changing lights and weathers, its cycle of days and seasons, are caught in the lives of its creatures. Their moments seem overheard, snatched in passing from the stream of time itself. Close-up, the imagination finds its human scale restored, and with it a way of reconciling the sense of continuity with the knowledge of transience. The rhythms of courtship are attuned to Egdon time. The 'true story' of the heath unfolds as interchange, echo, juxtaposition, between the human, animate and inanimate presences that share life

6. John Goode, *Thomas Hardy: The Offensive Truth* (Oxford: Blackwell, 1988), p. 41.
7. 'At Castle Boterel'.
8. *The Country and the City* (London: Chatto and Windus, 1973), pp. 205–6.

and death on Egdon: the mummied heath-bells 'washed colourless by Michaelmas rains, and dried to dead skin by October suns', their worn whisper, 'dry and papery', a parody of human song (p. 50); the fur of rabbits 'clotted into dark locks by the rain', the wind blowing the feathers of the finch 'until they stood on end, twisted round his little tail, and made him give up his song' (p. 179); the wasps rolling drunk with the juice of fallen apples, or 'creeping about the little caves in each fruit which they had eaten out before stupefied by its sweetness' (p. 233); the colony of ants, 'a never-ending heavy laden throng'; the heron struck into burnished silver by a shaft of sunbeams (p. 241); all are ephemerons 'passing their time in mad carousal' (p. 231).

It is this recognition of transient creatureliness that the 'customs of the country' express. Pagan in origin, grounded in the seasonal chronology of the heath, they celebrate 'homage to nature, self-adoration, frantic gaieties' (p. 318). Through this heath narrative Eustacia Vye finds a voice which transforms the potentially 'melodramatic Ur-text'[9] she sometimes seems to inhabit. Through what the narrator characterizes as the still-evolving 'instincts of Merrie England' (p. 318) the literary consciousness finds its own authentic voice. Returning to 'educate', Clym is himself changed by reimmersion in the Egdon community, most painfully by the breaking of societal bonds in his relationship with the two women whom in the end he believes he has silenced.

The story that unfolds in Book First, 'The Three Women', apparently made out of 'ruts and hair-pin bends',[1] provides a narrative direction for which The Quiet Woman is subject, emblem and destination. The thin thread of road that parts the heath from one horizon to the other bears the narrative of place as well as of person, connecting the story of the 'ruined maid' in Diggory Venn's cart with a folk culture reaching back into the history that made the road. There are 'tragical possibilities' suggested by Tamsin Yeobright's disgrace, but she is the bearer of narrative continuity: the solicitudes of Diggory Venn already anticipate the story's ending, despite Hardy's original intent, in marriage to the reddleman.

'Humanity Appears Upon the Scene, Hand in Hand with Trouble.' Trouble is what gives the scene its interest, as the sardonic relish of the second chapter's title indicates. The landscape is quickened into life as the human figures begin to individuate themselves. Narrative questions are voiced. The old man who walks the vicinal way wants to know the story the cart contains. But another

9. The phrase is Roger Ebbatson's, in The Evolutionary Self (Brighton: Harvester, 1982), p. 48.
1. Goode, op. cit., p. 41, argues that 'the opening of the novel has so many ruts and hairpin bends that the reader is almost forbidden to progress'.

quiet woman appears, silhouetted on top of a Celtic barrow, and
the reddleman, like 'the narrative demanding reader'[2] and the narrator, is speculative about her significance. In the silent drama that
follows, other figures join the scene, but

> the imagination of the observer clung by preference to that
> vanished, solitary figure, as to something more interesting,
> more important, more likely to have a history worth knowing
> than these newcomers, and unconsciously regarded them
> as intruders. But they remained, and established themselves.
> (p. 16)

It is a revealing narratorial comment. We are all cast in the observer's role here. Though it belongs most immediately to the observant Diggory Venn, a self-placing irony suggests that the literate
consciousness, with its romantic expectations, will be more likely to
see in the delicate female figure 'a history worth knowing' than in
the story unfolding in the procession of rural folk with their burden
of furze faggots. The point of the irony is in part that the novel will
show the two stories as continuously and necessarily interrelated.
While it is evident that the furze-cutters 'replace' the figure of Eustacia, the 'contradictory antithesis' to which George Wotton's
Bakhtinian reading would draw attention[3] is questioned rather than
affirmed in the replacements, appropriations, comparisons, between the popular and the literate, the folk and the 'thinking
classes' that are to follow. As Eustacia's story becomes implicated in
the true tale of Egdon, the gender and class implications of the interchange are by no means simple. These are among the equivocations towards which the Quiet Woman sign points. On the heath, it
is the folk who represent 'the ruling culture', and Eustacia who is
marginalized (both as an educated woman and as an outsider).
Hardy's notion of what represents 'thinking' is also elaborated in a
way that questions any valorizing of the intellect: lighting fires,
singing songs, having dreams, dancing or mumming, are equally
perceived as enlightening, and equally available to Eustacia and to
the folk. It is the folk culture attuned to the heath that now proceeds to gather in the stories of the quiet woman, both the hidden
shame of the 'quiet lady-like little body' Tamsin (p. 23), and the
'quiet eye' (p. 29) of Eustacia's bonfire, which represents Eustacia's
sexual call to Wildeve. The ancient ritual of the bonfire offers
itself for individual interpretation and revival: 'a spontaneous,
Promethean rebelliousness against the fiat that this recurrent sea-

2. The phrase is Goode's, ibid., p. 41.
3. George Wotton, *Thomas Hardy: Towards a Materialist Criticism* (Dublin: Gill & Macmillan, 1985), p. 63: 'here the workfolk represent the popular opposition to the "civilizing"
culture of the thinking world'.

son shall bring foul times, cold darkness, misery and death' (p. 18). The tufts that flicker near and far across the landscape, each locality distinguished by its particular fuel, celebrate in the heath's mid-winter story the renewal that follows. Personal and local enactments give the custom its contemporary meaning. Hardy's narrative, too, renews this story: Diggory Venn's cart may hold the story of failed mating between Tamsin and Wildeve, but it holds as well the promise of a new configuration between the male and the female figures on the road to the inn. Eustacia's fire expresses the passionate self-assertiveness that will rekindle out of the ashes of her relationship with Wildeve.

It is Eustacia, as much as Clym, who introduces 'a contemporary consciousness into Wessex',[4] but Hardy is generally perceived to be undecided about her value and significance: 'Queen of Night' or 'Courtly Pretender',[5] 'witch succubus' or 'the embodiment of philosophic idealism', 'biblical temptress, classical divinity, mythical witch, romantic heroine, perceiving subject',[6] both 'an expression and a critical placing of Hardy's anxious relationship to Romanticism'.[7] It may be not until Sue Bridehead that Hardy is able to give voice with confidence to what stirs in the much more limited Eustacia. Her implicit challenge to a traditionally masculine world of power and mobility blends the romantic recollections and theories and books of a girl's experience with the 'forwardness of mind' signalled in the hourglass and telescope by which she attempts to command her time and space. If she is 'Queen of Night' it is an honorific loaded with ironies within an Egdon that is her 'Hades'. 'To be loved to madness—such was her great desire' (p. 64). It is a will to power often melodramatically voiced in Eustacia's more extended thoughts and utterance, and somewhat ambivalently viewed by a narrative voice that sees her now as 'young girl', now as 'perfervid woman'.

It is when she is quietest that Eustacia is most interesting. Hardy's imagination is most responsive to the ways in which this urge for love, sexual need, boredom, frustration, expresses itself non-verbally. Here Hardy the pre-modernist and the sign-writer of folk culture are curiously at one, as becomes apparent in the lighting of Eustacia's bonfire, in her immersion in the mummers' play, and in the dream that pre-figures the play. When she lights her fire to summon Wildeve, she is undoubtedly using the ritual for her private ends, making a little fire 'that nobody else may enjoy it or come

4. Ian Gregor, *The Great Web: The Form of Hardy's Major Fiction* (London: Faber and Faber, 1974), p. 110: 'in introducing Clym, Hardy has introduced a contemporary consciousness into Wessex'.
5. David Eggenschwiler, 'Eustacia Vye, Queen of Night and Courtly Pretender', *Nineteenth-Century Fiction*, 25 (1971), p. 454.
6. Wotton, op. cit., p. 115.
7. Penny Boumelha, *Thomas Hardy and Women* (Brighton: Harvester, 1982), p. 50.

anigh it' (p. 29) as the heath folk observe. But to see her as 'trivial-
izing the traditional fertility rituals by divesting them of communal
significance'[8] is to miss the connection Hardy makes between Eustacia and the folk. She avails herself of the silent language of the
heath not only because it lies to hand, but because it is for her, as
it has been traditionally, a way of expressing feelings that cannot
readily be articulated in any other language. She is linked, then,
with the other fire-lighters on the heath and with the long tradition
that stretches back from Guy Fawkes to 'jumbled Druidical rites
and Saxon ceremonies' (p. 18). If it is an 'appropriation', it is one
that expresses the unruliness of her challenge to the traditional
male role as sexual initiator.

The courtship ritual enacted through Eustacia's fire is full of
equivocation: it represents a passion that is flickering out, its eddies
caught in the desultory, accusatory conversation with Wildeve in
which neither of them is sure whether Eustacia is victim or
temptress, and in which she is chafing against the constraints of
her role as wronged woman and her impulse to reassert the sexual
attraction that continues to draw Wildeve. It also represents the
self-assertion that will quicken into a new passion, new attraction,
new suffering. Hers is 'a history worth knowing' in the contemporary dimension it gives to the quiet woman story, in what Eustacia's
fire-lighting represents of the culture's restraints on female behaviour (challenging both the culture of middle-class respectability
and the culture of the heath), and in the class and gender-crossing
which is Eustacia's response to those constraints. Such apparent
mockery of traditional order is of course a recurring element in
popular festival, but it is Hardy's nineteenth century narrative that
effects the subversions here, and Eustacia's 'appropriation' of folk
tradition which continues the narrative interchange on which cultural tradition depends.

That interchange is almost immediately foregrounded in the
scene that follows, as the bonfire celebration modulates into a
village epithalamium. An old man lit by 'the beaming sight and
the penetrating warmth' articulates the meaning of the fires in
song and dance, igniting 'a cumulative cheerfulness which soon
amounted to delight' (p. 19) though not, it seems, among recent
readers who find the scene tedious:

> with his stick in his hand he began to jig a private minuet, a
> bunch of copper seals shining like a pendulum from under his
> waistcoat: he also began to sing, in the voice of a bee up a
> flue—

8. As Marjorie Garson does in *Hardy's Fables of Integrity: Woman, Body, Text* (Oxford:
Clarendon Press, 1991), p. 67.

'The king´ call'd down ´his no´-bles all´,
    By one´, by two´, by three´;
Earl Mar´-shal, I'll go shrive´ the queen´,
    And thou´ shalt wend ´with me´.

´A boon´, a boon´, quoth Earl´ Mar-shal´,
    And fell´ on his bend´-ded knee´,
That what´–so-e'er´ the queen ´ shall say´,
    No harm ´there-of´ may be´.' (p. 19)

What he sings is a version of The Earl Marshall Song, or Queen
Eleanor's Confession, still extant in rural Devon. Hardy joins a long
line of appropriators here, taking his version from Percy's *Reliques*,
which in turn recovers the story transcribed from 'recitation' by
Motherwell's Minstrelsey.[9] Onto the folk comedy of cuckolding has
been grafted in the twelfth century a story of high-life adultery put
about to slander Eleanor of Aquitaine on her marriage to Henry II
of England.[1] Hardy edits its long story down to the four verses
through which, intermittently, Grandfer Cantle releases the sinister
understated drama of another silenced woman. The Queen is given
no voice in the plot against her by husband and lover, temporarily
united and disguised in the authority of the church 'like friar and
his brother' to elicit her confession. The Earl's fealty to the King
and his terror of exposure are starkly rendered in the brevity of the
ballad line, but the masculine pact holds firm. The Earl's neck is
spared but the Queen will lose her character and her life.

The opening lines make clear why the Grandfer should rehearse
this apparently inappropriate ballad as his 'wedding stave' for the
newly married folks at the Quiet Woman. Like the men in the ballad, he is preparing himself for a journey to a queen. He celebrates
as well his own continuing vitality. The clearly marked rhythm of
body and voice which are primarily cues to the memory[2] also beat
out the pulse of communal renewal. There is no attempt in the ballad to question motives or assign blame: its rhythms give energy at
once to the self-assertion of the queen and to her victimization, to
the punitive determination of her husband and the terror of her se-
ducer. The ritual value of the ballad, like that of the bonfire, lies in
its assertion of the sexual energies through which the community
renews itself. Within Hardy's narrative sequence, the ballad takes
on an ironic appropriateness. Loss of character and the tacit collu-
sion of husband and lover in the woman's fate are to be played out

9. See Francis James Child ed., *The English and Scottish Popular Ballad*, (Cambridge,
    Massachusetts, 1890), Part VI, No. 156, version F, p. 263.
1. Ibid., p. 263.
2. Frances B. Gummere, *The Popular Ballad* (London: Constable, 1959), p. 248: 'when old
    folk tried to recite a ballad to the collectors without this stay in a monotonous rhythmic
    chant, they often made sad work of it.'

in contrasting ways in the lives of Tamsin and Eustacia, but, as in
the ballad, the gender stereotypes proposed in the quiet woman
story surface only to be relinquished. Victim or temptress, the
woman seems caught up in a drama that defies the labelling habit
of mind and all its polarities.

This is the habit of mind explored around the fireside as the
Egdon folk talk of marriage. There is no unease involved in Hardy's
unpatronizing perception that misogynist wit is alive and well in village anecdote: the conversation will move towards more complex
feelings about the relationship between man and woman. Nor is
Hardy selling out on the life and labour of the folk because its communal scenes are almost entirely devoted to holiday and festival:[3] it
is the burden of *The Return of the Native* (as elsewhere in Hardy)
that there are more fundamental determinants of human happiness
than the economic. If the narrative eye momentarily sees the fire-lit
faces of living furze-cutters as grotesque gargoyles this is not a sign
of detachment, but a perception of what it is that their festivity traditionally celebrates. The *memento mori* is what their gossip and
song about past lives makes living. Dead village faces they will one
day be, but their oral history is still in the present and still in the
making: 'work on it never stops'.[4] Hardy's mediation of dialect for
the metropolitan literary audience is currently heard as a defensive
'tidying up', in which parody lurks as the inevitable extreme of the
heteroglossic spectrum,[5] but it is linguistic gusto that expressively
individuates the voices of the Egdon community. Even those whose
names can only be signed by 'a terrible black cross' (p. 24) share
the narrator's respect for the talismanic power of words ('no moon,
no man', for example, passes around the fireside as ' "one of the
finest sayings ever spit out. The boy never comes to anything that's
born at new moon. A bad job for thee, Christian, that you should
have showed your nose then of all days in the month" ') (p. 27).
Grandfer Cantle, himself a returned native, mediates between past
and present, the exotic and the local, offering an engagingly
sprightly account of himself: still 'playward' and 'horn-piping', 'the
first in any spree that's going' (p. 20). The doleful utterance of the
hapless Christian Cantle, 'a man of the mournfullest make', keeps
up a contrast. Susan Nunsuch, 'a woman noisily constructed'
(p. 30) within her enclosing framework of whalebone and lath, has
her own noisiness of phrase: she means to make herself heard even
when her actions are most silently subversive. Olly Dowden, besom

---

3. As Roger Ebbatson suggests, in *Hardy: The Margin of the Unexpressed* (Sheffield:
   Sheffield Academic Press, 1993), p. 141.
4. John Berger, *Pig Earth* (London: Bloomsbury, 1979), p. 9.
5. See Ebbatson (1993), p. 139: 'argues, agrees, interrogates, eavesdrops . . . but also par-
   odically exaggerates'.

maker, has the civility and restraint of utterance consistent with gratitude to all the world 'for letting her remain alive' (p. 22). A more serious theological turn is given to the conversation by Humphrey, the solemn young furze-cutter, in his meditations on church going.

The village shrew is most effectively given voice in the story of Christian Cantle's failure as a suitor, drawn out of him by convivial talk. ' "Didst ever know a man, neighbour, that no woman at all would marry?" ' Humphrey asks (p. 25). Both Timothy Fairway and Christian Cantle assume that the general question has a particular answer known only to themselves. Reticence prevents Fairway from naming names, involuntary chattering teeth prevent Christian from remaining silent. It is one and the same story, the story of Christian's secret shame and of the words unleashed by his timorous proposal: ' "get out of my sight you slack-twisted, slim-looking maphrotight fool" '. ' "Not encouraging . . . rather a hard way of saying no" ', as Fairway dryly remarks, though he points out that time might have the last word, when ' "a few grey hairs show themselves in the hussy's head" ' (p. 26). And Fairway's recollections about the marriage of Humphrey's father suggest, perhaps, why the equivocations of the Quiet Woman sign may still be heard, though not so vividly, even in more politically correct times:

> 'all the time I was as hot as dog-days, what with the marriage, and what with the woman a-hanging to me, and what with Jack Changley and a lot more chaps grinning at me through church windows. But the next moment a strawmote would have knocked me down, for I called to mind that if thy father and mother had had high words once, they'd been at it twenty times since they'd been man and wife, and I zid myself as the next poor stunpoll to get into the same mess. . . .' (p. 24)

'As hot as dog-days . . . the next poor stunpoll': the woman remains the focus of masculine desire and bafflement: a catalyst for transformations all too apparent in the stories of marriages. But as Humphrey's question implies, conjugal life is the norm, an acknowledgement of mutual dependence that keeps at bay loneliness and the terrors of the night: ' 'tis not to married couples but to single sleepers that a ghost shows himself when 'a do come' (p. 27). Tamsin Yeobright's story, which has sparked off this discussion, is already being assimilated to folk memory as Fairway warms to a tale he has told more than once already, of how Mrs Yeobright's forbidding of the banns unsettled the parson:

> 'it fairly made my blood run cold to hear her. . . . Ah, her face was pale! Maybe you call to mind that monument in Weatherbury church—the cross-legged soldier that have had his arm

knocked away by the school-children? Well, he would about have matched that woman's face, when she said "I forbid the banns." ' (p. 22)

Mrs Yeobright may enter the scene at this point with a 'consciousness of superior communicative power' (p. 33) but nothing she says can match Fairway's poetic transformations of her moment of defiant pallor, a quiet woman indeed, into the permanent silence of the funerary monument. The image is proleptic. Mrs Yeobright's forthright speech is directly linked with her coming death. The dismembered body that figures so large in a train of images of decapitation and detached bodily parts[6] is the more chillingly represented here in stone. What Fairway senses is a relationship between Mrs Yeobright's forthrightness and her ultimate silencing. His awe in the face of this example of female unruliness is based not on class deference, but on the instinct that her words trespass into that territory of mysterious necessity that the conversation is opening up. This is the territory that Hardy's narrative will go on to explore.

Hardy's interest in the role of a late nineteenth century woman in the communal customs that celebrate Egdon's fertility is what draws 'the three women' into the foreground of Book First. In Book Second, when Eustacia once again avails herself of the anonymity of these customs, her involuntary silencing in the Christmas mummer's play is explored in terms of the contemporary (pre-Freudian) interest in the language of dreams. Eustacia's dream is the response of Egdon's queen to her experience of love and her desire to be loved to distraction. It follows her hearing the news of Clym Yeobright's return from Paris, and it takes its cue from her overhearing the village gossip that couples them as 'made o' purpose' (p. 95). In a kaleidoscope of shifting images, to the accompaniment of music that recalls her nostalgia for Budmouth, she dances with a partner in silver armour:

> Soft whisperings came into her ear from under the radiant helmet, and she felt like a woman in Paradise. Suddenly these two wheeled out from the mass of dancers, dived into one of the pools on the heath, and came out somewhere beneath into an iridescent hollow, arched with rainbows. 'It must be here,' said the voice at her side, and blushingly looking up she saw him removing his casque to kiss her. At that moment there was a cracking noise, and his figure fell into fragments like a pack of cards.
>
>   She cried aloud, 'O that I had seen his face. . . . 'Twas meant for Mr Yeobright.' (p. 104)

6. Garson, op. cit., draws attention to these.

It is a piece of classic dream work, in its privileging of the visual, its intense colouration, its apparently arbitrary movement from within to without. Until that last exclamation, which makes the bridge between sleeping and waking, it gives shape to the dreamer's voiceless longings. Its action appears to be generated by the heath, which becomes a permeable medium, concealing an edenic pastoral space, opening up promised gratifications. 'It must be here' reverberates ambiguously as to the what and the where, either closing in on a search or announcing the place for a consummation, establishing a tentatively indicative mood for the exchanged kiss. The indifference of Wildeve is replaced by new narrative configurations in the shape of a glamorous unknown lover. The figure with whom Eustacia dances is both an image of the desired other and an image of herself as she would like to be. It suggests a connection between her longings and the anticipated mummers' play and she proceeds to act on it. It refers backwards and forwards, it represents Wildeve or Yeobright. Eustacia's dalliance with Wildeve is recalled: 'how we roved among these bushes last year, when the hot days had got cool, and the shades of the hills kept us almost invisible in the hollows' (p. 77). Their 'gypsying' at the village picnic in Book Fourth is anticipated, when, escaping from her unhappiness with Clym to waft on Wildeve's arm, she becomes a silent woman 'rapt and statuesque, her soul passed away' (p. 219) like the ephemerons in their 'mad carousal'. The erotic space of the hollow, arched with rainbows, is the 'nest of vivid green' (p. 174) she inhabits, in successive summers, with lover and husband. The dive into the pool on the heath points forward to the mill pond in which she will drown with Wildeve. As in the ballad narrative of Queen Eleanor, the finer details of motivation and sequence are suppressed or obscured. What is affirmed in the succession of visual images is what is affirmed in the steady beat marked out by Grandfer Cantle: an on-driving energy in which the woman is subject or object, victim or temptress, in which moral judgement is suspended while process is unequivocally celebrated. But within the psychological context established in Hardy's narrative, the dream resonates as wish-fulfilling and narcissistic, its secret death-wish a subconscious recognition of Eustacia's self-destructive hazardings of self.

In the dream, as in the narrative interchanges the novel explores, the individual is required to play a role that is, and is not, authored by the self. Keeping up the annual tradition of the mummers' play, the furze-cutters seem stolid and perfunctory, 'moved by an inner compulsion to say and do their allotted parts whether they will or no' (p. 107). Hardy was later to rewrite the play from his recollection of local performances and from other extant versions, and the narrator's strictures about their 'unweeting manner of performance

. . . the true ring by which, in this refurbishing age, a fossilized survival may be known from a spurious reproduction' (p. 107), reflect
the criticism of the purist. The point of this episode, however, is
not to make a condescending judgement about 'mechanical and in-
competent survivals',[7] but to show the ancient play continuing to
serve its original purpose. That purpose is manifest in the play's
provenance, in yet another history of cultural appropriation. Onto
the ancient vegetation rite of summer's overcoming winter[8] a strong
and continuing folk tradition grafts the twelfth-century chivalric
narrative of St George overcoming the Turkish Knight. The mummers' play takes its place in the cyclic story of kindling and flowering and waning within which Clym and Eustacia's love is set. For
the village mummers too, the parts they play intersect with the unspoken drama of sexual competition and display acted out in the
matter of decorations and accoutrements by sisters and sweethearts.

The generalizing bent of this anonymous role play is suggested in
the etymology of the verb 'to mum'—'to mutter' and 'to be silent', as
well as 'disguise in a mask'.[9] The sign of the Quiet Woman now increasingly entangles issues of power and gender in the action of
keeping mum. Eustacia deploys sexual bribery to take over
Charley's role in the mummers' play, but her bold ploy to enter
Clym Yeobright's home renders her sexually impotent. (Tamsin,
'shining to advantage' in the audience, 'anxious, pale and interesting', (p. 125) seems to renew her role as Eustacia's sexual rival.) As
in her dream, Eustacia can neither see nor be seen. 'The power of
her face all lost' on 'the man for whom she had predetermined to
nourish a passion' (p. 124), her natural voice is silenced by the pebbles she holds in her mouth to disguise its female register. As well
as effectively silencing her as a woman, her role exposes her to ritual decapitation. Eustacia affirms her role as 'other', as exotic, as
scapegoat, but even as she does so, she takes further her challenge
to masculine strongholds. Her gender-crossing not only affronts
her grandfather's sense of decorum; it now more blatantly seizes
the sexual initiative conventionally assigned to the male. If there is
a carnivalesque exposure here of the idealisms and sublimation of
the bourgeois world,[1] it is as much the role adopted by Eustacia as
it is in that more routinely played by her fellow actors, and she is
exposed, as well as exposer. It is through the ancient ritual, however, that she achieves her final end, in which Clym's passion is ig-

---

7. As Goode, op. cit., p. 45, suggests it is.
8. Eggenschwiler, op. cit., p. 454.
9. J. Stevens Cox, *Mumming and the Mummers' Play of St. George* (Guernsey, 1970),
   p. 430.
1. Ebbatson (1993), p. 141.

nited by her revelation of gender ('I am a woman') and by the piquancy of 'a cultivated woman playing such a part as this' (p. 127).

The challenge for the modern story-teller, however, is to catch, in dialogue and plotting, the articulate surface of that forcefield of energies the ancient rituals celebrate. This includes making narrative space for what is not articulated (or articulable) as well as for what is said. Remarkably, Clym's wife and his mother, so aggressively unquiet in Books First and Second, choose to pursue their battle tacitly in Book Third, and it is by speech withheld that the narrative twists and turns we expect from a Hardy novel begin to shape themselves. Eustacia, like Queen Eleanor, is trapped into a series of tacit 'confessions' and the loss of 'character'. In effect, Mrs Yeobright forfeits her life to Eustacia's uncertain but unyielding power. Outspoken in her attempt to prevent her son's marriage as she has attempted to prevent that of her niece, (an interference that is balanced against her intuitive knowledge that both marriages are doomed to unhappiness), Mrs Yeobright chooses to reestablish communication with her son by similarly tacit means, sending his share of his father's guineas as a peace offering via the unreliable Christian Cantle. The dialogue that follows her discovery that the money has not reached its destination makes clear how her chosen mode of communicating feelings and intentions is likely to perpetuate misunderstanding:

> 'Have you received a gift from Thomasin's husband?'
> 'A gift?'
> 'I mean money!'
> 'What—I myself?'
> 'Well, I meant yourself, privately—though I was not going to put it in that way.'
> 'Money from Mr Wildeve? No—never! Madam, what do you mean by that?' Eustacia fired up all too quickly, for her own consciousness of the old attachment between herself and Mr Wildeve led her to jump to the conclusion that Mrs Yeobright also knew of it, and might have come to accuse her of receiving dishonourable presents from him now. (pp. 203–4)

We don't get far with conversations like this if we refuse to read them as the voices of 'real people, with an inner life which is amenable to analysis'.[2] Except for the whiff of Restoration drama in Eustacia's 'Madam, what do you mean by that?' which marks her shift into the language of conventional outrage, the dialogue is spare. What we have seen and heard of the two women in full flight

---

2. Garson's stated aim to treat characters instead as 'nodes or pressure points in the mythic structure', op. cit., p. 69, seems odd in view of the interesting psychological currents she goes on to note.

enables us to measure the degree of restraint and even appease-
ment Mrs Yeobright is attempting here, struggling against her suspicion of Eustacia and her anxieties about the fate of the money.
Speech commits her to the expression of these conflicting currents:
the baldness of her opening question elides past and present, so
that Eustacia's 'no-never' is prompted by the suspicion that Mrs
Yeobright is connecting a past history with a present situation. 'A
gift' is insultingly suggestive, and made further so by 'money' and by
'yourself, privately'. Interrogation takes on the aspect of a steadily
developing slander to which Eustacia can only reply with hostility.
What is activated in her is that moody consciousness of a secret
phase of her life that remains scarcely amenable to her understanding. The novel is reticent about Eustacia's premarital affair, but its
explosive legacy is fully apparent here: as a source of shame, humiliation and threatened disgrace. Voices rise into accusation and
rebuttal as the role of scold passes between mother and daughter-
in-law:

> 'You think me capable of every bad thing. Who can be worse
> than a wife who encourages a lover, and poisons her husband's
> mind against his relatives? Yet that is now the character given
> to me.' . . . 'I am only a poor old woman who has lost a son . . .
> only show my son one-half of the temper you have shown me
> today and you will find that though he is as gentle as a child
> with you he can be as hard as steel.' (p. 205)

Each woman is victim as well as scold, and those roles are established in terms of individual histories, particular personalities. The
gaps and leaps in the conversation direct attention to the significance of what is unsaid, as well as the power of what is said. The
intransigence that prevents Mrs Yeobright from attending her son's
wedding also prevents her from telling Eustacia at the outset what
she has done with the money. Checked by guilt, Eustacia's defensive sense of being judged unfairly prevents her from denying the
character given her, preparing the way for her turning again in the
direction of Wildeve.

From this confrontation flows the action that will silence both
women. What has been communicated and what has been withheld
exist in indeterminate relationship with the events that follow. As in
ballad narrative, connections are forcefully yet mysteriously felt.
The doctor is unable conclusively to say whether in her long trek
across the midsummer heath to heal the breach with Clym it is exhaustion that kills Mrs Yeobright, or heart attack, or the bite of the
adder. In Clym's mind, it is Eustacia's silence that kills his mother
when the narrative of her last journey is revealed in the image
she has left with Johnny Nunsuch: ' "a woman's face looking at me

through a window-pane" ' (p. 239). Compromised by the presence of Wildeve, and by the character given her by Mrs Yeobright, Eustacia can only preserve that silence, even to the point where she forfeits the love of Clym. But Mrs Yeobright speaks on out of the silence of death through the voice of Johnny in the message she sends to his mother: 'tell her you have seen a broken-hearted woman cast off by her son' (p. 240). Eustacia is made as vulnerable to the destructive power of the heath and her own recklessness as she has made Mrs Yeobright. The door is closed against her too.

Susan Nunsuch plays out through the ancient lore of witchcraft what activates those energies in which Clym's wife and mother are entangled. In this way, Hardy points to what remains mysterious, in terms of cause and effect, within his own narrative, and how equivocating its telling of the quiet woman story necessarily remains. Like Mrs Yeobright, Susan perceives Eustacia's sexual power as a threat to the sons of Egdon, her 'little slave' Johnny Nunsuch as well as the bewitched Clym. It is Susan's first offensive with hat-pin in church (yet another act of surreptitious unruliness), publicly exposing Eustacia as temptress, that makes Eustacia victim in Clym's eyes, and draws him to her. Susan's final act of ill-wishing, as she silently fashions her own quiet woman, the wax effigy of Eustacia, seems actively in touch with the forces that expel the weakened Eustacia from home and community. In the poignant sequences that dwell on her end, she becomes scapegoat and ritual victim.

It has already been so with Mrs Yeobright, in death. As she is gathered into Egdon's oral tradition by the weeping women, the slow procession towards Blooms-End, the voices of the heathfolk and the pageantry of the scene affirm her sacrificial role. Christian Cantle is rightly fearful of her, however, as a 'broomstick old woman' (p. 247), and superstitiously attuned to what is abroad on the heath:

> 'Neighbours, how do we know but that something of the old serpent in God's garden, that gied the apple to the young woman with no clothes, lives on in adders and snakes still? Look at his eye—for all the world like a villainous sort of black currant. 'Tis to be hoped he can't ill-wish us!' (p. 247)

Some readers of the novel would see Hardy indicting the serpent of sexuality, or the young woman; others, the mother calling into being all that is atavistic in Clym's initial return to the heath. In charting the psychological forces at work in the drama of man, wife, mother, mother-in-law, Hardy's narrative refuses to take sides or assign blame. It merely dramatizes the 'trouble' to which the quiet woman sign so inscrutably points, in the complex empowerment, sexual and maternal, set in motion by the fertility on which the ongoing life of the heath depends.

Through the storm that kills Eustacia, Tamsin walks sure-footedly, carrying her child, the little Eustacia. Abiding quietly, she survives the threat to her good name, and the deaths of Wildeve and Eustacia, to be assimilated in her own way into the story of the heath: 'the spring came and calmed her; the summer came and soothed her. Winter came round again' (p. 314). Come may-pole time, she is almost ready to hear once more the suit of the adaptable reddleman. Patience and adaptability are the survival skills she shares with him, but it is his superior cunning that warms her into life. The cycle of fertility begins again, and conjugal happiness is celebrated in talk that re-embraces Tamsin in its continuity. It is accompanied by the ceremony of bedmaking, a nice matter of stretching and waxing the tick and shaking the feathers:

> When the bed was in proper trim Fairway and Christian bought forward vast paper bags, stuffed to the full, but light as balloons, and began to turn the contents of each into the receptacle first prepared. As bag after bag was emptied, airy tufts of down and feathers floated about the room in increasing quantity till, through a mishap of Christian's, who shook the contents of one bag outside the tick, the atmosphere of the room became dense with gigantic flakes, which descended upon the workers like a windless snow-storm. (p. 329)

More practical than singing, the ancient craft carries with it generous, even profligate, well-wishing. ' "Beds be dear to fokes that don't keep geese" ', as Christian remarks, and though this couple may not be in want of a bed, it is deemed appropriate, by Fairway, ' "to show 'em a bit of friendliness in this great racketing vagary of their lives" ' (p. 328). This perception of marital vicissitude takes on a less strident aspect in the benison of fluttering feathers, image of abundance, warmth, solid comfort, ephemerons, vanished lives that make 'one year's accidental crop'[3] on Egdon. The new story is a reminder of old ones: Christian Cantle still puzzles over his lonely life, the Grandfer momentarily recognizes the waning of his powers, until assured by Fairway: 'though rather lean in the stalks you be a green-leaved old man still. There's time enough left to ye yet to fill whole chronicles'. Off he goes then, to ' "sing a wedding song. . . . 'Tis like me to do so, you know; and they'd see it as such" ' (p. 330). Into this rhythm of continuity and renewal Hardy's revised ending perfectly fits. Tamsin, seated with Diggory Venn, in an open fly hired for the occasion, passes by, 'fluttering her hand as quickly

3. D. H. Lawrence, 'Study of Thomas Hardy', *Phoenix* (London: Heinermann,1970), p. 415.

as a bird's wing towards them, and asking Diggory, with tears in her eyes, if they ought not to alight and speak to these kind neighbours' (p. 331). Her gesture, in its delicacy and grace, bears no greater weight than the fluttering feathers yielded by the denuded geese, but it is the happiness of her feelings, not the transience inseparable from them, that the moment holds.

Clym seems to have the final voice, as itinerant preacher on 'morally unimpeachable subjects' (p. 336). The wisdom he returned to preach, we are told, has been formed by 'the central town thinkers of his date' (p. 147). Among them, Hardy would have had in mind Joseph Arch and the French 'possibilists' who figure in his 1883 essay on 'The Dorsetshire Labourer', thinkers whose ameliorist approach to improving the lot of the rural labourer underlines the utopian quality of Clym's arguing 'culture before luxury to the bucolic world' (p. 148). This is consistent with the intransigence that makes him so clearly his mother's son and her opponent. Eustacia is right to resist Clym the furze-cutter, idyllically but myopically immersed in the life of the heath, unable to see how his commitment to her might pull in another direction. Yet she has made part of the vision he has of his own and Egdon's future, and it is his mother who is most alive to the incongruity.

The sign of the quiet woman points to what it is that Clym Yeobright encounters in his return and to the way in which, despite the new directions promised by his physical mobility and social and intellectual ambitions, he is finally made impotent by the drama in which he has been so deeply implicated. Hardy's re-reading of the sign is no more inclined to present Clym as a victim of the women or the agent of patriarchal oppression than it is to judge the women in terms of the gender stereotypes their behaviour seems to suggest. The sign stands as a mark of narrative repetitions, and the 'returns' they celebrate as renewals of the Egdon community. The tone of the final pages is unmistakeably, and self-consciously, ironic. Clym can do no more than transform the story he has inhabited into mythologizing literariness. As the heath-dwellers remark, 'it was well enough for a man to take to preaching who could not see to do anything else' (p. 336). Taking Eustacia's place on the barrow, he appropriates Egdon's oral tradition for ends of his own. But then, so does Hardy.

Thomas Hardy: A Chronology

1840 June 2	Hardy born at Higher Bockhampton ("Mellstock" in the novels), near Dorchester, the first of four children of Thomas Hardy, builder, and his wife Jemima, née Hand, some five months after their marriage. Three other children follow, all of whom remain unmarried: Mary (1841–1915), Henry (1851–1928), and Katharine, usually called Kate (1856–1940).
1848	Attends the newly established National School in Lower Bockhampton, recalled later in the poem "He Revisits His First School"; one of the founders of the school, Mrs. Julia Augusta Martin, takes a special interest in him.
1850	Enters the British School in Dorchester, run on Nonconformist lines by Isaac Last.
1853	Last starts an independent academy in Dorchester. Hardy's studies with him, including Latin, continue until 1856; thereafter he is mainly self-taught.
1856	Leaves school to join the Dorchester office of the architect, John Hicks, as an apprentice. Joins the crowd gathered outside Dorchester jail to watch the hanging of Martha Browne for the murder of her husband. Forms friendship with Horace Moule, son of the vicar of Fordington St. George in Dorchester; university-educated, eight years Hardy's senior, and already a published poet and critic, Moule encourages his studies but advises him to give up his hopes of entering university.
1858	The poem "Domicilium" probably written about this time, after the death of his grandmother, Mary Hardy, in January 1857.
1860	Completes his apprenticeship; stays on as Hicks's assistant.
1862 April	Moves to London, where he works in the office

of Arthur (later Sir Arthur) Blomfield, an architect specializing in church restoration and design. Hardy makes regular visits to the National Gallery, and soon begins his "Schools of Painting" notebook. The "Studies, Specimens &c" notebook, begun around this time, shows Hardy preparing himself to become a poet. Attends evening classes in French at King's College.

1863	Awarded an essay prize by the Royal Institute of British Architects. Forms a close relationship with Eliza Bright Nicholls, its course possibly reflected in the "She, to Him" sonnets. The relationship founders in 1867, when Hardy comes to prefer her younger sister Mary Jane; Eliza never marries.
1865 March	Hardy's short sketch "How I Built Myself a House" is published in *Chamber's Journal*, his first appearance as an author. About this time loses his religious faith, though throughout his life he retains an affection for the Church of England and its services.
1867	Leaves London to resume work with Hicks in Dorchester. Begins his first novel, *The Poor Man and the Lady*, which he later describes as "socialistic" and "a sweeping dramatic satire."
1868	Submits manuscript of *The Poor Man and the Lady* to Macmillan, unsuccessfully, and then at their suggestion to Chapman & Hall.
1869	In February Chapman & Hall agree to publish *The Poor Man and the Lady* if Hardy contributes £20 toward costs. Hardy meets George Meredith, who advises him to continue writing but not to begin his career with a novel likely to cause controversy.
April	Invited to join the architectural practice of G. R. Crickmay in Weymouth. Further efforts to place *The Poor Man and the Lady* are unsuccessful; the manuscript is later destroyed. Begins work on *Desperate Remedies*.
1870 March	Sent by Crickmay to examine the church at St. Juliot, Cornwall, where he meets and falls in love with the rector's sister-in-law, Emma Lavinia Gifford.
1871 March	*Desperate Remedies* published anonymously by Tinsley Brothers, after Hardy advances £75 to-

ward the costs of publication. A hostile and hurt-ful review in the *Spectator* ensures poor sales. Begins work on his next novel, *Under the Greenwood Tree*, and completes it by the summer.

1872 June   *Under the Greenwood Tree* published anonymously by Tinsley, who purchases the copyright; it does not sell, but receives a few sympathetic reviews. Hardy determines to become a full-time writer.

August   *A Pair of Blue Eyes* begins publication in *Tinsleys' Magazine*, in eleven monthly installments; it appears in volume form in May 1873, to mainly favorable reviews. All of Hardy's subsequent novels are first published in serial form.

1873   Visits Horace Moule in Cambridge (June); in September Moule commits suicide.

1874 January   Serialization of *Far from the Madding Crowd* begins in the *Cornhill Magazine*, under the editorship of Leslie Stephen. The volume publication, in November, brings Hardy his first major success.

September   Marries Emma Gifford at St. Peter's, Paddington, in London. After a honeymoon in France, they settle in the Paddington district.

1875   Moves to Swanage, Dorset; works on *The Hand of Ethelberta*, which begins serial publication in the *Cornhill* in July.

1876   Moves first to Yeovil, later to Sturminster Newton (in July); Hardy later describes this as his and Emma's happiest time together. They visit Holland and Germany in May.

1878 January   *The Return of the Native* begins serialization in *Belgravia*, after being rejected by both Leslie Stephen and John Blackwood as unsuitable for family reading.

March   The Hardys move to London; Hardy begins work on *The Trumpet-Major*. He is elected to the Savile Club.

1879   Hardy reviews William Barnes's *Poems of Rural Life*.

1880 January   Serialization begins of *The Trumpet-Major*, published in volume form in October.

October   Hardy falls ill, and believes himself close to death; he is unable to leave the house until April the following year. Much of *A Laodicean*, which

	begins serialization in December, is dictated to Emma.
1881 June	The Hardys leave London for Wimborne in Dorset. *A Laodicean* appears in volume form in November.
1882	Serialization begins of *Two on a Tower*, with volume publication in October.
1883	The Hardys move to Dorchester; construction of Max Gate begins in November.
1884	Hardy becomes a Justice of the Peace.
1885	*The Mayor of Casterbridge* is completed in April, ready for serial and volume publication in 1886. In June the Hardys move into Max Gate; this is their last move.
1887	*The Woodlanders* is published in volume form in March, when the Hardys take a holiday in Italy.
1888	Hardy publishes his first collection of short stories, *Wessex Tales*. The Hardys visit Paris.
1889	The opening chapters of *Tess of the d'Urbervilles* are turned down by several publishers.
1890	*A Group of Noble Dames* (short stories) begins serialization in December, with volume publication in May 1891. Hardy publishes his essay "Candour in English Fiction," urging the need for greater freedom of expression in the novel.
1891	*Tess of the d'Urbervilles* begins serial publication in July; volume publication follows in December, when the novel is attacked for its supposed indecency. It sells in large numbers, and helps to secure Hardy's financial independence.
1892 July	Death of Hardy's father.
October	Serial publication of *The Pursuit of the Well-Beloved* begins.
1893	While on a visit to Dublin with Emma, Hardy meets Florence Henniker, and begins the most intense of a number of close relationships with society women, often with literary interests.
1894	*Life's Little Ironies* (short stories) published in February. Serial publication of *Jude the Obscure* begins in December.
1895	*Jude* comes out in volume form in November; like *Tess*, the novel attracts some strongly hostile reviews. The first collected edition of Hardy's work, published by Osgood, McIlvaine, begins to appear.

1896	The Hardys visit the site of the Battle of Waterloo.
1897	*The Well-Beloved*, revised from *The Pursuit of the Well-Beloved*, published in volume form in March; Hardy writes no more novels after this date. The Hardys holiday in Switzerland.
1898 December	Hardy publishes his first poetry collection, *Wessex Poems*, with illustrations by himself, to mainly unsympathetic reviews.
1899	Hardy's dismay at the outbreak of the South African war is reflected in a number of poems, including "Drummer Hodge" and "The Souls of the Slain."
1901	*Poems of the Past and the Present* published in November, to mixed but broadly favorable reviews.
1904	Part First of *The Dynasts*, Hardy's epic-drama in verse about the Napoleonic Wars, is published. Hardy's mother Jemima, perhaps the most important figure in his life, dies in April.
1905 April	Hardy receives his first honorary degree, from Aberdeen University. Probably meets Florence Dugdale, his future wife, during this year.
1906	Part Second of *The Dynasts* is published.
1908	Part Third of *The Dynasts* is published in February.
1909	*Time's Laughingstocks* published in December. Hardy becomes President of the Society of Authors.
1910 July	Hardy awarded the Order of Merit by King George V; receives Freedom of Dorchester in November.
1911	Emma Hardy completes her *Some Recollections* (the last page is dated 4 January 1911).
1912	The Wessex Edition (Macmillan) begins to appear. In June Hardy receives the Gold Medal of the Royal Society of Literature.
November	Emma Hardy dies on November 27; Hardy begins the sequence of "Poems of 1912–13."
1913 March	Hardy visits scenes of his courtship of Emma in Cornwall. During the spring Florence Dugdale moves in to Max Gate. In July Hardy accepts an honorary fellowship at Magdalene College, Cambridge. *A Changed Man* (short stories) is published in October.

1914 February	Hardy marries Florence Dugdale (February 10). *Satires of Circumstance*, which includes "Poems of 1912–13," is published in November.
1915	Death of Hardy's sister Mary (November 24).
1916	Publication of *Selected Poems of Thomas Hardy*, chosen by Hardy himself.
1917	Hardy begins sifting papers in preparation for his autobiography, to be published after his death over the name of Florence Hardy. *Moments of Vision* (poems) appears in November.
1919	*Collected Poems* published. In October Hardy receives a "Poet's Tribute," a bound volume of holograph poems by 43 contemporary poets.
1920	Hardy receives a message of congratulation on his 80th birthday from King George V.
1922	Hardy receives honorary degree from University of St. Andrews and is made an honorary fellow of Queen's College, Oxford; *Late Lyrics and Earlier* published in May.
1923	Florence Henniker dies. Prince of Wales (later Edward VIII) visits Hardy at Max Gate. Hardy begins friendship with T. E. Lawrence; other visitors in the postwar years include Siegfried Sassoon, Robert Graves, and Virginia Woolf. Hardy's verse drama, *The Famous Tragedy of the Queen of Cornwall* is performed by the Hardy Players (December 28).
1924	Stage adaptation of *Tess* performed in Dorchester.
1925	*Human Shows* (poems) is published in November.
1928 January 11	Hardy, who has been ill since mid-December, dies in the evening of January 11. On January 16, in a double ceremony, his ashes are interred in Westminster Abbey, and his heart in the churchyard at Stinsford.
October	*Winter Words* is published. The first volume of his autobiography, *The Early Life of Thomas Hardy*, appears over his widow's name in this year; the second volume, *The Later Years of Thomas Hardy*, follows in 1930.
1940	Death of Kate Hardy, Hardy's youngest sibling and the last of the family line.

Selected Bibliography

• indicates works included or excerpted in this Norton Critical Edition.

BIBLIOGRAPHIES

Davis, W. Eugene, and Helmut E. Gerber. *Thomas Hardy: An Annotated Bibliography of Writings about Him*. De Kalb: Northern Illinois UP, 1973.
Davis, W. Eugene, and Helmut E. Gerber. *Thomas Hardy: An Annotated Bibliography of Writings about Him. Vol II: 1970–1978 and Supplement for 1871–1969*. De Kalb: Northern Illinois UP, 1983.
Draper, Ronald P., and Martin S. Ray. *An Annotated Critical Bibliography of Thomas Hardy*. London and New York: Macmillan, 1989.
Millgate, Michael. "Thomas Hardy." *Victorian Fiction: A Second Guide to Research*, ed. George H. Ford. New York: Modern Language Association of America, 1978.
Purdy, Richard Little. *Thomas Hardy: A Bibliographical Study*. Oxford: Clarendon Press, 1954.
Purdy, Richard Little. *Thomas Hardy: A Bibliographical Study*. Introduction and Supplement by Charles P. C. Pettit. London: The British Library, and New Castle, DE: Oak Knoll Press, 2002.

BIOGRAPHIES

Brennecke, Ernest. *The Life of Thomas Hardy*. New York: Greenpoint Press, 1925.
Gibson, James. *Thomas Hardy: A Literary Life*. London: Macmillan, 1996.
Gibson, James, ed. *Thomas Hardy: Interviews and Recollections*. London: Macmillan, 1999.
Gittings, Robert. *Young Thomas Hardy*. London: Heinemann, 1975.
Gittings, Robert. *The Older Thomas Hardy*. London: Heinemann, 1978.
Hands, Timothy. *A Hardy Chronology*. London: Macmillan, 1992.
Hardy, Evelyn. *Thomas Hardy: A Critical Biography*. London: Hogarth Press, 1954.
Millgate, Michael. *Thomas Hardy: A Biography*. New York: Random House, 1982.
Millgate, Michael. *Thomas Hardy: A Biography Revisited*. Oxford: OUP, 2004.
O'Sullivan, Timothy. *Thomas Hardy: An Illustrated Biography*. London: Macmillan, 1975.
Seymour-Smith, Martin. *Hardy*. London: Bloomsbury, 1994.
Stewart, J. I. M. *Thomas Hardy: A Critical Biography*. Harlow: Longman, 1971.
Turner, Paul. *The Life of Thomas Hardy*. Oxford: Blackwell, 1998.
Weber, Carl. *Hardy of Wessex: His Life and Literary Career*. New York: Columbia University Press, 1940; repr. 1966.

LIFE, LETTERS, AND NOTEBOOKS

Beatty, C. J. P., ed. *The Architectural Notebook of Thomas Hardy*. Dorchester: Dorset Natural History and Archaeological Society, 1966.
Björk, Lennart A., ed. *The Literary Notebooks of Thomas Hardy*. 2 vols. London: Macmillan, 1985.
• Millgate, Michael, ed. *The Life and Work of Thomas Hardy, by Thomas Hardy*. London: Macmillan, 1984.
• Millgate, Michael, ed. *Thomas Hardy's Public Voice: The Essays, Speeches, and Miscellaneous Prose*. Oxford: Clarendon Press, 2001.
Orel, Harold, ed. *Thomas Hardy's Personal Writings*. New York: St. Martin's Press, 1990.
Purdy, Richard Little, and Michael Millgate, eds. *The Collected Letters of Thomas Hardy*. 7 vols. Oxford: Clarendon Press, 1978–88.

Taylor, Richard H., ed. *The Personal Notebooks of Thomas Hardy*. London: Macmillan, 1979.

CRITICISM

Abercrombie, Lascelles. *Thomas Hardy: A Critical Study*. London: Secker, 1912.
Bayley, John. *An Essay on Hardy*. Cambridge: Cambridge UP, 1978.
Beach, Joseph Warren. *The Technique of Thomas Hardy*. Chicago, Ill.: University of Chicago Press, 1922; repr. New York: Russell & Russell, 1962.
Beer, Gillian. *Darwin's Plots: Evolutionary Narrative in Darwin, George Eliot and Ninteenth-Century Fiction*. Cambridge: CUP, 1983, 2nd ed., 2000.
• Beer, Gillian. *Open Fields: Science in Cultural Encounter*. Oxford: Clarendon Press, 1996.
Berger, Sheila. *Thomas Hardy and Visual Structures: Framing, Disruption, Process*. New York: New York UP, 1990.
Blunden, Edmund. *Thomas Hardy*. London: Macmillan, 1967.
Bloom, Harold, ed. *Modern Critical Interpretations of Thomas Hardy*. New York: Chelsea, 1987.
Boumelha, Penny. *Thomas Hardy and Women: Sexual Ideology and Narrative Form*. Brighton: Harvester, 1982.
Bradford, Andrew. *Thomas Hardy and the Survivals of Time*. Aldershot: Ashgate, 2003.
Brooks, Jean R. *Thomas Hardy: The Poetic Structure*. London: Elek Books, 1971.
Brown, Douglas. *Thomas Hardy*. London: Longmans, Green, 1954; rev. ed. 1961.
Bullen, J. B. *The Expressive Eye: Fiction and Perception in the Works of Thomas Hardy*. Oxford: Clarendon Press, 1986.
Butler, Lance St. J., ed. *Thomas Hardy after Fifty Years*. London: Macmillan, 1977.
Butler, Lance St. J., ed. *Alternative Hardy*. London: Macmillan, 1989.
Carpenter, Richard C. *Thomas Hardy*. New York: Twayne, 1964.
Casagrande, Peter. *Unity in Hardy's Novels: "Repetitive Symmetries."* London: Macmillan, 1982.
Chapman, Raymond, *The Language of Thomas Hardy*. London: Macmillan, 1990.
Clarke, Graham, ed. *Thomas Hardy: Critical Assessment of Writers in English*. 4 vols. Mountfield, East Sussex: Helm Information, 1993.
Collins, Deborah L. *Thomas Hardy and His God: A Liturgy of Unbelief*. London: Macmillan, 1990.
Cox, R. G., ed. *Thomas Hardy: The Critical Heritage*. London: Routledge and Kegan Paul, 1970.
Daleski, H. M. *Thomas Hardy and Paradoxes of Love*. Columbia and London: University of Missouri Press, 1997.
Draper, Ronald P., ed. *Hardy: The Tragic Novels*. London: Macmillan, 1975; rev. ed. 1991.
Ebbatson, Roger. *The Evolutionary Self: Hardy, Forster, Lawrence*. Brighton: Harvester, 1982.
Ebbatson, Roger. *Hardy: The Margin of the Unexpressed*. Sheffield: Sheffield Academic Press, 1993.
Elliott, Ralph W. V. *Thomas Hardy's English*. Oxford: Basil Backwell, 1984.
Elvy, Margaret. *Sexing Hardy: Thomas Hardy and Feminism*. London: Crescent Moon, 1998.
Enstice, Andrew. *Thomas Hardy: Landscapes of the Mind*. London: Macmillan, 1979.
Federico, Annette. *Masculine Identity in Hardy and Gissing*. London and Toronto: Associated University Presses, 1991.
Firor, Ruth. *Folkways in Thomas Hardy*. Philadelphia: University of Pennsylvania Press, 1931.
Fisher, Joe. *The Hidden Hardy*. London: Macmillan, 1992.
Garson, Marjorie. *Hardy's Fables of Integrity: Woman, Body, Text*. Oxford: Clarendon Press, 1991.
Gatrell, Simon. *Hardy the Creator: A Textual Biography*. Oxford: Clarendon Press, 1988.
Gatrell, Simon. *Thomas Hardy and the Proper Study of Mankind*. London: Macmillan, 1993.
Gatrell, Simon. *Thomas Hardy's Vision of Wessex*. London: Palgrave Macmillan, 2003.
Goode, John. *Thomas Hardy: The Offensive Truth*. Oxford: Blackwell, 1988.
Gregor, Ian. *The Great Web: The Form of Hardy's Major Fiction*. London: Faber and Faber, 1974.
Grundy, Joan. *Hardy and the Sister Arts*. London: Macmillan, 1979.
Guerard, Albert J. *Thomas Hardy: The Novels and Stories*. Cambridge: Harvard UP, 1949; rev. ed., London: New Directions, 1964.

Hardy, Barbara. *Thomas Hardy: Imagining Imagination: Hardy's Poetry and Fiction*. London: Athlone Press, 2000.

Hands, Timothy. *Thomas Hardy: Distracted Preacher? Hardy's Religious Biography and Its Influence on his Novels*. London: Macmillan, 1989.

Hands, Timothy. *Thomas Hardy*. London: Macmillan, 1995.

Higonnet, Margaret R., ed. *The Sense of Sex: Feminist Perspectives on Thomas Hardy*. Urbana: University of Illinois Press, 1993.

Howe, Irving. *Thomas Hardy*. New York: Macmillan, 1967.

Hughes, John. *"Ecstatic Sound": Music and Individuality in the Work of Thomas Hardy*. Aldershot: Ashgate, 2001.

Ingham, Patricia. *Thomas Hardy: A Feminist Reading*. Hemel Hempstead: Harvester, 1989.

Irwin, Michael. *Reading Hardy's Landscapes*. London: Palgrave Macmillan, 2000.

Jedzerewski, Jan. *Thomas Hardy and the Church*. London: Macmillan, 1996.

Kay-Robinson, Denis. *Hardy's Wessex Reappraised*. Newton Abbott: David and Charles, 1971.

King, Jeanette. *Tragedy in the Victorian Novel: Theory and Practice in the Novels of George Eliot, Thomas Hardy and Henry James*. Cambridge: Cambridge UP, 1978.

Kramer, Dale. *Thomas Hardy: The Forms of Tragedy*. Detroit: Wayne State UP, 1975.

Kramer, Dale, ed. *Critical Approaches to the Fiction of Thomas Hardy*. London: Macmillan, 1979.

Kramer, Dale, ed. *The Cambridge Companion to Thomas Hardy*. Cambridge: CUP, 1999.

Langbaum, Robert. *Thomas Hardy in Our Time*. London: Macmillan, 1995.

Lawrence, D. H. *Study of Thomas Hardy and Other Essays*, ed. Bruce Steele. Cambridge: Cambridge UP, 1985.

Lerner, Laurence, and John Holmstrom, eds. *Thomas Hardy and His Readers: A Selection of Contemporary Reviews*. London: Bodley Head, 1968.

Lucas, John. *The Literature of Change: Studies in the Nineteenth-Century Provincial Novel*. Brighton: Harvester, 1977.

Mallett, Phillip V., and Ronald P. Draper, eds. *A Spacious Vision: Essays on Thomas Hardy*. Penzance: Patten Press, 1994.

Mallett, Phillip, ed., *The Achievement of Thomas Hardy*. London: Macmillan, 2000.

Mallett, Phillip, ed., *Thomas Hardy: Texts and Contexts*. London: Palgrave Macmillan, 2002.

Mallett, Phillip, ed., *Palgrave Advances in Thomas Hardy Studies*. London: Palgrave Macmillan, 2004.

Meisel, Perry. *Thomas Hardy: The Return of the Repressed*. New Haven: Yale University Press, 1972.

Miller, J. Hillis. *Thomas Hardy: Distance and Desire*. Cambridge, MA: Harvard University Press, 1970.

Miller, J. Hillis. *Fiction and Repetition: Seven English Novels*. Cambridge, MA: Harvard University Press, 1982.

Millgate, Michael. *Thomas Hardy: His Career as a Novelist*. London: Bodley Head, 1971.

Moore, Kevin Z. *The Descent of the Imagination: Postromantic Culture in the Later Novels of Thomas Hardy*. New York: New York UP, 1990.

Morgan, Rosemarie. *Women and Sexuality in the Novels of Thomas Hardy*. London: Routledge, 1988.

Morrell, Roy. *Thomas Hardy: The Will and the Way*. Kuala Lumpur: University of Malaysia Press, 1965.

Page, Norman. *Thomas Hardy*. London: Routledge and Kegan Paul, 1977.

Page, Norman, ed. *Thomas Hardy: The Writer and His Background*. London: Bell and Hyman, 1980.

Page, Norman, ed. *Oxford Reader's Companion to Thomas Hardy*. Oxford: OUP, 2000.

Pettit, Charles P. C., ed. *New Perspectives on Thomas Hardy*. London: Macmillan, 1994.

Pettit, Charles P. C., ed. *Reading Thomas Hardy*. London: Macmillan, 1998.

Pinion, F. B. *A Hardy Companion*. London: Macmillan, 1968.

Pite, Ralph. *Hardy's Geography: Wessex and the Regional Novel*. London: Palgrave Macmillan, 2002.

Radford, Andrew. *Thomas Hardy and the Survivals of Time*. Aldershot: Ashgate, 2003.

Rutland, William R. *Thomas Hardy: A Study of His Writings and Their Background*. Oxford: Basil Blackwell, 1938.

Smith, Anne, ed. *The Novels of Thomas Hardy*. New York: Barnes and Noble, 1979.

Southerington, F. R. *Hardy's Vision of Man*. London: Chatto and Windus, 1971.

Springer, Marlene. *Hardy's Art of Allusion*. London: Macmillan, 1983.

Sumner, Rosemary. *Thomas Hardy: Psychological Novelist*. London: Macmillan, 1981.

Taylor, Dennis. *Hardy's Literary Language and Victorian Philology*. Oxford: Clarendon Press, 1993.

Vigar, Penelope. *The Novels of Thomas Hardy: Illusion and Reality*. London: Athlone Press, 1974.

White, R. J. *Thomas Hardy and History*. New York: Harper and Row, 1974.

Widdowson, Peter. *Hardy in History: A Study in Literary Sociology*. London and New York: Routledge, 1989.

Widdowson, Peter. *On Thomas Hardy: Late Essays and Earlier*. London: Macmillan, 1998.

Williams, Merryn. *Thomas Hardy and Rural England*. London: Macmillan, 1972.

Wing, George. *Thomas Hardy*. Edinburgh: Oliver and Boyd, 1963.

Wotton, George. *Thomas Hardy: Towards a Materialist Criticism*. Dublin: Gill & Macmillan, 1985.

Wright, T. R. *Hardy and the Erotic*. London: Macmillan, 1989.

THE RETURN OF THE NATIVE

Benvenuto, Richard. "*The Return of the Native* as a Tragedy in Six Books." *Nineteenth-Century Fiction* 26. 1 (1971): 83–93.

Benway, Ann M. B. "Oedipus Abroad: Hardy's Clym Yeobright and Lawrence's Paul Morel." *Thomas Hardy Yearbook* 13 (1986): 51–57.

Crompton, Louis. "The Sunburnt God: Ritual and Tragic Myth in *The Return of the Native*." *Boston University Studies in English* 4 (1960): 229–40.

• Dalziel, Pamela. "Anxieties of Representation: The Serial Illustrations to Hardy's *The Return of the Native*." *Nineteenth-Century Literature* 51 (1996): 84–110.

Deen, Leonard. "Heroism and Pathos in Thomas Hardy's *The Return of the Native*." *Nineteenth-Century Fiction* 15.3 (1960): 207–19.

Eggenschwiler, David. "Eustacia Vye, Queen of Night and Courtly Pretender." *Nineteenth-Century Fiction* 25.4 (1971): 444–54.

Evans, Robert. "The Other Eustacia." *Novel* 1 (1968): 251–59.

Garver, John. *Thomas Hardy: "The Return of the Native."* Harmondsworth: Penguin, 1988.

Giordano, Frank R. "Eustacia Vye's Suicide." *Texas Studies in Language and Literature* 30 (1980): 504–21.

• Gribble, Jennifer. "The Quiet Women of Egdon Heath." *Essays in Criticism* 46 (1996): 234–57.

Hagan, John. "A Note on the Significance of Diggory Venn." *Nineteenth-Century Fiction* 16.2 (1961): 147–55.

Jordan, Mary Ellen. "Thomas Hardy's *The Return of the Native*: Clym Yeobright and Melancholia." *American Imago* 39 (1982): 101–18.

May, Charles E. "The Magic of Metaphor in *The Return of the Native*." *Colby Library Quarterly* 22.2 (1986): 111–18.

McCann, Eleanor. "Blind Will or Blind Hero: Philosophy and Myth in Thomas Hardy's *The Return of the Native*." *Criticism* 3 (1961): 140–57.

Miller, J. Hillis. "Topography in *The Return of the Native*." *Essays in Literature* 8 (1981): 119–34.

• Nash, Andrew. "The Serialization and Publication of *The Return of the Native*: A New Thomas Hardy Letter." *The Library: The Transactions of the Bibliographical Society* 2.1 (2001): 53–59.

• Paterson, John. "*The Return of the Native* as Antichristian Document." *Nineteenth-Century Fiction* 14.2 (1959): 11–27.

Paterson, John. "The Poetics of *The Return of the Native*." *Modern Fiction Studies* 6 (1960): 214–22.

Paterson, John. *The Making of "The Return of the Native."* Berkeley: University of California Press, 1960.

Pinck, Joan B. "The Reception of Thomas Hardy's *The Return of the Native*." *Harvard Library Bulletin* 17 (1969): 291–300.

Robson, Peter, "Thomas Hardy's Play of Saint George." *Lore and Language* 17.1–2 (1999): 257–71.

Schweik, Robert. "Theme, Character and Perspective in Hardy's *The Return of the Native*." *Philological Quarterly* 41 (1962): 757–67.

Wheeler, Otis B. "Four Versions of *The Return of the Native*." *Nineteenth-Century Fiction* 14.1 (1959): 27–44.